Better Homes and Gardens®

ANNUAL • Recipes 1996

Better Homes and Gardens® Books
Des Moines, Iowa

Winter Squash-Apple Brunch Cake (page 69)

I am big on making links between past, present, and future. In fact, one of the first things I did as editor in chief was revisit our magazine's heritage. I started with the first issue published in 1922 and worked my way up to what would be my first issue at the helm. I'm a firm believer in knowing where you've been to find out where you should be going.

This year's annual is big on links between past, present, and future, too. First off, it's the second year of our redesign. We set out to create the kind of book you could truly use—again and again. Judging by your gratifying response, we succeeded.

The year 1996 has been a big year in food, too. In August, we proudly announced the 11th edition of the Better Homes and Gardens® *"red plaid" cookbook, an institution all its own. In the book and our story about it (see page 191), you'll find cherished classics, recipes for the way you cook today, and forecasts of the fun we're going to have with food in the future—especially as we toss more and more of our ethnic discoveries into the melting pot that continually keeps our traditions fresh and rich.*

At Better Homes and Gardens *magazine, we cherish food and all it means to home and family. In October, we reflected that philosophy in our story, "Dinner from the Heart: Home Cooking as the Tie that Binds" (for excerpts, see pages 227 and 241). The annual recipes cookbook is also a tie that bonds, a way to bring all of our recipes from the year together in one place for your convenience and pleasure.*

Speaking of connections, I can't help but want to tip you off: 1997 is our 75th anniversary, and we're already planning an eventful year.

So, to those of you who were with us last year, welcome back. And to those of you who are newcomers, welcome aboard.

Jean LemMon, *Editor in Chief*

the editors

*O*ur food editors possess a true love of food, and their commitment to quality marks every step of the process in producing a cookbook with the Better Homes and Gardens *name on the cover. Executive Food Editor Nancy Byal,* below, *and her staff bring years of experience to creating mouthwatering recipes and explaining new food trends with clarity.*

All of our recipes are expertly tested and retested in one of the 10 home-style kitchens in the Better Homes and Gardens Test Kitchen. At right, from left: Associate Editor Julia Martinusen and Home Economist Kay Springer examine the taste and appearance of a recipe under consideration. At top right, Senior Editor Joy Taylor and Associate Editor David Feder oversee food styling and photography to make the recipes eye-catching and realistic.

Only the best of the best survive this creative process. Our food editors, involved from the very seed of an idea through the finished page, make sure of it.

Better Homes and Gardens® Books
An Imprint of Meredith® Books

Better Homes and Gardens®
Annual Recipes 1996

Project Editor: *Jennifer Darling*
Contributing Editors: *Shelli McConnell, Gregory H. Kayko*
Associate Art Director: *Lynda Haupert*
Copy Chief: *Angela K. Renkoski*
Editorial and Design Assistants: *Judy Bailey, Jennifer Norris, Karen Schirm*
Test Kitchen Director: *Sharon Stilwell*
Illustrator: *Thomas Rosborough*
Electronic Production Coordinator: *Paula Forest*
Production Manager: *Douglas M. Johnston*
Prepress Coordinator: *Margie J. Schenkelberg*

Meredith® Books

Editor in Chief: *James D. Blume*
Managing Editor: *Christopher Cavanaugh*
Director, New Product Development: *Ray Wolf*

Better Homes and Gardens® **Magazine**

Editor in Chief: *Jean LemMon*
Executive Food Editor: *Nancy Byal*
Senior Editor: *Joy Taylor*
Associate Editors: *Julia Martinusen, David Feder, R.D.*

Meredith® Publishing Group

President, Publishing Group: *Christopher M. Little*
Vice President and Publishing Director: *John P. Loughlin*

Meredith® Corporation

Chairman of the Board and Chief Executive Officer: *Jack D. Rehm*
President and Chief Operating Officer: *William T. Kerr*

Chairman of the Executive Committee: *E. T. Meredith III*

Our seal assures you that every recipe in
Better Homes and Gardens Annual Recipes 1996 has been
tested in the Better Homes and Gardens Test Kitchen.
This means that each recipe is practical and
reliable, and meets our high standards of taste appeal.
We guarantee your satisfaction with this book for
as long as you own it.

Cover photograph: *Toffee-Apple Cheesecake (page 268)*
Page 1: *Angel Shortcake 'n' Lemon Cream (page 122)*
Page 2: *Winter Squash-Apple Brunch Cake (page 69)*

*Some of the images in this book are used by permission
of Zedcor, Inc., Tucson, AZ, from the 100,000 image and the
30,000 image DeskGallery® collections. 1-800-482-4567.*

All of us at Better Homes and Gardens Books are
dedicated to providing you with the information and ideas you
need to create tasty foods. We welcome your comments
and suggestions. Write to us at: Better Homes and Gardens Books,
Cookbook Editorial Department, 1716 Locust Street RW-240,
Des Moines, IA 50309-3023.

*If you would like to order additional copies
of this book, call 1-800-439-4119.*

CONTENTS

When this symbol appears with a recipe, rest assured that you can prepare the dish—start to finish—in 30 minutes or less.

Any recipe that bears this low-fat symbol has met our guideline of having no more than 10 grams of fat per serving (see page 8).

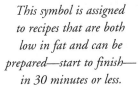

This symbol is assigned to recipes that are both low in fat and can be prepared—start to finish— in 30 minutes or less.

The recipes that display this blue-ribbon symbol have earned top honors in our monthly Prize Tested Recipes contest.

NUTRITION INFORMATION

With each recipe, we give you useful nutrition information you easily can apply to your own needs. First read "What You Need" (below) to determine your dietary requirements. Then refer to the Nutrition Facts listed with each recipe. You'll find the calorie count and the amount of fat, saturated fat, cholesterol, sodium, carbohydrates, fiber, and protein for each serving. In most cases, along with the Nutrition Facts per serving, you'll find the amount of vitamin A, vitamin C, calcium, and iron noted as a percentage of the Daily Values. The Daily Values are dietary standards set by the Food and Drug Administration. To stay in line with the nutrition breakdown of each recipe, follow the suggested number of servings.

HOW WE ANALYZE

The Better Homes and Gardens Test Kitchen computer analyzes each recipe for the nutritional value of a single serving.

◆ The analysis does not include optional ingredients.

◆ We use the first serving size listed when a range is given. For example: If we say a recipe "Makes 4 to 6 servings," the Nutrition Facts are based on 4 servings.

◆ When ingredient choices (such as margarine or butter) appear in a recipe, we use the first one mentioned for analysis. The ingredient order does not mean we prefer one ingredient over another.

◆ When milk is a recipe ingredient, the analysis is calculated using 2-percent milk.

WHAT YOU NEED

The dietary guidelines below suggest nutrient levels that moderately active adults should strive to eat each day. As your calorie levels change, adjust your fat intake, too. Try to keep the percentage of calories from fat to no more than 30 percent. There's no harm in occasionally going over or under these guidelines, but the key to good health is maintaining a balanced diet *most of the time.*

Calories:	About 2,000
Total fat:	Less than 65 grams
Saturated fat:	Less than 20 grams
Cholesterol:	Less than 300 milligrams
Carbohydrates:	About 300 grams
Sodium:	Less than 2,400 milligrams
Dietary fiber:	20 to 30 grams

LOW-FAT RECIPES

For recipes that meet our low-fat criteria, a main-dish serving must contain 10 or fewer grams of fat. For side dishes or desserts, the serving must contain 5 or fewer grams of fat. These recipes are flagged with a low-fat symbol.

JANUARY
Slices of Pleasure

30-minute recipes indicated in RED.
Low-fat recipes indicated with a ♥.

The skies may be gray and chill winds may howl, but inside you'll feel cozy with sweet smells wafting from the oven. A wedge of rich Double Chocolate-Mint Shortbread or a slice of Apricot and Toasted Pecan Torte will brighten anyone's mood. Pears are plentiful, so feature them in elegant desserts such as pretty Ginger Pear Tart or Warm Pear French Toast Sundae. Another midwinter restorative is warm pasta, bubbling with cheese and herbs. Many pasta dishes are low in fat, such as Shrimp and Fennel Fusilli, Pasta Pizza, and Chili-Sauced Pasta, studded with kidney beans and green peppers.

GINGER PEAR TART

The secret behind the no-cook filling? Instant pudding mix.

30 2-inch-wide gingersnaps
½ cup broken pecans
⅓ cup margarine or butter, melted

♦♦♦

¾ cup half-and-half or light cream
1 8-oz. carton dairy sour cream
1 4-serving-size pkg. instant vanilla pudding mix
1 Tbsp. chopped crystallized ginger, 2 tsp. grated gingerroot, or ¼ to ½ tsp. ground ginger
1 Tbsp. apricot brandy (optional)

♦♦♦

1 Tbsp. margarine or butter
3 Tbsp. sugar
1½ lb. pears (3 to 5 medium), peeled, halved, cored, and thinly sliced

♦♦♦

Fresh mint leaves (optional)

1 For crust, in a food processor bowl combine the gingersnaps and pecans. Cover and process till finely crushed. (Or, use a blender to crumb the gingersnaps, one-fourth at a time, adding pecans with the last portion.) You should have 2½ cups crumbs and nuts.

2 In a mixing bowl stir together crumb mixture and the ⅓ cup melted margarine or butter. Press firmly onto the bottom and up the sides of a 9½- to 11-inch round tart pan with a removable bottom or a 9-inch pie plate, forming a firm, even crust. Bake in a 350° oven for 8 minutes. Cool in pan on a wire rack.

3 When crust is cool, make filling. In a large mixing bowl gradually stir half-and-half or light cream into sour cream. Use a whisk or rotary beater to stir in pudding mix, ginger, and apricot brandy, if using. Beat for 1 to 2 minutes more or till thick and smooth. Spread in the baked crust. Cover and chill for several hours or overnight.

4 In a 10-inch skillet melt the 1 tablespoon margarine or butter; stir in sugar. Add pear slices. Cook, uncovered, over medium heat for 3 to 4 minutes or till pears are just tender, stirring gently. Use a slotted spoon to remove pears; drain on paper towels. Reserve liquid in skillet. Boil the liquid about 2 minutes or till reduced to 2 tablespoons. Cool pears and liquid.

5 Before serving, remove the sides of the tart pan. Arrange pear slices in overlapping circles on top of the pudding mixture. Brush the pear liquid onto pears. Cut into wedges and serve immediately. If desired, garnish with mint. Makes 8 servings.

Nutrition facts per serving: 439 cal., 24 g total fat (9 g sat. fat), 21 mg chol., 347 mg sodium, 53 g carbo., 3 g fiber, 3 g pro. *Daily values:* 21% vit. A, 7% vit. C, 6% calcium, 11% iron.

WHITE CHOCOLADAMIA BROWNIE PIE

1 recipe Flaky Pie Pastry (see page 11)

♦♦♦

¼ cup unsalted butter
3 oz. white baking bar, grated
1 cup all-purpose flour
¼ tsp. baking powder
3 eggs
¾ cup sugar
1 tsp. vanilla
1 cup chopped macadamia nuts, pecans, or almonds, toasted
3 oz. white baking bar, chopped

♦♦♦

Chocolate ice cream (optional)
1 recipe White Chocolate Sauce (optional) (see page 11)

1 For piecrust, on a lightly floured surface, use your hands to slightly flatten Flaky Pie Pastry dough. Roll dough to form a 12-inch circle. Carefully transfer pastry onto a 9-inch pie plate. Ease pastry into pie plate. Trim pastry to ½ inch beyond edge of pie plate. Fold under the extra pastry. Crimp edge. Do not prick pastry. Set aside.

2 For filling, in a saucepan melt butter. Remove from heat; cool. In a mixing bowl combine the 3 ounces grated baking bar, flour, and baking powder; set aside. Stir eggs, sugar, and vanilla into melted butter in saucepan. Use a wooden spoon to lightly beat egg mixture just till combined. Stir in flour mixture, nuts, and 3 ounces chopped baking bar.

3 Spread filling into pastry. Bake in a 350° oven for 50 to 55 minutes or till a toothpick inserted near center comes out clean. Serve warm or cooled with ice cream and White Chocolate Sauce, if desired. Serves 12.

Flaky Pie Pastry: Stir together 1¼ cups *all-purpose flour* and ¼ teaspoon *salt.* Cut in ⅓ cup *shortening* till pieces are the size of small peas. Sprinkle 1 tablespoon *water* over part of mixture, gently tossing with a fork. Push moistened dough to side of bowl. Repeat using 1 tablespoon water at a time, till all dough is moistened, using 4 to 5 tablespoons water total. Form into a ball.

Nutrition facts per serving: 385 cal., 24 g total fat, (8 g sat. fat), 64 mg chol., 82 mg sodium, 40 g carbo., 2 g fiber, 6 g pro. *Daily values:* 6% vit. A, 4% calcium, 9% iron.

White Chocolate Sauce: In a heavy saucepan bring ⅔ cup *whipping cream* and 1 teaspoon *vanilla* just to boiling, stirring often. Remove saucepan from heat. In a bowl beat 1 *egg yolk,* ⅓ cup *sugar,* and 2 to 4 tablespoons of the hot whipping cream mixture with an electric mixer on medium speed for 2 to 3 minutes or till thick and lemon-colored.

Gradually stir about half of the remaining whipping cream mixture into egg yolk mixture; return all to saucepan. Cook and stir over medium heat just till mixture returns to boiling; remove from heat. Stir in 2 ounces (½ cup) grated *white baking bar;* continue stirring till melted. Cover surface; cool 15 minutes. Stir before serving. Makes ¾ cup.

Nutrition facts per tablespoon: 98 cal., 7 g total fat (4 g sat. fat), 36 mg chol., 10 mg sodium, 9 g carbo., 0 g fiber, 1 g pro. *Daily values:* 8% vit. A, 1% calcium.

APRICOT AND TOASTED PECAN TORTE

1¼ **cups ground toasted pecans**
¼ **cup fine dry bread crumbs**

❖❖❖

3 **egg yolks**
¼ **cup granulated sugar**
3 **egg whites**
½ **tsp. cream of tartar**
3 **Tbsp. granulated sugar**

❖❖❖

¼ **cup dried apricots**
½ **cup water**
1 **Tbsp. granulated sugar**
1½ **tsp. lemon juice**
1 **3-oz. pkg. cream cheese, softened**
3 **Tbsp. granulated sugar**
  Sifted powdered sugar

1 Grease and lightly flour bottoms of two 8-inch round baking pans. In a bowl combine the ground pecans and bread crumbs. Set pans and nut mixture aside.

2 In a mixing bowl beat egg yolks and the ¼ cup granulated sugar with an electric mixer on high speed 5 minutes or till thick and lemon-colored. Thoroughly

wash beaters. In a large bowl beat egg whites and cream of tartar on medium to high speed till soft peaks form (tips curl). Gradually add the 3 tablespoons granulated sugar, beating till stiff peaks form (tips stand straight). Fold about 1 cup egg white mixture into yolk mixture. Fold yolk mixture into remaining egg white mixture. Sprinkle about one-third nut mixture at a time over batter; fold in.

3 Spread batter into prepared pans. Bake in a 350° oven 20 to 25 minutes or till cakes test done (cakes will not rise much). Cool cakes in pans on a wire rack 10 minutes. Remove cakes from pans; cool completely on the rack.

4 Meanwhile, for filling, in a small saucepan combine apricots, water, the 1 tablespoon granulated sugar, and lemon juice. Bring to boiling; reduce heat. Simmer, covered, 15 minutes or till apricots are tender. Remove from heat; cool slightly. Place apricot mixture in a blender container or food processor bowl. Cover; blend or process till smooth. Cool completely. In a mixing bowl beat cream cheese and 3 tablespoons granulated sugar till fluffy. Stir a small amount of apricot mixture into cream cheese. Fold in remaining apricot mixture. Place one cake layer on a serving plate. Spread with apricot mixture. Top with remaining cake layer. Sift powdered sugar over top. Cover and chill up to 4 hours. Serves 10.

Nutrition facts per serving: 213 cal., 14 g total fat (3 g sat. fat), 73 mg chol., 64 mg sodium, 21 g carbo., 1 g fiber, 4 g pro. *Daily values:* 15% vit. A, 1% vit. C, 2% calcium, 5% iron.

CITRUS ANGEL CAKE

The subtle lime, lemon, or orange flavor comes from frozen juice concentrate.

1½ **cups egg whites (10 to 12)**
1½ **cups sifted powdered sugar**
1 **cup sifted cake flour or sifted all-purpose flour**

♦♦♦

1 **tsp. cream of tartar**
3 **Tbsp. frozen limeade, lemonade, or orange juice concentrate, thawed**
¾ **cup granulated sugar**

♦♦♦

Whipped cream (optional)
Lime, lemon, and/or orange peel strips (optional)

1 Allow egg whites to stand at room temperature for 30 minutes. Sift powdered sugar and flour together 3 times; set aside.

2 In a large mixing bowl beat egg whites and cream of tartar with an electric mixer on medium speed till soft peaks form (tips curl). Add juice concentrate. Gradually add granulated sugar, about 2 tablespoons at a time, beating till stiff peaks form (tips stand straight).

3 Sift about one-fourth of the flour mixture over the beaten egg whites; fold in gently. (If the bowl is too full, transfer the mixture to a larger bowl.) Repeat, folding in the remaining flour mixture by fourths.

4 Pour the batter into an ungreased 10-inch tube pan; spread evenly. Bake on the lowest rack in a 350° oven for 40 to 45 minutes or till the top springs back when lightly touched. Immediately invert cake (leave in pan, but if cake has risen higher than the pan, invert it over a jar or bottle so the top does not touch countertop.) Cool thoroughly.

5 To serve, loosen sides and center from pan. Invert cake onto a serving plate. Use a serrated knife to cut into wedges. If desired, garnish each serving with whipped cream and citrus peel strips. Makes 12 servings.

Nutrition facts per serving: 150 cal., 0 g total fat, 0 mg chol., 46 mg sodium, 34 g carbo., 0 g fiber, 4 g pro.
Daily values: 4% iron.

CHOCOLATE TRUFFLE DESSERT

You can use our suggestions or another liqueur in these rich stars.

6 **oz. bittersweet or semisweet chocolate, chopped, or**
6 **oz. semisweet chocolate pieces**

♦♦♦

1 **cup whipping cream**
¼ **cup Irish cream liqueur, Kahlúa, or amaretto, or milk**

♦♦♦

2 **slightly beaten egg yolks**
2 **Tbsp. sugar**

♦♦♦

Melted white and/or dark chocolate (optional)
White chocolate shavings (optional)

1 Chill a small mixing bowl and the beaters of an electric mixer. Meanwhile, line an 8×8×2-inch pan with clear plastic wrap, extending plastic wrap over the edges of the pan; set aside.

2 In a heavy medium saucepan melt chopped chocolate or chocolate pieces over very low heat, stirring constantly till the chocolate begins to melt. Immediately remove from heat and stir till smooth; set aside.

3 In the chilled mixing bowl combine the whipping cream and 1 tablespoon of the liqueur. Beat with the chilled beaters on low speed till soft peaks form. Cover and refrigerate for up to 2 hours or till needed.

4 In a heavy small saucepan stir together the egg yolks, sugar, and remaining liqueur. Cook and stir with a wire whisk over medium-low heat till mixture is very thick (about 8 minutes). Remove from heat; pour mixture into a medium mixing bowl.

5 Add the melted chopped chocolate, 2 tablespoons at a time, to the hot mixture, beating on medium speed till combined (mixture will be thick). Add ½ cup of the whipped cream mixture; beat on low speed till smooth. Gently fold in remaining whipped cream mixture. Spoon the mixture into the prepared pan, spreading as necessary to make an even layer. Cover and freeze about 4 hours or till firm enough to cut.

6 Invert the frozen mixture onto a waxed-paper-lined baking sheet. Carefully remove plastic wrap. Using 1-, 2-, and 3-inch star-shaped cookie cutters, cut shapes from chocolate, dipping cutters into warm water between cuts to prevent sticking, if necessary. Cover and return the shapes to freezer till serving time.

7 To serve, if desired, drizzle plates with melted white and/or dark chocolate; top with the chocolate cutouts. If desired, sprinkle with shaved white chocolate. Makes 6 servings.

Nutrition facts per serving: 335 cal., 26 g total fat (16 g sat. fat), 123 mg chol., 27 mg sodium, 24 g carbo., 2 g fiber, 4 g pro. *Daily values:* 27% vit. A, 3% calcium, 8% iron.

TROPICAL PHYLLO TART

Overlap squares of phyllo dough to create the petals for the delicate crust. (See the photograph on page 41.)

8 sheets frozen phyllo dough (about 18×14-inch rectangles), thawed
¼ cup margarine or butter, melted
3 Tbsp. sugar

♦♦♦

⅓ cup sugar
1 envelope unflavored gelatin
¼ cup guava or passion fruit juice or cold water

♦♦♦

2 mangoes, peeled, seeded, and chopped, or refrigerated mango slices, drained and chopped (about 2½ cups)

1½ tsp. finely shredded lime peel
2 Tbsp. lime juice
1 cup whipping cream

♦♦♦

2 to 3 cups assorted sliced tropical fruits, such as mango, papaya, kiwifruit, pineapple, blood orange, kumquat, or carambola (star fruit)
⅓ cup orange marmalade

1 Chill a medium mixing bowl and the beaters of an electric mixer. Meanwhile, generously grease a 10-inch round tart pan with removable bottom. Trim phyllo sheets to 12-inch squares. Layer the phyllo sheets on the bottom of the pan, allowing ends to hang over the edge. Brush each sheet with melted margarine or butter and sprinkle with some of the 3 tablespoons sugar. Stagger the corners to create a petal effect. As you work, keep the remaining phyllo sheets covered with a damp cloth till ready to use.

2 Lightly press phyllo crust in pan to remove air bubbles. Line with a double thickness of heavy foil. Place on a baking sheet. Bake in a 375° oven for 10 minutes. Remove foil; bake for 5 to 7 minutes more or till puffed and golden. Cool in pan on a wire rack (crust will flatten upon cooling).

3 For filling, in a small saucepan stir together the ⅓ cup sugar and the gelatin. Stir in the fruit juice. Cook and stir over low heat till the sugar and gelatin dissolve. Remove from heat; cool.

4 Meanwhile, in a blender container or food processor bowl, combine chopped mango, lime peel, and lime juice. Cover and blend or process till smooth. Transfer mixture to a large bowl.

5 Stir cooled gelatin mixture into mango puree. Cover and chill to the consistency of corn syrup, stirring occasionally (about 1 hour). Remove from the refrigerator (gelatin mixture will continue to set).

6 In the chilled bowl beat the whipping cream with the chilled beaters on low speed till soft peaks form. When gelatin mixture is partially set (the consistency of unbeaten egg whites), fold the whipped cream into the gelatin mixture. Cover and chill till the mixture mounds when spooned (about 1 hour).

7 Spoon the gelatin mixture into the cooled crust. Cover and chill for 2 to 24 hours or till firm.

8 Before serving, arrange the fruit slices in a decorative pattern atop tart crust.

9 In a small saucepan heat the marmalade over low heat till just melted; drizzle over fruit. Makes 8 servings.

Nutrition facts per serving: 369 cal., 18 g total fat (8 g sat. fat), 41 mg chol., 176 mg sodium, 51 g carbo., 3 g fiber, 4 g pro. *Daily values:* 54% vit. A, 80% vit. C, 3% calcium, 6% iron.

CAPPUCCINO DECADENCE

Coffee, cinnamon, and orange zest flavor this tortelike dessert.

½ **cup finely crushed chocolate wafers**

❖❖❖

16 **oz. semisweet chocolate, chopped, or 16 oz. (2⅔ cups) semisweet chocolate pieces**
1 **cup whipping cream**
1 **Tbsp. instant coffee crystals**
½ **tsp. ground cinnamon**

❖❖❖

6 **beaten eggs**
¾ **cup granulated sugar**
⅓ **cup all-purpose flour**
½ **tsp. finely shredded orange peel**

❖❖❖

Powdered sugar (optional)
Unsweetened cocoa powder (optional)
Whipped cream (optional)
Chocolate-covered coffee beans (optional)
Chocolate candies (optional)
Edible flowers* (optional)

1 Grease a 9-inch springform pan. Lift and tilt the pan to coat the bottom and sides with chocolate wafer crumbs; set aside.

2 In a heavy medium saucepan combine the chocolate, whipping cream, coffee crystals, and cinnamon. Cook and stir over low heat till the chocolate is melted. Transfer the hot mixture to a medium mixing bowl.

3 In a large mixing bowl combine eggs, sugar, and flour. Beat with an electric mixer on medium speed about 10 minutes or till

TEST KITCHEN TIP

STORING FRESH CRANBERRIES

Refrigerate fresh cranberries in their original bag for up to 4 weeks. Or, to freeze them for up to 9 months, double-wrap the bag of cranberries with freezer wrap. (It's not necessary to thaw berries before using.)

thick and lemon-colored. Stir in orange peel. Fold one-fourth of the egg mixture into the chocolate mixture. Fold chocolate mixture into remaining egg mixture.

4 Pour mixture into prepared pan. Bake in a 325° oven 50 to 55 minutes or till edge is puffed halfway to center (center will be slightly soft). Cool in pan on a wire rack 20 minutes. Remove sides of pan. Cool at room temperature 4 hours. Cover and chill for 4 hours or till serving time.

5 Before serving, if desired, decorate plates by sifting a mixture of powdered sugar and cocoa powder over tops of plates. Add wedges of the dessert. Top with the whipped cream, chocolate-covered coffee beans, candies, and a flower. Serves 16.

*Note: To garnish food with flowers, choose those that have been grown without pesticides or other chemicals. They should be fresh and free of bruises. To be sure they're edible, look for small

packages in the produce section of your supermarket. Common edible varieties include violets, roses, pansies, and marigolds.

Nutrition facts per serving: 272 cal., 17 g total fat (10 g sat. fat), 101 mg chol., 50 mg sodium, 31 g carbo., 2 g fiber, 5 g pro. *Daily values:* 10% vit. A, 2% calcium, 9% iron.

STAR DESSERT CUPS

6 **to 8 (8-inch) flour tortillas**
Cooking oil for deep frying

❖❖❖

2 **oz. semisweet chocolate**
2 **tsp. shortening**

❖❖❖

Cinnamon ice cream
1 **Tbsp. sugar**
⅛ **tsp. ground cinnamon**
Cut-up fresh fruit

1 To soften tortillas, wrap in foil; warm in a 350° oven for 10 minutes. Cut into star shapes.

2 In a heavy large saucepan heat 3 inches of oil to 360°. Cook tortillas, one at a time, in oil 30 to 45 seconds or till golden and puffed, using a ladle to press tortillas in center to form cups. Remove; drain on paper towels.

3 Melt chocolate and shortening. Brush onto edges of tortilla cups; let dry. To serve, fill cups with ice cream. Top with sugar, cinnamon, and fruit. Makes 6 to 8 servings.

Nutrition facts per serving: 350 cal., 18 g total fat (4 g sat. fat), 11 mg chol., 34 mg sodium, 45 g carbo., 2 g fiber, 5 g pro. *Daily values:* 15% vit. A, 50% vit. C, 13% calcium, 12% iron.

Baked Star Dessert Cups: Soften tortillas and cut stars as directed on page 14. Spray four 10-ounce custard cups with *non-stick spray coating.* Press one tortilla star into each cup. Arrange on a baking sheet. Bake in a 350° oven about 15 minutes or till crisp. Cool in cups on a wire rack. Remove from cups. Brush with chocolate and serve as directed.

APPLE AND LEMON CHESS PIE

This recipe earned Carol Gillespie of Chambersburg, Pennsylvania, $200 in the magazine's monthly contest. (See the photograph on page 43.)

½ of a 15-oz. pkg. folded refrigerated unbaked piecrust (1 crust)

♦♦♦

4 eggs
1 cup sugar
1 cup unsweetened applesauce
1 tsp. finely shredded lemon peel
3 Tbsp. lemon juice
2 Tbsp. margarine or butter, melted
1 Tbsp. flaked coconut
⅛ tsp. ground cinnamon

♦♦♦

Whipped cream (optional)

1 Let piecrust stand at room temperature according to package directions. Unfold; fit crust into a 9-inch pie plate. Flute edges. Line with a double thickness of foil. Bake in a 450° oven 5 minutes. Remove foil; bake 5 minutes.

2 Meanwhile, for filling, in a medium mixing bowl beat eggs slightly. Stir in sugar, applesauce, peel, juice, margarine or butter, coconut, and cinnamon; mix well.

3 Place baked piecrust on oven rack. Pour in filling. Cover edge of pie with foil. Reduce oven temperature to 350°; bake for 20 minutes. Remove foil. Bake for 20 to 25 minutes more or till a knife inserted near center comes out clean. Cool pie on a wire rack. Cover; chill to store. If desired, top each serving with whipped cream. Makes 8 servings.

Nutrition facts per serving: 298 cal., 13 g fat (1 g sat. fat), 114 mg chol., 171 mg sodium, 42 g carbo., 1 g fiber, 4 g pro. *Daily values:* 8% vit. A, 6% vit. C, 1% calcium, 2% iron.

CRANBERRY CRUNCH DESSERT

½ cup all-purpose flour
½ cup rolled oats
⅓ cup packed brown sugar
¼ cup butter or margarine

♦♦♦

½ cup packed brown sugar
⅓ cup granulated sugar
3 cups cranberries
2 cups chopped, peeled cooking apples

♦♦♦

¼ cup sliced almonds
Vanilla ice cream (optional)

1 For topping, combine flour, oats, and ⅓ cup brown sugar. Cut in butter or margarine till crumbly; set aside.

2 In a large saucepan mix the ½ cup brown sugar, granulated

SAVE AND GRATE CITRUS

Why throw away squeezed lemons, oranges, or limes, when you can still use the peel? After squeezing out the juice, I store the halved rinds in a storage container in the freezer. When one of my recipes calls for finely shredded peel, I simply grate the frozen rind. That way, I get the fresh citrus flavor without having to keep the fresh fruits on hand. Using the fruit juice and peel saves money and cuts down on waste.

Carol White
Minneapolis, Minnesota

sugar, cranberries, and ½ cup *water.* Bring to boiling; reduce heat. Simmer, uncovered, for 3 to 4 minutes or till the cranberries pop. Stir in the apples.

3 Turn mixture into a 2-quart square baking dish. Sprinkle with topping then with almonds. Bake, uncovered, in a 375° oven about 30 minutes or till fruit is tender and topping is golden. If desired, serve warm with ice cream. Makes 6 servings.

Nutrition facts per serving: 339 cal., 11 g total fat (5 g sat. fat), 20 mg chol., 86 mg sodium, 61 g carbo., 4 g fiber, 4 g pro. *Daily values:* 7% vit. A, 15% vit. C, 4% calcium, 11% iron.

ALMOND BRICKLE CHEESECAKE

Gently tap through the brittle toffee topping to get to the rich reward beneath. (See the photograph on page 41.)

1¾ **cups finely crushed graham crackers (about 25 squares)**
1 **7½-oz. pkg. almond brickle pieces, finely chopped (about 1½ cups)**
½ **cup margarine or butter, melted**

❖❖❖

3 **8-oz. pkg. cream cheese, softened**
¾ **cup packed brown sugar**
2 **Tbsp. all-purpose flour**
3 **eggs**
¼ **cup milk**

1 For crust, in a mixing bowl combine graham crackers and ⅓ cup brickle pieces. Stir in melted margarine or butter. Press onto bottom and 2 inches up sides of an 8- or 9-inch springform pan.

2 In a medium mixing bowl combine the cream cheese, brown sugar, and flour. Beat with an electric mixer on medium speed till fluffy. Add the eggs all at once, beating on low just till combined. Stir in the milk and ⅔ cup brickle pieces.

3 Pour mixture into prepared pan. Place on a shallow baking pan in oven. Bake in a 375° oven till center appears nearly set when shaken, allowing 45 to 50 minutes for the 8-inch pan or 35 to 40 minutes for the 9-inch pan.

4 Cool in the pan on a wire rack for 15 minutes. Loosen sides. Cool 30 minutes more. Remove sides; cool completely. Cover and chill 4 hours or till serving time.

5 Before serving, place the cheesecake on a baking sheet. Sprinkle with remaining brickle pieces (about ½ cup). Broil 4 to 5 inches from heat 1 to 3 minutes or till pieces begin to melt and form a crust. Transfer to a serving plate and slice. Serves 12 to 16.

Nutrition facts per serving: 477 cal., 35 g total fat (15 g sat. fat), 121 mg chol., 416 mg sodium, 34 g carbo., 1 g fiber, 8 g pro. *Daily values:* 37% vit. A, 7% calcium, 11% iron.

PRIZE TESTED RECIPE WINNER

WARM PEAR FRENCH TOAST SUNDAE

This recipe earned Angela Gould of Union City, Georgia, $100 in the magazine's monthly contest.

¼ **cup packed brown sugar**
2 **Tbsp. margarine or butter**
¼ **tsp. ground cinnamon**
3 **pears, peeled, cored, and sliced**

❖❖❖

3 **eggs**
¾ **cup milk**
1 **tsp. vanilla**
3 **Tbsp. brown sugar**
1 **tsp. ground cinnamon**
¼ **tsp. ground nutmeg**

❖❖❖

6 **1-inch-thick French bread slices**
2 **Tbsp. margarine or butter**

❖❖❖

Light or regular ice cream

1 In a skillet combine ¼ cup brown sugar, 2 tablespoons margarine or butter, and ¼ teaspoon cinnamon. Cook and stir over medium-low heat till margarine is melted and sugar is dissolved. Add the pears and cook 5 minutes or till tender, stirring occasionally.

2 In a mixing bowl use a fork to beat eggs slightly. Beat in milk and vanilla. In a small bowl combine the 3 tablespoons brown sugar, 1 teaspoon cinnamon, and nutmeg; stir into egg mixture.

3 Dip bread into egg mixture, coating both sides. In a large skillet melt the 2 tablespoons margarine or butter. Cook bread on both sides over medium heat 2 to 3 minutes or till golden brown. Add more margarine as needed.

4 To serve, top each bread slice with pear mixture and scoop of ice cream. Makes 6 servings.

Nutrition facts per serving: 399 cal., 17 g total fat (8 g sat. fat), 138 mg chol., 349 mg sodium, 54 g carbo., 2 g fiber, 9 g pro. *Daily values:* 20% vit. A, 6% vit. C, 14% calcium, 14% iron.

30 MIN. NO FAT

WINTER-BRIGHT PEAR COMPOTE

⅓ **cup sugar**
¼ **cup dry white wine, orange juice, or white grapefruit juice**
1 **Tbsp. lemon juice**
3 **medium pears, peeled (if desired), cored, and quartered**
1½ **cups cranberries**

1 In a large skillet combine sugar, wine, lemon juice, and ¼ cup *water*. Bring to boiling; add pears. Return to boiling. Simmer, covered, 1 minute. Add cranberries and simmer, covered, 3 to 4 minutes or till berries pop. Remove from heat; cool. Serve warm or at room temperature. Serves 6.

Nutrition facts per serving: 112 cal., 0 g total fat, 0 mg chol., 1 mg sodium, 27 g carbo., 3 g fiber, 0 g pro.
Daily values: 13% vit. C, 1% calcium, 2% iron.

BAKED ALMOND-PEAR PUDDING

¾ **cup sliced almonds, toasted**
3 **eggs**
¾ **cup all-purpose flour**
¾ **cup milk**
½ **cup butter, melted**
½ **cup sugar**
½ **tsp. vanilla**
1 **tsp. baking powder**
1 **tsp. finely shredded lemon peel**
½ **tsp. salt**
⅛ **to ¼ tsp. ground nutmeg**
1 **29-oz. can sliced pears, drained and chopped**

♦♦♦

2 **Tbsp. sugar**
  Sweetened whipped cream

1 In a blender container or food processor bowl, blend or process ½ cup of the almonds till ground. Add eggs, flour, milk, 6 tablespoons of the butter, ½ cup sugar, vanilla, baking powder, lemon peel, salt, and nutmeg. Cover; blend till combined, scraping sides as necessary. Pour mixture into a bowl. Stir in pears.

THE CLEVER COOK

ON-THE-LEVEL WITH DRY INGREDIENTS

For a more accurate measure, I keep a clean wooden frozen dessert stick in my flour canister to level tops of measuring cups.

Mary Jean Scheuber
Ceres, California

2 Transfer mixture to a 2-quart rectangular baking dish. Sprinkle with remaining ¼ cup almonds and 2 tablespoons sugar. Drizzle with remaining 2 tablespoons butter. Bake in a 400° oven 25 minutes or till a knife inserted in center comes out clean; cool slightly. Serve warm with sweetened whipped cream. Makes 10 servings.

Nutrition facts per serving: 281 cal., 15 g total fat (7 g sat. fat), 90 mg chol., 268 mg sodium, 34 g carbo., 2 g fiber, 6 g pro.
Daily values: 12% vit. A, 2% vit. C, 8% calcium, 8% iron.

DOUBLE CHOCOLATE-MINT SHORTBREAD

Each tender wedge is so rich, it melts in your mouth.

¾ **cup butter**
1⅓ **cups all-purpose flour**
¾ **cup sifted powdered sugar**
¼ **cup unsweetened cocoa powder**
¼ **tsp. mint extract**

¾ **cup miniature semisweet chocolate pieces**

♦♦♦

  Chocolate and/or vanilla-flavored green candy coating, melted (optional)
  Crushed mint candies (optional)

1 In a large mixing bowl beat butter with an electric mixer on medium to high speed 30 seconds. Add about half of the flour, the powdered sugar, cocoa powder, and mint extract. Beat on low speed till combined, then on medium speed till blended. Stir in remaining flour. Stir in chocolate pieces. If necessary, chill dough 1 to 2 hours for easier handling.

2 On a lightly greased cookie sheet pat the dough into a 9-inch circle. Using your fingers, press and make a scalloped edge. Use a fork to prick dough deeply to make 16 wedges.

3 Bake in a 300° oven about 25 minutes or till edges are firm to the touch and center is set. Let cool 2 minutes on cookie sheet. Use a long, sharp knife to cut along the perforations of wedges. Remove to a wire rack to cool.

4 If desired, drizzle with the melted candy coating and sprinkle with the crushed candies before the coating dries. Makes 16 cookie wedges.

Nutrition facts per wedge: 164 cal., 11 g total fat (5 g sat. fat), 23 mg chol., 87 mg sodium, 14 g carbo., 0 g fiber, 2 g pro.
Daily values: 8% vit. A, 4% calcium, 7% iron.

HEAVENLY CUTOUT COOKIES

½ **cup butter**
1 **3-oz. pkg. cream cheese**
1¾ **cups all-purpose flour**
1½ **cups sifted powdered sugar**
1 **egg**
½ **tsp. baking powder**
½ **tsp. vanilla**

❖❖❖

1 **recipe Powdered Sugar Icing (optional) (see page 20)**

1 In a medium mixing bowl beat butter and cream cheese with an electric mixer on medium speed for 30 seconds. Add about half of the flour, the powdered sugar, egg, baking powder, and vanilla. Beat on low speed till combined. Beat on medium speed for 1 minute. Beat in remaining flour on low speed. Divide dough in half. Cover; chill 1 hour or till easy to handle.

2 On a lightly floured surface, roll dough, half at a time, to ⅛-inch thickness. Use assorted cutters to cut dough into desired shapes. Arrange dough shapes 1 inch apart on an ungreased noninsulated cookie sheet.

3 Bake in a 375° oven 8 to 9 minutes or till edges are set. Remove cookies and cool on a wire rack. If desired, glaze tops with Powdered Sugar Icing. Pipe icing on top, using a decorating bag fitted with a fine writing tip. Makes about 42 cookies.

Nutrition facts per cookie: 59 cal., 3 g total fat (2 g sat. fat), 13 mg chol., 34 mg sodium, 7 g carbo., 0 g fiber, 1 g pro. *Daily values:* 3% vit. A, 1% iron.

Heavenly Chocolate Cutouts: Prepare cookies as directed at left, except decrease the flour to 1½ cups and add ¼ cup *unsweetened cocoa powder* and ¼ teaspoon *ground cinnamon* with the first half of the flour.

Heavenly Citrus Cutouts: Prepare cookies as directed at left, except add 1 teaspoon finely shredded *lime, lemon, or orange peel* and substitute 1 tablespoon *lime, lemon, or orange juice* in place of the vanilla.

PRALINE COOKIES

Bits of sweet, crunchy praline candy make these cookies extra special.

1 **Tbsp. butter**

❖❖❖

⅓ **cup granulated sugar**
2 **Tbsp. water**
1 **cup chopped hazelnuts (filberts) or pecans, toasted**

❖❖❖

1 **cup butter**
2½ **cups all-purpose flour**
1 **cup packed brown sugar**
½ **cup granulated sugar**
2 **eggs**
1 **tsp. vanilla**
½ **tsp. baking soda**

❖❖❖

2 **oz. semisweet or bittersweet chocolate, chopped (optional)**
2 **Tbsp. finely chopped hazelnuts (filberts) or pecans (optional)**

1 Grease a large baking sheet with the 1 tablespoon butter. Set baking sheet aside. For praline, in a heavy medium saucepan stir together the ⅓ cup granulated sugar and the water. Cook and stir over medium-high heat till boiling. Cook for 2½ to 3½ minutes more or till syrup is a deep golden brown; remove from heat. Stir in 1 cup nuts. Immediately pour onto the prepared baking sheet. Cool completely on a wire rack till firm. When firm, transfer the praline to a heavy plastic bag. Using a rolling pin, crush the praline into small pieces; set aside.

2 For cookies, in a large mixing bowl beat the 1 cup butter with an electric mixer on medium to high speed about 30 seconds or till softened. Add about half of the flour, all of the brown sugar, ½ cup granulated sugar, eggs, vanilla, and baking soda. Beat till combined, scraping sides of bowl occasionally. Beat or stir in remaining flour. Stir in praline.

3 Drop rounded teaspoonsful of dough about 2 inches apart on an ungreased cookie sheet. Bake in a 375° oven for 8 to 10 minutes or till edges are lightly browned. Cool cookies on cookie sheet for 1 minute. Remove cookies and cool on a wire rack.

4 If desired, melt chocolate in a heavy small saucepan over very low heat, stirring constantly till chocolate begins to melt. Immediately remove the chocolate from the heat and stir till smooth. Drizzle chocolate over cookies and, if desired, sprinkle with the 2 tablespoons chopped nuts. Makes 72 cookies.

Nutrition facts per cookie: 70 cal., 4 g total fat (2 g sat. fat), 13 mg chol., 38 mg sodium, 9 g carbo., 0 g fiber, 1 g pro. *Daily values:* 2% vit. A, 2% iron.

WHITE CHOCOLATE-RASPBERRY COOKIES

8 oz. white chocolate baking
    squares

❖❖❖

½ cup butter
1 cup sugar
1 tsp. baking soda
2 eggs
2¾ cups all-purpose flour

❖❖❖

½ cup seedless raspberry jam
3 oz. white chocolate baking
    squares
½ tsp. shortening

1 Chop 4 ounces of the white chocolate baking squares; set aside. In a heavy small saucepan, melt remaining white chocolate baking squares over low heat, stirring constantly; cool.

2 In a bowl beat butter with an electric mixer on medium to high speed 30 seconds. Add sugar, soda, and ¼ teaspoon *salt*. Beat till combined. Beat in eggs and melted baking squares till combined. Beat in as much of the flour as you can. Stir in any remaining flour. Stir in chopped white chocolate baking squares.

3 Drop rounded teaspoonsful of dough 2 inches apart on greased cookie sheet. Bake in a 375° oven 7 to 9 minutes or till edges are lightly browned. Cool on cookie sheet l minute. Remove cookies; cool on a rack. Store in an airtight container at room temperature up to 3 days.

4 To serve, melt jam in a saucepan over low heat. Spoon about ½ teaspoon jam onto top of each cookie. In a heavy small saucepan combine 3 ounces white baking squares and shortening. Melt over low heat, stirring constantly. Drizzle melted mixture atop cookies. Chill 15 minutes to firm chocolate. Makes about 48.

Nutrition facts per cookie: 104 cal., 4 g total fat (2 g sat. fat), 14 mg chol., 66 mg sodium, 16 g carbo., 0 g fiber, 1 g pro. *Daily values:* 2% vit. A, 1% calcium, 2% iron.

TRIPLE-CHOCOLATE CHUNK COOKIES

2 oz. unsweetened
    chocolate, chopped

❖❖❖

1 cup butter or margarine,
    softened
¾ cup granulated sugar
¾ cup packed brown sugar
1 tsp. baking soda
2 eggs
1 tsp. vanilla
2 cups all-purpose flour
6 oz. white baking bar, cut
    into ½-inch pieces
6 oz. semisweet or
    bittersweet chocolate, cut
    into ½-inch pieces
1 cup chopped black walnuts
    or pecans (optional)

1 In a small saucepan melt unsweetened chocolate over very low heat till melted, stirring constantly. Set aside to cool.

2 In a large mixing bowl beat the butter or margarine with an electric mixer on medium to high speed 30 seconds. Add granulated sugar, brown sugar, soda, and cooled melted chocolate. Beat till well combined. Add eggs and vanilla; beat well. Gradually beat

WHAT IS "WHITE CHOCOLATE"?

Smooth, sweet, and creamy, "white chocolate" is carving a niche for itself in candy recipes. Here's what you need to know:

What it is. White chocolate contains milk or milk solids, sugar, fat (vegetable fat or cocoa butter), and vanilla flavoring. White chocolate that contains cocoa butter has a chocolatelike aroma. But white chocolate is not a true chocolate because it lacks chocolate liquor (the thick, rich brown paste that comes from ground cocoa beans).

Where to find it. White chocolate also goes by the names of white baking bar, candy coating, confectioners' coating, almond bark, and summer coating. It comes in bars, blocks, and small disks. Look for it on the grocery store shelf next to the baking chocolate or in a candy store.

in flour. Stir in the white baking bar, semisweet or bittersweet chocolate, and, if desired, nuts.

3 Drop rounded tablespoonsful of dough 3 inches apart on an ungreased cookie sheet. Bake in a 375° oven 9 to 11 minutes or till edges are firm. Cool on cookie sheet 1 minute. Remove and cool on a rack. Makes 45 cookies.

Nutrition facts per cookie: 126 cal., 7 g total fat (4 g sat. fat), 21 mg chol., 77 mg sodium, 15 g carbo., 0 g fiber, 1 g pro. *Daily values:* 4% vit. A, 1% calcium, 3% iron.

DIVINE ALMOND MOLDED COOKIES

Use your fingers or cookie stamps to shape almond paste dough into angels, harps, bells, stars, and suns.

1 cup butter, softened
2 oz. almond paste*, crumbled (¼ cup)
½ cup sugar
2½ cups all-purpose flour
♦♦♦
1 recipe Egg Paint (optional) (see at right)
♦♦♦
1 recipe Powdered Sugar Icing (optional) (see at right)

1 In a medium mixing bowl beat butter with an electric mixer on medium speed till fluffy. Add almond paste; beat till combined. Beat in sugar. Use a wooden spoon to stir in flour. (If necessary, knead in the remaining flour with hands.)

2 For each angel, shape dough into one 1¼-inch ball (for body), one ¾-inch ball (for head), two 1-inch balls (for wings), and two ¼-inch balls (for feet). On an ungreased noninsulated cookie sheet flatten the largest ball to ¼-inch thickness into a triangle for body. For the head, at the top point of the triangle attach the ¾-inch ball; flatten to a 1¼-inch circle. For feet, attach the ¼-inch balls to the base of the triangle. For wings, attach the 1-inch balls to opposite sides of triangle; shape into triangles. If desired, paint with Egg Paint.

3 Bake in a 325° oven about 15 minutes or till edges are light brown. Transfer to a wire rack;

cool completely. If desired, decorate with Powdered Sugar Icing, using a decorating bag and a fine writing tip. Makes about 20 cookies.

Egg Paint: In a small mixing bowl beat together 1 *egg yolk* and ¼ teaspoon *water*. Divide mixture among 3 or 4 small bowls. Add 2 or 3 drops *liquid or paste food coloring* to each bowl; mix well. Paint desired colors of egg yolk mixture onto unbaked cookies, using a small, clean paintbrush. If the egg paint thickens, stir in water, a drop at a time.

Powdered Sugar Icing: In a small mixing bowl stir together 1 cup sifted *powdered sugar* and ¼ teaspoon *vanilla*. Stir in *milk*, 1 teaspoon at a time, till icing is easy to pipe or drizzle.

***Note:** For best results, use an almond paste that is made without syrup or liquid glucose. Check ingredient label to be sure.

Nutrition facts per cookie: 164 cal., 10 g total fat (6 g sat. fat), 25 mg chol., 93 mg sodium, 17 g carbo., 0 g fiber, 2 g pro. *Daily values:* 8% vit. A, 5% iron.

Stamped Cookies: Form the dough into 1-inch balls. Arrange on an ungreased noninsulated cookie sheet. Using 2-inch-wide cookie stamps, press firmly to flatten dough and make patterns on tops. Bake in a 350° oven for 8 to 10 minutes or till edges are light brown. Remove cookies and cool on a wire rack. Makes about 36 cookies.

HAZELNUT CRINKLE COOKIES

In these chewy cookies, the flavor comes from two nutty ingredients—toasted hazelnuts and a creamy hazelnut-chocolate spread. You'll find this dark-colored spread either alongside the peanut butter or in the gourmet foods section of your supermarket.

3 cups all-purpose flour
2 tsp. baking powder
½ tsp. salt
♦♦♦
1 11-oz. jar chocolate-hazelnut spread
¼ cup shortening
1⅓ cups granulated sugar
1 tsp. vanilla
2 eggs
♦♦♦
⅓ cup milk
½ cup chopped hazelnuts (filberts), toasted
♦♦♦
Finely chopped hazelnuts (about 2 cups)
Sifted powdered sugar

1 In a medium mixing bowl stir together the flour, baking powder, and salt. Set aside.

2 In a large mixing bowl combine chocolate-hazelnut spread and shortening. Beat with an electric mixer on medium to high speed till combined. Add the granulated sugar; beat on medium speed till fluffy. Add vanilla and eggs; beat till combined.

3 Alternately add flour mixture and milk to creamed mixture, beating on medium speed just till combined. Use a spoon to stir in the ½ cup chopped hazelnuts. Cover and chill dough for several hours or till firm.

4 Shape the dough into 1- or 1½-inch balls. Roll the balls in finely chopped hazelnuts, then roll in powdered sugar. Place the balls 2 inches apart on a lightly greased cookie sheet (cookies will spread and crinkle as they bake). Bake in a 375° oven for 8 to 10 minutes or till surface is cracked and cookies are set. Remove cookies and cool on a wire rack. Makes about 72 cookies.

Nutrition facts per cookie: 92 cal., 5 g total fat (1 g sat. fat), 6 mg chol., 30 mg sodium, 11 g carbo., 0 g fiber, 1 g pro.
Daily values: 1% calcium, 2% iron.

CHOOSE-A-COOKIE DOUGH

Pick a flavor before you start baking because some ingredients will vary depending on which of our seven versions you follow.

 ½ **cup shortening**
 ½ **cup margarine or butter**
 1 **cup packed brown sugar**
 ½ **cup granulated sugar**
 ½ **tsp. baking soda**
 2 **eggs**
 1 **tsp. vanilla**
2½ **cups all-purpose flour**

1 In a large mixing bowl beat the shortening and margarine or butter with an electric mixer on medium to high speed for 30 seconds. Add brown sugar, granulated sugar, and baking soda. Beat till fluffy. Add eggs and vanilla; beat till combined. Beat or stir in flour. Use dough immediately or cover and chill for up to 24 hours.

2 Drop slightly rounded tablespoonsful of cookie dough 2 inches apart onto an ungreased cookie sheet.

3 Bake in a 375° oven for 10 to 12 minutes or till edges are light brown. Remove cookies and cool on a wire rack. Makes about 48 cookies.

Fruit Oatmeal Rounds: Prepare dough as directed at left, except substitute 1 cup *rolled oats* for 1 cup of flour. Stir 1 teaspoon *ground cinnamon* into flour mixture. Also, stir a 6-ounce package *mixed dried fruit bits* into dough.

Double Chocolate Delights: Prepare dough as directed at left, except substitute ⅓ cup *unsweetened cocoa powder* for ½ cup of the flour. Also, stir one 12-ounce package (2 cups) *semisweet chocolate pieces* into the dough.

Peanut Butter Buddies: Prepare dough as directed at left, except add ½ cup *peanut butter* with eggs and vanilla. Also, stir one 12-ounce package *peanut butter-flavored pieces* into dough.

Chocolate Candy Cookies: Prepare dough as directed at left, except stir 2 cups *candy-coated milk chocolate pieces* into dough.

Malted Milk Treats: Prepare dough as directed at left, except substitute ¼ cup *instant malted milk powder* for ¼ cup of the flour. Also stir 1½ cups chopped *malted milk balls* into the dough.

Macadamia Mania: Prepare dough as directed at left, except stir 2 cups coarsely chopped *white baking bar (or pieces)* and one 3½-ounce jar *macadamia nuts,* coarsely chopped, into the dough.

BEING EXACT

Ever wonder why the number of cookies you finish with is never the amount the recipe says you should have? There's an easy way to get the exact yield from a cookie recipe—as long as you don't sample too much of the dough or eat cookies before you count them.

Pat the dough into a square. Cut the dough square into the number of pieces the recipe should yield. If you want to make 48 cookies, cut the dough into six equal strips one way and eight equal strips the other way. Then shape the resulting pieces into 48 balls and bake them.

Super-Chunk Chippers: Prepare dough as directed at left, except stir 1 cup coarsely chopped *semisweet chocolate,* 1 cup coarsely chopped *milk chocolate,* and 1 cup chopped *pecans* into the dough. Drop dough from ¼-cup measure about 4 inches apart onto an ungreased cookie sheet. Flatten cookies slightly with a spoon. Bake for 13 to 15 minutes or till edges are light brown. Makes 18.

Nutrition facts per Fruit Oatmeal Round: 91 cal., 4 g total fat (1 g sat. fat), 9 mg chol., 42 mg sodium, 12 g carbo., 0 g fiber, 1 g pro. *Daily values:* 3% vit. A, 2% iron.

■ TO MAKE AHEAD ■

Wrap the dough in freezer wrap and freeze for up to 6 months. Before baking, thaw dough overnight in the refrigerator. Bake as directed.

BLACK BEAN LASAGNA

This recipe earned Mary C. Valentine of Santa Rosa, California, $200 in the magazine's monthly contest.

9 lasagna noodles (8 oz.)
2 15-oz. cans black beans, rinsed and drained

♦♦♦

Nonstick spray coating
½ cup chopped onion
½ cup chopped green sweet pepper
2 cloves garlic, minced
2 15-oz. cans low-sodium tomato sauce or tomato sauce with seasonings
¼ cup snipped fresh cilantro

♦♦♦

1 12-oz. container low-fat cottage cheese
1 8-oz. pkg. reduced-fat cream cheese (Neufchâtel), softened
¼ cup light dairy sour cream

♦♦♦

Halved tomato slices (optional)
Fresh cilantro (optional)

1 Cook noodles according to package directions; drain. Mash 1 can of beans; set aside.

2 Spray a large skillet with nonstick coating. Add the onion, sweet pepper, and garlic to skillet. Cook and stir over medium heat till tender but not brown. Add mashed beans, unmashed black beans, tomato sauce, and snipped cilantro; heat through.

3 In a large mixing bowl combine cottage cheese, cream cheese, and sour cream; set aside. Spray a 3-quart rectangular baking dish with nonstick coating. Arrange 3 of the noodles in the dish. Top with one-third of the bean mixture. Spread with one-third of the cheese mixture. Repeat layers twice, ending with bean mixture and reserving the remaining cheese mixture.

4 Bake, covered, in a 350° oven for 40 to 45 minutes or till heated through. Spoon reserved cheese mixture atop. Let stand for 10 minutes. If desired, garnish with tomato and cilantro. Makes 8 main-dish servings.

Nutrition facts per serving: 350 cal., 9 g total fat (5 g sat. fat), 27 mg chol., 589 mg sodium, 50 g carbo., 7 g fiber, 22 g pro. *Daily values:* 22% vit. A, 32% vit. C, 9% calcium, 21% iron.

VEGETABLE-MACARONI CASSEROLE

Try this healthy main dish instead of traditional macaroni and cheese. It's creamy and full of pasta—just the way the kids like it.

¾ cup elbow macaroni
1 10 oz. pkg. frozen mixed vegetables
1 medium zucchini, halved lengthwise and sliced

♦♦♦

1 12 oz. can (1½ cups) evaporated skim milk
½ cup reduced-sodium chicken broth
¼ cup all-purpose flour
½ tsp. dried oregano, crushed
¼ tsp. garlic salt
⅛ tsp. pepper

♦♦♦

Nonstick spray coating
1 medium tomato, sliced
3 Tbsp. grated Parmesan or Romano cheese

1 In a large saucepan cook macaroni according to package directions, except omit salt and add the mixed vegetables and zucchini the last 3 minutes of cooking. Drain. Return pasta mixture to saucepan.

2 Meanwhile, in a medium saucepan stir together the milk, chicken broth, flour, oregano, garlic salt, and pepper. Cook and stir till thickened and bubbly. Add to drained pasta mixture; toss to coat.

3 Spray a 2-quart square baking dish with nonstick coating. Spoon the macaroni mixture into the dish. Bake in a 375° oven for 10 minutes. Top with the sliced tomato and sprinkle with the Parmesan or Romano cheese. Bake about 5 minutes more or till mixture is heated through. Let stand for 5 minutes before serving. Makes 4 main-dish servings.

Nutrition information per serving: 256 cal., 3 g fat (1 g sat. fat), 6 mg chol., 423 mg sodium, 44 g carbo., 1 g fiber, 15 g pro. *Daily values:* 43% vit. A, 18% vit. C, 28% calcium, 15% iron.

PASTA PIZZA

This hybrid recipe combines popular casserole ingredients to create an outstanding dish that looks and tastes like pizza.

5 oz. corkscrew macaroni (rotini)

♦♦♦

1 beaten egg
¼ cup milk
2 Tbsp. grated Parmesan cheese

♦♦♦

8 oz. ground beef
⅓ cup chopped onion
1 clove garlic, minced
1 medium green and/or yellow sweet pepper, cut into 2-inch strips
1 14½-oz. can Italian-style stewed tomatoes
½ tsp. dried Italian seasoning, crushed
1 4½-oz. jar sliced mushrooms, drained
¼ tsp. crushed red pepper

♦♦♦

1 cup shredded mozzarella cheese (4 oz.)

1 Grease a 12-inch pizza pan; set aside. Cook the pasta according to package directions. Drain pasta; rinse with cold water. Drain again.

2 For pasta crust, in a large mixing bowl combine egg, milk, and Parmesan cheese. Stir in pasta. Spread pasta mixture evenly in the prepared pizza pan. Bake in a 350° oven for 20 minutes.

3 Meanwhile, in a large skillet cook ground beef, onion, and garlic over medium heat till meat is brown. Drain fat. Add sweet pepper strips, undrained tomatoes (cut up any large pieces of tomato), and Italian seasoning to meat mixture. Bring to boiling; reduce heat. Simmer, uncovered, for 10 to 12 minutes or till peppers are crisp-tender and most of the liquid is evaporated, stirring once or twice. Stir in mushrooms and crushed red pepper.

4 Spoon meat mixture over pasta crust. Sprinkle with mozzarella cheese. Bake for 10 to 12 minutes more or till heated through and cheese is melted. To serve, cut into wedges. Makes 6 main-dish servings.

Nutrition information per serving: 271 cal., 10 g fat (5 g sat. fat), 72 mg chol., 493 mg sodium, 27 g carbo., 1 g fiber, 18 g pro. *Daily values:* 12% vit. A, 29% vit. C, 16% calcium, 15% iron.

TEST KITCHEN TIP

COOKING WITH CHEESE

♦ Low temperatures and short cooking times are the secrets to successfully cooking with cheese. Also, use a thick-bottomed pan or double boiler to distribute heat more evenly.

♦ To speed up the cooking time when using cheese blends (such as process cheese), cut the cheese into 1-inch cubes, then bring to room temperature before using. For natural cheeses, finely shred to speed melting. A well-chilled cheese will shred more easily.

♦ After adding cheese to a hot mixture, stir the mixture constantly to speed melting.

♦ When adding natural cheese to a hot mixture, remove the pan from the heat. You'll avoid excessive heating, which toughens the cheese.

♦ Do not boil soups and sauces containing cheese. The protein in the cheese coagulates, or hardens and separates from the fat and water. The soup or sauce will end up watery and stringy or grainy.

♦ The more fat and moisture the cheese contains, the easier it will melt and blend with liquid. Therefore, many new lower-fat cheeses may not be suitable for certain dishes, such as soups and sauces.

♦ A sauce made with process cheese has a smooth consistency, but depending on the variety, may be slightly tacky or rubbery. A cheese sauce made with a natural cheese may seem grainier. Combining cheeses by using half process cheese and half natural cheese is a delicious way to get the best of both for a great-tasting dish that will be smooth, too.

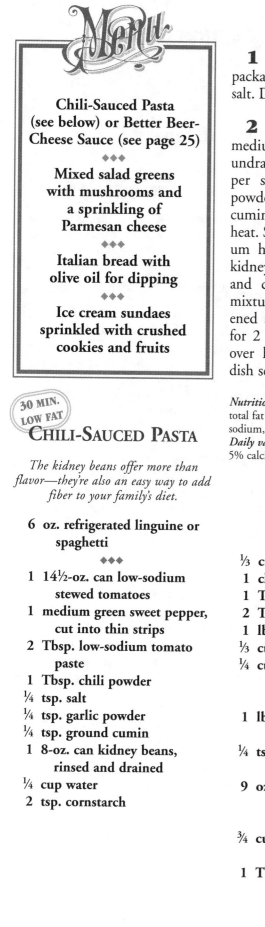

MENU

Chili-Sauced Pasta
(see below) or **Better Beer-
Cheese Sauce** (see page 25)

♦♦♦

**Mixed salad greens
with mushrooms and
a sprinkling of
Parmesan cheese**

♦♦♦

**Italian bread with
olive oil for dipping**

♦♦♦

**Ice cream sundaes
sprinkled with crushed
cookies and fruits**

*30 MIN.
LOW FAT*

CHILI-SAUCED PASTA

*The kidney beans offer more than
flavor—they're also an easy way to add
fiber to your family's diet.*

6 **oz. refrigerated linguine or
    spaghetti**

♦♦♦

1 **14½-oz. can low-sodium
    stewed tomatoes**
1 **medium green sweet pepper,
    cut into thin strips**
2 **Tbsp. low-sodium tomato
    paste**
1 **Tbsp. chili powder**
¼ **tsp. salt**
¼ **tsp. garlic powder**
¼ **tsp. ground cumin**
1 **8-oz. can kidney beans,
    rinsed and drained**
¼ **cup water**
2 **tsp. cornstarch**

1 Cook pasta according to package directions, except omit salt. Drain, cover, and keep warm.

2 Meanwhile, for sauce, in a medium saucepan combine the undrained tomatoes, sweet pepper strips, tomato paste, chili powder, salt, garlic powder, and cumin. Bring to boiling; reduce heat. Simmer, covered, over medium heat for 3 minutes. Stir in kidney beans. Stir together water and cornstarch; add to tomato mixture. Cook and stir till thickened and bubbly. Cook and stir for 2 minutes more. Serve sauce over hot pasta. Makes 3 main-dish servings.

Nutrition facts per serving: 279 cal., 2 g total fat (0 g sat. fat), 0 mg chol., 382 mg sodium, 58 g carbo., 8 g fiber, 12 g pro. *Daily values:* 22% vit. A, 58% vit. C, 5% calcium, 24% iron.

FRESH TOMATO
FETTUCCINE

⅓ **cup chopped onion**
1 **clove garlic, minced**
1 **Tbsp. olive oil**
2 **Tbsp. margarine or butter**
1 **lb. fresh mushrooms, sliced**
⅓ **cup dry white wine**
¼ **cup finely chopped
    prosciutto or fully
    cooked ham**
1 **lb. tomatoes, peeled, seeded,
    and chopped (2 cups)**
¼ **tsp. ground nutmeg**

♦♦♦

9 **oz. refrigerated spinach or
    plain fettuccine, cooked
    and drained**
¾ **cup finely shredded
    Parmesan cheese**
1 **Tbsp. margarine or butter**

SPAGHETTI
ETIQUETTE

Is there a proper way to eat spaghetti? That question has been argued for years. One school of thought says you should catch a few strands of pasta on a fork. Then, with the tines resting against a large spoon, twist the fork to wrap up the pasta. Others say you should spear a few strands on a fork. Then, with the tip of the fork resting against the plate (not a spoon), twirl the fork and pasta. Our advice is simple: Use whatever works best for you.

1 In a skillet cook onion and garlic in hot oil and 2 tablespoons margarine or butter till tender. Add mushrooms. Cook, uncovered, 10 minutes or till tender, stirring often. Stir in wine and prosciutto. Simmer, uncovered, for 10 minutes or till liquid is evaporated, stirring occasionally. Add tomatoes and nutmeg. Simmer for 15 minutes more, stirring occasionally.

2 Toss together cooked pasta, half of the cheese, and 1 tablespoon margarine or butter. Transfer to a platter. Ladle sauce over pasta. Sprinkle the remaining cheese atop. Makes 4 main-dish servings.

Nutrition facts per serving: 485 cal., 22 g total fat (6 g sat. fat), 61 mg chol., 639 mg sodium, 50 g carbo., 2 g fiber, 21 g pro. *Daily values:* 22% vit. A, 51% vit. C, 24% calcium, 25% iron.

BETTER BEER-CHEESE SAUCE

By substituting sharp cheddar cheese for mild, you will use less but still have lots of flavor.

1 cup bias-sliced carrots
1 cup chopped zucchini
1 cup fresh whole mushrooms, quartered

◆◆◆

1 cup skim milk
3 Tbsp. all-purpose flour
¼ cup light beer
¾ cup shredded reduced-fat sharp cheddar cheese (3 oz.)
8 oz. pasta (such as tricolor corkscrew macaroni (rotini) or rope macaroni (gemelli), cooked and drained

1 In a saucepan cook carrots, covered, in a small amount of boiling water for 6 minutes. Add zucchini and mushrooms. Cook, covered, 2 to 3 minutes or just till crisp-tender. Drain; set aside.

2 In a screw-top jar shake together milk and flour; add mixture to saucepan. Cook and stir over medium heat till thickened and bubbly. Add beer to saucepan and heat through. Remove pan from heat and stir in shredded cheddar cheese just till melted. Add cooked vegetables to cheese sauce. If desired, season to taste with *salt* and *pepper*. Serve over hot cooked pasta. Makes 4 main-dish servings.

Nutrition facts per serving: 363 cal., 5 g total fat (3 g sat. fat), 16 mg chol., 207 mg sodium, 59 g carbo., 2 g fiber, 17 g pro. *Daily values:* 92% vit. A, 5% vit. C, 21% calcium, 21% iron.

SPICED AND SAUCY SHELL DINNER

12 jumbo shell macaroni

◆◆◆

12 oz. ground beef, pork, or raw turkey
½ cup chopped onion
1 clove garlic, minced

◆◆◆

1 beaten egg
¼ cup fine dry bread crumbs
¼ tsp. ground cinnamon
¼ tsp. ground allspice
¼ tsp. pepper
1 15½-oz. jar (1⅔ cups) meatless spaghetti sauce

1 Cook jumbo shell macaroni according to package directions. Drain and set aside.

2 In a large skillet cook the ground meat, onion, and garlic over medium heat till the meat is browned and onion is tender. Drain off fat.

3 In mixing bowl combine egg, bread crumbs, cinnamon, allspice, and pepper. Stir in meat mixture and ¼ cup of the sauce; mix well. Stuff each shell with about 2 tablespoons of the meat mixture. Place ¼ cup sauce in each of four 12- to 16-ounce individual casseroles. Place three stuffed shells in each dish. Pour remaining sauce over shells. Wrap in moisture- and vapor-proof wrap. Seal, label, and freeze for up to 2 months.

4 To serve, unwrap. Cover frozen dinner(s) with foil. Bake in a 375° oven about 45 minutes or till heated through. Makes 4 main-dish servings.

THE CLEVER COOK

FREEZING LEFTOVER TOMATO PASTE

Store leftover tomato paste in an easy-to-use form. Spoon it into a freezer storage bag; flatten, remove the air, and freeze. Break off small chunks for sauces, stews, or soups.

Karen Niknami
Colorado Springs, Colorado

MICROWAVE DIRECTIONS

Prepare as directed at left, except combine meat, onion, and garlic in a 1-quart microwave-safe casserole. Micro-cook, covered, with waxed paper, on high for 3 to 5 minutes or till meat is browned, stirring once. Drain and continue as at left. Freeze in individual microwave-safe casseroles.

To reheat, unwrap one or two casseroles. Cover with vented plastic wrap. Micro-cook 1 serving on medium-high for 5 to 7 minutes (10 to 12 minutes for 2 servings) or till heated through, giving dish(es) a half-turn once.

Nutrition facts per serving: 426 cal., 18 g total fat (5 g sat. fat), 107 mg chol., 623 mg sodium, 43 g carbo., 1 g fiber, 24 g pro. *Daily values:* 15% vit. A, 22% vit. C, 5% calcium, 24% iron.

TURKEY-SAUCED PASTA

Buy cooked turkey breast for this tasty pasta main dish.

1½ cups bias-sliced celery
1½ cups bias-sliced carrots
 1 medium onion, cut into thin
   wedges
 1 cup water
 1 tsp. dried basil, crushed
 1 8-oz. carton dairy sour
   cream or plain yogurt
 1 10¾-oz. can condensed
   cream of mushroom soup
2½ cups cubed cooked turkey or
   chicken

♦♦♦

Hot cooked egg noodles or
whole wheat noodles
Grated Parmesan cheese

1 In a large saucepan combine the celery, carrots, onion, water, and basil. Bring to boiling; reduce heat. Simmer, covered, for 5 to 7 minutes or till vegetables are tender. Stir the sour cream or yogurt and soup into vegetable mixture. Add turkey. Cook and stir till heated through. Season to taste with *salt* and *pepper*.

2 To serve, arrange the hot noodles on a serving platter. Spoon the hot turkey mixture over the pasta. Sprinkle with Parmesan cheese. Makes 6 main-dish servings.

Nutrition facts per serving: 395 cal., 19 g total fat (8 g sat. fat), 102 mg chol., 531 mg sodium, 32 g carbo., 4 g fiber, 24 g pro. *Daily values:* 94% vit. A, 7% vit. C, 9% calcium, 21% iron.

SHRIMP AND FENNEL FUSILLI

 6 dried tomatoes
   (not oil-packed)
 6 oz. rippled fine noodles
   (fusilli) or fettuccine

♦♦♦

 1 large fennel bulb, halved
   lengthwise and sliced into
   thin strips
 2 cloves garlic, minced
 1 Tbsp. olive oil or cooking oil
 4 medium plum tomatoes,
   chopped (1½ cups)
 ¼ cup snipped fresh basil or
   1½ tsp. dried basil,
   crushed
 ¼ to ½ tsp. crushed red
   pepper
 1 cup chicken broth
 ¼ cup tomato paste
12 oz. medium shrimp, peeled,
   deveined, and halved
   lengthwise

1 Pour boiling water over dried tomatoes to cover; let stand 2 minutes. Drain; finely chop tomatoes. Cook pasta according to package directions; drain. Meanwhile, cook and stir fennel and garlic in hot oil 5 minutes or till crisp-tender. Add plum tomatoes, dried basil (if using), red pepper, and rehydrated tomatoes. Cook and stir 1 minute more. Stir in broth and tomato paste; bring to boiling. Add shrimp; cook 2 to 3 minutes or till shrimp are opaque. Stir in fresh basil, if using. Toss with pasta. Makes 4 main-dish servings.

Nutrition facts per serving: 314 cal., 6 g total fat (1 g sat. fat), 98 mg chol., 438 mg sodium, 47 g carbo., 2 g fiber, 20 g pro. *Daily values:* 14% vit. A, 50% vit. C, 5% calcium, 28% iron.

CHICKEN MARINARA WITH MUSHROOMS

This recipe earned Kim Harris of Columbus, Ohio, $100 in the magazine's monthly contest.

12 oz. linguine or spaghetti

♦♦♦

 4 cloves garlic, minced
 2 Tbsp. lower-fat margarine
 1 lb. skinless, boneless
   chicken breast halves, cut
   into thin bite-size strips
 ½ tsp. dried chervil, crushed
 ½ tsp. dried basil, crushed
 ¼ tsp. dried thyme, crushed
 6 oz. fresh mushrooms, sliced
 1 27½-oz. jar light spaghetti
   sauce
 ½ cup dry white wine
 2 tsp. sugar (optional)

1 Cook pasta according to package directions; drain.

2 Meanwhile, in a large skillet cook garlic in hot margarine for 30 seconds. Add half of the chicken, chervil, basil, and thyme. Cook and stir 3 to 4 minutes or till chicken is no longer pink. Remove chicken, reserving drippings in skillet. Repeat with remaining chicken and herbs. Add mushrooms to drippings in skillet. Cook and stir about 3 minutes or till tender. Add sauce, wine, and, if desired, sugar. Return chicken to skillet; heat through. Serve over hot pasta. Makes 6 main-dish servings.

Nutrition facts per serving: 426 cal., 7 g fat (1 g sat. fat), 40 mg chol., 128 mg sodium, 64 g carbo., 4 g fiber, 25 g pro. *Daily values:* 14% vit. A, 23% vit. C, 26% iron.

FEBRUARY
Comforts from the Kitchen

30-minute recipes indicated in RED.
Low-fat recipes indicated with a ♥.

Soups, stews, and casseroles star in many cuisines, and it's possible to take a global cook's tour without leaving your kitchen. An Italian osso buco, a country French garlic chicken, a Greek pastitsio, and a quick version of Russian borscht add zest to long winter days. Fuel yourself with hearty meat dishes—Pork Roast Cubano, Moroccan Lamb and Fruit Stew, and Bavarian Beef. Cabbage and root vegetables lend themselves to savory accompaniments. Peanut Butter Fudge or Marbled Biscotti is a sweet indulgence on a brisk February day, along with a steaming mug of Mocha Java.

FRENCH FARMHOUSE GARLIC CHICKEN

The classic version of this recipe requires stuffing and roasting a whole chicken. To speed dinner to the table, we've substituted chicken breasts cooked atop the stove.
(See the photograph on page 38.)

4 small skinless, boneless
  chicken breast halves
  (about 12 oz. total)
¼ tsp. salt
¼ tsp. pepper
1 Tbsp. cooking oil
40 small cloves unpeeled garlic*
  ◆◆◆
½ cup dry white wine or
  chicken broth
½ cup chicken broth
1 Tbsp. lemon juice
1 tsp. dried basil, crushed
½ tsp. dried oregano, crushed
  ◆◆◆
4 tsp. all-purpose flour
2 Tbsp. dry white wine or
  chicken broth
  Hot mashed potatoes or
  cooked rice
  Cooked zucchini, sliced
  (optional)

1 Rinse chicken; pat dry. Season with the salt and pepper. In a 10-inch skillet heat oil over medium-high heat. Add chicken and garlic cloves. Cook chicken for 2 to 3 minutes on each side or just till brown, turning once. Slowly add ½ cup white wine or broth, ½ cup broth, lemon juice, basil, and oregano. Simmer, covered, for 6 to 8 minutes or till chicken is tender and no longer pink. Use a slotted spoon to transfer the chicken and garlic to a warm serving platter; keep warm.

THE GLORY OF GARLIC

Forty cloves of garlic in a recipe may read like a misprint, even to those who believe the old tales that garlic repelled evil spirits and kept vampires at bay. But cooking the cloves makes them far more sweet and tender than raw ones, so a large number doesn't overwhelm foods.

Choose firm, plump heads with no soft, dark spots. Store them whole in a cool, dark, dry place. Garlic can also be purchased minced and bottled as a fresh paste, minced and dried, and as garlic juice and garlic powder. For one fresh clove you may substitute ⅛ teaspoon dried minced garlic or garlic powder, or ½ teaspoon bottled minced garlic. The flavor of the dried products is sharper and less sweet.

2 In a small bowl stir together flour and the 2 tablespoons dry white wine or broth. Stir into pan juices. Bring to boiling. Cook and stir for 1 minute more. Spoon sauce atop chicken. Serve with potatoes or rice and, if desired, zucchini. Makes 4 servings.

Note: Halve any large garlic cloves. If time allows, peel the garlic before cooking; otherwise, as you eat the cooked cloves, simply slip the skins off them with the tip of your dinner knife.

Nutrition facts per serving: 327 cal., 7 g total fat (2 g sat. fat), 48 mg chol., 755 mg sodium, 40 g carbo., 2 g fiber, 22 g pro. *Daily values:* 1% vit. A, 36% vit. C, 9% calcium, 12% iron.

COLD-WEATHER OSSO BUCO

This stew has been a mainstay of hungry, thrifty folks for ages. Ours revisits the family favorite with squash and Brussels sprouts. (See the photograph on pages 38–39.)

2 Tbsp. olive oil
4 veal shank crosscuts (2 lb.)
  or 1½ lb. boneless beef
  short ribs
¼ tsp. pepper
  ◆◆◆
1 large onion, chopped
3 cloves garlic, minced
1 10¾-oz. can condensed
  chicken broth
8 whole tiny new potatoes,
  halved
  ◆◆◆
1½ cups cubed, peeled
  butternut squash
  (1- to 1½-inch cubes)
  (about 1 lb. unpeeled)
1 10-oz. pkg. frozen Brussels
  sprouts*
1 Tbsp. prepared horseradish
2 Tbsp. cornstarch
2 Tbsp. cold water
  Snipped fresh parsley
  (optional)

1 In a 10-inch skillet heat oil over medium-high heat. Brown the veal shanks or beef ribs, half at a time, in hot oil. Transfer meat to a 3½- to 4-quart crockery cooker, reserving drippings in the skillet. Sprinkle meat with pepper.

2 Add the onion and garlic to the skillet. Add more oil if necessary. Reduce heat to medium; cook till onion is tender, stirring occasionally. Carefully add chicken broth, scraping bottom of the pan to loosen any browned bits.

3 Transfer the onion mixture with juices to the crockery cooker. Add potatoes. Cover and cook on the low-heat setting for 8 to 9 hours or on high-heat setting for 4 to 4½ hours, or till meat is nearly tender.

4 Add the squash, Brussels sprouts, and horseradish to cooker, rearranging so vegetables are in cooking liquid. Stir together cornstarch and water. Stir cornstarch mixture into the mixture in slow cooker. Increase the heat to high. Cook, covered, for 45 to 60 minutes more or till vegetables are just tender. Transfer meat and vegetables to a serving platter. If desired, sprinkle with parsley. Makes 4 servings.

*Note: If necessary, run the Brussels sprouts under water to separate them.

Nutrition facts per serving: 474 cal., 14 g total fat (4 g sat. fat), 139 mg chol., 626 mg sodium, 42 g carbo., 7 g fiber, 46 g pro. *Daily values:* 72% vit. A, 125% vit. C, 8% calcium, 29% iron.

30 MIN. LOW FAT

BORSCHT FOR BUSY PEOPLE

This chill-banishing soup took grandmothers in Russia hours to prepare. Ours is ready almost as fast as you can set the table, thanks to canned broth, veggies, and coleslaw mix.

6 cups packaged shredded cabbage with carrot (coleslaw mix)
1 cup vegetable or beef broth
1 15-oz. can great Northern beans, rinsed and drained
1 14½-oz. can tomatoes, cut up

1 14½-oz. can sliced beets
1 8-oz. can tomato sauce
1 large onion, sliced and separated into rings
¼ cup sugar
2 Tbsp. vinegar
¼ tsp. dillweed (optional)
¼ tsp. pepper

◆◆◆

6 Tbsp. light dairy sour cream (optional)
6 sprigs fresh dill (optional)

1 In a large pot stir together the cabbage with carrot, broth, beans, undrained tomatoes, undrained beets, tomato sauce, onion, sugar, vinegar, dillweed (if desired), and pepper. Bring to boiling; reduce heat. Simmer, covered, for 20 minutes.

2 To serve, ladle into soup bowls. If desired, garnish with sour cream and dill. Serves 6.

Nutrition facts per serving: 195 cal., 2 g total fat (1 g sat. fat), 2 mg chol., 758 mg sodium, 41 g carbo., 6 g fiber, 9 g pro. *Daily values:* 36% vit. A, 95% vit. C, 11% calcium, 19% iron.

30 MIN. LOW FAT

SALMON IN GOOD COMPANY

Japanese buckwheat (soba) noodles, found with the Asian foods in supermarkets, add a subtle earthy flavor. Substitute whole wheat noodles if you wish.

1¼ lb. fresh or frozen skinless salmon fillet, about 1 inch thick
¼ cup olive oil
¼ cup balsamic vinegar
1 Tbsp. cracked black pepper

◆◆◆

½ lb. buckwheat (soba) noodles or whole wheat noodles
⅓ cup orange juice
2 oranges, peeled, sectioned, and chopped
1 clove garlic, minced
¼ cup chopped red onion and/or sliced green onion
2 tsp. anise seed, crushed Fresh fennel tops (optional)

1 Thaw salmon, if frozen. In a 2-quart baking dish combine 1 tablespoon of the olive oil, 1 tablespoon of the balsamic vinegar, and the cracked pepper. Place fish in the mixture, turning to coat both sides. Marinate at room temperature for 10 minutes.

2 Place salmon on the unheated rack of a broiler pan. Broil 4 inches from the heat for 4 to 6 minutes per ½-inch thickness of fish or just till fish flakes easily when tested with a fork. Turn fish after half of the broiling time.

3 Meanwhile, in a large saucepan cook buckwheat noodles in boiling water 4 minutes or whole wheat noodles 8 to 10 minutes, or till just slightly chewy. Drain; place in a large bowl. Add remaining oil, vinegar, orange juice and sections, garlic, onion, and anise seed; toss to coat.

4 To serve, divide the noodle mixture among 4 dinner plates. Top each serving with a piece of salmon. If desired, garnish with a fresh fennel top. Serves 4.

Nutrition facts per serving: 372 cal., 6 g total fat (1 g sat. fat), 25 mg chol., 538 mg sodium, 55 g carbo., 2 g fiber, 29 g pro. *Daily values:* 3% vit. A, 51% vit. C, 5% calcium, 25% iron.

RAVIOLI LASAGNA

Lasagna in a skillet? Can do, thanks to our trick with ravioli. Fair warning: Once kids taste this lasagna, they'll clamor for it often. (See the photograph on page 38.)

2 cups light chunky-style spaghetti sauce

⅓ cup water

1 9-oz. pkg. refrigerated meat-or cheese-filled ravioli

♦♦♦

1 beaten egg

1 5-oz. carton fat-free ricotta cheese

¼ cup grated Romano or Parmesan cheese

1 10-oz. pkg. frozen chopped spinach, thawed and drained

1 In a 10-inch skillet combine spaghetti sauce and water; bring to boiling. Stir in the ravioli. Cover; cook mixture over medium heat about 5 minutes or till ravioli are nearly tender, stirring mixture once to prevent sticking.

2 In a medium mixing bowl combine the egg, ricotta cheese, and Romano or Parmesan cheese with a fork. Dot ravioli with spinach. Spoon ricotta mixture atop. Cook, covered, over low heat about 10 minutes more or till ricotta layer is set and pasta is just tender. Makes 4 servings.

Nutrition facts per serving: 433 cal., 14 g total fat (3 g sat. fat), 131 mg chol., 501 mg sodium, 49 g carbo., 3 g fiber, 36 g pro. *Daily values:* 74% vit. A, 30% vit. C, 39% calcium, 22% iron.

PORK ROAST CUBANO

Stir together a carton of guacamole with a bit of fresh diced pineapple—a Cuban preference—to serve with this marinated pork.

1 3-lb. boneless pork shoulder roast, rolled and tied

♦♦♦

⅓ cup frozen orange juice concentrate, thawed

2 tsp. finely shredded lime peel

⅓ cup lime juice

2 Tbsp. cooking oil

4 cloves garlic, minced

1 Tbsp. dried oregano, crushed

PARMESAN: THE GRATE ONE

Any way it's shredded, shaved, grated, cut, or crumbled, true Parmesan cheese arouses the Italian in pastas, pizzas, breads, and soups. The genuine Parmesan cheese, called Parmigiano-Reggiano (Pahr-muh-ZHAH-nah Rej-JYAH-noh) in Italian, may cost more than other grated cheeses, but the extra pennies are worth a bundle in flavor. Why is it so special? Only one region in northeast Italy has the right combination of ingredients—the cows, the grass, and the precise cheesemaking techniques—to produce this cheese. Hard cheeses made elsewhere may grate like the original, but they cannot be labeled Parmigiano-Reggiano, although they may be called Parmesan.

BUYING AND STORING

You'll know a cheese is genuine Parmigiano-Reggiano if it carries the oval seal of the Parma-Reggio region. The words Parmigiano-Reggiano and the month and year the cheese was made should be stamped on the rind. Parmesan peaks at two years, so think twice about buying cheese aged longer. The age affects the color, which may vary from pale cream to straw yellow. The color within a wedge should be uniform. The surface should be smooth and dry, not oily.

Keeping Parmesan on hand makes sense because it stores so well. Tightly sealed in plastic wrap and kept in a cool, dry place, Parmesan will stay fresh for up to four weeks. You can freeze small amounts, but the texture and flavor will change. Thaw it in the refrigerator before using.

SHAVING, SHREDDING, OR GRATING

Shave, shred, or grate Parmesan shortly before serving and use it as a topper for pasta, risotto, casseroles, vegetable or bean soups, salads, and cooked vegetables. Or, sprinkle a little Parmesan onto polenta or sliced bread and broil for a minute or two. When you pop a few shavings of Parmesan into your mouth, expect a slightly tangy, nutty taste. Parmigiano-Reggiano should not be salty, sharp, bitter, or excessively tart.

1 Unroll roast; butterfly it by making a lengthwise cut almost through the roast, then spreading it out to lie flat. Pierce meat on all sides with the tines of a fork. For marinade, combine juice concentrate, lime peel and juice, oil, garlic, oregano, 1 teaspoon *pepper,* and ¼ teaspoon *salt.*

2 Place meat in a plastic bag in a shallow dish. Pour marinade over meat, turning to coat all sides. Seal bag; chill 4 hours or overnight, turning once.

3 Remove meat from bag, reserving marinade. Reroll and tie roast; place on a rack in a roasting pan. Insert a meat thermometer. Roast, uncovered, in 325° oven 2¾ to 3½ hours or till the thermometer registers 165°, basting frequently with reserved marinade during first 2 hours of cooking. Remove from oven. Let the roast stand for 10 minutes before slicing. Makes 10 servings.

Nutrition facts per serving: 270 cal., 17 g total fat (5 g sat. fat), 89 mg chol., 125 mg sodium, 5 g carbo., 0 g fiber, 24 g pro. *Daily values:* 30% vit. C, 1% calcium, 10% iron.

BLACK AND WHITES

Serve this lively meld of beans and rice with Pork Roast Cubano, page 30.

½ **cup chopped onion**
½ **cup chopped green sweet pepper**
2 **cloves garlic, minced**
2 **tsp. ground cumin**
1 **tsp. chili powder**
1 **Tbsp. cooking oil**
1 **cup rice**

♦♦♦

2 **15-oz. cans black beans, rinsed and drained**
Chopped tomato
Sliced green onion

1 In a saucepan cook onion, sweet green pepper, garlic, cumin, chili powder, and ½ teaspoon *salt* in hot oil 2 minutes. Slowly add 2½ cups *water;* bring to boiling. Stir in rice. Transfer to a 2-quart casserole. Bake, covered, in a 325° oven 30 minutes. Pour beans over rice. Do not stir. Return to oven. Bake, covered, 5 to 10 minutes or till rice is tender and liquid is absorbed. Stir in beans. Garnish with tomato and green onion. Makes 10 side-dish servings.

Nutrition facts per serving: 143 cal., 2 g total fat (0 g sat. fat), 0 mg chol., 323 mg sodium, 28 g carbo., 4 g fiber, 7 g pro. *Daily values:* 1% vit. A, 7% vit. C, 3% calcium, 15% iron.

SPICE MARKET PASTITSIO

Some call this dish (pronounced pah-STEET-see-o) "the Greek lasagna." Kasseri, a firm Greek cheese, lends a pungent, nutty taste; if unavailable, Parmesan can fill its role.

8 **oz. corkscrew macaroni**
8 **oz. ground lamb or lean ground beef**
1 **14-oz. jar spaghetti sauce with onion and garlic**
1 **tsp. ground cinnamon**
¼ **tsp. fennel seed, crushed**

♦♦♦

1 **1.8-oz. envelope white sauce mix**
1 **cup milk**
2 **slightly beaten eggs**
¼ **cup crumbled feta cheese**
½ **tsp. ground nutmeg**

♦♦♦

¼ **cup grated kasseri or Parmesan cheese**
Greek or ripe olives (optional)
Fresh marjoram (optional)

1 Lightly grease a 2-quart-square baking dish; set aside. Cook pasta according to package directions; drain well. In a medium skillet cook meat till no longer pink. Drain off fat. In a mixing bowl combine cooked meat, spaghetti sauce, cinnamon, and fennel seed; set aside.

2 In a medium saucepan combine white sauce mix and milk. Cook and stir till thickened and bubbly. Remove from heat. Gradually stir half of the sauce into eggs; return all to saucepan. Stir in feta cheese and nutmeg.

3 To assemble, layer half of the pasta in prepared baking dish. Spread meat mixture over pasta; top with remaining pasta. Evenly spread the white sauce mixture atop. Sprinkle with kasseri cheese. Bake, uncovered, in a 350° oven about 35 minutes or till set. Let stand 10 minutes. If desired, garnish with olives and fresh marjoram. Makes 6 servings.

TO MAKE AHEAD

Assemble casserole as at left, except do not bake. Seal, label, and freeze for up to 2 months. To serve, unwrap the baking dish. Bake, covered, in a 350° oven for 1½ to 1¾ hours or till casserole is heated through.

Nutrition facts per serving: 417 cal., 16 g total fat (6 g sat. fat), 112 mg chol., 848 mg sodium, 46 g carbo., 0 g fiber, 20 g pro. *Daily values:* 20% vit. A, 5% vit. C, 21% calcium, 20% iron.

BAVARIAN BEEF

1 2½- to 3-lb. boneless beef
  chuck pot roast
1 Tbsp. cooking oil
♦♦♦
2 cups sliced carrots
2 cups chopped onions
1 cup sliced celery
¾ cup chopped kosher-style
  dill pickles
½ cup dry red wine or
  beef broth
⅓ cup German-style mustard
½ tsp. coarse ground black
  pepper
¼ tsp. ground cloves
2 bay leaves
♦♦♦
2 Tbsp. all-purpose flour
2 Tbsp. dry red wine or
  beef broth
  Hot cooked spaetzle or
  cooked noodles
  Chopped kosher-style dill
  pickle (optional)
  Crumbled cooked bacon
  (optional)

1 Trim fat from roast. If necessary, cut roast to fit into a 3½-
or 4-quart crockery cooker;
reserve trimmings for another
use. In a large skillet brown the
roast slowly on all sides in hot oil.

2 Meanwhile, in the crockery
cooker place the carrots, onions,
celery, and ¾ cup pickles. Place
the meat atop the vegetables. In a
small bowl combine the red wine
or beef broth, mustard, pepper,
cloves, and bay leaves. Pour over
meat. Cover and cook on the low-
heat setting for 8 to 10 hours or
on the high-heat setting for 4 to
5 hours. Remove the meat from
the cooker and place on a serving
platter; keep warm.

3 For gravy, transfer vegetables and cooking liquid to a 2-
quart saucepan. Skim off fat.
Remove bay leaves. Stir together
flour and the 2 tablespoons wine
or beef broth. Stir into the mixture in saucepan. Cook and stir
over medium heat till thickened
and bubbly. Cook and stir for
1 minute more. Serve meat and
vegetables with gravy and hot
cooked spaetzle or noodles. If
desired, top with additional
chopped pickle and bacon. Makes
8 servings.

Nutrition facts per serving: 454 cal., 15 g
total fat (5 g sat. fat), 158 mg chol., 548 mg
sodium, 35 g carbo., 4 g fiber, 41 g pro.
Daily values: 89% vit. A, 7% vit. C,
7% calcium, 42% iron.

MOROCCAN LAMB AND FRUIT STEW

1 to 2 tsp. crushed red pepper
¾ tsp. ground turmeric
¾ tsp. ground ginger
¾ tsp. ground cinnamon
½ tsp. salt
2 lb. boneless leg of lamb or
  beef bottom round roast,
  well trimmed and cut into
  1- to 1½-inch pieces
2 Tbsp. olive oil or
  cooking oil
2 large onions, chopped
3 cloves garlic, minced
1 14½-oz. can beef broth
♦♦♦
1 Tbsp. cornstarch
2 Tbsp. cold water
1 cup pitted dates
1 cup dried apricots
♦♦♦
  Hot cooked couscous or rice
¼ cup slivered almonds,
  toasted

1 In a shallow mixing bowl
combine crushed red pepper,
turmeric, ginger, cinnamon, and
salt. Coat meat with seasoning
mixture. In a large skillet heat oil
over medium-high heat. Brown
meat, a third at a time, in the hot
oil. Transfer meat to a 3½- to
4-quart crockery cooker. Add

onions and garlic; stir to combine. Pour beef broth over all. Cover and cook on low-heat setting for 7 to 9 hours or on high-heat setting for 3½ to 4½ hours or till meat is tender.

2 Skim fat from the surface of the juices in the crockery cooker. Stir cornstarch into water; stir into crockery cooker. Add dates and apricots; stir to combine. If using low-heat setting, turn to high-heat setting. Cover and cook 30 minutes more or till mixture is slightly thickened and bubbly.

3 To serve, spoon stew atop hot couscous or rice. Top with almonds. Makes 6 to 8 servings.

Nutrition facts per serving: 550 cal., 14 g total fat (3 g sat. fat), 76 mg chol., 475 mg sodium, 75 g carbo., 12 g fiber, 34 g pro. *Daily values:* 18% vit. A, 7% vit. C, 6% calcium, 29% iron.

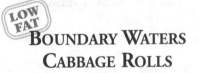

Boundary Waters Cabbage Rolls

Wild rice, turkey, cranberries, and a can of mushroom soup join our Midwestern translation of this treasured old-world classic. (See the photograph on page 42.)

1 4½-oz. pkg. long grain and wild rice mix
½ cup finely chopped onion
8 oz. ground raw turkey
⅓ cup dried cranberries or raisins, coarsely chopped
8 large green cabbage leaves

◆◆◆

1 10¾-oz. can golden mushroom soup or one 12-oz. jar turkey gravy
⅓ cup plain low-fat yogurt

1 In a medium saucepan cook rice mix according to package directions, adding the onion with the rice. Cool completely; transfer to a large bowl. Mix in turkey and cranberries or raisins. Trim the heavy center vein from each cabbage leaf. In a large amount of boiling water cook cabbage leaves, uncovered, 3 to 5 minutes or till just tender. Drain well; set aside.

2 Place about ½ cup of the filling in the center of a cabbage leaf. Fold over both sides and roll up; secure with a wooden toothpick, if necessary. Repeat with remaining leaves and filling. If desired, place rolls in an airtight container; chill up to 24 hours.

3 To serve, in a 12-inch skillet combine the soup or gravy and yogurt. Arrange cabbage rolls, seam side down, in sauce. Bring to boiling; reduce heat. Cook, covered, over low heat 20 to 25 minutes or till no pink remains in filling. Spoon the sauce onto serving plates. Set rolls atop. Makes 8 rolls or 4 servings.

Nutrition facts per serving: 305 cal., 7 g total fat (2 g sat. fat), 23 mg chol., 1,208 mg sodium, 48 g carbo., 5 g fiber, 15 g pro. *Daily values:* 11% vit. A, 48% vit. C, 7% calcium, 16% iron.

Root Cellar Bouillabaisse

8 frozen, cleaned baby clams and/or frozen mussels in shells
4 oz. fresh or frozen peeled and deveined shrimp with tails

12 oz. fresh or frozen firm white-fleshed fish, such as cod, haddock, or grouper

◆◆◆

2 medium onions, sliced and separated into rings
1 tsp. bottled minced garlic
2 Tbsp. olive oil
2 cups chicken broth or clam juice
1 cup dry white wine or chicken broth
1 14½-oz. can stewed tomatoes, cut up
1 tsp. finely shredded orange peel
1 tsp. dried thyme, crushed
1 tsp. fennel seed
⅛ tsp. ground saffron
1 7-oz. can sweet potatoes, drained and cut up

◆◆◆

6 slices French bread, toasted (optional)

1 Thaw seafood, if frozen. Cut fish into 1½-inch pieces. In a large saucepan cook the onions and garlic in hot oil 3 minutes or till just tender, stirring frequently. Add the broth, wine, undrained tomatoes, orange peel, thyme, fennel, saffron, ½ teaspoon *salt*, and ½ teaspoon *pepper*. Bring to boiling; add seafood and fish. Return to boiling; reduce heat. Simmer, covered, for 3 to 5 minutes. Add sweet potatoes; heat through, stirring gently.

2 To serve, remove and discard clams or mussels that have not opened. If desired, ladle soup into bowls atop bread. Serves 6.

Nutrition facts per serving: 334 cal., 7 g total fat (1 g sat. fat), 61 mg chol., 889 mg sodium, 40 g carbo., 3 g fiber, 22 g pro. *Daily values:* 72 % vit. A, 62% vit. C, 8% calcium, 48% iron.

The Cheeses of Mexico

Mexican food is hot, and we're not just talking jalapeños. Aficionados of authentic south-of-the-border flavor long for true Mexican cheeses to create the dream dishes they've read about or tasted on the road. The good news is that a growing number of American-made Mexican cheese is available in supermarkets this side of the customs booth. So save the Parmesan for pasta and say "queso."

Fresh Cheeses

The most popular varieties of Mexican cheeses are fresh cheeses, prized by cook and diner alike because they refuse to melt. When you stuff a chile relleno or an enchilada, the cheese minds its manners and doesn't ooze across your plate. The cheeses are quite similar to each other in appearance, though, so here's help in choosing the variety that will suit your needs.

Queso blanco (pronounced KAY-so BLONK-o), a mild, salty-sweet, slightly nutty cheese as white as its name suggests, has a somewhat rubbery texture. Try this versatile performer in any dish where cheese must retain its shape and character; use it in breads and desserts, too.

Queso fresco (KAY-so FRESK-o), or "fresh cheese," is delicious crumbled over salads and refried beans, nibbled as a snack, or layered into lasagna. Brands vary in texture from smooth to grainy and in flavor from mild to salty; some resemble ricotta, others feta.

Queso para freir (KAY-so PAR-ah fray-EER), a saltier cousin, has a creamy texture similar to ricotta. This cheese is ideal for cutting into fingers and breading for frying—the Latin American version of mozzarella sticks. Serve them straight from the skillet as an appetizer or dust the fried fingers with powdered sugar and serve them as dessert, the way they're enjoyed in Mexico.

Melting Cheeses

Imagine a quesadilla, the Mexican grilled cheese sandwich, pocked with unyielding lumps—not a pleasant thought. To avoid this fiasco, Mexican cheeses such as *queso quesadilla* (KAY-so kay-sa-DEE-yah), the slightly tinted, smooth and buttery *chihuahua* (chee-WHA-wha), and the smooth, pale *asadero* (ah-sah-DAY-ro), are prime candidates for melting evenly.

They all perform like cheeses born to melt, without separating into gummy hunks and pools of oil. With flavors similar to Muenster or Monterey Jack, these are the numero uno choices for nachos—they stay put on top of the chips. And they're just as well-behaved in quesadillas. Try them, too, in enchiladas and baked chiles rellenos.

Hard Cheeses

Cheeses such as the strong-tasting *cotija* (ko-TEE-yah), the Parmesan of Mexico with its dry and crumbly texture, and *anejo enchilado* (ah-NAY-ho en-cheel-AH-doh), a similarly pungent cheese, are excellent grated to enhance the flavor of many a Mexican dish. Use these assertive cheeses in chilaquiles (chee-lah-KEY-lehs), a casserole of tortillas, cheese, and salsa verde; sprinkled on tacos, soups, or pizzas; or to top a cheeseburger.

Monterey Tortilla Casseroles

In Mexico, this dish is served for breakfast; stateside families enjoy it most often as a quick and tasty dinner. (See the photograph on page 39.)

Nonstick spray coating
6 6-inch corn tortillas, each cut into 6 wedges

◆◆◆

2 cups cubed cooked chicken
1 cup loose-pack frozen whole kernel corn
1 16-oz. jar salsa verde
3 Tbsp. light dairy sour cream
3 Tbsp. snipped fresh cilantro
1 Tbsp. all-purpose flour
1 cup crumbled Mexican chihuahua or farmer cheese (4 oz.)
   Light dairy sour cream (optional)
   Jalapeño pepper, thinly sliced (optional)
   Snipped fresh cilantro (optional)
   Chopped tomato (optional)

1 Spray four 10- to 12-ounce baking dishes with nonstick spray. Place 5 tortilla wedges in bottom of each dish. Place remaining pieces on a baking sheet; bake in a 350° oven 10 minutes or till crisp.

2 Meanwhile, combine chicken, corn, salsa verde, the 3 tablespoons sour cream, cilantro, and flour. Divide mixture among dishes. Bake, uncovered, in a 350° oven 20 minutes. Arrange baked tortilla pieces atop casseroles. Top with cheese; bake for 5 to 10 minutes more or till heated through. If desired, garnish with additional sour cream, jalapeño slices, cilantro, and tomato. Serves 4.

Assemble casseroles as directed on page 34 except do not top with baked tortilla pieces. Place baked pieces in a moisture- and vapor-proof plastic bag. Freeze casseroles and pieces up to 2 months.

To serve, bake, covered, in a 350° oven 25 minutes. Uncover; bake 20 minutes more or till heated through. Top with tortilla pieces and cheese; bake 5 to 10 minutes or till cheese melts.

Nutrition facts per serving: 479 cal., 21 g total fat (3 g sat. fat), 98 mg chol., 1,247 mg sodium, 45 g carbo., 7 g fiber, 34 g pro. *Daily values:* 22% vit. A, 73% vit. C, 27% calcium, 11% iron.

BLACK BEAN AND SAUSAGE POSOLE

This recipe earned Millie Hawkins of Colorado Springs, Colorado, $200 in the magazine's monthly contest. (See the photograph on page 43.)

1 12-oz. pkg. light ground turkey-and-pork sausage
2 14½-oz. cans reduced-sodium chicken broth
1 15-oz. can black beans, rinsed and drained
1 14½-oz. can golden hominy, rinsed and drained
1 14½-oz. can Mexican-style stewed tomatoes
1 cup frozen loose-pack diced hash brown potatoes
½ cup chopped green sweet pepper
⅓ cup chopped onion
1 clove garlic, minced
1 tsp. dried oregano, crushed
½ tsp. chili powder

1 In a large saucepan brown the sausage; drain fat. Add the remaining ingredients; bring to boiling. Reduce heat; simmer, covered, for 30 minutes. Makes 6 main-dish servings.

Nutrition facts per serving: 292 cal., 14 g total fat (1 g sat. fat), 45 mg chol., 1,295 mg sodium, 26 g carbo., 4 g fiber, 17 g pro. *Daily values:* 7% vit. A, 30% vit. C, 3% calcium, 15% iron.

LOW FAT

SWEET POTATO AND ROSEMARY SOUP

⅓ cup finely chopped onion
1 clove garlic, minced
1 Tbsp. olive oil
4 cups peeled and finely chopped sweet potatoes
⅔ cup finely chopped carrots
½ cup finely chopped celery
1 tsp. snipped fresh rosemary or ¼ tsp. dried rosemary, crushed
½ tsp. snipped fresh thyme or ⅛ tsp. dried thyme, crushed
4 cups chicken or vegetable broth

♦♦♦

Dairy sour cream (optional)

1 In a saucepan cook onion and garlic in oil till tender. Add potatoes, carrots, celery, rosemary, and thyme. Cook and stir 5 minutes. Add broth. Bring to boiling; reduce heat. Simmer, covered, for 30 minutes. Cool slightly.

2 Place a third of the vegetable mixture in a blender container. Cover and blend till smooth. Repeat with the remaining mixture. Return all soup to saucepan; heat through.

3 To serve, ladle into bowls. If desired, spoon sour cream atop each serving. Makes 6 to 8 side-dish servings.

Nutrition facts per serving: 137 cal., 3 g total fat (1 g sat. fat), 1 mg chol., 550 mg sodium, 22 g carbo., 4 g fiber, 5 g pro. *Daily values:* 217% vit. A, 32% vit. C, 3% calcium, 6% iron.

EASY SAUSAGE-CORN CHOWDER

8 oz. bulk sweet Italian sausage or bulk pork sausage
2½ cups milk
2 cups frozen loose-pack diced hash brown potatoes
1 15-oz. can cream-style corn
¾ tsp. dried thyme, crushed
¼ tsp. garlic powder
¼ tsp. pepper
2 Tbsp. snipped fresh parsley
¼ cup shredded cheddar cheese (1 oz.) (optional)

1 In a large saucepan cook sausage till browned. Drain sausage; pat dry to remove excess fat. Wipe pan dry. Return sausage to pan. Stir in milk, potatoes, corn, thyme, garlic powder and pepper. Bring to boiling; reduce heat. Simmer, covered, about 20 minutes or till potatoes are tender.

2 To serve, ladle soup into bowls. Sprinkle with parsley and, if desired, cheddar cheese. Makes 4 main-dish servings.

Nutrition facts per serving: 374 cal., 15 g total fat (6 g sat. fat), 44 mg chol., 786 mg sodium, 46 g carbo., 3 g fiber, 18 g pro. *Daily values:* 11% vit. A, 30% vit. C, 17% calcium, 16% iron.

CREAMY CARROT SOUP WITH PESTO

Elizabeth B. Gallucci of Poughquag, New York, earned $100 in the magazine's monthly contest for this recipe. (See the photograph on page 37.)

½ **cup chopped onion**
1 **Tbsp. margarine or butter**
1 **cup sliced carrots**
¼ **tsp. dried thyme, crushed**
1 **clove garlic, crushed**
3 **cups chicken broth**
1 **cup cubed, peeled potatoes**
1 **small bay leaf**

♦♦♦

2 **Tbsp. buttermilk**
2 **Tbsp. pesto**

1 In a large saucepan cook the onion in hot margarine 1 minute. Add carrots, thyme, and garlic; cook 10 minutes or till tender. Carefully add broth, potatoes, and bay leaf. Bring to boiling; reduce heat. Simmer, covered, about 20 minutes or till vegetables are tender. Remove bay leaf.

2 Transfer about half of the mixture to a blender container or food processor bowl. Cover and blend or process till smooth. Repeat with remaining soup. Return all soup to saucepan; add buttermilk and heat through. To serve, ladle into soup bowls. Top each serving with pesto; swirl to mix. Makes 4 side-dish servings.

Nutrition facts per serving: 134 cal., 6 g total fat (3 g sat. fat), 10 mg chol., 655 mg sodium, 15 g carbo., 2 g fiber, 6 g pro. *Daily values:* 92% vit. A, 11% vit. C, 6% calcium, 7% iron.

MUSTARD 101

For added zest, paint this mustard onto meats before broiling or grilling. (See the photograph on page 37.)

⅓ **cup dry mustard**
¼ **cup packed brown sugar**
3 **Tbsp. white wine vinegar**

1 In a small mixing bowl stir together the dry mustard, brown sugar, and wine vinegar till smooth. Transfer to a clean jar. Store, covered, in the refrigerator for 2 weeks to mellow flavors. Use within 1 year. Makes ½ cup.

Nutrition facts per tablespoon: 34 cal., 1 g total fat (0 g sat. fat), 0 mg chol., 2 mg sodium, 6 g carbo., 0 g fiber, 1 g pro.

SAUERKRAUT AND SAUSAGE ROLLS

Apple cider, orange peel, and cardamom add new flavor surprises to this two-fisted sandwich, made extra-hearty with dark, full-bodied beer.

4 **fully cooked knockwurst or other mild-flavored sausage**
1 **12-oz. bottle dark beer**

♦♦♦

1 **14½-oz. jar sauerkraut, rinsed and well drained**
2 **Tbsp. apple cider or apple juice**
2 **tsp. finely shredded orange peel**
½ **tsp. ground cardamom**

♦♦♦

4 **hoagie buns**
  German-style or sweet-hot mustard

1 Use a fork to pierce each knockwurst 2 or 3 times. In a saucepan heat beer till simmering; add knockwursts. Simmer, uncovered, about 10 minutes or till hot.

2 Meanwhile, in a medium saucepan combine sauerkraut, apple cider or juice, orange peel, and cardamom. Heat through. To serve, split buns, cutting to within ½ inch of edge. If desired, toast buns under broiler. Spread bottom half with mustard. Drain knockwursts; place one in each bun. Divide sauerkraut mixture among buns. Makes 4 servings.

Nutrition facts per serving: 517 cal., 13 g total fat (4 g sat. fat), 19 mg chol., 1,749 mg sodium, 82 g carbo., 6 g fiber, 17 g pro. *Daily values:* 27% vit. C, 9% calcium, 33% iron.

HONEY DIJON-STYLE MUSTARD

Try this stirred into vinaigrettes. (See the photograph on page 37.)

½ **cup honey**
⅓ **cup mustard seed**
⅓ **cup white wine vinegar**
¼ **cup dry mustard**
½ **tsp. dried thyme, crushed**
½ **tsp. dried tarragon, crushed**
2 **cloves garlic, minced**

1 Combine all ingredients in a blender container. Cover; blend about 2 minutes or till seeds are ground. Transfer to a clean jar. Store, covered, in the refrigerator for 2 weeks to mellow flavors. Use within 1 year. Makes about 1 cup.

Nutrition facts per tablespoon: 55 cal., 1 g total fat (0 g sat. fat), 0 mg chol., 1 mg sodium, 10 g carbo., 0 g fiber, 1 g pro.

Mustard 101, on left, and Honey Dijon-Style Mustard (page 36)

Creamy Carrot Soup with Pesto (page 36)

Top: *French Farmhouse Garlic Chicken (page 28)*
Above: *Ravioli Lasagna (page 30)*
Right: *Cold-Weather Osso Buco (page 28)*
Page 39, top: *Monterey Tortilla Casseroles (page 34)*

Page 40: *Pineapple Cake with Rum-Caramel Sauce (page 49)*
Top: *Almond Brickle Cheesecake (page 16)*
Left: *Tropical Phyllo Tart (page 13)*

Above: *Boundary Waters Cabbage Rolls (page 33)*
Page 43, top: *Apple and Lemon Chess Pie (page 15)*
Page 43, bottom: *Black Bean and Sausage Posole (page 35)*

Top: *Spiced Bran Muffins (page 45)*
Above: *Farmer's Casserole (page 45)*

SPICED BRAN MUFFINS

Mix ¾ cup fresh or frozen blueberries into the batter with the nuts for 15 fruit-filled muffins.
(See the photograph on page 44.)

1½ cups all-purpose flour
1 cup whole bran cereal or
    1½ cups toasted wheat
    bran
2½ tsp. baking powder
1 tsp. ground cinnamon
¼ tsp. ground nutmeg
1 beaten egg
1 cup milk
½ cup packed brown sugar
¼ cup cooking oil
1 tsp. finely shredded lemon
    or orange peel
½ cup chopped nuts

1 In a large mixing bowl combine flour, bran cereal or wheat bran, baking powder, cinnamon, nutmeg, and ¼ teaspoon *salt*. Make a well in center. In another bowl combine egg, milk, brown sugar, oil, and peel. Add egg mixture all at once to flour mixture. Stir just till moistened (batter will be lumpy). Fold in nuts. Bake immediately or store, covered, in the refrigerator for up to 3 days.

2 To bake, gently stir chilled batter. Grease muffin cups or line with paper bake cups; fill cups ⅔ full. Bake in a 400° oven for 15 to 20 minutes or till muffins are golden. Remove from pans; serve warm. Makes 12 muffins.

MICROWAVE DIRECTIONS

Prepare batter as directed above. Line 1 or 2 microwave muffin cups or 6-ounce custard cups with paper bake cups. Gently stir batter. Spoon 2 rounded tablespoons of batter into each cup.

For 1 muffin, microwave, uncovered, on high 20 to 60 seconds or till done. For 2 muffins, cook on high for 45 to 90 seconds or till done. (If using a 1,000-watt microwave oven, check muffins 5 to 10 seconds sooner.) To test doneness, scratch the slightly wet surface with a wooden toothpick. The muffin should looked cooked underneath. Remove from cups. Let stand on a wire rack for 5 minutes.

Nutrition facts per muffin: 177 cal., 9 g total fat (1 g sat. fat), 19 mg chol., 177 mg sodium, 25 g carbo., 2 g fiber, 4 g pro. *Daily values:* 2% vit. A, 9% vit. C, 9% calcium, 12% iron.

FARMER'S CASSEROLE

See the photograph on page 44.

3 cups frozen shredded hash
    brown potatoes
¾ cup shredded Monterey Jack
    cheese with jalapeño
    peppers or shredded
    cheddar cheese (3 oz.)
1 cup diced fully cooked ham
    or Canadian-style bacon
¼ cup sliced green onions

♦♦♦

4 beaten eggs or 1 cup frozen
    egg product*
1 12-oz. can evaporated milk
    or evaporated skim milk*
    (1½ cups)
¼ tsp. pepper
⅛ tsp. salt

1 Grease a 2-quart-square baking dish. Arrange the potatoes evenly in the bottom of the dish. Sprinkle with cheese, ham, and green onions.

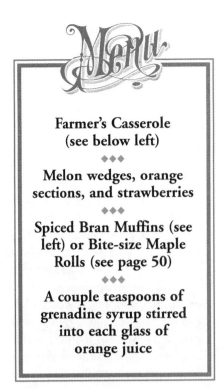

Menu

Farmer's Casserole (see below left)

♦♦♦

Melon wedges, orange sections, and strawberries

♦♦♦

Spiced Bran Muffins (see left) or Bite-size Maple Rolls (see page 50)

♦♦♦

A couple teaspoons of grenadine syrup stirred into each glass of orange juice

2 In a medium mixing bowl combine eggs, milk, pepper, and salt. Pour the egg mixture over potato mixture in dish. Bake, uncovered, in a 350° oven for 40 to 45 minutes or till center appears set. Let stand 5 minutes before serving. Makes 6 servings.

***Note:** Save 50 calories, 6 grams fat, and 150 milligrams cholesterol per serving by using evaporated skim milk and frozen egg product.

TO MAKE AHEAD

Prepare the casserole as directed at left, except do not bake. Cover and chill several hours or overnight. To serve, bake, uncovered, in a 350° oven for 55 to 60 minutes or till heated and center appears set.

Nutrition facts per serving: 297 cal., 18 g total fat (9 g sat. fat), 183 mg chol., 516 mg sodium, 18 g carbo., 1 g fiber, 18 g pro. *Daily values:* 15% vit. A, 15% vit. C, 23% calcium, 11% iron.

Baby Those Buttons

For a shy, rather plain-looking little fellow who prefers the gloom and hates bathing, the lowly button mushroom has quite a few friends in high places. In fact, wealthy Romans in Caesar's time prized the fungi so mightily, they decreed who could eat them. Today, mushrooms know no such limits. Cooks all over the world can savor the sponginess of these tender, meaty morsels. However, cooks know mushrooms crave tender care during storing and cooking because the thin skins of these bashful buttons bruise easily.

Mushroom Hunting

The best button mushrooms are firm and plump. Some have an off-white or creamy color; others may be brown. Size is a matter of preference not quality. Small or young mushrooms often have a closed veil, meaning the membrane between the stem and cap is still attached. Open-veiled mushrooms are more mature, softer, and often more flavorful. Avoid bruised, spotted, or slimy mushrooms.

Storing Fresh Mushrooms

Store fresh mushrooms in the refrigerator crisper drawer. Keep them unwashed, in paper or damp cloth bags, which allow them to breathe and stay fresh longer. Plastic bags restrict airflow and cause deterioration.

Cleaning and Cutting

Wipe fresh mushrooms with a clean, damp cloth or mushroom brush before using. Or, rinse them lightly, then gently dry with paper towels. Never soak fresh mushrooms; it ruins their texture.

Small or medium mushrooms are best in salads, soups, sauces, pizzas, pastas, and casseroles. Large mushrooms make great caps for stuffing or are perfect for broiling or grilling.

To trim button mushrooms, slice ¼ inch from the stem. An egg slicer works well for slicing.

Expect 1 pound of fresh uncooked mushrooms to measure about 6 cups sliced or 4 cups chopped. When cooked, a pound of sliced fresh mushrooms will equal about 2 cups.

---

2 Pour oil into a wok. Preheat over medium-high heat. Stir-fry cabbage in hot oil for 2 minutes. (Add more oil as necessary during cooking.) Add pea pods and mushrooms. Stir-fry 2 minutes more. Stir sauce; add to center of wok. Cook and stir till bubbly; cook and stir 1 minute more. Makes 4 side-dish servings.

Nutrition facts per serving: 93 cal., 4 g total fat (1 g sat. fat), 0 mg chol., 13 mg sodium, 14 g carbo., 3 g fiber, 3 g pro.
Daily values: 86% vit. C, 4% calcium, 12% iron.

Chinese Noodles and Mushroom Salad

  2 **oz. Chinese egg noodles or fine egg noodles**
  2 **cups fresh snow pea pods**

♦♦♦

  2 **cups thinly sliced fresh brown, shiitake, and/or oyster mushrooms**
  1 **Tbsp. cooking oil**
  1 **cup thinly sliced red, yellow, and/or green sweet pepper**
  2 **Tbsp. sliced green onion**

♦♦♦

  1 **Tbsp. rice vinegar**
  1 **Tbsp. soy sauce**
  2 **tsp. grated gingerroot**
  1 **tsp. toasted sesame oil**
  1 **clove garlic, minced**
  ½ **cup enoki mushrooms**
  1½ **tsp. toasted sesame seed**

1 Slightly break up Chinese egg noodles, if using. Cook Chinese egg noodles or egg noodles in lightly salted water according to package directions. Drain; rinse with cold water. Drain well.

Sweet 'n' Sour Cabbage Stir-Fry

  1 **cup fresh snow pea pods or ½ of a 6-oz. pkg. frozen snow pea pods, thawed**
  ⅓ **cup apple juice**
  1 **Tbsp. brown sugar**
  2 **Tbsp. white wine vinegar**
  ½ **tsp. cornstarch**

  1 **Tbsp. cooking oil**
  3 **cups shredded red and/or green cabbage**
  2 **cups halved fresh mushrooms**

1 Rinse fresh pea pods, if using; cut ends and remove strings. For sauce, in a small bowl combine apple juice, brown sugar, wine vinegar, and cornstarch; set aside.

2 Remove tips and strings from pea pods. Cook in boiling water 1 minute. Drain; rinse with cold water. Drain and chill.

3 Cook the mushrooms in oil over medium-high heat 4 to 5 minutes or till tender, stirring occasionally. In a bowl combine noodles, mushrooms, sweet peppers, and green onion; toss to mix.

4 In a screwtop jar combine vinegar, soy sauce, gingerroot, sesame oil, and garlic. Cover; shake well. Pour dressing over mushroom mixture, tossing to coat. Cover; chill 3 to 24 hours, stirring occasionally. Stir in half of the pea pods. Arrange remaining pea pods on 6 to 8 salad plates. Divide salad evenly among plates. Top with enoki mushrooms and sprinkle with sesame seed. Makes 6 to 8 side-dish servings.

Nutrition facts per serving: 98 cal., 4 g total fat (1 g sat. fat), 8 mg chol., 177 mg sodium, 13 g carbo., 2 g fiber, 4 g pro. *Daily values:* 13% vit. A, 84% vit. C, 2% calcium, 13% iron.

BLUE CHEESE AND BROCCOLI SOUFFLÉ

You can create your own soufflé using the same basic ingredients: Substitute up to 1½ cups of your favorite ingredients for the blue cheese and broccoli to experiment with different seasoning combinations.

　　4　egg yolks
　¼　cup margarine or butter
　¼　cup all-purpose flour
　⅛　tsp. salt
　　　Dash ground red pepper

　　　Dash dry mustard
　1　cup milk

◆◆◆

　1　cup finely chopped, cooked broccoli flowerets, drained
　½　cup crumbled blue cheese or finely shredded cheddar cheese (2 oz.)

◆◆◆

　4　egg whites
　½　tsp. cream of tartar

1 Attach a foil collar to a 1½-quart soufflé dish. (For collar, measure enough foil to go around the dish plus a 2- to 3-inch overlap. Fold the foil into thirds

lengthwise. Lightly butter one side of foil. With the buttered side in, position foil around the soufflé dish, letting collar extend 2 inches above top of dish; fasten foil with masking tape; set aside.)

2 Use a fork to lightly beat the egg yolks; set aside. In a medium saucepan melt the margarine or butter over medium-high heat. Stir in flour, salt, red pepper, and mustard. Stir in the milk. Cook and stir till thickened and bubbly. Cook and stir for 1 to 2 minutes more. Remove from heat.

3 Add the cooked broccoli and the blue or cheddar cheese to the milk mixture, stirring until the cheese is melted. Slowly add the broccoli mixture to the egg yolks, stirring constantly. Cool mixture slightly.

4 In a large mixing bowl beat the egg whites and cream of tartar with an electric mixer on high speed till stiff peaks form (tips stand straight). Gradually pour the yolk mixture over the beaten egg whites, folding to combine.

5 Pour the egg mixture into the ungreased soufflé dish. Bake in a 350° oven for 35 to 40 minutes or till the soufflé jiggles when gently shaken. Test soufflé for doneness while it's still in the oven. Serve soufflé immediately. Makes 4 main-dish servings.

Nutrition facts per serving: 296 cal., 22 g total fat (7 g sat. fat), 228 mg chol., 501 mg sodium, 12 g carbo., 2 g fiber, 13 g pro. *Daily values:* 58% vit. A, 49% vit. C, 16% calcium, 8% iron.

INDIAN CAULIFLOWER

Savor the spices of India—coriander, turmeric, and cumin.

1 head cauliflower (about
  1½ lb.)

◆◆◆

½ tsp. dry mustard
¼ tsp. ground turmeric
¼ tsp. ground cumin
⅛ tsp. ground coriander
⅛ tsp. ground red pepper

◆◆◆

1 Tbsp. cooking oil
4 green onions, bias-sliced into
  1-inch pieces (¾ cup)
1 small red or green sweet
  pepper, cut into 1-inch
  squares
¼ cup chicken broth

1 Rinse the cauliflower; remove leaves and woody stem. Break into flowerets, slicing any large pieces. (You should have about 4 cups.)

2 In a bowl combine mustard, turmeric, cumin, coriander, and red pepper; set aside.

3 Heat oil in a wok or large skillet over medium-high heat. (Add more oil as necessary.) Add cauliflower; stir-fry for 3 minutes. Add green onions and sweet pepper; stir-fry for 1 to 1½ minutes. Reduce heat to medium. Add spice mixture. Cook and stir for 30 seconds. Carefully stir in broth. Cook and stir about 1 minute more or till heated through. Serve immediately. Makes 4 side-dish servings.

Nutrition facts per serving: 71 cal., 4 g total fat (1 g sat. fat), 0 mg chol., 58 mg sodium, 7 g carbo., 3 g fiber, 3 g pro.
Daily values: 139% vit. C.

CARROT-CITRUS MARMALADE

Make this sensational breakfast spread from fresh produce even in the deep of winter.

½ of a lemon
½ of an orange

◆◆◆

2 cups coarsely shredded
  carrots (about 8 oz.)
1¼ cups sugar
½ cup water

◆◆◆

1½ tsp. grated gingerroot or
  ½ tsp. ground ginger
½ tsp. ground cinnamon

1 Remove the end from the lemon; discard. Remove the center core from the lemon and orange halves; discard. Cut each half into 4 lengthwise wedges; remove seeds. *Do not peel.*

2 In a 3-quart saucepan combine the lemon and orange wedges, carrots, sugar, and water. Bring to boiling, stirring to dissolve sugar. Reduce heat; simmer, uncovered, about 15 minutes or till mixture begins to thicken, stirring occasionally. Remove from heat; cool slightly.

3 Transfer carrot mixture to a food processor bowl. Cover and process till almost smooth. Return the carrot mixture to saucepan; add gingerroot and cinnamon. Simmer, uncovered, for 5 minutes or till mixture becomes very thick, stirring frequently.

4 Ladle at once into 2 hot, sterilized half-pint jars, leaving ¼-inch headspace. Adjust lids.

5 Store in refrigerator for up to 2 weeks. For longer storage, immediately process in boiling water bath 15 minutes (start timing after water boils). Makes about 2 half-pints.

Nutrition facts per tablespoon: 41 cal., 0 g total fat, 0 mg chol., 7 mg sodium, 11 g carbo., 0 g fiber, 0 g pro.
Daily values: 24% vit. A, 4% vit. C.

GINGER COOKIES

1⅓ cups all-purpose flour
½ tsp. cream of tartar
½ tsp. ground ginger
¼ tsp. baking soda
½ cup butter, softened
⅓ cup sugar
⅓ cup packed brown sugar
1 egg
½ tsp. vanilla
¼ cup finely chopped
  Candied Ginger (see
  page 49) or purchased
  candied ginger

1 Combine flour, cream of tartar, ground ginger, soda, and ⅛ teaspoon *salt;* set aside. In a large mixing bowl combine butter and sugars. Beat with an electric mixer on medium to high speed till fluffy. Add egg and vanilla; beat on medium speed till combined. Beat in as much of the flour mixture as you can. Stir in any remaining flour mixture and Candied Ginger. Cover; chill dough 1 hour or till easy to handle.

2 With lightly floured hands, shape dough into 1½-inch balls. Place balls at least 3 inches apart on an ungreased cookie sheet. If desired, flatten with bottom of a glass dipped into sugar. (The cookies will spread more during baking.) Bake in a 375° oven for

8 to 10 minutes or till cookies are pale gold and edges are firm. Remove cookies from cookie sheet; cool completely on a wire rack. Makes about 36 cookies.

Nutrition facts per cookie: 56 cal., 3 g total fat (2 g sat. fat), 13 mg chol., 44 mg sodium, 7 g carbo., 0 g fiber, 1 g pro. *Daily values:* 2% vit. A, 1% iron.

CANDIED GINGER

The Victorians served crystallized ginger as candy. Try our homemade version in Ginger Cookies, page 48.

1 **cup peeled, finely chopped gingerroot**

◆◆◆

1⅓ **cups sugar**
⅓ **cup water**
2 **Tbsp. sugar**

1 In a 1½-quart saucepan combine gingerroot and enough *water* to cover; bring to boiling. Reduce heat; simmer, covered, for 15 minutes. Drain the ginger through a wire strainer. Discard cooking liquid; set ginger aside.

2 In the same saucepan combine the 1⅓ cups sugar and ⅓ cup water. Bring to boiling, stirring constantly to dissolve sugar. Add the gingerroot. Return to boiling; reduce heat. Cook, uncovered, over medium-low heat 20 minutes, stirring often. (The mixture should boil at a moderate, steady rate over entire surface.)

3 Drain ginger through a wire strainer into a bowl; discard syrup. Spread ginger in a single layer on waxed paper. Let stand till cool enough to handle. Add ginger to plastic bag with 2 tablespoons sugar; shake to coat.

Spread on clean waxed paper. Dry for 1 to 2 hours. Cover tightly; store up to 1 week in refrigerator or up to 6 months in freezer. Makes about ⅔ cup.

PINEAPPLE CAKE WITH RUM-CARAMEL SAUCE

See the photograph on page 40.

1 **cup butter or margarine**
5 **eggs**
1 **cup pineapple or lemon yogurt**

◆◆◆

2½ **cups all-purpose flour**
½ **cup yellow or white cornmeal**
1 **tsp. baking powder**
¼ **tsp. baking soda**

◆◆◆

2 **cups sugar**
1 **tsp. vanilla**
1 **8-oz. can crushed pineapple (juice pack)**

◆◆◆

1 **recipe Rum-Caramel Sauce (see below)**

1 Allow butter or margarine, eggs, and yogurt to stand at room temperature for 30 minutes. Grease and flour a 10-inch fluted tube pan. In a medium mixing bowl stir together flour, cornmeal, baking powder, and baking soda. Set pan and flour mixture aside.

2 In a very large mixing bowl beat butter or margarine with an electric mixer on medium to high speed 30 seconds. Gradually add sugar, beating on medium to high speed for 10 minutes or till light and fluffy. Add vanilla. Add the eggs, one at a time, beating for 1 minute after each addition and

THE COLORS OF CORNMEAL

Made from dried corn kernels, cornmeal was the flour used by early Native American cooks. Today, cornmeal may be yellow, white, or blue, depending on the color of corn used in grinding. Use yellow and white interchangeably in cooking and baking; use blue cornmeal for a dark color.

scraping sides of bowl often. Alternately add flour mixture and yogurt to egg mixture, beating on low to medium speed after each addition just till combined. Drain pineapple, reserving juice for sauce. Stir pineapple into batter.

3 Pour batter into prepared tube pan. Bake in a 325° oven about 65 minutes or till wooden toothpick inserted near the center comes out clean. Cool in pan on a wire rack 10 minutes. Remove from pan; cool completely. Serve cake with warm Rum-Caramel Sauce. Makes 18 servings.

Rum-Caramel Sauce: In a saucepan combine one 12-ounce jar *caramel ice-cream topping* and 1 to 2 tablespoons *dark rum or reserved pineapple juice;* heat just till bubbly. Makes 1 cup.

Nutrition facts per serving: 339 cal., 12 g total fat (7 g sat. fat), 87 mg chol., 233 mg sodium, 55 g carbo., 1 g fiber, 5 g pro. *Daily values:* 12% vit. A, 2% vit. C, 5% calcium, 8% iron.

BITE-SIZE MAPLE ROLLS

¼ cup packed brown sugar
3 Tbsp. margarine or butter, softened
2 Tbsp. all-purpose flour
1 Tbsp. ground cinnamon

◆◆◆

1 1-lb. loaf frozen sweet bread dough, thawed
⅓ cup finely chopped pecans

◆◆◆

1 Tbsp. milk

◆◆◆

1 recipe Maple Icing (see below)

1 Grease a baking sheet; set aside. For filling, stir together brown sugar, margarine or butter, flour, and cinnamon. Set aside.

2 On a lightly floured surface, roll thawed dough to a 12×10-inch rectangle. Spread filling atop, leaving a ¼-inch plain border. Sprinkle with nuts. Cut rectangle in half lengthwise (two 12×5-inch rectangles). Roll up each rectangle, jelly-roll style, starting from a long side. Moisten edges; pinch to seal. Cut each log crosswise into 16 pieces. Arrange the pieces, cut side up, 1 inch apart on the prepared baking sheet. Cover and let rise in a warm place till nearly double (about 25 minutes).

3 Brush the sides of the rolls with milk. Bake, uncovered, in a 350° oven for 10 to 15 minutes or till golden. Remove from baking sheet; cool on wire rack. Drizzle with Maple Icing. Makes 32 rolls.

Maple Icing: In a saucepan heat 3 tablespoons *margarine or butter* over medium-low heat 7 to 10 minutes or till light brown.

THE CLEVER COOK

FASTER RISING BREAD

I fill a bowl with hot water. After emptying, drying, and greasing it, I have a warm bowl that speeds bread rising.

Pat Grootveld
Ames, Iowa

Remove pan from heat. Stir in 1½ cups sifted *powdered sugar* and 3 tablespoons *maple syrup*. Stir in enough *milk* (1 to 2 teaspoons) to make icing easy to drizzle.

Nutrition facts per roll: 91 cal., 3 g total fat (1 g sat. fat), 3 mg chol., 31 mg sodium, 14 g carbo., 1 g pro.

SPICE TWISTS

3 Tbsp. sugar
½ tsp. grated orange peel
⅛ tsp. ground nutmeg

◆◆◆

1 16-oz. loaf frozen sweet bread dough, thawed
1 Tbsp. margarine or butter, melted
½ cup miniature semisweet chocolate pieces

◆◆◆

1 recipe Chocolate Glaze (see above right)

1 Grease a baking sheet. For filling, combine sugar, orange peel, and nutmeg. Set baking sheet and filling aside.

2 On a lightly floured surface, roll thawed dough to an 18×10-inch rectangle. Brush margarine or butter onto dough, leaving a ½-inch plain border. Sprinkle filling and chocolate pieces atop, pressing pieces lightly into dough. Starting with a long side, fold a third of the dough over center third. Fold over again, forming 3 equal layers; seal edges. Cut crosswise into eighteen 1-inch-wide strips. Twist each strip; place twists 1 inch apart on a prepared sheet, pressing ends down. Cover; let rise in a warm place till nearly double (about 30 minutes).

3 Bake in a 350° oven 20 to 25 minutes or till golden. Remove from baking sheet; cool slightly on a wire rack. Spread with Chocolate Glaze. Makes 18.

Chocolate Glaze: Stir together 1 cup sifted *powdered sugar,* 2 tablespoons *unsweetened cocoa powder,* 1 teaspoon *vanilla,* and enough *milk* to make glaze easy to spread.

Nutrition facts per twist: 120 cal., 3 g total fat (0 g sat. fat), 0 mg chol., 21 mg sodium, 22 g carbo., 0 g fiber, 2 g pro.

PRIZE TESTED RECIPE WINNER

PEANUT BUTTER TWISTS

This recipe earned Joanne Seck of Bucyrus, Kansas, $200 in the magazine's monthly contest.

4½ to 5 cups all-purpose flour
2 pkg. active dry yeast
½ cup sugar
½ cup shortening

⅓ cup nonfat dry milk powder

2 eggs

♦♦♦

1 recipe Peanut Butter Filling
(see below)

1 recipe Powdered Sugar Glaze
(see right)

¼ cup chopped peanuts

1 Stir together 2 cups flour and the yeast; set aside. Heat and stir sugar, shortening, milk powder, 1 cup *water*, and ½ teaspoon *salt* till warm (120° to 130°) and shortening is almost melted; add to flour mixture. Add eggs; beat 30 seconds, scraping bowl. Beat for 3 minutes. Stir in as much remaining flour as you can. On a floured surface, knead in enough flour to make a soft dough that is elastic (3 to 5 minutes). Shape into a ball. Place in a greased bowl; turn once. Cover; let rise in a warm place till double (1 hour).

2 Punch dough down; divide in half. Cover; let rest 10 minutes. Chill one portion. Roll remaining portion to a 16×9-inch rectangle; spread with half the filling. Fold in half lengthwise; cut crosswise into 16 equal pieces. Hold ends and twist, pinching firmly. Repeat with remaining dough and filling. Arrange on a lightly greased foil-lined baking sheet, pressing ends down. Bake in a 350° oven 15 minutes or till golden. Drizzle with white and/or chocolate glaze. Top with nuts. Serve warm or cool. Makes 32 twists.

Peanut Butter Filling: Combine 1 cup *peanut butter*, ½ cup sifted *powdered sugar*, and ⅓ cup softened *margarine or butter*. Stir till smooth and spreadable.

Powdered Sugar Glaze: Stir together 2 cups sifted *powdered sugar* and, if desired, ¼ cup *unsweetened cocoa powder*. Stir in 2 tablespoons softened *margarine or butter*. Stir in 3 to 4 tablespoons *warm water*, 1 tablespoon at a time, till easy to drizzle.

Nutrition facts per twist: 215 cal., 11 g total fat (2 g sat. fat), 13 mg chol., 112 mg sodium, 26 g carbo., 1 g fiber, 5 g pro. *Daily values:* 4% vit. A, 1% calcium, 7% iron.

PEANUT BUTTER FUDGE

Who says fudge has to be made of chocolate? You'll find this peanutty version utterly delicious.

Butter

2 cups sugar

½ cup milk

⅓ cup creamy peanut butter

2 Tbsp. light-colored corn
syrup

♦♦♦

2 Tbsp. butter or margarine

1 tsp. vanilla

♦♦♦

½ cup coarsely chopped honey
roasted peanuts

♦♦♦

1 oz. chocolate-flavored candy
coating

2 Tbsp. finely chopped honey
roasted peanuts

1 Line a 9×5×3-inch loaf pan with foil, extending foil over edges of pan. Butter foil; set aside.

2 Butter the sides of a heavy 2-quart saucepan. In saucepan combine sugar, milk, peanut butter, and corn syrup. Cook over medium-high heat to boiling, stirring constantly with a wooden spoon to dissolve sugar. This should take about 5 minutes. When stirring, avoid splashing the mixture up the sides of pan.

3 Carefully clip candy thermometer to side of pan. Cook mixture over medium-low heat, stirring frequently, till thermometer registers 234°, soft-ball stage. The mixture should boil at a moderate, steady rate over entire surface. Reaching soft-ball stage should take about 8 to 10 minutes. Remove the saucepan from the heat. Add the 2 tablespoons butter or margarine and vanilla *(do not stir)*. Cool, without stirring, to 110°, or lukewarm. This should take about 55 minutes.

4 Remove the thermometer from the saucepan. Use a wooden spoon to beat fudge vigorously till mixture just begins to thicken. Stir in the ½ cup nuts. Continue beating till the fudge becomes very thick, but is still glossy. This should take 6 to 7 minutes total. Immediately turn fudge into prepared pan; spread evenly. (Candy will lose its gloss after it's turned into the pan.) While fudge is warm, score into 1-inch squares.

5 When fudge is firm, drizzle with melted chocolate-flavored candy coating and sprinkle with additional peanuts. Use foil to lift it out of pan; cut into squares. Store in a tightly covered storage container in a cool, dry place up to 3 weeks. Makes 45 pieces.

Nutrition facts per piece: 70 cal., 3 g total fat (1 g sat. fat), 2 mg chol., 16 mg sodium, 11 g carbo., 0 g fiber, 1 g pro.

PEANUT BUTTER CHOCOLATE CHIP POUND CAKE

3 eggs
1 cup buttermilk
¾ cup butter or margarine

♦♦♦

¾ cup peanut butter
1½ cups sugar
1 tsp. vanilla

♦♦♦

3 cups all-purpose flour
1½ tsp. baking powder
½ tsp. baking soda
1 cup miniature semisweet chocolate pieces (6 oz.)
Sifted powdered sugar (optional)

1 Let eggs, buttermilk, and butter or margarine stand at room temperature 30 minutes. Grease and flour a 10-inch fluted tube pan; set aside.

2 In a large mixing bowl beat butter and peanut butter with an electric mixer on medium speed for 30 seconds or till softened. Gradually add the sugar, beating on medium speed till light and fluffy. Beat in vanilla. Add eggs, one at a time, beating about 1 minute after each addition. Beat 2 minutes more.

3 Stir together the flour, baking powder, and soda. Add flour mixture and buttermilk alternately to creamed mixture, beating just till blended after each addition. Stir in chocolate pieces. Turn into the prepared tube pan. Bake in a 350° oven 50 to 60 minutes or till a wooden toothpick inserted comes out clean. Cool cake in pan on a wire rack

for 15 minutes. Remove cake from pan; cool completely. If desired, sprinkle with powdered sugar. Makes 16 servings.

Nutrition facts per serving: 376 cal., 19 g total fat (7 g sat. fat), 64 mg chol., 247 mg sodium, 46 g carbo., 1 g fiber, 7 g pro. *Daily values:* 10% vit. A, 0% vit. C, 5% calcium, 11% iron.

PEANUT BUTTER AND CHOCOLATE BREAD PUDDING

6 ¾-inch-thick-slices French bread, toasted
⅓ cup peanut butter
½ cup miniature semisweet chocolate pieces

♦♦♦

2 beaten eggs
1½ cups milk
½ cup sugar
Sweetened whipped cream (optional)

1 Grease a 2-quart-square baking dish. Spread toasted bread slices with peanut butter. Cut the slices into 1-inch squares. Arrange squares in the prepared dish. Sprinkle with chocolate pieces.

2 In a medium mixing bowl combine eggs, milk, and sugar. Pour mixture over bread squares. Bake in a 325° oven about 45 minutes or till a knife inserted near the center comes out clean. Cool slightly. If desired, serve warm with sweetened whipped cream. Makes 6 servings.

Nutrition facts per serving: 279 cal., 14 g total fat (3 g sat. fat), 76 mg chol., 140 mg sodium, 34 g carbo., 1 g fiber, 9 g pro. *Daily values:* 7% vit. A, 7% calcium, 6% iron.

PEANUT BUTTER BISCOTTI

2 cups all-purpose flour
½ tsp. baking powder
½ tsp. baking soda
¼ tsp. salt

♦♦♦

3 eggs
1 cup sugar
¾ cup crunchy peanut butter
½ tsp. vanilla
1 egg white, slightly beaten
½ cup milk chocolate pieces or semisweet chocolate pieces (optional)
1 Tbsp. shortening (optional)

1 Lightly grease a cookie sheet. In a large mixing bowl combine the flour, baking powder, soda, and salt. Make a well in the center. Set cookie sheet and flour mixture aside.

2 In a small bowl beat together the eggs, sugar, peanut butter, and vanilla with a fork till well combined. Pour the peanut butter mixture into the flour mixture. Stir to make a smooth dough. (Dough will be sticky.) Divide the dough into 3 portions. Use lightly oiled hands to shape each portion of dough into a 5½×2½-inch loaf. Place loaves about 4 inches apart on the prepared cookie sheet. Brush egg white over loaves.

3 Bake in a 375° oven for 25 minutes. Remove from oven; place cookie sheet on a cooling rack. Reduce oven temperature to 325°. Cool loaves on the cookie sheet 30 minutes. Cut each loaf diagonally into ½-inch-thick slices. Lay slices, cut side down, on cookie sheet. Bake in the 325°

oven 8 minutes. Turn slices over. Bake for 8 to 10 minutes more or till dry and crisp. Remove cookies and cool on wire racks.

4 If desired, in a heavy small saucepan melt chocolate pieces and shortening over low heat, stirring occasionally. Place cooled cookies, flat side up, on waxed paper. Use a spoon to drizzle chocolate atop cookies or dip one end of each cookie into melted chocolate. Let stand till chocolate is set. Makes about 36 cookies.

Nutrition facts per cookie: 83 cal., 3 g total fat (1 g sat. fat), 18 mg chol., 70 mg sodium, 12 g carbo., 1 g fiber, 3 g pro. *Daily values:* 3% iron.

MARBLED BISCOTTI

Because of the twisting, no two cookies are alike. Their size and good looks suit them for a tea or to accompany a dessert.

⅔ **cup butter or margarine**
1⅓ **cups sugar**
1 **Tbsp. baking powder**
¼ **tsp. salt**
4 **eggs**
1 **tsp. vanilla**
4 **cups all-purpose flour**
♦♦♦
1½ **cups semisweet chocolate pieces, melted and cooled**
1 **cup finely chopped hazelnuts (filberts)**
1 **Tbsp. finely shredded orange peel**

1 In a large mixing bowl beat butter or margarine with an electric mixer on medium to high speed for 30 seconds. Add sugar, baking powder, and salt; beat till combined. Beat in the eggs and

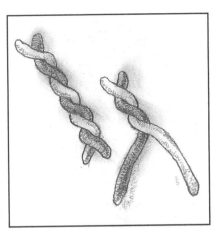

vanilla till combined. Beat in as much flour as you can with the mixer. Use a wooden spoon to stir in any remaining flour.

2 Divide dough in half; place half in another bowl. Into half of the dough, stir the melted chocolate and ½ cup of the nuts. Into the other half of the dough, stir in orange peel and remaining nuts.

3 Divide each half of dough into 3 equal portions. With lightly floured hands, shape each portion into a rope about 14 inches long. Place a rope of each color side by side on an ungreased cookie sheet. Twist ropes around each other several times. Flatten slightly to a 2-inch width (see illustration, above). Repeat with the other ropes, placing twists about 4 inches apart on the cookie sheet.

4 Bake in a 375° oven about 25 minutes or till lightly browned. Cool on cookie sheet about 1 hour or till completely cool. Transfer to a cutting board. Cut each loaf crosswise into ½-inch-thick slices. Lay slices, cut side down, on the cookie sheet. Bake in a 325° oven for 10 minutes. Turn slices to the other side

and bake 10 to 15 minutes more or till dry and crisp. Remove cookies and cool on wire rack. Makes about 70 cookies.

Nutrition facts per cookie: 86 cal., 4 g total fat (1 g sat. fat), 17 mg chol., 52 mg sodium, 12 g carbo., 0 g fiber, 1 g pro. *Daily values:* 2% vit. A, 1% calcium, 3% iron.

LOW FAT BANANA SPLIT CHOCOLATE PUDDING

½ **cup sugar**
¼ **cup unsweetened cocoa powder**
3 **Tbsp. cornstarch**
⅛ **tsp. salt**
2½ **cups skim milk**
1½ **tsp. vanilla**
♦♦♦
2 **small bananas, sliced**
4 **fresh strawberries (optional)**

1 In a heavy medium saucepan combine sugar, cocoa powder, cornstarch, and salt. Stir in milk. Cook and stir over medium heat till thickened and bubbly. Cook and stir 2 minutes more. Remove from heat. Stir in vanilla. Pour pudding into a bowl. Cover surface with plastic wrap. Chill without stirring.

2 To serve, divide half of the pudding among 4 dessert dishes. Top with banana slices, then remaining pudding. If desired, garnish each serving with a fresh strawberry. Makes 4 servings.

Nutrition facts per serving: 251 cal., 1 g total fat (0 g sat. fat), 3 mg chol., 147 mg sodium, 53 g carbo., 1 g fiber, 7 g pro. *Daily values:* 21% vit. C, 21% calcium.

AFTER-DINNER CHOCOLATE

True chocoholics will want to use bittersweet chocolate, which carries a more pronounced flavor than semisweet.

2 cups water
4 oz. bittersweet or semisweet chocolate, chopped
3 Tbsp. Grand Marnier or amaretto, or 4 tsp. vanilla

❖❖❖

¼ cup whipping cream

❖❖❖

Finely shredded orange peel (optional)

1 In a small saucepan combine the water and chocolate. Cook and stir just till boiling. Remove from heat; stir in liqueur.

2 In a small chilled mixing bowl beat the whipping cream with an electric mixer on low to medium speed till soft peaks form (tips curl).

3 To serve, divide chocolate mixture among 4 mugs. Top each serving of cocoa with a spoonful of whipped cream and, if desired, sprinkle with orange peel. Makes 4 servings (4 ounces each).

Nutrition facts per serving: 214 cal., 14 g total fat (9 g sat. fat), 20 mg chol., 10 mg sodium, 21 g carbo., 2 g fiber, 2 g pro.

COCOA CARIBE

Cocoa powder offers more concentrated chocolate taste than baking chocolate—and it's lower in fat and calories.

1 Tbsp. sugar
1 Tbsp. unsweetened cocoa powder
1 Tbsp. water
1 cup milk
⅛ tsp. ground cinnamon
Several dashes ground cardamom
Cinnamon stick (optional)

1 In a small saucepan combine the sugar, cocoa powder, and water. Cook and stir over medium heat till sugar is dissolved. Reduce heat. Stir in milk, ground cinnamon, and cardamom; heat through. Use a wire whisk to beat till frothy. Pour into a mug. If desired, serve with a cinnamon stick. Makes 1 serving (8 ounces).

Nutrition facts per serving: 193 cal., 5 g total fat (3 g sat. fat), 18 mg chol., 123 mg sodium, 27 g carbo., 0 g fiber, 9 g pro.

MOCHA JAVA

Coffee and chocolate often are served side by side. This elegant drink combines them in a single, satisfying cup.

1 cup strong coffee
2 Tbsp. semisweet chocolate pieces
1 Tbsp. sugar

❖❖❖

¼ cup half-and-half or light cream
Sugar (optional)

CHOOSE A COCOA

Choices abound in today's supermarkets and the baking aisle is no exception. Here's a comparison of cocoa powders:

Unsweetened cocoa powder is made by pressing most of the cocoa butter from pure chocolate, and it has no added ingredients. Dutch-process cocoa powder is cocoa treated with alkali to partially neutralize the natural acids in the cocoa bean. It is also called European-style cocoa powder and may be used in recipes calling for unsweetened cocoa powder. The flavor is more mellow and the color darker than unsweetened cocoa powder.

Both varieties will keep for several years if tightly covered and stored in a cool, dry place.

1 In a small saucepan combine coffee, chocolate pieces, and sugar. Cook and stir over medium heat for 2 to 3 minutes or till the chocolate is melted and sugar is dissolved.

2 In another small saucepan heat the half-and-half or light cream till steaming, stirring occasionally. Pour the coffee mixture into a mug. Add the warm half-and-half. If desired, stir in additional sugar to taste. Makes 1 serving (12 ounces).

Nutrition facts per serving: 165 cal., 9 g total fat (4 g sat. fat), 22 mg chol., 30 mg sodium, 21 g carbo., 0 g fiber, 2 g pro.

MARCH
A Late Winter Harvest

30-minute recipes indicated in RED.
Low-fat recipes indicated with a ♥.

Tangy, fresh dishes made with citrus fruits, tropical fruits, and a bounty of cold weather produce jazz up a jaded palate. Ingredients at their peak now are featured in Roasted Potato and Garlic Soup, Winter Risotto with broccoli raab, and an eye-catching mixture of Mustard-Glazed Brussels Sprouts and Oranges. Mushrooms as a main dish? Sure. Try Portobello Mushroom Fajitas or Italian Sausage and Mushroom Bread. Late winter produce makes it easy for dishes to look original. Create lemon curd with tangerines and serve apple crisp using pears. No falling into a rut this month.

WINTER PRODUCE PRIMER

Brighten the waning days of winter by serving in-season fruits and vegetables. Most of the produce in your market from about mid February through March comes from U.S. farms. Some of these fruits and vegetables (such as potatoes, apples, and root vegetables) have been held in cold or controlled-atmosphere storage since summer or fall when they were harvested. Other crops (including citrus and tropical fruits, salad greens, and lettuces) are picked during the winter months in fields, groves, and hothouses. Either way, the following fruits and vegetables are smart buys because they're in plentiful supply and in prime condition.

Apples—Grocery stores today offer many appealing options, not just red or green. In late winter, the most popular ones include Cortland, Empire, Golden Delicious, Granny Smith, Jonathan, McIntosh, Red Delicious, Rome Beauty, Stayman, Winesap, and York Imperial. Do a side-by-side apple tasting, and you'll immediately notice a difference in flavor and juiciness. Some taste best fresh (uncooked); others are the perfect choice for cooking. Check the chart on page 69 to identify the best uses for each. Keep apples in a plastic bag with ventilation holes in your refrigerator crisper or in a cold, moist place. Treat cut apples with lemon juice or ascorbic acid color-keeper to prevent browning.

Cabbage family—Large, round heads of green and red cabbage, petite Brussels sprouts, leafy broccoli raab (pronounced rob), and bok choy are all related. Of these, you may not be familiar with either bok choy or broccoli raab (also called rapini), which looks like stalks of broccoli with sprouting spinach leaves. Bok choy (a variety of Chinese cabbage) has long, white celerylike stalks and large, dark green leaves. When shopping, avoid vegetables with shriveled leaves. If you're concerned about pesticide residues, remove loose outer leaves of cabbage and Brussels sprouts before cooking. Store in plastic bags in the refrigerator for up to a week.

Chayote—You'll find fields of chayote (chaw-YOTE-ee) in sunny California, but it might be called mirliton, the preferred name, when used in Cajun and Southern cuisines. Chayote is a pear-shaped squash with a delicate green- or white-ridged skin. Inside, you'll find a single, large seed that can be easily removed with a spoon. The moist flesh tastes like a cross between an apple and a cucumber. Use chayote in cooking as you would zucchini or other summer squash. The skin is edible. Refrigerate chayote in a plastic bag for up to two weeks.

Citrus Fruits—In winter, Northerners especially welcome a gift of sunshine in the form of numerous varieties of oranges (including red-fleshed blood oranges and seedless navel oranges), grapefruits, easy-to-peel tangerines, tangelos, limes, lemons, and bite-size kumquats. All these juicy wonders keep well for two to three weeks in the refrigerator.

Fennel—This bulbous vegetable with celerylike stalks and feathery, bright green leaves has a light licorice flavor that mellows upon cooking. Look for firm, smooth bulbs that are free of cracks or brown spots. The stalks should be crisp. Store the bulb in a plastic bag in the refrigerator for up to four days. Discard the tough upper stalks. Save the leaves for a delicate garnish.

Greens and Lettuces—In winter, sturdy greens such as Belgian endive, escarole, radicchio, and romaine are plentiful. Belgian endive grows in a small, cone-shaped head with tightly packed, slender leaves. Escarole has irregularly shaped, dark green leaves; it's an ideal choice for wilted salads. Radicchio, an Italian red chicory, has ruby leaves with thick, white veins. Romaine, the classic choice for Caesar salad, features large, long, dark green leaves. Belgian endive, escarole, and radicchio leaves are slightly bitter tasting; romaine tastes mild. Choose heads that are crisp and unblemished. Rinse and drain before storing; chill in plastic bags up to a week.

Pears—Choose the pear variety from the chart on page 73 that works best for your recipe or eating fresh. Best pear buys in cold months include Anjou, Bosc, Comice, and Nelis. For optimum flavor and texture, pears are picked mature, yet not fully ripe. Select fresh pears without bruises or cuts. Don't judge ripeness by the skin color—with some varieties, the skin color doesn't change as the fruit ripens. To ripen pears at home, place unripe fruit in a paper bag and let stand at room temperature for a few days. When the pear yields to gentle thumb pressure at the slender stem end, eat or refrigerate. Treat cut-up pears with ascorbic acid color-keeper or lemon juice to prevent browning.

Potatoes—Red, white, round, oblong, all potato varieties are in plentiful supply year-round. Choose russets for baking or mashing and long whites for potato salad and casseroles. Or, call on round whites for any recipe. Choose potatoes with clean, smooth skins, free of green or soft spots. Store them in a well-ventilated place that is cool and slightly humid. Avoid refrigeration because chilled potatoes can become overly sweet and may darken when cooked. Also, keep them in the dark; bright light causes greening of the skin, resulting in a bitter flavor.

Root Vegetables—These are so named because the edible portion is the root rather than the leafy tops. Carrot is the most popular root vegetable, followed by parsnip, rutabaga, and turnip, all of which are often confused with one another. Just remember, parsnips resem-

ble white, sweet carrots; turnips are the tinier version of rutabagas. Store them in the refrigerator for a week or more. Sometimes parsnips, rutabagas, and turnips are covered with a wax coating to extend storage. Simply cut off this coating before cooking.

Tropical Fruits—Regions in Florida, California, and Hawaii have the right climate for growing many tropical fruits, including cherimoya, papaya, guava, kiwifruit, carambola (star fruit), and mango. You'll most likely find unripened fruit in stores. To ripen, store fruit at room temperature a few days until it yields to gentle pressure. Other ripeness tests: Carambola should be yellow with slight browning on the ribs (points of stars). A cherimoya may turn dull, brownish green when ripe. Once ripened, these fruits need gentle handling and refrigeration.

Winter Squash—These hard-shelled beauties mature in fall and are stored for cooking through the winter. Acorn, butternut, spaghetti, and turban squash are the most popular varieties, but look for other shapes, names, and colors in your store. Avoid cracked or bruised squash. At home, store whole squash in a cool, dry place for up to two months. If you purchase cut squash, store it wrapped in plastic wrap for up to four days in the refrigerator.

HERB-ROASTED CORNISH HENS WITH ROOT VEGETABLES

This savory dinner comes together easily in one pan with a minimum of fussing while it's roasting.
(See the photograph on page 83.)

2 1- to 1½-lb. Cornish game hens
4 medium carrots, peeled and cut into 2-inch lengths
4 medium parsnips, peeled and cut into 2-inch lengths
2 small turnips, peeled and cut into wedges
1 onion, cut into wedges

◆◆◆

3 Tbsp. olive oil or cooking oil
1 clove garlic, minced
2 tsp. dried rosemary, crushed
2 tsp. dried oregano, crushed
½ tsp. salt

1 Rinse hens and pat dry. Skewer neck skin to back; tie legs to tail. Twist wings under back. Place birds, breast up, on a rack in a large shallow roasting pan. Place the vegetables around the hens in pan. Combine oil, garlic, rosemary, oregano, and salt; brush onto birds and vegetables.

2 Roast, uncovered, in a 375° oven for 1¼ to 1½ hours or till hens are no longer pink and the drumsticks move easily in their

sockets. During roasting, turn the vegetables occasionally. Transfer hens from roasting pan to serving platter; cover and keep warm. Remove rack from roasting pan. Stir vegetables. Increase oven temperature to 450°. Continue roasting vegetables 15 to 20 minutes more or till tender and brown.

3 To serve, use a slotted spoon to spoon the vegetables around the hens on the platter. Makes 4 servings.

Nutrition facts per serving: 422 cal., 26 g total fat (5 g sat. fat), 80 mg chol., 406 mg sodium, 25 g carbo., 7 g fiber, 26 g pro. *Daily values:* 171% vit. A, 28% vit. C, 6% calcium, 8% iron.

PORK WITH PEAR, FENNEL, AND CABBAGE

Fennel bulbs and stalks have a celerylike texture with feathery green tops or leaves. The stalks should be crisp and the leaves bright green and fresh-looking.

- 2 **medium fennel bulbs**
- 4 **boneless pork loin chops, cut 1½ inches thick (America's Cut)**
- 1 **small onion, sliced**
- 1 **Tbsp. olive oil**

◆◆◆

- ½ **of a small head cabbage, coarsely chopped (2½ cups)**
- ½ **cup pear nectar or apple juice**
- ¼ **cup balsamic vinegar**
- ½ **tsp. caraway seed**
- ½ **tsp. dried thyme, crushed**
- ¼ **tsp. salt**
- ¼ **tsp. pepper**
- ⅛ **tsp. ground nutmeg**

◆◆◆

- **Pear nectar**
- 2 **Tbsp. cold water**
- 1 **Tbsp. cornstarch**
- 1 **large pear, cored and sliced**

1 Trim fennel; cut into thin wedges. Season pork with *salt* and *pepper*. In a 10-inch skillet brown the chops with the onion in hot oil about 4 minutes per side. Drain off fat.

2 Arrange the fennel and cabbage on top of meat. In a small bowl stir together the ½ cup pear nectar or apple juice, vinegar, caraway seed, thyme, the ¼ teaspoon salt, ¼ teaspoon pepper, and nutmeg; pour into skillet. Cover and simmer for 12 to 15 minutes or till tender. Use a slotted spoon to transfer the pork and vegetables to a serving platter. Cover with foil to keep warm.

3 For sauce, measure the pan juices. If necessary add enough additional pear nectar to pan juices to make 1¼ cups total; return to skillet. Blend together the water and cornstarch; stir into skillet juices. Cook and stir over medium heat till thickened and bubbly. Stir in pear slices; heat through. Spoon pear slices and sauce over pork and vegetables. Makes 4 servings.

Nutrition facts per serving: 334 cal., 15 g total fat (4 g sat. fat), 77 mg chol., 229 mg sodium, 25 g carbo., 2 g fiber, 26 g pro. *Daily values:* 1% vit. A, 62% vit. C, 5% calcium, 14% iron.

PASTA WITH FENNEL

See the photograph on page 81.

- 8 **oz. penne, rigatoni, or mostaccioli**

◆◆◆

- 2 **medium fennel bulbs**

◆◆◆

- 3 **cloves garlic, minced**
- ½ **tsp. crushed red pepper**
- 2 **Tbsp. olive oil or cooking oil**
- 2 **Tbsp. margarine or butter**
- 1 **cup red and/or green sweet pepper strips**
- 1 **15-oz. can great Northern beans, drained and rinsed**
- ¼ **tsp. dried thyme, crushed Cracked black pepper**
- ¼ **cup shaved or shredded Parmesan cheese**

1 In a 4-quart Dutch oven or large saucepan cook the pasta according to package directions; drain. Return to pan and cover. Trim fennel, reserving leaves for garnish, if desired. Cut the fennel crosswise into thin strips.

2 In a medium skillet cook garlic and crushed red pepper in olive oil and margarine or butter for 30 seconds. Add fennel to skillet; cook and stir 5 minutes. Add sweet pepper strips; cook 3 minutes more. Add beans and thyme; cook 2 minutes to heat through. Add fennel mixture to pasta; toss gently. Season to taste with pepper. Serve with Parmesan cheese. Makes 4 servings.

Nutrition facts per serving: 512 cal., 16 g total fat (2 g sat. fat), 5 mg chol., 179 mg sodium, 74 g carbo., 1 g fiber, 20 g pro. *Daily values:* 27% vit. A, 81% vit. C, 28% iron.

Spiced Roast with
Dijon Sauce (see below)

♦♦♦

Boiled new potatoes
drizzled with butter and
sprinkled with chives

♦♦♦

Steamed green beans

♦♦♦

Iceberg lettuce wedges
with Italian salad dressing

CARBONNADE OF BEEF AND VEGETABLES

Classic carbonnade, a French beef stew, usually contains beer, onions, and brown sugar.

2 lb. boneless beef top round steak, cut into 1-inch cubes
2 Tbsp. cooking oil
3 large leeks or medium onions, sliced
2 12-oz. cans beer (3 cups)
¼ cup red wine vinegar
3 Tbsp. brown sugar
2 Tbsp. instant beef bouillon granules
4 cloves garlic, minced
2 bay leaves
2 tsp. dried thyme, crushed
2 tsp. Worcestershire sauce
½ tsp. pepper
1 lb. carrots, peeled and cut diagonally into ½-inch slices
4 parsnips, peeled and cut diagonally into ½-inch slices

♦♦♦

¼ cup water
2 Tbsp. quick-cooking tapioca

♦♦♦

Hot cooked wide noodles
Fresh thyme (optional)

1 In a 4-quart Dutch oven brown the meat, half at a time, in hot oil. Drain off fat. Return all meat to Dutch oven. Add leeks or onions, beer, red wine vinegar, brown sugar, bouillon, garlic, bay leaves, thyme, Worcestershire sauce, and pepper. Bring mixture to boiling; reduce heat. Cover; simmer for 45 minutes, stirring occasionally. Add carrots and parsnips. Cook, covered, 35 to 40 minutes more or till tender.

2 Remove bay leaves; skim off any fat from the sauce. Combine water and tapioca. Stir tapioca mixture into the meat mixture; cook and stir over medium heat till thickened and bubbly. Cook and stir for 2 minutes more.

3 To serve, divide mixture into 2 equal portions. Serve half over hot noodles. If desired, garnish with fresh thyme. (Cool remaining half slightly. Transfer to a storage container. Cover and refrigerate up to 3 days. Or, place in a freezer container and freeze up to 6 months.) Serves 8.

Reheating directions: For refrigerated stew, place in a medium saucepan. Cook, covered, over medium-low heat 10 to 15 minutes or till heated through, stirring occasionally.

For frozen stew, place the unthawed stew in a medium saucepan. Cook, covered, over low heat for 45 to 50 minutes or till heated, stirring occasionally.

Nutrition facts per serving: 393 cal., 9 g total fat (2 g sat. fat), 79 mg chol., 755 mg sodium, 48 g carbo., 4 g fiber, 26 g pro. *Daily values:* 161% vit. A, 18% vit. C, 10% calcium, 34% iron.

SPICED ROAST WITH DIJON SAUCE

½ tsp. fennel seed
½ tsp. mustard seed
½ tsp. whole black pepper
1 2½-lb. boneless beef round rump roast

♦♦♦

1 cup sliced fresh mushrooms
1 Tbsp. margarine or butter
2 Tbsp. all-purpose flour
1 cup milk
2 Tbsp. coarse-grain brown mustard
1 tsp. snipped fresh chives

1 Using a mortar and pestle, crush the fennel seed, mustard seed, and pepper; set aside. Trim excess fat from meat. Place roast, fat side up, on a rack in a 13×9×2-inch baking pan. Rub half of the seed mixture over top and sides of roast. Insert a meat thermometer in center of roast. Roast, uncovered, in a 325° oven 1¼ to 1¾ hours or till meat thermometer registers 150° to 170°.

2 For sauce, in a saucepan cook mushrooms in margarine till tender. Stir in remaining seed mixture, flour, and ¼ teaspoon *salt*. Add milk all at once. Cook and stir till thickened and bubbly. Cook 1 minute more. Stir in mustard and chives. Serve with roast. Serves 8.

Nutrition facts per serving: 193 cal., 7 g total fat (2 g sat. fat), 70 mg chol., 198 mg sodium, 4 g carbo., 0 g fiber, 27 g pro. *Daily values:* 37% vit. A, 1% vit. C, 4% calcium, 18% iron.

The New Sweet-and-Sour Pork

Save 280 calories and 19 grams of fat per serving with this slimmed-down Oriental favorite.

1 cup long grain rice
◆◆◆
12 oz. lean boneless pork
½ cup fine dry bread crumbs
2 Tbsp. margarine or butter, melted
1 clove garlic, minced
◆◆◆
1 cup reduced-sodium chicken broth
⅓ cup sugar
⅓ cup red wine vinegar
4 tsp. cornstarch
1 Tbsp. reduced-sodium soy sauce
◆◆◆
Nonstick spray coating
1 clove garlic, minced
3 medium carrots, thinly bias-sliced (½ cup)
1 medium green sweet pepper, cut into 1-inch squares (1 cup)
1 medium red sweet pepper, cut into 1-inch squares (1 cup)
3 green onions, bias-sliced into 1-inch pieces
◆◆◆
1 8-oz. can pineapple chunks (juice pack), drained

1 Cook rice according to the package directions, except omit the margarine or butter and the salt. Keep rice warm while preparing the pork and vegetables.

2 Meanwhile, trim any visible fat from the pork. Cut the pork into ¾-inch cubes; set aside. Place bread crumbs in a shallow dish. In a medium mixing bowl stir together the melted margarine or butter and the 1 clove minced garlic. Add the pork and toss to coat. Roll pork cubes in bread crumbs to coat evenly.

3 Arrange the pork in an ungreased 15×10×1-inch baking pan. Bake in a 375° oven for 10 to 12 minutes or till pork is tender and no pink remains. (It's not necessary to turn pork during baking.) Cover and keep pork warm while preparing the sauce and vegetables.

4 For sauce, in a small mixing bowl stir together the chicken broth, sugar, red wine vinegar, cornstarch, and soy sauce. Set sauce aside.

5 Spray a cold wok or large skillet with nonstick coating. Preheat the wok or skillet over medium heat. Add the 1 clove minced garlic to the wok or skillet and stir-fry for 15 seconds. Add the sliced carrots; cover and cook for 3 minutes. Add the green and red sweet peppers and green onions; stir-fry for 3 to 4 minutes more or till vegetables are crisp-tender. (If necessary, add a small amount of water during cooking to prevent sticking.)

6 Remove the cooked vegetables from the wok or skillet. Stir sauce mixture; add to the wok. Cook and stir sauce till thickened and bubbly. Cook and stir 2 minutes more. Stir in the pineapple chunks and cooked vegetables.

Cook and stir about 1 minute more or till heated through.

7 To serve, spoon hot cooked rice onto 4 dinner plates. Top rice with pork; spoon vegetable mixture over pork. Serve immediately. Makes 4 main-dish servings.

Nutrition facts per serving: 447 cal., 13 g total fat (3 g sat. fat), 38 mg chol., 502 mg sodium, 65 g carbo., 3 g fiber, 19 g pro. *Daily values:* 203% vit. A, 46% vit. C, 8% calcium, 25% iron.

Bean Soup With Rutabaga and Bok Choy

For a speedier version, you can skip the dry beans and their soaking. Instead, use two rinsed and drained cans of great Northern beans.

1 cup dry navy beans
4 cups water
◆◆◆
4 cups chicken broth
½ cup chopped onion
1 clove garlic, minced
¾ tsp. dried sage, crushed
¼ tsp. pepper
1½ cups rutabaga, peeled and cubed (about 8 oz.)
◆◆◆
1 14½-oz. can tomatoes, cut up
2 cups thinly sliced bok choy*

1 Rinse beans. In a 3-quart saucepan combine beans and the 4 cups water. Bring to boiling; reduce heat. Simmer for 2 minutes; remove from heat. Cover and let stand for 1 hour. (Or, soak beans in water overnight.) Drain and rinse beans.

2 In the same pan combine chicken broth, onion, garlic, sage, pepper, and drained beans. Bring to boiling; reduce heat. Simmer, covered, for 40 minutes. Add rutabaga. Return to boiling; reduce heat. Simmer, covered, for 20 to 25 minutes or till beans are tender. Slightly mash beans.

3 Stir in undrained tomatoes and bok choy. Cook for 4 to 5 minutes or till bok choy is crisp-tender. Makes 8 cups (4 main-dish servings).

***Note:** You can use both the stalks and the green leaves of bok choy in this soup. To prepare, trim the base and pull the stalks apart. Slice the stalks, then slice or shred the leaves.

Nutrition facts per serving: 255 cal., 2 g total fat (1 g sat. fat), 1 mg chol., 960 mg sodium, 42 g carbo., 3 g fiber, 17 g pro. *Daily values:* 10% vit. A, 77% vit. C, 13% calcium, 30% iron.

ROASTED POTATO AND GARLIC SOUP

4 medium red potatoes
1 large onion, coarsely chopped
2 tsp. snipped fresh rosemary or 1 tsp. dried rosemary, crushed
1 bulb garlic
1 Tbsp. olive oil
  ♦♦♦
1 14½-oz. can chicken broth
1 Tbsp. all-purpose flour
¼ tsp. pepper
  ♦♦♦

1 cup half-and-half or light cream
1 recipe Homemade Croutons (see below right) (optional)
 Fresh rosemary (optional)

1 Peel and cube 2 of the potatoes. Cube remaining 2 potatoes, leaving skin on. Place peeled potatoes on one side of a 9×9×2-inch baking pan and unpeeled potatoes on the other side. Sprinkle onion and snipped rosemary evenly over all. Peel away the dry outer leaves of skin from bulb of garlic. Leave skins of cloves intact. Snip off the pointed top with scissors, leaving the bulb intact, but exposing the cloves. Place the garlic bulb, cut side up, on top of the potatoes. Drizzle olive oil over all. Bake, covered, in a 400° oven about 50 minutes or till garlic cloves feel soft and potatoes are tender; cool slightly.

2 Squeeze the garlic bulb to remove the paste from the cloves. In a blender container or food processor bowl, combine about half the onion, garlic paste, and peeled potatoes, and half the chicken broth, all of the flour, and the pepper. Cover and blend or process till nearly smooth.

3 Pour the pureed mixture into a medium saucepan. Stir in the unpeeled cooked potato, remaining onion and broth, and half-and-half. Cook and stir over medium heat till slightly thickened and bubbly. Cook and stir for 1 minute more. If necessary, stir in additional half-and-half to make the soup the desired consistency. To serve, ladle into soup bowls. If desired, top each serving

Bean Soup with Rutabaga and Bok Choy (see page 60)

♦♦♦

Rye rolls with butter

♦♦♦

Carrot cake or apple cake

with Homemade Croutons and a sprig of rosemary. Makes 5 cups (4 side-dish servings).

Nutrition facts per serving: 285 cal., 11 g total fat (5 g sat. fat), 23 mg chol., 361 mg sodium, 40 g carbo., 3 g fiber, 8 g pro. *Daily values:* 7% vit. A, 26% vit. C, 8% calcium, 7% iron.

HOMEMADE CROUTONS

2 cups cubed sourdough bread or rye bread
2 Tbsp. margarine or butter, melted
½ tsp. Italian seasoning, crushed

1 Spread the sourdough or rye bread cubes in a single layer in a shallow baking dish. Stir together melted margarine or butter and Italian seasoning; pour over bread cubes. Bake in a 400° oven for 5 minutes; stir. Bake for 5 to 10 minutes more or till crisp and brown. Makes 2 cups.

Nutrition facts per ¼ cup: 43 cal., 3 g total fat (1 g sat. fat), 0 mg chol., 72 mg sodium, 3 g carbo., 0 g fiber, 1 g pro. *Daily values:* 3% vit. A, 1% iron.

WINTER SQUASH SOUP

A surprising blend of tomato and orange juices adds snap to this pureed soup. If you like, chill the smooth soup overnight, then just reheat to serve.

1¼ **lb. butternut squash**
♦♦♦
2 **stalks celery, chopped (1 cup)**
1 **medium onion, chopped (½ cup)**
1 **Tbsp. margarine or butter**
1 **tart medium apple (such as Granny Smith or McIntosh), peeled, cored, and chopped (1 cup)**
1¼ **cups water**
1¼ **cups tomato juice**
¼ **tsp. apple pie spice**
¼ **tsp. salt**
♦♦♦
¾ **cup orange juice**
Poached apple slices (optional)
Snipped fresh chives (optional)

1 Peel, seed, and cube squash (should have about 3 cups). Set squash aside.

2 In a 3-quart saucepan cook celery and onion in hot margarine or butter about 5 minutes or till nearly tender. Add the apple, water, tomato juice, apple pie spice, salt, and cubed squash. Bring to boiling; reduce heat. Simmer, covered, about 20 minutes or till squash is tender. Cool the mixture slightly.

3 Place mixture, half at a time, in a blender container or food processor bowl. Cover and blend or process till smooth. Return mixture to saucepan. Stir in orange juice; heat through. Season to taste with *pepper*. If desired, garnish each serving with poached apple slices and snipped chives. Makes about 5 cups (4 side-dish servings).

Nutrition facts per serving: 145 cal., 3 g total fat (1 g sat. fat), 0 mg chol., 350 mg sodium, 30 g carbo., 5 g fiber, 3 g pro. *Daily values:* 82% vit. A, 85% vit. C, 7% calcium, 10% iron.

WINTER RISOTTO

Arborio rice is a short Italian grain that contributes to the creamy quality of risotto. This rice is worth looking for in specialty food shops if you can't find it in your supermarket.

½ **cup chopped onion**
2 **cloves garlic, minced**
1 **Tbsp. margarine or butter**
1 **cup Arborio rice or medium grain rice**
♦♦♦
2 **cups water**
1 **14½-oz. can chicken broth**
♦♦♦
8 **oz. broccoli raab, torn into bite-size pieces (about 2¾ cups), or 4 oz. broccoli, cut into 1-inch pieces, plus 4 oz. torn fresh spinach**
⅓ **cup finely shredded Parmesan cheese**
¼ **tsp. pepper**
Dash ground nutmeg
¼ **cup chopped toasted pecans**
Cracked black pepper
Finely shredded Parmesan cheese (optional)

1 In a 3-quart saucepan cook onion and garlic in hot margarine or butter till onion is tender. Add uncooked rice. Cook and stir 2 minutes more.

2 Carefully stir water and broth into rice mixture. Bring to boiling; reduce heat. Simmer, covered, for 20 minutes (do not lift cover). Remove from heat.

3 Stir in broccoli raab or broccoli and spinach, ⅓ cup Parmesan cheese, ¼ teaspoon pepper, and nutmeg. Cover; let stand 10 minutes. To serve, top with pecans, cracked pepper, and, if desired, additional cheese. Makes 2½ cups (4 side-dish servings).

Nutrition facts per serving: 317 cal., 11 g total fat (1 g sat. fat), 8 mg chol., 494 mg sodium, 43 g carbo., 2 g fiber, 11 g pro. *Daily values:* 38% vit. C, 11% calcium, 18% iron.

CHAYOTE AND POTATO AU GRATIN

To fix ahead, prepare the filling and spoon it into the chayote halves; cover and refrigerate for up to 4 hours. Simply add a few extra minutes to the baking time to heat through.

2 **medium chayotes**
♦♦♦
2 **medium red potatoes, chopped (about 2 cups)**
♦♦♦
2 **Tbsp. margarine or butter**
4 **tsp. all-purpose flour**
¼ **tsp. salt**
⅛ **tsp. ground nutmeg**
1 **cup milk**
1 **Tbsp. chopped pimiento**
♦♦♦
¾ **cup soft bread crumbs (1 slice)**
¼ **cup finely shredded or grated Parmesan cheese**
1 **Tbsp. margarine or butter, melted**

1 In a large saucepan cook whole chayotes, covered, in enough boiling salted water to cover, about 40 minutes or till tender; drain. When cool enough to handle, halve chayotes lengthwise; remove seeds. Scoop out pulp to within ½ inch of skin; discard pulp. Set halves aside.

2 Meanwhile, in a medium saucepan cook potatoes, uncovered, in boiling salted water for 5 to 7 minutes or till tender. Drain and set aside.

3 In the same medium saucepan melt the 2 tablespoons margarine or butter. Stir in the flour, salt, and nutmeg. Add milk all at once. Cook and stir till thickened and bubbly. Cook and stir for 1 minute more. Stir in pimiento and potatoes.

4 Season the insides of chayote halves lightly with *salt* and *pepper*. Place the halves, cut side up, in a 2-quart square baking dish. Spoon potato mixture into halves. In a small bowl toss together the bread crumbs, Parmesan cheese, and the 1 tablespoon melted margarine. Sprinkle atop the chayote halves (can refrigerate them at this point). Bake in a 350° oven, uncovered, about 25 minutes or till light brown and heated. Makes 4 side-dish servings.

Nutrition facts per serving: 268 cal., 12 g total fat (2 g sat. fat), 9 mg chol., 396 mg sodium, 34 g carbo., 3 g fiber, 8 g pro. *Daily values:* 65% vit. A, 39% vit. C, 15% calcium, 14% iron.

MUSTARD-GLAZED BRUSSELS SPROUTS AND ORANGES

You'll win converts to Brussels sprouts when you serve this slightly sweet dish. (See the photograph on page 83.)

3 medium oranges (such as blood and/or navel)

◆◆◆

1 lb. fresh Brussels sprouts (about 4 cups)

◆◆◆

1 Tbsp. margarine or butter
2 tsp. cornstarch
¼ tsp. five-spice powder or dried dillweed
2 Tbsp. honey mustard

1 Finely shred portion of peel of one orange to make ½ teaspoon peel; set aside. Halve orange; squeeze juice. Working over a bowl to catch juices, peel and section remaining oranges (see illustration, below right); set aside. Combine juices to make ⅓ cup (add water, if necessary).

2 Rinse the Brussels sprouts. Halve any large sprouts. In a medium saucepan cook sprouts, uncovered, in a small amount of boiling water for 10 to 12 minutes or till tender. Drain and transfer sprouts to a serving bowl. Gently stir in the orange sections; cover and keep warm.

3 In the same saucepan melt margarine or butter. Stir in cornstarch and five-spice powder or dillweed. Stir in mustard, reserved orange peel, and orange juice. Cook and stir till thickened and

bubbly. Cook and stir for 1 minute more. Pour sauce over sprouts and oranges, tossing gently to coat. Makes 3½ cups (5 to 6 side-dish servings).

Nutrition facts per serving: 103 cal., 3 g total fat (1 g sat. fat), 0 mg chol., 87 mg sodium, 19 g carbo., 5 g fiber, 3 g pro. *Daily values:* 11% vit. A, 148% vit. C, 4% calcium, 9% iron.

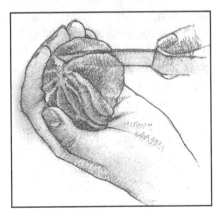

MUSHROOM CROUSTADES

This recipe earned Beth Labant of Elk Grove Village, Illinois, $100 in the magazine's monthly contest.

24 slices firm-textured white bread

♦♦♦

3 Tbsp. chopped shallots or onion
¼ cup margarine or butter
3 cups finely chopped fresh mushrooms
2 Tbsp. all-purpose flour
1 cup whipping cream
2 Tbsp. snipped fresh chives
1 Tbsp. snipped fresh parsley
½ tsp. lemon juice
¼ tsp. salt
⅛ tsp. ground red pepper
Dash ground black pepper

♦♦♦

2 Tbsp. grated Parmesan cheese
Dairy sour cream (optional)
Snipped fresh chives (optional)

1 Lightly grease twenty-four 2½-inch muffin cups. Cut a 2½-inch round from each slice of bread.* Carefully press each round into prepared muffin cups. Bake in a 400° oven about 10 minutes or till golden.

2 Meanwhile, for filling, in a medium saucepan cook shallots or onion in hot margarine or butter for 4 minutes. Stir in mushrooms; cook, uncovered, about 15 minutes or till most of the liquid has evaporated. Stir in flour. Add whipping cream all at once. Cook and stir till thickened and bubbly. Cook and stir for 1 minute more; remove from heat. Stir in the 2 tablespoons chives, parsley, lemon juice, salt, red pepper, and black pepper.

3 Place bread shells in a shallow baking pan. Spoon filling into shells; sprinkle with Parmesan cheese. Bake, uncovered, in 350° oven 15 minutes. If desired, top with sour cream and chives. Makes 24 appetizers.

***Note:** You can use the bread scraps to make soft bread crumbs for toppings and stuffings.

▐ TO MAKE AHEAD ▌

Prepare the baked bread shells as directed. Place in a freezer container or bag and freeze for up to 3 months. To serve, thaw bread shells, fill, and bake as directed.

Nutrition facts per appetizer: 93 cal., 6 g total fat (3 g sat. fat), 14 mg chol., 126 mg sodium, 8 g carbo., 0 g fiber, 2 g pro. *Daily values:* 8% vit. A, 1% vit. C, 2% calcium, 4% iron.

MUSHROOM TARTS

1 cup all-purpose flour
⅓ cup unsalted butter
2 Tbsp. sesame seed or poppy seed
3 to 4 Tbsp. water

♦♦♦

3 cups chopped fresh button, shiitake, oyster, or other mushrooms
½ cup chopped green onions
2 cloves garlic, minced
2 Tbsp. unsalted butter
2 tsp. soy sauce
1 Tbsp. cognac or brandy (optional)

⅔ cup whipping cream
2 tsp. cornstarch
½ tsp. dried thyme, crushed
Salt and pepper
Finely chopped red sweet pepper or green onion, or snipped fresh chives or parsley

1 In a bowl stir together the flour and ¼ teaspoon *salt*. Cut in the ⅓ cup butter till size of small peas. Stir in sesame or poppy seed and enough water to moisten. On a lightly floured surface, knead lightly till dough becomes a smooth ball. Divide dough into 24 balls. Place each ball in an ungreased 1¾-inch muffin cup. Press dough evenly against the bottom and sides of cups. Bake in a 375° oven for 12 to 15 minutes or till lightly golden brown. Cool in pan 5 minutes. Remove from cups and cool completely on a wire rack.

2 Meanwhile, for filling, in a large skillet cook the mushrooms, green onions, and garlic in the 2 tablespoons butter for 3 minutes. Add soy sauce and, if desired, cognac or brandy; cook 1 minute more. Stir together the whipping cream, cornstarch, and thyme. Add to skillet and cook and stir till thickened and bubbly. Cook and stir 2 minutes more. Season to taste with salt and pepper. Spoon about 1 tablespoon filling into each baked tart shell. Sprinkle with red pepper, green onion, chives, or parsley; serve warm. Makes 24 appetizers.

Nutrition facts per appetizer: 75 cal., 6 g total fat (3 g sat. fat), 17 mg chol., 54 mg sodium, 5 g carbo., 0 g fiber, 1 g pro. *Daily values:* 6% vit. A, 1% vit. C, 3% iron.

PORTOBELLO MUSHROOM FAJITAS

This recipe earned Lisa Keys of Middlebury, Connecticut, $200 in the magazine's monthly contest.

- 3 Tbsp. lime juice
- 1 Tbsp. olive oil or cooking oil
- 2 large cloves garlic, minced
- ½ tsp. ground cumin
- ¼ tsp. dried oregano, crushed
- 10 oz. fresh portobello mushrooms, thinly sliced
- 1 medium red, green, or yellow sweet pepper, cut into thin strips
- 4 green onions, cut into 1½-inch pieces

◆◆◆

- 6 7-inch flour tortillas
  Lime wedges (optional)

1 Combine lime juice, oil, garlic, cumin, oregano, and 3 tablespoons *water*. Add mushrooms, sweet pepper, and onions; toss. Marinate at room temperature for 15 to 30 minutes. Wrap tortillas in foil; heat in 350° oven 10 minutes.

2 For filling, in a large nonstick skillet cook undrained vegetables over medium-high heat about 5 minutes or till sweet pepper is tender and most of the liquid has evaporated, stirring occasionally. To serve, spoon mushroom filling onto tortillas; roll up. If desired, serve with lime wedges. Makes 6 side-dish servings.

Nutrition facts per serving: 156 cal., 5 g total fat (1 g sat. fat), 0 mg chol., 169 mg sodium, 24 g carbo., 1 g fiber, 4 g pro. *Daily values:* 2% vit. A, 24% vit. C, 4% calcium, 15% iron.

MAGNIFICENT MUSHROOMS

Mushrooms are one of the hottest happenings on today's food scene. These magnificent morsels have hit the produce shelves in all shapes and sizes. Besides being available in several varieties year-round, they're good for you, have lots of flavor, and are quick to cook. Familiarize yourself with the various mushrooms, then add some to your favorite dishes.

Shiitake—This Oriental mushroom has a smoky, woodsy flavor. Cook only the floppy, spongy caps; discard the stems.

Brown—Also called crimini, this mushroom has an earthy but mild flavor that distinguishes it from the white mushroom. Enjoy it raw or cooked.

Enoki—This Oriental variety with a long, slender stem and tiny cap has an extremely mild flavor and is good raw. Trim ½ to 1 inch off the base to separate.

White—The most popular all-purpose mushroom, also called button, it has caps from ½ inch to 3 inches in diameter. Cooked or raw, it has a delicate, mild flavor.

Oyster—This Oriental variety tastes like oysters and has a cream color, silky texture, and large flowerlike cap. Cooking enhances its flavor.

Portobello—This giant mushroom is actually a mature brown mushroom. Cooking brings out its hearty beef flavor.

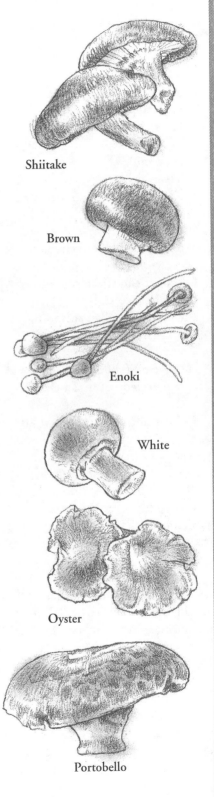

Shiitake

Brown

Enoki

White

Oyster

Portobello

ITALIAN SAUSAGE AND MUSHROOM BREAD

5¾ to 6¼ cups all-purpose flour
1 pkg. active dry yeast
3 cups coarsely chopped fresh mushrooms
8 oz. bulk Italian sausage
¼ cup chopped onion
1 large clove garlic, minced

❖❖❖

2 cups milk
2 Tbsp. sugar
1 Tbsp. margarine, butter, or olive oil
1¼ tsp. salt
½ cup shredded mozzarella cheese (2 oz.)
1 2¼-oz. can sliced ripe olives (about ½ cup)
2 tsp. dried Italian seasoning, crushed

❖❖❖

Olive oil (about 2 Tbsp.)
¼ cup grated Parmesan cheese

1 In a large mixing bowl stir together 2½ cups of the flour and the yeast; set aside. Reserve 1 cup of the mushrooms; set aside. In a medium skillet cook the sausage, onion, garlic, and remaining mushrooms till sausage is browned. Drain and set aside.

2 In a medium saucepan heat the milk, sugar, margarine, and salt till warm (120° to 130°) and margarine almost melts. Add to flour mixture and beat with an electric mixer on low speed for 30 seconds. Beat on high speed for 3 minutes, scraping bowl constantly. Use a wooden spoon to stir in the mozzarella, olives, Italian seasoning, and sausage mixture. Stir in as much of the remaining flour as possible.

3 Turn dough out onto a lightly floured surface. Knead in enough of the remaining flour to make a moderately stiff dough (6 to 8 minutes total). Shape dough into a ball. Place in a large, lightly greased bowl, turning once to grease surface. Cover and let rise in a warm place till double (about 1 hour).

4 Punch dough down. Divide dough in half. Cover and let rest 10 minutes. Grease two 12-inch pizza pans or large baking sheets. Place a dough portion on each. Pat dough into an even round, 12 inches in diameter. Use your fingertips to poke the dough to dimple surface all over. Cover loosely and let rise till nearly double (about 30 minutes).

5 Brush each round with a little olive oil. Sprinkle each with Parmesan cheese and reserved mushrooms. Bake in a 400° oven about 25 minutes or till golden brown. Cut into wedges and serve warm. To store, cool completely, cover, and chill. To reheat, place on a pizza pan or baking sheet. Bake in a 350° oven 8 minutes or till warm. Makes 24 servings.

```
TO MAKE AHEAD
```

Prepare and bake bread as directed; cool completely. Place in a freezer container or bag and freeze for up to 3 months. To serve, place frozen bread on a pizza pan or baking sheet. Cover loosely with foil. Bake in 350° oven for 15 to 20 minutes or till warm.

Nutrition facts per serving: 171 cal., 5 g total fat (2 g sat. fat), 9 mg chol., 239 mg sodium, 24 g carbo., 1 g fiber, 6 g pro. *Daily values:* 2% vit. A, 1% vit. C, 5% calcium, 11% iron.

MIXED CITRUS SALAD

1 pink or red grapefruit
1 blood or navel orange

❖❖❖

¼ cup salad oil
½ tsp. finely shredded lemon peel
2 Tbsp. lemon juice
1 tsp. sugar
2 tsp. Dijon-style mustard

❖❖❖

2 cups thinly sliced Belgian endive*
2 cups torn escarole
½ of a small jicama, peeled and cut into matchsticks (about 1 cup)

1 Peel and section grapefruit and orange, reserving any juices (see illustration, page 63). Cover and set aside or chill till needed.

2 In a screw-top jar combine oil, lemon peel, lemon juice, sugar, mustard, grapefruit and orange juices, and ¼ teaspoon *pepper.* Cover and shake well.

3 Place Belgian endive and escarole on salad plates. Arrange grapefruit and orange sections and jicama atop greens; drizzle with dressing. Makes 4 to 6 side-dish servings.

*Note: To prepare Belgian endive, pull apart leaves to reveal core. Use a knife to remove this bitter core. Thinly slice cone-shaped bunch of leaves crosswise.

Nutrition facts per serving: 191 cal., 14 g total fat (2 g sat. fat), 0 mg chol., 70 mg sodium, 17 g carbo., 2 g fiber, 2 g pro. *Daily values:* 7% vit. A, 90% vit. C, 2% calcium, 4% iron.

COASTAL FRUIT BOWL

Try some of the tropical fresh fruits now being grown in Florida and California. Soak them in a Caribbean-style rum and lime syrup, then serve them icy cold.

⅓ cup water
¼ cup sugar
1 Tbsp. lime juice
1 to 2 Tbsp. light rum (optional)
   Few dashes aromatic bitters (optional)

❖❖❖

2 cups desired cut-up fresh fruit, such as cherimoya, carambola (star fruit), guava, kiwifruit, mango, banana, and/or papaya, chilled*
   Lime peel curls (optional)
   Lime wedges (optional)

1 In a small saucepan bring water and sugar to boiling, stirring till sugar is dissolved. Reduce heat to low. Simmer, uncovered, for 1 minute; remove from heat. Stir in lime juice and, if desired, rum and bitters. Transfer to a storage container; cover and chill.

2 To serve, place fruit in bowls. Spoon the chilled syrup over fruit. If desired, garnish each serving with a lime peel curl and serve with a lime wedge. Makes 4 side-dish servings.

***Note:** Some fruit skins and seeds are edible, but others aren't. You'll want to peel cherimoya, mango, and papaya, and discard their seeds. The carambola doesn't require peeling before slicing, but

you may want to strip off the brownish fibers on the ridges. The skins and seeds of guava and kiwifruit are edible.

Nutrition facts per serving: 84 cal., 0 g total fat, 0 mg chol., 4 mg sodium, 21 g carbo., 3 g fiber, 1 g pro.
Daily values: 6% vit. A, 128% vit. C, 1% calcium, 1% iron.

30 MIN.

WARM WINTER SALAD

Serve this easy wilted salad as a companion to broiled fish and chicken. Keep your cooked entrée warm while you quickly toss together this fanciful medley. (See the photograph on page 84.)

2 cups torn romaine
2 cups coarsely shredded radicchio and/or Belgian endive
2 cups torn escarole
1 medium onion, thinly sliced and separated into rings
1 Tbsp. sugar
3 Tbsp. olive oil or salad oil
2 Tbsp. pine nuts or slivered almonds

❖❖❖

2 cloves garlic, minced
¼ tsp. dried tarragon, crushed
   Toasted baguette slices (optional)
   Fresh ground black pepper
   Lemon wedges

1 In a large bowl toss together the romaine, radicchio and/or Belgian endive, and escarole; set aside. In a 10-inch skillet cook and stir onion and sugar in hot oil about 5 minutes or till onion is tender. Add pine nuts or almonds. Cook and stir for 1 to 2 minutes more or till nuts are toasted.

FRESH FRUIT IN WINTER?

More and more supermarkets are stocking favorite summer fruits, even in the dead of winter. That's because, on the other side of the equator (especially in Chile), summer fruits are now being picked and shipped north. If you're craving fresh plums, peaches, grapes, and berries in January, however, you'll pay dearly. Here are a couple of tips on enjoying your imported treasures:

◆ Nectarines, plums, and peaches are harvested and shipped when mature but still unripe. That means they need ripening at room temperature in a paper bag before you sink your teeth into them. Once the fruit feels soft and fleshy, store in a plastic bag in the refrigerator for several days.

◆ Reserve your imported gems for fresh fruit bowls, lunch-box treats, and dessert garnishes. In winter, when you prepare a baked dessert (such as cobbler or pie) that requires cupfuls of fruit, choose frozen fruits.

2 Add garlic, tarragon, and greens to skillet. Toss 30 to 60 seconds or till just wilted (do not overcook). If desired, serve over baguette slices. Sprinkle with pepper. Pass lemon to squeeze over salad. Makes 4 servings.

Nutrition facts per serving: 151 cal., 13 g total fat (2 g sat. fat), 0 mg chol., 13 mg sodium, 9 g carbo., 1 g fiber, 3 g pro.
Daily values: 12% vit. A, 19% vit. C, 3% calcium, 7% iron.

PRIZE
TESTED
RECIPE
WINNER

HERBED HAM AND
VEGETABLE QUICHE

*This recipe earned Laurie Wethington
of Farmington, Michigan, $200 in the
magazine's monthly contest.*

2   cups thinly sliced zucchini
     and/or yellow summer
     squash
1   cup chopped onions
½   cup sliced fresh mushrooms
½   cup chopped red sweet
     pepper
1   Tbsp. margarine or butter

♦♦♦

¼   cup snipped fresh parsley or
     1 Tbsp. dried parsley
2   Tbsp. snipped fresh basil or
     1 tsp. dried basil, crushed
1   tsp. snipped fresh oregano or
     ¼ tsp. dried oregano,
     crushed
¼   tsp. garlic powder
⅛   tsp. pepper
2   beaten eggs

1   cup diced cooked ham
1   cup shredded mozzarella
     cheese (4 oz.)
½   cup shredded fontina
     cheese (2 oz.)

♦♦♦

1   17½-oz. pkg. (8) refrigerated
     biscuits

1 Grease a 10-inch quiche
dish; set aside. For filling, in a
large skillet cook the zucchini
and/or summer squash, onions,
mushrooms, and sweet pepper in
hot margarine or butter about
6 minutes or just till tender,
stirring occasionally. Remove
from heat. Stir in parsley, basil,
oregano, garlic powder, and pepper. Stir in eggs, ham, mozzarella,
and fontina cheese; set aside.

2 For crust, in prepared
quiche dish arrange 7 slightly flat-
tened biscuits around edge, allowing dough to extend over sides.
Place the remaining biscuit in
bottom of dish. Pinch edges to
seal. Flatten slightly to form an
even crust.

3 Spread filling evenly in
crust. Bake in a 375° oven about
25 minutes or till a knife inserted
near center comes out clean, covering edge with foil the last 5 to
10 minutes to prevent overbrowning. Let stand 10 minutes.
To serve, cut into wedges. Makes
6 servings.

Nutrition facts per serving: 438 cal., 23 g
total fat (8 g sat. fat), 105 mg chol.,
1,290 mg sodium, 39 g carbo., 2 g fiber,
20 g pro. *Daily values:* 20% vit. A, 42%
vit. C, 22% calcium, 18% iron.

PRIZE
TESTED
RECIPE
WINNER

BAKED ITALIAN OMELET

*This recipe earned Dawn K. Murphy
of Hercules, California, $100
in the magazine's monthly contest.*

8   beaten eggs
1   cup ricotta cheese
½   cup milk
½   tsp. dried basil, crushed
¼   tsp. salt
¼   tsp. fennel seed, crushed
¼   tsp. pepper
1   10-oz. pkg. frozen chopped
     spinach, thawed and well
     drained
1   cup chopped tomatoes
1   cup shredded mozzarella
     cheese (4 oz.)
½   cup thinly sliced green
     onions
½   cup diced salami

1 Grease a 3-quart rectangular
baking dish; set aside. In a large
mixing bowl combine eggs and
ricotta cheese; beat just till combined. Stir in milk, basil, salt, fennel seed, and pepper. Fold in
spinach, tomatoes, mozzarella,
green onions, and salami.

2 Spread mixture evenly in
the prepared dish. Bake in a 325°
oven for 30 to 35 minutes or till a
knife inserted near center comes
out clean. Let stand for 10 minutes. Makes 6 to 8 servings.

Nutrition facts per serving: 281 cal., 18 g
total fat (8 g sat. fat), 318 mg chol., 620 mg
sodium, 8 g carbo., 1 g fiber, 22 g pro.
Daily values: 51% vit. A, 21% vit. C,
28% calcium, 14% iron.

WINTER SQUASH-APPLE BRUNCH CAKE

No one will guess the secret ingredient that makes this so moist and golden. (See the photograph on page 2.)

2¼ cups all-purpose flour
2 tsp. baking powder
½ tsp. baking soda
½ tsp. ground cinnamon
¼ tsp. ground nutmeg

♦♦♦

½ cup margarine or butter
1⅓ cups granulated sugar
½ tsp. vanilla
3 eggs

♦♦♦

¾ cup mashed, cooked acorn or butternut squash (about 6 oz.)
½ cup buttermilk

♦♦♦

3 to 4 medium tart cooking apples (such as Granny Smith or McIntosh)
1 cup finely chopped walnuts
1 cup golden raisins
¼ cup granulated sugar
½ tsp. ground cinnamon

♦♦♦

1 recipe Powdered Sugar Icing (see right) or powdered sugar

1 Grease a 10-inch springform pan or 13×9×2-inch baking pan; set aside. Combine flour, baking powder, baking soda, ½ teaspoon cinnamon, and nutmeg; set aside.

2 In a large mixing bowl beat margarine or butter 30 seconds. Add the 1⅓ cups granulated sugar and vanilla; beat till combined. Add the eggs, one at a time, beating well after each addition.

3 Combine mashed squash and buttermilk. Add squash mixture and dry ingredients alternately to the egg mixture; mix well. Peel, core, and chop enough of the apples to make 1½ cups. Stir chopped apples, walnuts, and ½ cup of the raisins into the batter. Spoon batter into prepared pan. Peel, core, and thinly slice enough of the remaining apples to equal 1 cup. Combine the ¼ cup sugar and ½ teaspoon cinnamon; toss with sliced apples. Arrange apples on top of batter. Sprinkle with remaining raisins.

4 Bake in 325° oven 1 to 1¼ hours for springform pan (55 to 60 minutes for 13×9×2-inch pan) or till cake tests done with a toothpick. Cool on rack 10 minutes. If using springform pan, loosen sides of pan; cool on rack. Serve slightly warm or cool. Drizzle with Powdered Sugar Icing or sprinkle with powdered sugar. Makes 12 to 14 servings.

Powdered Sugar Icing: Stir together 1 cup sifted *powdered sugar* and enough *buttermilk* to make icing easy to drizzle.

Nutrition facts per serving: 434 cal., 16 g total fat (3 g sat. fat), 54 mg chol., 234 mg sodium, 71 g carbo., 2 g fiber, 6 g pro. *Daily values:* 12% vit. A, 5% vit. C, 9% calcium, 13% iron.

TEST KITCHEN TIP

WINTER APPLE VARIETIES

You'll find the following apples in markets during the winter months. Choose the variety that is best suited for your recipe.

VARIETY	FLAVOR	USES
Cortland	slightly tart	eating, baking
Empire	mildly tart	eating, salads
Golden Delicious	tangy, sweet	all-purpose
Granny Smith	tart	all-purpose
McIntosh	tart	eating, salads, sauces
Red Delicious	rich, sweet	eating, salads
Rome Beauty	slightly tart	baking, cooking
Stayman	rich, mildly tart	eating, cooking
Winesap	tangy, winelike	all-purpose
York Imperial	slightly tart	baking, cooking

STRAWBERRY-PAPAYA BREAKFAST SHAKE

½ cup skim milk
½ cup plain fat-free yogurt
½ cup fresh strawberries, hulled
½ of a medium papaya, seeded, peeled, and chopped (about ¾ cup)
1 Tbsp. honey

♦♦♦

3 large ice cubes or ⅓ cup crushed ice

1 In a blender container combine skim milk, plain yogurt, strawberries, papaya, and honey.

Cover and blend till smooth. With the blender running, add ice cubes, one at a time, through the opening in lid. Blend till smooth. Pour into tall glasses; serve immediately. Makes 2 (10-ounce) servings.

Nutrition Facts per serving: 117 cal., 0 g total fat (0 g sat. fat), 2 mg chol., 78 mg sodium, 24 g carbo., 1 g fiber, 6 g pro. *Daily values:* 14% vit. A, 91% vit. C, 17% calcium, 2% iron.

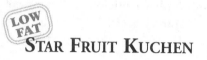

STAR FRUIT KUCHEN

Star fruit, also called carambola, is named for its star-shaped slices. Its slightly tart flavor tastes like a combination of lemon, pineapple, and apple.

½ cup all-purpose flour
½ cup yellow cornmeal
⅓ cup quick-cooking rolled oats
1 tsp. baking powder
⅛ tsp. baking soda

♦♦♦

2 egg whites
½ cup plain fat-free yogurt
⅓ cup packed brown sugar
2 Tbsp. dark molasses
2 Tbsp. margarine or butter, melted
1 tsp. finely shredded lemon peel

♦♦♦

1 large star fruit (carambola),* cut into 12 slices

♦♦♦

2 tsp. granulated sugar

1 In a large bowl combine flour, cornmeal, oats, baking powder, and baking soda. In another bowl combine egg whites, yogurt, brown sugar, molasses, margarine, and lemon peel.

2 Add egg white mixture to flour mixture, stirring just till combined. Spread batter into a lightly greased 8-inch round quiche pan or cake pan. Top batter with fruit slices.

3 Bake in a 350° oven about 30 minutes or till a toothpick inserted near the center comes out clean. Sprinkle with granulated sugar. Cool slightly in pan on a wire rack. Serve warm. Serves 8.

*Note: You can substitute one 8½-ounce can sliced peaches for the star fruit. Drain the syrup from the peaches and pat the fruit dry with paper towels before placing on top of the batter.

Nutrition facts per serving: 159 cal., 4 g total fat (1 g sat. fat), 0 mg chol., 131 mg sodium, 28 g carbo., 1 g fiber, 4 g pro. *Daily values:* 4% vit. A, 8% vit. C, 9% calcium, 12% iron.

BREAKFAST COUSCOUS WITH ORANGES AND CRANBERRIES

Special couscous topped with this honey-sweetened fruit sauce offers a new twist on hot breakfast cereal.

1 cup skim milk
¼ tsp. ground cinnamon
Dash ground nutmeg
1 cup couscous
2 Tbsp. dried currants
⅓ cup orange juice

♦♦♦

¾ cup cranberries
2 Tbsp. honey
2 Tbsp. water
1 11-ounce can mandarin orange sections, drained
1 Tbsp. slivered almonds, toasted

1 In a medium saucepan combine skim milk, cinnamon, and nutmeg. Bring to boiling over medium heat. Add couscous and currants. Cover; remove from heat. Let stand for 5 minutes. Stir in orange juice. Fluff with a fork.

2 Meanwhile, in a small saucepand combine cranberries, honey, and water. Cook over low heat for 4 to 5 minutes or till the cranberry skins begin to pop. Remove from heat. Gently stir in orange sections and almonds.

3 To serve, spoon the warm couscous into individual serving bowls. Top each serving with warm cranberry-orange mixture. Makes 4 servings.

Nutrition Facts per serving: 304 cal., 1 g total fat (0 g sat. fat), 1 mg chol., 42 mg sodium, 65 g carbo., 9 g fiber, 9 g pro. *Daily values:* 4% vit. A, 23% vit. C, 8% calcium, 6% iron.

COTTAGE BREAD

Use any pan you have on hand—a loaf pan, a round pan, or a casserole.

2 cups all-purpose flour
1 pkg. active dry yeast

❖❖❖

½ cup cream-style cottage cheese
½ cup water
1 Tbsp. sugar
1 Tbsp. margarine or butter
1 tsp. dried minced onion
¾ tsp. salt
1 egg
½ cup toasted wheat germ

1 Grease an 8×1½-inch round baking pan, 8×4×2-inch loaf pan, or a 1-quart casserole. Stir together 1 cup of the flour and the yeast. Set the baking pan and flour mixture aside.

2 In a medium saucepan heat and stir the cottage cheese, water, sugar, margarine or butter, onion, and salt till warm (120° to 130°) and margarine or butter is almost melted. Add cottage cheese mixture to the flour mixture. Add the egg. Beat with an electric mixer on low speed 30 seconds, scraping bowl constantly. Beat on high speed for 3 minutes more. Use a wooden spoon to stir in the wheat germ and the remaining flour (batter will be stiff). Spoon batter into the prepared pan or casserole. Cover; let rise in a warm place till nearly double (50 to 60 minutes).

3 Bake in a 375° oven 25 to 30 minutes for round baking pan or casserole (30 to 35 minutes for loaf pan) or till bread sounds hollow when lightly tapped. If necessary, cover with foil for the last 10 minutes to prevent overbrowning. Remove from pan or casserole. Serve warm or cool. Makes 1 loaf (12 servings).

■ TO MAKE AHEAD

Prepare and bake the bread as directed; cool completely. Place bread in a freezer container or bag and freeze for up to 3 months. Before serving, thaw the bread at room temperature.

Nutrition facts per serving: 118 cal., 2 g total fat (1 g sat. fat), 19 mg chol., 186 mg sodium, 19 g carbo., 1 g fiber, 5 g pro. *Daily values:* 3% vit. A, 1% calcium, 9% iron.

Cinnamon and Raisin Bread: Prepare and bake bread as directed below left, except add 2 teaspoons *ground cinnamon* with yeast, increase sugar to ¼ cup, omit the onion, and add ¾ cup *raisins* with wheat germ.

Feta-Spinach Bread: Prepare and bake bread as directed below left, except substitute ½ cup crumbled *feta cheese* and ¼ cup *milk* for cottage cheese. With the egg, add half of a 10-ounce package *frozen chopped spinach,* thawed and drained, and ½ tsp. *dried oregano,* crushed.

RICOTTA FRUIT DIP

Cut-up fruit from the produce section of your grocery store are great timesavers in this easy recipe.

⅓ cup fat-free ricotta cheese
2 Tbsp. powdered sugar
1 Tbsp. orange juice
½ tsp. vanilla
⅓ cup vanilla or peach low-fat yogurt

❖❖❖

2 cups strawberries, melon balls, and/or other cut-up fresh fruit

1 In a blender container or food processor bowl combine the ricotta cheese, powdered sugar, orange juice, and vanilla. Cover and blend or process till smooth. Stir into yogurt. Cover and chill for up to 24 hours, if desired. Serve with strawberries, melon, and/or other fruit. Serves 4.

Nutrition Facts per serving: 70 cal., 1 g total fat (0 g sat. fat), 3 mg chol., 23 mg sodium, 13 g carbo., 1 g fiber, 4 g pro. *Daily values:* 2% vit. A, 73% vit. C, 5% calcium, 2% iron.

CRANBERRY MUFFINS

2 cups all-purpose flour
2 tsp. baking powder
¼ tsp. baking soda

♦♦♦

½ cup unsweetened applesauce
½ cup sugar
¼ cup refrigerated or frozen
    egg product, thawed
3 Tbsp. unsweetened
    pineapple juice or
    orange juice
2 Tbsp. cooking oil
1 cup cranberries, coarsely
    chopped

♦♦♦

2 Tbsp. sugar
½ tsp. ground cinnamon

1 Line twelve 2½-inch muffin cups with paper bake cups or spray with *nonstick spray coating;* set aside. In a large mixing bowl stir together flour, baking powder, baking soda, and ⅛ teaspoon *salt.* Make a well in the center.

2 Stir together applesauce, the ½ cup sugar, the egg product, pineapple juice, and oil. Add to flour mixture and stir just till moistened. Fold in cranberries.

3 Spoon batter into prepared muffin cups, filling about three-fourths full. Stir together the 2 tablespoons sugar and the cinnamon. Sprinkle over batter. Bake in a 375° oven 20 to 25 minutes or till golden. Cool in cups 5 minutes. Remove and cool slightly on wire rack. Serve warm. Makes 12.

Nutrition facts per muffin: 146 cal., 3 g total fat (0 g sat. fat), 0 mg chol., 119 mg sodium, 29 g carbo., 1 g fiber, 3 g pro. *Daily values:* 1% vit. A, 3% vit. C, 5% calcium, 7% iron.

CHOCOLATE-SAUCED PEARS

Go ahead and splurge: A serving of this luscious pear dish contains fewer than 120 calories and only 1 gram of fat.

4 small pears

♦♦♦

2 Tbsp. lemon juice
2 tsp. vanilla
½ tsp. ground cinnamon

♦♦♦

2 Tbsp. chocolate-flavored
    syrup

1 Core pears from bottom end, leaving stems intact. Peel pears. If necessary, cut a thin slice from bottoms of pears to help them stand upright.

2 Place the pears in a 2-quart square baking dish. In a small bowl stir together the lemon juice, vanilla, and cinnamon. Brush mixture onto pears. Pour any extra juice mixture over pears.

3 Bake, covered, in a 375° oven for 30 to 35 minutes or till pears are tender. Cool slightly.

4 To serve, place the warm pears, stem end up, on dessert plates. Strain baking liquid; pour liquid into a small bowl. Stir in the chocolate-flavored syrup. Drizzle the sauce over the pears. Makes 4 servings.

Nutrition facts per serving: 116 cal., 1 g total fat (0 g sat. fat), 0 mg chol., 5 mg sodium, 29 g carbo., 4 g fiber, 1 g pro. *Daily values:* 15 % vit. C, 1% calcium, 4% iron.

PEAR CRISP WITH LEMON SAUCE

A crunchy oat and almond topping with warm, tender fruit underneath is capped with a rich lemon sauce. (See the photograph on page 82.)

5 cups sliced, peeled, and
    cored baking pears
1 Tbsp. granulated sugar
¼ tsp. finely shredded
    lemon peel

♦♦♦

⅔ cup regular rolled oats
⅓ cup packed brown sugar
⅓ cup all-purpose flour
¼ tsp. ground cardamom
¼ tsp. finely shredded
    lemon peel
¼ cup butter or margarine
⅓ cup sliced almonds

♦♦♦

1 recipe Lemon Sauce
    (see page 73)

1 In a 2-quart square baking dish toss the sliced pears with granulated sugar and ¼ teaspoon lemon peel.

2 For topping, in a medium bowl combine oats, brown sugar, flour, cardamom, and ¼ teaspoon lemon peel. Cut in butter or margarine till the mixture resembles coarse crumbs. Stir in almonds. Sprinkle topping over pears.

3 Bake in a 375° oven for 30 to 35 minutes or till pears are tender and topping begins to brown. Serve warm with Lemon Sauce. Makes 6 servings.

Nutrition facts per serving: 339 cal., 15 g total fat (6 g sat. fat), 62 mg chol., 103 mg sodium, 51 g carbo., 4 g fiber, 5 g pro. *Daily values:* 14% vit. A, 10% vit. C, 5% calcium, 11% iron.

LEMON SAUCE

You also can spoon this zippy sauce over poached pears or apples or slices of pound cake. Refrigerate any leftover sauce until needed.

¼ **cup sugar**
2 **tsp. cornstarch**
½ **cup water**

♦♦♦

1 **beaten egg yolk**
1 **Tbsp. butter or margarine**
¼ **tsp. finely shredded lemon peel**
1 **Tbsp. lemon juice**

1 In a 1-quart saucepan stir together the sugar and cornstarch. Add the water; stir till combined. Cook and stir over medium heat till thickened and bubbly. Cook and stir for 2 minutes more. Remove the saucepan from heat.

2 Stir a little of the hot mixture into the beaten egg yolk. Return all of the mixture to the saucepan. Cook and stir over low heat till nearly bubbly. Cook and stir for 1 minute more. Remove from heat. Stir in the butter or margarine, shredded lemon peel, and lemon juice. Serve sauce warm. Makes about ⅔ cup.

Nutrition facts per 2 tablespoons: 76 cal., 3 g total fat (2 g sat. fat), 48 mg chol., 26 mg sodium, 11 g carbo., 0 g fiber, 1 g pro. *Daily values:* 9% vit. A, 2% vit. C.

IRISH COFFEE ICE CREAM

Inspiration for this indulgence came from the popular beverage that blends coffee, Irish whiskey, and cream. Irish whiskey is less pungent than Scotch whisky and sweeter and cleaner in taste than American bourbon whiskey. Omit the whiskey if you wish, or use Irish Mist, a liqueur made of whiskey and honey, for a slightly sweeter note.

1 **cup sugar**
1 **envelope unflavored gelatin**
4 **cups half-and-half or light cream**

♦♦♦

3 **beaten eggs**
¼ **cup instant coffee crystals**
¼ **cup whiskey or Irish Mist liqueur**

1 In a large saucepan combine the sugar and gelatin. Stir in the half-and-half or light cream. Cook and stir over medium heat till mixture almost boils and sugar dissolves. Remove from heat.

2 Stir about 1 cup of the hot mixture into beaten eggs; return all to saucepan. Cook and stir for 2 minutes or till slightly thickened. Do not boil. Stir in the instant coffee crystals and whiskey or liqueur; cool. Transfer the mixture to a 4-quart ice-cream maker and freeze according to the manufacturer's directions. (Or, transfer the mixture to a 9×9×2-inch baking pan. Cover and freeze for 2 to 3 hours or till almost firm. Break frozen mixture into chunks. Transfer to a chilled bowl. Beat with an electric mixer till smooth but not melted. Return to pan. Cover and freeze till firm.) To serve, scoop into dessert dishes. Makes about 1½ quarts (12 to 16 servings).

Nutrition facts per ½ cup serving: 205 cal., 11 g total fat (6 g sat. fat), 83 mg chol., 50 mg sodium, 21 g carbo., 0 g fiber, 5 g pro. *Daily values:* 12% vit. A, 1% vit. C, 7% calcium, 2% iron.

Tangerine-Vanilla Curd

Slather this buttery and zesty spread onto scones, biscuits, toasted English muffins, or sourdough toast. Or, use it to fill tart shells or layer cakes. Make the vanilla sugar about a week beforehand so the vanilla bean has a chance to flavor the sugar.

¼ cup vanilla sugar (see tip, right)
1 Tbsp. cornstarch
1½ tsp. finely shredded tangerine peel (set aside)
1½ tsp. finely shredded lemon peel (set aside)
½ cup tangerine juice
1 Tbsp. lemon juice

◆◆◆

3 beaten egg yolks
2 Tbsp. margarine or butter, cut up

1 In a small saucepan combine vanilla sugar and cornstarch. Stir in tangerine juice and lemon juice. Cook and stir over medium heat till thickened and bubbly. Cook and stir for 1 minute more.

2 Stir about half of the hot mixture into egg yolks. Return all to saucepan. Cook and stir just till mixture begins to bubble. Remove from heat. Stir in tangerine peel, lemon peel, and margarine or butter just till melted (do not overmix). Cover surface with plastic wrap. Cool, then chill up to 2 weeks. Stir before serving. Makes about ⅞ cup.

Nutrition facts per tablespoon: 48 cal., 3 g total fat (1 g sat. fat), 46 mg chol., 21 mg sodium, 5 g carbo., 0 g fiber, 1 g pro. *Daily values:* 9% vit. A, 6% vit. C, 1% iron.

Vanilla Biscuits

Warm and tender, these delicate biscuits are a delicious choice for breakfast or brunch. We think they taste best when made with real butter.

1¾ cups all-purpose flour
⅓ cup vanilla sugar (see tip, right)
2 tsp. baking powder
¼ tsp. baking soda
¼ tsp. salt
⅓ cup butter

◆◆◆

1 egg
⅓ cup dairy sour cream
½ cup milk

◆◆◆

Powdered sugar

1 Lightly grease a baking sheet; set aside. In a medium mixing bowl stir together the flour, vanilla sugar, baking powder, baking soda, and salt. Using a pastry blender, cut in the butter till the mixture resembles coarse crumbs. Make a well in the center; set aside.

2 In a small mixing bowl beat egg slightly with a fork. Stir the sour cream into the egg till smooth. Stir in the milk. Add the egg mixture all at once to the flour mixture. Use a fork to stir just till moistened.

Vanilla Sugar

Split a vanilla bean lengthwise; store it in 1 to 2 cups sugar in a covered container about a week. Before using the sugar, discard bean. Use vanilla sugar in custards, breads, or in recipes such as those at left.

3 Drop dough by slightly rounded tablespoonsful onto the prepared baking sheet. Bake in a 375° oven for 12 to 15 minutes or till golden. Cool on the baking sheet for 5 minutes. Transfer the biscuits to a wire rack. Sift powdered sugar over tops. Serve warm. Makes about 12 biscuits.

TO MAKE AHEAD

Prepare and bake biscuits as directed, except cool completely and do not sprinkle with powdered sugar. Place biscuits in a freezer container or bag and freeze for up to 3 months. To serve, wrap frozen biscuits in foil; heat in a 300° oven for 20 to 25 minutes or till warm. Sprinkle with powdered sugar.

Nutrition facts per biscuit: 154 cal., 7 g total fat (4 g sat. fat), 35 mg chol., 197 mg sodium, 20 g carbo., 0 g fiber, 3 g pro. *Daily values:* 7% vit. A, 6% calcium, 6% iron.

APRIL
Fresh Meals in a Flash

30-minute recipes indicated in RED.
Low-fat recipes indicated with a ♥.

The secret to lighter, fresher, faster meals can be boiled down to a single word—pasta. From no-mess manicotti to no-cook noodles, pasta is the utility infielder of the spring kitchen. Angel Hair with Asparagus, Tomatoes, and Fresh Basil is a speedy choice, as is Orzo Pasta with Mushrooms and Leeks. Some pastas can be served warm or cold. Pasta salads such as Penne Salad with Italian Green Beans and Gorgonzola become main dishes by adding grilled lamb or chicken. Artichokes and rhubarb appear in April, just in time for Artichoke Sauté and an old favorite, Rhubarb Upside-Down Cake.

FETTUCCINE WITH SHRIMP, ARTICHOKES, AND RED CHILI PEPPERS

A flavored pasta, such as saffron or cayenne, will complement the shrimp. If using plain pasta, add a pinch of saffron or ground red pepper to the cooking water. (See the photograph on page 77.)

1¼ lb. fresh or frozen medium to large shrimp, peeled and deveined, and, if deveined, with tails intact

6 fresh baby artichokes or one 10-oz. pkg. frozen artichoke hearts, thawed

¾ tsp. finely shredded lemon peel (set aside)

2 Tbsp. lemon juice

♦♦♦

8 oz. fettuccine or other long, flat noodle, such as tagliatelle, mafalda, or linguine

♦♦♦

2 large shallots, peeled and finely chopped (⅓ cup)

½ cup chicken broth

2 tsp. snipped fresh thyme or ½ tsp. dried thyme, crushed

½ tsp. crushed red pepper

¼ tsp. salt

♦♦♦

½ cup whipping cream

1 Tbsp. butter*

♦♦♦

Lemon wedges (optional)

1 Thaw shrimp, if frozen. If using fresh artichokes, rinse well and trim stems. Remove the outer leaves; snip off sharp leaf tips about ¼ inch from top. Cut artichokes into quarters and dip into lemon juice to prevent browning. (If using frozen artichokes, cut in half and set aside.) Cook the pasta according to the package directions; drain and return to pan. Keep warm.

2 Meanwhile, in a large skillet combine the artichokes, shallots, chicken broth, thyme, red pepper, and salt; bring to boiling. Reduce heat; simmer, covered, till artichokes are tender. Allow 8 to 10 minutes for fresh artichokes or 5 minutes for frozen artichokes. Use a slotted spoon to remove the artichokes and shallots, reserving the liquid in skillet. Add shrimp to skillet and cook, uncovered, over medium heat for 2 to 3 minutes or till pink, stirring often. Use a slotted spoon to transfer shrimp to artichoke mixture, reserving liquid in skillet.

3 Reduce any liquid left in skillet to about 1 tablespoon. Add the whipping cream and boil gently for 2 to 3 minutes or till thickened, stirring constantly. Remove from heat; stir in butter and lemon peel.

4 Stir shrimp-artichoke mixture into sauce; heat through. Pour the sauce over the pasta and toss gently. If serving shrimp with tails on, use cooking tongs to arrange them on plate. If desired, serve with lemon wedges. Makes 4 main-dish servings.

*Note: Butter is used in this recipe to bind the sauce; margarine might not be an effective substitute in this pasta dish.

Nutrition facts per serving: 486 cal., 16 g total fat (9 g sat. fat), 223 mg chol., 535 mg sodium, 55 g carbo., 4 g fiber, 30 g pro. *Daily values:* 35% vit. A, 22% vit. C, 8% calcium, 40% iron.

Fettuccine with Shrimp, Artichokes, and
Red Chili Peppers (page 76)

Top: *Bow Ties with Sausage and Sweet Peppers*
(page 85)
Above: *Orzo Pasta with Mushrooms and Leeks*
(page 88)
Right: *Angel Hair with Asparagus, Tomatoes, and*
Fresh Basil (page 87)
Page 79, inset: *Soup with Mixed Pastas*
(page 88)

Page 80: *Wide Ribbon Noodles with Chicken and Baby Lima Beans (page 93)*
Above left: *Manicotti and Shells with Turkey and Lentils (page 86)*
Above: *Pasta with Fennel (page 58)*
Left: *Crab and Pasta Cakes with Cilantro-Lime Mayonnaise (page 91)*

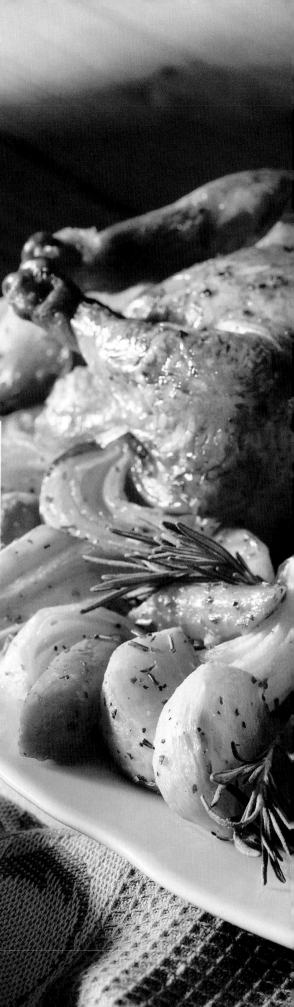

Page 83, inset: *Mustard-Glazed Brussels Sprouts and Oranges (page 63)*
Right: *Herbed-Roasted Cornish Hens with Root Vegetables (page 57)*
Below: *Pear Crisp with Lemon Sauce (page 72)*

Left: *Warm Winter Salad (page 67)*
Below: *Rigatoni with Eggplant and Dried Tomato Pesto (page 85)*

RIGATONI WITH EGGPLANT AND DRIED TOMATO PESTO

Serve this country-style pasta warm with cheese as a main dish, or take it on a picnic as a cold pasta salad.
(See the photograph on page 84.)

1 medium onion
1 Tbsp. olive oil
♦♦♦
1 medium eggplant
   (about 1 lb.)
1 Tbsp. olive oil
♦♦♦
6 oz. rigatoni or other short
   pasta, such as penne or
   rotini
⅓ of a recipe Dried Tomato
   Pesto (see right)
¼ tsp. fresh ground pepper
♦♦♦
2 Tbsp. crumbled semisoft
   goat cheese or feta cheese
   (optional)
   Fresh Italian parsley
   (optional)

1 Cut onion into 8 wedges. Place in a 13×9×2-inch baking pan; brush with 1 tablespoon olive oil. Roast in a 425° oven for 10 minutes.

2 Cut stem end off eggplant; discard. Cut eggplant in half lengthwise. Brush with 1 tablespoon olive oil. Stir onion in pan; place eggplant in pan, cut side down. Continue roasting 15 minutes more or till onion is golden brown and eggplant is just tender.

3 Meanwhile, cook the pasta according to package directions; drain well. Toss pasta with Dried Tomato Pesto and pepper.

4 Transfer pasta to a serving bowl; keep warm. Transfer eggplant to a cutting board. Use a serrated knife to cut eggplant into ½-inch-thick slices (use a fork to steady eggplant as you slice). Toss eggplant and onion with pasta; season to taste with *salt.* If desired, sprinkle with the goat cheese and Italian parsley. Makes 6 to 8 side-dish servings or 4 main-dish servings.

Nutrition facts per side-dish serving: 249 cal., 13 g total fat (2 g sat. fat), 0 mg chol., 75 mg sodium, 29 g carbo., 2 g fiber, 5 g pro. *Daily values:* 11% vit. C, 1% calcium, 10% iron.

DRIED TOMATO PESTO

¾ cup oil-packed dried
   tomatoes (about ¾ of a
   7-oz. jar)
   Olive oil
♦♦♦
8 cloves garlic, chopped
¼ cup pine nuts or slivered
   almonds
¼ cup snipped fresh basil or
   1 Tbsp. dried basil,
   crushed
½ tsp. salt

1 Drain the tomatoes; reserve oil. Add olive oil to reserved oil to equal ½ cup.

2 In a food processor bowl or blender container, combine tomatoes, garlic, pine nuts, basil, and salt. Cover and process or blend till finely chopped. With machine running, gradually add the ½ cup oil, processing till almost smooth and stopping to scrape down sides

as needed. Divide the pesto into thirds; refrigerate for up to 1 month. Makes approximately three ⅓-cup portions.

Nutrition facts per tablespoon: 86 cal., 9 g total fat (1 g sat. fat), 0 mg chol., 81 mg sodium, 2 g carbo., 0 g fiber, 1 g pro. *Daily values:* 9% vit. C, 1% iron.

BOW TIES WITH SAUSAGE AND SWEET PEPPERS

For a lower-fat version, use Italian-style ground turkey sausage.
(See the photograph on page 78.)

8 oz. bow-tie pasta
12 oz. fresh hot Italian sausage
   links
2 medium red sweet peppers,
   cut into ¾-inch pieces
♦♦♦
½ cup vegetable or beef broth
¼ tsp. black pepper
¼ cup snipped fresh Italian
   parsley

1 Cook pasta according to package directions. Cut sausage into 1-inch pieces. In a skillet cook sausage and sweet peppers till sausage is brown. Drain fat.

2 Add broth and black pepper to skillet. Bring to boiling; reduce heat. Simmer, uncovered, 5 minutes. Remove from heat. When pasta is cooked, drain well. Toss pasta with sausage mixture and parsley. Makes 4 servings.

Nutrition facts per serving: 397 cal., 18 g total fat (6 g sat. fat), 94 mg chol., 713 mg sodium, 38 g carbo., 3 g fiber, 24 g pro. *Daily values:* 31% vit. A, 114% vit. C, 4% calcium, 19% iron.

30 MIN. LOW FAT

SPAGHETTI WITH VEGETARIAN "SAUCE BOLOGNESE"

The cereal in the sauce gives a texture that is remarkably similar to ground meat. Serve it as you would regular spaghetti—with hot, crusty bread.

- 8 oz. spaghetti
- 1 Tbsp. olive oil
- ½ cup finely chopped carrot
- ½ cup thinly sliced celery
- ½ cup finely chopped onion
- ½ tsp. dried oregano, crushed
- ¼ tsp. pepper
- 3 cloves garlic, minced
- ¾ cup Grape Nuts cereal
- 1 14½-oz. can Italian-style stewed tomatoes
- 1 8-oz. can tomato sauce
- ¼ to ½ cup water

♦♦♦

- 1 Tbsp. olive oil
  Grated Parmesan or Romano cheese (optional)
  Fresh oregano (optional)

1 Cook pasta according to package directions. Meanwhile, in a medium saucepan heat 1 tablespoon olive oil over medium-high heat. Add carrot, celery, onion, dried oregano, and pep-

per; cook till onion is tender. Add garlic; cook for 1 minute more. Stir in the cereal. Add the undrained tomatoes, tomato sauce, and desired amount of water. Bring to boiling; reduce heat. Simmer, covered, for 5 to 10 minutes or till desired thickness.

2 Drain the cooked pasta. Toss pasta with 1 tablespoon olive oil. Divide the hot pasta among 4 dinner plates. Top with sauce. If desired, sprinkle with the Parmesan or Romano cheese and garnish with fresh oregano. Makes 4 main-dish servings.

TO MAKE AHEAD

Prepare sauce as directed, except cool completely. Transfer to a freezer container; seal, label, and freeze for up to 2 months. To serve, transfer the frozen sauce to a heavy saucepan. Add 1 to 2 tablespoons *water*. Cook, covered, over low heat 20 to 25 minutes or just till bubbly, stirring occasionally. Serve as directed.

Nutrition facts per serving: 416 cal., 8 g total fat (1 g sat. fat), 0 mg chol., 907 mg sodium, 76 g carbo., 3 g fiber, 12 g pro. *Daily values:* 87% vit. A, 32% vit. C, 8% calcium, 24% iron.

MANICOTTI AND SHELLS WITH TURKEY AND LENTILS

If you wish, prepare this specialty of northern Italy using 4 manicotti and 8 jumbo shells. (See the photograph on page 81.)

- 8 manicotti or 12 to 15 jumbo shell pasta
- 8 oz. ground raw turkey

- 1 small onion, finely chopped
- 3 large plum (Roma) tomatoes, seeded and finely chopped
- 1 Tbsp. dried Italian seasoning, crushed
- ½ tsp. ground nutmeg
- 1 cup cooked lentils* or canned lentils, rinsed and drained
- 1 15-oz. container refrigerated fresh Alfredo sauce (about 2 cups)
- ½ cup ricotta or cream-style cottage cheese
- ¼ cup shredded reduced-fat mozzarella cheese (1 oz.)
- ¼ cup snipped fresh parsley

♦♦♦

- ¼ cup shredded reduced-fat mozzarella cheese (1 oz.)
- ¼ cup grated Parmesan cheese
  Fresh oregano (optional)

1 Lightly grease a 2-quart rectangular baking dish; set aside. Cook pasta according to package directions. Meanwhile, for filling, in a large saucepan brown turkey and onion. Add the tomatoes, Italian seasoning, nutmeg, and ¼ teaspoon *pepper;* reduce heat. Simmer, uncovered, 5 minutes, stirring often. Stir in lentils; remove from heat. Stir in ½ cup of the Alfredo sauce, the ricotta cheese, ¼ cup mozzarella cheese, and parsley. Spoon ⅓ cup filling into each manicotti or about 2 tablespoons into each shell.

2 Arrange filled pastas in the prepared dish. Bake, covered, in a 375° oven for 15 minutes. Sprinkle with ¼ cup mozzarella and Parmesan cheeses. Bake for 10 minutes more or till cheese is golden brown.

3 Meanwhile, in a saucepan heat remaining sauce. Spoon sauce onto plates; top with pasta. If desired, garnish with fresh oregano. Makes 4 or 5 servings.

*Note: To make 1 cup cooked lentils, sort through ⅓ cup *dried lentils;* discard any pebbles or discolored lentils. Rinse sorted lentils and place in a medium saucepan. Add ⅔ cup *water or chicken, beef, or vegetable broth.* Bring to boiling; reduce heat. Simmer, covered, 15 minutes or till almost tender; drain and rinse under cool running water.

▌TO MAKE AHEAD ▐

Fill pasta as directed; arrange in the baking dish. Pour remaining sauce over top. Seal, label, and freeze for up to 1 month. (Freeze cheese mixture separately.) Before cooking, thaw overnight in refrigerator. Bake, covered, in a 350° oven 55 minutes. Uncover; sprinkle with cheese mixture. Bake 10 minutes more or till cheese is golden and pasta is heated.

Nutrition facts per manicotti: 327 cal., 14 g total fat (7 g sat. fat), 45 mg chol., 591 mg sodium, 34 g carbo., 2 g fiber, 17 g pro. *Daily values:* 12% vit. A, 19% vit. C, 23% calcium, 16% iron.

ANGEL HAIR WITH ASPARAGUS, TOMATOES, AND FRESH BASIL

This light and elegant dish goes from the grocery bag to the table in about 20 minutes. (See the photograph on page 79.)

1 lb. asparagus spears

♦♦♦

1 Tbsp. olive oil
4 cloves garlic, thinly sliced or minced
¼ tsp. pepper
6 medium plum (Roma) tomatoes, seeded and chopped (2¼ cups)
¼ cup dry white wine
¼ tsp. salt
1 Tbsp. butter*

♦♦♦

1 9-oz. pkg. refrigerated angel hair pasta
¼ cup shredded fresh basil

1 Trim the asparagus and rinse in cold water. Remove the tips; set aside. Bias-slice the remaining portions of asparagus spears into 1- to 1½-inch pieces and set them aside.

2 In a large skillet heat oil over medium heat. Add the garlic and pepper; cook and stir for 1 minute. Add the tomatoes and cook for 2 minutes more, stirring often. Add the asparagus spears, wine, and salt to the mixture in the skillet. Cook, uncovered, for 3 minutes. Add the asparagus tips and cook, uncovered, for 1 minute more. Add butter and stir till melted.

3 Meanwhile, cook the pasta according to package directions. Drain pasta; return to pan. Add asparagus mixture and basil to pasta, tossing to coat. Makes 3 main-dish servings.

*Note: Butter is used in this recipe to bind the sauce; margarine might not be an effective substitute in this pasta dish.

Nutrition facts per serving: 484 cal., 11 g total fat (3 g sat. fat), 10 mg chol., 238 mg sodium, 81 g carbo., 4 g fiber, 15 g pro. *Daily values:* 19% vit. A, 86% vit. C, 5% calcium, 31% iron.

PORTOBELLISSIMO!

Intriguing giants of the mushroom world, portobellos are popping up everywhere like, well, mushrooms.

Lately, these dessert-plate-size mushrooms have been seen muscling in on the more familiar variety, button mushrooms, at supermarkets nationwide. If you've been curious about whether their taste lives up to their size, be assured in this case that bigger is better. These meaty monsters often are grilled and for an excellent reason: Grilling brings out their rich, steak-like flavor and texture.

Thankfully, as their popularity has escalated, portobello's asking price has come down. They are still more expensive than their siblings, the button mushroom and the brown cremini, but now they have become an affordable treat guaranteed to impress. Choose specimens that are firm, with dry gills, and no soft spots on the cap. Refrigerate them as you would button mushrooms, unwashed and in paper bags or with a paper towel in a porous plastic bag. They'll keep this way for several days to a week.

For classic grilled portobellos, simply cut off the stem, gently brush off any crumbs of the porous material in which they grew, and rub them gently with olive oil, softened butter, or margarine. To highlight their earthy flavor, add salt, fresh ground pepper, and a little dried thyme. Grill over medium heat for 2 or 3 minutes per side or till just tender. Serve with other grilled vegetables or as a deluxe side-dish to accompany grilled meats.

To stop the show at a party, you can remove the stems and bake them, topped with a little tomato sauce, oregano, and cheese, as portobello "pizzas." Bake on a non-stick baking sheet in a 350° oven for 10 to 15 minutes or till the cheese bubbles.

In recipes, use portobellos wherever you would any other mushroom. To showcase portobellos in salads, on sandwiches, and in pastas, slice them in thick strips and cook in olive oil or butter with minced garlic, just a shake of salt, and fresh ground pepper.

½ tsp. instant beef or chicken
   bouillon granules
   Grated Romano cheese
   (optional)

1 Cook orzo or rosamarina pasta according to package directions; drain well. Meanwhile, in a large skillet heat margarine or butter over medium-high heat. Stir in the mushrooms, leek, garlic, pepper, and salt. Cook, uncovered, 5 minutes. Add water, marjoram, and bouillon. Reduce heat; cook about 6 minutes or till liquid is almost absorbed. Toss the mushroom mixture with pasta. If desired, sprinkle with Romano cheese. Makes 4 to 6 side-dish servings.

Nutrition facts per serving: 167 cal., 4 g total fat (2 g sat. fat), 8 mg chol., 209 mg sodium, 29 g carbo., 2 g fiber, 5 g pro. *Daily values:* 2% vit. A, 4% vit. C, 1% calcium, 14% iron.

*30 MIN.
LOW FAT*
SOUP WITH MIXED PASTAS

*With this recipe, you can make creative use of any extra pastas tucked away in your pantry.
(See the photograph on page 79.)*

*30 MIN.
LOW FAT*
ORZO PASTA WITH MUSHROOMS AND LEEKS

*Enjoy this simple side dish with grilled or roasted beef or chicken.
(See the photograph on page 78.)*

¾ cup orzo or rosamarina
   pasta
1 Tbsp. margarine or butter

4 oz. fresh assorted
   mushrooms, such as
   cremini, chanterelle,
   shiitake, or button, sliced
   or quartered
1 leek or 2 large green onions,
   chopped (about ⅓ cup)
1 clove garlic, minced
¼ tsp. pepper
⅛ tsp. salt
¼ cup water
½ to 1 tsp. snipped fresh
   marjoram or ¼ tsp. dried
   marjoram, crushed

4 cups reduced-sodium
   chicken broth
1 cup water
3 bay leaves
1 large onion, chopped
1 large carrot, chopped
4 cloves garlic, minced
♦♦♦
4 oz. skinless, boneless
   chicken breasts, coarsely
   chopped
1 tsp. olive oil or cooking oil

2 oz. various small pastas,
    such as shells, rotini,
    ditalini, alphabetini,
    and/or broken spaghetti
Fresh sage leaves

1 In a large saucepan bring chicken broth and water to boiling. Add bay leaves, onion, carrot, and garlic. Reduce heat and simmer, uncovered, 10 minutes.

2 In a skillet cook and stir chicken in hot oil 3 minutes or till no longer pink. Add chicken, pastas, and sage to soup. Simmer, uncovered, for 8 to 10 minutes or till larger pieces of pasta are tender but slightly firm. Remove the bay leaves. Makes 3 main-dish or 6 side-dish servings.

Nutrition facts per main-dish serving: 220 cal., 6 g total fat (1 g sat. fat), 20 mg chol., 896 mg sodium, 28 g carbo., 2 g fiber, 14 g pro. *Daily values:* 79% vit. A, 8% vit. C, 3% calcium, 11% iron.

ZUCCHINI LASAGNA WITH WALNUTS

2 **medium zucchini**
1 **tsp. olive oil**
        ◆◆◆
1 **Tbsp. olive oil**
2 **large carrots, finely chopped**
2 **large onions, finely chopped**
4 **cloves garlic, minced**
2 **cups purchased marinara sauce**
1 **Tbsp. snipped fresh basil or 1 tsp. dried basil, crushed**
        ◆◆◆
1½ **cups shredded mozzarella cheese (6 oz.)**
½ **cup grated Parmesan cheese**
        ◆◆◆
6 **no-boil lasagna noodles***
½ **cup chopped walnuts**

THE CLEVER COOK

NO-COOK NOODLES

I discovered that you do not need to cook lasagna noodles if you make the lasagna the night before. Simply assemble your recipe as directed but use uncooked noodles and do not bake. Cover and chill overnight (this softens the noodles), then cook as directed in your recipe. You'll save time and avoid working with wet, slippery noodles.

LeeAnn Mancini
Boca Raton, Florida

1 Trim ends off zucchini. Thinly slice zucchini lengthwise. (You should have 9 slices total, about ⅛ inch thick.) Place in a single layer on a lightly greased baking sheet; brush lightly with 1 teaspoon olive oil. Broil 3 to 4 inches from heat about 5 minutes or till crisp-tender, turning once; cool. Grease a 2-quart square baking dish; set aside.

2 In a large saucepan heat the 1 tablespoon olive oil over medium-high heat. Add the carrots, onions, and garlic; cook and stir about 5 minutes or till tender. Add marinara sauce, basil, and ⅛ teaspoon *pepper*. Bring to boiling; reduce heat. Simmer, covered, for 10 minutes, stirring occasionally.

3 In a small mixing bowl toss together the mozzarella cheese and Parmesan cheese; set aside.

4 In the prepared baking dish arrange 2 noodles. Spread with a third of the sauce. Sprinkle with a third of the nuts. Top with a third of the zucchini, then sprinkle with a third of the cheese mixture. Repeat layering, alternating direction of the zucchini in each layer and finishing with the zucchini; set remaining cheese aside.

5 Bake, covered, in a 375° oven for 20 minutes. Uncover and sprinkle with the remaining cheese mixture. Bake, uncovered, about 20 minutes more or till heated through. Let stand for 15 minutes before serving. Makes 6 main-dish servings.

*Note: All brands of no-boil lasagna are not the same size. Use enough noodles to have 3 even, single layers.

TO MAKE AHEAD

Prepare lasagna as directed, except do not bake. Wrap, label, and freeze for up to 1 month. Freeze cheese for topping separately. To serve, thaw in the refrigerator overnight. Bake, covered, in a 350° oven for 1 hour. Sprinkle with reserved cheese. Bake, uncovered, about 15 minutes more or till heated through. Let stand 15 minutes before serving.

Nutrition facts per serving: 358 cal., 19 g total fat (6 g sat. fat), 23 mg chol., 839 mg sodium, 33 g carbo., 3 g fiber, 17 g pro. *Daily values:* 100% vit. A, 28% vit. C, 29% calcium, 12% iron.

CRAB: A TRUE SEA TREASURE

Blue Crab

Dungeness Crab

Stone Crab

Snow Crab

King Crab

Dinner turns into a treasure hunt when crab is served. With a crab cracker or nutcracker in hand and bib in place, your search begins. Rich, succulent crabmeat is your just reward. Learn more about America's crab varieties and how to enjoy them in this primer.

Blue Crab: For Atlantic coast crab fanciers, the blue crab ritual includes a plateful of spicy boiled crabs served piping hot on newspaper-laden tables. These crabs are small, so plan to eat several. Purchase 1 pound of live whole crabs per person. (Or, look for fresh, pasteurized, canned, or chilled meat. The meat does not freeze well.) This species also produces the coveted soft-shell crab. During molting (late spring through early fall), blue crabs shed their shells. During this time, they are edible except for the face, intestines, and gills. To try soft-shell crabs at home, coat in seasoned flour and sauté in butter. Or, steam or boil the crabs.

Dungeness Crab: The favorite of the West Coast, Dungeness crabs fork over large chunks of buttery,

fine-textured crabmeat, straight from the shell. Fortunately, the hefty size of these Pacific crabs (up to 4 pounds) means there usually is a lot of meat. It's all hidden beneath their large bodies and in their legs and claws. Because the prized meat is so plentiful and easy to retrieve, the Dungeness is prized by cooks and diners alike, whether it's served hot or cold. Dungeness crabs may be sold whole, either fully cooked or live. Figure on ½ to 1 crab for each person.

King Crab: Because these North Pacific giants reach up to 25 pounds, you won't find them whole in your market. Instead, scout the freezer case for fully cooked split or whole legs, clusters (shoulder, legs, and claws), claws, or shelled meat. The secret to frozen king crab is a slow thaw in the refrigerator (1 or 2 days). This ensures firm, moist meat instead of a mushy, watery texture. Steam, microwave, broil, or grill king crab just till heated through. Or, serve precooked crab cold. Count on 8 ounces crab legs or 3 to 4 ounces meat per serving.

Snow Crab: Harvested in the icy waters of the Northwest, snow crabs take their name from their snow-white-colored meat. Other names include tanner, spider, and queen crab. The flavor resembles the scarcer, more expensive king crab, but with their smaller size (average 1½ to 3 pounds), you'll need a little more patience when picking the meat from the shells. Thaw and prepare legs, claws, and clusters as you would king crab. Serve 6 to 8 claws per serving (2 to 3 claws per appetizer serving).

Stone Crab: Florida lays claim to this crab species. Only the claws can be harvested. Since the claws regenerate, this restriction helps to conserve the stone crab population. As the name hints, you'll need a crab cracker or nutcracker (or a hammer) to crack the stone-hard shells of the cooked claws. Inside, the meat is rich and sweet, with a firmer, more fibrous texture than other kinds of crab. Serve stone crab cold as an appetizer with the meat still attached to the main pincer or pick the meat out of the claws for use in recipes. Plan on 3 large claws per serving.

PENNE SALAD WITH ITALIAN GREEN BEANS AND GORGONZOLA

This salad is at its best with crisp, fresh beans and radicchio. Add grilled lamb or chicken for a more filling salad.

6 oz. penne, ziti, elbow macaroni, or other short pasta

8 oz. fresh Italian green beans, trimmed and bias-sliced into 1-inch pieces, or one 9-oz. pkg. frozen Italian green beans, thawed

◆◆◆

⅓ cup nonfat Italian salad dressing

1 Tbsp. snipped fresh tarragon or ½ tsp. dried tarragon, crushed

½ tsp. fresh ground pepper

2 cups torn radicchio or 1 cup finely shredded red cabbage

◆◆◆

4 cups fresh sorrel or spinach leaves, cleaned, trimmed and, if desired, shredded

½ cup crumbled Gorgonzola or other blue cheese (2 oz.)

1 Cook pasta according to package directions, adding fresh green beans to pasta the last 5 to 7 minutes of cooking. (Or, add thawed beans the last 3 to 4 minutes.) Rinse pasta and beans well under cold running water; drain.

2 In a large mixing bowl combine the Italian dressing, tarragon, and pepper. Add radicchio or cabbage, pasta, and beans; toss gently to coat.

3 To serve, divide the shredded sorrel or spinach among 8 salad plates. Top with the pasta mixture and sprinkle with the Gorgonzola cheese. Makes 8 side-dish servings.

Nutrition facts per serving: 130 cal., 3 g total fat (1 g sat. fat), 5 mg chol., 264 mg sodium, 21 g carbo., 2 g fiber, 6 g pro. *Daily values:* 22% vit. A, 19% vit. C, 7% calcium, 13% iron.

CRAB AND PASTA CAKES WITH CILANTRO-LIME MAYONNAISE

These delicate crab cakes show off a different use for pasta, putting an Adriatic twist on an Atlantic seaboard favorite. (See the photograph on page 81.)

8 oz. lump fresh crabmeat, flaked, or crab-flavored salad-style fish, finely chopped

1 cup cooked spaghetti or linguine

◆◆◆

2 beaten eggs

3 green onions, finely chopped

¼ cup fine dry bread crumbs

2 Tbsp. snipped fresh cilantro

2 fresh serrano peppers, finely chopped, or 2 Tbsp. chopped green sweet pepper

2 tsp. olive oil or cooking oil

¼ tsp. salt

¼ tsp. pepper

◆◆◆

2 Tbsp. cooking oil

1 recipe Cilantro-Lime Mayonnaise (see right)

Lime and/or lemon wedges (optional)

Chive blossoms (optional)

1 Clean the crabmeat carefully, removing any shell or cartilage pieces and discarding them. Cut the cooked pasta into 1-inch pieces. Set aside.

2 In a large mixing bowl combine eggs, green onions, bread crumbs, cilantro, serrano peppers or sweet pepper, olive oil, salt, and pepper. Add crabmeat and cooked pasta; mix well. Using 2 tablespoons of mixture for each crab cake, shape into 12 patties, about ½ inch thick.

3 In a heavy large skillet heat the 2 tablespoons cooking oil (add a little more oil if necessary during cooking). Cook a few patties at a time over medium heat about 3 minutes on each side or till golden brown. Drain on paper towels. Cover and keep warm in a 300° oven while preparing the remaining cakes. Serve the crab cakes warm with the Cilantro-Lime Mayonnaise. If desired, serve with lime and/or lemon wedges and use chive blossoms for garnish. Makes 12 crab cakes.

Cilantro-Lime Mayonnaise: In a small mixing bowl stir together ¼ cup *reduced-calorie mayonnaise or salad dressing,* 1 tablespoon finely snipped *fresh cilantro,* ½ teaspoon finely shredded *lime peel,* and 1 tablespoon fresh *lime juice.* Cover and chill till serving time. Makes ½ cup.

Nutrition facts per 2 cakes with 2 teaspoons Cilantro-Lime Mayonnaise: 203 cal., 12 g total fat (2 g sat. fat), 109 mg chol., 497 mg sodium, 12 g carbo., 1 g fiber, 11 g pro. *Daily values:* 4% vit. A, 16% vit. C, 4% calcium, 6% iron.

MIXED PASTAS WITH FRESH HERBS

Use interesting pasta shapes in this simple recipe. Try shapes that have similar cooking times so you can cook them together.

**8 oz. assorted pastas
2 Tbsp. walnut oil or olive oil
2 Tbsp. coarsely snipped mixed fresh herbs (such as sage, rosemary, and basil)
¼ tsp. salt
¼ tsp. coarsely ground black pepper**

1 Cook pasta according to package directions; drain. Toss the hot pasta with the oil, herbs, salt, and pepper. Makes 8 side-dish servings.

Nutrition facts per serving: 170 cal., 7 g total fat (1 g sat. fat), 0 mg chol., 67 mg sodium, 22 g carbo., 0 g fiber, 4 g pro. *Daily values:* 7% iron.

CHILI-RUBBED CHICKEN WITH HORSERADISH

**1   3- to 5-lb. whole roasting chicken
½   cup peeled and finely shredded horseradish root
2   Tbsp. pure maple syrup
2   tsp. olive oil or cooking oil**

♦♦♦

**1   tsp. chili powder
¼   tsp. salt**

1 Rinse chicken; pat dry. Cut slits in skin of breast and drumsticks. Stir together horseradish and syrup; stuff mixture in slits and rub into meat, spreading evenly under skin. Brush the chicken with oil.

2 Combine the chili powder and salt; rub mixture over chicken and inside body cavity. Pull neck skin to back and fasten with a small metal skewer. Tie legs to tail. Twist wing tips under back. Place chicken, breast side up, on a rack in a shallow roasting pan. Roast, uncovered, in a 375° oven for 1¼ to 2 hours or till the drumsticks move freely and the juices run clear. Makes 6 servings.

Nutrition facts per serving: 262 cal., 14 g total fat (4 g sat. fat), 79 mg chol., 168 mg sodium, 8 g carbo., 1 g fiber, 25 g pro. *Daily values:* 5% vit. A, 27% vit. C, 4% calcium, 10% iron.

ITALIAN POT ROAST

**2   Tbsp. fennel seed, crushed
2   Tbsp. dried parsley, crushed
4   tsp. dried Italian seasoning, crushed
1½ tsp. garlic salt
1   tsp. pepper
1   3- to 4-lb. boneless pork shoulder roast**

♦♦♦

**1   Tbsp. cooking oil
5   carrots, quartered
6   small potatoes, peeled (about 1½ lb.)
1   large fennel bulb, trimmed and cut into wedges**

♦♦♦

¼   cup instant-type flour

1 Combine the fennel seed, parsley, Italian seasoning, garlic salt, and pepper; set aside. Untie pork roast and unroll; trim fat. Rub seasoning mixture over roast, roll up, and retie.

2 In a Dutch oven heat oil. Brown pork roast on all sides; drain fat. Pour ¾ cup *water* over meat. Roast, covered, in a 325° oven 1½ hours. Arrange vegetables around roast. Cover and roast 50 to 60 minutes more or till vegetables and meat are tender, adding water, if necessary. Transfer meat to serving platter; cover and let stand 15 minutes. Remove strings and carve. Use a slotted spoon to transfer vegetables to a serving bowl; keep warm.

3 For gravy, skim fat from pan juices; strain juices. Add *water* to juices, if necessary, to make 1½ cups. Cook juices in Dutch oven over medium-high heat till bubbly. Combine ½ cup *cold water* and flour; stir till smooth. Add flour mixture gradually to hot pan juices, whisking till smooth and bubbly. Cook and stir 1 minute. Serve with roast. Serves 6 to 8.

Nutrition facts per serving: 552 cal., 26 g total fat (8 g sat. fat), 149 mg chol., 686 mg sodium, 35 g carbo., 4 g fiber, 43 g pro. *Daily values:* 143% vit. A, 21% vit. C, 7% calcium, 30% iron.

WIDE RIBBON NOODLES WITH CHICKEN AND BABY LIMA BEANS

Broad ribbon noodles generously hold the delicate tomato-cream sauce. (See the photograph on page 80.)

1 14½-oz. can Italian-style stewed tomatoes
8 oz. pappardelle, mafalda, or fettuccine
1 10-oz. pkg. frozen baby lima beans

A ROOT TO TASTE

It may be called horseradish, but it has a kick like a mule. Used for thousands of years as a curative for everything from colds to impotence, this piquant relative of mustard and kale is enjoying a rediscovery of its kitchen roots.

No longer relegated to subservience as just a table-top condiment, fresh horseradish is galloping out of the starting gate in new uses. Boil diced horseradish with potatoes to give some springtime zing to mashed spuds. A little shredded horseradish will go a long way in scrambled eggs, marinades, chutneys, tuna salad, and slaws. In baking, adding horseradish to a savory bread dough gets a rise out of the flavor.

Fresh horseradish arrives in the supermarket in March, and prime season lasts through June. Roots should be creamy beige and extremely firm. The smaller roots are the most tender. To store before using, wrap horseradish loosely in a paper towel and seal in an airtight plastic bag. Store for up to two months. To use, scrub the root clean with a brush under cold running water. Peel and grate or shred as desired.

To make an easy horseradish condiment, finely shred the peeled root. Add a little beet juice for color, if desired, and enough white wine or rice vinegar to cover it. Also, adding a little sugar will take some of the sting out. Store in an airtight, glass container. The condiment will keep for a month or more in the refrigerator, but try to use it up in a week or two, because the longer you store it, the weaker it becomes.

2 small skinless, boneless chicken breasts, cut into bite-size pieces
1 small onion, cut into wedges
¼ tsp. cracked black pepper
2 Tbsp. olive oil
¼ cup chicken broth
½ cup whipping cream
   Snipped fresh chives (optional)
   Shredded Parmesan cheese (optional)

1 Place tomatoes with their juice in a blender container or food processor bowl. Cover and blend or process till pureed. Cook pasta according to the package directions, adding lima beans to boiling water with pasta.

2 Meanwhile, in a large skillet cook chicken, onion, and pepper in hot oil over medium-high heat for 2 to 4 minutes or till chicken is no longer pink. Reduce heat; stir in broth and tomato puree. Simmer, uncovered, about 5 minutes or till liquid is reduced by half. Stir in cream; simmer 2 to 3 minutes more or till sauce is of desired consistency. To serve, drain pasta and beans. Toss pasta gently with sauce. If desired, sprinkle with the chives and Parmesan cheese. Serves 4.

Nutrition facts per serving: 683 cal., 21 g total fat (9 g sat. fat), 71 mg chol., 451 mg sodium, 90 g carbo., 5 g fiber, 34 g pro. *Daily values:* 21% vit. A, 21% vit. C, 7% calcium, 47% iron.

FIRE UP—IT'S SPRING

Spring is in the air, and you can almost smell the burgers. But before you fire up your gas grill, ensure top performance by giving it a quick spring cleaning.

Greasy drippings can clog the burner's gas ports and short out the ignition flame. Following your manual's instructions, slip off gas tubes and remove the burner unit. Use a soft cloth and soapy water to remove dirt and grease. Towel-dry, then clear out gas ports with a toothpick. Clean tubes with a nonmetallic bottle brush.

Cover the gas orifices beneath the control panel with foil to keep out water, then scrub all surfaces with a brass-bristle brush and soapy water. Rinse with a hose and towel-dry.

Dented or badly rusted fuel tanks must be replaced. Reconnect your propane tank by removing its safety plug and attaching the grill's rubber gas lines. If you didn't use a plug when you removed the propane cylinder, clean out possible opening blockages with a cotton swab. Test the connections for leaks by brushing them with soapy water and turning on the gas. If you see growing bubbles or detect a gas odor, shut off the tank and tighten the connections.

To remove cooking grease, flip the briquettes so the greasy sides face the burner and replace the cooking grids. Light the grill, close the lid, and set the flame on high for 15 minutes. The heat will burn off the grease. When cool, remove the grids and briquettes. Using a brass-bristle brush and soapy water, scrub the grids; rinse, and towel-dry. To help prevent corrosion, coat them with cooking oil. Put the briquettes back in place and bring on the burgers.

GRILLED ROSEMARY LAMB

⅓ cup dry red wine
⅓ cup lemon juice
⅓ cup cooking oil
¼ cup Dijon-style mustard
3 Tbsp. snipped fresh rosemary or 2 tsp. dried rosemary, crushed
4 cloves garlic, minced
½ tsp. salt
½ tsp. pepper

❖❖❖

1 3- to 4-lb. boneless leg of lamb roast or portion, tied

1 For marinade, combine wine, lemon juice, oil, mustard, rosemary, garlic, salt, and pepper; mix well.

2 Untie roast and remove fell (paper-thin, pinkish-red layer) from outer surface of lamb; discard. Trim fat from lamb. Reroll and retie. Place lamb in a plastic bag in a shallow dish. Pour marinade over lamb, turning lamb to coat all sides. Seal bag and marinate in the refrigerator for 6 hours or overnight, turning once. Remove the lamb from marinade, reserving marinade. Brush excess herb from meat.

3 In a covered grill arrange medium coals around a drip pan. Test for medium-low heat above pan. Insert a meat thermometer into the lamb. Place lamb, fat side up, on the grill rack over the drip pan. Lower grill hood. Grill for 1½ to 2 hours or till meat thermometer registers 145°, brushing several times with marinade during the first half of grilling time. Discard remaining marinade. Let lamb stand for 15 minutes before carving. Makes 8 servings.

Nutrition facts per serving: 285 cal., 17 g total fat (4 g sat. fat), 86 mg chol., 384 mg sodium, 2 g carbo., 0 g fiber, 28 g pro. *Daily values:* 0% vit. A, 8% vit. C, 1% calcium, 14% iron.

PRIZE TESTED RECIPE WINNER

SWEET POTATO ENCHILADAS

This recipe earned Karen Sheer of Demarest, New Jersey, $100 in the magazine's monthly contest.

3 cups cubed, peeled sweet potatoes
1 Tbsp. cooking oil

❖❖❖

1 Tbsp. cooking oil
1 large onion, sliced and separated into rings
2 medium red, yellow, and/or green sweet peppers, thinly sliced
1 cup fresh or frozen whole kernel corn
4 cloves garlic, minced
½ tsp. dried oregano, crushed
½ tsp. ground cumin
½ tsp. chili powder
Dash crushed red pepper
1 14½-oz. can diced tomatoes

LEAN ON LAMB

Mary had a leg of lamb—well, maybe she never ate it for Sunday dinner, but many of us love lamb so much we reserve it for a special treat once or twice a year. But these days a lean and tasty leg of lamb is easier than ever to prepare since the new, smaller boneless roasts often come already seasoned.

The convenient mini roast allows you to trot out lamb any time you're looking for a way to shepherd new flavors to your table. The meat is tender and delicately flavored because USDA regulations require that lamb in your supermarket come from an animal less than 1 year old. It's leaner than ever, too, and delivers essential nutrients.

6 8-inch flour tortillas
½ cup shredded Monterey Jack cheese
Nonstick spray coating
Dairy sour cream (optional)
Fresh hot chili peppers (optional)

1 In a shallow roasting pan combine sweet potatoes and 1 tablespoon oil. Bake, uncovered, in a 425° oven 35 minutes or till tender and golden brown, stirring once. Grease a 3-quart rectangular baking dish; set aside.

2 Meanwhile, for filling, in a large skillet heat 1 tablespoon oil over medium-high heat. Add onion; cook and stir about 3 minutes or till tender. Add sweet pepper strips; cook and stir about

5 minutes more or till tender. Add corn, garlic, oregano, cumin, chili powder, red pepper, and a dash *salt* and *black pepper.* Cook and stir 1 minute more. Carefully add the undrained tomatoes. Simmer, uncovered, for about 10 minutes or till most of the juices have evaporated.

3 Fill each tortilla with about ⅓ cup sweet potatoes, ½ cup filling, and 1 rounded tablespoon cheese; roll up. Place in the prepared baking dish. Spray enchiladas with nonstick coating. Bake, uncovered, in a 375° oven for 20 to 25 minutes or till crisp. If desired, serve with sour cream and hot peppers. Makes 6 main-dish servings.

Nutrition facts per serving: 310 cal., 11 g total fat (3 g sat. fat), 8 mg chol., 363 mg sodium, 48 g carbo., 3 g fiber, 9 g pro. *Daily values:* 155% vit. A, 116% vit. C, 13% calcium, 17% iron.

PICADILLO TACOS

This recipe earned Alice Hutson of San Antonio, Texas, $200 in the magazine's monthly contest.

½ cup raisins
¼ cup tequila

◆◆◆

8 oz. bulk pork sausage
8 oz. lean ground beef
½ cup chopped onion
3 cloves garlic, minced
1 14½-oz. can whole tomatoes, cut up
1 4-oz. can diced green chili peppers, drained
2 Tbsp. sugar
1 tsp. ground cinnamon

Menu

Picadillo Tacos (see below)

◆◆◆

Salad of sliced avocado and orange sections

◆◆◆

Orange or lemon sherbet

◆◆◆

Iced tea with lemon wedges

¼ tsp. ground cumin
Dash ground cloves

◆◆◆

12 7-inch flour tortillas
⅓ cup finely chopped pecans
Shredded lettuce (optional)

1 In a small saucepan combine the raisins and tequila. Bring to boiling; remove from heat. Do not drain. Let stand 5 minutes.

2 For filling, in a large skillet cook sausage, beef, onion, and garlic over medium heat till meat is brown. Drain off fat. Stir in undrained tomatoes, green chili peppers, sugar, cinnamon, cumin, cloves, and undrained raisins. Bring to boiling; reduce heat. Simmer, uncovered, 30 minutes or till most of the liquid is evaporated.

3 Meanwhile, wrap tortillas in foil. Heat in a 350° oven about 10 minutes or till warm. Stir pecans into meat mixture. To serve, if desired, top warm tortillas with lettuce. Spoon filling atop; fold or roll up. Makes 6 main-dish servings.

Nutrition facts per serving: 479 cal., 19 g total fat (5 g sat. fat), 39 mg chol., 706 mg sodium, 55 g carbo., 2 g fiber, 18 g pro. *Daily values:* 4% vit. A, 30% vit. C, 12% calcium, 27% iron.

Greek Chicken Tortilla Roll-Ups

1 lb. skinless, boneless, chicken breasts, cut into thin, bite-size pieces
2 Tbsp. olive oil
2 Tbsp. lemon juice
1 Tbsp. Dijon-style mustard
2 cloves garlic, minced
1 tsp. dried oregano, crushed
⅛ tsp. pepper

❖❖❖

½ cup plain low-fat yogurt
¾ cup peeled, seeded, and coarsely chopped cucumber
1 clove garlic, minced
¼ tsp. dried dillweed

❖❖❖

10 7-inch flour tortillas
3 cups shredded lettuce
  Chopped red onion (optional)

1 Rinse chicken; pat dry. Place chicken in a plastic bag set in a deep bowl. For marinade combine oil, lemon juice, mustard, 2 cloves garlic, oregano, and pepper. Pour marinade over chicken in bag. Seal bag; turn to coat chicken. Refrigerate 3 to 24 hours, turning bag occasionally.

2 For sauce, combine the yogurt, cucumber, 1 clove garlic, and dillweed. Cover and chill till serving time.

3 Heat a large nonstick skillet over medium-high heat. Add half of the chicken and marinade. Cook and stir for 2 to 3 minutes or till chicken is no longer pink; drain. Repeat with remaining chicken and marinade.

4 Meanwhile, wrap tortillas in foil. Heat in a 350° oven 10 minutes. To serve, place a scant ⅓ cup of the chicken and a generous tablespoon of sauce on each flour tortilla. Top with shredded lettuce and, if desired, onion; roll up. Makes 5 main-dish servings.

Nutrition facts per serving: 379 cal., 13 g total fat (2 g sat. fat), 49 mg chol., 439 mg sodium, 39 g carbo., 1 g fiber, 25 g pro. *Daily values:* 2% vit. A, 9% vit. C, 12% calcium, 20% iron.

Oriental Cashew Asparagus

This recipe earned Donna Holland of Ketchum, Oklahoma, $100 in the magazine's monthly contest.

1 lb. asparagus spears, trimmed and bias-sliced into 1-inch pieces
1½ cups quartered fresh mushrooms
1 medium onion, cut into thin wedges
¼ cup chopped red sweet pepper

❖❖❖

2 Tbsp. margarine or butter
1 tsp. cornstarch
⅛ to ¼ tsp. pepper
1 Tbsp. teriyaki sauce
1 Tbsp. dry sherry
2 Tbsp. cashew halves

1 Place asparagus in steamer basket over, but not touching, gently boiling water. Cover; reduce heat. Steam for 2 minutes. Add mushrooms, onion, and red pepper. Cover; steam for 2 to 5 minutes more or till crisp-tender. Remove basket; discard liquid.

Good to Know

Sweet onions arrive in late spring and can be found well into autumn. Vidalias, a popular variety, come from Georgia. Maui onions, flat-shaped and golden, grow in the rich volcanic soil of Hawaii. A new variety, Texas Sweets, is nicknamed "1015" because the best day for planting these onions is October 15.

2 In the same saucepan melt margarine; stir in cornstarch and pepper. Add teriyaki sauce, sherry, and 2 teaspoons *water*. Cook and stir till thickened and bubbly. Return vegetables to saucepan, tossing gently to coat; heat through. Top each serving with nuts. Makes 4 side-dish servings.

Nutrition facts per serving: 121 cal., 8 g total fat (2 g sat. fat), 0 mg chol., 269 mg sodium, 10 g carbo., 2 g fiber, 4 g pro. *Daily values:* 17% vit. A, 50% vit. C, 8% iron.

Mushroom-and-Nut-Stuffed Onions

6 large sweet onions (see tip above)
1 tsp. cooking oil

❖❖❖

¾ cup chopped fresh mushrooms
1 small carrot, finely chopped
¼ tsp. pepper
2 Tbsp. margarine or butter
½ cup apple cider or apple juice
1 tart baking apple, cored and finely chopped

½ cup cooked wild rice or
    long grain rice
⅓ cup finely chopped
    hazelnuts (filberts)
1 cup soft whole wheat bread
    crumbs
1 Tbsp. snipped fresh basil

◆◆◆

⅓ cup apple cider or apple
    juice

1 Cut a thin slice from bottom and top of onions, leaving skins on. Scoop out onion centers, leaving ¼-inch-thick shells. Finely chop enough removed onion centers to measure ⅓ cup. Brush onions with oil.

2 For filling, in a large skillet cook mushrooms, carrot, pepper, and the ⅓ cup reserved onion centers in 1 tablespoon of the margarine 5 minutes. Slowly add ½ cup cider. Stir in apple, rice, nuts, and ¼ teaspoon *salt;* cook for 1 minute more. Remove from heat. Stir in ½ cup of the bread crumbs and the basil. Spoon the filling into each onion shell.

3 Arrange stuffed onions in a 2-quart rectangular baking dish. Pour ⅓ cup cider around stuffed onions. Bake, covered, in a 350° oven 40 minutes or till onions are tender. Melt the remaining 1 tablespoon margarine; stir in remaining ½ cup bread crumbs; sprinkle over onions. Bake, uncovered, 5 to 15 minutes more or till onions are tender. Remove the outer skins before eating. Makes 6 side-dish servings.

Nutrition facts per serving: 230 cal., 9 g total fat (1 g sat. fat), 0 mg chol., 177 mg sodium, 35 g carbo., 5 g fiber, 5 g pro. *Daily values:* 30% vit. A, 20% vit. C, 6% calcium, 9% iron.

ARTICHOKE SAUTÉ

If fresh baby artichokes aren't available, substitute a 9-ounce package frozen artichoke hearts. Cook them according to package directions and proceed with step two.

10 baby artichokes
    Lemon juice

◆◆◆

1 medium red onion, cut into
    thin wedges
2 cloves garlic, minced
2 tsp. olive oil or cooking oil
1 tsp. cornstarch
¼ cup chicken broth
¼ cup dry white wine or
    chicken broth
4 oil-pack dried tomatoes,
    cut into thin strips
1 oz. thinly sliced prosciutto
    or cooked ham, cut in
    thin strips
2 Tbsp. snipped fresh basil
    and/or oregano

1 Trim stems; cut off top fourth of artichokes. Remove outer leaves till you reach pale green parts. Halve or quarter artichokes. Cut out fuzzy center, if necessary. Brush cut surfaces with lemon juice. Cook artichokes in a large amount of boiling water 15 minutes or till tender; drain.

2 In a skillet cook onion and garlic in hot oil till tender. Stir in cornstarch; add broth and wine. Cook and stir till thickened and bubbly. Cook and stir 2 minutes more. Add tomatoes, prosciutto, herb, and artichokes; heat through. Makes 4 or 5 side-dish servings.

Nutrition facts per serving: 112 cal., 5 g total fat (0 g sat. fat), 0 mg chol., 250 mg sodium, 12 g carbo., 3 g fiber, 5 g pro. *Daily values:* 1% vit. A, 26% vit. C, 3% calcium, 6% iron.

ARTICHOKE FETA TORTILLA WRAP

1 14-oz. can artichoke hearts,
    drained and finely chopped
3 green onions, thinly sliced
½ of an 8-oz. tub cream cheese
    (about ½ cup)
¼ cup crumbled feta cheese
¼ cup grated Parmesan cheese
1 Tbsp. grated Romano or
    Parmesan cheese
3 Tbsp. pesto

◆◆◆

8 8-inch flour tortillas
    Nonstick spray coating
    (optional)

◆◆◆

1 8-oz. carton plain yogurt
1 Tbsp. snipped fresh cilantro

1 Grease a 3-quart rectangular baking dish; set aside. For filling, in a mixing bowl stir together the artichoke hearts; green onions; cream cheese; feta, Parmesan, and Romano cheeses; and pesto.

2 Place about ¼ cup filling onto each tortilla; roll up. Arrange tortillas in the prepared baking dish. Use a sharp knife to make decorative slits in top of tortilla rolls. If desired, spray rolls with nonstick spray coating. Bake, uncovered, in a 350° oven about 15 minutes or till heated through.

3 Meanwhile, stir together the yogurt and cilantro. Cut each tortilla into thirds and arrange on a serving platter. Serve with yogurt mixture. Makes 24 appetizers.

Nutrition facts per appetizer: 90 cal., 5 g total fat (1 g sat. fat), 8 mg chol., 143 mg sodium, 9 g carbo., 1 g fiber, 3 g pro. *Daily values:* 1% vit. A, 2% vit. C, 5% calcium, 3% iron.

RASPBERRY-CRANBERRY SPINACH SALAD

This recipe earned Carol Roessing of Findlay, Ohio, $200 in the magazine's monthly contest.

1 10-oz. pkg. frozen red raspberries in syrup, thawed

◆◆◆

¼ cup sugar
2 tsp. cornstarch
½ cup cranberry-raspberry juice cocktail
¼ cup red wine vinegar
¼ tsp. celery seed
¼ tsp. ground cinnamon
⅛ tsp. ground cloves

◆◆◆

1 10-oz. pkg. pre-washed fresh spinach
½ cup broken walnuts
⅓ cup dried cranberries
¼ cup shelled sunflower seeds
3 green onions, thinly sliced

1 For dressing, place raspberries in a blender container or food processor bowl. Cover and blend or process till raspberries are smooth. Strain through a sieve to remove the seeds; discard seeds.

2 In a medium saucepan stir together the sugar and cornstarch. Stir in the cranberry-raspberry juice cocktail, wine vinegar, celery seed, cinnamon, cloves, and strained raspberries. Cook and stir over medium heat till thickened and bubbly. Cook and stir for 2 minutes more. Transfer mixture to a nonmetal container; cover and chill till serving time.

Menu

Grilled or broiled turkey tenderloins

◆◆◆

Whole tiny new potatoes drizzled with butter and sprinkled with fresh dill

◆◆◆

Raspberry-Cranberry Spinach Salad (see left)

◆◆◆

Whole wheat rolls

3 To serve, in a salad bowl toss together spinach, walnuts, dried cranberries, sunflower seeds, and green onions. Drizzle with half of the dressing, tossing to coat. Cover and chill the remaining dressing in a nonmetal container for up to 1 week to use in other salads. Makes 6 to 8 side-dish servings.

Nutrition facts per serving: 178 cal., 9 g total fat (1 g sat. fat), 0 mg chol., 82 mg sodium, 23 g carbo., 3 g fiber, 4 g pro. *Daily values:* 33% vit. A, 31% vit. C, 5% calcium, 13% iron.

SPRING GREENS AND VEGETABLE SALAD

Mesclun, also known as spring greens or gourmet salad mix, is a mixture of young, tender salad greens. If your supermarket does not carry mesclun, try a mixture of Bibb lettuce, arugula, radicchio, and curly endive.

8 cups mesclun or other torn mixed greens
2 medium tomatoes, cut into thin wedges
1 medium cucumber, halved lengthwise and thinly sliced
1 15-oz. can garbanzo beans, drained and rinsed
½ of a small onion, finely chopped
¼ cup snipped fresh cilantro
2 Tbsp. snipped fresh mint or 1 tsp. dried mint, crushed
2 Tbsp. snipped fresh basil or 1 tsp. dried basil, crushed

◆◆◆

½ to ¾ cup Herbed Vinaigrette (see below)
Nasturtium blossoms (optional)

1 In a large salad bowl toss together the salad greens, tomatoes, cucumber, garbanzo beans, onion, cilantro, mint, and basil. Add desired amount of vinaigrette, tossing gently to coat. If desired, garnish with nasturtiums. Makes 8 side-dish servings.

Herbed Vinaigrette: In a screw-top jar combine ¼ cup *red wine vinegar or vinegar;* ¼ cup *olive oil;* 1½ teaspoons *Worcestershire sauce;* 1 teaspoon snipped *fresh basil or oregano or* ¼ teaspoon *dried basil or oregano,* crushed; 1 teaspoon snipped *fresh mint or* ¼ teaspoon *dried mint,* crushed; 1 large clove *garlic,* minced; ½ teaspoon *dry mustard;* ¼ teaspoon *salt;* and ⅛ teaspoon *pepper.* Cover and shake well to mix. Chill for 2 to 24 hours. Shake well before serving.

Nutrition facts per serving: 111 cal., 6 g total fat (1 g sat. fat), 0 mg chol., 258 mg sodium, 13 g carbo., 4 g fiber, 4 g pro. *Daily values:* 9% vit. A, 30% vit. C, 3% calcium, 14% iron.

Just-for-Kids Vegetables

Kids think they know all the tricks to avoid eating their vegetables—but you can outfox them with these creative ideas. If your kids are feeding peas to Fido on the sly, be ready with a few stunts of your own. These fun-to-fix vegetable recipes will charm your kids into asking for seconds instead of hiding their firsts.

Cool-as-a-Cucumber Dip: Combine ½ of a 1-ounce package ranch salad dressing mix (milk recipe), ½ cup milk, ½ cup nonfat mayonnaise dressing, ¼ cup chopped cucumber, and ¼ teaspoon dried dillweed. Serve with cut-up raw vegetables.
Nutrition facts: Each spoonful has only 13 calories.

Chunky Gazpacho Salsa: For salsa, in a blender combine 1 cut-up medium tomato, 1 sliced green onion, 1 tablespoon water, 2 teaspoons lemon juice, ½ teaspoon sugar, ¼ teaspoon salt, and a dash bottled hot pepper sauce. Cover; blend till nearly smooth. Stir in ⅓ cup each of finely chopped cucumber, green sweet pepper, and celery; set aside.

For tortilla chips, cut three 8-inch flour tortillas into 8 wedges each. Arrange the tortilla wedges in a single layer on an ungreased baking sheet. Bake in a 350° oven for 8 to 10 minutes or till dry and crisp. Serve tortilla chips with salsa.
Nutrition facts: Colorful vegetables mean lots of vitamins A and C. Tortillas promise B vitamins.

Corn-Patch Packages: Wrap a stack of six 8-inch flour tortillas in foil. Heat in a 350° oven 10 minutes. Cook a 10-ounce package frozen whole kernel corn according to package directions; drain. Stir in ⅓ cup process cheese sauce and ¼ cup salsa; heat. Spoon corn mixture onto centers of tortillas; fold in sides and roll up.
Nutrition facts: Enough protein for a meal, plus iron and carbohydrates.

Bumpy Stumps and Toadstools: Cook one 16-ounce package frozen vegetables (cauliflower, broccoli, and carrots) and 1 cup halved fresh mushrooms according to the vegetable package directions; drain. For sauce, combine half of a 10¾-ounce can condensed cheddar cheese soup and ⅓ to ½ cup salsa. Cook and stir till smooth and heated through. Serve over vegetables.
Nutrition facts: Plan on 90 calories per serving, plus vitamins A and C.

Stars and Stripes Forever: Using a star-shaped hors d'oeuvre cutter, cut 2 small red, yellow, and/or green sweet peppers into stars. (Save the pepper trimmings for another recipe.) Drain an 8-ounce can sliced bamboo shoots; slice shoots lengthwise into thin strips. Cook peppers, covered, in a small amount of boiling salted water about 2 minutes or till crisp-tender; drain. Stir in bamboo shoots and ¼ cup bottled sweet-and-sour sauce; heat through.
Nutrition facts: High in vitamins A and C; no fat.

Mock Spaghetti: Halve spaghetti squash lengthwise; scoop out seeds. Place halves, cut side down, in a baking dish. Bake in a 350° oven for 30 to 40 minutes or till tender. Using two forks, remove stringy pulp from squash. Top with your favorite spaghetti sauce.
Nutrition facts: Low in calories; high in vitamin C.

Vegetable Garden Bread: Take a slice of whole wheat bread and spread with cream cheese with chives and onion. Finely chop some fresh vegetables, such as carrots, broccoli, green sweet pepper, celery, spinach, radish, and cauliflower. Sprinkle a spoonful or two of the vegetables onto the cream cheese. To make a sandwich, top with another slice of whole wheat bread spread with some cream cheese.
Nutrition facts: With carrots, one slice of bread provides a vitamin A punch.

Super Spud Crisps: Scrub 2 unpeeled small baking potatoes. Using a sharp paring knife, thinly slice (you should have about 1½ cups sliced potatoes). On a well-greased 15×10×1-inch baking pan arrange potato slices in a single layer. In a small custard cup microwave a spoonful of margarine or butter on high for 15 to 30 seconds or till melted. Brush the melted margarine or butter onto the potato slices. Combine ¼ cup grated Parmesan cheese and a dash pepper; sprinkle onto potato slices. Bake, uncovered, in a 450° oven for 8 minutes. Turn potato slices and bake for 8 to 10 minutes more or till the edges are brown and crisp. Serve warm on a plate with catsup.
Nutrition facts: High in vitamin C and calcium, with enough protein for a satisfying mini-meal.

POTASSIUM POWER

When you head for your next workout, remember to take along a potassium-rich snack as well as your water bottle. Foods such as bananas and melon replenish potassium lost when you perspire from heavy exercise or hot weather. Potassium plays an important role in balancing the water in your cells, strengthening blood vessels, and decreasing high blood pressure.

Foods, rather than supplements, are the source of choice. Foods provide your body with additional nutrients—not to mention fiber. Also, taking in too much potassium (which is easier to do with supplements), can be dangerous. Although no recommendations exist for potassium intake, a range of 1,800 to 5,600 mg is considered safe for adults.

BEST SOURCES

Food	Potassium (mg)
Potato, with skin, baked (1)	844
Dried figs (5)	666
Beet greens, cooked (½ cup)	654
Cantaloupe (1 cup cubed)	494
Honeydew melon (1 cup cubed)	461
Great Northern beans (½ cup)	460
Banana (1 medium)	451
Orange juice (1 cup)	436
Yogurt, low-fat (1 cup)	402
Grapefruit juice (1 cup)	378
Milk (1 cup)	377

SWEET BANANA DESSERT TACOS

⅔ cup dairy sour cream
2 Tbsp. powdered sugar
6 8-inch flour tortillas
3 medium bananas, thinly sliced
2 Tbsp. granulated sugar
½ cup milk chocolate pieces
⅓ cup chopped pecans, toasted

◆◆◆

2 Tbsp. margarine or butter
2 Tbsp. packed brown sugar
2 Tbsp. water

1 Combine sour cream and powdered sugar; set aside. Wrap tortillas in foil. Heat in a 350° oven for 10 minutes. Meanwhile, toss together bananas, granulated sugar, chocolate pieces, and nuts.

2 To assemble, spoon about ⅓ cup banana mixture near one edge of each tortilla. Fold edge nearest filling up and over the filling just till mixture is covered. Fold in the two sides; roll up. Fasten with a wooden toothpick.

3 In a large skillet melt the margarine or butter; stir in brown sugar and water till well blended. Heat just till mixture comes to boil; add half of the filled tortillas. Cook about 2 minutes per side or till golden. Use a slotted spatula to remove tortillas from skillet. Repeat with remaining tortillas. Serve warm topped with sour cream mixture. Makes 6 servings.

Nutrition facts per serving: 401 cal., 21 g total fat (8 g sat. fat), 11 mg chol., 241 mg sodium, 53 g carbo., 1 g fiber, 6 g pro. *Daily values:* 12% vit. A, 9% vit. C, 9% calcium, 11% iron.

PEANUT BUTTER PIZZA

It's hard to improve on pizza's perfection, but adding another juvenile favorite—peanut butter—and turning it into dessert just might push pizza off the chart.

½ cup margarine or butter
½ cup peanut butter
½ cup packed brown sugar
⅓ cup granulated sugar
1 egg
1 tsp. vanilla
1 cup all-purpose flour

◆◆◆

½ cup semisweet chocolate pieces
½ cup peanut butter pieces
¾ cup tiny marshmallows
⅔ cup peanuts
½ cup miniature candy-coated semisweet chocolate pieces

1 In a bowl beat margarine and peanut butter with an electric mixer on medium to high speed 30 seconds. Beat in brown sugar, granulated sugar, egg, and vanilla. Beat in the flour on low speed.

2 Spread dough evenly in an ungreased 12- or 13-inch pizza pan. Bake in a 350° oven 15 to 18 minutes or till golden. Remove from oven and sprinkle with chocolate and peanut butter pieces. Let stand 1 to 2 minutes or till softened. Spread melted pieces over crust. Top with the marshmallows, peanuts, and miniature candy pieces. Bake 5 minutes more or till the marshmallows are golden. Cool pan on wire rack. Makes 12 servings.

Nutrition facts per serving: 384 cal., 23 g total fat (5 g sat. fat), 19 mg chol., 215 mg sodium, 41 g carbo., 2 g fiber, 7 g pro. *Daily values:* 10% vit. A, 1% calcium, 8% iron.

THE CREAM CHEESE OF CHOICE

Once upon a time, a toasted bagel made no demands. You simply reached for cream cheese. Now, buying cream cheese is almost like buying a car with a lot of options available—more or less fat, firm or soft texture, flavored or plain? It's enough to make the most dedicated cream cheese loyalist waver. To help you choose, our Test Kitchen put cream cheese through its paces. A few rounds of cheese later, we came up with the following guidelines.

BAKE WITH THE BRICK

For an all-purpose cream cheese, stash away a brick of regular, Neufchâtel, or fat-free cream cheese. With easy-to-measure cutting marks on the package, brick-style cream cheese is designed for cooking. Use any of the three varieties in recipes for cheesecakes, dips, sauces, breads, and other desserts. Side by side, you might notice slight differences among the options. But if you want to cut fat, you'll be happy with the lower-fat choices. Brick-style cream cheese also works as a spread. Just let it stand a few minutes at room temperature to soften.

Regular: Made with whole milk, cream, and cheese culture, this product is the familiar, rich, smooth, original cream cheese. You also can buy regular brick cheese with chives, perfect for topping baked potatoes and using in appetizer cheesecakes.
Nutrition facts per ounce plain: 100 cal., 10 g fat (6 sat. fat), 30 mg chol.

Neufchâtel (⅓ less fat): This product is made with the same ingredients as regular cheese, only with different amounts to lower the fat, calories, and cholesterol by a third.
Nutrition facts per ounce: 70 cal., 6 g fat (4 g sat. fat), 20 mg chol.

Fat-Free: Skim milk and sugar replace whole milk and cream. Fat-free cream cheese has a firmer texture and shinier surface than the other brick-style cheeses. As a spread, it lacks tang. Top it with jam or fruit for extra flavor.
Nutrition facts per ounce: 25 cal., 0 g fat, less than 5 mg chol.

RUB-A-DUB WITH THE TUB

For cream cheese to top bagels that comes in a convenient container, the tub is your best choice. Even straight from the refrigerator, tub-style cream cheeses are soft enough to spread without tearing the bread. They also produce softer results in recipes, so they should not be used for cooking.

Regular: With the same ingredients as brick-style cheese, this has the familiar flavor. It just spreads a little easier. Soft-style regular cream cheese comes in several flavors.
Nutrition facts per 2 tablespoons plain: 100 cal., 10 g fat (7 g sat. fat), 30 mg chol.

Light: This soft, creamy cheese is made with milk, skim milk, cream, and sometimes gelatin. A little lighter-textured than regular cream cheese, this version still has a tangy, satisfying flavor.
Nutrition facts per 2 tablespoons plain: 70 cal., 5 g fat (3 g sat. fat), 15 mg chol.

Fat-Free: Skim milk replaces almost all of the cream. Because of thickeners, tub-style fat-free cream cheese seems firmer and shinier than the other tub-style cheeses. Like its fat-free brick-style counterpart, this spread lacks the tang and creamy texture of regular cream cheese. Serve it with a little jam to boost the flavor or try the flavored varieties.
Nutrition facts per 2 tablespoons plain: 30 cal., 0 g fat, less than 5 mg chol.

RHUBARB UPSIDE-DOWN CAKE

If fresh rhubarb is unavailable, measure 2 cups frozen sliced rhubarb; thaw slightly, and chop. Before using rhubarb, thaw completely.

½ cup quick-cooking
     rolled oats
2 Tbsp. margarine or butter
1 cup granulated sugar
2 cups diced rhubarb
1 cup all-purpose flour
1 tsp. baking powder
¼ tsp. baking soda
½ tsp. ground cinnamon
½ cup packed brown sugar
¼ cup cooking oil
1 egg

1 Pour ⅔ cup *boiling water* over oats; cover and let stand for 20 minutes. Place margarine in an 8×8×2-inch baking pan and heat in a 350° oven 2 minutes or till melted; stir in ⅓ cup of the granulated sugar. Top with rhubarb.

2 Combine flour, baking powder, soda, cinnamon, and ¼ teaspoon *salt;* set aside. In a bowl combine remaining ⅔ cup granulated sugar, brown sugar, oil, and egg; beat till combined. Add oat mixture; beat well. Add flour mixture to oat mixture; beat just till combined. Carefully pour batter atop rhubarb. Bake in 350° oven 50 minutes or till a wooden toothpick inserted in center comes out clean. Cool on wire rack 5 minutes. Run a knife along sides of pan to loosen; invert onto serving plate. Serve warm. Serves 9.

Nutrition facts per serving: 278 cal., 10 g total fat (2 g sat. fat), 24 mg chol., 177 mg sodium, 46 g carbo., 1 g fiber, 3 g pro. *Daily values:* 4% vit. A, 3% vit. C, 6% calcium, 8% iron.

TEST KITCHEN TIP

RHUBARB TIPS

When choosing rhubarb, select firm and tender stalks; avoid those that are extra thick or wilted. To preserve its crisp texture, wrap raw rhubarb in plastic wrap and chill up to 1 week. One pound of rhubarb yields 3 cups sliced fruit.

BLUEBERRY-RHUBARB CRUMBLE

Warm-from-the oven, old-fashioned fruit desserts are everyone's favorite. Serve this one with whipped cream or light cream.

1½ cups rolled oats
 ⅔ cup packed brown sugar
 ½ cup all-purpose flour
 ½ cup butter or margarine
        ◆◆◆
 3 cups blueberries
 2 cups rhubarb cut into
        1-inch pieces
 ½ cup granulated sugar
 2 Tbsp. all-purpose flour

1 Combine oats, brown sugar, and ½ cup flour. Cut in butter or margarine till mixture resembles coarse crumbs. Reserve ⅔ cup crumb mixture. Pat remaining crumb mixture into bottom of a greased 9×1½-inch round baking pan. Bake in a 350° oven 10 to 15 minutes or till light brown.

---

2 Meanwhile, combine the blueberries and rhubarb. Add granulated sugar and 2 tablespoons flour; toss to coat. Spoon atop crust. Sprinkle with reserved crumb mixture. Bake in 45 to 50 minutes or till golden. Serves 6.

Nutrition facts per serving: 443 cal., 17 g total fat (10 g sat. fat), 41 mg chol., 168 mg sodium, 71 g carbo., 5 g fiber, 5 g pro. *Daily values:* 15% vit. A, 21% vit. C, 6% calcium, 13% iron.

30 MIN. LOW FAT

RHUBARB CHUTNEY

Looking for a way to perk up a basic ham slice, pork chops, or chicken pieces? Give this spunky fruited condiment a try.

¼ cup water
½ cup sugar
4 cups fresh or frozen rhubarb
     cut into ½-inch pieces
½ cup golden raisins or raisins
3 Tbsp. vinegar
1 tsp. grated gingerroot
1 tsp. curry powder
⅛ tsp. salt
     Dash bottled hot pepper
     sauce

1 In a large saucepan bring water and sugar to boiling, stirring to dissolve sugar. Add rhubarb; return to boiling. Reduce heat; simmer, uncovered, 3 to 5 minutes or till rhubarb is tender but holds its shape. Add remaining ingredients. Return to boiling; cook for 1 minute more. Serve warm or cover and chill up to 1 week. Makes 2½ cups.

Nutrition facts per 41 tablespoon servings: 19 cal., 0 g total fat, 0 mg chol., 8 mg sodium, 5 g carbo., 0 g fiber, 0 g pro. *Daily values:* 1% vit. C, 1% calcium.

MAY
The Spice of Life

*H*elp the temperatures
climb with a rich
mélange of herbs, spices,
and peppers that
transform old standbys
into spectaculars. Cases
in point: Cumin Mayo,
sesame-cilantro pesto,
chocolate torte with a
hint of ancho chili
pepper, and Fish Tacos
with Mango Salsa.
Lemongrass is the
defining ingredient in
breezy Lemon-Light
Spring Soup.
Gingerroot and lemon
peel utterly transform
plain strawberries in
no-fat Ginger Berry
Sorbet. May is made for
pungent boiled crawfish
and shrimp salad
enlivened with avocado
slices and feta cheese.
And there's no better
time to savor ripe
berries resting on a
cloud of angel cake.

30-minute recipes indicated in RED.
Low-fat recipes indicated with a ♥.

Cumin (pronounced COME-in) is the spice that makes it hard to say no when walking by a taco stand. Its nutty, earthy aroma spells comfort food, Mexican style. This tiny, toast-colored seed of an annual herb in the parsley family is grown mainly in India and the Middle East. Spaniards brought cumin to the New World, where it quickly took fire and became an anchor of Mexican cooking.

Cumin's slightly bitter, spicy (but not hot) flavor is the backbone of chili and curry powders. It also works its magic in Caribbean food. Try it with ground meats, sausages, stews, and bean dishes. Or, use it to season veggies, chutneys, dips, and salad dressings.

Toasting the seeds releases their pleasant, smoky essence. To toast, place them in a small frying pan over low heat; cook, stirring, for 5 minutes. Or, spread them in a shallow baking pan and toast, stirring occasionally, in a 350° oven for about 10 minutes or till brown and aromatic.

Most spices retain their flavor better when stored whole in airtight containers; this is especially true of cumin. Use the seeds whole or grind in a coffee grinder (clean it carefully after use, unless you're a fan of cumin-flavored coffee), a blender, or with a mortar and pestle, or a hammer and cutting board.

SIZZLING VEGETABLE SANDWICHES

A bun's worth of grilled veggies graduates from ho-hum to hurrah with a gloss of Cumin Mayo. (See the photograph on page 119.)

1 **small eggplant, cut lengthwise into ½-inch slices**
1 **medium zucchini, cut lengthwise into ¼-inch slices**
1 **medium yellow summer squash, cut lengthwise into ¼-inch slices**
1 **medium red sweet pepper, seeded and cut into ½-inch strips**
1 **small onion, cut into ½-inch slices**
⅓ **cup olive oil**

◆◆◆

4 **poppy seed kaiser rolls, split**
¼ **cup Cumin Mayo (see right) or Easy Cumin Mayo (see page 105)**

1 Brush the vegetables with some of the olive oil. Place onion slices on a long metal skewer. Grill the onion over medium coals for 5 minutes. Add remaining vegetables and grill for 12 to 15 minutes more or till vegetables are tender, turning once. (If some vegetables cook more quickly than others, remove and keep warm.) (Or, to broil, place half of the vegetables on the rack of a broiler pan. Broil 3 to 4 inches from heat 12 to 15 minutes or till vegetables are tender, turning once. Remove vegetables; keep warm. Repeat with remaining vegetables. Toast rolls under broiler about 1 minute.)

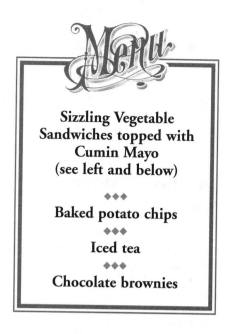

Menu

Sizzling Vegetable Sandwiches topped with Cumin Mayo (see left and below)

◆◆◆

Baked potato chips

◆◆◆

Iced tea

◆◆◆

Chocolate brownies

2 Brush split sides of rolls with remaining olive oil. Grill rolls, split sides down 1 minute or till toasted. Layer vegetables atop bottom halves of rolls. Spread top layer of vegetables with 1 tablespoon Cumin Mayo; cover with roll tops. Makes 4 servings.

Nutrition facts per serving: 405 cal., 25 g total fat (3 g sat. fat), 0 mg chol., 347 mg sodium, 40 g carbo., 3 g fiber, 8 g pro. *Daily values:* 16% vit. A, 60% vit. C, 6% calcium, 17% iron.

CUMIN MAYO

Make this spread from scratch or just spice up a prepared version. (See the photograph on page 119.)

¼ **cup refrigerated or frozen egg product, thawed**
2 **Tbsp. lime juice**
1 **clove garlic, cut up**
1 **tsp. cumin seed, crushed**
¼ **tsp. salt**
¾ **cup salad oil**

1 In a blender container or small food processor bowl, combine the egg product, lime juice, garlic, cumin seed, and salt. Cover and blend or process a few seconds or till combined. With the blender or processor running, gradually add oil in a thin, steady stream. When necessary, stop machine and scrape down sides of the container. Transfer mayonnaise to an airtight container and store in the refrigerator for up to 2 weeks. Makes about 1¼ cups.

Nutrition facts per tablespoon: 76 cal., 8 g total fat (1 g sat. fat), 0 mg chol., 32 mg sodium, 0 g carbo., 0 g fiber, 0 g pro.

Easy Cumin Mayo: In a bowl stir together 1 cup *reduced-calorie mayonnaise;* 2 tablespoons *lime juice;* 1 clove *garlic,* minced; and 1 teaspoon *cumin seed,* crushed.

Nutrition facts per tablespoon: 41 cal., 4 g total fat (1 g sat. fat), 0 mg chol., 88 mg sodium, 1 g carbo., 0 g fiber, 0 g pro.

ORIENTAL-SPICED FLANK STEAK

Anise seed, two kinds of pepper, and garlic make for a spicy marinade. Add some pineapple slices and sweet pepper wedges to the grill for accompaniments.

¼ cup soy sauce
2 Tbsp. water
1 Tbsp. brown sugar
½ tsp. anise seed, crushed
¼ tsp. cracked black pepper
¼ tsp. crushed red pepper
2 small bay leaves
2 tsp. cooking oil
1 tsp. toasted sesame oil
1 large clove garlic, minced
♦♦♦
1 1¼- to 1½-lb. beef flank steak, about ¾ inch thick

1 For marinade, in a saucepan combine the soy sauce, water, brown sugar, anise seed, black pepper, red pepper, bay leaves, cooking oil, sesame oil, and garlic. Bring to boiling, stirring to dissolve sugar. Let mixture stand for 15 minutes. Remove bay leaves.

2 Place the meat in a plastic bag set in a shallow bowl. Add the cooled marinade to the bag. Seal bag and refrigerate for 8 to 24 hours, turning bag occasionally.

3 Drain meat, reserving marinade. Grill meat on the grill rack of an uncovered grill directly over medium coals for 12 to 14 minutes or to desired doneness, turning meat once halfway through grilling time.

4 Meanwhile, place reserved marinade in a small saucepan. Bring to boiling. To serve, thinly slice meat across the grain. Spoon warm marinade over sliced meat. Makes 6 servings.

Nutrition facts per serving: 146 cal., 8 g total fat (3 g sat. fat), 35 mg chol., 732 mg sodium, 3 g carbo., 0 g fiber, 15 g pro. *Daily values:* 12% iron.

ALBUQUERQUE CHICKEN SALAD

For a sizzling fast supper, stir up the Southwestern salsa the night before, then fry chicken just before serving.

1 15-oz. can black beans or small red beans, rinsed
1 10-oz. package frozen whole kernel corn, cooked
1 cup cubed, peeled jicama
3 Tbsp. canned diced green chili peppers
♦♦♦

⅓ cup lime juice
⅓ cup salad oil
2 Tbsp. honey or sugar
1 tsp. dried oregano, crushed
½ tsp. ground cumin
¼ tsp. ground black pepper
¼ tsp. salt
♦♦♦
8 oz. skinless, boneless chicken breast halves
½ tsp. paprika
¼ tsp. salt
⅛ to ¼ tsp. ground red pepper
♦♦♦
Nonstick spray coating
1 large red or green sweet pepper, cut into bite-size strips
Leaf lettuce

1 In a nonmetal bowl combine beans, corn, jicama, and chili peppers. In a screw-top jar combine lime juice, oil, honey or sugar, oregano, cumin, black pepper, and ¼ teaspoon salt; shake well. Add to vegetables; toss. Cover; chill 4 to 24 hours.

2 Rinse chicken and pat dry. Cut chicken into ½-inch-wide strips. Stir together the paprika, ¼ teaspoon salt, and ground red pepper. Coat the chicken with the spice mixture.

3 Spray a large skillet with nonstick coating. Preheat over medium heat for 1 minute. Add the chicken and stir-fry for 3 to 4 minutes or till chicken is no longer pink. Stir in sweet pepper strips. To serve, arrange sweet pepper and chicken on 4 lettuce-lined plates. Top with bean and vegetable mixture. Serves 4.

Nutrition facts per serving: 429 cal., 22 g total fat (3 g sat. fat), 30 mg chol., 625 mg sodium, 48 g carbo.

COYOTE PIZZA WITH RED PEPPER SAUCE

Pizza takes on a Southwestern tingle with avocado, Mexican cheese, and a roasted pepper sauce.

1 **16-oz. Italian bread shell (Boboli brand) (12-inch)**
1 **recipe Red Pepper Sauce (see below right)**
2 **cups coarsely shredded deli roasted or rotisserie chicken (about 8 oz.)**
¼ **cup sliced green onions**
¾ **cup crumbled or shredded queso fresco cheese* and/or Monterey Jack cheese**
1 **avocado, halved, seeded, peeled, and sliced**
½ **cup dairy sour cream**
   Fresh serrano pepper or jalapeño pepper, thinly sliced (optional)
   Fresh cilantro sprigs (optional)

1 Place bread shell on a preheated baking stone or a 12-inch pizza pan. Spread with Red Pepper Sauce. Bake in a 425° oven 5 minutes. Top with the chicken, onions, and cheese. Bake 5 minutes more. Top with avocado and sour cream. Sprinkle with serrano or jalapeño pepper and cilantro, if desired. Serves 6.

*Note: Queso fresco is a mildly salty, white Mexican cheese found in supermarkets or in Mexican groceries (see page 34).

Nutrition facts per serving: 562 cal., 33 g total fat (9 g sat. fat), 69 mg chol., 724 mg sodium, 40 g carbo., 3 g fiber, 29 g pro. *Daily values:* 31% vit. A, 90% vit. C, 19% calcium, 19% iron.

CHILI PEPPERS

Chili peppers were mentioned in a Ladies Aid cookbook, circa 1922, as a source of the "peculiar but delicious flavor" behind Mexican sauces. Today, with salsa rivaling catsup in popularity, it's evident that the "delicious" part of the equation is winning the vote.

The potency of chili peppers soars from mild to lethal. The jalapeño is our most commonly used hot pepper. If it proves too fiery for your liking, replace it with a milder green chili such as the New Mexico or Anaheim. The serrano pepper, kin to the jalapeño, is more potent. Hottest of all is the habañero.

As green chili peppers mature, they become redder, mellower, and sweeter, but not milder. Some chili peppers are roasted and canned. Others, such as the mild to medium-hot poblano, are allowed to dry, then packaged whole, crushed, or ground. When dried, the dark green poblano becomes a mahogany-toned pepper now called ancho. What's sold as chili powder is actually a blend of ground mild chili pepper and other spices.

You can grow chili peppers as you would a sweet green pepper, or find them in the produce section of your supermarket. Choose firm-fleshed, unblemished peppers; remove the stems, seeds, and inner ribs to temper the fire somewhat, if desired.

To work with chili peppers, wear rubber gloves and refrain from touching your eyes or other sensitive body parts. After use, wash your knife and the cutting surface thoroughly with warm, soapy water.

Some chili peppers, especially the young, green ones, can be eaten raw. Call on these peppers to add pizzazz to guacamole and tomato sauces, mustard, mayonnaise, corn bread, eggs, beans, and ground meat.

RED PEPPER SAUCE

To ease last-minute preparations, roast the peppers ahead of time, then freeze. When needed, simply thaw them in your microwave oven on high for 3 to 5 minutes, then proceed.

2 **medium red sweet peppers**
1 **fresh Anaheim pepper**
   ♦♦♦
1 **clove garlic, cut up**
⅓ **cup olive oil**
½ **tsp. salt**
½ **tsp. cumin seed, crushed**

1 Halve the red sweet peppers and the Anaheim pepper; remove seeds and membranes. To roast, place peppers, cut side down, on a greased, foil-lined baking sheet. Bake in a 425° oven about 20 minutes or till skins are blistered. Place in a clean paper sack or container; seal and let stand for 10 minutes to steam. Use a paring knife to gently peel off the skins. Coarsely chop peppers.

2 In a blender container or food processor bowl, combine the peppers, garlic, olive oil, salt, and cumin seed. Cover and blend or process till nearly smooth. Transfer to an airtight container and store in the refrigerator for up to 10 days. Makes about ¾ cup.

Nutrition facts per tablespoon: 58 cal., 6 g total fat (1 g sat. fat), 0 mg chol., 90 mg sodium, 1 g carbo., 0 g fiber, 0 g pro. *Daily values:* 9% vit. A, 41% vit. C, 1% iron.

HOTCHA CHOCOLATE TORTE

Dense, rich chocolate tortes are all the rage. What gets your attention here is a hidden hint of ancho pepper—just enough to make you sit up and smile. (See the photograph on page 120.)

8 oz. bittersweet or semisweet chocolate, cut up
1 to 2 Tbsp. fresh ground ancho pepper* or purchased ancho chili powder

◆◆◆

6 egg yolks
2 Tbsp. all-purpose flour

◆◆◆

6 egg whites
⅓ cup granulated sugar

◆◆◆

Powdered sugar (optional)
1 recipe Raspberry Sauce (see right)
Fresh raspberries (optional)

1 Grease and lightly flour a 10-inch springform pan. In a heavy small saucepan melt the chocolate over low heat, stirring constantly. Remove from heat and

stir in the ancho pepper or chili powder. Set the springform pan and chocolate mixture aside.

2 In a medium mixing bowl beat the egg yolks with an electric mixer on high speed about 5 minutes or till thick and lemon-colored. Fold the cooled chocolate mixture into the egg yolk mixture. Gently fold in flour; set aside.

3 Wash beaters thoroughly. In a large mixing bowl beat the egg whites with the electric mixer on medium speed till soft peaks form (tips curl). Gradually add the granulated sugar, 1 tablespoon at a time, beating till stiff peaks form (tips stand straight).

4 Stir about 1 cup of the beaten egg white mixture into the chocolate mixture to lighten. Fold the chocolate mixture into the remaining egg white mixture. Turn the batter into the prepared

pan. Bake in a 350° oven for 25 to 30 minutes or till set and a wooden toothpick inserted near the center comes out clean. Cool on a wire rack (the center will fall during cooling).

5 Use a knife to loosen the edge of the torte from the sides of the pan. Remove sides of the springform pan. To serve, sift powdered sugar over torte, if desired. Cut torte into thin wedges. Serve each wedge atop a pool of Raspberry Sauce and garnish with fresh berries, if desired. Makes 12 to 16 servings.

*Note: Remove the stem and seeds from ancho peppers; snip peppers into bits. Place in a coffee grinder and grind till the size of finely ground pepper. (One large ancho pepper yields about 2 teaspoons ground pepper.) Clean coffee grinder thoroughly.

Raspberry Sauce: In a blender container or food processor bowl, combine 4 cups *fresh or frozen loose-pack raspberries,* thawed, and ¼ cup sifted *powdered sugar.* Cover and blend or process till smooth. Use a wire sieve to strain mixture to remove seeds. Cover the sauce and refrigerate till serving time. Makes about 1¼ cups.

Nutrition facts per serving: 184 cal., 9 g total fat (5 g sat. fat), 107 mg chol., 38 mg sodium, 25 g carbo., 3 g fiber, 5 g pro. *Daily values:* 19% vit. A, 17% vit. C, 2% calcium, 9% iron.

FLANK STEAK WITH CALIENTE CATSUP

This recipe earned Donald E. Collings of Pawcatuck, Connecticut, $200 in the magazine's monthly contest. (See the photograph on page 118.)

1   16-oz. can whole Italian-
     style tomatoes, cut up
½   cup wine vinegar
¼   cup chopped onion
¼   cup chopped celery
¼   cup chopped green sweet
     pepper
3   Tbsp. brown sugar
2   fresh jalapeño peppers,
     seeded and finely chopped
6   cloves garlic, minced
½   tsp. ground cinnamon
¼   tsp. salt
¼   tsp. ground ginger
¼   tsp. crushed red pepper

♦♦♦

1   Tbsp. chili powder
1½ tsp. ground cumin
¼   tsp. salt
1   1¼- to 1½-lb. beef flank
     steak or sirloin steak, cut
     about 1 inch thick

1 For catsup, in a medium saucepan combine tomatoes, wine vinegar, onion, celery, sweet pepper, brown sugar, jalapeño peppers, garlic, cinnamon, ¼ teaspoon salt, ginger, and red pepper. Bring to boiling; reduce heat. Simmer, uncovered, about 20 minutes or till of desired consistency, stirring occasionally.

2 Meanwhile, combine chili powder, cumin, and ¼ teaspoon salt. Rub onto both sides of steak. Grill steak on the grill rack of an uncovered grill directly over medium coals for 14 to 16 minutes or to desired doneness. Remove from grill; let stand for 5 minutes. To serve, thinly slice meat across the grain; serve with the catsup. Makes 6 servings.

Nutrition facts per serving: 195 cal., 7 g total fat (3 g sat. fat), 44 mg chol., 382 mg sodium, 14 g carbo., 2 g fiber, 20 g pro. *Daily values:* 10% vit. A, 47% vit. C, 4% calcium, 23% iron.

30 MIN.
LOW FAT

FISH TACOS WITH MANGO SALSA

Vibrant with cilantro and jalapeño peppers, this fruity salsa takes on a Jamaican beat with jerk-spiced fish. (See the photograph on page 119.)

8   6-inch flour tortillas
1   lb. fresh or frozen swordfish
     or halibut steaks, cut
     1 inch thick
½   tsp. Jamaican jerk seasoning

♦♦♦

2   cups shredded fresh spinach
     or lettuce
1   recipe Mango Salsa
     (see right)
     Fresh spinach leaves
     (optional)

1 Wrap tortillas in foil; place at the edge of the grill. Heat for 10 minutes over medium-hot coals, turning occasionally. Meanwhile, slice fish into ¾-inch slices; sprinkle with Jamaican jerk seasoning. Place strips in a lightly greased grill basket. Grill directly over medium-hot coals for 8 to 10 minutes or till fish flakes easily, turning the basket once. (Or, to broil, place seasoned fish slices on the greased unheated rack of a broiler pan. Broil 4 inches from the heat for 5 minutes; turn fish.

THE CLEVER COOK

EASY-FILL TACOS

To make tacos easier to fill, turn a muffin pan over and put the shells between the slots. This way, you can fill them faster and with less mess.

Laurie Guasti
*Truth or Consequences,
New Mexico*

Broil for 3 to 7 minutes more or till fish just flakes easily with a fork. Meanwhile, wrap tortillas in foil. Heat package on lower rack of oven for final 5 to 7 minutes.)

2 To serve, fill each tortilla with shredded spinach, fish, and Mango Salsa. If desired, serve on spinach leaves. Makes 8 tacos (4 main-dish servings).

Mango Salsa: In a large mixing bowl combine 1 large *mango*, peeled and chopped; 1 large *tomato*, seeded and chopped; 1 small *cucumber*, seeded and chopped; 1 thinly sliced *green onion*; 2 to 4 tablespoons snipped *fresh cilantro*; 1 *fresh jalapeño pepper*, seeded and chopped; and 1 tablespoon *lime juice.* Cover and refrigerate till serving time. Use a slotted spoon to serve. Makes about 3 cups.

Nutrition facts per serving: 418 cal., 10 g total fat (2 g sat. fat), 45 mg chol., 463 mg sodium, 52 g carbo., 3 g fiber, 30 g pro. *Daily values:* 46% vit. A, 63% vit. C, 11% calcium, 28% iron.

SINGAPORE BEEF SLAW

Our slaw of crunchy veggies is topped with marinated beef. Toasted cumin seed adds another new dimension. (See the photograph on page 119.)

12 oz. boneless beef sirloin steak, cut 1 inch thick

♦♦♦

¼ cup snipped fresh cilantro
3 Tbsp. salad oil
2 Tbsp. cider vinegar
1 clove garlic, minced
1 tsp. sugar
⅛ to ¼ tsp. crushed red pepper (optional)
4 cups shredded cabbage
1 cup peeled, thin jicama strips
1 medium red sweet pepper, cut into thin bite-size strips
½ to 1 tsp. cumin seed, toasted*
Coarsely shredded carrot (optional)
Lime wedges (optional)
Fresh cilantro leaves (optional)

1 Place meat on the unheated rack of a broiler pan. Broil 3 inches from heat 13 to 17 minutes or to desired doneness, turning once. When meat is cool enough to handle, cut into bite-size strips.

2 For marinade, in a non-metal bowl combine cilantro, salad oil, cider vinegar, garlic, sugar, and, if desired, crushed red pepper. Add steak slices; stir to moisten. Cover and marinate in the refrigerator for 6 to 24 hours. To serve, in a large serving bowl combine meat with the marinade, cabbage, jicama, and sweet pepper; toss gently to coat. Sprinkle toasted cumin seed atop salad.

Garnish with shredded carrot and serve with lime wedges and cilantro leaves, if desired. Serves 4.

*Note: To toast cumin seed, see "Cumin" tip on page 104.

Nutrition facts per serving: 292 cal., 18 g total fat (5 g sat. fat), 57 mg chol., 59 mg sodium, 12 g carbo., 2g fiber, 21 g pro. *Daily values:* 22% vit. A, 143% vit. C, 4% calcium, 21% iron.

NOUVEAU PESTO

Serve this sesame-cilantro take-off atop grilled chicken, meaty fish, or vegetables, or toss it with cooked pasta.

¼ cup sesame seed, toasted
2 cups firmly packed fresh cilantro or 1 cup each of fresh cilantro and parsley
2 cloves garlic, quartered
2 tsp. lime juice
¼ tsp. salt
¼ tsp. pepper
⅓ cup olive oil

1 Place sesame seed in a blender container or food processor bowl. Cover and blend or process 30 seconds or till almost ground. Add cilantro, garlic, lime juice, salt, and pepper; blend or process with several on-off turns. With machine running, gradually add olive oil, blending till mixture is smooth. Transfer to an airtight container and store in the refrigerator up to 1 week or freeze up to 6 months. To serve, bring to room temperature; stir. Makes ½ cup.

Nutrition facts per tablespoon: 106 cal., 11 g total fat (1 g sat. fat), 0 mg chol., 69 mg sodium, 1 g carbo., 0 g fiber, 1 g pro. *Daily values:* 9% vit. A, 1% vit. C, 1% calcium, 3% iron.

CILANTRO

Cilantro is the name given to the thin, lacy leaves of the coriander plant—a daintier version of its kissing cousin, parsley. Some say cilantro's flavor is like parsley's but more pungent. To others, it recalls a robust blend of sage and citrus. Naysayers of this love-it-or-loathe-it leaf claim it tastes like soap. Whatever. Cilantro adds a fresh taste to Indian, Chinese, and Latin American cooking when snipped into dishes as you would parsley. Left whole, its frilly leaves make a beautiful garnish.

It's easy to grow cilantro in a garden plot or windowsill pot. Or you can find it, bunched like parsley, in the produce section. Look for leaves that appear perky and have no brown discoloration. Before using, wash stems and leaves, then shake dry.

You can store cilantro for up to 1 week in the refrigerator by giving the stems a fresh cut, then plunging them into a jar of water 2 inches deep; cover the leaves loosely with a plastic bag or wrap. Or, simply store the bunch in a plastic bag in your refrigerator's vegetable drawer. Freeze the excess in a freezer container or moisture- and vapor-proof plastic bag (the herb may lose some of its bright color). No need to thaw before using—just add directly to the dish you're cooking. To substitute dried cilantro for fresh herb, use one-third the amount.

Enjoy cilantro in guacamole, salsa, soups, stir-fries, curries, bean dishes, and salads. Also use it to add flavor to vegetables such as tomatoes, onions, corn, and cauliflower.

Pork Chops with Spicy Peanut Sauce (see below)

❖❖❖

Hot cooked rice tossed with snipped fresh cilantro

❖❖❖

Lime wedges

❖❖❖

Soft pita bread

❖❖❖

Fruit sorbet

PRIZE TESTED RECIPE WINNER

Pork Chops with Spicy Peanut Sauce

This recipe earned Annette Rivers of Pickens, South Carolina, $100 in the magazine's monthly contest.

⅓ **cup milk**
⅓ **cup shredded coconut**
¼ **cup creamy peanut butter**
¼ **cup chicken broth**
2 **Tbsp. canned diced green chili peppers**
1 **Tbsp. diced pimiento**
1 **Tbsp. reduced-sodium soy sauce**
2 **cloves garlic, minced**
1 **tsp. sugar**
½ **tsp. ground ginger**
½ **tsp. ground coriander**

❖❖❖

4 **boneless pork loin chops, cut ¾ inch thick**
1 **Tbsp. cooking oil**
   Green onion slivers (optional)

1 In a small saucepan heat milk till almost boiling; remove from heat. Stir in coconut; let stand for 10 minutes. Strain milk, discarding coconut; return milk to pan. Stir in peanut butter, chicken broth, chili peppers, pimiento, soy sauce, garlic, sugar, ginger, and coriander. Cook and stir over medium heat till thickened and smooth.

2 Sprinkle pork with *salt* and *pepper*. In a large skillet cook chops in hot oil 10 to 12 minutes or till slightly pink in center, turning once. Serve with sauce. If desired, top with green onion. Makes 4 servings.

Nutrition facts per serving: 269 cal., 20 g total fat (6 g sat. fat), 37 mg chol., 323 mg sodium, 8 g carbo., 2 g fiber, 17 g pro. *Daily values:* 10% vit. C, 4% calcium, 8% iron.

30 MIN. LOW FAT

Brandied Apricot Chops

Serve a simple side of hot cooked couscous tossed with a little parsley.

1 **Tbsp. cooking oil**
1 **cup chopped red sweet pepper**
1 **cup sliced green onions**
1 **cup snipped dried apricots**
2 **tsp. dried parsley, crushed**
1 **tsp. dried thyme, crushed**

❖❖❖

4 **pork loin or rib chops, cut 1¼ inches thick**
1 **Tbsp. Worcestershire sauce**
⅛ **tsp. salt**
⅛ **tsp. pepper**

❖❖❖

¼ **cup apricot brandy or brandy**
¾ **cup apricot preserves**

1 In a 12-inch skillet heat oil over medium-high heat. Add sweet pepper, onions, and apricots. Cook and stir for 2 to 3 minutes or till vegetables are just tender. Stir in the parsley and thyme. Remove from skillet.

2 Brush both sides of chops with Worcestershire sauce. Sprinkle with salt and pepper. Cook chops in skillet over medium-high heat 8 minutes or till browned, turning once. Return vegetable mixture to skillet. Add 2 tablespoons *water;* reduce heat. Simmer, covered, for 8 minutes or till chops are no longer pink.

3 To serve, transfer chops and vegetable mixture to a serving platter; keep warm. Carefully add brandy to hot skillet. Use a wooden spoon to scrape the bottom of the skillet to loosen browned bits. Bring to boiling; add preserves. Heat through. Pour over chops. Makes 4 servings.

Nutrition facts per serving: 188 cal., 8 g total fat (1 g sat. fat), 36 mg chol., 296 mg sodium, 5 g carbo., 1 g fiber, 24 g pro. *Daily values:* 31% vit. C, 6% calcium, 10% iron.

LOW FAT

Chilly Fruit Soup

The pretty hue of this cool bowl of pleasure comes from the blending of rhubarb and cantaloupe.

½ **cup sugar**
¼ **cup water**
1 **Tbsp. grated gingerroot**
⅛ **tsp. pepper**
2 **cups fresh or frozen rhubarb, cut into ½-inch-thick slices**

❖❖❖

1 medium cantaloupe, peeled, seeded, and cut up (about 4 cups)
¾ cup orange juice
1 8-oz. carton plain low-fat yogurt

♦♦♦

Fresh mint (optional)

1 In a medium saucepan combine sugar, water, gingerroot, and pepper; bring to boiling. Add rhubarb. Return to boiling; reduce heat. Simmer, covered, about 5 minutes or till rhubarb is tender. Do not drain. Remove from heat; let cool.

2 In a blender container or food processor bowl,* place about half of the cantaloupe and half of the orange juice. Cover and blend or process till smooth. Add about half of the cooled rhubarb mixture and half of the yogurt. Cover and blend till smooth. Transfer to a large bowl. Repeat with remaining rhubarb mixture, cantaloupe, orange juice, and yogurt.

3 Transfer soup to a large bowl. Cover and chill soup in the refrigerator for several hours or till cold. To serve, ladle soup into individual bowls. If desired, garnish with fresh mint. Makes 6 cups (6 side-dish servings).

***Note:** If using a food processor, you may need to process one-third at a time, especially if the bowl has a smaller capacity.

Nutrition facts per serving: 149 cal., 1 g total fat (0 g sat. fat), 2 mg chol., 39 mg sodium, 34 g carbo., 2 g fiber, 4 g pro. *Daily values:* 36% vit. A, 106% vit. C, 9% calcium, 2% iron.

GINGERROOT

Gingerroot is to Chinese food what garlic is to Italian. This dried root of a tropical Asian plant was praised by Confucius as early as 500 B.C. By 1650, it had reached the New World, where its slightly hot, spicy taste made a hit in cakes and cookies. But its zippy flavor and aroma are too wonderful to stop there.

Fresh gingerroot is more hot and spicy than ginger in its ground form. In your grocer's produce section, look for a root with firm "fingers" that contains no soft spots.

Dice, sliver, mince, or grate the root as your recipe directs; peeling isn't necessary. Refrigerate any unused portion in a paper bag for several days. Or, place the gingerroot in a moisture- and vapor-proof plastic bag and freeze. Then grate or slice the frozen root as needed and immediately return unused portion to the freezer.

Here are some ideas for using gingerroot: Grate it into salad dressings, barbecue sauces, stir-fries, and curries. Chop it for marinades or rub the root directly onto pork, beef, and chicken before roasting. Add a few thin slices to hot tea. Call on gingerroot to awaken soups and vegetables. Add it to baked items. Use gingerroot to flavor an ice cream or sorbet recipe, and doll up a sundae by adding some to a hot fudge or custard sauce.

To substitute gingerroot for ground ginger, use 1 teaspoon grated gingerroot in place of ¼ teaspoon ground ginger.

JUMPIN' GINGER BUTTER

You've enjoyed garlic butter on everything from crusty bread to escargot. As a change of pace, trade up to ginger and bring new zest to grilled fowl, fish, vegetables, rice, and pasta. We love it slathered on corn muffins.

½ cup butter, softened
2 Tbsp. thinly sliced green onion
1 Tbsp. grated gingerroot
1 tsp. bottled minced garlic
1 tsp. reduced-sodium soy sauce

1 In a small mixing bowl stir together the softened butter, sliced green onion, gingerroot, garlic, and soy sauce. Cover and chill the butter mixture till almost firm, allowing about 1 hour in the refrigerator or about 20 minutes in the freezer.

2 On plastic wrap or waxed paper, shape the chilled mixture with a knife into two 4-inch-long logs. Fold wrap over logs and push logs into round shapes, using one hand to keep the plastic wrap taut while the other does the shaping. Wrap in the plastic wrap. If necessary, chill again and roll logs till smooth.

3 Rewrap the logs and chill till serving time. Store in the refrigerator for up to 1 week. To serve, cut into ¼-inch-thick slices. Makes ½ cup.

Nutrition facts per tablespoon: 102 cal., 11 g total fat (7 g sat. fat), 31 mg chol., 138 mg sodium, 0 g carbo., 0 g fiber, 0 g pro. *Daily values:* 10% vit. A.

GINGER BERRY SORBET

While the strawberries steep in sugar and lemon juice, the gingerroot and lemon peel impart their zest to boiling water.

- 1 cup sliced fresh strawberries
- ½ cup sugar
- 4 thin strips lemon peel (about 2×½ inches each)
- 3 Tbsp. lemon juice
- ½ cup boiling water
- 3 Tbsp. grated gingerroot

♦♦♦

- 1½ cups cold water
- 2 Tbsp. light-colored corn syrup
  Few drops red food coloring (optional)

♦♦♦

  Fresh sliced strawberries (optional)

1 In a medium mixing bowl combine the 1 cup strawberries, sugar, and lemon juice. Cover and refrigerate for at least 1 hour. Meanwhile, in a small mixing bowl pour boiling water over gingerroot and lemon peel; let stand for 15 minutes. Strain the mixture, pressing to extract liquid. Discard the solids; refrigerate the liquid about 1 hour or till chilled.

2 Place the strawberry mixture in a blender container or food processor bowl. Cover and blend or process mixture till smooth. If necessary, transfer mixture to another bowl. Stir in the chilled gingerroot liquid, the cold water, corn syrup, and red food coloring, if desired.

3 Freeze mixture in a 2-, 4-, or 5-quart ice-cream freezer according to manufacturer's directions.* To serve, garnish with fresh strawberries, if desired. Makes 5 cups (ten ½-cup servings).

*Note: If you desire, double the recipe and freeze in a 4- or 5-quart ice-cream freezer.

FREEZER DIRECTIONS

Turn mixture into a 9×9×2-inch pan. Cover; freeze till firm. Break mixture into chunks with a large metal spoon. Turn into a chilled mixing bowl. Beat with electric mixer on low speed till slightly slushy, then on medium to high speed till smooth and fluffy. Return to pan; cover and freeze till firm.

Nutrition facts per serving: 58 cal., 0 g total fat, 0 mg chol., 5 mg sodium, 15 g carbo., 0 g fiber, 0 g pro.
Daily values: 19% vit. C, 1% iron.

SUNBELT SHRIMP SALAD

Use the remainder of this zesty dressing as a marinade for meat, poultry, and fish. Or, toss it with robust greens and vegetables for another salad option.

- ½ cup rice vinegar
- ⅓ cup salad oil
- 2 Tbsp. brown sugar
- 1 Tbsp. chopped lemongrass
- 2 tsp. toasted sesame oil

♦♦♦

- 8 cups torn mild-flavored lettuce, such as Bibb or leaf
- 12 oz. peeled and deveined cooked shrimp with tails attached, chilled (about 16)
- 1 large avocado, halved, seeded, peeled, and sliced lengthwise
- 1 large mango, halved, seeded, peeled, and cubed
- ¼ cup chopped green onions
- ¼ cup crumbled feta cheese or shredded farmer cheese (1 oz.)

1 For dressing, in a small bowl combine rice vinegar, salad oil, brown sugar, lemongrass, and sesame oil; set aside.

2 Divide lettuce among 4 individual salad plates. Arrange shrimp, avocado, and mango atop lettuce. Drizzle each serving with 2 tablespoons dressing. (Chill and reserve remaining dressing for another use.) Sprinkle with green onions and cheese. Serves 4.

Nutrition facts per serving: 355 cal., 20 g total fat (3 g sat. fat), 173 mg chol., 238 mg sodium, 24 g carbo., 5 g fiber, 23 g pro.
Daily values: 54% vit. A, 71% vit. C, 15% calcium, 32% iron.

LEMONGRASS

Lemongrass, found in Asian markets, could pass for an ugly green onion. The leaves and stem are tough and fibrous, and sprout from a white, juicy, slightly bulbous base. Choose firm and unbroken stalks.

Traditionally, only the inner portions of the white bulb are used to impart its signature light, lemony flavor to foods. Chop and use the tender inner section in meat and vegetable dishes, salsas, vinaigrettes, and marinades. A 2-inch stalk portion yields about 1 tablespoon finely chopped lemongrass.

Some cooks also use the tougher green portions in recipes where the herb will be removed before serving. For easy removal, wrap the chopped herb in 100-percent cotton cheesecloth and use it as a bouquet garni in soups.

Use the fibrous stems (pound them with the blade of a knife or mallet to release their essence) to flavor fish, shellfish, and chicken; in dishes with a southeast Asia accent; or when lemon flavoring is wanted.

Fresh lemongrass may be stored in the refrigerator for up to 3 weeks or frozen in a moisture- and vapor-proof plastic bag or container. Dried lemongrass is available in packets of diced stems, which you must soak in water before using. Or, you can find it in shredded or powdered form. Dried forms have a stronger peppery bite and taste less lemony than fresh stalks. If you can't find lemongrass, you may substitute lemon peel (½ teaspoon peel for 1 tablespoon chopped lemongrass).

LEMON-LIGHT SPRING SOUP

After imparting a slightly spicy citrus flavor, the woody stalks of lemongrass are strained out, leaving a light broth to showcase delicate enoki mushrooms and spring's best asparagus.

- **3 cups chicken broth**
- **2 large stalks lemongrass, cut into 2-inch pieces**
- **2 Tbsp. snipped fresh cilantro**
- **⅛ to ¼ tsp. pepper**

◆◆◆

- **8 oz. asparagus spears, trimmed and cut into bite-size pieces**
- **1 cup fresh enoki mushrooms (3.5-oz. pkg.) or sliced button mushrooms**
- **½ cup sliced green onions**

1 In a medium saucepan combine the chicken broth, lemongrass, cilantro, and pepper; bring mixture to boiling. Reduce heat to low and simmer, covered, for 15 minutes. Strain broth, discarding solids. Return broth to pan.

2 Return broth to boiling. Add asparagus, button mushrooms, if using, and green onions. Cover and simmer about 5 minutes or till asparagus is tender. Remove from heat. Stir in the enoki mushrooms, if using. Serve the soup immediately. Makes 4 appetizer servings.

Nutrition facts per serving: 55 cal., 1 g fat (0 g sat. fat), 1 mg chol., 585 mg sodium, 6 g carbo., 1 g fiber, 6 g pro. *Daily values:* 6% vit. A, 31% vit. C, 2% calcium, 5% iron.

LEMONY FISH WITH ASPARAGUS

- **1 lb. fresh or frozen orange roughy, trout, red snapper, or salmon fillets**
- **1 lb. asparagus spears**
- **2 large stalks lemongrass, trimmed and cut in half crosswise**

◆◆◆

- **1 tsp. instant chicken bouillon granules**
-    **Pinch ground or thread saffron, crushed**
- **1 medium yellow sweet pepper, cut into bite-size strips**
- **½ cup dry white wine**
- **2 tsp. cornstarch**
- **2 Tbsp. sliced almonds, toasted**

1 Thaw fish, if frozen. Rinse fish; pat dry. Cut fillet into 4 pieces; set aside. Trim asparagus; set aside. Pound lemongrass lightly with a meat mallet to bruise.

2 In a skillet combine lemongrass, bouillon, saffron, 1 cup *water,* and ⅛ teaspoon *pepper.* Bring to boiling; reduce heat. Add fish; cook, covered, 2 minutes. Place asparagus and sweet pepper atop fish; simmer, covered, 4 to 6 minutes or till fish just flakes easily. Transfer all to a serving platter, reserving liquid in skillet; discard lemongrass. Combine wine and cornstarch; stir into liquid. Cook and stir till thickened and bubbly. Cook and stir 2 minutes more. Serve sauce with fish; sprinkle with almonds. Makes 4 servings.

Nutrition facts per serving: 210 cal., 6 g total fat (1 g sat. fat), 65 mg chol., 253 mg sodium, 8 g carbo., 2 g fiber, 27 g pro. *Daily values:* 8% vit. A, 177% vit. C, 9% calcium, 19% iron.

Menu

Olive Relish with Halibut
Steaks (see below)

❖❖❖

Hot cooked orzo pasta
with a bit of lemon peel

❖❖❖

Romaine hearts with a
citrus vinaigrette

❖❖❖

Rye rolls with butter

30 MIN. LOW FAT

OLIVE RELISH WITH HALIBUT STEAKS

This refreshing citrus and olive relish pairs well with pork or chicken, too.

¼ cup sliced pitted ripe olives
¼ cup sliced pimiento-stuffed green olives
½ tsp. finely shredded orange peel
2 medium oranges, peeled, sectioned, and chopped
1 Tbsp. snipped fresh parsley
1 Tbsp. snipped fresh mint
1 clove garlic, minced
¼ tsp. pepper
1 Tbsp. white wine vinegar

❖❖❖

1 lb. fresh or frozen halibut steaks, cut 1 inch thick, thawed
1 Tbsp. olive oil

1 For relish, in a medium mixing bowl combine the ripe and green olives, orange peel, chopped orange, parsley, mint, garlic, ¼ teaspoon pepper, and wine vinegar. Cover and refrigerate for up to 1 hour.

2 Brush both sides of halibut steaks with olive oil. Sprinkle with *salt* and *pepper*. Grill fish on the grill rack of an uncovered grill directly over medium-hot coals for 4 minutes. Turn fish and grill 4 to 8 minutes more or till fish just flakes easily with a fork. Serve with relish. Makes 4 servings.

Nutrition facts per serving: 188 cal., 8 g total fat (1 g sat. fat), 36 mg chol., 296 mg sodium, 5 g carbo., 1 g fiber, 24 g pro. *Daily values:* 6% vit. A, 31% vit. C, 6% calcium, 10% iron.

CRAWFISH ÉTOUFFÉE

Étouffée (AY-too-FAY) in Cajun cooking refers to simmering seafood smothered in onions, green pepper, and celery. The name comes from the French word étouffer, which means "to smother."

1 lb. fresh or frozen, peeled, cooked crawfish tails
¼ cup all-purpose flour
¼ cup cooking oil, butter, or margarine
1 cup finely chopped onions
1 cup finely chopped celery
½ cup finely chopped green sweet pepper
3 cloves garlic, minced

❖❖❖

1 Tbsp. butter or margarine
¾ cup water
½ cup sliced green onions
¼ cup snipped fresh parsley
½ to ¾ tsp. salt
¼ to ½ tsp. ground red pepper
¼ tsp. ground black pepper
Hot cooked rice

CRAWFISH TALES

Every spring, Cajuns in Louisiana look to the swampy bayous to find their favorite shellfish: crawfish, or as they like to call them, crawdads. You don't have to be Cajun to love crawfish, and you certainly don't need to catch your own. Crawfish farming has made these freshwater crustaceans available throughout the country almost year-round. If you prefer not to boil your own live crawfish (see directions on page 115), look for cooked crawfish still in the shell, either refrigerated or frozen, and frozen or canned crawfish tail meat.

1 Thaw crawfish tails, if frozen. In a heavy 3-quart saucepan stir together flour and oil till smooth. Cook over medium-high heat 3 minutes, stirring constantly. Reduce heat to medium. Cook and stir 5 to 8 minutes or till reddish brown roux forms. Add onions, celery, green pepper, and garlic. Cook and stir 5 minutes.

2 Add butter to mixture in saucepan; stir till melted. Stir in water, green onions, parsley, salt, red pepper, and black pepper. Bring to boiling. Add crawfish. Return to boiling; reduce heat. Simmer 5 minutes or till heated. Serve with rice. Serves 4.

Nutrition facts per serving: 397 cal., 18 g total fat (3 g sat. fat), 125 mg chol., 412 mg sodium, 37 g carbo., 2 g fiber, 21 g pro. *Daily values:* 11% vit. A, 45% vit. C, 7% calcium, 18% iron.

BOILED CRAWFISH

Cooked crawfish can be frozen and used later in dishes such as Crawfish Étouffée on page 114.

4 lb. live crawfish
8 qt. cold water
⅓ cup salt

❖❖❖

8 qt. water
1 cup purchased or 1 recipe Crab Boil Seasoning (see below)
2 tsp. salt

1 Rinse crawfish under cold running *water*. In a 12- to 16-quart kettle combine 8 quarts cold water and ⅓ cup salt; add crawfish. Soak for 15 minutes. Rinse and drain.

2 In the same kettle combine 8 quarts water, the Crab Boil Seasoning, and 2 teaspoons salt; bring to boiling. Add live crawfish. Return to boiling; reduce heat. Simmer, uncovered, about 5 minutes or till the shells are a bright reddish orange; drain. Discard crawfish with straight tails. (A straight tail means the crawfish was dead before cooking and could be spoiled.) Makes 1 pound cooked crawfish tails.

Crab Boil Seasoning: In a double layer of 100-percent cotton cheesecloth, combine 6 tablespoons *mustard seed,* 6 tablespoons *whole coriander,* 12 *bay leaves,* 2 tablespoons *whole allspice,* 4 teaspoons *whole cloves,* and 2 to 3 teaspoons *crushed red pepper.* Bring up the corners of the cheesecloth and tie into a bag.

PRIZE TESTED RECIPE WINNER

SMOKED SALMON CHEESECAKE

This recipe earned Joseph A. Divita of Tonawanda, New York, $100 in the magazine's monthly contest.

2 cups soft bread crumbs
2 Tbsp. margarine or butter, melted

❖❖❖

3 eggs
1 15-oz. carton ricotta cheese
1½ cups shredded Swiss cheese (6 oz.)
½ cup evaporated skim milk
4 oz. smoked salmon, finely flaked, with skin and bones removed
1 tsp. dried dillweed
⅛ tsp. salt
⅛ tsp. white pepper

❖❖❖

Dairy sour cream (optional)
Fresh dill (optional)

1 For crust, in a small mixing bowl combine the bread crumbs and melted margarine or butter. Press the crumb mixture onto the bottom of a 9-inch quiche dish; set aside.

2 For filling, in a large mixing bowl use a fork to beat eggs slightly. Stir in ricotta cheese and Swiss cheese. Stir in evaporated skim milk, salmon, dillweed, salt, and white pepper. (You can cover and chill this mixture for up to 6 hours.)

THE CLEVER COOK

SEARCH NO MORE

If you highlight the recipe titles in the index of your cookbook after you've made the recipes, you'll be able to find your favorites quickly and easily. For example, I highlight the ones my family likes in yellow and the ones we don't like in red.

Debbie Arnote
California City, California

3 Pour filling into the prepared quiche dish. Bake in a 350° oven for 35 to 40 minutes or till the center is nearly set when shaken. Remove and cool slightly in pan on a wire rack; serve warm.

4 To serve, cut cheesecake into wedges. If desired, top with sour cream and fresh dill. Cover and store any leftovers in the refrigerator for up to 3 days.* Makes 16 appetizer servings.

*Note: To reheat a slice of chilled cheesecake in a microwave oven, place slice on a microwave-safe plate. Cover loosely with microwave-safe plastic wrap. Micro-cook on 50% power (medium) for about 40 seconds or till warm.

Nutrition facts per serving: 133 cal., 8 g total fat (4 g sat. fat), 60 mg chol., 200 mg sodium, 6 g carbo., 0 g fiber, 10 g pro. *Daily values:* 10% vit. A, 17% calcium, 3% iron.

PEAR DUMPLINGS WITH LEMONGRASS

Spices often work well in tandem, which solves the problem of finding other uses for leftover seasonings. Here, gingerroot joins lemongrass in both the stuffing and the syrup.
(See the photograph on page 117.)

1¾ cups water
¼ cup packed brown sugar
¼ cup finely chopped lemongrass*
½ tsp. grated gingerroot
2 Tbsp. margarine or butter

♦♦♦

2¼ cups all-purpose flour
2 tsp. grated gingerroot
¼ tsp. salt
⅔ cup shortening
6 to 8 Tbsp. water

♦♦♦

6 small pears, such as Anjou or Bartlett, or apples, such as Cortland or Rome Beauty (about 4 oz. each)
¼ cup packed brown sugar
2 Tbsp. finely chopped lemongrass*
½ tsp. grated gingerroot

♦♦♦

1 beaten egg
1 Tbsp. water

1 For syrup, in a medium saucepan combine 1¾ cups water, brown sugar, ¼ cup lemongrass, and ½ teaspoon gingerroot. Bring to boiling; reduce heat. Simmer, uncovered, for 5 minutes. Remove from heat; strain, discarding solids. Stir the margarine or butter into syrup; set aside.

2 For pastry, in a medium mixing bowl combine flour, 2 teaspoons gingerroot and salt. Cut in shortening till pieces are

the size of small peas. Sprinkle 1 tablespoon water at a time (6 to 8 tablespoons total) over part of mixture; gently toss with a fork. Push dough to side of bowl. Repeat till all is moistened. Form into a ball. On a lightly floured surface, roll dough into a 20×13-inch rectangle. Cut the rectangle into six 6½-inch squares.

3 Peel and core pears or apples from bottoms, leaving the stems attached. If necessary, trim the bottom of the fruit so it sits flat. Combine the ¼ cup brown sugar, 2 tablespoons lemongrass, and ½ teaspoon gingerroot. Spoon about 1 tablespoon mixture into each cored fruit. Place each stuffed fruit on a pastry square. Moisten pastry edges. If desired, decorate corners with the tines of a fork. Fold corners to center near top of fruit; press sides of pastry edges to seal and fold points back (see below).

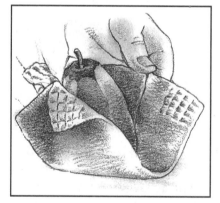

4 Arrange dumplings in a 3-quart rectangular baking dish. Pour syrup around pastry. Combine egg and 1 tablespoon water; brush onto pastry. Bake in a 375° oven for 30 to 40 minutes or till fruit is tender and pastry is golden. Cool slightly before serving. Makes 6 servings.

*Note: Remove the tough outer lemongrass leaves; save for another use or discard. Thinly slice the inner stalks crosswise, then chop.

Nutrition facts per serving: 532 cal., 28 g total fat (7 g sat. fat), 36 mg chol., 150 mg sodium, 66 g carbo., 4 g fiber, 6 g pro. *Daily values:* 6% vit. A, 7% vit. C, 3% calcium, 18% iron.

CARAMEL CRUNCH ICE-CREAM SAUCE

You just can't buy this delicious homemade taste.
(See the photograph on page 117.)

¼ cup margarine or butter
⅓ cup chopped or sliced almonds

♦♦♦

⅓ cup light-colored corn syrup
⅓ cup packed brown sugar
1 Tbsp. water
⅓ cup crisp rice cereal, coarsely crushed
Ice cream

1 In a medium skillet melt margarine or butter. Add the almonds; cook and stir over medium-low heat about 5 minutes or till almonds are browned.

2 Add the corn syrup, brown sugar, and water to the skillet. Cook and stir till bubbly and the brown sugar is dissolved (about 4 minutes). Stir in the rice cereal. Serve immediately over ice cream. Makes about 1 cup.

Nutrition facts per 2 tablespoons sauce: 159 cal., 9 g total fat (1 g sat. fat), 0 mg chol., 92 mg sodium, 21 g carbo., 1 g fiber, 1 g pro.

Left: *Pear Dumplings with Lemongrass (page 116)*
Below: *Caramel Crunch Ice-Cream Sauce (page 116)*

Page 118: *Flank Steak with Caliente Catsup (page 108)*
Top: *Fish Tacos with Mango Salsa (page 108)*
Above left: *Singapore Beef Slaw (page 109)*
Above right: *Sizzling Vegetable Sandwich with Cumin Mayo (page 104)*

Above: *Berries on a Cloud (page 121)*
Inset: *Hotcha Chocolate Torte (page 107)*

BERRIES ON A CLOUD

If you have a berry patch in your yard (and haven't treated it with pesticides), harvest the tiny berry leaves and blooms to top each serving. (See the photograph on page 120.)

1 recipe White Chocolate
   Meringue Shells
   (see below)
¾ of an 8-oz. pkg. (6 oz.)
   reduced-fat cream cheese
   (Neufchâtel), softened
½ cup light dairy sour cream
2 Tbsp. sugar
½ tsp. vanilla
¼ of an 8-oz. container frozen
   light dessert whipped
   topping, thawed

◆◆◆

1 oz. semisweet chocolate,
   cut up
½ tsp. shortening
3 to 4 cups hulled small fresh
   strawberries
¼ cup strawberry jelly

1 Prepare and bake White Chocolate Meringue Shells. Beat together the cream cheese, sour cream, sugar, and vanilla till smooth. Fold in thawed topping. Spread evenly in meringue shells. Cover and chill about 1 hour.

2 In a heavy small saucepan melt semisweet chocolate with shortening; cool. Drizzle over tops and sides of filled shells. Arrange berries, hulled end down, atop cream cheese filling. In a small saucepan heat jelly just till melted. Add 1 to 2 teaspoons *water* to thin. Drizzle over berries. Makes 8 servings.

White Chocolate Meringue Shells: Let 3 *egg whites* stand in a large mixing bowl at room

---

SODA FOUNTAIN FAVORITES

Just like saddle shoes, the jukebox, and your favorite after-school hangout, these golden oldie beverages are just too good to forget. Plus, they're a breeze to stir together. Savor the '50s with each sip.

◆ **Red River:** A stream of cherry syrup* flows through this classic fountain drink. To make a river, in a tall glass stir a 12-ounce can of carbonated water or club soda into a couple of spoonfuls of cherry-flavored syrup. Cool it all off with ice cubes.

◆ **Cherry Phosphate:** A phosphate is like a river drink, only with a tart flavoring added, usually citric acid or lemon juice. In a tall glass stir a can of carbonated water or club soda into a spoonful or two of cherry syrup* and lemon juice. Plunk in some ice cubes.

◆ **Cherry Cola:** In a tall glass stir a can of cola into a splash of cherry syrup.* Add a few ice cubes and a couple of bright red maraschino cherries.

◆ **Root Beer Float:** Plop vanilla ice cream into root beer and watch it float. Start with a tall glass and figure on 2 scoops of ice cream for each 12-ounce can of root beer.

◆ **Chocolate Soda:** A soda is a cross between a fizzy drink, a float, and a milk shake. In a tall, wide-mouthed glass stir some carbonated water or club soda into a couple of spoonfuls of chocolate-flavored syrup. Add a scoop of vanilla ice cream. Stir till the ice cream is almost melted. Add the rest of the can of soda to fill. Top with another scoop of ice cream.

◆ **Chocolate Malt:** This malt is so thick you'll need a spoon to eat it. The malt flavor comes from malted milk powder. In a blender container combine 2 scoops of vanilla ice cream, ½ cup milk, a couple of spoonfuls of chocolate-flavored syrup, and a spoonful of malted milk powder. Cover and blend till smooth. Serve the malt in a tall glass.

*Note: You'll find cherry syrup for Red River, Cherry Phosphate, and Cherry Cola near the ice-cream toppings at the supermarket.

---

temperature 30 minutes. Cover a baking sheet with clean plain brown paper or foil; draw eight 3-inch circles on paper or foil.

Add ½ teaspoon *vanilla* and ¼ teaspoon *cream of tartar* to egg whites. Beat with an electric mixer on medium speed till soft peaks form (tips curl). Add 1 cup *sugar,* a tablespoon at a time, beating on high speed till very stiff peaks form (tips stand straight) and sugar is almost dissolved. Fold in 1 ounce of grated *white chocolate baking square.* Spread or pipe meringue over circles on paper and shape into shells. Bake in a 300° oven for 30 minutes. Turn oven off; let meringues dry in oven with door closed at least 1 hour (do not open door). Peel off paper. Store in an airtight container. Makes 8 shells.

Nutrition facts per serving: 288 cal., 9 g total fat (4 g sat. fat), 19 mg chol., 134 mg sodium, 48 g carbo., 1 g fiber, 5 g pro. *Daily values:* 10% vit. A, 53% vit. C, 4% calcium, 3% iron.

ANGEL SHORTCAKE 'N' LEMON CREAM

For the lightest, highest angel cake, add the granulated sugar gradually to the beaten egg whites. Also, don't rush folding in the flour-powdered sugar mixture. This batter needs a tender touch to keep it airy. (See the photograph on page 1.)

1½ cups egg whites (10 to 12 large eggs)
1½ cups sifted powdered sugar
1 cup sifted cake flour or sifted all-purpose flour

◆◆◆

1½ tsp. cream of tartar
1 tsp. vanilla
1 cup granulated sugar

◆◆◆

1 recipe Lemon Cream (see top right)
4 cups sliced fresh strawberries

1 In a very large mixing bowl let the egg whites stand at room temperature for 30 minutes. Sift the powdered sugar and flour together 3 times. Set the flour mixture aside.

2 Beat egg whites, cream of tartar, and vanilla with an electric mixer on medium speed till soft peaks form (tips curl). Gradually add the granulated sugar, about 2 tablespoons at a time, beating on high speed till stiff peaks form (tips stand straight).

3 Sift about one-fourth of the flour mixture over egg whites. Lightly and gently fold the flour mixture into the beaten egg whites. Repeat the sifting over and folding in of remaining flour mixture by fourths.

THE CLEVER COOK

PUTTING THE STRAW IN STRAWBERRIES

To remove the stem from strawberries, take a plastic drinking straw (large core) and push it into the bottom of the berry. Keep pushing it into the tip through to the stem, so the stem and core come away clean.

Gretchen Bubnik
Thiensville, Wisconsin

4 Pour the batter into an ungreased 10-inch tube pan. Use a narrow metal spatula or knife to gently cut through batter to remove air bubbles. Bake on the lowest rack in a 350° oven for 40 to 45 minutes or till golden brown and top springs back when lightly touched. Immediately invert cake in the pan, standing the tube pan on its legs or resting the center tube over a tall-necked bottle (leave cake in pan). Cool completely. Use a narrow metal spatula to loosen cake from pan; gently invert onto serving plate.

5 To serve, use a serrated knife to slice cake into wedges. Top each serving with Lemon Cream and strawberries. Makes 12 servings.

Nutrition facts per serving (with 2 tablespoons cream): 228 cal., 4 g total fat (2 g sat. fat), 14 mg chol., 56 mg sodium, 44 g carbo., 1 g fiber, 5 g pro. *Daily values:* 4% vit. A, 47% vit. C, 2% calcium, 5% iron.

LEMON CREAM

No time to bake? Enjoy this fluffy topping spooned over berries.

½ cup whipping cream
¼ cup sifted powdered sugar
½ cup lemon low-fat yogurt

1 In a chilled mixing bowl beat whipping cream and sugar just till soft peaks form. By hand, fold in yogurt. Serve immediately or cover and refrigerate for up to 4 hours. Makes 1⅓ cups.

Nutrition facts per tablespoon: 30 cal., 2 g total fat (1 g sat. fat), 8 mg chol., 5 mg sodium, 2 g carbo., 0 g fiber, 0 g pro. *Daily values:* 2% vit. A.

HEAVENLY CHEESECAKE

Celebrate spring with slices of this sweet sensation (just remember to start the Yogurt Cheese a day ahead).

2½ cups Yogurt Cheese (see page 123)

◆◆◆

1 cup finely crushed gingersnaps (about 20 cookies)
1 cup finely crushed vanilla wafers (about 25 cookies)
1 Tbsp. all-purpose flour
¼ cup margarine or butter, melted

◆◆◆

¾ of an 8-oz. pkg. (6 oz.) reduced-fat cream cheese (Neufchâtel), softened
1 cup sugar
1½ tsp. finely shredded orange peel (set aside)
1 Tbsp. orange juice

3 eggs or ¾ cup refrigerated or frozen egg product, thawed
1½ tsp. grated gingerroot

❖❖❖

⅓ cup strawberry jelly
2 cups sliced fresh strawberries
1 cup orange sections

1 Prepare the Yogurt Cheese at least 1 day ahead.

2 For crust, in a mixing bowl combine crushed gingersnaps, vanilla wafers, and flour. Drizzle with melted margarine or butter, tossing to mix well. Press the crumb mixture onto the bottom and 1½ inches up the sides of an 8-inch springform pan. Bake in a 350° oven for 5 minutes.

3 For filling, in a mixing bowl combine the Yogurt Cheese, cream cheese, sugar, and orange juice; beat with an electric mixer on medium speed till smooth.

Add eggs or egg product; beat on low speed just till combined. Stir in the orange peel and gingerroot. Pour the batter into the crust.

4 Place the springform pan in a shallow baking pan on the oven rack. Bake in a 350° oven about 50 minutes or till the center appears nearly set when shaken. Remove springform pan from baking pan and cool for 15 minutes on a wire rack. Use a flexible metal spatula to loosen the crust from the sides of the pan. Cool for 30 minutes more; remove the sides of the pan. Cool on a wire rack. Chill for at least 4 hours.

5 For topping, melt jelly in a small saucepan over low heat; cool slightly. In a bowl stir together strawberries and orange sections. To serve, slice cheesecake. Top each serving with fruit. Drizzle with cooled jelly. Store any remaining cheesecake in the refrigerator for up to 3 days. Makes 10 servings.

Yogurt Cheese: Spoon 56 ounces *plain nonfat yogurt** into a 100-percent cotton cheesecloth-lined sieve or colander set over a large bowl. Let yogurt stand in refrigerator about 15 hours or overnight. Discard liquid in bowl. To store, wrap Yogurt Cheese in plastic wrap and chill for up to 4 days. Makes about 2½ cups.

*Note: Be sure to read the ingredient list on the yogurt carton to make sure it is gelatin-free. Yogurt with gelatin won't separate into curds and whey (the

curds are the cheese) the way you need it to for this recipe. You also can use this cheese in dips and spreads or in other recipes calling for cream cheese.

Nutrition facts per serving: 404 cal., 13 g total fat (5 g sat. fat), 85 mg chol., 342 mg sodium, 59 g carbo., 1 g fiber, 14 g pro. *Daily values:* 15% vit. A, 48% vit. C, 29% calcium.

CARAMEL APPLE CHEESECAKE

This recipe earned Jeanmarie Bond of San Diego, California, $200 in the magazine's monthly contest.

1½ cups crushed graham
    crackers (about 20 cracker
    squares)
2 Tbsp. sugar
¼ cup butter, melted
    ♦♦♦
2 8-oz. pkg. cream cheese,
    softened
1 cup sugar
¾ tsp. ground cinnamon
½ tsp. apple-pie spice
1 16-oz. can applesauce
2 Tbsp. lemon juice
5 eggs
    ♦♦♦
1 recipe Caramel-Pecan Sauce
    (see above right)

1 For crust, combine crushed crackers and 2 tablespoons sugar. Stir in butter. Press onto bottom and 1 inch up sides of a 9-inch springform pan. Bake in a 375° oven 10 minutes or till edges begin to brown. Cool slightly.

2 For filling, beat the cream cheese, 1 cup sugar, cinnamon, and apple-pie spice till fluffy. Beat in applesauce and lemon juice. Beat in eggs just till combined.

3 Pour filling into crust. Bake on a shallow baking pan in a 375° oven 40 to 45 minutes or till center is nearly set. Cool 15 minutes on a wire rack. Loosen sides of the pan. Cool for 30 minutes more; remove sides of pan. Cool

completely. Chill for at least 4 hours. Serve with the Caramel-Pecan Sauce. Serves 12 to 16.

Caramel-Pecan Sauce: In a heavy small saucepan melt ½ cup *sugar* over medium-high heat till sugar begins to melt, shaking pan often. Do not stir. Reduce heat; cook 5 minutes more or till sugar is melted and golden. Stir as necessary after sugar begins to melt (only when mixture bubbles). Remove from heat. Carefully pour in ½ cup *whipping cream.* Add 1 tablespoon *butter.* Cook and stir 1 to 2 minutes or till smooth. Stir in ⅓ cup chopped *pecans;* cool. Makes 1 cup.

Nutrition facts per serving: 443 cal., 27 g total fat (15 g sat. fat), 157 mg chol., 251 mg sodium, 46 g carbo., 1 g fiber, 7 g pro. *Daily values:* 29% vit. A, 5% calcium, 10% iron.

ORANGE DELIGHT CHEESECAKE

1½ cups crushed chocolate
    graham crackers (about
    20 cracker squares)
¼ cup sugar
2 Tbsp. all-purpose flour
¼ cup butter or margarine,
    melted
    ♦♦♦
3 8-oz. packages fat-free cream
    cheese or reduced-fat
    cream cheese (Neufchâtel)
1 cup sugar
2 Tbsp. all-purpose flour
1 cup refrigerated or frozen
    egg product, thawed or
    4 eggs
1 tsp. vanilla
1½ tsp. finely shredded orange
    peel
    ♦♦♦

⅓ cup orange marmalade, or
    apricot or peach
    preserves,* melted
¼ cup semisweet chocolate
    pieces
½ tsp. shortening

1 For crust, combine crushed crackers, ¼ cup sugar, and 2 tablespoons flour. Stir in melted butter or margarine. Press onto bottom and 1½ inches up sides of a 9-inch springform pan. Bake in a 350° oven 8 minutes; set aside.

2 For filling, in a large mixing bowl beat the cream cheese for 30 seconds. Add the 1 cup sugar and 2 tablespoons flour; beat well. Add egg product or eggs and vanilla. Beat on low speed just till combined. Stir in orange peel.

3 Pour filling into crust. Bake on a shallow baking pan in a 350° oven 45 to 50 minutes or till center appears nearly set when shaken. Cool 15 minutes. Loosen crust from sides of pan. Cool 30 minutes more; remove sides of pan. Cool completely. Cover and chill at least 4 hours.

4 To serve, drizzle melted marmalade or preserves over cheesecake. In a heavy small saucepan cook and stir the chocolate pieces and shortening over low heat till melted. Drizzle chocolate over cheesecake. Makes 12 to 16 servings.

*Note: Snip any large pieces of fruit in preserves.

Nutrition facts per serving: 262 cal., 7 g total fat (4 g sat. fat), 19 mg chol., 103 mg sodium, 40 g carbo., 1 g fiber, 11 g pro. *Daily values:* 28% vit. A, 1% vit. C, 17% calcium, 5% iron.

JUNE
Outdoor Appetite

Picnics. Campfires. Lunch al fresco. Dinner on the deck, screened-in porch, or patio. June is meant to be enjoyed outside. The garden is thriving, so dress tender greens with Herbed Balsamic Vinaigrette, Summer Fruit Vinegar, or Rosemary Wine Vinegar. Get creative with the grill, slicing loin chops into a fast Ginger Pork Salad and stuffing a sirloin roast with fresh basil leaves. Desserts are unfussy, such as low-fat Chocolate Malted Cupcakes and Fresh Summer Fruit Tart with a no-cook filling and no-roll crust. This is the month to try an open-air breakfast of Skillet Sausage and Potatoes and Green Chili Muffins.

HOMINY CHICKEN SALAD

This recipe earned Beth P. Sanborn of Mililani, Hawaii, $200 in the magazine's monthly contest.

4 medium skinless, boneless chicken breast halves
½ cup chopped onion
6 cups shredded romaine lettuce
2 14½-oz. cans hominy, drained
1 cup cubed Monterey Jack cheese (4 oz.)

❖❖❖

¾ cup light dairy sour cream
¾ cup green salsa
Milk (optional)

❖❖❖

4 6-inch corn tortillas
2 Tbsp. cooking oil

❖❖❖

1 ripe avocado, halved, seeded, peeled, and sliced

1 In a 10-inch skillet combine chicken breasts and onion; add water to cover. Bring to boiling; reduce heat. Simmer, covered, for 15 to 20 minutes or till no longer pink; drain. Remove chicken and onion; cool slightly. Cut into bite-size pieces. In a large mixing bowl toss together chicken and onion, romaine, hominy, and cheese. Cover and chill till ready to serve.

2 For dressing, in a small mixing bowl stir together the sour cream and salsa. If necessary, stir in enough milk to make a dressing of desired consistency. Cover and chill till ready to serve.

3 Before serving, cut tortillas in half; cut crosswise into ¼-inch-wide strips. In a large skillet heat oil over medium heat. Add the tortilla strips. Cook and stir about 5 minutes or till crisp and golden. Remove strips and drain on paper towels; cool slightly.

4 To serve, divide chicken mixture among 6 dinner plates; add avocado slices. Top with tortilla strips; drizzle with dressing. Makes 6 main-dish servings.

Nutrition facts per serving: 418 cal., 21 g total fat (7 g sat. fat), 60 mg chol., 513 mg sodium, 35 g carbo., 3 g fiber, 26 g pro. *Daily values:* 30% vit. A, 45% vit. C, 20% calcium, 17% iron.

TROPICAL LUNCHEON SALAD

4 medium skinless, boneless chicken breast halves

❖❖❖

½ cup low-calorie seedless blackberry spread
⅓ cup salad oil
3 Tbsp. white wine vinegar
2 Tbsp. pineapple juice
2 Tbsp. dry white wine

❖❖❖

8 cups mixed salad greens
1 medium banana, sliced
1 orange, peeled and sliced
1 cup sliced strawberries
2 kiwifruit, peeled and sliced
1 recipe Caramelized Walnuts (see right)

1 Rinse chicken; pat dry. Grill chicken on the grill rack of an uncovered grill directly over medium-hot coals for 15 to 18 minutes or till tender and no longer pink, turning once. (Or, to broil, place chicken on the unheated rack of a broiler pan. Broil 3 to 4 inches from heat for 12 to 15 minutes or till tender and no longer pink, turning once.)

2 For dressing, whisk together blackberry spread, oil, vinegar, pineapple juice, and wine. Cover; chill till ready to serve.

3 To serve, slice chicken diagonally into strips. Divide greens among 4 dinner plates. Arrange chicken and fruit atop. Drizzle with dressing and sprinkle with Caramelized Walnuts. Makes 4 main-dish servings.

Caramelized Walnuts: In a small skillet combine ½ cup broken *walnuts* and 2 tablespoons *sugar.* Cook over medium heat, shaking skillet occasionally, till sugar begins to melt. Do not stir. Reduce heat to low and cook till sugar is golden brown, stirring occasionally. Turn onto buttered foil to cool.

Nutrition facts per serving: 588 cal., 31 g total fat (3 g sat. fat), 60 mg chol., 88 mg sodium, 56 g carbo., 6 g fiber, 27 g pro. *Daily values:* 30% vit. A, 160% vit. C, 8% calcium, 19% iron.

GINGER PORK SALAD

Before grilling or broiling, brush the chops with hoisin, a thick, spiced Oriental sauce. While you wait for the meat to cook, toss the vegetables with a ginger-soy dressing.

1 lb. boneless pork loin chops, cut 1 inch thick (America's cut)
2 Tbsp. hoisin sauce or apple butter

❖❖❖

3 cups shredded Chinese
   cabbage
1 cup sliced celery
1 medium carrot, cut into
   matchstick-size strips
1 medium red onion, thinly
   sliced and separated
   into rings
⅓ cup clear Italian salad
   dressing
3 Tbsp. orange juice
2 Tbsp. reduced-sodium
   soy sauce
½ tsp. ground ginger
⅛ tsp. pepper
❖❖❖
1 cup chow mein noodles or
   rice crackers, broken

1 Brush pork chops with hoisin sauce or apple butter. Arrange chops on the unheated rack of a broiler pan. Broil 4 inches from the heat to desired doneness, allowing 9 to 13 minutes for medium (slightly pink in center) or 14 to 16 minutes for well done (no pink remains), turning once. (Or, grill, uncovered, directly over medium coals for 9 to 13 minutes for medium or 14 to 16 minutes for well done, turning once.) Thinly slice the meat crosswise; cover and keep warm.

2 Meanwhile, in a salad bowl toss together the cabbage, celery, carrot, and red onion. For dressing, in a screw-top jar combine the Italian salad dressing, orange juice, soy sauce, ginger, and pepper; cover and shake well to mix. Add the dressing to the vegetables, tossing to coat.

3 To serve, arrange cabbage mixture and meat on 4 dinner plates. Sprinkle with chow mein noodles or broken rice crackers. Makes 4 main-dish servings.

SLIM SALAD DRESSINGS

All dressed up, these salad toppers have everywhere to go. Low in fat and calories, they give your salads a delicious lift without forking over your light eating plans. Each dressing contains less than 2 grams of fat per tablespoon. Compared to 9 grams in a regular salad dressing, that's quite a nutrition bargain. Try them on your favorite salads and see for yourself.

HERBED
TOMATO VINAIGRETTE
In a blender combine ½ cup water; 3 tablespoons vinegar; 2 tablespoons snipped, oil-packed dried tomatoes; 2 tablespoons oil from tomatoes or olive oil; 2 teaspoons snipped fresh oregano or ½ teaspoon dried oregano, crushed; 1½ teaspoons sugar; and a dash salt. Cover and blend till smooth. Chill up to 1 week. Shake before serving. Serve over seafood or green salads. Makes 1 cup.

Nutrition facts per tablespoon: 18 cal., 2 g total fat (0 g sat. fat), 0 mg chol., 11 mg sodium, 1g carbo., 0 g fiber.

CREAMY
CILANTRO DRESSING
In a small bowl stir together ½ cup buttermilk, 2 tablespoons thinly sliced green onion, 2 tablespoons nonfat dairy sour cream, 1 tablespoon snipped fresh cilantro, and 1 tablespoon Dijon-style mustard.

Cover and chill for up to 1 week. Stir before serving. Serve over seafood or chicken salads or Tex-Mex salads. Makes about ⅔ cup.

Nutrition facts per tablespoon: 9 cal., 0 g total fat, 0 mg chol., 48 mg sodium, 1 g carbo., 1 g pro.

CREAMY
LEMON-MINT DRESSING
In a small bowl stir together an 8-ounce container plain low-fat yogurt; 1 to 2 tablespoons lemon juice; 2 teaspoons snipped fresh mint or ½ teaspoon dried mint, crushed; ½ teaspoon finely shredded lemon peel; and ¼ teaspoon salt. Cover; chill up to 1 week. Stir before serving. Serve over fruit or meat salads. Makes 1 cup.

Nutrition facts per tablespoon: 9 cal., 0 g total fat, 1 mg chol., 43 mg sodium, 1 g carbo., 0 g fiber, 1 g pro.

HONEY-CANTALOUPE
DRESSING
In a blender container or food processor bowl, cover and blend 1 cup cut-up cantaloupe till smooth. Stir in ½ cup vanilla low-fat yogurt and 1 tablespoon honey. Cover; chill till serving time or up to 2 days. Stir before serving. Serve over fruit salads. Makes 1¼ cups.

Nutrition facts per tablespoon: 12 cal., 0 g total fat, 0 mg chol., 4 mg sodium, 2 g carbo., 0 g fiber, 0 g pro.

Nutrition facts per serving: 263 cal., 14 g total fat (3 g sat. fat), 51 mg chol., 818 mg sodium, 17 g carbo., 3 g fiber, 19 g pro. *Daily values:* 73% vit. A, 44% vit. C, 9% calcium, 13% iron.

Jasmine Rice Salad With Gingered Tea Vinaigrette

There's something light and lemony, and something unique about this salad. Who would ever guess it's lemon tea that gives the dressing its hint of citrus?

1 cup jasmine, basmati, or
  long grain rice

♦♦♦

2 lemon tea bags
⅓ cup boiling water
¼ cup salad oil
2 Tbsp. rice vinegar or white
  wine vinegar
2 tsp. sugar
½ tsp. grated gingerroot

♦♦♦

4 oz. fresh snow peas, trimmed
  (about 1¼ cups)
¼ cup finely chopped or
  shredded carrot
¼ cup sliced green onions
2 cups watercress or other
  torn salad greens
1 tsp. toasted sesame seed
  Red and/or yellow sweet
  pepper strips or rings
  (optional)
  Sliced green onion (optional)

1 Prepare rice according to package directions, cooking till the liquid is absorbed and the rice is tender. Transfer to a large mixing bowl.

2 Meanwhile, in a measuring cup combine the tea bags and boiling water. Let stand for 5 minutes. With the back of a spoon, press bags against a side of the cup to extract liquid. Discard tea bags. For dressing, in a screw-top jar combine the brewed tea, oil, vinegar, sugar, and gingerroot. Cover and shake well to mix. Pour over cooked rice, tossing gently. Set aside to cool.

3 Place snow peas in a colander. Pour boiling water over peas; rinse with cold water. Cut pea pods in half diagonally. Add pea pods, carrots, and ¼ cup green onions to the rice, tossing to mix. Cover; chill or serve at room temperature. To serve, arrange watercress around edge of a large serving platter. Spoon rice mixture onto center of platter. Sprinkle with sesame seed. If desired, garnish with sweet pepper and sprinkle with additional green onion. Makes 6 side-dish servings.

Nutrition facts per serving: 212 cal., 10 g total fat (1 g sat. fat), 0 mg chol., 12 mg sodium, 28 g carbo., 1 g fiber, 3 g pro. *Daily values:* 19% vit. A, 35% vit. C, 5% calcium, 17% iron.

Not-Your-Lunch-Box Tuna Salad

The dressing can be made ahead and stored, covered, in the refrigerator. Rub the fish with herbs shortly before grilling. To retain juiciness and flavor, do not overcook the fish.

12 oz. fresh or frozen tuna
  steak, cut about 1 inch
  thick
8 oz. fresh green beans,
  trimmed
1 Tbsp. olive oil
2 to 3 Tbsp. snipped fresh
  rosemary or ½ to 1 tsp.
  dried rosemary, crushed
1 tsp. cracked black pepper

♦♦♦

1 10-oz. pkg. torn mixed salad
  greens or mesclun mix
8 medium radishes, sliced
1 medium cucumber, sliced
1 recipe Sesame-Soy Dressing
  (see below)
  Lemon wedges

1 Thaw fish, if frozen. In a medium saucepan cook beans, covered, in a small amount of *boiling salted water* for 20 to 25 minutes or till crisp-tender. Drain and set aside. Meanwhile, brush both sides of tuna lightly with olive oil. Sprinkle both sides of the fish with rosemary and pepper, pressing to adhere. Grill tuna on the greased rack of an uncovered grill directly over medium coals for 8 to 12 minutes or till the fish just begins to flake easily, turning once.

2 Divide the greens among 4 dinner plates; place tuna atop. Arrange cooked beans, radish slices, and cucumber slices around tuna. Drizzle dressing over salads. Serve with lemon wedges. Makes 4 main-dish servings.

Sesame-Soy Dressing: In a screw-top jar combine 2 tablespoons *salad oil*, 2 tablespoons *lime juice*, 1 tablespoon *toasted sesame oil*, 1 tablespoon *reduced-sodium soy sauce*, 1 tablespoon *water*, ½ teaspoon *sugar*, and ½ teaspoon grated *gingerroot or* ¼ teaspoon *ground ginger*. Cover and shake well. Use immediately or chill till needed.

Nutrition facts per serving: 302 cal., 19 g total fat (3 g sat. fat), 35 mg chol., 306 mg sodium, 10 g carbo., 3 g fiber, 24 g pro. *Daily values:* 67% vit. A, 35% vit. C, 5% calcium, 17% iron.

TURN A NEW LEAF

Start fresh with your salad bowl by tossing in something other than lettuce. You already may have tasted some of these leafy alternatives without knowing them by name because they're often included in packaged mixed greens. Besides looking prettier than plain lettuce, they have more flavor, adding a pinelike or spicy note to salads. Another plus: Their bright colors are an indication of the nutrition punch they pack. Look over the choices below, then mix and match them with more common salad greens.

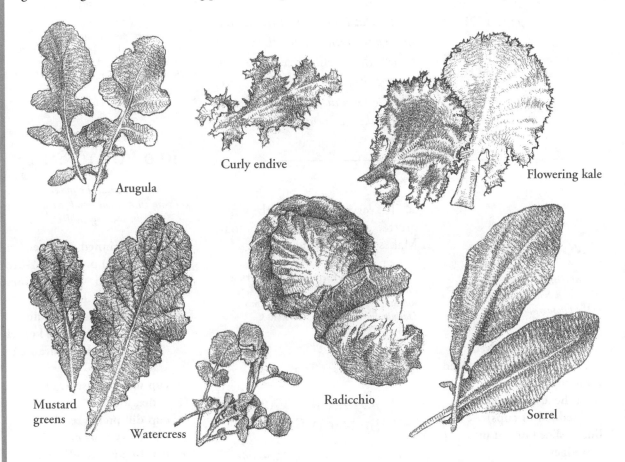

Arugula

Curly endive

Flowering kale

Mustard greens

Watercress

Radicchio

Sorrel

1. Arugula (ah-ROO-guh-lah): Also known as rocket. Long green leaves that are notched. Zesty, peppery flavor.

2. Curly endive: Otherwise known as chicory. Frilly, narrow, prickly leaves. A pleasantly bitter tang. Baby endive is softer than mature curly endive.

3. Flowering kale: Large, frilly leaves that may be purple, pink, green, or creamy white. Cabbage-like flavor.

4. Mustard greens: Round frilly-edged green leaves. Spicy mustard flavor.

5. Radicchio (rah-DEE-kee-oh): Looks like a small red cabbage, with purplish red leaves and white veins. Tangy, slightly bitter flavor.

6. Sorrel (SOR-uhl): Also known as sourgrass. Looks like garden spinach, with smaller, lighter green leaves and pointed notches at the base. Lemony, sweet-sour flavor.

7. Watercress: Tiny round green leaves with delicate stems that grow in clumps. Slightly pungent, peppery flavor. Darker and larger leaves are better.

Salad Picnic in the Woods

Orange-Pear Spinach Salad

♦♦♦

Avocado Slaw

♦♦♦

Corn and Red Potato Salad

♦♦♦

Pepper-Olive Pasta Salad
(see recipe, page 132)

♦♦♦

Parmesan Corn Bread Twists
(see recipe, page 132)

♦♦♦

Lemonade

Before you head to the woods: Bake the bread twists. Fix the dressing for each salad and chill. Prepare the salad ingredients and chill. Make lemonade; freeze some in cubes.

To tote: Place cooled twists in a storage container. Pack the chilled salads and dressings separately in storage containers and chill on ice. Pack lemonade with ice cubes in an insulated vacuum container.

AVOCADO SLAW

Avocados, limes, and cilantro give coleslaw a Southwestern spin. (See the photograph on page 158.)

3 small avocados, halved, seeded, peeled, and sliced
   Lime juice
1 small head red cabbage, shredded (4 cups)
2 limes, sliced or cut into wedges
4 cups shredded lettuce
   Fresh cilantro (optional)
1 recipe Lime Vinaigrette (see page 131)

1 Brush cut edges of avocado with lime juice. On a serving platter arrange rows of shredded cabbage, lime slices or wedges, shredded lettuce, and avocado slices. If desired, garnish with cilantro. (To tote, cover the serving platter with plastic wrap; chill for up to 4 hours. Pack with ice.)

2 To serve, drizzle with vinaigrette, tossing gently to coat. Makes 10 side-dish servings.

Nutrition facts per serving: 170 cal., 14 g total fat (3 g sat. fat), 0 mg chol., 11 mg sodium, 13 g carbo., 3 g fiber, 2 g pro. *Daily values:* 6% vit. A, 48% vit. C, 2% calcium, 7% iron.

ORANGE-PEAR SPINACH SALAD

If your pears are firm, ripen them at room temperature in a paper bag until they yield to gentle pressure. (See the photograph on page 158.)

2 medium red or yellow pears, such as Bartlett
   Lemon juice
4 cups fresh spinach leaves
4 cups leaf lettuce
3 oranges, peeled, halved, and sectioned
1 recipe Herbed Balsamic Vinaigrette (see page 131)

1 Slice pears; brush cut edges with lemon juice. On a serving platter arrange spinach and lettuce. Top with orange and pear slices. (To tote, cover with plastic wrap; chill for up to 4 hours. Pack with ice.) To serve, drizzle with dressing, tossing to coat. Makes 8 to 10 side-dish servings.

Nutrition facts per serving: 112 cal., 7 g total fat (1 g sat. fat), 0 mg chol., 26 mg sodium, 12 g carbo., 3 g fiber, 1 g pro. *Daily values:* 20% vit. A, 39% vit. C, 3% calcium, 9% iron.

CORN AND RED POTATO SALAD

Save on cleanup by making the dressing in a salad bowl, then tossing in the vegetables.

2 lb. red-skinned potatoes (about 6) or two 14½-oz. cans sliced white potatoes, rinsed and drained
2 fresh ears of corn or one 15¼-oz. can whole kernel corn, rinsed and drained

♦♦♦

½ cup mayonnaise or salad dressing*
⅓ cup dill pickle relish
¼ cup dairy sour cream*
½ tsp. finely shredded lemon peel
1 Tbsp. lemon juice
¼ tsp. salt
⅛ tsp. pepper

♦♦♦

½ cup sliced green onions
   Milk (optional)
½ cup cherry tomatoes, quartered or halved
   Fresh dill (optional)

1 If using fresh potatoes and corn, scrub potatoes; remove husks and silks from corn. In a 4-quart pot cook potatoes in boiling water for 15 minutes. Add corn; cook 10 minutes more or till potatoes are tender. Drain potatoes and corn; cool. Use a sharp knife to slice potatoes and to cut kernels from corn.

2 Meanwhile, for dressing, in a large salad bowl or storage container, combine the mayonnaise or salad dressing, pickle relish, sour cream, lemon peel, lemon juice, salt, and pepper.

3 Add the potatoes, corn, and green onions to dressing, tossing gently to coat. Cover and chill. (To tote, pack in the storage container. Chill on ice.) If necessary to moisten, stir in 1 to 2 tablespoons milk. Top with tomatoes. If desired, garnish with fresh dill. Makes 10 to 12 side-dish servings.

Nutrition facts per serving: 209 cal., 10 g total fat (2 g sat. fat), 9 mg chol., 217 mg sodium, 28 g carbo., 2 g fiber, 3 g pro. *Daily values:* 4% vit. A, 28% vit. C, 2% calcium, 12% iron.

*Note: Use low-fat versions of mayonnaise and sour cream to cut the fat in half and the calories to 166 per serving. With nonfat ingredients, you can cut the fat completely and reduce the calories to 134.

HERBED BALSAMIC VINAIGRETTE

One dressing has many uses. Serve the vinaigrette variations as suggested on the Avocado Slaw (see recipe, page 130), Pepper-Olive Pasta Salad (see recipe, page 132), and Orange-Pear Spinach Salad (see recipe, page 130), or on your own green salads.

¼ cup olive oil
¼ cup balsamic vinegar or wine vinegar
1 to 2 Tbsp. sugar (optional)
1 tsp. snipped fresh basil or ¼ to ½ tsp. dried basil, crushed
1 tsp. snipped fresh thyme or ¼ to ½ tsp. dried thyme, crushed
½ tsp. snipped fresh marjoram or ¼ to ½ tsp. dried marjoram, crushed

1 For dressing, in a screw-top jar combine olive oil; balsamic vinegar or wine vinegar; sugar, if desired; basil; thyme; and marjoram. Cover and shake well to mix.

2 Chill the dressing till serving time or for up to 1 week. (To tote, pack in the jar or in a plastic storage container; chill on ice.) Makes ½ cup (eight 1-tablespoon servings) vinaigrette.

Nutrition facts per tablespoon: 67 cal., 7 g total fat (1 g sat. fat), 0 mg chol., 1 mg sodium, 2 g carbo., 0 g fiber, 0 g pro. *Daily values:* 2% vit. C, 2% iron.

Lime Vinaigrette: Prepare Herbed Balsamic Vinaigrette as directed above, except omit the marjoram. Instead, add ½ teaspoon finely shredded *lime peel*. Store or serve as directed.

Lemon-Dijon Vinaigrette: Prepare Herbed Balsamic Vinaigrette as directed at left, except substitute 2 tablespoons *lemon juice* for 2 tablespoons of the balsamic vinegar. Add 1 tablespoon *Dijon-style mustard*, ½ teaspoon finely shredded *lemon peel*, and ¼ teaspoon *pepper*. Store or serve as directed.

JICAMA SLAW

If you have leftover jicama, wrap the portion in plastic wrap and refrigerate for up to 1 week.

2 cups shredded cabbage
1 cup julienned peeled jicama
1 medium apple, chopped
¼ cup chopped red onion
◆◆◆
3 Tbsp. reduced-calorie mayonnaise dressing or salad dressing
2 Tbsp. snipped fresh cilantro or parsley
1 Tbsp. cider vinegar
1½ tsp. sugar
Dash to ⅛ tsp. ground red pepper

1 In a large mixing bowl combine the cabbage, jicama, apple, and red onion. Set aside.

2 In a mixing bowl combine mayonnaise dressing, cilantro, vinegar, sugar, and red pepper. Pour dressing over cabbage mixture, tossing to coat. Cover and chill for 2 to 24 hours. To serve, transfer mixture to a salad bowl.

Nutrition facts per serving: 91 cal., 4 g total fat (1 g sat. fat), 0 mg chol., 91 mg sodium, 14 g carbo., 2 g fiber, 1 g pro. *Daily values:* 52% vit. C, 2% calcium, 4% iron.

PEPPER-OLIVE PASTA SALAD

A collage of shapes turns simple pasta salad into something extraordinary. Our favorite combination is penne and radiatore pasta, but you can use whatever small pastas you happen to have in the pantry.
(See the photograph on page 158.)

3 cups small pasta, such as penne, radiatore, wagon wheel, and/or corkscrew

❖❖❖

2 yellow, red, and/or green sweet peppers, cut into thin strips
½ cup pitted green olives, drained and halved
½ cup thinly sliced green onions
1 recipe Lemon-Dijon Vinaigrette (see page 131)

1 In a large saucepan cook the desired pasta in lightly *salted boiling water* according to package directions; drain. Rinse with cold water; drain again.

2 In a large salad bowl combine the pepper strips, olives, green onions, and pasta. (To tote, pack in a storage container; chill on ice.) To serve, add dressing, tossing gently to coat. Makes 8 to 10 side-dish servings.

Nutrition facts per serving: 193 cal., 8 g total fat (1 g sat. fat), 0 mg chol., 211 mg sodium, 26 g carbo., 1 g fiber, 4 g pro. *Daily values:* 12% vit. A, 106% vit. C, 1% calcium, 9% iron.

PARMESAN CORN BREAD TWISTS

The kids will have fun shaping and coating this refrigerated dough fix-up.

2 11½-oz. pkg. refrigerated corn bread twists
3 Tbsp. yellow cornmeal
3 Tbsp. grated Parmesan cheese
1 tsp. poppy seed

1 Separate the refrigerated dough into 32 strips. In a shallow dish stir together the cornmeal, Parmesan cheese, and poppy seed. Roll the dough strips in the cornmeal mixture.

2 On an ungreased baking sheet shape strips into twists according to the package directions. Bake in a 375° oven for 11 to 13 minutes or till golden. Serve warm. Or, cool completely on a wire rack. (To tote, pack cooled twists in a covered storage container.) Makes 16 twists.

High-altitude directions: Call the refrigerated dough manufacturer for high-altitude directions. The coated bread twists may take a few more minutes to bake.

Nutrition facts per twist: 152 cal., 8 g total fat (2 g sat. fat), 1 mg chol., 322 mg sodium, 17 g carbo., 1 g fiber, 3 g pro. *Daily values:* 1% calcium, 5% iron.

GREEK LENTIL SALAD

This recipe earned Jennifer G. Sweemer of Cincinnati, Ohio, $100 in the magazine's monthly contest.

3 cups water
½ cup dry lentils
½ cup bulgur

❖❖❖

½ cup sliced, pitted ripe olives
½ cup snipped fresh parsley
½ cup crumbled feta cheese (2 oz.)
¼ cup sliced green onions
¼ cup sliced pepperoncini (salad peppers)
2 Tbsp. snipped fresh basil or 1 tsp. dried basil, crushed

❖❖❖

2 Tbsp. olive oil or salad oil
2 Tbsp. lemon juice
½ to 1 tsp. coarsely ground black pepper
⅛ tsp. salt
⅛ tsp. onion powder
⅛ tsp. garlic powder
Leaf lettuce (optional)

1 In a medium saucepan combine water and lentils. Bring to boiling; reduce heat. Simmer, covered, for 10 minutes. Add bulgur; simmer for 12 to 15 minutes more or till just tender. Drain and rinse with cold water; drain again.

2 In a large mixing bowl combine lentil mixture, olives, parsley, feta cheese, green onions, pepperoncini, and basil. Set aside.

3 For dressing, in a small bowl combine oil, lemon juice, pepper, salt, onion powder, and garlic powder. Add dressing to lentil mixture, gently tossing to coat. Cover and chill at least 2 hours. If desired, garnish with lettuce. Makes 6 side-dish servings.

Nutrition facts per serving: 234 cal., 13 g total fat (4 g sat. fat), 19 mg chol., 735 mg sodium, 21 g carbo., 3 g fiber, 9 g pro. *Daily values:* 6% vit. A, 17% vit. C, 11% calcium, 17% iron.

SUMMER GARDEN VEGETABLE SALAD

To take this salad to a picnic, pack the vegetables in a storage container and chill on ice. Add the dressing just before serving.

2   **medium eggplant**
2   **medium zucchini, sliced ½ inch thick**
2   **Tbsp. olive oil**
2   **medium tomatoes, chopped**
4   **green onions, sliced**
♦♦♦
¼   **cup olive oil**
¼   **cup red wine vinegar**
2   **tsp. lemon juice**
½   **tsp. salt**
½   **tsp. sugar**
½   **tsp. ground cumin**
¼   **tsp. ground cinnamon**
1   **clove garlic, minced**
♦♦♦
4   **cups shredded romaine lettuce**
2   **Tbsp. snipped fresh parsley**

1 Peel eggplant, if desired. Slice eggplant, crosswise, into ¼-inch-thick slices. Arrange eggplant and zucchini on 2 baking sheets; brush with 2 tablespoons olive oil. Bake in a 350° oven 15 to 20 minutes or just till tender. Cut eggplant slices into quarters and zucchini slices in half. In a bowl combine eggplant, zucchini, tomatoes, and green onions.

2 For dressing, in a screw-top jar combine the ¼ cup olive oil, vinegar, lemon juice, salt, sugar, cumin, cinnamon, and garlic. Cover and shake till well combined. Pour dressing over eggplant mixture, tossing to coat. Cover; chill 1 to 4 hours.

3 To serve, place romaine on a large serving platter or 8 salad plates. Top with eggplant mixture and sprinkle with parsley. Makes 8 side-dish servings.

Nutrition facts per serving: 135 cal., 11 g total fat (1 g sat. fat), 0 mg chol., 143 mg sodium, 11 g carbo., 4 g fiber, 2 g pro. *Daily values:* 12% vit. A, 30% vit. C, 2% calcium, 8% iron.

STRAWBERRY SPINACH SALAD

Add your personal touch to purchased salad dressing by mixing in orange peel and juice. To lower the calories and fat in this salad, use low-calorie or nonfat dressing.

1   **lb. asparagus spears**
♦♦♦
½   **cup bottled poppy seed dressing or Italian dressing**
1   **tsp. grated orange peel**
1   **Tbsp. orange juice**
♦♦♦
8   **cups torn fresh spinach or mixed salad greens**
2   **cups sliced strawberries and/or whole blueberries**
¾   **to 1 lb. cooked turkey, cut into ½-inch cubes**
¼   **cup pecan halves**

1 Snap off and discard woody bases from asparagus. If desired, scrape off scales. Cut into 1-inch pieces. Cook the asparagus pieces, covered, in a small amount of

boiling water for 4 to 6 minutes or just till crisp-tender. Rinse with *cold water*. Let stand in cold water till cool; drain.

2 Meanwhile, for dressing, in a medium mixing bowl stir together the poppy seed or Italian dressing, orange peel, and orange juice; set aside.

3 In a salad bowl, combine the spinach or salad greens, strawberries or blueberries, turkey, and asparagus. Add the dressing mixture, tossing to coat. To serve, divide mixture among 4 dinner plates. Sprinkle with pecans. Makes 4 main-dish servings.

Nutrition facts per serving: 437 cal., 30 g total fat (3 g sat. fat), 85 mg chol., 616 mg sodium, 14 g carbo., 7 g fiber, 31 g pro. *Daily values:* 82% vit. A, 170% vit. C, 14% calcium, 37% iron.

Sunset Supper

Southwestern Antipasto Platter

♦♦♦

Basil-Stuffed Beef

♦♦♦

Broccoli, Corn, and Tomato
Skillet

♦♦♦

Cheese-Stuffed Grilled Potatoes

♦♦♦

Bakery breads

♦♦♦

Peach-Apricot Crisp
(see recipe, page 137)

♦♦♦

Red wine, iced tea, or
fruit punch

Putting it all together: Ahead of time, bake and stuff the potatoes. Freeze the stuffed potatoes, if desired. Stuff the meat and tie to secure. Roast the peppers for the antipasto platter. Cover and chill for up to 24 hours.

To cook: Roast the meat and potatoes over the coals or in the oven. As they cook, prepare and bake the peach crisp. Assemble the antipasto platter. When the meat is done, cook the vegetables.

SOUTHWESTERN ANTIPASTO PLATTER

While dinner is on the grill, set out this platter of vegetable bites.

- **2 cups broccoli and/or cauliflower flowerets**
- **1 jicama, peeled and cut into sticks**
- **4 medium red and/or yellow sweet peppers, roasted and cut into strips***
- **16 to 20 radishes**
- **16 to 20 pitted green olives Lettuce leaves**

1 Arrange vegetables on a lettuce-lined serving platter. Makes 8 to 10 appetizer servings.

***Note:** To roast peppers, cut the peppers lengthwise into quarters. Remove the stems and seeds. Cut small slits in the ends of the pepper pieces to make them lie flat. Place the pepper pieces, cut sides down, on a foil-lined baking sheet. Bake in a 425° oven for 20 to 25 minutes or till the skins are bubbly. Immediately place the pepper pieces in a clean brown paper bag. Close the bag tightly; cool. When the peppers are cool enough to handle, remove the pepper skins. Cut into strips.

Nutrition facts per serving: 32 cal., 1 g total fat (0 g sat. fat), 0 mg chol., 173 mg sodium, 5 g carbo., 1 g fiber, 1 g pro. Daily values: 3% vit. A, 65% vit. C, 1% calcium, 4% iron.

BASIL-STUFFED BEEF

*Take your pick: Add smoky flavor by grilling the meat over indirect coals, or roast it in the oven.
(See the photograph on page 156.)*

- **1 3- to 3½-lb. boneless beef sirloin roast, cut 1¾ inches thick**
- **¼ tsp. salt**
- **¼ tsp. pepper**
- **2 cups loosely packed fresh basil leaves, snipped**
- **8 to 10 cloves garlic, minced**
- **2 tsp. olive oil**

1 Make five or six 5-inch-long slits along the top of the roast, cutting almost through the roast. Sprinkle with salt and pepper.

2 For filling, in a mixing bowl combine basil and garlic. Stuff filling into slits in the meat. Tie the meat with heavy-duty string to hold slits closed. Drizzle with olive oil. Roast, using the following indirect grilling, quick oven-roasting, or slow oven-roasting directions. Let the meat stand, covered, for 10 minutes before slicing. (The meat temperature will rise slightly upon standing.) Slice against the grain. Makes 10 to 12 main-dish servings.

INDIRECT GRILLING

In a covered grill arrange medium coals around a drip pan. Test for medium-low heat above the pan. Place meat on grill rack over drip pan but not over coals. Insert a meat thermometer and lower the grill hood. Grill for 45 minutes to 1½ hours or till meat thermometer registers the desired temperature (140° for rare, 155° for medium, 165° for well done). Add more coals as necessary.

QUICK OVEN-ROASTING

Place roast on a rack in a shallow roasting pan. Insert a meat thermometer. Roast, uncovered, in a 425° oven for 15 minutes. Reduce oven temperature to 350°; roast for 35 to 45 minutes more or till thermometer registers 140° or to desired doneness.

Place the roast on a rack in a shallow roasting pan. Insert a meat thermometer. Roast, uncovered, in a 325° oven 1½ to 1¾ hours, till the meat thermometer registers 140°, or to desired doneness.

Nutrition facts per serving: 255 cal., 13 g total fat (5 g sat. fat), 91 mg chol., 121 mg sodium, 1 g carbo., 0 g fiber, 31 g pro. *Daily values:* 1% vit. C, 2% calcium, 23% iron.

LOW FAT

CHEESE-STUFFED GRILLED POTATOES

If you like, you can grill and stuff the potatoes ahead of time, then freeze. Add about 20 minutes to the baking time for frozen potatoes. (See the photograph on page 156.)

5 large baking potatoes (6 to 8 oz. each) Cooking oil

♦♦♦

1½ cups shredded reduced-fat or regular cheddar or Monterey Jack cheese
½ cup light dairy sour cream
¼ to ⅓ cup milk

1 Scrub potatoes; pat dry. Rub with oil. Halve the potatoes lengthwise; wrap both halves of each potato loosely in heavy foil. Bake in a 400° oven about 1 hour or till tender. (Or, grill directly over medium-hot coals for 45 to 50 minutes or till tender, turning potatoes occasionally. You also can put wrapped potatoes directly onto coals, checking for doneness after 30 minutes.) Cool slightly.

2 Gently scoop out each potato half, leaving ¼-inch-thick shell and spooning pulp into a large

mixing bowl (you should have 3½ to 4 cups pulp). With an electric mixer on low speed or a potato masher, beat or mash potato pulp. Add *1 cup* of the cheese and the sour cream; beat till smooth. If necessary, stir in enough milk to make of desired consistency. Season to taste with *salt* and *pepper*. Spoon mashed potato mixture into potato shells. Place in a greased 13×9×2-inch baking pan. (If desired, cover and freeze.)

3 Bake, uncovered, in a 425° oven 25 minutes or till light brown. (Or, cover pan with foil; grill directly over medium-hot coals 25 minutes or till heated.) Sprinkle with remaining cheese. Makes 10 side-dish servings.

High-altitude directions: Bake raw potatoes in 400° oven or over medium-hot coals 1½ hours or till tender. Continue as directed.

Nutrition facts per serving: 161 cal., 4 g total fat (2 g sat. fat), 14 mg chol., 157 mg sodium, 23 g carbo., 1 g fiber, 8 g pro. *Daily values:* 4% vit. A, 21% vit. C, 12% calcium, 7% iron.

30 MIN. LOW FAT

BROCCOLI, CORN, AND TOMATO SKILLET

Fresh corn cut from the cob can't be beat, but canned corn is a great substitute when corn season ends. (See the photograph on page 156.)

5 cups broccoli flowerets
2 Tbsp. olive oil
2½ cups fresh cut sweet corn (3 large or 5 medium ears) or one 15¼-oz. can whole kernel corn, rinsed and drained

THE CLEVER COOK

POP BOTTLES FOR ICE PACKS

To recycle empty plastic pop containers, we wash them, fill them with water or a favorite fruit drink, then freeze them. When we go on a picnic or trip, we use them as the ice in our cooler. Once they melt, we have ice-cold water or a fruit drink to quench our thirst.

Lynette Kittle
Spring Hill, Florida

2 medium tomatoes, peeled, seeded, and cut up (1¼ cups)
1 to 2 Tbsp. margarine or butter
1 Tbsp. snipped fresh marjoram or 1 tsp. dried marjoram, crushed
½ tsp. garlic salt

1 In a heavy, large ovenproof skillet cook and stir broccoli in hot oil over medium-high heat for 4 minutes. Add the fresh or canned corn, tomatoes, and enough margarine or butter to moisten. Cook and stir about 4 minutes more or till vegetables are crisp-tender. Stir in marjoram, garlic salt, and ¼ teaspoon *pepper*. Makes 10 side-dish servings.

Nutrition facts per serving: 103 cal., 5 g total fat (1 g sat. fat), 0 mg chol., 145 mg sodium, 15 g carbo., 4 g fiber, 4 g pro. *Daily values:* 14% vit. A, 108% vit. C, 3% calcium, 6% iron.

Sweet Potato Shortcakes with Mountain Berries

Lucky you, if you stumble upon a patch of wild strawberries to top this shortcut shortcake. They're usually smaller than those found at the market but just as juicy. Whatever berry you use, you're sure to fall in love with this sweet potato version of an old-fashioned summer favorite. Biscuit mix is its secret timesaver.

1   16-oz. can sweet potatoes
     (in syrup)

♦♦♦

½   cup milk
2   Tbsp. margarine or butter,
     melted
2½ cups packaged biscuit mix
2   Tbsp. sugar
¼   tsp. ground cinnamon

♦♦♦

6   to 8 cups strawberries, sliced
     (if desired); red
     raspberries; blackberries;
     and/or blueberries
3   Tbsp. sugar
1   to 1½ cups whipping cream
2   Tbsp. sugar

♦♦♦

     Salvia or mint sprigs
     (optional)

1 Chill a medium mixing bowl and the beaters of an electric mixer. Grease a baking sheet; set aside. Drain sweet potatoes, reserving 2 tablespoons of the syrup. Mash enough of the sweet potatoes to make ½ cup; set aside. (Cover and chill any remaining sweet potatoes and syrup to heat later as a side dish.)

TEST KITCHEN TIP

Cooking on High

Mountain retreats are high on the list of favorite summer vacation spots, yet they pose a puzzle for folks who are used to cooking at sea level. Higher altitudes and lower air pressure can affect the way food cooks. Water boils at a lower temperature, meaning vegetables, rice, and pasta take more time to cook. Baked products rise higher and need less leavening. Liquids evaporate quicker, so you might need more to start with. Baked potatoes and thick roasts take longer, too.

If you're heading for the hills, use the high-altitude directions given on these pages for the recipe you want to make. The adjustments are suitable for 6,000 feet above sea level. To adjust your own sea-level recipes (especially baked goods), try them as is first. You may find only some of the following changes are necessary.

♦ For shortening-type cakes and quick breads, slightly decrease the shortening, sugar, and baking powder or soda. Add an egg and a little liquid.

♦ For cakes and cookies, increase oven temperature by about 20 degrees and shorten the time.

♦ For yeast doughs, use the least amount of flour called for. Let the dough rise twice before shaping.

♦ For cooking in boiling water, increase the cooking time.

♦ For deep-fat frying, fry foods at a lower temperature for a longer period of time (3 degrees lower for each 1,000 feet in elevation).

♦ Check food packages for high-altitude directions.

♦ For information on high-altitude cooking, contact a county extension agent or write the Colorado State University Food Sciences Extension Office, Fort Collins, CO 80523.

2 In a medium mixing bowl combine the mashed sweet potatoes, reserved syrup, milk, and melted margarine or butter; stir till blended. Sprinkle biscuit mix, 2 tablespoons sugar, and cinnamon over sweet potato mixture. Stir just till dough clings together. (The batter may have some lumps and will be thick.) Drop batter in 8 equal portions onto the prepared baking sheet. Bake in a 425° oven about 12 minutes or till golden. Transfer to a wire rack to cool slightly. (To tote, place cooled cakes in storage container.)

3 Meanwhile, in a large mixing bowl combine strawberries, raspberries, blackberries, and/or blueberries and 3 tablespoons sugar; set aside. In the chilled mixing bowl beat the whipping cream and 2 tablespoons sugar with an electric mixer on medium speed till soft peaks form. (To tote, pack the berries and whipped cream in separate storage containers and chill on ice for a couple of hours.)

4 To serve, split each shortcake in half crosswise. Place the bottom halves on 8 dessert plates. Top with some of the berries and whipped cream. Add shortcake tops and top with more whipped cream and berries. If desired, garnish with salvia or mint. Makes 8 servings.

High-altitude directions: Prepare as directed, except bake the shortcakes in a 425° oven about 15 minutes or till golden.

Nutrition facts per serving: 415 cal., 15 g total fat (8 g sat. fat), 42 mg chol., 704 mg sodium, 65 g carbo., 5 g fiber, 6 g pro. *Daily values:* 52% vit. A, 127% vit. C, 22% calcium, 14% iron.

PEACH-APRICOT CRISP

A combination of canned and fresh fruit carries a double promise—convenience plus juicy, just-picked flavor. (See the photograph on page 157.)

2 29-oz. cans peach slices in light syrup
4 cups sliced, peeled fresh apricots and/or peaches

◆◆◆

1 cup rolled oats
1 cup all-purpose flour
1 cup packed brown sugar
1 tsp. ground cinnamon
½ cup butter or margarine, melted
    Half-and-half or light cream (optional)

1 Drain the canned peaches, reserving ¼ cup syrup. In a 3-quart rectangular baking dish combine the canned peaches, reserved syrup, and fresh apricots and/or peaches.

2 For topping, in a large bowl stir together the rolled oats, flour, brown sugar, and cinnamon. Add melted butter or margarine; stir till mixed. Sprinkle atop fruit. Bake in a 350° oven about 30 minutes or till hot and bubbly. If desired, serve warm with half-and-half or light cream. Serves 10.

High-altitude directions: Prepare as directed, except use ½ cup of the syrup and bake crisp in a 350° oven 35 to 40 minutes.

Nutrition facts per serving: 336 cal., 10 g total fat (6 g sat. fat), 25 mg chol., 108 mg sodium, 62 g carbo., 4 g fiber, 4 g pro. *Daily values:* 29% vit. A, 16% vit. C, 3% calcium, 15% iron.

FULL-OF-FRUIT MUFFINS

½ cup pitted whole dates, snipped
½ cup dried apricots, snipped
½ cup raisins
½ cup unpitted prunes, snipped
1 cup apple juice
⅓ cup margarine or butter, cut up

◆◆◆

1 cup all-purpose flour
2 tsp. baking powder
1 tsp. ground cinnamon
¼ tsp. baking soda
2 eggs, slightly beaten
1 tsp. vanilla

1 Grease twelve 2½-inch muffin cups or line with paper bake cups; set aside. In a saucepan combine fruits and apple juice. Bring to boiling; reduce heat. Simmer, covered, for 5 minutes. Remove from heat; stir in margarine or butter. Set aside to cool.

MUFFINS AND QUICK BREAD TIPS

◆ To keep the edges of your muffins and quick breads nicely rounded, grease the muffin cups or baking pans on the bottoms and only ½ inch up the sides.

◆ After adding the liquid mixture to the flour mixture, stir just till moistened. If you stir till the batter is smooth, your muffins and quick breads will have a tough texture.

◆ Be sure to bake muffin and quick bread batter right away. Batters with baking powder and/or baking soda lose their leavening power if they're not baked immediately.

◆ To avoid soggy sides and bottoms, cool muffins and quick breads in baking pans only as long as directed in the recipe.

2 In a mixing bowl combine flour, baking powder, cinnamon, and soda. Make a well in center. Stir eggs and vanilla into fruit mixture. Add fruit mixture to flour mixture. Stir just till moistened (batter should be lumpy).

3 Spoon batter into prepared cups, filling each three-fourths full. Bake in a 400° oven for 15 to 20 minutes or till golden. Cool in cups on a wire rack for 5 minutes. Remove from cups. Serve warm. Makes 12 muffins.

Nutrition facts per muffin: 172 cal., 6 g total fat (1 g sat. fat), 36 mg chol., 159 mg sodium, 28 g carbo., 2 g fiber, 3 g pro. *Daily values:* 13% vit. A, 1% vit. C, 6% calcium, 9% iron.

Campfire Breakfast

Skillet Sausage and Potatoes

♦♦♦

Fresh melon and berries

♦♦♦

Green Chili Muffins

♦♦♦

Juice, coffee, or
hot chocolate

The night before: Bake the muffins to reheat on the campfire while cooking breakfast.

To tote: Pack the turkey sausage and fruit in storage containers with an ice pack. Pack muffins in a storage container or wrap in foil. Pour coffee, juice, or hot chocolate into insulated vacuum containers.

GREEN CHILI MUFFINS

The canned green chilies used in these buttery muffins can vary in hotness. Use more or less, depending on your family's preference.

- 2 **cups all-purpose flour**
- ¼ **cup sugar**
- 2 **tsp. baking powder**
- ¼ **to ½ tsp. salt**
- 2 **slightly beaten eggs**
- 1 **cup milk**
- ¼ **cup margarine or butter, melted**
- 1 **4-oz. can diced green chili peppers, rinsed and drained**

1 Lightly grease ten to twelve 2½-inch muffin cups; set aside. In a small mixing bowl combine the flour, sugar, baking powder, and salt. In another mixing bowl combine the eggs, milk, melted margarine or butter, and green chili peppers. Add the flour mixture all at once to the egg mixture. Stir just till moistened (the batter will be lumpy).

2 Spoon batter into prepared muffin cups, filling each two-thirds full. Bake in a 400° oven for 20 to 25 minutes or till golden. Cool in the muffin cups on a wire rack for 5 minutes. Remove from cups. Serve warm. (To tote, wrap the cooled muffins in foil and reheat over medium coals.) Makes 10 to 12 muffins.

Nutrition facts per muffin: 173 cal., 6 g total fat (3 g sat. fat), 57 mg chol., 229 mg sodium, 24 g carbo., 1 g fiber, 5 g pro. *Daily values:* 7% vit. A, 6% vit. C, 10% calcium, 9% iron.

SKILLET SAUSAGE AND POTATOES

Gung-ho outdoor lovers will opt for cooking breakfast over the coals. Indoor campers can follow the range-top directions.

- 3 **Tbsp. olive oil or cooking oil**
- 1¾ **lb. unpeeled red-skinned potatoes, cut into ½-inch cubes (5 cups)**
- 2 **medium onions, cut into thin wedges and/or chopped (1½ cups)**

♦♦♦

- 8 **oz. fully cooked smoked turkey sausage, diagonally sliced ¼ inch thick**
- 1 **Tbsp. olive oil or cooking oil**
- 2 **Tbsp. snipped fresh thyme or 1 tsp. dried thyme, crushed**
- 1½ **to 2 tsp. cumin seed, slightly crushed**

1 (To tote, pack ingredients, keeping sausage on ice.) Pour 3 tablespoons oil into a heavy 12-inch ovenproof skillet. Place

skillet directly over hot coals or on the range top. Lift and tilt to cover bottom of skillet with oil. Cook the potatoes and onions, uncovered, in hot oil over medium-high heat about 12 minutes or till potatoes are nearly tender, stirring occasionally.

2 Add sausage and 1 tablespoon oil, if necessary, to prevent sticking. Cook, uncovered, about 10 minutes more or till potatoes and onions are tender and slightly brown, stirring often. Stir in thyme, cumin seed, ¼ teaspoon *salt*, and ¼ teaspoon *pepper;* cook and stir for 1 minute more. Makes 6 main-dish servings.

High-altitude directions: Prepare as directed, except increase the cooking times. Allow 15 to 20 minutes for potatoes and onions, 12 minutes after adding the sausage, and 2 to 3 minutes after adding the seasonings.

Nutrition facts per serving: 270 cal., 10 g total fat (2 g sat. fat), 24 mg chol., 419 mg sodium, 36 g carbo., 2 g fiber, 10 g pro. *Daily values:* 35% vit. C, 5% calcium, 18% iron.

CRUNCHY BANANA OATMEAL MUFFINS

Crowned with a sweet sesame seed and pecan topping, these oaty muffins are wonderful served warm. If you wish, eat them plain or slather them with butter or a spoonful of marmalade.

Nonstick spray coating
¼ cup packed brown sugar
2 Tbsp. chopped pecans
2 Tbsp. all-purpose flour
1 Tbsp. sesame seed
1 Tbsp. margarine or butter, softened
¼ tsp. ground cinnamon

❖❖❖

1½ cups all-purpose flour
¾ cup quick-cooking rolled oats
¼ cup packed brown sugar
2 tsp. baking powder
½ tsp. salt
½ tsp. ground cinnamon

❖❖❖

2 medium ripe bananas, mashed (about ⅔ cup)
1 cup milk
1 slightly beaten egg
2 Tbsp. cooking oil
1 tsp. vanilla

1 Spray twelve 2½-inch muffin cups with nonstick spray coating; set aside. For topping, in a small bowl stir together the ¼ cup brown sugar, chopped pecans, 2 tablespoons flour, sesame seed, margarine or butter, and ¼ teaspoon cinnamon till well combined. Set aside.

THE CLEVER COOK

MIX-AND-MATCH CEREALS

Coax your family into eating less sugar for breakfast. Encourage everyone to use unsweetened cereals to fill their bowls and presweetened cereals only as a topper.

Denise Jawor
Tinley Park, Illinois

2 In a large mixing bowl stir together the 1½ cups flour, the rolled oats, ¼ cup brown sugar, baking powder, salt, and ½ teaspoon cinnamon. Make a well in the center.

3 In a medium mixing bowl stir together the bananas, milk, egg, oil, and vanilla. Add the banana mixture to the flour mixture. Stir just till moistened (batter should be lumpy).

4 Spoon batter into prepared muffin cups, filling each nearly full. Sprinkle topping over each. Bake in a 400° oven about 20 minutes or till golden. Cool in cups on a wire rack for 5 minutes. Remove from cups. Serve warm. Makes 12 muffins.

Nutrition facts per muffin: 180 cal., 6 g total fat (1 g sat. fat), 19 mg chol., 179 mg sodium, 29 g carbo., 1 g fiber, 4 g pro. *Daily values:* 3% vit. A, 3% vit. C, 8% calcium, 9% iron.

PEAR-WALNUT MUFFINS

This recipe earned Meri Villane of Colorado Springs, Colorado, $200 in the magazine's monthly contest.

1½ cups all-purpose flour
½ cup packed brown sugar
2 tsp. baking powder
1 tsp. ground cinnamon
½ tsp. ground ginger
1 slightly beaten egg
½ cup cooking oil
½ cup plain low-fat yogurt
½ tsp. vanilla
1 pear, cored and finely chopped

❖❖❖

3 Tbsp. finely chopped walnuts
2 Tbsp. brown sugar

1 Lightly grease twelve 2½-inch muffin cups or line with paper bake cups; set aside. In a bowl combine flour, ½ cup brown sugar, baking powder, cinnamon, ginger, and ⅛ teaspoon *salt.* Make a well in center. In a bowl combine egg; oil, yogurt, and vanilla; add to flour mixture. Stir just till moistened. Fold in pear.

2 Spoon batter into prepared muffin cups, filling each two-thirds full. For topping, combine walnuts and 2 tablespoons brown sugar; sprinkle over batter. Bake in a 400° oven 20 minutes or till golden. Cool in cups on wire rack for 5 minutes. Remove from cups; serve warm. Makes 12 muffins.

Nutrition facts per muffin: 206 cal., 11 g total fat (2 g sat. fat), 18 mg chol., 77 mg sodium, 26 g carbo., 1 g fiber, 3 g pro. *Daily values:* 7% calcium, 7% iron.

Trail-Ride Lunch

Deli cheeses and meats

◆◆◆

Pesto-Cream-Cheese Spread

◆◆◆

Dilled Hummus Spread

◆◆◆

**Honey Whole Wheat Bread
or bakery bread**

◆◆◆

Fresh vegetable dippers

◆◆◆

**Saddlebag Trail Mix
(see page 142)**

◆◆◆

Chocolate Toffee Bars

◆◆◆

Soft drinks

Before you hit the trail: Bake bars and bread, combine trail mix, and prepare vegetables. Buy French bread for the cheese spread, pita bread for the hummus spread, and sliced bread for sandwiches. Pick up sliced meats and cheeses. Let everyone make their own sandwiches at lunchtime.

To tote: Pack meats, cheeses, spreads, and vegetables in storage containers on ice. Place breads in plastic storage containers. Pack trail mix in resealable plastic bags. Cover bars with plastic wrap.

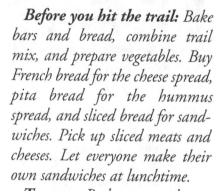

1 In a blender container or food processor bowl, combine garbanzo beans, tahini or peanut butter and sesame oil, lemon juice, olive or cooking oil, garlic, dill, salt, and red pepper. Cover and blend or process till the mixture is smooth, stopping and scraping the sides as necessary.

2 Transfer mixture to a storage container; cover and chill till ready to serve or for up to 1 week. (To tote, chill storage container on ice.) Stir before serving. Makes about 1½ cups (24 one-tablespoon servings).

Nutrition facts per tablespoon: 36 cal., 2 g total fat (0 g sat. fat), 0 mg chol., 89 mg sodium, 3 g carbo., 1 g fiber, 1 g pro. *Daily values:* 3% vit. C, 3% iron.

PESTO-CREAM-CHEESE SPREAD

1 **8-oz. pkg. cream cheese, softened**
1 **7-oz. container refrigerated pesto sauce**

1 In a storage container or bowl combine cream cheese and pesto sauce; stir till mixed. Cover and chill till ready to serve or up to 1 week. (To tote, pack in storage container on ice.) Let stand 30 minutes for easier spreading. Stir before using. Spread on French bread. Makes 1½ cups (24 one-tablespoon servings).

Nutrition facts per tablespoon: 76 cal., 7 g total fat (2 g sat. fat), 11 mg chol., 73 mg sodium, 1 g carbo., 0 g fiber, 1 g pro. *Daily values:* 4% vit. A.

DILLED HUMMUS SPREAD

Your blender makes quick work of this Middle Eastern sandwich spread. Serve it with pita bread.

1 **15-oz. can garbanzo beans, rinsed and drained**
¼ **cup tahini (sesame paste) or 3 Tbsp. creamy peanut butter plus 1 Tbsp. sesame oil**
3 **Tbsp. lemon juice**
1 **Tbsp. olive oil or cooking oil**
2 **cloves garlic, minced**
2 **tsp. snipped fresh dill or ½ tsp. dried dillweed**
¼ **tsp. salt**
   Dash ground red pepper

LOW FAT
HONEY WHOLE WHEAT BREAD

Homemade bread makes picnic sandwiches taste just that much better. However, when time is too short for baking, a stop by the bakery on the way will net some hearty, crusty loaves to round out your picnic.

3 **to 3½ cups all-purpose flour**
1 **pkg. active dry yeast**

◆◆◆

1¾ **cups water**
3 **Tbsp. honey or ¼ cup packed brown sugar**
3 **Tbsp. butter or margarine**
1 **tsp. salt**
2 **cups whole wheat flour**

◆◆◆

Milk
Toasted wheat germ (optional)

1 In a large mixing bowl stir together *2 cups* of the all-purpose flour and the yeast; set aside.

2 In a medium saucepan heat and stir water, honey or brown sugar, butter or margarine, and salt just till warm (120° to 130°) and butter is almost melted. Add to the flour mixture. Beat on medium speed for 30 seconds, scraping bowl. Beat on high speed for 3 minutes. Stir in whole wheat flour and as much of the remaining all-purpose flour as you can.

3 On a lightly floured surface, knead in enough remaining all-purpose flour to make a moderately stiff dough that is smooth and elastic (6 to 8 minutes total). Shape into a ball. Place in a lightly greased bowl; turn once. Cover and let rise in a warm place till double (about 1 hour).

4 Punch dough down. Divide in half. Cover and let rest for 10 minutes. Lightly grease 2 baking sheets. Shape each portion into a round loaf. Place on prepared baking sheets. Cover and let rise in a warm place till nearly double (about 45 minutes).

5 Brush loaves with milk. If desired, sprinkle with wheat germ. Bake in a 375° oven for 40 to 45 minutes or till bread sounds hollow when tapped with fingers. If necessary, cover loosely with foil the last 15 minutes to prevent overbrowning. Cool on wire racks. (To tote, place cooled breads in storage containers.) Makes 2 loaves (32 servings).

High-altitude directions: Prepare the bread as directed, except knead the dough for 8 minutes. Punch down dough 30 minutes into the first rising and again at the end of 1 hour.

Nutrition facts per serving: 80 cal., 1 g total fat (1 g sat. fat), 3 mg chol., 79 mg sodium, 15 g carbo., 1 g fiber, 2 g pro.
Daily values: 5% iron.

CHOCOLATE TOFFEE BARS

Skip a mixing bowl by stirring the batter in the saucepan used for melting.

½ **cup butter or margarine**
1 **cup packed brown sugar**
2 **slightly beaten eggs**
2 **tsp. vanilla**
1½ **cups all-purpose flour**
1½ **tsp. baking powder**
¼ **tsp. salt**
1 **6-oz. pkg. (1 cup) semisweet chocolate pieces**

♦♦♦

Powdered sugar (optional)

1 Grease an 11×7×½-inch baking pan. In a medium saucepan melt the butter or margarine and brown sugar; cool to lukewarm. Stir in the eggs and vanilla. Sprinkle flour, baking powder, and salt over the butter mixture. Stir just till mixture is smooth. Stir in all but 2 tablespoons of the chocolate pieces. Spread batter into prepared baking pan. Sprinkle with reserved chocolate pieces.

2 Bake in a 350° oven for 25 to 30 minutes or till a wooden toothpick inserted near center comes out clean. Cool in pan on a wire rack. If desired, sprinkle with powdered sugar. Cut into bars. (To tote, cover pan with plastic wrap.) Makes 18 bars.

Nutrition facts per bar: 170 cal., 8 g total fat (3 g sat. fat), 37 mg chol., 122 mg sodium, 23 g carbo., 0 g fiber, 2 g pro.
Daily values: 5% vit. A, 3% calcium, 6% iron.

TEST KITCHEN TIP

PACKING FOR PICNICS

The perfect picnic spot may be important, but it's not the only key to a picnic's success. Packing to protect food from breaking, leaking, or spoiling is a top priority, too. Several of the recipes on these pages are designed with toting in mind. When appropriate, recipes give directions, but two guidelines apply to all:

◆ For carrying most picnic foods, choose sturdy plastic containers with tight-sealing lids. They protect foods from getting crushed and from leaking. Plus, they do not create litter that you can inadvertently leave behind.

◆ Some foods, including salads, meats, cheeses, and dairy products, need to be kept chilled. Pack these cold foods with an ice pack in an insulated bag or cooler. You also can freeze cold juices to act as ice. By picnic time, the drinks will still be cold but thawed enough for drinking.

LAID-BACK SUMMER COOKING

For many, the simple life is the only life, especially during summer. Whether you retreat to a cabin in the woods, a cottage on the beach, or a camper at a lake, it's great to take the time to kick back and indulge in a back-to-nature lifestyle.

Though eating is a necessity, when you're away from the accommodations that your own kitchen offers, you shouldn't be burdened with cumbersome cooking. So, to help keep cooking on your outing easy, we've put together a few hints.

◆ Stock up on mixes that can be fixed up to taste like homemade. That way, you don't need a lot of from-scratch ingredients. Use biscuit mix and refrigerated dough for making muffins, quick breads, toppers, pancakes, and desserts.

◆ Use ready-made condiments, such as pickle relish, pesto, and mustard, to flavor sauces and salad dressings. For example, add relish to potato salad dressing and pesto to cream cheese for a sandwich spread.

◆ Pick up versatile canned fruits and vegetables, such as tomatoes and peaches, to use in salads and desserts and skip chopping or peeling.

◆ Mix batters and salads in the pan or serving bowl to save on dishes.

◆ Take along a bottle of clear Italian salad dressing to use on salad greens or as a marinade for poultry or meat.

SADDLEBAG TRAIL MIX

Let the kids stir together a batch of this high-energy snack mix. It's perfect for hiking, biking, and backyard munching.

2 cups raisins
2 cups dried banana chips
2 cups unsalted dry roasted peanuts
1 6-oz. pkg. mixed dried fruit bits (1⅓ cups)

1 In a storage container combine the raisins, banana chips, peanuts, and fruit. Store in a cool, dry place for up to 1 week. (To tote, take the container or divide among small resealable plastic bags.) Makes about 7 cups (twenty-eight, ¼-cup servings).

Nutrition facts per ¼ cup: 172 cal., 9 g total fat (4 g sat. fat), 0 mg chol., 6 mg sodium, 22 g carbo., 1 g fiber, 3 g pro.
Daily values: 1% vit. A, 2% vit. C, 3% iron.

CHOCOLATE MALTED CUPCAKES

With the help of a cake mix and some malted milk powder, you can whip up some spectacular cupcakes as easy as you can turn a shake into a malt.

1 pkg. 2-layer-size chocolate cake mix
¼ cup instant malted milk powder
1 recipe Chocolate Malted Frosting (see above right)
Crushed malted milk balls (optional)

1 Line muffin pans with paper bake cups; set aside. Prepare cake mix according to package directions, except stir malted milk powder into dry ingredients. Spoon batter into cups, filling each about two-thirds full. Bake in a 350° oven 20 to 25 minutes or till a toothpick inserted in the centers comes out clean. Cool in cups on a wire rack for 5 minutes. Remove from cups; cool completely. Frost with Chocolate Malted Frosting. If desired, garnish with malted milk balls. Makes 24 to 28 cupcakes.

Chocolate Malted Frosting: In a mixing bowl beat ⅓ cup softened *butter,* ⅓ cup *unsweetened cocoa powder,* 3 tablespoons *instant malted milk powder,* and 1⅓ cups sifted *powdered sugar.* Slowly beat in ¼ cup *milk* and 1 teaspoon *vanilla.* Gradually beat in ¾ cup sifted *powdered sugar* till frosting is easy to spread.

Nutrition facts per cupcake with frosting: 171 cal., 5 g total fat (3 g sat. fat), 8 mg chol., 265 mg sodium, 30 g carbo., 0 g fiber, 2 g pro.
Daily values: 2% vit. A, 5% calcium, 4% iron.

APPLE BUTTER CUPCAKES

This recipe earned Mrs. Robert L. St. Clair of Covington, Virginia, $100 in the magazine's monthly contest.

1¾ cups all-purpose flour
1½ tsp. baking powder
1 tsp. baking soda
¼ tsp. salt

½ **cup margarine or butter**
1 **cup sugar**
1 **egg**
1 **cup apple butter**
1 **tsp. vanilla**
2 **Tbsp. lemon juice**
1 **5-oz. can evaporated milk**
   (⅔ cup)

◆◆◆

1 **recipe Penuche Frosting**
   (optional) (see below)

1 Grease twenty-four 2½-inch muffin cups or line with paper bake cups; set aside. In a small mixing bowl stir together the flour, baking powder, soda, and salt; set aside. In a medium mixing bowl beat the margarine or butter with an electric mixer on medium speed for 30 seconds. Add sugar and beat till fluffy. Add egg; beat well. Beat in apple butter and vanilla. Stir lemon juice into milk (mixture will curdle). Add the flour mixture and milk mixture alternately to apple butter mixture, beating on low to medium speed after each addition just till combined.

2 Spoon batter into prepared cups, filling each two-thirds full. Bake in a 350° oven for 20 to 25 minutes or till a wooden toothpick inserted in the centers comes out clean. Cool in cups on a wire rack for 5 minutes. Remove from cups and cool completely. If desired, frost with Penuche Frosting. Makes 24 cupcakes.

Penuche Frosting: In a small saucepan melt ½ cup *margarine or butter.* Stir in 1 cup packed *brown sugar.* Cook and stir till bubbly; remove from heat. Add ¼ cup *milk;* stir till smooth. Add 3½ cups *powdered sugar;* beat by

hand till frosting is of spreading consistency. Frost cooled cupcakes immediately. (If frosting thickens, stir in hot water, a few drops at a time, till it's of spreading consistency again.)

Nutrition facts per cupcake without frosting: 134 cal., 5 g total fat (1 g sat. fat), 11 mg chol., 151 mg sodium, 22 g carbo., 0 g fiber, 2 g pro.
Daily values: 5% vit. A, 1% vit. C, 3% calcium, 3% iron.

CROSS-COUNTRY COOKIES

½ **cup butter or margarine**
½ **cup peanut butter**
¾ **cup granulated sugar**
¾ **cup packed brown sugar**
1 **tsp. baking powder**
¼ **tsp. baking soda**
2 **eggs**
1 **tsp. vanilla**
1½ **cups all-purpose flour**
1¾ **cups rolled oats**
1 **cup candy-coated chocolate**
   pieces
½ **cup peanuts**
½ **cup raisins**
¼ **cup wheat germ**

1 In a large mixing bowl beat butter or margarine and peanut butter with an electric mixer on medium to high speed about 30 seconds or till combined. Add the granulated sugar, brown sugar, baking powder, and baking soda. Beat till combined. Beat in eggs and vanilla till combined. Beat in as much of the flour as you can with the mixer. Using a wooden spoon, stir in any remaining flour. Stir in the rolled oats, chocolate pieces, peanuts, raisins, and wheat germ.

2 Drop dough by rounded teaspoonful 2 inches apart on an ungreased cookie sheet. Bake in a 375° oven about 9 minutes or till edges are lightly browned. Cool on cookie sheet for 1 minute. Remove the cookies from cookie sheet and cool on a wire rack. Store cookies in an airtight container or plastic bag at room temperature for up to 3 days. Makes about 60 cookies.

Nutrition facts per cookie: 92 cal., 4 g total fat (1 g sat. fat), 11 mg chol., 40 mg sodium, 12 g carbo., 1 g fiber, 2 g pro.
Daily values: 1% vit. A, 1% calcium, 2% iron.

Cross-Country Megacookies: Prepare cookies as directed, except drop dough in ¼-cup mounds 4 inches apart on an ungreased cookie sheet and flatten slightly. Bake in a 375° oven for 10 to 12 minutes or till edges are lightly browned. Makes 25 cookies.

VEGETARIAN-STYLE EATING

Pass the beans and rice, please. And, forgo the meat, at least for today. Whether you call it meatless dining, vegetarianism, or just plain and simple cooking, this manner of eating is becoming almost as popular as Big Macs. Many families today are balancing their burgers with meat-free meals on other days. Here's a simple guide to vegetarian dining, so you, too, can go meatless every once in a while or every day.

BOUNTIFUL BENEFITS

Vegetarian-style eating can help you and your family meet the goal of eating low-fat, high-fiber, vitamin-rich meals as recommended by health authorities. The abundance of fruits, vegetables, legumes, and grains in vegetarian dishes provides familiar nutrients such as vitamins, minerals, and fiber. These foods also contain compounds called phytochemicals, which appear to help fend off heart disease and cancer. Examples of these increasingly appreciated substances include beta-carotene from deep green and yellow-orange fruits and vegetables and the isoflavone genistein found in foods made from soybeans.

The American Dietetic Association reports that vegetarians, especially "vegans," also have lower mortality rates from several chronic diseases and conditions, including heart disease, hypertension, certain cancers, diabetes, and obesity. Their diet as well as other lifestyle factors may play a beneficial role.

GETTING STARTED

Even with so many good things in the foods that make up vegetarian meals, devotees do not automatically eat a healthful diet. A recent study found that vegetarians eat nearly as much fat as meat-eaters. This could be attributed to cheeses and nuts, which are concentrated sources of both protein and fat. Also, meal planning requires special attention (especially of strict vegetarians) to ensure that the menu provides a variety of nutrients.

To help people make the most of vegetarian-style eating, Dr. Arlene Spark, professor of nutrition at New York Medical College, designed The Vegetarian Pyramid, *above*. This guide can help you plan plant-based meals that provide all of the 40 or so nutrients known to be crucial to good health. Spark suggests that vegetarians "eat a variety of foods as well as the appropriate number of servings from each group." Like the USDA's Food Guide Pyramid, The Vegetarian Pyramid has six groups:

The Vegetarian Pyramid

6 Special needs for Vegans
4 Milk and Milk substitutes
5 Meat/Fish/Poultry substitutes
2 All other Vegetables
3 Fruits
1 Grains and Starchy Vegetables

1. Grains and starchy vegetables: The foundation of meals, vegetarian or not, should include 6 to 11 daily servings of breads, cereals, rice, and pasta plus starchy vegetables such as potatoes, corn, and green beans. These foods provide energy-rich carbohydrates, fiber, B vitamins, and iron; grains such as wheat, corn, oats, and rice also add protein.

2. All other vegetables: 3 or more servings a day provide important vitamins, minerals, and fiber.

3. Fruits: Plan on 2 to 4 servings each day to meet your need for vitamins A and C. Eating foods containing vitamin C (such as citrus fruit) at the same time as an iron-containing food (such as beans) will help your body absorb the iron more efficiently.

4. Milk and milk substitutes: If you regularly consume milk, cheese, yogurt, and even ice cream, your calcium intake should be adequate. If you avoid dairy products, reach for green leafy vegetables, calcium-fortified orange juice, and fortified soy milk and cheese.

5. Meat/fish/poultry substitutes: To meet your minimum protein needs include 2 to 3 servings of dry beans, nuts, seeds, peanut butter, tofu, or eggs throughout a day. Contrary to popular belief, vegans don't need to carefully mix and match their plant sources of protein as long as a variety of foods is eaten.

6. Special needs for vegans: When you eat only plant foods, you come up short on some nutrients. Here's how to compensate each day: 1 tablespoon blackstrap molasses contributes iron and calcium; 1 tablespoon brewer's yeast is rich in vitamin B12; and 3 to 5 teaspoons vegetable oil contributes vitamin E and calories (should you need extra).

AS-YOU-LIKE-IT PILAF

Let your family members decide—with chicken or without? This recipe is made to accommodate both requests without any extra hassle.

1   14½-oz. can vegetable broth
1   medium onion, chopped
½   cup dry lentils, rinsed and drained
½   cup long grain rice
¾   tsp. dried basil, crushed
1   tsp. finely shredded lemon peel
¼   cup water
1½ cups small broccoli flowerets
2   stalks celery, thinly sliced

◆◆◆

3   medium skinless, boneless chicken breast halves (12 oz.)
1   Tbsp. olive oil
2   plum tomatoes, chopped
¾   tsp. dried basil, crushed

◆◆◆

    Romaine or spinach leaves
    Finely shredded Parmesan cheese (optional)
    Sliced cucumbers and tomatoes (optional)

1 In a 3-quart saucepan combine the vegetable broth, chopped onion, lentils, uncooked rice, ¾ teaspoon basil, the lemon peel, water, ⅛ teaspoon *salt,* and ⅛ teaspoon *pepper.* Bring to boiling; reduce heat. Cover and simmer for 20 minutes, adding broccoli flowerets and celery during the last 5 minutes of cooking.

2 Meanwhile, in a 10-inch skillet brown the chicken on both sides in olive oil. Sprinkle the chicken with *half* of the chopped tomatoes, ¾ teaspoon basil, and

additional *salt* and *pepper,* as desired. Cover and cook over medium-low heat 12 minutes or till chicken is no longer pink.

3 Remove lentil mixture from heat; let stand 5 minutes. Stir remaining chopped tomato into pilaf. To serve, divide lentil mixture among romaine- or spinach-lined plates, allowing 1½ cups for a vegetarian entrée or ⅔ cup mixture for a chicken-pilaf entrée. Arrange chicken on smaller pilaf portions. If desired, serve with Parmesan cheese and garnish with sliced cucumbers and tomatoes. Makes 5 cups pilaf (enough for 2 vegetarian entrées plus 3 chicken and pilaf entrées).

Nutrition facts per vegetarian serving: 219 cal., 1 g total fat (0 g sat. fat), 0 mg chol., 641 mg sodium, 47 g carbo., 5 g fiber, 9 g pro. *Daily values:* 9% vit. A, 58% vit. C, 7% calcium, 28% iron.

Nutrition facts per serving with chicken: 175 cal., 4 g total fat (1 g sat. fat), 24 mg chol., 320 mg sodium, 23 g carbo., 3 g fiber, 14 g pro. *Daily values:* 11% vit. A, 30% vit. C, 4% calcium, 18% iron.

GARDEN CHEDDAR CROCK

1   8-oz. tub cream cheese
¼   cup margarine or butter, softened
3   Tbsp. milk
1   Tbsp. spicy brown or Dijon-style mustard
1   cup finely shredded cheddar cheese (4 oz.)
¼   cup thinly sliced green onions
¼   cup drained and chopped oil-pack dried tomatoes
    Dash bottled hot pepper sauce

◆◆◆

VEGETARIANISM: FROM STRICT TO SOMETIMES

Vegan: Eats only foods that are plant based.
Lacto-Vegetarian: Includes milk and milk products in the diet.
Ovo-Vegetarian: Includes eggs.
Lacto-Ovo Vegetarian: Includes milk, milk products, and eggs.
Pollo-Vegetarian: Includes poultry in addition to the above.
Pesca-Vegetarian: Includes fish and other seafood in the diet but no poultry or meat products.
The Sometimes Vegetarian: Chooses mainly a plant-centered diet with small amounts of animal-derived products consumed less frequently.

    Sliced green onion
    Sweet pepper strips, jicama strips, breads, and/or crackers (optional)

1 In a small bowl stir together cream cheese and margarine. Stir in milk and mustard. Stir in the cheddar cheese, ¼ cup green onions, dried tomatoes, and hot pepper sauce. Transfer to a small crock or serving dish. Cover and chill for 4 to 24 hours.

2 To serve, sprinkle additional green onion atop cheese mixture. If desired, serve with sweet pepper or jicama strips, breads, and/or crackers. Makes 2 cups (32 one-tablespoon servings).

Nutrition facts per tablespoon: 55 cal., 5 g total fat (2 g sat. fat), 11 mg chol., 73 mg sodium, 1 g carbo., 0 g fiber, 2 g pro. *Daily values:* 4% vit. A, 1% vit. C, 2% calcium.

POACHED SALMON WITH DILLED SOUR CREAM

Easier to fix than it seems, this elegant dish can be made the evening before and kept chilled.

1½ lb. fresh or frozen salmon
   fillets
⅛ tsp. white pepper

♦♦♦

⅔ cup dry white wine
⅓ cup water
1 tsp. coriander seed
3 star anise or ½ tsp. anise
   seed
½ of a lemon, cut into thick
   slices

♦♦♦

1 large cucumber, peeled
1 head Bibb or Boston lettuce,
   torn
1 recipe Dilled Sour Cream
   (see right)
   Fresh dill (optional)
   Cucumber slices (optional)

1 Thaw fish, if frozen. Remove any skin from fish. Cut fish into 4 portions, if necessary. Measure thickness of fish. Sprinkle fish with white pepper.

2 In a large skillet combine the wine, water, coriander, star anise or anise seed, and lemon slices. Bring to boiling; reduce heat. Gently add the fish fillets. Simmer, covered, for 4 to 6 minutes for each ½ inch of thickness or till fish just flakes when tested with a fork. Carefully remove the fish fillets with a slotted spatula. Cover and chill for several hours or overnight.

3 Use a sharp vegetable peeler to peel cucumber lengthwise into wide, paper-thin slices. Wrap fish

in cucumber slices. Serve on lettuce-lined plates. Spoon Dilled Sour Cream over each serving. If desired, garnish with the fresh dill and cucumber slices. Makes 4 servings.

Dilled Sour Cream: In a bowl combine ½ cup *light dairy sour cream,* 1 tablespoon snipped *fresh dill,* and 1 tablespoon *lime juice.* Add *salt* and *pepper* to taste. Cover and chill before serving.

Nutrition facts per serving: 217 cal., 8 g total fat (2 g sat. fat), 35 mg chol., 141 mg sodium, 8 g carbo., 1 g fiber, 27 g pro. *Daily values:* 12% vit. A, 16% vit. C, 6% calcium, 10% iron.

FRESH SUMMER FRUIT TART

This recipe is especially easy to make—even for first-time bakers. No rolling pin required!

1 cup all-purpose flour
¼ cup packed brown sugar
½ cup butter
1 Tbsp. water

♦♦♦

2 3-oz. pkg. cream cheese,
   softened
½ cup dairy sour cream
¼ cup sifted powdered sugar
1 tsp. vanilla

♦♦♦

1½ tsp. snipped fresh mint or
   lemon verbena
2 cups desired fresh fruit, such
   as blueberries, raspberries,
   sliced strawberries,
   nectarine slices, or
   mandarin orange segments
¼ cup apricot or seedless
   raspberry preserves

1 In a medium mixing bowl stir together the flour and brown sugar. Using a pastry blender, cut butter into the flour mixture till mixture resembles coarse crumbs. Sprinkle the water over the mixture. Toss with a fork till all is moistened. Shape mixture into a ball. Press dough firmly and evenly onto the bottom and up the sides of a 9-inch tart pan with removable bottom or a 9-inch pie plate. Bake in a 400° oven for 10 to 15 minutes or till light brown. Cool completely in pan on a wire rack.

2 In a medium mixing bowl stir together the cream cheese, sour cream, powdered sugar, and vanilla till smooth. Cover and chill for up to 4 hours or till ready to fill tart shell.

3 Just before serving, sprinkle mint or lemon verbena onto pastry. Using a spoon, spread the cream filling evenly over the tart shell. Arrange fresh fruit atop filling. In a small saucepan heat preserves just till melted; cool. Drizzle melted preserves over fruit. Remove from tart pan. Cut into wedges to serve. Cover and store any leftovers in the refrigerator and use within 1 day. Makes 8 servings.

Nutrition facts per serving: 342 cal., 22 g total fat (14 g sat. fat), 61 mg chol., 209 mg sodium, 33 g carbo., 1 g fiber, 4 g pro. *Daily values:* 28% vit. A, 16% vit. C, 4% calcium, 8% iron.

LACTOSE-FREE VANILLA ICE CREAM

You can fix this dessert in an ice-cream maker or in your freezer. The ice-cream maker creates a creamier texture.

¾ **cup sugar**
1 **tsp. unflavored gelatin**
4 **cups milk substitute (see tip, right)**
1 **vanilla bean or 2 tsp. vanilla**
4 **beaten egg yolks**

1 In a large saucepan combine sugar and gelatin. Stir in milk substitute and vanilla bean, if using. Cook and stir over medium heat till mixture almost boils and sugar dissolves. Stir ½ cup of the hot mixture into yolks; return to saucepan. Cook and stir for 2 minutes more. Do not boil (mixture may curdle). Remove from heat; cool. Stir in vanilla extract, if using. Remove vanilla bean. Slit the bean lengthwise; scrape seeds into egg mixture. Discard bean.

2 Transfer mixture to a 13×9×2-inch baking pan. Cover and freeze about 4 hours or till almost firm. Break into chunks. Transfer to a chilled mixing bowl. Beat with an electric mixer just till smooth but not melted. Return to pan. Cover and freeze till firm.

(Or, freeze mixture in a 4-quart ice-cream maker according to the manufacturer's directions.) Makes about 1½ quarts (twelve ½-cup servings).

Nutrition facts per serving: 111 cal., 2 g total fat (1 g sat. fat), 71 mg chol., 33 mg sodium, 21 g carbo., 0 g fiber, 1 g pro. *Daily values:* 19% vit. A, 4% vit.C, 10% calcium, 2% iron.

Cinnamon Ice Cream: Prepare ice cream as directed, except add 1 teaspoon *ground cinnamon* with the gelatin. Continue as directed.

Hazelnut Praline Ice Cream: For praline, in a heavy skillet cook ½ cup chopped *hazelnuts (filberts)* and ¼ cup *sugar* over medium-high heat till sugar begins to melt; do not stir but shake skillet occasionally. Reduce heat to low; cook till sugar turns golden, stirring frequently. Spread on buttered foil. Cool; break into pieces. Prepare ice cream as directed, stirring in praline chunks before freezing. (If using freezer method, fold praline into ice cream after beating.) Continue as directed.

Mocha Ice Cream: Prepare ice cream as directed, except stir 3 ounces melted and cooled *unsweetened chocolate* and 1 teaspoon *instant coffee crystals* into gelatin mixture after heating. Beat with a rotary beater till combined. Continue as directed.

Lactose-Reduced Ice Cream: Prepare any of the above ice-cream flavors as directed, except substitute *lactose-reduced milk* for the milk substitute (see tip, right) and 3 *whole eggs* for the 4 egg yolks. Continue as directed.

MILK SUBSTITUTE SAVVY

Some people suffer from severe lactose intolerance. Others can handle a little lactose. Consult your doctor to pinpoint your tolerance level.

For individuals with severe intolerance, a lactose-free milk substitute, such as Rice Dream, can be a dream come true. Made from organic brown rice, this product is a nondairy beverage and contains 1 percent fat. Unlike cow's milk, rice milk is not a source of calcium, nor of vitamins A and D (an enriched product is available). Look for it in health food stores or next to the canned milk in your supermarket in a 32-ounce, shelf-stable box.

Or, look for lactose-free non-fat milk (Lactaid brand), which contains 80 calories per cup and meets 30 percent of an adult's daily calcium requirements. This milk tastes a lot like regular milk and contains no fat. It is fortified with vitamins A and D.

If you have a mild lactose intolerance, try a lactose-reduced milk, such as Dairy Ease. It is available in nonfat or 2 percent milk fat and contains 70 percent less lactose than regular milk. Dairy Ease is fortified with vitamins A and D, contains 90 calories per cup (nonfat) or 130 calories per cup (2 percent milk fat). It also provides about 30 percent of the total calcium required for the day. You'll find it in the dairy case next to regular milk.

VINEGAR VARIETIES

You can alter the taste or color of a recipe simply by using one of the many different vinegars available. Here's what you can expect from each kind.

◆ Cider vinegar is a good choice when a recipe calls for "vinegar." Made from fermented apples, it has a slightly fruity flavor and tawny color. Use it for pickles, chutneys, relishes, and salad dressings, when its darker color won't affect your recipe.

◆ Distilled vinegar, also called white vinegar, tastes extra sharp. Try this colorless variety in place of cider vinegar.

◆ Malt vinegar is best known as the companion to English fish and chips. Fermented potatoes or grain make the base for this brownish vinegar.

◆ Wine vinegars taste smoother than cider or distilled vinegars. Try using white wine vinegar in salad dressings or sprinkled over cooked fish. Use red wine vinegar when you need a little color added to a sauce.

◆ Rice wine and sherry vinegars are specific types of wine vinegar. Rice wine vinegar starts with sake (Japanese rice wine), lending a mild flavor. Long aging gives sherry vinegars a smoky flavor.

◆ Fruit and herb vinegars are made from either cider, distilled, or wine vinegars to which the natural flavor of fruits or herbs is added. Use in marinades or mix with olive oil in dressings.

◆ Balsamic vinegar starts with highly sugared grapes that are cooked in copper cauldrons. This rich Italian vinegar ages in wooden barrels, which results in a smooth, mellow taste.

SUMMER FRUIT VINEGAR

2 large peaches, peeled, pitted, and chopped, or 2 cups pitted tart red cherries, blueberries, raspberries, or small strawberries
4 cups cider vinegar
2 cups dry white wine
Peach wedges, cherries, or berries

1 In a nonreactive saucepan (such as stainless steel or glass) combine fruit, vinegar, and wine. Stir with a spoon to slightly bruise fruit (do not mash). Bring to boiling; reduce heat. Simmer gently, uncovered, for 3 minutes. Remove from heat; cool.

2 Strain vinegar through 2 layers of 100-percent cotton cheesecloth. Pour into sterilized bottles. Place fruit (a peach wedge or a few berries) in the bottles for identification. Cap bottles tightly. Let stand in a cool, dark place for 2 to 4 weeks. Store in a cool, dry, dark place for up to 6 months. Makes about 6 cups.

Nutrition facts per tablespoon: 6 cal., 0 g fat, 0 mg chol, 0 mg sodium, 1 g carbo, 0 g fiber, 0 g protein.

CRANBERRY VINEGAR

Slightly sweet, this vinegar is best in salad dressings for green or fruit salads.

1 12-oz. pkg. cranberries
1 750-ml. bottle champagne (3¼ cups)
3 cups white wine vinegar
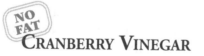
Cranberries (optional)

1 In a large nonreactive saucepan (such as stainless steel or glass), combine the cranberries, champagne, and vinegar. Bring to boiling; reduce heat. Simmer gently, uncovered, for 3 minutes. Remove from heat; cool. Pour mixture into a sterilized 3-quart jar. Cover jar tightly with a non-metal lid (or cover with plastic wrap and tightly seal with a metal lid). Let stand in a cool, dark place for 2 weeks.

2 Strain vinegar; discard the cranberries. Transfer the strained vinegar to sterilized decorative bottles. If desired, add a few additional cranberries to each bottle. Store vinegar in a cool, dark place for up to 6 months. Makes about 6 cups.

Nutrition facts per tablespoon: 8 cal., 0 g total fat, 0 mg chol., 0 mg sodium, 1 g carbo., 0 g fiber, 0 g pro.

ROSEMARY WINE VINEGAR

For a perfect gift, tuck a sprig of fresh rosemary into each bottle before wrapping. Tie on a ribbon and card suggesting that the vinegar be used in lamb dishes or pasta salads.

1 cup tightly packed fresh rosemary sprigs
4 tiny fresh red hot peppers, such as cayenne
6 cups white wine vinegar

1 Rinse rosemary sprigs; pat dry with paper towels. In a nonreactive saucepan (such as stainless steel or glass), combine the rosemary sprigs, hot peppers, and vinegar. Crush rosemary lightly with the back of a spoon. Bring mixture almost to boiling. Remove from heat; cool. Pour the mixture into a sterilized 2-quart jar. Cover the jar tightly with a nonmetal lid (or cover the jar with plastic wrap and then tightly seal with a metal lid). Let stand in a cool, dark place for 2 weeks.

2 Strain vinegar; discard rosemary and peppers. Transfer the strained vinegar to sterilized decorative bottles. Store in a cool, dark place for up to 6 months. Makes about 6 cups.

Nutrition facts per tablespoon: 11 cal., 0 g total fat, 0 mg chol., 1 mg sodium, 3 g carbo., 0 g fiber, 0 g pro.
Daily values: 3% vit. C, 1% iron.

APRICOT-RASPBERRY FREEZER JAM

2   12-oz. pkg. (6 cups) frozen unsweetened red raspberries
3   cups sugar
1   21-oz. can apricot or peach pie filling
1   3-oz. pkg. lemon-flavored gelatin

1 In a 4½-quart pot cook and stir the raspberries and sugar over low heat till sugar is dissolved. Bring to boiling; reduce heat. Boil gently, uncovered, for 10 minutes, stirring often. Cut up any large fruit in pie filling. Stir pie filling and gelatin into raspberry mixture. Return to boiling, stirring constantly. Remove from heat. Ladle at once into hot, clean half-pint jars or freezer containers, leaving ¼-inch headspace. Seal

and label. Store in the refrigerator for up to 1 month or in the freezer for up to 1 year. Makes about 6 half-pints.

Nutrition facts per tablespoon: 43 cal., 0 g total fat, 0 mg chol., 5 mg sodium, 11 g carbo., 1 g fiber, 0 g pro.
Daily values: 4% vit. C.

CHERRY-BERRY FREEZER JAM

Crystallized ginger, also called candied ginger, is bits of gingerroot that are cooked in a sugar syrup then coated with sugar.

3   cups pitted tart red cherries
2   cups blueberries
4¼ cups sugar
2   Tbsp. finely chopped crystallized ginger
1   cup water
1   1¾-oz. pkg. powdered fruit pectin

1 Halve cherries. Crush blueberries slightly. In a bowl combine cherries, blueberries, sugar, and ginger. Let stand for 10 minutes.

2 In a small saucepan combine water and pectin. Bring to a full, rolling boil (a boil that cannot be stirred down). Boil hard 1 minute, stirring constantly. Stir pectin mixture into fruit mixture. Stir constantly 3 minutes. Ladle at once into hot, clean half-pint jars or freezer containers, leaving a ¼-inch headspace. Seal and label. Let stand at room temperature 24 hours. Store in refrigerator up to 3 weeks or in freezer for up to 1 year. Makes about 6 half-pints.

Nutrition facts per tablespoon: 46 cal., 0 g total fat, 0 mg chol., 1 mg sodium, 12 g carbo., 0 g fiber, 0 g pro.

COMPANY-BEST SWEET PICKLES

This all-time favorite recipe from years gone by, came from a reader in 1952. The pickling process takes up to eight days, but the results are worth it.

4   lbs. pickling cucumbers
8   cups sugar
4   cups cider vinegar
2   Tbsp. mixed pickling spices
5   tsp. salt

1 Wash cucumbers; place in a large bowl. Add *boiling water* to cover. Let stand, covered, at room temperature for 12 to 24 hours. Drain and repeat the procedure 3 times.

2 On the fifth day, drain cucumbers and cut into ½-inch slices; place in an 8-quart nonmetal container. In a medium saucepan combine the sugar, vinegar, pickling spices, and salt. Bring to boiling; cook and stir to dissolve sugar. Pour hot mixture over cucumber pieces. Cover and let stand for 24 to 48 hours.

3 Transfer the cucumber mixture to an 8- to 10-quart pot or kettle. Heat to boiling; remove from heat. Fill hot, sterilized pint canning jars, leaving ½-inch headspace. Remove air bubbles, wipe jar rims, and adjust lids. Process the filled jars in a boiling-water canner for 10 minutes. Remove jars from canner; cool on racks. Makes 8 pints.

Nutrition facts per ¼ cup: 101 cal., 0 g total fat, 0 mg chol., 168 mg sodium, 27 g carbo., 0 g fiber, 0 g pro.
Daily values: 3% vitamin C, 1% iron.

BABY VEGETABLE PICKLES

Low Fat

Baby zucchini, squash, and carrots may come with flowers or tops, which should be discarded before pickling. Though available year-round, peak season for baby zucchini and squash is May through October.
(See the photograph on page 159.)

8   oz. tiny whole carrots
½   cup pearl onions
8   oz. whole tiny zucchini
8   oz. whole tiny yellow squash

◆◆◆

½   cup pickling salt
8   cups water
1   small head cauliflower,
      broken into flowerets
      (1¾ cups)

◆◆◆

8   sprigs fresh thyme,
      marjoram, or oregano, or
      four 2-inch sprigs fresh
      tarragon
4 to 8 small hot red peppers or
      jalapeño peppers

◆◆◆

3   cups white vinegar
1   cup sugar

1 Scrub carrots. Remove onion skins. Cook carrots and onions, covered, in a small amount of *boiling water* for 5 minutes; drain. If desired, halve squash lengthwise.

2 In a large nonmetal container dissolve pickling salt in water. Add drained carrots and onions, zucchini, yellow squash, and cauliflower. Let stand for 3 hours. Drain; rinse and drain well.

TEST KITCHEN TIP

PICKLE PRINCIPLES

These practical tips for pickling baby vegetables ensure your pints will be safe and delicious.

◆ Select fresh, firm baby vegetables without bruises or blemishes. Using overripe vegetables may cause the pickles to be soft.

◆ Use pure granulated pickling salt or uniodized table salt for the brine. Iodized table salt can cause pickles to turn dark.

◆ Choose utensils made of stoneware, aluminum, glass, or stainless steel. Other metals can cause the acid in the vinegar to rust or oxidize the utensil surface.

◆ To heat and sterilize jars before canning, cover them with water and boil for 15 minutes.

◆ When filling the hot sterilized jars, leave a ½-inch headspace at the top to allow the food or liquid to expand and to form the vacuum that seals the jars.

◆ After filling jars, use a flexible spatula or table knife to work out any air bubbles that could be trapped around vegetables.

◆ Wipe rims of filled jars with a damp cloth or paper towel.

Food particles on the rim could interfere with proper sealing.

◆ Top with the lids, following the manufacturer's directions.

◆ Place each jar in the canner of boiling water after tightening the lid, making sure the jars do not touch each other. After the last jar has been added, fill the canner with additional boiling water so the water is at least 1 inch above tops of jars.

◆ After processing, check each jar to be sure it has sealed. To check, turn it upside down to see if it leaks; look for a dip in the lid indicating the vacuum. Or, tap the lid with a metal spoon; a sealed lid with no food touching it has a clear ringing sound. An unsealed jar must be repacked and reprocessed with a new lid. If just 1 jar didn't seal, refrigerate and serve it within a week.

◆ Once you are satisfied that the jar is sealed, remove the metal screw band. Wipe with a clean, damp cloth and label with the product name and date. Store in a cool, dark place.

3 Pack vegetables into 4 hot, sterilized pint jars, with 1 or 2 sprigs of desired herb and 1 or 2 red peppers in each, leaving ½-inch headspace.

4 In a large saucepan combine vinegar and sugar. Bring to boiling. Pour the hot vinegar-sugar mixture over vegetables, leaving ½-inch headspace. Wipe jar rims; adjust lids. Process in a boiling water bath for 10 minutes. (Start timing when the water boils.) Makes 4 pints.

Nutrition facts per ¼ cup: 13 cal., 0 g total fat, 0 mg chol., 404 mg sodium, 3 g carbo., 0 g fiber, 0 g pro.
Daily values: 1% vit. A, 16% vit. C.

JULY
Thrill of the Grill

30-minute recipes indicated in RED.
Low-fat recipes indicated with a ♥.

Ready the marinades, pat on the rubs, and dip a brush into sauces. With tempting choices such as Spanish Olive Rub, Apple Butter Barbecue Sauce, and Ginger-Rum Marinade, your grill will be glowing all month long. Go beyond steaks and burgers and conquer grilled fajitas and Indonesian satés. Finish fish steaks and poultry with memorable toppers such as Plum Chutney and Apricot-Rosemary Salsa. Too many garden vegetables? Light a fire under them with Ratatouille on a Skewer. There are recipes aplenty for zucchini and a generous selection of fabulous treats using fresh summer berries.

Menu

Pork loin roast with
Honey-Peach Sauce
(see below)

◆◆◆

Buttered fresh green beans

◆◆◆

Fresh peach slices

◆◆◆

French rolls with butter

◆◆◆

Homemade ice cream

HONEY-PEACH SAUCE

*Barbecue goes uptown with this
smooth fruit sauce. Pool it
around pork loin roast and serve
with fresh garden vegetables.
(See the photograph on page 153.)*

4 medium peaches, peeled
    (if desired), or nectarines,
    pitted
2 Tbsp. lemon juice
2 Tbsp. honey
½ tsp. cracked black pepper

◆◆◆

1 to 2 tsp. snipped fresh thyme
    or ¼ to ½ tsp. dried
    thyme, crushed

1 For sauce, cut up *3* peaches or nectarines. In a blender container or food processor bowl, combine cut-up fruit, lemon juice, honey, and pepper. Cover and blend or process till smooth. Transfer blended fruit mixture to a saucepan. Bring to boiling; reduce heat. Simmer, uncovered, about 15 minutes or till slightly thickened, stirring occasionally.

2 Meanwhile, finely chop the remaining peach or nectarine; stir into sauce with thyme. Brush sauce onto meat the last 15 minutes of grilling. (For grilling information, see pages 166 and 167.) Heat remaining sauce just till bubbly; serve with meat. Makes about 1¾ cups sauce, enough for 2 to 3 pounds of meat.

▌ TO MAKE AHEAD ▐

Cover and chill sauce for up to 24 hours. To serve, reheat the sauce in a saucepan over low heat, stirring occasionally.

Nutrition facts per tablespoon: 15 cal., 0 g total fat, 0 mg chol., 0 mg sodium, 4 g carbo., 0 g fiber, 0 g pro.
Daily values: 1% vit. A, 2% vit. C.

PEANUT SATÉ SAUCE

*Brush this sauce on skewers of
chicken, pork, or beef cubes for an
Indonesian-style taste sensation.
(See the photograph on page 153.)*

¼ cup creamy peanut butter
2 Tbsp. rice vinegar or white
    vinegar
2 Tbsp. soy sauce
2 cloves garlic, minced
½ tsp. toasted sesame oil
⅛ tsp. crushed red pepper
2 Tbsp. thinly sliced green
    onion

1 For sauce, in a small bowl stir together the peanut butter, rice vinegar or white vinegar, soy sauce, garlic, toasted sesame oil, and crushed red pepper. Stir in the green onion.

SPOON ON THE SAUCE

Dabbed, brushed, or slathered, it's the sauce that defines great barbecue. The easy sauces are here, ready to serve alongside or brush on during cooking.

◆ Sweetening the sauce pot with sugar, honey, or preserves can cause sauce to burn on the meat's exterior before the meat inside can cook. To avoid burning the meat, wait until the last 5 or 10 minutes of grilling to brush on sweet sauces.

◆ Keep the sauce you're brushing onto raw meat separate from the remaining sauce you're serving at the table. Or, boil the brush-on sauce for 2 minutes just before passing.

◆ Store homemade sauces in the refrigerator for up to a week and boil before using.

◆ A long-handled brush is the safest tool for applying your secret sauce. After every cookout, clean it in hot, sudsy water or in the dishwasher.

2 Brush sauce onto meat kabobs the last 5 minutes of grilling. (For grilling information, see pages 166 and 167.) Heat and stir any remaining sauce just till bubbly; serve with kabobs. Makes about ½ cup sauce, enough for 1 to 2 pounds of meat.

Nutrition facts per tablespoon: 53 cal., 4 g total fat (1 g sat. fat), 0 mg chol., 296 mg sodium, 3 g carbo., 1 g fiber, 2 g pro.
Daily values: 1% iron.

Top: *Peanut Saté Sauce on chicken kabobs (page 152)*
Above: *Honey-Peach Sauce on pork (page 152)*

Above: *Coconut-
Cherry Crisp
(page 172)*
Near right: *Triple
Cherry Trifle
(page 172)*
Far right: *Strawberry-
White-Chocolate
Dessert (page 173)*

Left: *Clockwise from top: Broccoli, Corn, and Tomato Skillet (page 135), Basil-Stuffed Beef (page 134), Cheese-Stuffed Grilled Potatoes (page 135)*
Inset: *Peach-Apricot Crisp (page 137)*

Page 158: *Clockwise from top: Orange-Pear Spinach Salad (page 130), Avocado Slaw (page 130), Pepper-Olive Pasta Salad (page 132)*
Top: *Baby Vegetable Pickles (page 150)*
Above: *Sweet and Spicy Rub on lamb chops (page 162)*

Top left: *Spicy Barbecue Sauce on ribs (page 161)*
Center left: *Apple Butter Barbecue Sauce (page 161)*
Bottom: *Spanish Olive Rub on beef (page 161)*

APPLE BUTTER BARBECUE SAUCE

Purchased apple butter plus tomato sauce equals a sweet, easy combo for burgers. Pickapeppa sauce, a Jamaican condiment similar to Worcestershire sauce, adds a little punch.
(See the photograph on page 160.)

1 **8-oz. can tomato sauce**
½ **cup apple butter**
1 **Tbsp. Pickapeppa sauce or Worcestershire sauce**

1 For sauce, in a small saucepan combine tomato sauce, apple butter, and Pickapeppa or Worcestershire sauce. Bring just to boiling; remove from heat.

2 Brush sauce onto burgers the last 10 minutes of grilling. (For grilling information, see page 166.) Heat any remaining sauce just till bubbly, stirring occasionally; serve with burgers. Makes about 1⅓ cups sauce, enough for 1 to 2 pounds of meat.

Nutrition facts per tablespoon sauce: 18 cal., 0 g total fat, 0 mg chol., 75 mg sodium, 4 g carbo., 0 g fiber, 0 g pro.
Daily values: 1% vit. A, 5% vit. C, 1% iron.

SPICY BARBECUE SAUCE

What goes best with finger-lickin' sauces? Pork ribs, of course.
(See the photograph on page 160.)

⅓ **cup sugar**
½ **cup finely chopped onion**
1½ **cups boiling water**
1 **6-oz. can tomato paste**
¼ **cup Worcestershire sauce**
¼ **cup vinegar**
1 to 2 **tsp. chili powder**
1 **tsp. dry mustard**
¼ **tsp. salt**

1 For sauce, in a medium saucepan cook sugar over medium-high heat till it begins to melt, shaking pan occasionally (do not stir). Reduce heat to low; add onion. Cook and stir about 5 minutes more or till sugar is golden brown. Carefully and gradually add the boiling water to sugar mixture, stirring constantly. Whisk in the tomato paste, Worcestershire sauce, vinegar, chili powder, mustard, and salt. Bring to boiling; reduce heat. Simmer, uncovered, for 10 to 15 minutes or to desired consistency.

2 Brush sauce onto both sides of ribs the last 10 minutes of grilling. (For grilling information, see page 167.) Heat remaining sauce till bubbly; serve with meat. Makes 2½ cups sauce, enough for 3 pounds of meat.

Nutrition facts per tablespoon: 13 cal., 0 g total fat, 0 mg chol., 32 mg sodium, 3 g carbo., 0 g fiber, 0 g pro.
Daily values: 1% vit. A, 7% vit. C, 1% iron.

SPANISH OLIVE RUB

Olives, capers, and garlic meet their match with beef steak and lamb chops.
(See the photograph on page 160.)

½ **cup pimiento-stuffed green olives**
3 **cloves garlic, chopped**
1 **Tbsp. capers, drained**
1½ **tsp. finely shredded orange peel**
½ **tsp. pepper**

HERE'S THE RUB

A bold blend of seasonings rubbed right onto the meat promises a direct hit of flavor. Take a bite and let your taste buds tingle.

◆ Wet rubs for meat often feature condiments such as mustard, horseradish, and yogurt. Dry rubs play up fresh and dried herbs and spices.

◆ Slightly crush spices, seeds, and dried herbs before rubbing to release the flavors.

◆ To allow the flavor to penetrate more deeply, cut slits in the meat. Or, rub the seasonings under the skin of poultry.

◆ When using dry rubs, brush a little cooking oil, olive oil, or melted butter on the meat before rubbing.

◆ The oils in the peppers may burn your skin and eyes. For protection, when rubbing fresh or dried peppers onto meats, wear rubber gloves or wash your hands well with soap and water afterward.

1 In a blender container or food processor bowl, combine olives, garlic, capers, orange peel, and pepper. Cover and blend or process till chunky. Rub mixture onto steak or chop. If desired, cut a pocket in meat and stuff. Grill according to charts on pages 166 and 167. Makes about ⅓ cup, enough for 1 pound of meat.

Nutrition facts per tablespoon: 28 cal., 2 g total fat (0 g sat. fat), 0 mg chol., 480 mg sodium, 2 g carbo., 1 g fiber, 1 g pro.
Daily values: 1% vit. A, 7% vit. C, 1% calcium, 3% iron.

Menu

Lamb chops with Sweet and Spicy Rub (see below)

◆◆◆

Sliced cucumber

◆◆◆

Rice pilaf

◆◆◆

Fresh figs

SWEET AND SPICY RUB

Team red and black pepper with six spices for a Middle Eastern-style coating for lamb chops, beef roasts, and steaks. (See the photograph on page 159.)

2 Tbsp. margarine or butter
1 tsp. ground cinnamon
½ tsp. salt
½ tsp. ground cumin
½ tsp. ground turmeric
½ tsp. ground red pepper
½ tsp. ground black pepper
¼ tsp. ground cardamom
⅛ tsp. ground cloves
⅛ tsp. ground nutmeg
1 Tbsp. sugar

1 In a small saucepan melt margarine or butter. Stir in the remaining ingredients, except sugar. Remove from heat. Stir in sugar; cool. Rub mixture onto meat. Grill according to chart on page 166. Makes about ¼ cup, enough for 4 pounds of meat.

Nutrition facts per tablespoon: 70 cal., 6 g total fat (1 g sat. fat), 0 mg chol., 335 mg sodium, 5 g carbo., 0 g fiber, 0 g pro. *Daily values:* 8% vit. A, 1% vit. C, 1% calcium, 5% iron.

HERBED PECAN RUB

Pecans, lemon, and fresh herbs make a delicate coating for firm-fleshed fish steaks (such as halibut, swordfish, or tuna) or chicken pieces.

½ cup broken pecans
½ cup fresh oregano leaves
½ cup fresh thyme leaves
3 cloves garlic, cut up
½ tsp. finely shredded lemon peel
½ tsp. pepper
¼ tsp. salt
¼ cup cooking oil

1 In a blender container or food processor bowl, combine the pecans, oregano, thyme, garlic, lemon peel, pepper, and salt. Cover and blend or process with several on-off turns till a paste forms, stopping the machine several times and scraping the sides. With the blender running, gradually add oil till mixture forms a paste. Rub onto fish or chicken. Grill according to chart on page 167. Makes ½ cup, enough for 3 pounds of meat.

Nutrition facts per tablespoon: 108 cal., 11 g total fat (1 g sat. fat), 0 mg chol., 67 mg sodium, 2 g carbo., 0 g fiber, 1 g pro.

GINGER-RUM MARINADE

Chicken pieces and pork chops really take to the flavors of this tropically inspired marinade. Use dark rum for a more intense taste. Keep the meal light by serving grilled pineapple or papaya slices alongside the meat.

½ cup unsweetened pineapple juice
⅓ cup light rum
¼ cup soy sauce

MARINADE MASTERY

Soaking in a tangy bath gives meat a double bonus. It tenderizes the meat and permeates it with mouthwatering flavor at the same time.

◆ Put the meat in a plastic bag with the marinade to coat the meat more evenly and make cleanup easier. Set the bag in a nonmetal bowl.

◆ Marinate in the refrigerator, never at room temperature.

◆ For tenderizing, marinades must contain an acid, such as vinegar or lemon juice.

◆ To tenderize meats, plan on marinating at least 4 hours. To add flavor, 30 minutes may be enough.

◆ The texture of some meats, poultry, and fish can change if they're marinated too long. When the recipe suggests a time limit, follow the guideline.

1 Tbsp. grated gingerroot
2 cloves garlic, minced
1 Tbsp. brown sugar
¼ tsp. ground red pepper

1 For marinade, in a mixing bowl stir together the pineapple juice, rum, soy sauce, gingerroot, garlic, brown sugar, and red pepper. Place meat in a plastic bag set in a deep bowl. Pour marinade over meat; seal bag. Marinate in the refrigerator for 4 to 8 hours, turning the bag occasionally. Remove meat from the bag, reserving marinade.

2 Grill meat according to chart on page 167, brushing occasionally with the reserved marinade. Discard the remaining marinade. Makes about 1¼ cups marinade, enough for 1 to 2 pounds of meat.

Nutrition facts per tablespoon: 17 cal., 0 g total fat, 0 mg chol., 206 mg sodium, 2 g carbo., 0 g fiber, 0 g pro. *Daily values:* 1% vit. C.

CITRUS MARINADE

This delightful orange and lemon combination perfectly complements salmon and halibut steaks. To complete the meal, serve couscous tossed with toasted pecans, finely shredded orange peel, and snipped fresh parsley; a salad of mixed greens, tomato wedges, and sliced red onion; and whole grain dinner rolls with butter.

¼ **cup frozen orange juice concentrate, thawed**
2 **Tbsp. cooking oil**
2 **tsp. finely shredded lemon peel**
2 **Tbsp. lemon juice**
2 **cloves garlic, minced**

1 For marinade, in a small mixing bowl stir together the orange juice concentrate, cooking oil, shredded lemon peel, lemon juice, and garlic. Place the salmon or halibut steaks in a plastic bag set in a deep bowl. Pour the marinade over salmon or halibut steaks; seal bag. Marinate in the refrigerator about 2 hours, turning bag occasionally. Remove salmon or halibut steaks from bag, reserving the marinade.

CUTTING UP AT THE GRILL

Don't leave food safety inside when you're cooking outside. Follow these simple rules of using cutting boards:

◆ It's best to use only nonabsorbent cutting boards of plastic or marble.

◆ If you do use a hardwood board, designate one cutting board for raw meat, poultry, and fish. Do not use this board for produce, bread, or cooked meat, even after cleaning.

◆ After each use, wash any cutting board used for raw meat in hot, soapy water, then rinse and air dry.

◆ Frequently disinfect the cutting boards with a solution of 2 teaspoons bleach to 1 quart warm water. Rinse under cold running water.

◆ Replace old, nicked, or scarred cutting boards with new ones.

◆ Use only cutting boards that are made of materials approved for food usage.

---

2 Grill salmon or halibut steaks according to the chart on page 167, brushing with marinade halfway through grilling. Makes ½ cup marinade, enough for 1½ to 2 pounds of fish.

Nutrition facts per tablespoon: 47 cal., 3 g total fat (1 g sat. fat), 0 mg chol., 0 mg sodium, 4 g carbo., 0 g fiber, 0 g pro. *Daily values:* 26% vit. C.

FAJITA MARINADE

Grill your own fajitas at home using beef flank steak or boneless, skinless chicken breast halves and this six-ingredient marinade. Slice the grilled meat and serve with warm tortillas, grilled onion and sweet peppers, avocado, and cilantro.

½ **cup clear Italian salad dressing**
½ **cup salsa**
1 **tsp. finely shredded lime peel**
2 **Tbsp. lime juice**
1 **Tbsp. snipped fresh cilantro**
¼ **tsp. bottled hot pepper sauce**

1 For marinade, in a small mixing bowl stir together salad dressing, salsa, lime peel, lime juice, snipped cilantro, and hot pepper sauce. Place the beef or chicken in a plastic bag set in a deep bowl. Pour the marinade over beef or chicken; seal bag. Marinate in the refrigerator about 4 hours for chicken or overnight for beef, turning bag occasionally. Remove beef or chicken from bag, reserving marinade.

2 Grill beef or chicken and vegetables for fajitas according to the charts on pages 166 and 167, brushing occasionally with the reserved marinade. Slice to serve beef or chicken as a fajita filling. Heat any remaining marinade to boiling; serve with fajitas. Makes 1 cup marinade, enough for 1 to 2 pounds of meat.

Nutrition facts per tablespoon: 37 cal., 4 g total fat (1 g sat. fat), 0 mg chol., 86 mg sodium, 2 g carbo., 0 g fiber, 0 g pro. *Daily values:* 1% vit. A, 5% vit. C.

Tarragon Vinaigrette

Grilled vegetables are the rage dish at summer cookouts these days, and this fresh herb marinade does them justice. (It's also mighty tasty on grilled turkey and chicken.)

⅓ cup white wine vinegar
¼ cup olive oil or cooking oil
¼ cup white wine Worcestershire sauce
1 Tbsp. snipped fresh tarragon or thyme or 1 tsp. dried tarragon or thyme, crushed
1 Tbsp. honey
¼ tsp. salt
⅛ tsp. pepper

1 For marinade, in a small mixing bowl stir together wine vinegar, olive oil or cooking oil, Worcestershire sauce, tarragon or thyme, honey, salt, and pepper. Place vegetables or poultry in a plastic bag set in a deep bowl. Pour marinade over vegetables or poultry; seal bag. Marinate in the refrigerator about 4 hours, turning bag occasionally. Remove vegetables or poultry from bag, reserving the marinade.

2 Grill the vegetables or poultry according to the charts on page 167, brushing occasionally with the reserved marinade. Discard any remaining marinade. Makes about 1 cup marinade, enough for 1 to 2 pounds of vegetables or poultry.

How Hot Is Hot?

To judge the hotness of coals, hold your hand, palm side down, where your food will cook and at the same height as the food will be grilled. Count "one thousand one, one thousand two," etc., for each second you can hold your hand there. You'll need to remove your hand after two seconds if the coals are hot; three seconds for medium-hot, four seconds for medium, five seconds for medium-slow, and six seconds or more for a slow fire.

Note: For vegetables, good choices include cut-up carrots, zucchini, red or yellow sweet peppers, kohlrabi, yellow summer squash, and new potatoes. Precook firm or starchy vegetables such as carrots and potatoes in a little boiling water for a few minutes (see chart, page 167).

Nutrition facts per tablespoon: 36 cal., 3 g total fat (0 g sat. fat), 0 mg chol., 65 mg sodium, 2 g carbo., 0 g fiber, 0 g pro.

Beer-Mustard Marinade

This German-style marinade makes pork chops and fresh bratwurst taste better than ever. Prick the sausages first to let the flavors penetrate. Serve with Orange-Walnut Cabbage Slaw (see recipe, page 169).

1 cup beer or nonalcoholic beer
¼ cup Dijon-style mustard or stone-ground mustard
3 Tbsp. light-flavored molasses
2 tsp. white wine Worcestershire sauce
½ tsp. ground nutmeg
¼ tsp. ground cloves

1 In a small mixing bowl stir together the beer, Dijon-style mustard or stone-ground mustard, molasses, Worcestershire sauce, nutmeg, and cloves. Place meat in a plastic bag set in a deep bowl. Pour marinade over meat; seal bag. Marinate in the refrigerator for 8 to 24 hours, turning bag occasionally. Remove meat from bag, reserving marinade.

2 Grill the meat according to the chart on page 167, brushing occasionally with reserved marinade. Discard the remaining marinade. Makes 1½ cups marinade, enough for 2 to 3 pounds of meat.

Nutrition facts per tablespoon: 14 cal., 0 g total fat, 0 mg chol., 64 mg sodium, 2 g carbo., 0 g fiber, 0 g pro.

BLACK BEAN AND CORN SALSA

Season red snapper or white fish fillets with a little lime juice and garlic powder before grilling. Then spoon this colorful salsa atop the grilled fish. If you have any leftover salsa, you can store it in the refrigerator for three to five days and serve it atop grilled steaks and chops.

2　large tomatoes, seeded and chopped (1½ cups)
½　of a 15-oz. can black beans, rinsed and drained (¾ cup)
½　cup frozen loose-pack whole kernel corn, thawed
3　Tbsp. thinly sliced green onions
2　Tbsp. snipped fresh cilantro
2　Tbsp. olive oil or cooking oil
1　fresh jalapeño pepper, chopped
1　Tbsp. lime juice
¼　tsp. salt
¼　tsp. ground cumin
⅛　tsp. pepper

1 In a medium mixing bowl stir together the tomatoes, black beans, corn, green onions, cilantro, olive oil or cooking oil, jalapeño pepper, lime juice, salt, ground cumin, and pepper. Cover and chill in the refrigerator for 6 to 24 hours. Stir before serving. Makes about 3 cups.

Nutrition facts per ¼ cup: 59 cal., 3 g total fat (0 g sat. fat), 0 mg chol., 122 mg sodium, 7 g carbo., 2 g fiber, 2 g pro.
Daily values: 3% vit. A, 23% vit. C, 1% calcium, 3% iron.

RELISH ON THE SIDE

Salsas, chutneys, relishes, and other condiments are a great way to add flavor to grilled foods once they're on your plate.

◆ Use your blender or food processor to keep the chopping to a minimum.

◆ Splash a little lemon juice onto the fresh fruits you use in salsas and relishes to keep their colors bright.

◆ Keep storage in mind when deciding how much is enough to make. Without processing in cans or jars, most fresh relishes will keep in the refrigerator for up to a week.

APRICOT-ROSEMARY SALSA

Tomato salsa, make room for this impudent upstart—a great topper for grilled fish steaks and chicken pieces. Make it up to a day before serving; much more than that and the salsa loses its pretty color.

½　cup chopped, peeled apricots or peaches
¼　cup chopped, seeded, and peeled avocado
¼　cup chopped tomato
½　tsp. finely shredded lime peel or lemon peel
2　Tbsp. lime juice or lemon juice
1　Tbsp. thinly sliced green onion
1　tsp. snipped fresh rosemary or ½ tsp. dried rosemary, crushed

1 In a medium mixing bowl stir together the apricots or peaches, avocado, tomato, lime or lemon peel, lime or lemon juice, green onion, and rosemary. Cover and chill in the refrigerator for up to 24 hours. Stir before serving. Makes about 1 cup.

Nutrition facts per ¼ cup: 37 cal., 2 g total fat (0 g sat. fat), 0 mg chol., 3 mg sodium, 5 g carbo., 1 g fiber, 1 g pro.
Daily values: 6% vit. A, 14% vit. C, 2% iron.

PLUM CHUTNEY

Lightly season turkey, chicken, lamb, or pork before grilling, then serve with this plum-dandy relish.

1　lb. red or yellow plums, seeded and chopped (2½ cups)
¼　cup sugar
¼　cup chopped onion
3　Tbsp. orange juice or water
2　Tbsp. golden raisins
2　Tbsp. vinegar
2　cloves garlic, minced
½　tsp. ground allspice
¼　tsp. salt

1 In a large saucepan combine plums, sugar, onion, orange juice or water, raisins, vinegar, garlic, allspice, and salt. Bring to boiling; reduce heat. Simmer, covered, for 30 minutes, stirring occasionally. Uncover; cook about 10 minutes more or till chutney is of desired consistency. Cool to room temperature. Cover and chill in refrigerator up to 1 week. Stir before serving. Makes about 1½ cups.

Nutrition facts per ¼ cup: 92 cal., 1 g total fat (0 g sat. fat), 0 mg chol., 90 mg sodium, 23 g carbo., 2 g fiber, 1 g pro.
Daily values: 2% vit. A, 19% vit. C, 1% iron.

OUTDOOR GRILLING GUIDE

When you're craving a perfectly cooked steak, a juicy burger,
flaky fish, or crisp grilled vegetables, look to these handy charts for grilling times and
temperatures. Summer never tasted so good!

INDIRECT-GRILLING MEAT, POULTRY, AND FISH

Indirect grilling means that food is cooked by hot air circulating around the food, much like an oven. It's a slower cooking method than direct grilling because less heat is provided. Also with indirect grilling, flare-ups from dripping fat are minimized so the food doesn't char. You can grill food indirectly in both gas grills and charcoal grills with a lid.

For charcoal grills: Light the coals and bring to desired heat. You'll need hot coals to provide medium-high heat; medium-hot coals for medium heat; medium coals for medium-slow heat, and so forth. Place a disposable foil drip pan or heavy foil in the center of the fire box and arrange the hot coals around the pan using long tongs. Test for the heat above the pan (see tip, page 164). Place food on the grill rack over the drip pan, not over the coals. Cover and grill for the time given below and on page 167 or till food reaches desired doneness, adding more briquettes to maintain heat as necessary.

For gas grills: Refer to your owner's manual for specific directions on indirect cooking. Usually, if you have a two-burner gas grill, after preheating with both burners on, you'll turn one off and place the food over the unit side, away from the heat source. For three-burner gas grills, you'll usually turn off the middle burner after preheating and place the food in the center of the grill. For single-burner gas grills, after preheating, the burner usually is turned down to low.

MEAT: *For roasts, insert a meat thermometer and grill until the thermometer registers 5° below the specified temperature.*

CUT	THICKNESS/ WEIGHT	TEMPERATURE ABOVE PAN	DONENESS	INDIRECT- GRILLING TIME
BEEF				
Boneless sirloin roast	4 to 6 pounds	Medium-slow	145° (medium rare)	1¾ to 2¼ hours
			160° (medium)	2¼ to 2¾ hours
Boneless sirloin steak	1 inch	Medium	Medium rare	22 to 26 minutes
			Medium	26 to 30 minutes
Flank steak	¾ to 1 inch	Medium	Medium	18 to 22 minutes
Ground meat patties	¾ inch (4 per pound)	Medium	No pink remains	20 to 24 minutes
Steak (porter- house, rib, rib	1 inch	Medium	Medium rare	16 to 20 minutes
			Medium	20 to 24 minutes
eye, sirloin,	1¼ to 1½	Medium	Medium rare	20 to 22 minutes
T-bone, top loin)	inches		Medium	22 to 26 minutes
Tenderloin roast	2 to 3 pounds	Medium-hot	145° (medium rare)	¾ to 1 hour
	4 to 6 pounds	Medium-hot	145° (medium rare)	1¼ to 1½ hours
Tenderloin steak	1 inch	Medium	Medium rare	16 to 20 minutes
			Medium	20 to 22 minutes
	1½ inches	Medium	Medium rare	18 to 22 minutes
			Medium	22 to 26 minutes
LAMB				
Boneless rolled leg roast	4 to 7 pounds	Medium-slow	160° (medium)	2¼ to 3¾ hours
Chop	1 inch	Medium	Medium rare	16 to 18 minutes
			Medium	18 to 20 minutes
PORK*				
Boneless top loin roast	2 to 4 pounds (single loin)	Medium-slow	160°	1 to 1¼ hours
	3 to 5 pounds (double loin, tied)	Medium-slow	160°	1¼ to 2¼ hours

Pork should be cooked until juices run clear.

CUT	THICKNESS/ WEIGHT	TEMPERATURE ABOVE PAN	DONENESS	INDIRECT-GRILLING TIME
Bratwurst, Polish, and Italian sausages (fresh link)	3 to 4 per pound	Medium	Well-done	20 to 25 minutes
Chop	¾ inch 1¼ to 1½ inches	Medium-hot Medium	Medium Medium	20 to 24 minutes 35 to 40 minutes
Ribs, loin-back and spareribs	2 to 4 pounds	Medium	Well-done	1¼ to 1½ hours
POULTRY				
Chicken breast, half (skinned and boned)	4 to 5 ounces	Medium	Tender; no longer pink	15 to 18 minutes
Meaty chicken pieces	2 to 2½ pounds total	Medium	Tender; no longer pink	50 to 60 minutes
Turkey breast tenderloin steak	4 to 6 ounces	Medium	Tender; no longer pink	15 to 18 minutes

FISH
For fish fillets, place in a well-greased grill basket. For fish steaks and whole fish, grease the grill rack. Place the fish on the greased grill rack over the drip pan. Cover and grill until the fish just begins to flake easily when tested with a fork. If desired, brush with melted margarine or butter, or olive oil.

FORM OF FISH	THICKNESS	TEMPERATURE ABOVE PAN	DONENESS	INDIRECT-GRILLING TIME
Fillets, steaks, cubes (for kabobs)	½ to 1 inch thick	Medium	Flakes	4 to 6 minutes per ½-inch thickness

DIRECT-GRILLING VEGETABLES

Before grilling, rinse, trim, cut up, and precook vegetables as directed. To precook vegetables, in a saucepan bring a small amount of water to boiling; add desired vegetable and simmer, covered, for the time specified in the chart. Drain well. Generously brush vegetables with olive oil or melted margarine or butter before grilling to prevent vegetables from sticking to the grill rack. Test for medium or medium-hot coals. To grill, place vegetables on a piece of heavy foil or on the grill rack directly over the preheated coals. If putting vegetables directly on grill rack, lay them perpendicular to wires of the rack so they won't fall into the coals. Grill, uncovered, for the time given or till tender, turning occasionally. Monitor grilling so vegetables don't char.

VEGETABLE	PREPARATION	PRECOOKING TIME	DIRECT-GRILLING TIME
Carrots	Cut off tops; wash and peel carrots. Halve lengthwise.	3 to 5 minutes	3 to 5 minutes
Corn on the cob	Peel husks back, but do not remove. Remove silk. Pull husks back up. Soak corn in cold water for 1 hour. Drain and shake off excess water. Grill corn with husks on.	Do not precook.	25 to 30 minutes
Onions	Cut crosswise into ¾-inch slices. Brush with oil and wrap in foil.	Do not precook.	20 to 25 minutes
New potatoes	Halve potatoes.	10 minutes or until almost tender	10 to 12 minutes
Sweet peppers	Remove stems. Quarter peppers. Remove seeds and membranes. Cut into 1-inch-wide strips.	Do not precook.	8 to 10 minutes
Zucchini or yellow summer squash	Wash; cut off ends. Quarter lengthwise.	Do not precook.	5 to 6 minutes

RATATOUILLE ON A SKEWER

Grill the skewers alongside steaks or chops flavored with Spanish Olive Rub (see page 161).

1 small eggplant, peeled and cut into 1-inch chunks
2 medium zucchini, cut into 1-inch chunks
2 green and/or yellow sweet peppers, seeded and cut into 1-inch pieces
2 small onions, peeled and quartered
½ cup French salad dressing
¼ cup grated Parmesan cheese
¼ cup fine dry bread crumbs

♦♦♦

16 cherry tomatoes

1 Alternately thread eggplant, zucchini, peppers, and onions onto 8 skewers. Brush with salad dressing. Combine Parmesan cheese and bread crumbs; place on a piece of waxed paper. Roll the kabobs in the crumb mixture to coat evenly.

2 Grill kabobs directly over medium coals 10 to 12 minutes or till zucchini is crisp-tender, turning frequently. Place tomatoes on end of skewers during the last 2 minutes of grilling. Makes 8 side-dish servings.

Nutrition facts per serving: 127 cal., 8 g total fat (2 g sat. fat), 4 mg chol., 301 mg sodium, 13 g carbo., 3 g fiber, 3 g pro.
Daily values: 4% vit. A, 36% vit. C, 5% calcium, 4% iron.

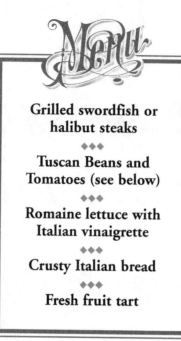

Menu

Grilled swordfish or halibut steaks

♦♦♦

Tuscan Beans and Tomatoes (see below)

♦♦♦

Romaine lettuce with Italian vinaigrette

♦♦♦

Crusty Italian bread

♦♦♦

Fresh fruit tart

---

30 MIN.
LOW FAT

TUSCAN BEANS AND TOMATOES

This simple dish tastes as if it's straight from the Italian countryside, yet it's from canned beans and tomatoes.

1 19-oz. can cannellini beans or one 16-oz. can great Northern beans, rinsed and drained
1 14½-oz. can Italian-style or pasta-style stewed tomatoes
1 Tbsp. balsamic vinegar
1 tsp. snipped fresh rosemary or ½ tsp. dried rosemary, crushed
½ tsp. crushed red pepper
Cracked black pepper (optional)
Fresh rosemary (optional)

1 In a large saucepan combine the beans, undrained tomatoes, balsamic vinegar, rosemary, and red pepper; heat to boiling. Serve with a slotted spoon.

2 If desired, sprinkle with pepper and garnish with rosemary. Makes 4 side-dish servings.

Nutrition facts per serving: 110 cal., 0 g total fat, 0 mg chol., 569 mg sodium, 26 g carbo., 6 g fiber, 9 g pro.
Daily values: 9% vit. A, 21% vit. C, 4% calcium, 12% iron.

SALSA-BEAN SALAD

Mom's three-bean salad goes Tex-Mex—with spicy salsa, corn, and jicama. Fix ahead and chill thoroughly to serve with ribs brushed with Spicy Barbecue Sauce (see page 161).

3 15-oz. cans beans, such as red kidney, garbanzo, and/or black beans, rinsed and drained
1 8-oz. can whole kernel corn, drained
½ cup chopped, peeled jicama or water chestnuts
⅓ cup sliced green onions
¾ cup salsa
⅓ cup French salad dressing

1 In a large mixing bowl combine the beans, corn, jicama or water chestnuts, and green onions. For the dressing, stir together the salsa and French dressing. Add to vegetable mixture, tossing gently to coat. Cover and chill in the refrigerator for 2 to 24 hours. Toss before serving. Makes 10 side-dish servings.

Nutrition facts per serving: 95 cal., 4 g total fat (1 g sat. fat), 1 mg chol., 308 mg sodium, 15 g carbo., 3 g fiber, 4 g pro.
Daily values: 3% vit. A, 15% vit. C, 1% calcium, 5% iron.

ORANGE-WALNUT CABBAGE SLAW

What a nutty and nice fix-up for a package of preshredded coleslaw.

5 cups shredded cabbage with carrot (coleslaw mix)
1 small orange, peeled, sliced crosswise, and quartered
2 green onions, thinly sliced
3 Tbsp. vinegar
3 Tbsp. salad oil
2 Tbsp. sugar
1½ tsp. finely shredded orange peel
2 Tbsp. orange juice
1 tsp. walnut oil (optional)
⅛ tsp. salt

◆◆◆

¼ cup chopped walnuts, toasted

1 In a large mixing bowl combine shredded cabbage with carrot, orange pieces, and green onions. For salad dressing, in a screw-top jar combine the vinegar, salad oil, sugar, orange peel, orange juice, walnut oil (if desired), and salt. Cover and shake well to mix.

2 Pour the dressing over the cabbage-orange mixture, tossing gently to coat. Cover and chill in the refrigerator 2 to 4 hours or till thoroughly chilled. Before serving, add chopped walnuts; toss again. Makes 6 side-dish servings.

Nutrition facts per serving: 142 cal., 10 g total fat (1 g sat. fat), 0 mg chol., 61 mg sodium, 13 g carbo., 2 g fiber, 2 g pro.
Daily values: 28% vit. A, 80% vit. C, 4% calcium, 4% iron.

PRIZE TESTED RECIPE WINNER

ZUCCHINI WITH BALSAMIC VINAIGRETTE

This recipe earned Lisa Perry of Hampton, New Jersey, $200 in the magazine's monthly contest.

2 medium zucchini
1 small red sweet pepper
1 small yellow sweet pepper
1 Tbsp. olive oil
¼ tsp. salt

◆◆◆

⅓ cup olive oil
¼ cup balsamic vinegar
1 clove garlic, minced
2 Tbsp. snipped fresh parsley

◆◆◆

2 Tbsp. snipped fresh basil
1 Tbsp. pine nuts, toasted
8 ½-inch-thick slices French bread (baguette), toasted
2 oz. provolone cheese, cut up (½ cup)

1 Halve zucchini crosswise; slice lengthwise into ¼-inch-thick pieces. Halve and seed sweet peppers; cut into ¾-inch-thick strips. Line a 15×10×1-inch baking pan with foil. Arrange the zucchini and pepper strips on the pan. Combine the 1 tablespoon olive oil and the salt; brush onto vegetables. Bake, uncovered, in a 325° oven for 15 to 20 minutes or till vegetables are just tender.

2 Meanwhile, for dressing, in a blender container or food processor bowl, combine the ⅓ cup olive oil, balsamic vinegar, and garlic; cover and blend or process till smooth. Stir in parsley.

3 To serve, arrange the zucchini and pepper strips on 4 salad plates; drizzle with some of the dressing. Sprinkle with the basil and pine nuts. Serve with bread slices and cheese. Makes 4 appetizer servings.

Nutrition facts per serving: 318 cal., 18 g total fat (4 g sat. fat), 10 mg chol., 498 mg sodium, 32 g carbo., 1 g fiber, 9 g pro.
Daily values: 14% vit. A, 42% vit. C, 13% calcium, 14% iron.

HERB-GRILLED TOMATOES

4 small tomatoes
3 Tbsp. dairy sour cream or plain yogurt
1 Tbsp. snipped fresh basil or 1 tsp. dried basil, crushed
1 Tbsp. fine dry bread crumbs
1 Tbsp. finely shredded or grated Parmesan cheese

1 Remove cores and cut the tomatoes in half crosswise. Spread cut side of each tomato with sour cream or yogurt. Sprinkle each with basil. Sprinkle bread crumbs and Parmesan cheese atop tomatoes. Arrange tomato halves in a foil pie pan.

2 Arrange preheated coals around a drip pan in a covered grill. Test for medium heat above the pan. Place the foil pan containing tomatoes on grill over drip pan. Cover and grill for 10 to 15 minutes or till tomatoes are heated through. Makes 4 servings.

Nutrition facts per serving: 56 cal., 3 g total fat (1 g sat. fat), 6 mg chol., 46 mg sodium, 6 g carbo., 1 g fiber, 2 g pro.
Daily values: 8% vit. A, 29% vit. C, 2% calcium, 3% iron.

CAJUN BUTTER

Pour this zesty blend over cooked vegetables, such as carrots, zucchini, cauliflower, broccoli, and corn.

¼ tsp. chili powder
¼ tsp. ground black pepper
⅛ tsp. garlic powder
⅛ tsp. ground red pepper
2 Tbsp. butter
1 tsp. cornstarch
¼ cup chicken broth

1 In a small bowl stir together the chili powder, black pepper, garlic powder, and red pepper. In a small saucepan cook spice mixture in hot butter for 1 minute. Stir in the cornstarch. Carefully add the chicken broth. Cook and stir over medium heat till thickened and bubbly. Cook and stir for 2 minutes more. Serve warm over cooked vegetables. Makes enough for 4 servings.

Nutrition facts per serving: 56 cal., 6 g total fat, (4 g sat. fat), 16 mg chol., 99 mg sodium, 0 g carbo., 0 g fiber, 0 g pro. *Daily value:* 8% vit. A, 0% vit. C, 1% iron.

ZUCCHINI CRESCENT PIE

Refrigerated rolls make an easy crust for this quiche-like pie.

1 pkg. refrigerated crescent rolls (8)

♦♦♦

2 Tbsp. margarine or butter
4 cups thinly sliced zucchini (about 1 lb.)
1 cup sliced fresh mushrooms
1 clove garlic, minced

1 Tbsp. snipped fresh oregano or 1 tsp. dried oregano, crushed
1 Tbsp. snipped fresh basil or 1 tsp. dried basil, crushed
¼ tsp. salt
¼ to ½ tsp. pepper
½ cup shredded mozzarella cheese (2 oz.)

♦♦♦

2 eggs, slightly beaten
½ cup milk

1 Separate crescent rolls into 8 triangles and press into the bottom and up the sides of a lightly greased 11-inch quiche dish or 10-inch deep-dish pie plate to form a crust; set aside.

2 In a large skillet heat margarine or butter over medium heat. Add zucchini, mushrooms, garlic, oregano, basil, salt, and pepper. Cook and stir over medium-high heat 5 to 7 minutes or till zucchini is tender. Spread mixture into prepared crust. Sprinkle cheese over zucchini mixture.

3 In a small bowl stir together eggs and milk. Pour evenly over zucchini mixture in dish. Bake in a 375° oven for 20 to 25 minutes or till center is set and top is golden. Let stand for 10 minutes before serving. Cut into wedges. Makes 8 main-dish servings.

Nutrition facts per serving: 198 cal., 9 g total fat (5 g sat. fat), 92 mg chol., 336 mg sodium, 21 g carbo., 3 g fiber, 10 g pro. *Daily values:* 14% vit. A, 27% vit. C, 14% calcium, 8% iron.

GOT-EXTRA-ZUCCHINI SPOON BREAD

This recipe earned Georgetta Tomlinson of Enid, Oklahoma, $100 in the magazine's monthly contest.

1 cup fresh or frozen loose-pack whole kernel corn
½ cup chopped onion (1 medium)
½ cup green sweet pepper strips (1 medium)
½ cup water
1 cup chopped zucchini
1 cup chopped tomato (2 small)
1 cup shredded cheddar cheese (4 oz.)
½ cup cornmeal

♦♦♦

2 eggs, slightly beaten
½ cup milk
½ tsp. salt
¼ tsp. pepper
Several dashes bottled hot pepper sauce

1 Grease a 1½-quart casserole; set aside. In a large saucepan combine corn, onion, pepper strips, and water. Bring to boiling; reduce heat. Simmer, covered, 5 minutes. Do not drain. Stir in the zucchini, tomato, cheddar cheese, and cornmeal.

2 In a small mixing bowl combine the eggs, milk, salt, pepper, and hot pepper sauce. Stir the egg mixture into the vegetable mixture in the saucepan. Turn mixture into prepared casserole. Bake, uncovered, in a 350° oven about 40 minutes or till set. Let stand 5 minutes before serving. Makes 6 side-dish servings.

Nutrition facts per serving: 198 cal., 9 g total fat (5 g sat. fat), 92 mg chol., 336 mg sodium, 21 g carbo., 3 g fiber, 10 g pro. *Daily values:* 14% vit. A, 27% vit. C, 14% calcium, 8% iron.

ZUCCHINI SQUASH RELISH
NO FAT

Do you have more zucchini than you know what to do with? If so, make some of this mixed vegetable relish and savor the garden fresh flavors all winter long.

4 **medium zucchini (1 lb.)**
3 **medium onions**
1 **small red sweet pepper**
1 **small green sweet pepper**
2 **Tbsp. salt**

♦♦♦

1⅓ **cups sugar**
4 **tsp. cornstarch**
¼ to ½ **tsp. curry powder**
¼ **tsp. celery seed**
¼ **tsp. ground turmeric**
¼ **tsp. pepper**
¾ **cup vinegar**

1 Process each vegetable in a food processor with several on/off turns till chopped, or chop by hand. (You should have about 3 cups zucchini, 1½ cups onions, and ½ cup of each sweet pepper.) In a large bowl combine all vegetables; sprinkle with salt and stir till combined. Let stand at least 4 hours or overnight in a cool place, stirring once or twice. Drain in a colander; rinse thoroughly under cold water to remove excess salt.

2 In a large saucepan combine the sugar, cornstarch, curry powder, celery seed, turmeric, and pepper. Stir in the vinegar. Cook and stir till thickened and bubbly. Add drained vegetables. Return to boiling; reduce heat. Boil gently, uncovered, about 15 minutes or till vegetables are crisp-tender. Cool slightly.

3 Ladle relish into hot, sterilized half-pint canning jars or freezer containers, leaving a ½-inch headspace. Adjust lids or seals, and cool. Store in the refrigerator for up to 2 weeks or in the freezer for up to 6 months. Before serving, thaw, if necessary, and stir. Makes 3 half pints (24 two-tablespoon servings).

Nutrition facts per 2 tablespoons: 52 cal., 0 g total fat, 0 mg chol., 179 mg sodium, 14 g carbo., 0 g fiber, 0 g pro. *Daily values:* 2% vit. A, 10% vit. C, 1% iron.

ZUCCHINI SNACK CAKE

It's important to finely shred the zucchini for this fruit and vegetable cake.

¾ **cup all-purpose flour**
¼ **cup whole wheat flour**
½ **tsp. baking soda**
¼ **tsp. salt**
¼ **tsp. ground nutmeg**

♦♦♦

1 **egg, slightly beaten**
1¼ **cups finely shredded zucchini (8 oz.)**
¾ **cup packed brown sugar**
¼ **cup margarine or butter, melted**
¼ **cup cooking oil**
½ **tsp. vanilla**
¾ **cup whole bran cereal**
½ **cup coconut**

THE CLEVER COOK

RECIPE FINDER
To avoid searching through my cookbook collection for a favorite recipe, I place a blank recipe card in each category of my recipe file box. When I find a recipe my family likes, I jot the source on that card for easy reference.

Beth Garner
Jefferson City, Missouri

½ **cup snipped, pitted whole dates or raisins**
Powdered sugar (optional)

1 Grease an 8×8×2-inch baking pan. In a medium bowl stir together the all-purpose flour, whole wheat flour, baking soda, salt, and nutmeg. Set aside.

2 In a large mixing bowl combine egg, zucchini, brown sugar, margarine or butter, oil, and vanilla. Stir in flour mixture. Add bran cereal, coconut, and dates or raisins, stirring just till combined. Pour into prepared pan. Bake in a 350° oven 30 to 35 minutes or till a wooden toothpick inserted near the center comes out clean. Cool on a wire rack. Sift powdered sugar over the top, if desired. Makes 12 servings.

Nutrition facts per serving: 169 cal., 6 g total fat (2 g sat. fat), 18 mg chol., 212 mg sodium, 30 g carbo., 3 g fiber, 3 g pro. *Daily values:* 12% vit. A, 4% vit. C, 2% calcium, 11% iron.

COCONUT-CHERRY CRISP

If fresh tart cherries are hard to find, use frozen ones.
(See the photograph on page 154.)

5 cups fresh or frozen unsweetened, pitted tart red cherries
¼ cup granulated sugar
4 tsp. cornstarch

❖❖❖

¾ cup regular or quick-cooking rolled oats
½ cup packed brown sugar
⅓ cup all-purpose flour
¼ tsp. ground cardamom, nutmeg, or ginger
⅓ cup butter
½ cup coconut
¼ cup chopped pecans or walnuts
 Ice cream or light cream (optional)

1 Pit fresh cherries over a bowl to catch juices. (If using frozen fruit, thaw but do not drain.) In a large saucepan combine sugar and cornstarch; stir in cherries and 2 tablespoons reserved cherry liquid or *water.* Cook and stir till thickened and bubbly. Pour into a 2-quart square baking dish; set aside.

2 For topping, combine oats, brown sugar, flour, and spice. Cut in butter till mixture resembles coarse crumbs. Stir in coconut and nuts. Sprinkle topping over filling. Bake in a 375° oven 25 minutes or till golden. Serve warm with ice cream or light cream, if desired. Serves 6.

Nutrition facts per serving: 368 cal., 16 g total fat (9 g sat. fat), 27 mg chol., 114 mg sodium, 55 g carbo., 2 g fiber, 4 g pro. *Daily values:* 25% vit. A, 21% vit. C, 3% calcium, 11% iron.

PRIZE TESTED RECIPE WINNER

CHOCOLATE-BERRY COBBLER

This recipe earned Viola Roberts of Salina, Kansas, $100 in the magazine's monthly contest.

3 cups fresh or frozen berries, such as strawberries, raspberries, blackberries, or blueberries
1 cup sugar
⅓ cup margarine or butter
1 cup all-purpose flour
1 Tbsp. baking powder
1 cup milk

❖❖❖

¼ cup chocolate-flavored syrup
 Vanilla ice cream (optional)

1 Thaw berries if frozen, but do not drain. Combine berries, *¼ cup* of the sugar, and 2 tablespoons *water;* let stand 5 minutes.

In a 9×9×2-inch baking pan melt the margarine in a 350° oven. Stir together flour, remaining sugar, and baking powder; stir in milk.

2 Remove pan from oven. Pour the batter atop melted margarine or butter. Drizzle with chocolate syrup. Spoon undrained berries atop. Bake in a 350° oven about 40 minutes or till a wooden toothpick comes out clean. Cool slightly. If desired, serve warm with ice cream. Makes 6 servings.

Nutrition facts per serving: 360 cal., 12 g total fat (2 g sat. fat), 3 mg chol., 329 mg sodium, 63 g carbo., 2 g fiber, 4 g pro. *Daily values:* 15% vit. A, 71% vit. C, 19% calcium, 11% iron.

TRIPLE CHERRY TRIFLE

See the photograph on page 154.

1 recipe Stirred Custard (see page 173)
1 10¾-oz. loaf frozen pound cake, thawed

❖❖❖

¼ cup cherry preserves
3 Tbsp. cherry liqueur or unsweetened cherry or orange juice
2 cups halved, pitted fresh dark or light sweet cherries
2 Tbsp. sliced almonds, toasted

❖❖❖

½ cup whipping cream
1 Tbsp. sugar
½ tsp. vanilla

1 Prepare Stirred Custard; cool and chill. Cut the pound cake into ½-inch cubes (you should have about 5 cups).

2 In 8 dessert dishes or a 1½-quart bowl, layer *half* of the preserves, cake, and liqueur or juice. Dot with remaining preserves. Top with *half* of the cherries, almonds, and Stirred Custard. Repeat layers without preserves. Cover and chill for 3 to 24 hours. Chill a mixing bowl and beaters of an electric mixer.

3 Before serving, in the chilled bowl combine whipping cream, sugar, and vanilla; beat with an electric mixer on medium speed till soft peaks form. Top trifle with whipped cream. Serves 8.

Stirred Custard: In a heavy medium saucepan combine 3 beaten *eggs;* 2 cups *milk, half-and-half, or light cream;* and ¼ cup *sugar.* Cook and stir over medium heat till mixture just coats a metal spoon. Remove from heat. Stir in 1 teaspoon *vanilla.* Quickly cool by placing saucepan in a sink or bowl of *ice water* for 1 to 2 minutes, stirring constantly. Cover surface with clear plastic wrap; chill.

Nutrition facts per serving: 361 cal., 18 g total fat (6 g sat. fat), 105 mg chol., 175 mg sodium, 43 g carbo., 1 g fiber, 7 g pro. *Daily values:* 14% vit. A, 4% vit. C, 8% calcium, 4% iron.

BERRIES, COOKIES, AND CREAM PARFAITS

- 1 **8-oz. carton dairy sour cream**
- 3 **Tbsp. sugar**
- 2 **Tbsp. crème de cassis or orange juice**
- ½ **tsp. finely shredded lemon peel**

- ⅛ **tsp. ground nutmeg**
- ½ **cup whipping cream**
- 1½ **cups coarsely crumbled shortbread cookies (about ½ of a 10-oz. pkg.)**

◆◆◆

- 2 **cups desired fresh berries, such as blueberries, raspberries, and/or halved strawberries**

1 In a large mixing bowl stir together sour cream, sugar, crème de cassis or orange juice, lemon peel, and nutmeg; set aside. In a chilled mixing bowl beat cream with an electric mixer on medium speed till soft peaks form. Fold whipped cream into sour cream mixture. Fold in crumbled cookies.

2 In 6 parfait glasses or wineglasses layer half the berries, all of the cream mixture, and remaining berries. Before serving, cover and chill about 2 hours. Serves 6.

Nutrition facts per serving: 332 cal., 21 g total fat (11 g sat. fat), 50 mg chol., 136 mg sodium, 32 g carbo., 1 g fiber, 3 g pro. *Daily values:* 18% vit. A, 25% vit. C, 6% calcium, 5% iron.

PRIZE TESTED RECIPE WINNER

STRAWBERRY-WHITE-CHOCOLATE DESSERT

This recipe earned Lisa Molnar of Kissimmee, Florida, $200 in the magazine's monthly contest. (See the photograph on page 155.)

- 2 **6-oz. pkg. white baking bars, cut up**
- 1½ **cups whipping cream**
- 1 **cup brewed espresso or strong coffee**

- 2 **Tbsp. brandy (optional)**
- 1 **3-oz. pkg. cream cheese, softened**

◆◆◆

- 2½ **3-oz. pkg. ladyfingers, split (30)**
- 3 **cups sliced fresh strawberries**
- 2 **cups halved fresh strawberries**

1 In a medium saucepan combine baking bars and *¼ cup* of the cream; heat and stir over low heat till bars are melted. Cool slightly. Stir together espresso or coffee and, if desired, brandy; set aside.

2 For filling, in a chilled mixing bowl beat remaining cream with an electric mixer on medium speed till soft peaks form; set aside. In a large mixing bowl beat cream cheese till fluffy. Add baking bar mixture to cream cheese; beat on medium speed till smooth. Fold whipped cream into cream cheese mixture; set aside.

3 To assemble, line sides of a 9-inch springform pan with *some* of the ladyfinger halves, flat side in. Arrange *half* of the remaining ladyfingers on the bottom of the pan. Drizzle *half* of the espresso mixture over ladyfingers in bottom of pan. Spoon a third of the filling over ladyfingers. Top with sliced strawberries. Top with remaining ladyfingers. Drizzle with remaining espresso mixture. Top with the remaining filling. Cover and chill for 3 to 4 hours. To serve, arrange halved berries atop filling. Serves 10 to 12.

Nutrition facts per serving: 434 cal., 29 g total fat (17 g sat. fat), 137 mg chol., 101 mg sodium, 40 g carbo., 1 g fiber, 6 g pro. *Daily values:* 23% vit. A, 72% vit. C, 10% calcium, 8% iron.

BLUEBERRY CREAM PIE

1½ cups fresh blueberries
⅓ cup orange juice
¼ cup sugar
1 Tbsp. cornstarch
1 baked 9-inch pastry shell

◆◆◆

⅔ cup sugar
3 Tbsp. cornstarch
2 cups milk
3 egg yolks, beaten
2 Tbsp. margarine or butter
1 tsp. vanilla
1 cup whipping cream,
    whipped (optional)
¼ cup toasted coconut

1 In a blender container combine *½ cup* of the blueberries, the orange juice, ¼ cup sugar, and 1 tablespoon cornstarch; process till smooth. Transfer to a medium saucepan; add remaining berries. Cook and stir over medium-high heat till thickened and bubbly; cook and stir 2 minutes more. Pour into the baked pastry shell.

2 In a saucepan combine ⅔ cup sugar, 3 tablespoons cornstarch, and dash *salt.* Slowly stir in milk. Cook and stir over medium-high heat till thickened and bubbly. Reduce heat; cook and stir 2 minutes more. Gradually stir 1 cup hot mixture into egg yolks. Return mixture to saucepan; cook and stir 2 minutes more. Remove from heat; stir in margarine and vanilla. Pour atop blueberry mixture; cool. Cover; chill at least 4 hours. Top with whipped cream, if desired, and coconut. Serves 8.

Nutrition facts per serving: 360 cal., 16 g total fat (4 g sat. fat), 84 mg chol., 142 mg sodium, 50 g carbo., 1 g fiber, 5 g pro. *Daily values:* 19% vit. A, 15% vit. C, 7% calcium, 8% iron.

BLUEBERRY COFFEE CAKE

1¼ cups all-purpose flour
½ cup granulated sugar
½ tsp. baking powder
½ tsp. baking soda
½ tsp. ground cinnamon
⅛ tsp. salt
⅔ cup buttermilk
1 beaten egg
3 Tbsp. cooking oil
½ tsp. vanilla
1 cup fresh or frozen
    blueberries

◆◆◆

2 Tbsp. brown sugar
1 Tbsp. all-purpose flour
¼ tsp. ground cinnamon
2 tsp. margarine or butter

1 Lightly grease and flour a 9×1-inch round baking pan; set aside. In a large mixing bowl stir together the 1¼ cups flour, granulated sugar, baking powder, baking soda, the ½ teaspoon cinnamon, and the salt. In a small mixing bowl stir together buttermilk, egg, oil, and vanilla. Add to dry ingredients. Stir till smooth. Pour batter into prepared pan. Sprinkle berries over batter.

2 In a small bowl combine brown sugar, the 1 tablespoon flour, and ¼ teaspoon cinnamon. Cut in the margarine or butter. Sprinkle over top of berries. Bake in a 350° oven for 30 to 35 minutes or till a wooden toothpick inserted near center comes out clean. Cool slightly; serve warm. Makes 8 servings.

Nutrition facts per serving: 200 cal., 6 g total fat (1 g sat. fat), 27 mg chol., 166 mg sodium, 33 g carbo., 1 g fiber, 3 g pro.

RASPBERRY-LEMON BREAKFAST BISCUITS

2 cups all-purpose flour
2 Tbsp. sugar
1 Tbsp. baking powder
1 Tbsp. finely shredded lemon
    peel
½ tsp. cream of tartar
¼ tsp. salt
¼ tsp. baking soda
½ cup margarine or butter
1 cup buttermilk or sour milk
1 cup red raspberries
1 recipe Lemon Butter
    Frosting (see below)

1 In a medium mixing bowl stir together flour, sugar, baking powder, lemon peel, cream of tartar, salt, and baking soda. Using a pastry blender, cut in margarine or butter till mixture resembles coarse crumbs. Make a well in center of dry ingredients; add buttermilk or sour milk all at once. Using a fork, stir just till moistened. Gently fold in raspberries. Drop dough by tablespoonsful 1 inch apart on a greased baking sheet. Bake in a 450° oven for 10 to 12 minutes or till golden. Cool biscuits on a wire rack while preparing Lemon Butter Frosting. Frost tops of biscuits. Serve warm. Makes 12 biscuits.

Lemon Butter Frosting: In a small mixing bowl stir together 1 cup sifted *powdered sugar* and 1 tablespoon softened *margarine or butter.* Stir in ¼ teaspoon finely shredded *lemon peel* and enough *water or lemon juice* to make the frosting of spreading consistency.

Nutrition facts per biscuit: 201 calories, 9 g total fat (2 g sat. fat), 1 mg chol., 284 mg sodium, 28 g carbo., 1 g fiber, 3 g pro.

AUGUST
Garden in Glory

30-minute recipes indicated in RED.
Low-fat recipes indicated with a ♥.

The air grows crisp, the colors mellow, and gardens everywhere show off a last burst of productivity. Vegetable demand will equal supply if you turn your jackpot into Summer Vegetable Paella or low-fat Asian Gazpacho. Teach roasting ears new tricks in Corn with Savory-Lime Butter. Ditto for tomatoes with Fresh Mozzarella and Tomato Salad. A tasty counterpoint to late summer produce is fish. Poached Fish with Sherry-Spinach Sauce makes a dazzling presentation, but any fish is company-worthy when served with a fresh fruit salsa.

TAVERNA VEGGIE SANDWICHES

In just 20 minutes, bake and layer eggplant and tomato on bread; add herb and feta cheese to carry out the Grecian theme. A zesty tabbouleh salad adds to the summer-fresh scenario.

1 large eggplant, sliced lengthwise into ½-inch-thick pieces (4 to 8 slices)
¼ cup roasted garlic oil*
3 medium tomatoes, cut into ½-inch-thick slices

♦♦♦

4 large slices sourdough, Italian, or French bread, about ¾ inch thick
2 Tbsp. snipped fresh oregano
½ cup crumbled feta cheese (about 2 oz.)

1 Place eggplant slices on a lightly greased, foil-lined baking sheet; brush with a little of the oil. Bake, uncovered, in a 450° oven for 10 minutes; add tomato slices to baking sheet, brush lightly with oil. Bake about 5 minutes more or till vegetables are just tender and eggplant is lightly browned. Lift foil with vegetables from baking sheet; set aside to cool slightly.

2 Place bread slices on same baking sheet. Brush the top side of each bread slice with some oil. Bake in 450° oven about 4 minutes or till lightly browned. For each sandwich, place 1 slice bread, browned side down. Brush each unbrowned side with some more of the oil. Top each bread slice with some tomato slices and 1 or 2 roasted eggplant slices. Place more tomato slices atop eggplant.

Sprinkle sandwiches with oregano and feta cheese. Makes 4 servings.

*Note: Roasted garlic oil is a flavored olive oil available in specialty sections of many supermarkets. If unavailable, do not attempt to make your own flavored oil; only those prepared commercially are sure to be safe to eat. Instead, substitute ⅛ teaspoon *garlic puree* or *minced garlic* and ¼ cup *salad oil*.

Nutrition facts per serving: 310 cal., 22 g total fat (7 g sat. fat), 28 mg chol., 517 mg sodium, 23 g carbo., 3 g fiber, 8 g pro. *Daily values:* 10% vit. A, 30% vit. C, 15% calcium, 10% iron.

FRESH MOZZARELLA AND TOMATO SALAD

Fresh mozzarella is worth hunting for to make this salad a standout (you'll find it in specialty cheese shops or deli cases). Sold in balls, its texture is soft and spongy and its flavor mild and sweet.

Fresh spinach leaves
4 medium ripe tomatoes, cut into wedges
6 oz. fresh mozzarella cheese or fresh smoked mozzarella cheese, sliced
2 Tbsp. extra-virgin olive oil*
2 Tbsp. balsamic vinegar
¼ cup snipped fresh basil
1 tsp. cracked pepper

1 Line a platter or individual salad plates with spinach leaves. Arrange tomato wedges and mozzarella slices atop spinach. Combine oil and vinegar; drizzle over salad. Sprinkle basil and cracked pepper over all. Makes 4 main-dish or 8 side-dish servings.

Menu

Grilled beef tenderloin, chilled and sliced thin

♦♦♦

Breadsticks

♦♦♦

Fresh Mozzarella and Tomato Salad (see below left)

♦♦♦

Steamed green beans and wax beans

♦♦♦

Red wine

♦♦♦

Chocolate cheesecake

*Note: Extra-virgin olive oil has an intensely fruity flavor and aroma. If unavailable, substitute virgin olive oil.

Nutrition facts per main-dish serving: 220 cal., 16 g total fat (7 g sat. fat), 33 mg chol., 193 mg sodium, 10 g carbo., 2 g fiber, 10 g pro. *Daily values:* 36% vit. A, 54% vit. C, 21% calcium, 11% iron.

MIDWESTERN TABBOULEH

Great bowls of grain. Bulgur, made from cracked wheat, is found in the rice aisle of your supermarket. It takes on a homespun flavor when tossed with zucchini as well as its traditional allies—tomatoes, parsley, and mint.

1 cup bulgur
1½ cups red and/or yellow cherry tomatoes, halved or quartered
¼ cup thinly sliced green onions (2)
1 cup shredded zucchini
½ cup snipped fresh parsley

¼ cup snipped fresh mint
¼ cup olive oil
¼ cup lemon juice
½ tsp. salt
½ to 1 tsp. pepper
   Kale leaves (optional)

1 Rinse bulgur in a colander with cold water; drain. In a large bowl combine bulgur, tomatoes, green onions, zucchini, parsley, and mint. Combine ½ cup *water,* the oil, lemon juice, salt and pepper; pour over bulgur mixture and stir to combine. Cover and chill 4 to 24 hours. If desired, serve on kale leaves and garnish with additional *fresh mint.* Makes 8 to 10 side-dish servings (about 5 cups).

Nutrition facts per serving: 132 cal., 7 g total fat (1 g sat. fat), 0 mg chol., 142 mg sodium, 16 g carbo., 5 g fiber, 3 g pro. *Daily values:* 5% vit. A, 29% vit. C, 1% calcium, 9% iron.

ZUCCHINI IN MIXED COMPANY

This simple side-dish grill of onions, zucchini, and summer squash needs just a gloss of scented oils to showcase the veggies at their best.

2 Tbsp. walnut oil or olive oil
1 Tbsp. olive oil
1 tsp. snipped fresh rosemary
   or ½ tsp. dried rosemary,
   crushed
½ tsp. bottled minced garlic
½ to 1 tsp. crushed red pepper
¼ tsp. salt
2 medium onions, cut
   crosswise into ¾-inch-
   thick slices
   ❖❖❖
2 medium zucchini, cut
   lengthwise into ¼-inch-
   thick strips

2 medium yellow summer
   squash, cut lengthwise
   into ¼-inch-thick strips
   ❖❖❖
Fresh rosemary sprig
   (optional)

1 In a small bowl stir together walnut oil, olive oil, rosemary, minced garlic, red pepper, and salt. Tear off a 36×18-inch piece of heavy foil. Fold in half crosswise to make a double thickness of foil. Place onion slices in a single layer in center of foil. Brush some of the oil mixture over onions; seal foil with a double fold. Fold ends to completely enclose onions, leaving space in packet for steam to build. Place foil packet on grill rack.

2 Grill directly over medium-hot coals for 20 to 25 minutes or till onions are almost tender, turning packet occasionally. Using a wide metal spatula, carefully lift onion slices from the foil packet and place directly on grill over medium-hot coals (discard foil).

3 Brush zucchini and yellow squash slices with some of the remaining oil mixture; add to grill. Cook vegetables over coals for 3 to 4 minutes or till just tender and lightly browned, turning once and carefully brushing with any remaining oil mixture.

4 Transfer vegetables to a serving platter; if desired, garnish with a fresh rosemary sprig. Makes 4 side-dish servings.

Nutrition facts per serving: 149 cal., 11 g total fat (1 g sat. fat), 0 mg chol., 139 mg sodium, 13 g carbo., 4 g fiber, 2 g pro. *Daily values:* 6% vit. A, 21% vit. C, 4% calcium, 6% iron.

ZUCCHINI-BASIL SALAD DRESSING

This thick, tangy dressing clings well to salad greens.

¾ cup coarsely chopped
   zucchini
½ cup mayonnaise or salad
   dressing
¼ cup dairy sour cream
2 Tbsp. buttermilk
1 Tbsp. snipped fresh basil or
   1 tsp. dried basil, crushed
¼ tsp. garlic powder
¼ tsp. onion powder
¼ tsp. pepper
   ❖❖❖
¼ cup finely chopped zucchini
   (optional)

1 In a blender container or food processor bowl, combine the ¾ cup chopped zucchini, mayonnaise or salad dressing, sour cream, buttermilk, basil, garlic powder, onion powder, and pepper. Cover and blend or process till mixture is almost smooth.

2 If desired, stir in the ¼ cup chopped zucchini. Cover and store in the refrigerator for up to 1 week. Makes about 1 cup.

Nutrition facts per tablespoon: 59 cal., 6 g total fat, (1 g sat. fat), 6 mg chol., 43 mg sodium, 1 g carbo., 0 g fiber, 0 g pro. *Daily values:* 1% vit. A, 1% vit. C.

ZUCCHINI MADRAS CURRY

In India, the home of curry, spices are used to dispel summer heat as well as to impart flavor. That's the only control over August's heat wave we can offer. With only a few minutes on the stove, this dish won't wilt the cook.

2 cloves garlic, minced
1 Tbsp. cooking oil
1 Tbsp. curry powder
2 cups zucchini cut into matchsticklike strips
1 medium tart green apple (such as Granny Smith), cored and sliced into thin wedges
1 cup peeled, cubed, cooked potato*
1 cup frozen peas

❖❖❖

1 8-oz. carton plain yogurt
¼ tsp. salt
2 cups hot cooked rice

1 In a large skillet cook garlic in hot oil over medium heat for 1 minute or till golden. Add curry powder; cook and stir the mixture for 1 minute. Add zucchini and apple. Cook and stir about 3 minutes or till almost tender. Gently stir in cooked potato and peas; heat through.

2 In a large mixing bowl gently toss vegetable mixture with yogurt and salt. If desired, season to taste with additional *salt* and *pepper*. Serve immediately with rice. Makes 4 side-dish servings.

*Note: To prepare potato, peel and cut into cubes. Cook, covered, in lightly salted boiling water for 15 to 20 minutes or till tender; drain. To prepare in a microwave oven, in a small microwave-safe baking dish combine cubed potato and 1 tablespoon *water*. Microwave, covered, for 5 to 7 minutes, stirring after 3 minutes; drain.

Nutrition facts per serving: 266 cal., 5 g total fat (1 g sat. fat), 3 mg chol., 206 mg sodium, 48 g carbo., 4 g fiber, 8 g pro. *Daily values:* 21% vit. C, 12% calcium, 16% iron.

SUMMER VEGETABLE PAELLA

Just as the original Spanish dish cleans the larder of scraps of roasts and sausages, our vegetarian version cuts a swath through the garden, creating a mosaic of what's ripe and ready.

1 6-oz. jar marinated artichoke hearts
4 cloves garlic, minced
1 large onion, cut into wedges
2 14½-oz. cans (3½ cups total) reduced-sodium chicken broth or vegetable broth
⅓ cup water
½ tsp. pepper
¼ tsp. ground saffron
1 cup Arborio or long grain rice
2 cups green beans cut into 1-inch pieces

❖❖❖

2 fresh ears of corn, husked and cut crosswise into 2-inch pieces
2 medium zucchini, cut into ½-inch-thick slices
1 medium red sweet pepper, cut into strips
½ tsp. finely shredded lemon peel
1 15-oz. can garbanzo beans, drained

1 Drain marinade from the artichokes into a 12-inch skillet; set artichokes aside. Heat marinade over medium heat. Add garlic and onion. Cook, stirring frequently, for 5 minutes. Add chicken or vegetable broth, water, pepper, and saffron. Bring to boiling. Stir in *uncooked* rice and green beans. Return to boiling. Reduce heat and simmer, covered, for 8 minutes.

2 Add corn, zucchini, sweet pepper, and lemon peel; cook, covered, for 7 to 8 minutes more or till vegetables and rice are tender. Stir in garbanzo beans and artichoke hearts; heat through. Makes 4 to 6 main-dish servings.

Nutrition facts per serving: 409 cal., 6 g total fat (0 g sat. fat), 1 mg chol., 1,125 mg sodium, 79 g carbo., 8 g fiber, 14 g pro. *Daily values:* 22% vit. A, 97% vit. C, 9% calcium, 39% iron.

KITCHEN GARDEN RATATOUILLE

Ratatouille (ra-tuh-TOO-ee) is a rich vegetable medley devised by housewives in the south of France to translate the goods of a teeming garden into premier table fare. We like it served with Cheesy Polenta, but purchased polenta or cooked rice stands in nicely.

1 recipe Cheesy Polenta (see page 179) or one 16-oz. pkg. refrigerated cooked polenta or 3 cups hot cooked rice

❖❖❖

1 small green sweet pepper, seeded and cut into strips
1 small onion, thinly sliced
1 clove garlic, minced

1 Tbsp. cooking oil
½ small eggplant, cut into
    ½-inch pieces

♦♦♦

1 large yellow summer squash
    or zucchini, sliced
1 large tomato, peeled (if
    desired) and cut into
    wedges
1 Tbsp. snipped fresh basil
⅛ tsp. salt
⅛ to ¼ tsp. pepper
3 Tbsp. snipped fresh parsley
    Shredded Parmesan cheese
    (optional)
    Fresh flowering basil sprig
    (optional)

1 Prepare Cheesy Polenta (or warm purchased polenta according to package directions, if using). Cover and keep warm.

2 Meanwhile, in a 4-quart pot cook the sweet pepper, onion, and garlic in hot oil over medium heat for 5 minutes, stirring frequently. Add eggplant; cook 5 minutes more, stirring frequently.

3 Stir in summer squash or zucchini, tomato, snipped basil, salt, and pepper. Cover and cook for 5 to 7 minutes more or till vegetables are tender, stirring occasionally. Stir in snipped parsley. To serve, top warm polenta or rice with ratatouille mixture. If desired, sprinkle Parmesan cheese over each serving and garnish with flowering basil. Makes 4 to 6 main-dish servings.

Nutrition facts per serving with Cheesy Polenta: 255 cal., 8 g total fat (1 g sat. fat), 10 mg chol., 570 mg sodium, 37 g carbo., 5 g fiber, 10 g pro.
Daily values: 9% vit. A, 47% vit. C, 16% calcium, 15% iron.

HOW TO RIPEN TOMATOES INDOORS

When tomatoes fall before their time or the first frost spurs you to pick them earlier than their prime, store them at room temperature in a brown paper bag or in a fruit-ripening bowl with other fruits. Keep them in the refrigerator only after they've turned ripe. Don't stand tomatoes in the sun or they'll turn mushy. When ripe, tomatoes will feel slightly soft.

Cheesy Polenta: In a large saucepan bring 2¾ cups *water* to boiling. In a bowl combine 1 cup *cornmeal,* ½ teaspoon *salt,* and 1 cup *cold water.* Slowly add cornmeal mixture to boiling water in saucepan, stirring constantly. Cook and stir till mixture returns to boiling. Add ½ cup shredded *Parmesan cheese;* cook, uncovered, over low heat about 5 minutes or till thick, stirring occasionally. Makes 3 cups.

OUR FAVORITE TORTILLA SOUP

Anaheims and poblano peppers add a lively beat to fresh corn and tomatoes in this aromatic broth.

1 large onion, chopped
4 cloves garlic, minced
2 to 4 fresh Anaheim or
    poblano peppers, seeded
    and chopped
1 Tbsp. cumin seed

2 Tbsp. cooking oil
1½ cups (about 3 ears) fresh cut
    corn kernels
3 medium tomatoes, chopped
2 14½-oz. cans (3½ cups total)
    reduced-sodium chicken
    broth
1½ cups coarsely shredded
    cooked chicken
½ cup snipped fresh cilantro

♦♦♦

2 cups coarsely crushed tortilla
    chips
1 cup shredded Monterey Jack
    cheese (4 oz.) (optional)
    Tortilla chips (optional)
    Lime wedges (optional)
    Fresh cilantro sprigs
    (optional)

1 In a large pot cook onion, garlic, Anaheim or poblano peppers, and cumin seed in hot oil about 5 minutes or till tender, stirring constantly. Add corn kernels, tomatoes, chicken broth, shredded cooked chicken, and the snipped cilantro. Bring mixture to boiling; reduce heat. Simmer, covered, for 10 minutes.

2 To serve, divide crushed tortilla chips among 6 soup bowls. Ladle soup atop chips. If desired, garnish each serving with cheese, extra tortilla chips, lime wedge, and fresh cilantro sprig. Makes 6 main-dish servings.

Nutrition facts per serving: 274 cal., 13 g total fat (2 g sat. fat), 29 mg chol., 504 mg sodium, 26 g carbo., 4 g fiber, 16 g pro. *Daily values:* 7% vit. A, 78% vit. C, 3% calcium, 14% iron.

Freezer-Fresh Vegetables

Freeze garden fresh vegetables and enjoy them up to eight to 12 months later. Follow these tips:

◆ Start with fresh, unbruised produce (straight from the garden is best). Wash thoroughly in cold water.

◆ Prepare vegetables as suggested in chart below. Blanch vegetables to stop or slow the enzymes that can cause loss of flavor and color and toughen the vegetables. To blanch, in a large kettle or pot, bring at least 4 quarts of water to a rapid boil. Place 1 pound of prepared vegetables in a wire basket; lower into water and cover. Start timing immediately (see chart below for timing). Cook on high heat. (Add 1 minute if you live 5,000 feet above sea level or higher). Remove the vegetables and plunge into ice-cold water to chill quickly. Chill for about the same length of time vegetables were boiled; drain.

◆ Transfer vegetables to a freezer container or freezer bag; label and freeze, keeping freezer at 0° or below.

Vegetable	Preparation	Blanching/Freezing
Asparagus	Allow 2½ to 4½ pounds per quart. Wash; scrape off scales. Break off woody bases where spears snap easily. Wash again. Sort by thickness. Leave whole or cut into 1-inch lengths.	Blanch medium spears 3 minutes; cool quickly. Fill containers; shake down, leaving ½-inch headspace.
Beans, green or wax	Allow 1½ to 2½ pounds per quart. Wash; remove ends and strings. Leave whole or snap or cut into 1-inch pieces.	Blanch 3 minutes; cool quickly. Fill containers; shake down, leaving ½-inch headspace.
Broccoli	Allow about 1 pound per pint. Wash; remove outer leaves and tough parts of stalks. Wash again. Cut lengthwise into spears. Cut to fit containers.	Blanch 3 minutes; cool quickly. Package, leaving no headspace.
Cauliflower	Allow 1 to 1½ pounds per pint. Wash; remove leaves and woody stems. Break into 1-inch pieces.	Blanch 3 minutes; cool quickly. Package, leaving no headspace.
Corn, whole kernel	Allow 4 to 5 pounds per quart. Remove husks; scrub with a vegetable brush to remove silks. Wash and drain. Do not cut corn off cobs.	Blanch 6 ears at a time for 4 minutes; cool quickly. Cut corn from cobs at two-thirds depth of kernels; do not scrape. Fill containers, shaking to pack lightly and leaving ½-inch headspace.
Peas	Allow 2 to 2½ pounds per pint. Wash, shell, rinse and drain.	Blanch 1½ minutes; cool quickly. Fill containers; shake down, leaving ½-inch headspace.
Sweet peppers	Wash. Remove stems, seeds, and membranes. Cut into large pieces or leave whole.	Do not blanch. Spread peppers in a single layer on a baking sheet; freeze firm. Fill container, shaking to pack closely and leaving no headspace.
Winter squash and pumpkin	Allow 1½ to 3 pounds per quart. Peel and cut into 1-inch cubes.	Instead of blanching, simmer cubes in 1 to 2 inches of water about 15 minutes or till tender. Drain; place pan in ice water to cool quickly. Mash. Fill containers; shake to pack lightly. Leave ½-inch headspace.

GRILLED VEGETABLES MEDITERRANEAN

Grill this vegetable combo alongside your entrée.

6 dried tomatoes
  (not oil-packed)
2 medium eggplants, peeled
  (if desired) and cut into
  ¾-inch-thick slices
2 medium tomatoes, halved
2 medium onions, cut into
  ½-inch-thick slices
2 medium green sweet
  peppers, halved and
  seeded
¼ cup olive oil or cooking oil

❖❖❖

1 large clove garlic, minced
3 Tbsp. red wine vinegar
2 Tbsp. olive oil or cooking oil
1 to 2 Tbsp. snipped fresh
  parsley
¼ tsp. salt
⅛ tsp. pepper

1 Soak dried tomatoes in *boiling water* for 2 minutes. Drain, finely chop, and set aside.

2 Brush cut surfaces of sliced eggplant, halved tomatoes, sliced onions, and halved sweet peppers with the ¼ cup oil. Place on the grill rack of an uncovered grill. Grill over hot coals about 5 minutes per side or till charred and cooked, turning once. Remove peel from peppers and skin tomatoes. Coarsely chop grilled vegetables and combine in a large bowl.

3 Combine dried tomatoes, garlic, red wine vinegar, the 2 tablespoons oil, parsley, salt, and pepper; mix with vegetables. Serve at room temperature. If making vegetables ahead, chill,

---

TEST KITCHEN TIP

INGREDIENT KNOW-HOW

These tips will help you become familiar with the makings for Asian Gazpacho (see right):

Bitter melon: This green vegetable may remind you of a pebbly skinned cucumber. Scrape out the seeds with a spoon and enjoy the meaty, bitter-tasting skin raw or cooked as you would zucchini.

Daikon: Also called Japanese radish, this large, white vegetable has a peppery flavor. To use, peel off the outer layer as you would a carrot. Chop, slice, or shred to enjoy raw or stir-fried.

Rice vinegar: Compared to most other vinegars, rice vinegar is mild and slightly sweet. Substitute white or cider vinegar, if desired.

Cilantro: This green leafy herb (also known as fresh coriander or Chinese parsley) has a stronger flavor and fragrance than American parsley. Use it sparingly when you first try it. Rinse and snip, as for other herbs, before using. As with all fresh herbs, cilantro is highly perishable; store it in a plastic bag in the refrigerator.

covered. Remove from refrigerator 1 hour before serving to bring to room temperature. Makes 12 side-dish servings.

Nutrition facts per serving: 92 cal., 7 g total fat (1 g sat. fat), 0 mg chol., 72 mg sodium, 8 g carbo., 2 g fiber, 1 g pro.
Daily values: 2% vit. A, 25% vit. C, 3% iron.

LOW FAT

ASIAN GAZPACHO

Serve bowls of this chilled soup as an appetizer or as a light meal along with a sandwich or salad.

4 oz. bitter melon or 1 small
  zucchini

❖❖❖

4 cups chicken broth
1 cup chopped cucumber
1 cup chopped red or green
  sweet pepper
½ cup thinly sliced green
  onions (4)
½ cup chopped celery
½ cup chopped daikon
⅓ cup rice vinegar or white
  wine vinegar
¼ cup snipped fresh cilantro
  (optional)
1 Tbsp. soy sauce
1½ tsp. sesame oil
  Few dashes bottled hot
  pepper sauce
½ cup enoki mushrooms
  (optional)

1 Halve bitter melon lengthwise; remove seeds. Cut bitter melon into thin strips (you should have about 1 cup).

2 In a large bowl combine bitter melon or zucchini, broth, cucumber, sweet pepper, onions, celery, daikon, vinegar, cilantro (if desired), soy sauce, sesame oil, and pepper sauce. Cover and chill 4 hours or overnight. To serve, ladle into soup bowls. If desired, sprinkle with enoki mushrooms. Makes 6 to 8 side-dish servings.

Nutrition facts per serving: 52 cal., 2 g total fat (0 g sat. fat), 1 mg chol., 703 mg sodium, 5 g carbo., 1 g fiber, 4 g pro.
Daily values: 15% vit. A, 58% vit. C, 1% calcium, 5% iron.

CORN WITH SAVORY-LIME BUTTER

8 fresh ears of corn, husked

❖❖❖

½ cup butter or margarine, softened
1 Tbsp. snipped fresh savory or 1 tsp. dried savory or thyme, crushed
1 tsp. finely shredded lime peel

1 Scrub corn with a stiff brush to remove silks. Rinse. Cook, uncovered, in enough lightly salted *boiling water* to cover for 5 to 7 minutes or till tender.

2 Meanwhile, in a small bowl thoroughly combine the butter or margarine, savory, and lime peel. Serve herb butter with hot corn. Store any remaining butter or margarine, covered, in the refrigerator. Makes 8 servings.

Nutrition facts per serving: 184 cal., 12 g total fat (7 g sat. fat), 31 mg chol., 129 mg sodium, 19 g carbo., 3 g fiber, 3 g pro. *Daily values:* 12% vit. A, 8% vit. C, 3% iron.

PARTY FLORENTINE CHICKEN ROLL-UPS

The curry in the stuffing and the basil in the creamy sauce lend interesting flavor to these phyllo-wrapped, stuffed chicken rolls.

6 medium skinless, boneless chicken breast halves

❖❖❖

¼ cup finely chopped fresh mushrooms
2 Tbsp. margarine or butter
2 cups herb-seasoned stuffing mix
¼ cup grated Parmesan cheese
½ tsp. curry powder
⅛ tsp. garlic powder
⅛ tsp. pepper
Chicken broth

❖❖❖

6 sheets frozen phyllo dough (18×14-inch rectangles), thawed
¼ cup margarine or butter, melted

❖❖❖

1⅓ cups half-and-half, light cream, or milk
2 Tbsp. all-purpose flour
¼ tsp. salt
⅛ tsp. pepper
¼ cup shredded fresh spinach
1 Tbsp. snipped fresh basil or ½ tsp. dried basil, crushed

1 Rinse chicken; pat dry. Place chicken breasts between 2 pieces of plastic wrap. Using the flat side of a meat mallet, pound lightly from the center to edges till chicken is ¼ inch thick. Set aside.

2 In a large saucepan cook mushrooms in the 2 tablespoons margarine or butter till tender. Stir in the stuffing mix, Parmesan cheese, curry powder, garlic powder, and the ⅛ teaspoon pepper. Stir in enough chicken broth to moisten (⅓ to ½ cup).

3 To assemble, divide stuffing among chicken breasts. Roll up chicken breasts around stuffing, tucking in sides as you roll.

4 Brush 1 sheet of phyllo with some of the ¼ cup melted margarine or butter. Fold in half crosswise. Brush again with some of the margarine or butter. Place 1 chicken roll on the edge of a short side of the phyllo sheet; roll up, tucking in sides while rolling. Repeat with remaining phyllo sheets and chicken rolls.

5 Place wrapped chicken breasts, seam side down, in a shallow baking pan. Brush each with any remaining melted margarine or butter. Bake in a 375° oven about 45 minutes or till browned and chicken is no longer pink.

6 Meanwhile, for sauce, in a screw-top jar combine half-and-half, cream or milk; flour; salt; and the ⅛ teaspoon pepper. Cover and shake till mixed. Pour into a small saucepan. Cook and stir till mixture is thickened and bubbly; cook and stir for 1 minute more. Stir in spinach and basil. Serve some of the sauce over each chicken roll-up. Makes 6 servings.

Nutrition facts per serving: 456 cal., 24 g total fat (8 g sat. fat), 83 mg chol., 880 mg sodium, 30 g carbo., 0 g fiber, 30 g pro. *Daily values:* 24% vit. A, 2% vit. C, 12% calcium, 16% iron.

TOUCH-OF-GOLD CHICKEN-RICE SALAD

This recipe earned Sally Vog of Springfield, Oregon, $100 in the magazine's monthly contest.

2 cups chicken broth
¾ cup long grain rice
1 Tbsp. margarine or butter
½ tsp. curry powder
2 dashes bottled hot pepper sauce
½ cup sliced celery
¼ cup sliced green onions (2)
2 Tbsp. finely chopped crystallized ginger
2 Tbsp. snipped fresh cilantro

◆◆◆

1½ lb. skinless, boneless chicken breast halves, cut into bite-size strips
1 Tbsp. cooking oil

◆◆◆

Fresh spinach leaves
1 cup sliced, peeled peaches or sliced nectarines
1 recipe Poppy Seed Dressing (see above right)
⅓ cup pistachio nuts, coarsely chopped

1 In saucepan combine broth, *uncooked* rice, margarine, curry powder, and pepper sauce. Bring to boiling; reduce heat. Cover; simmer for 15 minutes or till tender. Remove from heat. Stir in celery, onions, ginger, and cilantro. Cover and let stand for 5 minutes.

2 Season chicken with *salt* and *pepper.* In a large skillet cook chicken, half at a time, in oil over medium-high heat for 2 to 3 minutes or till no longer pink.

Remove from pan. To serve, line plates with spinach. Place rice mixture atop. Arrange chicken and peaches or nectarines on rice. Drizzle with dressing; sprinkle with nuts. Makes 6 main-dish servings.

Poppy Seed Dressing: In a small mixing bowl whisk together ⅓ cup *orange juice,* 3 tablespoons *salad oil,* 1 tablespoon *Dijon-style mustard,* 1 teaspoon *poppy seed,* and 2 to 3 dashes *bottled hot pepper sauce.* Makes about ½ cup.

Nutrition facts per serving: 398 cal., 19 g total fat (3 g sat. fat), 60 mg chol., 416 mg sodium, 29 g carbo., 2 g fiber, 27 g pro. *Daily values:* 12% vit. A, 22% vit. C, 4% calcium, 17% iron.

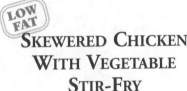

SKEWERED CHICKEN WITH VEGETABLE STIR-FRY

4 medium skinless, boneless chicken breast halves (about 12 oz. total)
¼ cup light teriyaki sauce
¼ cup orange juice
2 Tbsp. rice vinegar
¼ tsp. ground ginger
Dash ground red pepper

◆◆◆

2 tsp. cornstarch
1 Tbsp. cooking oil
2 medium leeks, thinly sliced
4 cups shredded Chinese cabbage
1 small red sweet pepper, chopped
3 cups hot cooked rice

1 Rinse chicken; pat dry. Cut each chicken breast into 4 lengthwise strips. Thread chicken, accordion-style, on 4 skewers. Place in a 2-quart rectangular

Touch-of-Gold
Chicken-Rice Salad
(see left)

◆◆◆

Corn muffins

◆◆◆

Iced tea with lemon

◆◆◆

Strawberry ice cream with sugar cookies

baking dish. Combine teriyaki sauce, orange juice, vinegar, ginger, and ground red pepper; pour over chicken. Cover and refrigerate for 2 to 6 hours, turning occasionally. Remove chicken from marinade; reserve marinade.

2 Place skewers on unheated rack of a broiler pan. Broil 4 to 5 inches from heat 5 minutes. Turn; broil 3 to 5 minutes more or till chicken is tender and not pink.

3 Meanwhile, stir cornstarch into reserved marinade; set aside. Heat oil in a wok or large skillet. Add leeks; stir-fry 2 minutes. Add cabbage and sweet pepper; stir-fry 2 to 3 minutes more or till sweet pepper is crisp-tender. Push vegetables from center of wok; add reserved marinade mixture. Cook and stir till thickened and bubbly. Cook and stir 2 minutes more. Stir all together to coat. Serve vegetables and chicken atop hot cooked rice. Makes 4 servings.

Nutrition facts per serving: 337 cal., 6 g total fat (1 g sat. fat), 45 mg chol., 375 mg sodium, 48 g carbo., 3 g fiber, 22 g pro. *Daily values:* 19% vit. A, 86% vit. C, 8% calcium, 20% iron.

CITRUS-GRILLED CHICKEN

This recipe earned Dolores McSpadden of Grapevine, Texas, $200 in the magazine's monthly contest.

½ tsp. coriander seed
¼ tsp. anise seed

♦♦♦

⅓ cup honey
¼ cup lemon juice
3 Tbsp. orange juice
3 Tbsp. lime juice
2 green onions, thinly sliced
1 tsp. snipped fresh sage
1 tsp. snipped fresh thyme
½ tsp. snipped fresh rosemary
¼ tsp. salt
⅛ tsp. coarsely ground pepper

♦♦♦

1½ lb. skinless, boneless chicken breast halves
Lemon, lime, and/or orange slices (optional)
Fresh rosemary (optional)

1 In a small skillet cook and stir the coriander and anise seed over medium heat for 5 to 7 minutes or till seeds are fragrant and toasted, stirring constantly. Remove skillet from heat. Let cool. Grind spices with a mortar and pestle. Set aside.

2 For marinade, in a large nonmetal bowl combine honey, lemon juice, orange juice, lime juice, green onions, sage, thyme, snipped rosemary, salt, and pepper. Stir in toasted coriander and anise seed.

3 Rinse chicken; pat dry. Add chicken to marinade; turn to coat. Let stand at room temperature for 30 minutes, turning chicken occasionally. Remove chicken from marinade; reserve marinade.

4 Place chicken on the grill rack of an uncovered grill. Grill directly over medium coals for 12 to 15 minutes or till chicken is tender and no longer pink, turning once and brushing occasionally with remaining marinade during the first 10 minutes. If desired, garnish with citrus slices and rosemary. Makes 6 servings.

Nutrition facts per serving: 188 cal., 3 g total fat (1 g sat. fat), 59 mg chol., 144 mg sodium, 18 g carbo., 0 g fiber, 22 g pro. *Daily values:* 1% vit. A, 19% vit. C, 1% calcium, 6% iron.

30 MIN.

CHICKEN CARIBBEAN

Coconut and orange mesh in this simple sauce spiced with Jamaican jerk seasoning.

4 medium skinless, boneless chicken breast halves (about 12 oz. total)
1 Tbsp. margarine or butter

♦♦♦

¼ cup orange juice
½ cup purchased coconut milk
2 Tbsp. snipped fresh basil
½ tsp. Jamaican jerk seasoning

♦♦♦

2 cups hot cooked rice or couscous
1 tsp. finely shredded orange peel (optional)

1 Rinse chicken; pat dry. In a large skillet cook chicken over medium heat in hot margarine or butter about 10 minutes or till tender and no longer pink, turning once. Remove the chicken, reserving pan drippings; keep chicken warm.

2 Carefully stir orange juice into pan, scraping up any browned bits. Stir in coconut milk, basil, and Jamaican jerk seasoning. Bring to boiling; reduce heat. Simmer gently, uncovered, for 2 minutes or till reduced to ½ cup. Return chicken to skillet. Heat through, spooning sauce over chicken.

3 If desired, combine hot cooked rice or couscous and orange peel. Serve chicken and sauce over rice or couscous. Makes 4 servings.

Nutrition facts per serving: 306 cal., 14 g total fat (7 g sat. fat), 45 mg chol., 101 mg sodium, 25 g carbo., 0 g fiber, 19 g pro. *Daily values:* 5% vit. A, 13% vit. C, 2% calcium, 13% iron.

30 MIN.
LOW FAT

POACHED FISH WITH SHERRY-SPINACH SAUCE

Choose a mild-flavored fish, such as orange roughy or sole, for this dish.

12 oz. fresh or frozen, skinless white-fleshed fish fillets, ½ inch thick
Salt

♦♦♦

¼ cup chicken broth
2 Tbsp. dry sherry or chicken broth
2 tsp. rice vinegar or vinegar

♦♦♦

2 Tbsp. water
1 Tbsp. cornstarch
½ cup finely chopped fresh
   spinach
1 Tbsp. diced pimiento

❖❖❖

**Fresh spinach leaves, cut into
thin strips (optional)**

1 Thaw fish, if frozen. Divide the fish fillets into 4 serving-size portions. Rinse fish; pat dry. Sprinkle fish lightly with salt.

2 In a 2-quart square microwave-safe baking dish stir together the chicken broth, sherry or additional chicken broth, and vinegar. Add fish pieces. Turn under any thin portions of fish so total thickness is about ½ inch.

3 Cover dish with microwave-safe plastic wrap, venting 1 corner. Microwave for 3 to 5 minutes or till the fish flakes easily when tested with a fork, giving dish a half turn once. With a slotted spoon, remove fish from baking dish and keep warm, reserving cooking liquid.

4 For the sauce, transfer cooking liquid in the baking dish to a 1-cup microwave-safe measure. In a small dish combine water and cornstarch. Stir cornstarch mixture into chicken broth mixture. Microwave, uncovered, for 1 to 2 minutes or till thickened and bubbly, stirring once or twice. Stir in the ½ cup finely chopped spinach and the pimiento.

5 To serve, line 4 dinner plates with remaining spinach, if desired. Place warm fish atop and spoon on the spinach sauce. Makes 4 servings.

Nutrition facts per serving: 84 cal., 1 g total fat (0 g sat. fat), 32 mg chol., 135 mg sodium, 3 g carbo., 0 g fiber, 14 g pro. *Daily values:* 6% vit. A, 8% vit. C, 1% calcium, 4% iron.

OVEN-FRIED TROUT

4 8- to 10-oz. fresh or frozen
   pan-dressed trout or 1 lb.
   fresh or frozen trout fillets
Nonstick spray coating

❖❖❖

¼ cup skim milk
⅓ cup fine dry bread crumbs
3 to 4 Tbsp. yellow cornmeal
½ tsp. paprika
¼ tsp. garlic powder
¼ tsp. salt
⅛ tsp. pepper
2 Tbsp. margarine or butter,
   melted
1 Tbsp. lemon juice

1 Thaw fish, if frozen. If using fillets, separate fillets, or cut into 4 serving-size portions. Rinse fish; pat dry. Measure thickness of fillets. Set aside. Spray shallow baking pan with nonstick coating.

2 Pour milk into a shallow bowl. In another shallow bowl combine bread crumbs, cornmeal, paprika, garlic powder, salt, and pepper. Dip fish into milk, then roll in crumb mixture. Place fish in prepared pan. Combine melted margarine or butter and lemon juice; drizzle over fish.

FISH AND SEAFOOD BUYING PRIMER

You don't need to be a marine specialist to make smart fish and seafood choices. Here are a few tips to keep in mind at the fresh fish counter.

Whole Fish: Eyes should be clear, bright, and not sunken. The gills should be bright red or pink, the skin should be shiny and elastic, and the scales should be tightly in place.

Fish Fillets and Steaks: Make sure the fish is displayed on a bed of ice. It should have a mild smell not a fishy odor. Avoid fish that is dry around the edges.

Scallops: Select firm, sweet-smelling scallops in thin, cloudy liquid. Don't buy scallops if they are in a thick liquid or have a strong sulfur odor.

Shrimp: Pick fresh shrimp that are moist and firm with translucent flesh and a fresh aroma. Avoid shrimp with an ammonia smell.

3 Bake pan-dressed fish in a 500° oven for 8 to 10 minutes or till golden and fish flakes easily with a fork. For fillets, bake 4 to 6 minutes for each ½ inch of thickness. Makes 4 servings.

Nutrition facts per serving: 209 cal., 9 g total fat (2 g sat. fat), 45 mg chol., 290 mg sodium, 12 g carbo., 1 g fiber, 19 g pro. *Daily values:* 11% vit. A, 7% vit. C, 7% calcium, 14% iron.

PLANNER'S GUIDE TO OUTDOOR GATHERINGS

Parties take a bit of planning in modern America. Yet entertaining crowds outdoors can allow for more relaxed standards than serving smaller numbers at a sit-down dinner party in the dining room. Guests dress more casually and enjoy more casual fare, and you don't have to dust the grass. By following our checklist, your biggest problem should be fending off the compliments.

LOCATION, LOCATION

If you're expecting a cast of hundreds, you might consider reserving space in a local park, state recreation facility, zoo, botanical garden, or other public place; this way, you're usually assured of a shelter in case of rain as well as rest rooms, parking facilities, tables, and water. If guests will number in the dozens, using your own backyard or development's commons makes transportation of food, drink, and decorations easier—and the bad weather back-up plan is built-in. If you have particularly agreeable neighbors, it may be possible to negotiate overflow use of their lawn.

ALL EQUIPPED

Party rental companies can ease the burden of rounding up the props—equipment few households have on hand in large quantities. For orders of $100 or more, or for a slight charge, many will deliver and retrieve rentals. It's wise to place your order at least a month in advance.

Such companies rent tables and chairs (about $120 covers accommodations for 100 guests), tents (a 20×20-foot tent should rent for around $90), beverage stations (about $25 each), portable toilet (about $50), large serving equipment (about $15 each), grills (8-foot length, about $50 each), and urns for coffee or lemonade (about $12 each). Buy, rent, or borrow trash containers. You might check with your church, public library, or school to see if it rents or lends equipment. Consider hiring some teenagers, too—warm bodies to mow the grass, help serve, clear, keep an eye on the ice supply, stash umbrellas, (heaven forbid you should need them), remove trash, and even act as parking valets. Ask neighbors' permission to use their curbs and driveways; if you invite them over, how can they say no? If you are planning music or strings of decorative lights,

corral extra extension cords. Extend invitations well in advance (3 to 4 weeks wins you points from Miss Manners) so people have sufficient time to respond; that way you'll have a better idea about numbers of guests and won't prepare too much or too little food.

STAGE SETTING

Purchase table coverings (inexpensive bedsheets or vinyls are fine; paper is cheaper and makes cleanup easier), plates (remember, those flimsy numbers may be gone with the wind), napkins, cutlery, and cups. Select centerpieces that won't topple in a breeze.

Consider the vital issue of how to keep hot food hot and cold food cold, so memories will center on the good time had and not the trip to the emergency room. Rent hot trays and coolers as needed. Camping coolers filled with ice come in handy to keep beverages and cold dishes chilled, or you can fill washtubs or other large containers. Buy lots of ice—more than you think you'll ever need, because you will.

Ask if the neighbors have empty freezers. Plan activities and stake out turf where people can enjoy them. If your guests include children, a separate play space or napping corner (and a teenager as "camp counselor") can be a blessing. And don't forget to stock up on bug spray or citronella candles.

THE FOOD'S THE THING

In calculating the amount of food you'll need, consider the time of day, length of the party, and ages of the guests. Plan foods that can be presented in large quantities, such as casseroles, fruit bowls, and sheet cakes, rather than a sea of individual servings.

Opt for dishes that don't require precise serving times; skip the ice cream and soufflé. Plan food you can prepare—and properly store at the required temperature—a day or two in advance. Choose items such as beef roast or turkey in sizes that will fit on your grill or into your oven, cook with minimal tending, and slice easily, if required.

Shop a week or more in advance for nonperishable items such as chips and pickles. Many supermarkets have a section with institutional-size containers of foods such as baked beans, potato products, salad dressings, salsa, tomato sauce, and cooked vegetables you might choose to toss into marinated salads.

Cooking for large numbers of people is also a great reason to call on convenience products such as frozen chopped onions, minced garlic, cake and biscuit mixes, bite-size fruits and vegetables that you'll find on your supermarket's salad bar, or the whole chickens spinning on the rotisserie. (Call ahead to reserve, especially if your event falls on a holiday weekend when other cooks want to take a break from cooking.)

When planning to purchase large quantities of cheese or cold cuts, you may save money if you buy several pounds in bulk form (rather than the presliced packages), and then have the deli attendants slice them to your specifications. The supermarket is also a good source for giant sheet cakes and brownies.

Unless you've inherited a talent for multiplying loaves and fishes, you may need some guidelines on quantities to purchase. Count on 1 gallon of fruit juice to produce 32 (4-ounce) servings; 2 gallons of iced tea and lemonade produces 32 (8-ounce) glasses. One pound of coffee makes 56 cups.

Figure on 1 ounce per serving for potato chips, corn chips, mixed nuts, creamy dip, and pretzels.

Stock up on beverages well in advance. If you plan to serve alcoholic beverages, your dealer can help you figure the quantities you'll need and also can offer advice on what's popular (at parties, white wine usually disappears twice as fast as red wine, for instance). Ask if the store will take back unopened bottles as a safeguard against running short. Be sure to offer a selection of juices, soft drinks, and bottled waters.

List any preparation equipment, serving dishes, and utensils that will be needed, and make a grocery list for perishable ingredients. Should you feel comfortable drafting friends to help, supply them with the recipes you've chosen for the party.

COUNTDOWN

Day Before: Mow the lawn. Assemble food and beverage serving stations, and set out nonfood items. Position trash containers. Set up chairs and tables. Prepare cold food and get a start on hot items, or pull prepared dishes from the freezer to thaw in the refrigerator. Contact any assistants to run through their responsibilities. Take the kids out for pizza so they won't mess up your kitchen.

Party Day: Attach table coverings with clips or tape. Position centerpieces and other decorations. Complete food preparation. Spray the yard or set out candles. Shower and change. Practice saying, "Oh, it was nothing; glad you enjoyed yourselves."

LOW FAT

LIME-SHRIMP KABOBS

Brighten up your buffet table with a trayful of colorful fruit and tangy, lime-marinated shrimp skewers.

12 oz. fresh or frozen peeled, deveined, and cooked large shrimp
1 tsp. finely shredded lime peel
1/3 cup lime juice
1/4 cup salad oil
2 Tbsp. snipped fresh cilantro or parsley

1 fresh jalapeño pepper, seeded and finely chopped, or 1 Tbsp. canned chopped jalapeño peppers
1 clove garlic, minced

♦♦♦

2 cups assorted fruit pieces, such as papaya chunks, kiwifruit chunks, red grapes, and/or orange sections

1 Thaw shrimp, if frozen. For marinade, in a medium mixing bowl stir together lime peel, lime juice, salad oil, cilantro or parsley, jalapeño pepper, and garlic. Add shrimp to marinade; toss to coat. Cover and chill for 2 hours.

2 Drain shrimp, reserving marinade. On each of twelve 6-inch skewers, thread 2 or 3 pieces of shrimp and 2 or 3 pieces of fruit. Drizzle with remaining marinade. Serve immediately or cover and chill for up to 2 hours. Makes 12 kabobs.

Nutrition facts per kabob: 85 cal., 5 g total fat (1 g sat. fat), 55 mg chol., 64 mg sodium, 4 g carbo., 0 g fiber, 6 g pro. *Daily values:* 4% vit. A, 33% vit. C, 1% calcium, 6% iron.

CHAMPAGNE SAUCE

This recipe earned Claire Karl, of Sparta, Wisconsin, $200 in the magazine's monthly contest.

1 cup champagne*
½ cup whipping cream
♦♦♦
2 beaten egg yolks
1 Tbsp. snipped fresh chives
⅛ tsp. salt
⅛ tsp. coarsely ground pepper

1 In a 2-quart saucepan bring champagne to boiling; reduce heat. Simmer, uncovered, about 8 minutes or till liquid measures ½ cup. Add whipping cream; cook over medium heat about 8 minutes more or till reduced to ⅔ cup. (Watch carefully to be sure the mixture does not boil over.)

2 Gradually stir hot mixture into egg yolks; return all to saucepan. Cook and stir just till boiling. Add chives, salt, and pepper. Serve over fish or chicken. Makes about ¾ cup.

***Note:** Use a 375-milliliter bottle of champagne (about 1½ cups) to make this sauce.

Nutrition facts per tablespoon: 57 cal., 5 g total fat (3 g sat. fat), 49 mg chol., 27 mg sodium, 1 g carbo., 0 g fiber, 1 g pro. *Daily values:* 9% vit. A.

HORSERADISH CREAM SAUCE

If you like, double the amount of sauce and serve the fluffy mixture with a roast beef dinner.

2 to 3 Tbsp. grated fresh horseradish or well-drained prepared horseradish
1 Tbsp. mayonnaise or salad dressing
1 clove garlic, minced
½ tsp. dry mustard
½ tsp. vinegar
¼ tsp. sugar
⅛ tsp. salt
⅛ tsp. ground black pepper
♦♦♦
¼ cup whipping cream

1 In a medium mixing bowl stir together the horseradish, mayonnaise or salad dressing, garlic, dry mustard, vinegar, sugar, salt, and pepper.

2 In a small mixing bowl beat whipping cream with an electric mixer till soft peaks form. Fold into the horseradish mixture. Cover and chill at least 1 hour before serving. Serve with sliced, chilled cooked meat, poultry, or salmon, or steamed vegetables. Makes 1 cup.

Nutrition facts per tablespoon: 21 cal., 2 g total fat (1 g sat. fat), 6 mg chol., 23 mg sodium, 1 g carbo., 0 g fiber, 0 g pro. *Daily values:* 1% vit. A, 2% vit. C.

THE CLEVER COOK

A NATURAL CENTERPIECE

For a recent shower, I needed a flower arrangement. To keep the costs down, I took a basket with me to the local nursery and filled it with little pots of herbs, flowers, and ground covers for around $20. It was a hit at the party and better yet, I planted everything afterward, so now I can enjoy it all summer long.

Dale Craft
Wawarsing, New York

FRESH SALSA

Remove the thin, papery brown husk before chopping the tomatillos.

2 tomatoes, chopped (1½ cups)
2 tomatillos, chopped (½ cup)
½ cup chopped roasted red pepper
¼ cup chopped fresh cilantro
¼ cup chopped red onion
1 fresh jalapeño pepper, seeded and finely chopped
1 fresh small serrano chili pepper, seeded and finely chopped
2 tsp. olive oil
2 tsp. red wine vinegar
1 tsp. lime juice
1 tsp. lemon juice
½ tsp. ground cumin
⅛ tsp. salt

1 In a large mixing bowl combine tomatoes, tomatillos, roasted red pepper, cilantro, onion, jalapeño pepper, serrano pepper, oil, red wine vinegar, lime juice, lemon juice, cumin, and salt. Cover and chill for at least 1 hour. Makes about 2½ cups.

Nutrition facts per tablespoon: 6 cal., 0 g total fat, 0 mg chol., 8 mg sodium, 1 g carbo., 0 g fiber, 0 g pro.
Daily values: 1% vit. A, 13% vit. C.

Zesty Avocado Salsa

1 medium avocado, halved, seeded, peeled, and finely chopped
1 large tomato, peeled and finely chopped
2 green onions, finely chopped
1 tsp. finely shredded lemon peel
2 Tbsp. lemon juice
2 Tbsp. snipped fresh cilantro
1 fresh small Anaheim pepper, seeded and finely chopped
1 fresh jalapeño pepper, seeded and finely chopped
⅛ tsp. salt
⅛ tsp. pepper
Tortilla chips (optional)

1 In a medium mixing bowl combine avocado, tomato, green onions, lemon peel, lemon juice, snipped cilantro, Anaheim pepper, jalapeño pepper, salt, and pepper. Cover and chill for 1 to 2 hours. If desired, serve with tortilla chips. Makes about 2 cups.

Nutrition facts per tablespoon: 12 cal., 1 g total fat (0 g sat. fat), 0 mg chol., 9 mg sodium, 1 g carbo., 0 g fiber, 0 g pro.
Daily values: 1% vit. A, 6% vit. C.

COFFEE: ICED IS NICE

Refresh with a tall, cool glass of iced coffee, the "hot" drink for warm weather. Drink the beverage straight on the rocks or make the creamy variations.

ICED COFFEE

3 cups hot strong coffee
2 to 3 Tbsp. sugar (optional)
Ice cubes

Pour hot coffee into a nonmetal container. Cover; cool to room temperature. (Do not refrigerate or coffee may become cloudy.) To serve, stir desired amount of sugar into cooled coffee. Pour over ice in tall glasses. If desired, garnish each glass with a wedge of *orange.* Makes 4 (6-ounce) servings.

Nutrition facts per serving: 0 cal., 0 g total fat, 0 mg chol., 2 mg sodium, 0 g carbo., 0 g fiber, 0 g pro.

Iced Cappuccino: Add 1 teaspoon *vanilla* to the cooled coffee. Sweeten to taste. Pour the beverage over ice in glasses. Pour about 3 tablespoons *half-and-half* or *light cream* into each glass. Makes 4 (6-ounce) servings.

Nutrition facts per serving: 63 cal., 5 g total fat (3 g sat. fat), 15 mg chol., 24 mg sodium, 4 g carbo., 0 g fiber, 2 g pro.

Iced Café Mocha: Add ½ cup *half-and-half* or *light cream* and ¼ cup *chocolate-flavored syrup* to the cooled coffee. Sweeten to taste. Serve the beverage over ice. Makes 4 (7-ounce) servings.

Nutrition facts per serving: 88 cal., 4 g total fat (2 g sat. fat), 11 mg chol., 29 mg sodium, 14 g carbo., 0 g fiber, 2 g pro.

SOUTHWEST CANTALOUPE SALSA

1⅓ cups finely chopped cantaloupe
½ cup peeled and finely chopped jicama
⅓ cup finely chopped red or green sweet pepper
3 Tbsp. lime juice
4 tsp. finely chopped red onion
1 to 2 Tbsp. snipped fresh cilantro
1 fresh serrano chili pepper, seeded and finely chopped
¼ tsp. sugar

1 In a medium mixing bowl combine cantaloupe, jicama, sweet pepper, lime juice, red onion, cilantro, serrano pepper, sugar, dash *salt,* and, if desired, a few dashes *bottled hot pepper sauce.* Cover and chill for 2 to 24 hours. Serve with grilled fish, pork, or chicken. Makes about 2¼ cups.

Nutrition facts per tablespoon: 4 cal., 0 g total fat, 0 mg chol., 4 mg sodium, 1 g carbo., 0 g fiber, 0 g pro.
Daily values: 3% vit. A, 9% vit. C

30 MIN. LOW FAT

FRUIT BRÛLÉE

4 cups seeded watermelon balls
1 cup sliced nectarines
1 banana, bias-sliced
¼ cup orange liqueur or orange juice
1 8-oz. carton light dairy sour cream
2 tsp. finely shredded lime peel
½ cup sugar

1 Arrange fruit in 4 dessert bowls. Drizzle with orange liqueur or orange juice. Combine sour cream and lime peel; spoon ¼ cup onto each serving.

2 Place sugar in a heavy medium skillet. Cook over medium-high heat, uncovered, without stirring, just till the sugar begins to melt and bubble, shaking the skillet occasionally to heat evenly. Reduce heat to medium-low; cook about 5 minutes more or till sugar is melted and golden; stir occasionally with a wooden spoon after sugar begins to melt. Remove skillet from heat. Quickly and carefully drizzle caramelized sugar atop each serving. Serve immediately. Serves 4.

Nutrition facts per serving: 294 cal., 5 g total fat (2 g sat. fat), 7 mg chol., 68 mg sodium, 57 g carbo., 1 g fiber, 5 g pro. *Daily values:* 14% vit. A, 33% vit. C, 6% calcium, 2% iron.

PRIZE TESTED RECIPE WINNER

FRESH PEACH SALSA

This recipe earned Ellen M. Forgett of Seattle, Washington, $100 in the magazine's monthly contest.

2 cups chopped, peeled peaches
¼ cup chopped onion
3 Tbsp. lime juice
2 to 3 Tbsp. finely chopped, seeded fresh jalapeño peppers
1 Tbsp. snipped fresh cilantro
1 clove garlic, minced
½ tsp. sugar

1 In a mixing bowl combine peaches, onion, lime juice, jalapeño peppers, cilantro, garlic, and sugar. Cover and chill for 1 to 2 hours. Serve with tortilla chips, grilled pork, chicken, fish, or Mexican dishes. Makes 2 cups.

Nutrition facts per tablespoon: 6 cal., 0 g total fat, 0 mg chol., 0 mg sodium, 2 g carbo., 0 g fiber, 0 g pro. *Daily values:* 4% vit. C.

IS IT RIPE?

Thumping a watermelon will leave you clueless. Instead, look for an even coat of pale-to-dark-green rind with a creamy yellow patch on the underside. A watermelon's shape should be symmetrical; avoid fruit with soft ends. If you buy slices, choose those with firm, brightly colored, juicy flesh; avoid sections with white streaks, holes, cracks, or a mealy look.

30 MIN. LOW FAT

BELLA MELONE

It simply means "beautiful melon," but the Italians say it best. The secret is in the vinegar, and not just any kind will do. Balsamic vinegar boasts a rich, mellow note that wakes up summer's lazy taste buds.

2 cups chilled, seeded, and cubed watermelon
2 cups chilled, seeded, and cubed cantaloupe
1 to 2 tsp. sugar
¼ cup balsamic vinegar
1 tsp. fresh ground pepper (optional)

1 Divide chilled watermelon and cantaloupe among 4 dessert dishes. Stir sugar into vinegar till dissolved. Drizzle some of the vinegar mixture over each serving. Sprinkle with fresh ground pepper, if desired. Serves 4.

Nutrition facts per serving: 73 cal., 1 g total fat (0 g sat. fat), 0 mg chol., 11 mg sodium, 17 g carbo., 1 g fiber, 1 g pro. *Daily values:* 28% vit. A, 73% vit. C, 1% calcium, 5% iron.

SEPTEMBER
Home Cooking at Its Best

IN THIS CHAPTER

30-minute recipes indicated in RED.
Low-fat recipes indicated with a ♥.

America's best-selling cookbook, the red plaid Better Homes and Gardens® New Cook Book *celebrates its 11th edition this year. Readers depend on it for yesterday's favorites such as Chicken Potpies, German Chocolate Cake, and Fried Green Tomatoes. For today's lifestyles, we've updated many classics, such as Low-Fat Berry Marble Cheesecake and Grilled Chicken Salad. And we're always looking to tomorrow's flavors, with recipes such as Onion and Olive Focaccia and Orange-Rosemary Pound Cake.*

Favorites from Yesterday

There are certain recipes that both newlyweds and mothers-in-law expect to find in a kitchen resource like our red plaid Better Homes and Gardens® New Cook Book. *So the 1996 edition stands by tradition with plenty of golden oldies ready to nourish your cravings for comfort food.*

CHICKEN POTPIES

See the photograph on page 193.

1 recipe Pastry for Double-Crust Pie or Pastry for Single-Crust Pie (see right)
♦♦♦
1 10-oz. pkg. frozen mixed vegetables
½ cup chopped onion
½ cup chopped fresh mushrooms
¼ cup margarine or butter
⅓ cup all-purpose flour
¾ tsp. dried sage, marjoram, or thyme, crushed
½ tsp. salt
⅛ to ¼ tsp. pepper
2 cups chicken broth
¾ cup milk
3 cups cubed cooked chicken or turkey (1 lb.)
¼ cup snipped fresh parsley
¼ cup chopped pimiento
Milk
Sesame seed (optional)

1 Prepare Pastry for Double-Crust Pie to make 6 individual casseroles or Pastry for Single-Crust Pie to make 1 casserole; set aside.

2 Cook frozen vegetables according to package directions; drain. In a medium saucepan cook onion and mushrooms in hot margarine or butter till tender. Stir in the flour; sage, marjoram, or thyme; salt; and pepper. Add broth and ¾ cup milk all at once. Cook and stir till thickened and bubbly. Stir in the chicken, parsley, pimiento, and vegetables; cook and stir till bubbly. Pour chicken mixture into six 10-ounce casseroles or a 2-quart round casserole.

3 For the 6 individual casseroles, roll out double-crust pastry to a 15×10-inch rectangle; cut into six 5-inch circles. For the 2-quart casserole, roll out single-crust pastry to a 10-inch circle. Cut out shapes or cut slits in center(s) of pastry circle(s). Place crusts on top of casserole(s). Flute edges. Brush with milk; top with cutouts, if using. If desired, sprinkle with sesame seed.

4 Bake in a 450° oven till pastry is golden brown, allowing 12 to 15 minutes for individual casseroles or 15 to 20 minutes for large casserole. Makes 6 servings.

Nutrition facts per serving: 638 cal., 38 g total fat (9 g sat. fat), 70 mg chol., 820 mg sodium, 43 g carbo., 3 g fiber, 31 g pro. *Daily values:* 52% vit. A, 25% vit. C, 6% calcium, 27% iron.

Biscuit-Topped Chicken Pot-pies: Prepare potpies as directed at left, except omit pastry. Cut dough rounds from 1 package (6) *refrigerated biscuits* into quarters; arrange atop bubbly chicken mixture in casserole(s). Bake in a 400° oven 15 minutes or till biscuits are golden.

PASTRY FOR DOUBLE-CRUST PIE

Make the two-crust pastry for the individual potpies or the single crust for the casserole. Or, save a little time and use one or two refrigerated piecrusts.

2 cups all-purpose flour
½ tsp. salt
⅔ cup shortening
6 to 7 Tbsp. cold water

1 In a mixing bowl stir together flour and salt. Using a pastry blender, cut in shortening till pieces are the size of small peas. Sprinkle 1 tablespoon of the cold water over part of the mixture; gently toss with a fork. Push to side of bowl. Repeat, using 1 tablespoon water at a time, till all is moistened. Divide in half. Form each half into a ball.

Pastry for Single-Crust Pie: Prepare pastry as directed above, except only use 1¼ cups all-purpose flour, ¼ teaspoon salt, ⅓ cup shortening, and 4 to 5 tablespoons cold water.

Inset: *Espresso Chocolate Pots de Crème (page 211) and Lemon-Poppy Seed Biscotti (page 212)*
Below: *Chicken Potpies (page 192)*

Above: *Fried Green Tomatoes*
(page 202)
Right: *Grilled Chicken Salad (page 204)*
with Ginger Vinaigrette (page 205)

Above: *Low-Fat Berry Marble Cheesecake (page 203)*
Left: *Cracked Wheat Bread (page 204)*

Page 198: *Swiss Steak (page 202)*
Top: *Fresh Tomato Soup with cilantro (page 206)*
Above: *Grilled Fish Sandwich on focaccia (page 205)*

Above: *German Chocolate Cake (page 201)*
Right: *Orange-Rosemary Pound Cake (page 207)*

GERMAN CHOCOLATE CAKE

Make this classic temptation extra-yummy by frosting the sides of the cake with creamy chocolate frosting. (See the photograph on page 200.)

1 4-oz. pkg. sweet baking chocolate
1½ cups all-purpose flour
¾ tsp. baking soda
¼ tsp. salt

♦♦♦

1 cup sugar
¾ cup shortening
3 eggs
1 tsp. vanilla
¾ cup buttermilk or sour milk*
1 recipe Coconut-Pecan Frosting (see right)
1 recipe Chocolate Butter Frosting (see right) (optional)

1 In a heavy saucepan heat chocolate and ½ cup *water* over low heat till chocolate is melted, stirring to blend; cool. Grease and flour two 8×1½- or 9×1½-inch round baking pans. Combine flour, soda, and salt; set aside.

2 In a large mixing bowl beat sugar and shortening with an electric mixer on medium speed till fluffy. Add eggs and vanilla; beat on low speed till combined. Beat 1 minute on medium speed. Beat in chocolate mixture. Add flour mixture alternately with buttermilk, beating on low speed after each addition till combined.

3 Spread batter evenly in prepared pans. Bake in a 350° oven about 30 minutes for 9-inch layers, 35 to 40 minutes for 8-inch layers, or till a toothpick inserted near center comes out clean. Cool in pans 10 minutes on wire racks. Remove from pans; cool completely on wire racks.

4 To assemble, place 1 cake layer on a serving plate. Spread *half* the Coconut-Pecan Frosting on top; repeat layers. If desired, frost sides with Chocolate Butter Frosting. Chill till ready to serve. Makes 12 servings.

*Note: To make sour milk, place 1 tablespoon *lemon juice or vinegar* in a glass measuring cup. Add enough *milk* to make 1 cup total liquid; stir. Let stand for 5 minutes before using.

Coconut-Pecan Frosting: In a saucepan slightly beat 1 *egg*. Stir in one 5-ounce can (⅔ cup) *evaporated milk*, ⅔ cup *sugar*, and ¼ cup *butter or margarine*. Cook and stir over medium heat 12 minutes or till thickened and bubbly. Remove from heat. Stir in 1⅓ cups *coconut* and ½ cup chopped *pecans*. Cool slightly; cover and cool thoroughly.

Nutrition facts per serving with Coconut-Pecan Frosting only: 470 cal., 29 g total fat (11 g sat. fat), 85 mg chol., 214 mg sodium, 51 g carbo., 2 g fiber, 6 g pro. *Daily values:* 7% vit. A, 3% vit. C, 5% calcium, 9% iron.

Chocolate Butter Frosting: Beat ⅓ cup *butter or margarine* with an electric mixer till fluffy. Slowly add 2 cups sifted *powdered sugar* and ½ cup *unsweetened cocoa powder*. Beat in ¼ cup *milk* and 1½ teaspoons *vanilla*. Beat in 2 cups sifted *powdered sugar*. Beat in additional *milk*, if needed, to make the frosting easy to spread.

BAKING POWDER BISCUITS

Who can resist a flaky biscuit warm from the oven? This comfort food is easy to re-create and quicker, too, when you use the drop biscuit version, below.

2 cups all-purpose flour
1 Tbsp. baking powder
¼ to ½ tsp. salt
⅓ cup shortening
¾ cup milk

1 In a mixing bowl combine flour, baking powder, and salt. Cut in shortening till mixture resembles coarse crumbs. Make a well in center. Add milk all at once. Stir just till moistened.

2 Turn dough out onto a lightly floured surface. Quickly knead dough by gently folding and pressing dough 10 to 12 strokes or till nearly smooth. Pat or lightly roll dough to ½-inch thickness. Cut dough with a floured 2½-inch biscuit cutter. Place biscuits 1 inch apart on an ungreased baking sheet. Bake in a 450° oven 10 to 12 minutes or till golden. Remove from baking sheet; serve warm. Makes 10.

Nutrition facts per biscuit: 153 cal., 7 g total fat (2 g sat. fat), 1 mg chol., 225 mg sodium, 19 g carbo., 1 g fiber, 3 g pro. *Daily values:* 1% vit. A, 10% calcium, 8% iron.

Drop Biscuits: Prepare biscuits as directed above, except increase milk to 1 cup. Do not knead, roll, or cut dough. Using a large spoon, drop dough into 12 mounds on a greased baking sheet. Bake as directed. Makes 12.

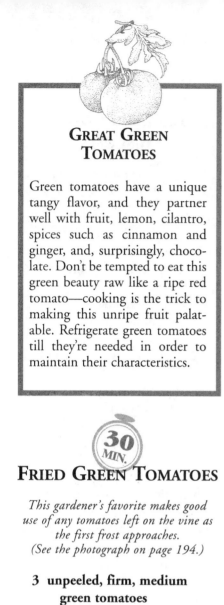

GREAT GREEN TOMATOES

Green tomatoes have a unique tangy flavor, and they partner well with fruit, lemon, cilantro, spices such as cinnamon and ginger, and, surprisingly, chocolate. Don't be tempted to eat this green beauty raw like a ripe red tomato—cooking is the trick to making this unripe fruit palatable. Refrigerate green tomatoes till they're needed in order to maintain their characteristics.

30 MIN.
FRIED GREEN TOMATOES

This gardener's favorite makes good use of any tomatoes left on the vine as the first frost approaches.
(See the photograph on page 194.)

3 unpeeled, firm, medium
    green tomatoes
¼ to ⅓ cup milk
½ cup all-purpose flour
2 eggs, beaten
¾ cup fine dry bread crumbs
   ♦♦♦
¼ cup cooking oil

1 Cut tomatoes into ½-inch-thick slices. Sprinkle both sides of each slice with *salt* and *pepper*. Dip slices into milk, then into flour. Dip into eggs, then into bread crumbs.

2 In a 10-inch skillet cook *half* of the slices at a time in hot oil over medium heat 8 to 10 minutes on each side or till brown. (If tomatoes begin to

brown too quickly, reduce heat to medium-low.) Add more *oil*, if needed. Season with *salt* and *pepper*. Makes 6 servings.

Nutrition facts per serving: 176 cal., 11 g total fat (2 g sat. fat), 72 mg chol., 87 mg sodium, 14 g carbo., 1 g fiber, 5 g pro. *Daily values:* 7% vit. A, 24% vit. C, 2% calcium, 7% iron.

SWISS STEAK

Convenient oven and crockery cooker directions update this favorite. Also, we've reduced the salt and fat content. (See the photograph on page 198.)

1 lb. boneless beef round
    steak, cut ¾ inch thick
2 Tbsp. all-purpose flour
¼ tsp. salt
¼ tsp. pepper
   ♦♦♦
1 Tbsp. cooking oil
1 14½-oz. can tomatoes,
    cut up
1 small onion, sliced and
    separated into rings
½ cup sliced celery (1 stalk)
½ cup sliced carrot (1 medium)
½ tsp. dried thyme, crushed
2 cups hot cooked noodles
    or rice

1 Trim fat from meat. Cut into 4 serving-size pieces. Combine flour, salt, and pepper. Using the notched side of a meat mallet, evenly pound the flour mixture into the meat.

2 In a large skillet brown meat on both sides in hot oil. Drain off fat. Add undrained tomatoes, onion, celery, carrot, and thyme. Bring to boiling; reduce heat. Simmer, covered, about 1¼ hours or till meat is tender. Skim off fat.

Menu

Swiss Steak with hot cooked noodles (see left)
♦♦♦
Buttered julienned carrots
♦♦♦
Mixed salad greens with your choice of dressing
♦♦♦
Fruit crisp à la mode

Serve with hot cooked noodles or rice. Makes 4 servings.

Nutrition facts per serving with noodles: 352 cal., 9 g total fat (2 g sat. fat), 72 mg chol., 404 mg sodium, 34 g carbo., 2 g fiber, 31 g pro. *Daily values:* 49% vit. A, 33% vit. C, 5% calcium, 31% iron.

OVEN DIRECTIONS

Prepare and brown meat as directed at left. Transfer meat to a 2-quart square baking dish. In same skillet combine undrained tomatoes, onion, celery, carrot, and thyme. Bring to boiling, scraping up any browned bits in pan. Pour over meat. Cover and bake in a 350° oven about 1 hour or till tender. Serve as directed.

CROCKERY COOKER

Omit flouring and pounding meat. Brown meat in hot oil. In a 3½- or 4-quart electric crockery cooker place onion, celery, and carrot. Sprinkle with thyme, 2 tablespoons *quick-cooking tapioca*, salt, and pepper. Pour undrained tomatoes over vegetables; add meat. Cover and cook on low-heat setting for 10 to 12 hours. Serve as directed.

Eating for Today

*N*o question about it—great taste at mealtime is an
absolute must. But today we'd also like our cooking
to be healthful, fast, fresh, and convenient. And,
because we don't want to give up our favorite foods, we
search for ways to cut the fat but not the flavor.
Take cheesecake. By relying on low-fat ingredients, a
classic dessert becomes guilt-free.

CHEESECAKE SUPREME

*When cheesecake came on the scene in
the 1940s, who'd have believed it
would someday surpass apple pie as
America's favorite dessert?
(See the photograph on page 197.)*

1¾ **cups finely crushed graham
     crackers**
¼ **cup finely chopped walnuts**
½ **tsp. ground cinnamon**
½ **cup butter, melted**
◆◆◆
3 **8-oz. pkg. cream cheese**
1 **cup sugar**
2 **Tbsp. all-purpose flour**
1 **tsp. vanilla**
½ **tsp. finely shredded lemon
    peel (optional)**
2 **eggs**
1 **egg yolk**
¼ **cup milk**

1 For crust, in a medium
mixing bowl stir together crushed
graham crackers, walnuts, and
cinnamon. Stir in butter. If
desired, reserve ¼ *cup* for topping.
Press remaining crumb mixture
onto   bottom   and   about
2 inches up sides of an 8- or
9-inch springform pan; set aside.

2 For filling, soften cream
cheese. In a large mixing bowl
combine cream cheese, sugar,
flour, vanilla, and lemon peel (if
using); beat with an electric mixer
on medium speed till combined.
Add whole eggs and egg yolk all at
once, beating on low speed just
till combined (do not overbeat).
Stir in milk.

3 Pour filling into crust-lined
pan. If desired, top with reserved
crumbs. Place on a shallow baking
pan. Bake in a 375° oven for 45 to
50 minutes for 8-inch pan, 35 to
40 minutes for 9-inch pan, or till
center appears nearly set when
shaken gently.

4 Cool in the pan on a wire
rack for 15 minutes. Use a sharp,
thin bladed knife to loosen the
crust from the sides of the pan;
cool for 30 minutes more.
Remove the sides of the pan; cool
cheesecake completely. Cover and
chill at least 4 hours before
serving. Makes 12 to 16 servings.

Nutrition facts per serving: 429 cal., 32 g
total fat (18 g sat. fat), 137 mg chol., 329
mg sodium, 30 g carbo., 1 g fiber, 7 g pro.
Daily values: 35% vit. A, 5% calcium,
10% iron.

**Low-Fat Berry Marble Cheese-
cake:** Prepare cheesecake as
directed at left, except for crust
reduce graham crackers to ⅓ cup;
omit walnuts and butter. Sprinkle
cracker mixture onto bottom and
sides of a well-greased 8- or 9-inch
springform pan.

For filling, substitute three
8-ounce packages *nonfat cream
cheese* for the regular cream
cheese; ½ cup *refrigerated or frozen
egg product (thawed)* for the eggs
and egg yolk. Continue as directed. If desired, top cheesecake with
nonfat sour cream; spoon on
seedless red raspberry preserves and
swirl with a spoon.

Chocolate Cheesecake: Prepare cheesecake as directed at left,
except omit lemon peel. Melt
4 ounces *semisweet chocolate.* Beat
melted chocolate into filling
mixture just before adding eggs.

Chocolate Swirl Cheesecake:
Prepare cheesecake as directed at
left, except omit lemon peel. Melt
2 ounces *semisweet chocolate.* Stir
the melted chocolate into *half* of
the filling. Pour chocolate filling
into the crust; pour plain filling
into the crust. Use a spatula to
gently swirl fillings.

Sour Cream Cheesecake: Prepare cheesecake as directed at left,
except reduce cream cheese to
2 packages and omit the milk.
Add three 8-ounce cartons *dairy
sour cream* with the eggs. Bake
about 55 minutes for an 8-inch
pan (about 50 minutes for a
9-inch pan).

CRACKED WHEAT BREAD

With today's increased focus on fiber, eating a combination of new and different grains in familiar foods is an easy way to boost fiber in your diet. (See the photograph on page 196.)

2 cups boiling water
1 cup cracked wheat or bulgur

♦♦♦

3¾ to 4¼ cups all-purpose flour
1 pkg. active dry yeast
1¾ cups water
¼ cup sugar
1 Tbsp. margarine or butter
1 tsp. salt
1¼ cups whole wheat flour
¼ cup unprocessed wheat bran

1 In a medium saucepan combine the 2 cups boiling water and cracked wheat or bulgur. Let stand, covered, for 5 minutes. Drain well, discarding liquid. Set cracked wheat or bulgur aside.

2 In a large mixing bowl combine *1½ cups* of the all-purpose flour and the yeast; set aside. In a medium saucepan heat and stir 1¾ cups water, sugar, margarine or butter, and salt just till warm (120° to 130°) and margarine or butter is almost melted. Add water mixture to flour mixture. Beat with an electric mixer on low speed 30 seconds, scraping sides of bowl. Beat on high speed for 3 minutes. Using a wooden spoon, stir in cracked wheat or bulgur, whole wheat flour, and bran. Stir in as much remaining all-purpose flour as you can.

3 Turn the dough out onto a lightly floured surface. Knead in enough of the remaining all-purpose flour to make a moderately

stiff dough that is smooth and elastic (6 to 8 minutes total). Shape the dough into a ball. Place the dough in a lightly greased bowl, turning once to grease the dough surface. Cover and let rise in a warm place till double in size (about 1¼ hours).

4 Punch dough down. Turn dough out onto a lightly floured surface. Divide dough in half. Cover and let rest for 10 minutes.

5 Lightly grease two 8×4×2-inch loaf pans. Shape each portion of dough into a loaf. Place in the prepared loaf pans. Cover and let the dough rise in a warm place till nearly double in size (30 to 40 minutes).

6 Bake in a 375° oven for 35 to 40 minutes or till the bread sounds hollow when you tap the top with your fingers (if necessary, cover the bread loosely with foil the last 10 minutes of baking to prevent overbrowning). Immediately remove the bread from pans. Cool on wire racks. Makes 2 loaves (32 servings).

Nutrition facts per serving: 80 cal., 1 g total fat (0 g sat. fat), 0 mg chol., 71 mg sodium, 16 g carbo., 1 g fiber, 2 g pro.
Daily values: 6% iron.

Menu

Grilled Chicken Salad (see right)

♦♦♦

Crisp breadsticks

♦♦♦

Angel food cake slices with raspberry sorbet

GRILLED CHICKEN SALAD

The buzzwords today are fresh, fast, tropical, and grilled. This sizzling chicken salad has it all. (See the photograph on page 194.)

4 small boneless, skinless chicken breast halves
2 cups green and/or yellow wax beans (optional)

♦♦♦

4 to 6 cups torn or shredded mixed greens, such as leaf lettuce, flowering kale, curly endive, or spinach
4 cups cut-up fresh fruit, such as mango, carambola (star fruit), peaches, nectarines, kiwifruit, strawberries, or grapes
¼ cup chopped red onion (optional)
Toasted coconut (optional)
Cracked black pepper (optional)
1 recipe Ginger Vinaigrette or Creamy Honey-Lime Dressing (see page 205)

1 Rinse chicken; pat dry. Grill chicken on an uncovered grill directly over medium coals 12 to 15 minutes, turning once. (Or, place chicken on the unheated rack of a broiler pan. Broil 4 to 5 inches from heat 9 minutes or till no longer pink, turning once.)

2 Meanwhile, if desired, cook beans, covered, in a small amount of boiling water for 8 to 10 minutes or till crisp-tender; drain.

3 To serve, slice each grilled chicken breast crosswise into thin pieces. Line 4 plates with mixed greens. Top with chicken, cooked

Flavors for Tomorrow

*W*hat we cook and how we season it evolve over time. The future looks incredibly delicious, thanks to an influx of new ethnic ingredients, innovative and influential chefs, and agricultural advances. Five years ago, you would have had to visit faraway places to taste Jamaican jerk seasoning or focaccia. Now this Caribbean seasoning and Italian flat bread are almost as common as pepper and white bread.

beans (if using), and fruit. If desired, top with onion, coconut, and black pepper. Serve with Ginger Vinaigrette or Creamy Honey-Lime Dressing. Makes 4 main-dish servings.

Ginger Vinaigrette: In a blender container or food processor bowl, combine 1 cup *papaya nectar or apricot nectar,* ⅓ cup *rice wine vinegar or white wine vinegar,* 4 teaspoons grated *gingerroot,* ½ teaspoon *toasted sesame oil,* and ¼ to ½ teaspoon *ground red pepper.* Cover and blend till mixed. With the blender or food processor running, slowly add ⅓ cup *olive oil or salad oil* through the hole in the top, blending till smooth. Transfer to a storage container. Cover and store in the refrigerator till ready to serve or for up to 2 weeks. Shake before using. Makes 1¾ cups.

Creamy Honey-Lime Dressing: In a small mixing bowl combine ⅓ cup *plain low-fat or fat-free yogurt,* ⅓ cup *regular or light dairy sour cream,* 2 tablespoons *honey,* 1½ teaspoons finely shredded *lime peel or lemon peel,*

2 teaspoons *lime juice or lemon juice,* ¼ teaspoon *salt,* and ¼ teaspoon *pepper.* Cover and store in the refrigerator till ready to serve or for up to 1 week. Stir before using. Makes about 1 cup.

Nutrition facts per serving with 3 tablespoons Ginger Vinaigrette: 294 cal., 13 g total fat (2 g sat. fat), 45 mg chol., 61 mg sodium, 29 g carbo., 4 g fiber, 18 g pro. *Daily values:* 42% vit. A, 128% vit. C, 6% calcium, 13% iron.

GRILLED FISH SANDWICHES

Pick your choice of tongue-tingling seasoning to rub onto the fish—each yields a distinctly different flavor. It's like getting three recipes in one. (See the photograph on page 199.)

4 **fresh or frozen fish fillets (about 4 oz. each)**
1 **Tbsp. lemon or lime juice**
1 **tsp. lemon-pepper seasoning, Jamaican jerk seasoning, or Cajun seasoning**

♦♦♦

½ **cup mayonnaise or salad dressing**
4 **tsp. Dijon-style mustard**
1 **to 3 tsp. honey**

♦♦♦

4 **slices Onion and Olive Focaccia (see page 206) or purchased focaccia, or 4 hamburger buns or kaiser rolls, split and toasted**
   Watercress or lettuce leaves (optional)
   Roasted sweet red pepper strips or fresh tomato slices (optional)

1 Thaw fish, if frozen. Brush fish fillets with lemon or lime juice. Rub desired seasoning evenly onto all sides of fish. Place the seasoned fish fillets in a well-greased wire grill basket. Grill in the wire basket on an uncovered grill directly over medium coals for 4 to 6 minutes for each ½-inch thickness of fish or just till fish begins to flake easily when tested with a fork.

2 Meanwhile, for spread, in a small mixing bowl stir together mayonnaise or salad dressing, mustard, and honey to taste.

3 To serve, spread cut sides of focaccia or buns with spread. Top bottom halves of focaccia slices or buns with watercress or lettuce (if desired), fish, additional spread, red pepper strips or tomato slices (if desired), and top halves of focaccia slices or buns. Makes 4 servings.

Nutrition facts per serving with bun: 311 cal., 14 g total fat (2 g sat. fat), 51 mg chol., 676 mg sodium, 24 g carbo., 1 g fiber, 22 g pro. *Daily values:* 2% vit. A, 4% vit. C, 3% calcium, 10% iron.

30 MIN. LOW FAT

FRESH TOMATO SOUP

Tomato soup is nothing fancy, but, when made with fresh tomatoes and seasoned with cilantro, it's a whole new bowl game. (See the photograph on page 199.)

3 medium tomatoes, peeled and quartered, or one 14½-oz. can tomatoes, cut up
1½ cups water
½ cup chopped onion (1 medium)
½ cup chopped celery (1 stalk)
½ of a 6-oz. can (⅓ cup) tomato paste
2 Tbsp. snipped fresh cilantro or parsley
2 tsp. instant chicken bouillon granules
2 tsp. lime juice or lemon juice
1 tsp. sugar
  Few dashes bottled hot pepper sauce
  Snipped fresh cilantro or parsley (optional)

1 If desired, seed tomatoes. In a large saucepan combine the fresh or undrained canned tomatoes, water, onion, celery, tomato paste, the 2 tablespoons cilantro or parsley, bouillon granules, lime juice or lemon juice, sugar, and hot pepper sauce. Bring to boiling; reduce heat. Simmer, covered, about 20 minutes or till celery and onion are extremely tender. Cool slightly.

2 Place *half* of the tomato mixture into a blender container or a food processor bowl. Cover and blend or process till smooth. Repeat with remaining mixture. Return all to pan; heat through or serve chilled. Ladle soup into bowls. If desired, garnish with additional cilantro or parsley. Makes 4 side-dish servings.

Nutrition facts per serving: 59 cal., 1 g total fat (0 g sat. fat), 0 mg chol., 480 mg sodium, 13 g carbo., 3 g fiber, 2 g pro. *Daily values:* 11% vit. A, 52% vit. C, 2% calcium, 8% iron.

LOW FAT

ONION AND OLIVE FOCACCIA

Serve flat Italian focaccia (foh-KAH-chee-ah) plain or turn a ho-hum sandwich into a new rave meal.

3¼ to 3¾ cups bread flour or all-purpose flour
1 pkg. active dry yeast
1¼ cups warm water (120° to 130°)
1 Tbsp. olive oil or cooking oil
1 tsp. salt

1½ cups chopped onions
2 cloves garlic, minced
2 Tbsp. olive oil or cooking oil

1 cup sliced pitted ripe olives and/or snipped oil-packed dried tomatoes, drained (optional)

◆◆◆

2 Tbsp. snipped fresh rosemary or 2 tsp. dried rosemary, crushed

1 In a large mixing bowl stir together *1¼ cups* of the flour and the yeast. Add warm water, 1 tablespoon olive oil or cooking oil, and salt to the dry mixture. Beat with an electric mixer on low to medium speed for 30 seconds, scraping sides of the bowl constantly. Beat on high speed for 3 minutes. Stir in as much of the remaining flour as you can.

2 Turn dough onto a lightly floured surface. Knead in enough remaining flour to make a stiff dough that is smooth and elastic (8 to 10 minutes total). Shape dough into a ball. Place in a lightly greased bowl; turn once. Cover and let rise in a warm place till double (about 1 hour).

3 Lightly grease 2 baking sheets. Punch dough down. Turn out onto a lightly floured surface. Divide in half. Shape each half into a ball. Place onto prepared baking sheets. Cover and let rest for 10 minutes.

4 For topping, in a medium skillet cook onions and garlic in the 2 tablespoons olive or cooking oil, covered, over low heat for 3 to 5 minutes or till onion is translucent, stirring occasionally. Uncover; cook and stir just till onion begins to brown. Remove from heat. Stir olives (if using) into onion mixture; set aside.

5 Using your hands, flatten each ball into a circle about 12 inches in diameter. With your fingers, press ½-inch-deep indentations about 2 inches apart on surface. Spoon onion mixture atop. Sprinkle with rosemary. Cover; let rise in a warm place till nearly double (about 20 minutes).

6 Bake in a 375° oven about 25 minutes or till golden. Sprinkle dried tomatoes (if using) atop bread during last 5 minutes of baking. Remove from baking sheet; cool on wire racks. Makes 2 rounds (24 servings).

Nutrition facts per serving: 87 cal., 2 g total fat (0 g sat. fat), 0 mg chol., 90 mg sodium, 15 g carbo., 1 g fiber, 3 g pro.
Daily values: 5% iron.

Blue Cheese and Walnut Focaccia: Prepare bread as directed on page 206, except omit the onion, garlic, olives or tomatoes, and rosemary. Instead, brush shaped dough with the 2 tablespoons olive oil or cooking oil. Sprinkle with 1½ cups chopped *walnuts* and 1 cup crumbled *blue cheese or* shredded *Swiss cheese.* Continue as directed.

SOUR CREAM POUND CAKE

Start looking at herbs in a different way, making them leap from savory to sweet. The rosemary variation gives old-fashioned pound cake a flavor update.
(See the photograph on page 200.)

½ **cup butter**
3 **eggs**
½ **cup dairy sour cream**
1½ **cups all-purpose flour**
¼ **tsp. baking powder**
⅛ **tsp. baking soda**

◆◆◆

1 **cup sugar**
½ **tsp. vanilla**

◆◆◆

Dairy sour cream (optional)
Fresh berries (optional)

1 Let the butter, eggs, and ½ cup sour cream stand at room temperature for 30 minutes. Grease and lightly flour an 8×4×2-inch or 9×5×3-inch loaf pan. In a bowl stir together the flour, baking powder, and baking soda; set aside.

2 In a large mixing bowl beat butter with an electric mixer on medium speed for 30 seconds. Gradually add sugar, beating

about 10 minutes or till light and fluffy. Beat in vanilla. Add eggs, 1 at a time, beating for 1 minute after each addition and scraping bowl frequently. Add the flour mixture and sour cream alternately to beaten mixture, beating on low to medium speed after each addition just till combined. Pour the batter into the prepared pan, spreading evenly.

3 Bake in a 325° oven for 60 to 75 minutes or till a wooden toothpick inserted near the center comes out clean. Cool in the pan on a wire rack for 10 minutes. Remove cake from pan; cool on rack. If desired, serve cake with sour cream and fresh berries. Makes 10 servings.

Nutrition facts per serving: 260 cal., 12 g total fat (7 g sat. fat), 93 mg chol., 141 mg sodium, 34 g carbo., 0 g fiber, 4 g pro.
Daily values: 12% vit. A, 2% calcium, 7% iron.

Orange-Rosemary Pound Cake: Prepare cake as directed at left, except stir 1¼ teaspoons finely shredded *orange peel* and 1 teaspoon snipped *fresh rosemary* into the batter. If desired, garnish cake with *fresh rosemary.* Continue as directed.

Lemon-Poppy Seed Pound Cake: Prepare cake as directed at left, except substitute ½ cup *low-fat lemon yogurt* for the sour cream. Add 2 tablespoons *poppy seed,* 1 teaspoon finely shredded *lemon peel,* and 2 tablespoons *lemon juice* to the batter. Continue as directed.

QUICK FIXES FOR MIXES

Serving a home-cooked meal doesn't always mean starting from scratch. Tweaking a packaged food and combining it with other ingredients creates a new family favorite. Try these convenient combos the next time dinner has to be on the double.

SWEET-AND-SOUR FISH
Does Caribbean cuisine sound good tonight? No problem. Your at-home island adventure starts with sweet-and-sour sauce that's simmered with pineapple chunks and sweet pepper strips. Serve it over broiled fish or chicken.

BARBECUE PIZZA
Corral your family for a pizza that's faster than takeout. Slather equal amounts of salsa catsup and barbecue sauce onto a baked pizza crust. Round up your favorite pizza toppings, additional sauce, and shredded cheese. Bake in a 425° oven about 5 minutes or till the cheese melts and bubbles.

CITRUS CHICKEN MARINARA
Even a favorite pasta sauce benefits from a taste twist now and then. Heat together marinara pasta sauce, finely shredded orange peel, a splash of orange juice, and a dash of ground red pepper. Serve with sautéed chicken breasts, hot cooked pasta, and grated Parmesan cheese.

HAM JAMBALAYA
Rice goes spicy in this Cajun-style dinner. In a medium skillet heat a 10-ounce can of tomatoes with green chili peppers, a cup of uncooked rice, and ½ cup water. When the mixture boils, turn down the heat and turn up the flavor, stirring in some cubed cooked ham and enough chili powder to suit your taste. Cover and simmer till the liquid is absorbed. Stir before serving to fluff the cooked rice.

BEEF AND CURLY NOODLES
This fast fix-up uses your noodle—Oriental noodles, that is. In a large skillet brown 1 pound of ground meat. Stir in a drained 14-ounce can of stewed tomatoes, an undrained small can of whole kernel corn, and a 3-ounce package of Oriental noodles with pork flavor. (Break up the noodles, if you like.) Cover and simmer about 10 minutes or till the noodles are tender and the liquid is absorbed.

PORK CHOPS WITH APPLE PILAF
An apple a day goes a long way in this fix-and-forget-it combo. In a 3-quart casserole combine a 6-ounce package of long grain and wild rice mix, a can of sliced apples, a splash of vinegar, and a cup of water. Top with browned ¾-inch-thick pork chops. Bake, covered, in a 350° oven for 45 to 50 minutes or till tender.

PRIZE TESTED RECIPE WINNER

PASTA WITH FENNEL AND DRIED TOMATOES

This recipe earned Dr. Peter Darrigo of Buffalo, New York, $100 in the magazine's monthly contest.

- ¾ cup dried tomatoes (not oil-packed)
- 8 oz. penne or ziti pasta
- 2 cups loose-pack frozen cut broccoli

♦♦♦

- 1½ cups fennel bulb cut into strips
- ¾ cup red sweet pepper, cut into thin bite-size strips
- ½ cup chopped onion
- 2 cloves garlic, minced
- 1 Tbsp. olive oil
- ¼ cup tomato paste
- 1 tsp. sugar
- 1 tsp. instant vegetable bouillon granules
  Dash crushed red pepper (optional)
- 2 Tbsp. snipped fresh parsley
- ⅓ cup finely shredded Parmesan cheese
- ⅓ cup pine nuts, toasted
  Fresh fennel leaves (optional)

1 Pour 1½ cups *boiling water* over tomatoes. Let stand 5 minutes. Drain, reserving liquid. Snip tomatoes. Cook pasta according to package directions, except add broccoli the last 3 minutes of cooking. Drain; return to the pan. Cover and set aside.

2 Meanwhile, in a large skillet cook fennel, sweet pepper, onion, and garlic in hot olive oil about 5 minutes or just till tender. Add tomato paste, sugar, bouillon granules, crushed red pepper (if desired), snipped tomatoes, and reserved liquid. Add the fennel mixture to pasta mixture. Bring to boiling; reduce heat. Simmer, uncovered, for 2 to 3 minutes or till slightly thickened. (If too dry, stir in a little *hot water*.) Stir in parsley. Sprinkle with Parmesan cheese and pine nuts. If desired, garnish with fennel leaves. Makes 4 main-dish servings.

Nutrition facts per serving: 448 cal., 14 g total fat (3 g sat. fat), 7 mg chol., 712 mg sodium, 67 g carbo., 3 g fiber, 19 g pro. *Daily values:* 30% vit. A, 118% vit. C, 16% calcium, 30% iron.

(30 MIN.) CURRY-SAUCED VEGETABLES

2 Tbsp. olive oil or cooking oil
½ cup chopped red onion
4 cloves garlic, minced
1 small sweet potato, peeled and cut into ½-inch cubes
2 cups assorted fresh vegetables, such as broccoli or cauliflower flowerets, or coarsely chopped carrots or sweet peppers
1 15-oz. can garbanzo beans, drained
2 to 3 tsp. curry powder
1 tsp. ground cumin
½ tsp. crushed red pepper
¼ tsp. salt

♦♦♦

¾ cup unsweetened coconut milk or 1 cup evaporated milk*
⅓ cup golden raisins
3 cups hot cooked couscous
¼ cup chopped peanuts or cashews

1 In a large skillet heat oil over medium-high heat. Add onion and garlic; cook and stir about 3 minutes or till onion is tender. Add sweet potato; cook and stir for 3 minutes more. Add mixed vegetables, garbanzo beans, curry powder, cumin, crushed red pepper, and salt. Cook and stir for 1 minute more.

2 Carefully add coconut or evaporated milk to skillet. Bring to boiling; reduce heat. Simmer, covered, about 10 minutes or till the vegetables are tender. Stir in the raisins. Serve over couscous. Sprinkle with peanuts or cashews. Makes 4 main-dish servings.

***Note:** If using evaporated milk, sprinkle each serving with *toasted coconut* along with nuts.

Nutrition facts per serving: 662 cal., 31 g total fat (14 g sat. fat), 18 mg chol., 708 mg sodium, 30 g carbo., 16 g fiber, 21 g pro. *Daily values:* 64% vit. A, 111% vit. C, 23% calcium, 35% iron.

VEGETABLE PIE

Yellow cornmeal
2 6- or 6½-oz. pkg. pizza crust mix

♦♦♦

2 eggs, beaten
1 cup ricotta cheese
½ cup finely shredded Parmesan cheese

♦♦♦

¼ cup chopped onion
2 medium zucchini, halved lengthwise and thinly sliced (about 2½ cups)
1 7-oz. jar roasted red sweet peppers, well drained and coarsely chopped
1 Tbsp. olive oil or cooking oil

1 6-oz. can Italian-style tomato paste
⅛ tsp. crushed red pepper
6 oz. sliced mozzarella cheese
1 egg, beaten
2 tsp. sesame seed

1 Grease a 9-inch springform pan; sprinkle with cornmeal. Prepare pizza crust mixes according to package directions. Divide dough in half; cover half and set aside. On a lightly floured surface roll remaining half into a 15-inch circle. Fit crust into prepared pan letting edges extend over sides.

2 In a medium bowl stir together the 2 eggs and ricotta and Parmesan cheeses. Spoon *half* the mixture into the crust-lined pan.

3 In a large skillet cook and stir onion, zucchini, and roasted red peppers in hot oil 5 minutes or till vegetables are tender. Stir in tomato paste, crushed red pepper, and 1 cup *water*. Spoon *half* of the mixture atop ricotta layer. Layer with *half* of the mozzarella cheese. Repeat ricotta, vegetable, and mozzarella layers. On lightly floured surface roll out remaining crust to a 9-inch circle. Place atop filling; fold edge of bottom crust over top crust and seal. Combine egg and 1 tablespoon *water;* brush over crust. Cut slits in top crust. Sprinkle with sesame seed. Bake in a 375° oven 45 minutes. Cool in pan on a wire rack 15 minutes. Remove sides of pan. Cool about 30 minutes more. Cut in wedges. Makes 8 main-dish servings.

Nutrition facts per serving: 363 cal., 13 g total fat (5 g sat. fat), 106 mg chol., 743 mg sodium, 41 g carbo., 1 g fiber, 19 g pro. *Daily values:* 30% vit. A, 90% vit. C, 25% calcium, 19% iron.

JALAPEÑO CORN CHOWDER

6 fresh ears of corn or 3 cups loose-pack frozen whole kernel corn
1½ cups chicken broth
1 cup milk, half-and-half, or light cream
1 to 2 fresh jalapeño peppers, seeded and finely chopped
¼ of a 7-oz. jar roasted red sweet peppers, drained and chopped (¼ cup)
½ cup crumbled feta cheese

1 Cut kernels from ears of corn, if using. In a blender container combine *half* of the corn and the broth. Blend till nearly smooth. In a large saucepan combine broth mixture and remaining corn kernels. Stir in milk, jalapeños, and roasted peppers; heat through. Ladle soup into bowls. Sprinkle with feta cheese. Makes 4 side-dish servings.

Nutrition facts per serving: 210 cal., 6 g total fat, (3 g sat. fat), 17 mg chol., 499 mg sodium, 34 g carbo, 5 g. fiber, 10 g pro.
Daily values: 12% vit. A, 59% vit. C, 12% calcium, 7% iron.

CORN-STUFFED POBLANO CHILIES

5 to 6 large fresh poblano peppers (about 4 oz. each), halved lengthwise and membranes and seeds removed*
2 cups cooked rice
2 cups loose-pack frozen whole kernel corn
1 8-oz. carton dairy sour cream
1 cup shredded cheddar cheese

1 cup crumbled feta cheese
¼ cup finely chopped red onion
2 fresh jalapeño peppers, seeded and finely chopped
2 Tbsp. snipped fresh cilantro
3 Tbsp. pine nuts or slivered almonds

1 Immerse peppers into *boiling water* for 3 minutes. Invert onto paper towels to drain well. Stir together the rice, corn, sour cream, cheeses, onion, jalapeños, and cilantro. Spoon filling into each poblano pepper half. Place stuffed pepper halves in a 3-quart rectangular baking dish. Sprinkle with pine nuts or almonds. Bake, uncovered, in a 350° oven for 30 minutes or till heated through. Makes 5 to 6 main-dish servings.

*****Note:** If you prefer, substitute 5 or 6 small green sweet peppers.

Nutrition facts per serving: 470 cal., 26 g total fat, 64 mg chol., 429 mg sodium, 48 g carbo., 3 g fiber, 18 g pro.
Daily values: 32% vit. A, 571% vit. C, 30% calcium, 24% iron.

PRIZE TESTED RECIPE WINNER

LENTIL PASTITSIO

This recipe earned Wendy Leece of West Bend, Wisconsin, $200 in the magazine's monthly contest.

⅔ cup dry lentils
3 cloves garlic, minced
1 cup chopped onion
1 cup chopped green sweet pepper
1 30-oz. jar meatless spaghetti sauce with vegetables
¾ tsp. ground cinnamon

¼ tsp. pepper
1 egg, slightly beaten
¼ cup grated Parmesan cheese
¼ cup snipped fresh parsley
8 oz. mafalda or fettuccine, cooked and drained

◆◆◆

2 cups skim milk
¼ cup all-purpose flour
1 cup shredded mozzarella cheese (4 oz.)
2 egg whites
Ground cinnamon (optional)

1 In a saucepan bring 1⅓ cups *water* to boiling; add lentils and garlic. Return to boiling; reduce heat. Simmer, covered, 10 minutes. Add onion and sweet pepper. Cook, covered, 5 to 10 minutes or till tender. Drain; return to pan. Stir in sauce, cinnamon, and pepper. In a bowl combine egg, Parmesan cheese, and parsley. Add pasta; toss to coat. Set aside.

2 For topping, in a saucepan stir together milk and flour. Cook and stir till thickened and bubbly; remove from heat. Stir in *½ cup* of the mozzarella cheese. Beat egg whites till foamy. Fold egg whites into topping; set aside.

3 Grease a 3-quart rectangular baking dish. Layer *half* the lentil mixture and *half* the pasta mixture; repeat layers. Spoon topping over all. Bake, uncovered, in a 350° oven about 45 minutes or till hot. Top with remaining cheese and, if desired, additional cinnamon. Let stand for 10 minutes. Makes 8 main-dish servings.

Nutrition facts per serving: 390 cal., 7 g total fat, 38 mg chol., 576 mg sodium, 61 g carbo., 2 g fiber, 22 g pro.
Daily values: 28% vit. A, 61% vit. C, 23% calcium, 36% iron.

Chocolate Pots de Crème

Coffeehouses and espresso are hot and getting hotter. Espresso powder gives a java twist to this rich dessert. (See the photograph on page 193.)

1 cup half-and-half or light
    cream
1 4-oz. pkg. sweet baking
    chocolate, coarsely
    chopped
2 tsp. sugar

♦♦♦

3 beaten egg yolks
½ tsp. vanilla

1 In a heavy small saucepan combine half-and-half or light cream, chocolate, and sugar. Cook and stir over medium heat 10 minutes or till mixture reaches a full boil and thickens.

2 Gradually stir about half of the hot mixture into the beaten egg yolks. Stir egg yolk mixture into remaining hot mixture in pan. Cook and stir over low heat for 2 minutes more. Remove from heat. Stir in vanilla.

3 Pour the warm chocolate mixture into 4 to 6 pots de crème cups or small dessert bowls. Cover and chill for 2 to 24 hours. Makes 4 to 6 servings.

Nutrition facts per serving: 276 cal., 21 g total fat (11 g sat. fat), 182 mg chol., 31 mg sodium, 22 g carbo., 2 g fiber, 5 g pro. *Daily values:* 32% vit. A, 7% calcium, 7% iron.

Espresso Chocolate Pots de Crème: Prepare pots de crème as directed above, except add 2 teaspoons *instant espresso powder* along with the half-and-half.

Green Devil Cake

2½ cups all-purpose flour
1¾ cups packed brown sugar
1 tsp. baking powder
1 tsp. baking soda
1 tsp. ground cinnamon
4 oz. unsweetened chocolate,
    melted
1 cup buttermilk or sour milk
    (see note, page 201)
1 cup pureed green tomatoes
¾ cup butter, softened
2 eggs
1 Tbsp. grated orange peel
1 recipe Chocolate Glaze
    Whipped cream (optional)

1 Grease and flour a 13×9×2-inch baking pan; set aside. In a large bowl combine flour, brown sugar, baking powder, soda, and cinnamon. Add melted chocolate, buttermilk, tomatoes, butter, eggs, and grated orange peel. Beat with an electric mixer on low speed till combined. Beat on medium speed 2 minutes. Pour into prepared pan. Bake in a 350° oven for 35 to 40 minutes or till a wooden toothpick inserted near center comes out clean. Cool cake in pan on a wire rack. Drizzle glaze over each serving. If desired, serve with whipped cream. Makes 16 servings.

Chocolate Glaze: Melt 4 ounces *semisweet chocolate* and 3 tablespoons *butter* over low heat, stirring frequently; remove from heat. Stir in 1¼ cups sifted *powdered sugar* and 3 tablespoons *hot water.* Stir in more *hot water,* if needed, to make glaze easy to drizzle.

Nutrition facts per serving : 356 cal., 18 g total fat (10 g sat. fat), 56 mg chol., 235 mg sodium, 49 g carbo., 2 g fiber, 5 g pro.

Raspberry Cheesecake Cookie Pizza

¾ cup butter or margarine
¾ cup sugar
1 egg yolk
1 tsp. vanilla
1½ cups all-purpose flour

♦♦♦

1 8-oz. package cream cheese,
    softened
1 egg
1 Tbsp. sugar
⅓ cup seedless raspberry
    preserves
¼ cup sliced almonds, toasted

1 Beat the butter or margarine in a large mixing bowl with an electric mixer on medium to high speed for 30 seconds. Add the ¾ cup sugar and beat till combined. Beat in egg yolk and vanilla. Beat in as much of the flour as you can with the mixer. Stir in any remaining flour with a spoon.

2 Spread dough in a lightly greased 12- or 13-inch pizza pan. Bake in a 350° oven about 20 minutes or till golden.

3 Meanwhile, beat together cream cheese, 1 egg, and the 1 tablespoon sugar till smooth. Spread over hot crust to within ½ inch of the edge. Spoon preserves on top. With a knife, carefully swirl preserves to marble. Sprinkle with almonds. Bake 5 to 10 minutes more or till filling is set. Cool in pan on a wire rack. Cut into wedges. Store in refrigerator. Makes 12 to 16 servings.

Nutrition facts per serving: 320 cal., 20 g total fat (12 g sat. fat), 87 mg chol., 180 mg sodium, 32 g carbo., 1 g fiber, 4 g pro. *Daily values:* 22% vit. A, 2% calcium, 8% iron.

CUBING BREAD FOR BETTIES

Betties are made with soft bread cubes rather than dry cubes like bread puddings. Cubing bread for a betty is easier if the bread is frozen. Whether the bread is frozen or not, use a serrated knife and a gentle sawing motion to cut the bread into the ½-inch cubes.

PEACH-BERRY BETTY

The name could have been inspired by some frugal colonial cook whose dessert combines spiced fruit and thrifty leftover bread. Top it with ice cream.

- ½ cup sugar
- 1 Tbsp. all-purpose flour
- ½ tsp. ground nutmeg
- 3 cups sliced, peeled fresh peaches or nectarines
- 2 cups fresh raspberries or blueberries
- ¼ cup orange juice or water
- 4 cups soft bread cubes (5 slices)

♦♦♦

- ¼ cup coconut
- 2 Tbsp. butter or margarine, melted
- ⅛ tsp. ground nutmeg

1 For filling, stir together the sugar, flour, and the ½ teaspoon nutmeg. Add the peaches or nectarines and raspberries or blueberries. Stir in the orange juice or water. Add *2 cups* of the bread

cubes, tossing to mix. Transfer to an ungreased 2-quart square baking dish.

2 For topping, combine the remaining 2 cups bread cubes and the coconut. Stir together the melted butter or margarine and ⅛ teaspoon nutmeg; drizzle onto bread cube mixture. Toss gently to coat.

3 Sprinkle topping onto filling. Bake in a 375° oven for 25 to 35 minutes or till fruit is tender and topping is golden. Makes 6 servings.

Nutrition facts per serving: 232 cal., 6 g total fat (3 g sat. fat), 10 mg chol., 142 mg sodium, 44 g carbo., 4 g fiber, 3 g pro.
Daily values: 8% vit. A, 35% vit. C, 3% calcium, 7% iron.

CHERRY-PLUM SLUMP

New England's slump is topped with biscuit dumplings, which flatten or "slump" during cooking. In Cape Cod, a slump may be known as a grunt— presumably the sound the fruit makes as it bubbles on the stove.

- 2 cups sliced, pitted plums
- 1 cup pitted sweet cherries
- ¾ cup water
- ½ cup sugar

♦♦♦

- ¾ cup all-purpose flour
- ¼ cup sugar
- 1 tsp. baking powder
- 1 tsp. ground cinnamon
- ⅛ tsp. salt
- 3 Tbsp. butter or margarine
- ⅓ cup milk

1 In a 3-quart saucepan combine the plums, cherries, water, and the ½ cup sugar. Bring to boiling; reduce heat.

2 Meanwhile, for dumplings, stir together the flour, the ¼ cup sugar, baking powder, cinnamon, and salt. Using a pastry blender, cut in butter or margarine to resemble coarse crumbs. Add the milk, stirring just to moisten.

3 Spoon dough in 6 mounds atop hot filling. Cover and simmer about 15 minutes or till a wooden toothpick inserted in the dumplings comes out clean. Serve warm. Makes 6 servings.

Nutrition facts per serving: 229 cal., 6 g total fat (4 g sat. fat), 16 mg chol., 439 mg sodium, 43 g carbo., 1 g fiber, 2 g pro.
Daily values: 6% vit. A, 3% vit. C, 31% calcium, 9% iron.

LOW FAT
LEMON-POPPY SEED BISCOTTI

Along with coffee goes biscotti, (bee-SKAWT-tee), the low-fat, twice-baked Italian cookie that is traditionally dunked into a steaming cup of your favorite blend. (See the photograph on page 193.)

- ⅓ cup butter or margarine
- ⅔ cup sugar
- 4 tsp. finely shredded lemon peel
- 1 Tbsp. poppy seed
- 1 tsp. baking powder
- ½ tsp. baking soda
- 2 eggs
- 2½ cups all-purpose flour

1 In large mixing bowl beat butter or margarine with an electric mixer on medium to high speed about 30 seconds or till softened. Add sugar, shredded lemon peel, poppy seed, baking powder, and baking soda; beat till combined. Add eggs; beat till combined. Beat in as much of the flour as you can with the electric mixer. Using a wooden spoon, stir in any remaining flour.

2 Divide dough in half. Shape into two 9×1½-inch rolls. Place rolls on an ungreased cookie sheet, flattening each slightly. Bake in a 375° oven about 20 minutes or till a wooden toothpick inserted in the center comes out clean. Cool on cookie sheet on a wire rack for 1 hour.

3 Cut each roll crosswise into ½-inch-thick slices. Arrange the slices flat about 4 inches apart on the cooled cookie sheet. Bake in a 325° oven for 8 minutes; turn slices and bake about 8 minutes more or till surfaces are crisp and light brown. Remove biscotti from cookie sheet; cool on a wire rack. Makes about 36 cookies.

Nutrition facts per cookie: 64 cal., 2 g total fat (1 g sat. fat), 16 mg chol., 48 mg sodium, 10 g carbo., 0 g fiber, 1 g pro. *Daily values:* 2% vit. A, 1% calcium, 3% iron.

Almond Brickle Biscotti: Prepare biscotti as directed at left, except substitute *brown sugar* for the sugar. Omit the lemon peel and poppy seed. Stir in 1 cup *almond brickle pieces* after adding the flour. Continue shaping and baking as directed.

Orange-Cranberry Biscotti: Prepare biscotti as directed at left, except substitute finely shredded *orange peel* for the lemon peel. Omit poppy seed. Stir in ½ cup finely chopped *dried cranberries or dried tart red cherries* after adding the flour. Continue shaping and baking as directed.

RASPBERRY SWIRL BARS

"White chocolate" swirled with raspberry jam makes a decadent treat.

½ **cup butter or margarine**
½ **cup vanilla milk pieces**
⅓ **cup seedless raspberry jam**
1 **Tbsp. lemon juice**

♦♦♦

2 **eggs, beaten**
1 **cup all-purpose flour**
½ **cup sugar**
1 **tsp. vanilla**
½ **tsp. baking powder**
⅛ **tsp. salt**
¾ **cup vanilla milk pieces**

1 Generously grease an 11×7×1½-inch baking pan; set aside. In a small saucepan heat butter or margarine and the ½ cup vanilla milk pieces over medium-low heat till melted, stirring constantly. Cool slightly (about 5 minutes). In another small saucepan heat jam and lemon juice over low heat till jam is melted; set aside.

2 In a large mixing bowl stir together the eggs, flour, sugar, vanilla, baking powder, and salt. Fold in the ¾ cup vanilla milk pieces and melted vanilla piece mixture. Pour into prepared pan. Drizzle jam mixture atop. With a knife or narrow metal spatula, swirl jam into batter. Bake in a 350° oven about 30 minutes or till set. Cool in pan on wire rack. Cut into bars. Makes 20 bars.

Nutrition facts per bar: 160 cal., 8 g total fat (4 g sat. fat), 34 mg chol., 85 mg sodium, 20 g carbo., 0 g fiber, 2 g pro. *Daily values:* 5% vit. A, 3% calcium, 2% iron.

LIME-COCONUT TRIANGLES

This recipe earned Charselle Hooper of San Rafael, California, $100 in the magazine's monthly contest.

1 **cup all-purpose flour**
⅓ **cup sifted powdered sugar**
¼ **cup chopped pecans**
¼ **cup coconut**
⅓ **cup butter or margarine, melted**

♦♦♦

2 **eggs, slightly beaten**
1 **cup granulated sugar**
2 **tsp. finely shredded lime peel**
¼ **cup lime juice**
¼ **tsp. baking powder**
½ **cup coconut**
   Finely shredded lime peel (optional)

1 Grease an 8×8×2-inch baking pan. For crust, combine flour, powdered sugar, pecans, and ¼ cup coconut. Stir in butter or margarine. Press into prepared pan. Bake in a 350° oven for 20 minutes.

2 Meanwhile, combine eggs, granulated sugar, peel, juice, and baking powder. Stir in ½ cup coconut. Pour mixture atop baked crust. Bake in 350° oven about 20 minutes or till edges are light brown and center is set. Cool in pan on a wire rack. Cut into triangles. If desired, top with lime peel. Makes 18 triangles.

Nutrition facts per triangle: 137 cal., 6 g total fat (3 g sat. fat), 33 mg chol., 47 mg sodium, 20 g carbo., 2 g pro. *Daily values:* 4% vit. A, 2% vit. C, 3% iron.

BRANDIED CRANBERRY-APRICOT BARS

This recipe earned Sharon Davidson of Reno, Nevada, $200 in the magazine's monthly contest.

⅓ **cup golden raisins**
⅓ **cup dark raisins**
⅓ **cup dried cranberries**
⅓ **cup snipped dried apricots**
½ **cup brandy or water**

♦♦♦

1 **cup all-purpose flour**
⅓ **cup packed brown sugar**
½ **cup butter or margarine**

♦♦♦

2 **eggs**
1 **cup packed brown sugar**
½ **cup all-purpose flour**
1 **tsp. vanilla**
⅓ **cup chopped pecans**
   Powdered sugar

1 In a 4-cup glass measure or microwave-safe mixing bowl, combine the golden and dark raisins, cranberries, apricots, and brandy or water. Cover with microwave-safe plastic wrap; turn back a corner to vent. Microwave on high for 2 minutes. (Or, place fruit and brandy in a saucepan; bring to boiling. Remove from heat.) Let stand for 20 minutes; drain.

2 For crust, in a medium mixing bowl stir together 1 cup flour and ⅓ cup brown sugar. Using a pastry blender, cut in butter or margarine till mixture resembles coarse crumbs. Press into an ungreased 8×8×2-inch baking pan. Bake in 350° oven about 20 minutes or till golden.

THE CLEVER COOK

TREATS AWAITING

For every batch of cookies or brownies I bake, I freeze a dozen on a paper plate in a freezer bag. This way, I always have a home-baked treat to offer on special occasions, such as the birth of a baby, new neighbors, or a family celebration. The cookies thaw quickly at room temperature and are packed and ready to go whenever I need them.

Lynn J. Miller
Cozad, Nebraska

3 In a medium mixing bowl beat eggs with an electric mixer on low speed for 4 minutes; stir in the 1 cup brown sugar, the ½ cup flour, and vanilla just till combined. Add pecans and drained fruit; stir to mix. Pour mixture atop baked crust; spread evenly.

4 Bake about 40 minutes or till a wooden toothpick inserted in center comes out clean, covering with foil the last 10 minutes to prevent overbrowning. Cool in pan on a wire rack. Sprinkle with powdered sugar. Cut into squares. Makes 16 bars.

Nutrition facts per square: 222 cal., 8 g total fat (4 g sat. fat), 42 mg chol., 72 mg sodium, 32 g carbo., 1 g fiber, 2 g pro. *Daily values:* 8% vit. A, 2% calcium, 8% iron.

PUMPKIN SPICE SQUARES

1 **cup all-purpose flour**
½ **cup quick-cooking oats**
½ **cup packed brown sugar**
½ **cup chopped walnuts**
1 **tsp. ground cinnamon**
¼ **tsp. ground nutmeg**
½ **cup butter or margarine, melted**

♦♦♦

1 **cup canned pumpkin**
1 **egg**
¾ **cup evaporated milk**
½ **cup granulated sugar**
1 **tsp. ground cinnamon**
½ **tsp. ground allspice**

♦♦♦

1 **8-oz. pkg. cream cheese, softened**
¼ **cup orange marmalade**

1 Grease a 13×9×2-inch baking pan. For crust, combine the flour, oats, brown sugar, walnuts, 1 teaspoon cinnamon, and the nutmeg. Stir in melted butter or margarine. Press into bottom of prepared pan. Bake in a 350° oven for 20 minutes.

2 For filling, beat together pumpkin, egg, evaporated milk, granulated sugar, 1 teaspoon cinnamon, and the allspice. Pour atop crust. Bake 20 minutes more or till a knife inserted in center comes out clean. Cool on a rack.

3 For frosting, beat together the cream cheese and marmalade. Spread over cooled bars. Cut into squares. Cover and store in the refrigerator. Makes 20 squares.

Nutrition facts per square: 196 cal., 12 g total fat (6 g sat. fat), 38 mg chol., 97 mg sodium, 21 g carbo., 1 g fiber, 3 g pro. *Daily values:* 37% vit. A, 1% vit. C, 4% calcium, 6% iron.

OCTOBER
Dinner from the Heart

IN THIS CHAPTER

30-minute recipes indicated in ^RED.
Low-fat recipes indicated with a ♥.

Crisp fall days mean school schedules to juggle and a new resolve to eat more meals together as a family. We profile two families who regularly gather around the dinner table, and we share their treasured family recipes, such as Red Pepper Lasagna, Pork Roast with Sweet Potatoes, Granny Cake, and Chicken with Porcini Mushrooms. It's also harvest time. Audition apples for new roles in Apple Cream Scones, Apple Pudding Pie, and low-fat Apple-Cranberry Sorbet. Pick up an extra pumpkin at the orchard or roadside stand and turn it into Curried Pumpkin Soup, using the shell as a tureen.

APPLE OF YOUR PIE

A sweet and juicy Red Delicious apple wins the popularity poll of the lunchbox set, but put it in a pie and it turns to mush. Unlike the old testimony to a rose, "an apple is an apple is an apple" does not hold true. So when you crave to cook or bake the fruit, choose a variety with virtues that can stand up to the heat.

Cooking can be a blessing to disguise apples that are overripe or bruised; sautéing and simmering also bring out the best in hard, tart, under-ripened apples. Apples that don't make the cut for pies often are best for sauce.

Rome Beauty: Cooking and baking accentuate the rich but mellow flavor of this medium-tart, deep-red apple. It's called Queen of the Bakers, and holds up well when cooked whole. Enjoy this beauty in bread puddings, pies, quick breads, and sauces, too.

Golden Delicious: This huge, sweet golden globe is delicious raw, cooked, or baked. The fruit's rich flavor and tender flesh are boons in stir-fries, casseroles, cobblers, soups, stews, and sauces. The way it keeps its shape makes it a natural in pies.

Granny Smith: This bright green fruit is on the tart and tangy end of the barometer. The Granny is firm when bitten into but won't hold up to prolonged heat—yet its high acid content makes it the apple of many a pie-baker's eye. Also try Granny Smith sautéed with pork.

Cortland: The agreeable, slightly sweet, slightly tart all-purpose Cortland is ideal for baking whole (especially in the microwave) because it maintains its portly shape. Chopped or sliced, this apple is fine to fill a pie or strudel with and cooks up nicely in pancakes and muffins.

Newtown Pippin: Another all-purpose fruit, the green-gold Newtown Pippin is a good keeping apple. Its highly perfumed flesh is crisp and juicy and holds up well in the frying pan or oven. This apple's sweet-tart flavor makes it a favorite for baked desserts.

PRIZE TESTED RECIPE WINNER

APPLE PUDDING PIE

This recipe earned Dawn Veldhuis of Yuma, Arizona, $100 in the magazine's monthly contest.

1 **unbaked 9-inch pastry shell**

◆◆◆

3 **eggs**
1 **cup applesauce**
½ **cup granulated sugar**
½ **cup packed brown sugar**
½ **cup vanilla fat-free yogurt**
⅓ **cup rolled oats**
1 **tsp. ground cinnamon**
4 **slices bread, cut up (about 3 cups)**

2 **medium cooking apples, peeled, cored, and sliced**

◆◆◆

¼ **cup packed brown sugar**
¼ **cup all-purpose flour or whole wheat flour**
2 **Tbsp. butter**
½ **cup chopped walnuts, pecans, or almonds**

1 For crust, line the unbaked pastry shell with a double thickness of foil. Bake in a 450° oven for 8 minutes. Remove foil. Bake for 4 minutes more. Remove pastry from oven. Reduce oven temperature to 350°.

2 For filling, in a mixing bowl combine eggs, applesauce, granulated sugar, ½ cup brown sugar, yogurt, oats, and cinnamon. Stir in bread and apples; set aside.

3 For topping, in another bowl combine ¼ cup packed brown sugar and flour. Cut in butter till mixture resembles coarse crumbs. Stir in nuts. Pour filling into baked pastry. Sprinkle topping over filling. Cover edge of crust with foil. Bake 30 minutes. Remove foil; bake about 30 minutes more or till top is golden and fruit is tender. Makes 8 servings.

Nutrition facts per serving: 322 cal., 10 g total fat (3 g sat. fat), 88 mg chol., 137 mg sodium, 54 g carbo., 2 g fiber, 6 g pro. *Daily values:* 6% vit. A, 3% vit. C, 6% calcium, 11% iron.

APPLE-CHERRY PECAN TART

For a stunning tart top, take the pastry trimmings and cut them into hearts, stars, or leaves. Brush the cutouts with a little milk, sprinkle with sugar, and bake. Garnish the fruit filling with the pastry shapes.

½ of an 11-oz. pkg. piecrust mix (1⅓ cups)
½ cup finely chopped pecans
2 Tbsp. packed brown sugar
2 Tbsp. water
♦♦♦
2 Tbsp. margarine or butter
¾ cup granulated sugar
¾ cup apple juice
6 small cooking apples, peeled, cored, and thinly sliced (4 cups)
1½ cups frozen pitted tart red cherries
♦♦♦
4 tsp. cornstarch
2 Tbsp. water
1 tsp. vanilla
Whipped cream (optional)

1 Grease the bottom of a 10- or 11-inch tart pan with removable bottom. Combine piecrust mix, pecans, brown sugar, and 2 tablespoons water. Prepare according to piecrust package directions. On a lightly floured surface roll out dough to a 12- to 13-inch circle. Transfer to prepared pan, pressing bottom and sides gently to remove any air bubbles. Turn overlapping dough edges to inside and press against sides of pan. Line with a double thickness of foil. Bake in a 450° oven for 8 minutes. Remove foil. Bake for 5 to 6 minutes more or till golden. Cool on a wire rack.

2 In a large skillet melt the margarine or butter. Add granulated sugar and apple juice; cook and stir till sugar is dissolved. Add apples and cherries. Bring to boiling; reduce heat. Simmer, covered, about 5 minutes or till apples are just tender. Using a slotted spoon, transfer apples and cherries to the baked pastry shell, reserving liquid in skillet.

3 Combine cornstarch and 2 tablespoons water; add to liquid in skillet. Stir in vanilla. Return to heat; cook and stir till thickened and bubbly. Cook and stir for 2 minutes more. Spoon the thickened mixture atop fruit in pastry; cool.

4 To serve, cut tart into wedges. If desired, spoon whipped cream atop each wedge. Makes 12 servings.

Nutrition facts per serving: 228 cal., 9 g total fat (2 g sat. fat), 0 mg chol., 114 mg sodium, 36 g carbo., 2 g fiber, 2 g pro. *Daily values:* 5% vit. A, 7% vit. C, 1% calcium, 4% iron.

APPLE-RAISIN COMPOTE WITH SWEET TORTILLA CRISPS

Call it mock apple pie à la mode. Warm apple and raisin pielike filling is topped with cinnamon-sugared tortilla crisps and ice cream.

½ cup raisins or ⅓ cup dried tart red cherries
2 Tbsp. apricot brandy or apple juice
3 7-inch flour tortillas
1 Tbsp. butter or margarine, melted
1 Tbsp. sugar
¼ tsp. ground cinnamon
1 Tbsp. butter or margarine
4 medium cooking apples, peeled, cored, and thinly sliced
¼ cup sugar
2 tsp. cornstarch
½ cup apple juice
♦♦♦
1 pint cinnamon or French vanilla ice cream

1 Soak raisins or cherries in brandy or apple juice for 30 minutes. Meanwhile brush 1 side of each tortilla with melted butter. Combine 1 tablespoon sugar and the cinnamon; sprinkle atop buttered side of tortillas. Cut each tortilla into 6 wedges. Place wedges, buttered sides up, on a large baking sheet (do not overlap). Bake in a 350° oven for 10 to 15 minutes or till golden; cool.

2 In a large skillet melt 1 tablespoon butter or margarine; add apples. Cook, covered, 5 minutes or till apples are just tender, stirring occasionally. Combine ¼ cup sugar and cornstarch; sprinkle over apples. Stir in ½ cup apple juice and undrained raisins. Cook till bubbly, stirring gently as needed. Reduce heat; cook 2 minutes more. Remove from heat; cool 30 minutes.

3 To serve, spoon fruit mixture into 6 dessert bowls. Top with ice cream and some tortilla wedges. Makes 6 servings.

Nutrition facts per serving: 322 cal., 10 g total fat (6 g sat. fat), 30 mg chol., 160 mg sodium, 55 g carbo., 2 g fiber, 4 g pro. *Daily values:* 9% vit. A, 8% vit. C, 7% calcium, 7% iron.

APPLE-PICKIN' TIME

Our family loves to go apple picking in fall and usually comes home with several bushels to make apple pie. When we get home, we immediately slice and core the apples, then mix them in freezer bags with the sugar, flour, and spices called for in our apple pie recipe. In about 3 hours we have 2 bushels of apples turned into fillings that are neatly stacked in our freezer (enough for about 15 pies). When we crave apple pie, we just defrost a bag before continuing our recipe.

Ginger Gibson
Powell, Ohio

PRIZE
TESTED
RECIPE
WINNER

APPLE CREAM SCONES

This recipe earned Aime Inman-Cox of Escondido, California, $200 in the magazine's monthly contest.

- 2 cups chopped tart apples
- 2 Tbsp. butter
- 1 Tbsp. instant coffee crystals
- 1 tsp. hot water
- ½ cup whipping cream

❖❖❖

- 2¼ cups all-purpose flour
- ⅓ cup granulated sugar
- 1 Tbsp. baking powder
- ¼ tsp. salt
- ¼ cup butter

❖❖❖

- 2 Tbsp. coarse sugar

1 In a large skillet cook apples in 2 tablespoons butter till tender and liquid is almost evaporated, stirring often; cool slightly. Dissolve the coffee in hot water; stir in whipping cream.

2 In a large mixing bowl stir together the flour, granulated sugar, baking powder, and salt. Cut in ¼ cup butter till pieces resemble coarse crumbs. Add the apples and coffee mixture to flour mixture, stirring just till dough clings together.

3 Turn dough out onto a lightly floured surface. Gently knead by folding and pressing about 6 times. On an ungreased baking sheet pat dough into an 8-inch circle. Sprinkle with coarse sugar. Cut into 12 wedges; separate slightly. Bake in a 400° oven for 20 to 25 minutes or till golden. Cool slightly. Separate scones and serve warm. Makes 12 scones.

Nutrition facts per scone: 205 cal., 10 g total fat (6 g sat. fat), 29 mg chol., 198 mg sodium, 28 g carbo., 1 g fiber, 3 g pro. *Daily values:* 9% vit. A, 1% vit. C, 8% calcium, 8% iron.

LOW FAT

APPLE-CRANBERRY SORBET

- 4 medium tart apples, peeled, cored, and chopped
- ½ cup sugar
- 1½ cups cranberry juice cocktail
- ¼ tsp. ground cinnamon
- ¼ cup brandy or apple brandy (optional)*

1 In a medium saucepan combine apples, sugar, and cranberry juice cocktail. Bring to boiling; reduce heat. Simmer, covered, about 10 minutes or till apples are extremely tender; cool. Place cooled mixture in a blender container with cinnamon and, if desired, brandy. Blend till smooth. Freeze in a 1-quart ice-cream freezer according to the manufacturer's directions. Makes 1 quart (eight ½-cup servings).

*Note: If you use brandy or apple brandy, the sorbet will take longer to freeze.

Nutrition facts per serving: 112 cal., 0 g total fat, 0 mg chol., 2 mg sodium, 29 g carbo., 1 g fiber, 0 g pro. *Daily values:* 32% vit. C, 1% iron.

PHYLLO APPLES

- ½ cup mixed dried fruit bits
- ¼ cup amaretto or orange juice
- 6 medium tart baking apples
- 1 Tbsp. lemon juice
- 2 Tbsp. brown sugar
- ¼ cup chopped walnuts

❖❖❖

- 6 sheets phyllo dough
- ⅓ cup margarine or butter, melted

❖❖❖

- ⅔ cup whipping cream, half-and-half, or light cream
- ½ of a vanilla bean, split lengthwise, or ½ tsp. vanilla
- 1 beaten egg yolk
- ⅓ cup sugar
- 2 tsp. amaretto, white crème de menthe, or orange liqueur (optional)

1 In a small bowl combine mixed dried fruit bits and ¼ cup amaretto or orange juice. Let stand for 15 to 20 minutes or till most of the liquid is absorbed. Meanwhile, peel apples. Carefully core, leaving bottoms intact. Brush apples with lemon juice. Add brown sugar and walnuts to soaked fruit, stirring to mix. Spoon fruit mixture into the hollowed apples; set aside.

2 Brush 1 sheet of phyllo with *some* of the melted margarine or butter. Halve lengthwise, then crosswise to make 4 equal rectangles. Stack rectangles, staggering pieces of phyllo to create a jagged edge. Turn stack over and brush bottom with a little margarine or butter. Place an apple in center of phyllo stack. Lift phyllo up around apple, pressing slightly and leaving top open. Repeat with remaining phyllo and apples. Place apples in a foil-lined shallow baking pan. Place piece of foil over each apple. Bake in a 375° oven 45 to 55 minutes or till phyllo is golden and apple is tender.

3 Meanwhile, in a small heavy saucepan bring cream and vanilla bean (if using) just to boiling, stirring frequently. Remove from heat. In a mixing bowl combine egg yolk, sugar, and about *2 tablespoons* of the hot cream. Beat with an electric mixer on medium to high speed for 2 to 3 minutes or till thick and lemon-colored. Gradually stir about *half* of the remaining cream mixture into the egg yolk mixture. Return all of the egg yolk mixture to the saucepan. Cook and stir over medium heat just till bubbly. Remove from heat. Discard the

vanilla bean. Stir in liquid vanilla (if using). If desired, stir in liqueur. Cover surface with plastic wrap. Chill till serving time. Serve sauce over warm apples. Serves 6.

Nutrition facts per serving: 476 cal., 25 g total fat (9 g sat. fat), 72 mg chol., 232 mg sodium, 59 g carbo., 3 g fiber, 4 g pro. *Daily values:* 32% vit. A, 15% vit. C, 3% calcium, 8% iron.

CURRIED PUMPKIN SOUP

Choose a round pumpkin with a flat bottom so it won't tip as you serve.

1	7- to 8-lb. pumpkin

♦♦♦

3	14½-oz. cans chicken broth
2	baking apples, peeled, cored, and coarsely chopped
1	carrot, chopped
2	tsp. grated gingerroot
1	tsp. curry powder
½	tsp. ground cumin
6	slices bacon
¼	cup chopped onion
2	Tbsp. sugar
1	cup croutons

1 Slice off top fourth of pumpkin; set aside. Scoop out seeds and stringy pulp; replace top. Place pumpkin on a 15×10×1-inch baking pan. Bake in a 375° oven 50 to 60 minutes or till pumpkin flesh can be scooped out easily. (Pumpkin will not be tender.) Cool slightly. Scoop out and reserve pumpkin flesh, leaving about a ¾-inch thickness of flesh on pumpkin walls. Cut flesh into chunks (should have about 4 cups). Do not remove any flesh from bottom of shell. Discard pumpkin top.

2 In a large pot combine the 4 cups pumpkin flesh, broth, apples, carrot, gingerroot, curry powder, and cumin. Bring to boiling; reduce heat. Simmer, covered, 10 to 12 minutes or till vegetables are tender; cool slightly. In a blender or food processor, blend mixture, a third at a time, or till smooth. Place pumpkin shell in a 3-quart casserole. (If pumpkin is to be removed from the casserole before serving, line casserole with a double thickness of heavy foil.) Pour soup into shell. Bake, uncovered, in a 375° oven 20 minutes.

3 Meanwhile, cook bacon till crisp. Remove bacon, reserving 1 tablespoon drippings. Cook onion and sugar in drippings till onion is tender. Crumble bacon; stir bacon and croutons into onion. Sprinkle bacon mixture atop soup in pumpkin. Makes 8 to 10 side-dish serving.

Nutrition facts per serving: 135 cal., 4 g total fat (1 g sat. fat), 5 mg chol., 600 mg sodium, 20 g carbo., 4 g fiber, 6 g pro. *Daily values:* 32% vit. A, 16% vit. C, 38% calcium, 10% iron.

CHOCOLATE FUDGE CHEESECAKE

4 8-oz. cartons vanilla yogurt*

❖❖❖

1½ cups crushed chocolate wafer cookies (25)

¼ cup butter or margarine, melted

❖❖❖

2 8-oz. packages cream cheese, softened

6 oz. semisweet chocolate, melted and cooled

¾ cup sugar

2 Tbsp. all-purpose flour

1 tsp. vanilla

3 eggs

1 recipe Fudge Topping (see right)

1 Place yogurt in a colander lined with 100-percent cotton cheesecloth over a mixing bowl. Cover and let drain in the refrigerator overnight.

2 For crust, in a bowl combine crushed cookies and melted butter. Press onto bottom of a 9-inch springform pan; set aside.

3 For filling, in a large mixing bowl beat cream cheese, chocolate, sugar, flour, and vanilla with an electric mixer on medium to high speed till combined. Add eggs all at once. Beat on low speed just till combined. Do not overbeat. Stir in yogurt. Pour filling into crust-lined pan. Place on a shallow baking pan. Bake in a 375° oven 35 to 40 minutes or till center appears set when shaken. Cool 15 minutes. Loosen crust from sides of pan. Cool 30 minutes more; remove sides of pan. Cool completely. Cover and chill 4 hours or overnight.

4 To serve, spread Fudge Topping atop cheesecake. Cut into wedges. Makes 16 servings.

*Note: Use a yogurt that does not contain gelatin.

Fudge Topping: In a medium saucepan combine 1 cup sifted *powdered sugar*, one 5-ounce can (⅔ cup) *evaporated milk*, ⅓ cup *semisweet chocolate pieces*, and ¼ cup *butter or margarine*. Bring to boiling. Boil gently 6 minutes, stirring constantly. Remove from heat. Stir in ½ teaspoon *vanilla*; cool. Cover and store in refrigerator till serving time.

Nutrition facts per serving: 414 cal., 25 g total fat (14 g sat. fat), 92 mg chol., 270 mg sodium, 45 g carbo., 1 g fiber, 8 g pro. *Daily values:* 21% vit. A, 11% calcium, 10% iron.

MOCHA CHEESECAKE

1¼ cups crushed graham crackers (17 squares)

¼ cup granulated sugar

¼ cup unsweetened cocoa powder

⅓ cup butter or margarine, melted

❖❖❖

2 8-oz. pkg. cream cheese, softened

¾ cup granulated sugar

⅓ cup unsweetened cocoa powder

¼ cup packed brown sugar

3 eggs

¼ cup coffee liqueur or strong coffee

¼ cup strong coffee

2 tsp. vanilla

❖❖❖

1 8-oz. carton dairy sour cream

1 Tbsp. granulated sugar

1 For crust, in a bowl combine crushed graham crackers, ¼ cup granulated sugar, and ¼ cup cocoa powder. Stir in melted butter. Press onto bottom of a 9-inch springform pan. Bake in a 375° oven for 5 minutes; set aside.

2 For filling, in a large mixing bowl beat cream cheese, the ¾ cup granulated sugar, ⅓ cup cocoa powder, and brown sugar with an electric mixer on medium to high speed till combined. Add eggs all at once. Beat on low speed just till combined. Do not overbeat. Stir in liqueur or coffee, coffee, and *1 teaspoon* of the vanilla.

3 Pour filling into crust-lined pan. Bake in a 375° oven for 30 to 35 minutes or till center appears set when shaken.

4 For topping, in a small bowl combine sour cream, 1 tablespoon sugar, and remaining vanilla. Carefully spread atop hot cheesecake (topping will set as the cheesecake cools). Cool for 15 minutes.

5 Loosen crust from sides of pan. Cool 30 minutes more; remove sides of pan. Cool completely. Cover and chill at least 4 hours or overnight. To serve, cut into wedges. Makes 16 servings.

Nutrition facts per serving: 299 cal., 19 g total fat (11 g sat. fat), 88 mg chol., 181 mg sodium, 27 g carbo., 0 g fiber, 5 g pro. *Daily values:* 20% vit. A, 7% calcium, 8% iron.

BASIC CREPES

1¼ **cups milk**
1 **cup all-purpose flour**
1 **egg**
1 **tsp. cooking oil**
¼ **tsp. baking powder**

1 In a blender container combine milk, flour, egg, oil, and baking powder. For dessert crepes, add 1 teaspoon *vanilla* and 1 teaspoon *sugar*. For savory crepes, add ¼ teaspoon *salt*. If desired, flavor the batter (see tip, right). Cover; blend till smooth.

2 Heat a slightly greased 6- or 8-inch skillet with flared sides over medium-high heat. Remove from heat. Pour about 2 tablespoons batter into the center of the 6-inch skillet or 3 tablespoons batter into the 8-inch skillet; lift and tilt skillet to spread the batter. Return to heat. Cook about 1 minute or till brown. Turn with a spatula and cook second side for 30 seconds. Invert over paper towels; remove crepe. Repeat with remaining batter, greasing skillet occasionally and stirring batter occasionally, if needed. Makes about 16 (6-inch) or 12 (8-inch) crepes.

Nutrition facts per basic 6-inch crepe: 43 cal., 1 g total fat, 15 mg chol., 19 mg sodium, 6 g carbo., 0 g fiber, 2 g pro. *Daily values:* 1% vit. A, 2% calcium, 2% iron.

BUILD YOUR OWN CREPE

Using the basic crepe recipe below left, try the flavors and fillings suggested below to create your favorite combinations. For filled crepes, plan on 3 to 4 tablespoons filling per crepe. If serving warm, heat the filling before folding the crepe around it. Serve filled crepes immediately or warm the filled crepes in the microwave oven on high power for 3 to 5 minutes or till heated through.

DINNER CREPE IDEAS
Season the batter with one of the following ingredients.
◆ ½ tsp. dried thyme, crushed
◆ ½ tsp. curry powder
◆ ½ tsp. dried sage, crushed
◆ ½ tsp. five-spice powder
◆ ½ tsp. ground red pepper

Fill crepes with one of the following ingredients.
◆ Cut-up cooked boneless chicken with steamed broccoli moistened with light Alfredo sauce
◆ Steamed spinach and lentils with crumbled feta cheese
◆ Minced and cooked pork with finely chopped butternut squash topped with cranberry sauce
◆ Cooked shredded beef, bean sprouts, and a little hoisin sauce

DESSERT CREPE IDEAS
Flavor the basic batter with one or two of the following ingredients.
◆ 1 Tbsp. unsweetened cocoa powder
◆ 1 Tbsp. instant espresso coffee powder
◆ 2 Tbsp. mashed ripe banana
◆ 2 Tbsp. fresh blueberries
◆ ½ tsp. ground cinnamon

Fill crepes with one of the following ingredients.
◆ Sliced bananas, chopped toasted walnuts, and a touch of maple syrup
◆ Fresh fruit slices with plain or flavored low-fat yogurt
◆ Mixed fresh berries with whipped cream
◆ Soft-style cream cheese mixed with fruit preserves or lemon curd
◆ Bananas cooked with butter or margarine and a little brown sugar

THE SKINNY ON PEANUT BUTTER

No longer faced with a simple question of creamy or chunky, choosy peanut butter lovers have more choosing to do. Reduced-fat peanut butters offer PB fans a new way to experience that familiar stick-to-the-roof-of-your-mouth sensation—with less fat than the traditional spread. Is the trade worthwhile for the die-hard fanatic? Our Test Kitchen sampled the tried-and-true peanut butter cookie and some simple spreads using both versions. Here's what they found:

LESS FAT, EQUAL CALORIES

Making the switch to the light version of peanut butter to lose weight won't help. Reduced-fat peanut butter is just that—lower in fat but not in calories. To cut the calories, you'll still have to eat less of the reduced-fat peanut butter.

HOW THE COOKIE CRUMBLES

You can use reduced-fat peanut butter in cookies for moderate fat savings. Make your favorite recipe once, substituting the same amount of reduced-fat peanut butter for the regular version. If that's a success, next time try cutting the butter or margarine slightly. The lower-fat cookies may be slightly chewier.

BREAD SPREADS

Naturally, reduced-fat peanut butter works just fine in the quintessential lunch box commodity, the peanut-butter-and-jelly sandwich. In fact, we dare you to tell the difference.

Reduced-fat peanut butter also makes delicious spreadables for breads, waffles, bagels, toast, crackers, apple slices, celery, and carrots. Spread it on plain or make some of the spreads below. Store them in the refrigerator for up to a week.

Spicy Apple: Heat a little applesauce, then remove from heat. Stir in twice as much peanut butter as the applesauce and add a dash of apple pie spice.

Chocolate Peanut: Stir in a little chocolate-flavored syrup and a sprinkling of chopped peanuts.

Maple Cream: Combine peanut butter with an equal amount of tub cream cheese. Stir in enough maple syrup or honey to soften.

Honey Raisin: Stir in a few raisins and a little bit of honey.

Orange Ginger: Blend in a little grated gingerroot and finely shredded orange peel. Spread on raisin bread or toss with hot rice or pasta.

Top Banana: Mash a banana and stir in some peanut butter.

PEANUT BUTTER POUND CAKE

For a winning combination, drizzle this nutty pound cake with a duo of delectable frostings—peanut butter and chocolate.

- ¾ cup butter
- 3 eggs
- 3 cups all-purpose flour
- 1½ tsp. baking powder
- 1 tsp. baking soda
- ¼ tsp. salt

◆◆◆

- ¾ cup peanut butter
- 1½ cups sugar
- 1½ tsp. vanilla
- 1½ cups plain low-fat yogurt

◆◆◆

- 1 recipe Peanut Butter Glaze (see page 223)
- 1 recipe Cocoa Glaze (see page 223)

1 Let butter and eggs stand at room temperature for 30 minutes. Meanwhile, grease and lightly flour a 10-inch tube pan. Combine flour, baking powder, baking soda, and salt; set aside.

2 In a large mixing bowl beat butter and peanut butter with an electric mixer on medium to high speed about 30 seconds or till combined. Gradually add sugar, 2 tablespoons at a time, beating on medium speed about 6 minutes or till extremely light and fluffy. Add vanilla. Add eggs, 1 at a time, beating on low to medium speed 1 minute after each addition and scraping bowl frequently. Alternately add flour mixture and yogurt, beating on low speed just till combined. Pour batter into prepared pan.

Set the Pace for Breakfast

Eating is a balancing act: When you plan to indulge in a big juicy steak followed by a rich dessert at dinnertime, it's wise to dine lightly at breakfast. Likewise, if you crave bacon and eggs in the a.m., it's better to eat lighter during the rest of the day. Either way, breakfast is still your most important meal. To help you set the day's pace, study these calorie and fat comparisons of typical breakfast fare.

Note: Nutrition values of foods vary according to brand, so check the food label information. Values given are approximations.

All-American

2 strips bacon
2 eggs, scrambled
1 slice whole wheat toast with butter and jam
1 cup orange juice
1 cup coffee with sugar and milk
Total values: About 475 calories and 22 g fat

All-American Light

2 slices Canadian-style bacon
¼ cup egg substitute, scrambled
1 slice whole wheat toast plus jam
1 cup orange juice
Total values: About 300 calories and 5 g fat

On-the-Go

8 ounces chocolate milk
1 glazed doughnut
1 cappuccino
Total values: About 460 calories and 20 g fat

On-the-Go Light

1 banana
2 rice cakes with light cream cheese
1 cup grapefruit juice
Total values: About 280 calories and 3 g fat

The Usual Road Trip

1 7-inch waffle with butter and syrup
2 sausage links
1 egg, scrambled
1 cup orange juice
1 cup coffee with sugar and milk
Total values: About 700 calories and 27 g fat

A Better Road Trip

¾ cup raisin bran cereal with
    skim milk and strawberries
1 cup orange juice
1 cup cantaloupe pieces
Total values: About 350 calories and 2 g fat

---

3 Bake in a 325° oven about 65 minutes or till a wooden toothpick inserted in center comes out clean. Cool in pan on wire rack 15 minutes. Remove from pan. Cool completely on wire rack. Spoon Peanut Butter Glaze over top and down side of cake. Let stand 1 hour to set. Drizzle with Cocoa Glaze. Make 16 to 20 servings.

Peanut Butter Glaze: In a small bowl beat ¼ cup *peanut butter* till fluffy. Gradually beat in 1 cup sifted *powdered sugar,* 3 tablespoons *milk,* and 1 teaspoon *vanilla.* Beat in an additional ½ cup sifted *powdered sugar* and enough *milk* to make glaze easy to drizzle.

Cocoa Glaze: In a small bowl stir ¾ cup sifted *powdered sugar,* 1 tablespoon *unsweetened cocoa powder,* 1 tablespoon *melted butter or margarine,* and 1 tablespoon *water* till smooth. Stir in additional sifted *powdered sugar or water* to make the glaze easy to drizzle.

Nutrition facts per serving: 412 cal., 19 g total fat (7 g sat. fat), 64 mg chol., 348 mg sodium, 55 g carbo., 2 g fiber, 9 g pro. *Daily values:* 10% vit. A, 7% calcium, 10% iron.

Menu

California Quiche
(see below and right)

◆◆◆

Salad of cooked green
beans and whole tiny
potatoes with vinaigrette
on mesclun greens

◆◆◆

Iced tea

◆◆◆

Shortbread cookies with
pecan ice cream

FOUR-WAY QUICHE

½ of a 15-oz. pkg. folded
   refrigerated unbaked
   piecrust (1 crust)
3 eggs
1½ cups milk
¼ cup sliced green onions
1½ cups specified shredded
   cheese
1 Tbsp. all-purpose flour

1 Ease unbaked piecrust into
a 9-inch quiche dish or pie plate.
Trim to ½ inch beyond edge. Fold
under extra pastry; flute edge.
Line unpricked pastry with a
double thickness of foil. Bake in a
450° oven 8 minutes; remove foil.
Bake 4 to 5 minutes or till set.

2 Meanwhile, for filling, in a
mixing bowl combine eggs, milk,
green onions, ¼ teaspoon *salt,* and
⅛ teaspoon *pepper.* Stir in filling
and seasoning for variation. Toss
together cheese and flour. Add to
egg mixture; mix well.

3 Pour egg mixture into hot
pastry shell on oven rack. Cover

edge of quiche with foil. Bake in a
325° oven for 35 to 40 minutes or
till a knife inserted near the center
comes out clean, removing foil
after 20 minutes. Let stand for
10 minutes on a wire rack. Serve
warm. Makes 6 servings.

California Quiche: For filling
soak 6 dried *tomato halves* (not
oil-packed) in *boiling water* for
5 minutes; drain and chop. For
seasoning, use 1 tablespoon
snipped *fresh basil* and 2 cloves
garlic, minced. Use *smoked or
regular Gouda cheese.*

Nutrition facts per serving: 371 cal., 23 g
total fat (10 g sat. fat), 144 mg chol.,
525 mg sodium, 25 g carbo., 1 g fiber, 15 g
pro. *Daily values:* 14% vit. A, 4% vit. C,
25% calcium, 11% iron.

Greek Quiche: For filling, use
half of a 10-ounce package *frozen
chopped spinach,* thawed and well
drained, and ¼ cup sliced pitted
ripe olives. For seasoning, use
½ teaspoon each *dried rosemary
and mint,* crushed. Use 1 cup
shredded *mozzarella cheese* and
½ cup crumbled *feta cheese.*

Nutrition facts per serving: 376 cal, 24 g
total fat (10 g sat. fat), 141 mg chol.,
604 mg sodium, 25 g carbo., 1 g fiber,
16 g pro. *Daily values:* 28% vit. A, 6%
vit. C, 29% calcium, 14% iron.

Thai Quiche: For filling, use
1 cup chopped *cooked chicken or
pork.* For seasoning, use 1 tablespoon snipped *fresh cilantro,*
¼ teaspoon *ground ginger,* and
a dash *ground red pepper.* Use
brick cheese.

Nutrition facts per serving: 414 cal., 26 g
total fat (10 g sat. fat), 161 mg chol.,
421 mg sodium, 24 g carbo., 1 g fiber, 22 g
pro. *Daily values:* 19% vit. A, 2% vit. C,
23% calcium, 13% iron.

Cajun Quiche: For filling, in
an 8-inch skillet cook 4 ounces
bulk pork sausage, ½ cup chopped
red or green sweet pepper, and
¼ cup chopped *onion* till no
pink remains in meat; drain
on paper towels. For seasoning,
use ½ teaspoon *Cajun seasoning.*
Use *Monterey Jack cheese with
jalapeño peppers.*

Nutrition facts per serving: 405 cal., 27 g
total fat (11 g sat. fat), 144 mg chol.,
521 mg sodium, 24 g carbo., 1 g fiber,
17 g pro. *Daily values:* 22% vit. C, 25%
calcium, 13% iron.

FRESH MOZZARELLA WITH BASIL

*Fresh mozzarella has a texture that's
softer than that of cream cheese and a
singularly sweet, delicate taste. You'll
find balls of fresh mozzarella, often
packed in whey, in the deli case.*

1 lb. fresh mozzarella cheese
¼ cup roasted garlic oil or
   olive oil
1 to 2 tsp. balsamic vinegar
2 Tbsp. snipped fresh basil or
   1 tsp. dried basil, crushed
1 Tbsp. fresh cracked pepper
   Baguette slices (optional)

1 Cut cheese into 1-inch
cubes. Place cubes in a bowl. Add
oil, vinegar, basil, and pepper; toss
gently till cheese is well coated.
Serve immediately; or store, covered, in refrigerator up to several
days. Place toothpicks in each
cheese cube. If desired, serve with
baguette slices. Serves 14 to 16.

Nutrition facts per serving: 100 cal., 7 g
total fat (4 g sat. fat), 18 mg chol., 151 mg
sodium, 1 g carbo., 0 g fiber, 8 g pro.
Daily values: 5% vit. A, 17% calcium.

RATATOUILLE-STYLE CHILI

Spaghetti sauce gives this chunky vegetable chili a head start.

1½ lb. lean ground beef
1 cup chopped onion

♦♦♦

1 30-oz. jar spaghetti sauce
   with mushrooms
4 cups peeled and cubed
   eggplant and/or cubed
   zucchini
2 15-oz. cans red kidney beans
   and/or garbanzo beans,
   rinsed and drained
1 14½-oz. can tomatoes,
   cut up
1 cup water
1 4-oz. can diced green chili
   peppers, drained
2 to 3 Tbsp. chili powder
1 tsp. ground cumin

♦♦♦

6 slices American cheese, cut
   into triangles (optional)
   Chopped green onion
   (optional)

1 In a large pot cook beef and onion till beef is brown and onion is tender. Drain off fat.

2 Add spaghetti sauce, eggplant and/or zucchini, red kidney and/or garbanzo beans, undrained tomatoes, water, chili peppers, chili powder, and cumin to pot. Bring to boiling; reduce heat. Cover; simmer 20 minutes or till vegetables are tender. Season with *salt* and *pepper*.

3 To serve, ladle chili into bowls. If desired, top with cheese and green onion. Makes 12 main-dish servings.

■ TO MAKE AHEAD ■

Cool mixture slightly; ladle into three 4-cup freezer containers. Seal, label, and freeze. To reheat, transfer a container of chili to a large saucepan. Add ½ cup *water*. Cook, covered, over medium-low heat about 45 minutes or till hot, stirring often. (Or, transfer a container of chili to a 1½-quart microwave-safe casserole. Add ¼ cup *water*. Cover and cook on 70% power [medium] for 28 to 33 minutes or till hot, stirring often.) Serve as directed.

Nutrition information per serving: 251 cal., 10 g fat (3 g sat. fat), 36 mg chol., 611 mg sodium, 29 g carbo., 6 g fiber, 18 g pro. *Daily values:* 16% vit. A, 33% vit. C, 6% calcium, 21% iron.

SOUTHWEST HARVEST CASSEROLE

This chili-style casserole is hearty, full of vitamins, and low in fat. You'll find it satisfying and delicious.

1 2½- to 3-lb. turban squash
   or two 1½ to 2 lb.
   butternut squash*

♦♦♦

8 oz. ground raw turkey or
   chicken
2 green onions, sliced
1 to 2 tsp. chili powder
½ tsp. dried oregano, crushed
1 15-oz. can black beans or
   pinto beans, rinsed and
   drained
1 8-oz. can tomato sauce
1 fresh jalapeño pepper, seeded
   and chopped
¼ cup sliced pitted ripe olives
   Dairy sour cream or plain
   yogurt

1 Cut and reserve a thin slice from the top of the squash; remove seeds and discard. Hollow squash, leaving a ½-inch-thick shell. Finely chop ½ cup of the squash pulp; save remaining pulp for another use.

2 Place squash in a 2-quart rectangular baking dish; replace top. (Invert if using butternut squash.) Bake in a 350° oven about 40 minutes or till squash is tender.

3 In a large skillet cook turkey or chicken and finely chopped squash pulp till meat is browned. Stir in green onions, chili powder, and oregano. Cook and stir 2 minutes more. Stir in drained black beans or pinto beans, tomato sauce, jalapeño pepper, and olives. Bring to boiling. Spoon into baked squash. Return to oven and bake for 15 minutes more. To serve, spoon casserole from squash. Top each serving with sour cream or yogurt. Makes 4 to 6 main-dish servings.

*Note: If using butternut squash, cut the rounded base of the squash from the longer portion. Remove seeds and discard. Use the rounded portion for stuffing. Finely chop enough of the top portion to equal ½ cup. Save remaining squash for another use.

Nutrition facts per serving: 243 cal., 6 g total fat (1 g sat. fat), 21 mg chol., 695 mg sodium, 38 g carbo., 10 g fiber, 17 g pro. *Daily values:* 142% vit. A, 74% vit. C, 11% calcium, 24% iron.

CONFETTI BARLEY AND SAUSAGE

This recipe earned Becky Harrison of San Jose, California, $100 in the magazine's monthly contest.

½ cup pearl barley
8 oz. bulk pork sausage
1½ cups thinly sliced carrots
½ cup chopped onion
3 cloves garlic, minced

❖❖❖

1 10-oz. pkg. frozen chopped spinach, thawed and well drained
1 14¾-oz. can cream-style corn
1 4-oz. can sliced mushrooms, drained
3 green onions, thinly sliced
½ tsp. garlic powder
½ tsp. dried savory, crushed
½ tsp. dried thyme, crushed
¼ tsp. dried marjoram, crushed
⅛ tsp. pepper

❖❖❖

½ cup shredded Parmesan cheese
Fresh savory (optional)

1 Cook pearl barley according to package directions; drain. Meanwhile, in a large skillet cook the sausage, carrots, onion, and garlic till sausage is no longer pink. Drain off fat.

2 In a large mixing bowl stir together the spinach, corn, mushrooms, green onions, garlic powder, dried savory, thyme, marjoram, pepper, barley, and sausage mixture.

3 Place mixture in a 2-quart casserole. Bake, covered, in a 350° oven about 40 minutes or till heated through. Sprinkle with Parmesan cheese. Bake, uncovered, about 5 minutes more or till cheese is melted. If desired, garnish with fresh savory. Makes 4 main-dish servings.

Nutrition facts per serving: 359 cal., 13 g total fat (3 g sat. fat), 32 mg chol., 973 mg sodium, 47 g carbo., 7 g fiber, 18 g pro. *Daily values:* 169% vit. A, 24% vit. C, 20% calcium, 21% iron.

PRIZE
TESTED
RECIPE
WINNER

CREAMY CHICKEN AND TOMATO PASTA

This recipe earned Xan Pilgrim of Superior, Colorado, $200 in the magazine's monthly contest.

8 oz. pasta, such as linguine, farfalle (bow ties), penne, or rotelle (wagon wheel)
2 shallots, chopped
1 clove garlic, minced
1 Tbsp. olive oil
12 oz. skinless, boneless chicken breast halves, cut into bite-size pieces
¼ cup dry white wine or chicken broth
¼ cup snipped fresh basil
1 Tbsp. snipped fresh Italian parsley

❖❖❖

1 10-oz. container refrigerated light Alfredo sauce

¾ cup oil-packed dried tomatoes, drained and thinly sliced
⅓ cup milk
¼ cup grated Parmesan cheese
¼ tsp. pepper

❖❖❖

¼ cup grated Parmesan cheese
Fresh basil (optional)

1 Cook pasta according to package directions; drain. Meanwhile, in a large skillet cook shallots and garlic in hot olive oil over medium-high heat for 30 seconds. Add chicken; cook and stir for 3 to 4 minutes or till chicken is tender and no longer pink. Drain off fat. Carefully add white wine or chicken broth, snipped basil, and parsley. Cook for 1 minute more.

2 In a large mixing bowl combine the drained pasta, chicken mixture, Alfredo sauce, dried tomatoes, milk, ¼ cup Parmesan cheese, and pepper. Gently toss to mix.

3 Transfer mixture to a 2-quart rectangular baking dish. Sprinkle with ¼ cup Parmesan cheese. Bake, covered, in a 350° oven for 15 minutes. Uncover and bake for 10 to 15 minutes more or till heated through and top is slightly golden. If desired, garnish with fresh basil. Makes 6 main-dish servings.

Nutrition facts per serving: 428 cal., 16 g total fat (7 g sat. fat), 58 mg chol., 640 mg sodium, 45 g carbo., 0 g fiber, 24 g pro. *Daily values:* 15% vit. A, 31% vit. C, 22% calcium, 14% iron.

DINNER FROM THE HEART

There was a time, long before the days of fast-forward lifestyles, when families sat down together at the dinner table. One generation nurtured the next on a diet of comfort and support as well as tasty victuals.

Matt Brown is one serious cook who won't let the warm tradition of family mealtime die. "Food brings our family together," says Matt, who learned to cook from his dad and now shares the joy with his wife, Caitlin. Sunday night is the couple's favorite part of the week, a time when their extended family gathers around the butcher block or out in the California sunshine for an informal feast. "The whole family pitches in at our Sunday dinners," says Matt. And, more than likely, the recipes they're fixing come from a loose-leaf, three-ring binder. This homemade cookbook includes dishes for Italian, Croatian, and Midwestern specialties that embrace the family's roots. These are the foods Matt grew up eating. "When we were young, every dinner was a big deal," recalls Matt. And that's still true today. Home cooking, well-seasoned with laughter and love, is the glue that makes the Brown traditions endure.

CHICKEN WITH PORCINI MUSHROOMS

This rich mushroom-glazed chicken dish is perfect for a cool fall evening. (See the photograph on page 239.)

1 oz. dried porcini mushrooms
½ cup warm water
♦♦♦
1 Tbsp. butter
1 Tbsp. olive oil
2½ to 3 lb. meaty chicken pieces
   (skinned, if desired)
♦♦♦
½ cup dry white wine
½ tsp. salt
¼ tsp. pepper
½ cup chopped fresh tomatoes
♦♦♦
   Polenta* (optional)
   Sliced fresh tomatoes
      (optional)
   Grated Parmesan cheese
      (optional)
   Snipped fresh herb
      (optional)

1 Rinse and drain dried mushrooms. Soak mushrooms in the warm water for 20 to 30 minutes. Drain mushrooms, reserving liquid. Coarsely chop mushrooms; set aside.

2 In a 12-inch skillet heat butter and olive oil over medium-high heat. Add chicken pieces and cook about 10 minutes or till browned on all sides (add more oil, if necessary).

3 Carefully add the white wine, salt, and pepper to skillet. Simmer, uncovered, about 5 minutes or till most of the wine is evaporated. Add the chopped tomatoes and mushrooms. Slowly add reserved mushroom liquid.

4 Reduce heat to low. Simmer, covered, for 15 to 20 minutes or till chicken is tender and no longer pink. Transfer chicken to a warmed platter.

5 For sauce, skim fat from mixture in skillet. Bring mixture to boiling. Boil about 5 minutes or till of desired consistency. Pour over chicken. If desired, serve with polenta and sliced tomatoes sprinkled with Parmesan cheese and fresh herb. Makes 4 main-dish servings.

***Note:** Look for a tube of ready-to-heat polenta in your supermarket and cook according to package directions.

Nutrition facts per serving: 423 cal., 22 g total fat (7 g sat. fat), 137 mg chol., 414 mg sodium, 7 g carbo., 1 g fiber, 43 g pro. *Daily values:* 9% vit. A, 9% vit. C, 2% calcium, 14% iron.

LAMB AND VEGETABLE PLATTER

Matt Brown has been cooking since he was 8, but he got more serious about it at 15. That's when his dad told him cooking was a good way to impress girls. No matter what your age, you'll impress anyone visiting your dinner table if you fix this luscious dish. (See the photograph on page 234.)

8 baby artichokes* or
    4 medium artichoke
    bottoms*
1 Tbsp. olive oil
    ❖❖❖
1 lb. boneless leg of lamb roast
¼ cup all-purpose flour
    ❖❖❖
2 Tbsp. olive oil
3 anchovy fillets, chopped
    (optional)
2 cloves garlic, minced
1½ tsp. snipped fresh rosemary
    or ½ tsp. dried rosemary,
    crushed
¼ tsp. pepper
¾ cup chicken broth
2 Tbsp. red wine vinegar
    ❖❖❖
1 recipe Roasted Red Potatoes
    (see right) (optional)
    Steamed carrots (optional)
    Fresh rosemary sprigs
    (optional)

1 Prepare artichokes as directed.* In a large saucepan heat 1 tablespoon olive oil over medium heat. If using baby artichokes, cook and stir halved or quartered artichokes in the hot oil about 10 minutes or till nearly tender. If using artichoke bottoms, cook and stir artichoke pieces in the hot oil till heated through. Remove from heat; cover and keep warm.

2 Meanwhile, cut the lamb lengthwise into ¼-inch-thick slices (as in scallopini or thin cutlets). Coat with flour.

3 In a large skillet heat 2 tablespoons olive oil over medium-high heat. Cook the lamb in hot oil for 1½ to 2 minutes on each side or till done. Remove the lamb from skillet, reserving the drippings in pan.

4 Reduce heat to medium. For sauce, add anchovy fillets (if desired), garlic, rosemary, and pepper to skillet. Cook and stir for 30 seconds. Carefully add chicken broth and wine vinegar, scraping up browned bits. Bring to boiling; reduce heat. Simmer, uncovered, about 3 minutes or till mixture is reduced to about ½ cup. Return lamb to skillet; heat through.

5 Transfer lamb to serving platter; pour sauce over lamb. Serve with the artichokes and, if desired, Roasted Red Potatoes and steamed carrots. If desired, garnish platter with rosemary sprigs. Makes 4 main-dish servings.

***Note:** If using baby artichokes, cut off top ½ inch of each artichoke and trim stem. Remove tough outer leaves. Halve or quarter artichokes lengthwise. Brush cut edges with *lemon juice* or let stand in a bowl of *lemon juice* mixed with water to prevent browning; drain before using.

If using artichoke bottoms, remove loose outer leaves from 4 whole artichokes. Cook artichokes, covered, in a large amount of *boiling water* about 25 minutes or till a leaf pulls out

easily; drain and cool. Remove the leaves till the heart appears. Halve artichokes lengthwise. Remove and discard each fuzzy choke. Remove the heart of each artichoke and trim stem; reserve leaves and hearts for another use. Halve each bottom portion.

Roasted Red Potatoes: Quarter 8 small *red potatoes*. Toss with 1 tablespoon *olive oil*; 2 teaspoons snipped *fresh rosemary or* ¾ tsp. *dried rosemary,* crushed; and 2 cloves *garlic,* minced. Arrange potatoes in a single layer in a shallow baking pan. Roast in a 450° oven for 20 to 30 minutes or till tender and brown.

Nutrition facts per serving: 310 cal., 16 g total fat (3 g sat. fat), 58 mg chol., 304 mg sodium, 20 g carbo., 4 g fiber, 24 g pro. *Daily values:* 2% vit. A, 21% vit. C, 5% calcium, 24% iron.

THE ULTIMATE MINESTRONE

This recipe has evolved from Matt's discussions with fellow cooks and from reading Italian cookbooks. He claims sautéing the vegetables before adding the broth is the secret. (See the photograph on page 239.)

¼ cup olive oil
2 medium carrots, sliced
2 large stalks celery, chopped
1 medium onion, chopped
1 small head savoy or green
    cabbage, coarsely shredded
6 leaves Swiss chard, coarsely
    shredded
6 leaves kale, coarsely
    shredded
8 oz. green beans, trimmed
    and cut into 2-inch pieces

8 oz. potatoes, peeled and
   cubed (optional)
8 cups chicken broth
2 14½-oz. cans tomatoes, cut
   up, or 3 cups chopped
   fresh tomatoes
½ tsp. pepper
2 15-oz. cans white kidney
   (cannellini) beans,
   drained, or 1½ cups dry
   great Northern beans,
   cooked*
1 medium zucchini or yellow
   summer squash, quartered
   lengthwise and sliced
¾ cup snipped fresh basil

1 In a 6- to 8-quart pot heat olive oil over medium-high heat. Add carrots, celery, and onion. Cook and stir for 2 minutes. Add cabbage, Swiss chard, and kale. Cook and stir vegetables about 6 minutes more or till greens are wilted. Add green beans and potatoes, if desired. Cook and stir for 2 minutes more.

2 Add chicken broth, tomatoes, and pepper. Bring to boiling; reduce heat. Simmer, covered, for 20 minutes. Stir in white kidney or great Northern beans, and zucchini or squash. Return to boiling; reduce heat. Simmer, covered, 20 minutes more. Stir in basil. Makes 8 main-dish servings.

*Note: To cook dry beans, rinse beans. In a 4- to 5-quart pot combine rinsed beans and 5 cups *cold water.* Bring to boiling; reduce heat. Simmer, uncovered, for 2 minutes. Remove from heat. Cover and let stand for 1 hour. (Or, omit simmering; soak dry beans in *cold water* overnight in a covered pot.) Drain beans and rinse. In the same pot combine rinsed beans and 5 cups fresh *water.* Bring to boiling; reduce heat. Cover and simmer beans for 1 to 1½ hours or till beans are tender, stirring occasionally.

Nutrition tip: To reduce the sodium in this recipe, use reduced-sodium chicken broth and/or tomatoes.

Nutrition facts per serving: 213 cal., 9 g total fat (1 g sat. fat), 1 mg chol., 1,159 mg sodium, 27 g carbo., 8 g fiber, 14 g pro. *Daily values:* 63% vit. A, 55% vit. C, 10% calcium, 21% iron.

EGGPLANT ROLLATINI

All the pizza flavors your family loves are wrapped into this meal. (See the photograph on page 233.)

1 medium eggplant
2 Tbsp. olive oil
   ◆◆◆
1 clove garlic, minced
1 Tbsp. olive oil
1 14½-oz. can diced tomatoes
1 tsp. dried basil, crushed, or
   2 Tbsp. snipped fresh basil
1 Tbsp. tomato paste
   ◆◆◆
4 oz. Monterey Jack or
   mozzarella cheese
4 oz. thinly sliced prosciutto
   or cooked ham
¼ tsp. pepper
   ◆◆◆
¼ cup finely shredded
   Parmesan cheese

1 Trim and peel eggplant; cut lengthwise into eight ¼-inch-thick slices. In a 12-inch skillet heat 2 tablespoons olive oil over medium-high heat. Cook eggplant, 3 or 4 slices at a time, in oil about 2 minutes on each side or till browned (add oil to skillet as necessary). Remove eggplant and drain on paper towels. Set aside.

2 For sauce, in a medium saucepan cook garlic in 1 tablespoon olive oil over medium-high heat for 30 seconds. Stir in undrained tomatoes, dried basil (if using), and tomato paste. Bring to boiling; reduce heat. Simmer, uncovered, 15 minutes or till of desired consistency, stirring frequently. Stir in fresh basil (if using). Pour sauce into a 2-quart rectangular baking dish.

3 To assemble eggplant rolls, cut cheese into eight 3×½×½-inch spears. Divide prosciutto or ham and place atop eggplant slices. Place a spear of cheese on an end of each eggplant slice. Roll up each slice around the cheese. Arrange eggplant rolls, seam side down, atop sauce. Sprinkle rolls with pepper. Bake, uncovered, in a 450° oven for 8 to 10 minutes or till sauce is bubbly and cheese in rolls just starts to melt.

4 To serve, place 2 eggplant rolls on each dinner plate. Spoon sauce over rolls. Sprinkle with Parmesan cheese. Makes 4 main-dish servings.

■ TO MAKE AHEAD ■

Cool sauce before pouring into baking dish. Arrange rolls atop sauce. Cover; refrigerate for up to 24 hours. Bake, covered, in a 400° oven for 20 to 25 minutes or till sauce is bubbly and cheese just starts to melt. Serve as directed.

Nutrition facts per serving: 364 cal., 28 g total fat (7 g sat. fat), 30 mg chol., 906 mg sodium, 12 g carbo., 4 g fiber, 19 g pro. *Daily values:* 16% vit. A, 31% vit. C, 25% calcium, 9% iron.

Homemade Pasta Points

Homemade Egg Pasta (see right) is so versatile you can use the cooked pasta in any number of ways—with a sauce, in a casserole, or tossed as a salad. Whichever way you choose, follow our hints to use your fresh pasta to the best advantage.

Shaping Pasta
Once the pasta dough is rolled out, shape it according to the directions in a recipe or in one of these shapes:

Linguine or Fettuccine: Loosely roll up the rolled-out dough jelly-roll style. Cut it into ⅛-inch-wide slices for linguine or ¼-inch-wide slices for fettuccine. Shake out the strands to separate them. Cut the pasta strands into even lengths.

Farfalle: Cut the rolled-out dough into 2×1-inch rectangles. Pinch centers of the rectangles forming bow ties.

Tripolini: Cut the rolled-out dough into 1-inch circles. Pinch the centers of the circles forming butterfly shapes.

Storing Pasta
To prepare pasta for storage, hang ribbonlike shapes, such as linguine or fettuccine, from a pasta drying rack or clothes hanger. Spread small shapes, such as farfalle or tripolini, on a wire rack. Let pasta stand at room temperature overnight or till completely dry. Place pasta in airtight containers and refrigerate up to 3 days.

To freeze homemade pasta, let it dry as above at least 1 hour, then seal it in freezer bags or containers. Freeze for up to 8 months.

How Much Pasta to Serve
When serving homemade pasta with a sauce, use 4 ounces uncooked per person for a main dish and 2 ounces per person for a side dish.

To substitute homemade pasta for packaged dried pasta in a recipe, use twice as much homemade pasta as dried pasta. To substitute homemade pasta for refrigerated pasta in a recipe, use the same amount.

Cooking Pasta
In a 6- to 8-quart pot bring water (about 3 quarts of water for 4 to 8 ounces of pasta) to boiling. If desired, add 1 teaspoon cooking oil (to help keep the pasta separated) and 1 teaspoon salt. Add pasta a little at a time so the water does not stop boiling. Reduce the heat slightly. Boil pasta, uncovered, for 1½ to 2 minutes for linguine or fettuccine (2 to 3 minutes for farfalle or tripolini) or till the pasta is al dente (tender but slightly firm). Stir the pasta occasionally. Test the pasta often for doneness near the end of the cooking time.

Serving Pasta Hot
To make sure your pasta is warm when it comes to the table, plan to serve it in a warm serving bowl. Warm the bowl by filling it with hot water and letting it stand a few minutes to absorb the heat. Then, empty the bowl and wipe it dry. Next, drain the pasta quickly into a colander, giving the colander a few quick shakes. Transfer the pasta to the warm bowl and serve immediately.

LOW FAT
Homemade Egg Pasta

For the final rolling, Matt strongly suggests a pasta machine. But if you don't have one, a rolling pin will work.

   4 **eggs**
   2 **Tbsp. water**
2½ **cups all-purpose flour**
   ½ **tsp. salt**

◆◆◆

   ½ **cup all-purpose flour**

1 To prepare dough, in a food processor bowl combine eggs and water. Cover and process till combined. Add the 2½ cups flour and the salt. Cover and process till mixture forms a ball. (Or, to prepare by hand, in a large bowl stir together the 2½ cups flour and the salt. Make a well in the center of the mixture. Combine the eggs and water. Add egg mixture to the flour mixture; mix well.)

2 Sprinkle kneading surface with the ½ cup flour. Turn dough out onto floured surface. Knead about 4 minutes or till all the flour is incorporated. The dough should be firm but not stiff and dry. Cover and let rest for 15 to 20 minutes.

3 To roll out dough with a pasta machine, divide the dough into thirds. Pass each portion through pasta machine at widest roller opening. Repeat at same setting to smooth dough, if necessary. Set machine at the next narrower opening and pass each portion of dough through machine. Repeat at same setting till dough is smooth. If dough tears or pulls, fold dough and reroll. Continue resetting machine at narrower openings and rolling each portion of dough till it is about 1/16 inch thick. For easier handling, divide dough as it lengthens from successive rollings. (Or, to roll out dough with a rolling pin, divide dough into thirds. On a lightly floured surface, roll out each portion to a 16×12-inch rectangle. If dough seems too elastic while rolling, cover and let rest a few minutes.)

4 Shape pasta (see tip, page 230). Use pasta as directed in recipes. Makes about 1½ pounds (twelve 2-ounce servings).

Nutrition facts per 2-oz. serving: 130 cal., 2 g total fat (1 g sat. fat), 71 mg chol., 110 mg sodium, 22 g carbo., 1 g fiber, 5 g pro. *Daily values:* 3% vit. A, 1% calcium, 10% iron.

SQUASH-STUFFED TORTELLI

A drizzle of browned butter and sage is the crowning finish for these plump pasta pillows. Serve them on the side with grilled meats. (See the photograph on page 238.)

1 **2-lb. butternut squash**
1 **tsp. snipped fresh thyme or ¼ tsp. dried thyme, crushed**
1 to 2 **Tbsp. olive oil**
4 **cloves garlic**

♦♦♦

¼ **cup grated Parmesan cheese**
2 **Tbsp. fine dry bread crumbs**
¼ **tsp. ground nutmeg**

♦♦♦

1 **recipe Homemade Egg Pasta (see page 230)**

♦♦♦

¼ **cup butter**
½ **cup packed small fresh sage leaves**
   Ground nutmeg (optional)

1 For filling, halve squash; remove seeds. Sprinkle cut sides of squash with thyme and some *salt* and *pepper;* drizzle with olive oil. Place squash halves, cut sides down, on a baking sheet. Tuck 2 cloves of garlic under each half. Bake in a 350° oven for 35 to 40 minutes or till tender; cool.

2 Peel squash. In a bowl combine squash and garlic. Mash with a potato masher. Stir in the Parmesan cheese, bread crumbs, and ¼ teaspoon nutmeg; mix well. If the mixture is thin and wet, stir in additional *cheese.*

3 Prepare Homemade Egg Pasta. Roll out the dough. Using a fluted pastry wheel or sharp knife, cut the pasta dough into 3-inch-wide strips. Place about 1 tablespoon filling every 3 inches down the center of half of the strips. Using a pastry brush or your fingertips, brush *water* onto the dough around the mounds of filling.

4 Lay a second strip of dough atop the first. Using the side of your hand, press the pasta around each mound of filling so the 2 moistened strips of dough stick together. Using the pastry wheel or knife, cut the pasta between the mounds of filling to make about 24 evenly sized tortelli. (At this point, the filled pasta may be placed in an airtight container and stored in the refrigerator up to 2 days or in the freezer up to 3 months.)

5 To cook the pasta, bring a large pot of *salted water* to boiling. (Add 1 teaspoon *cooking oil* to

Menu

Grilled rib eye steaks

♦♦♦

Squash-Stuffed Tortelli (see below left)

♦♦♦

Salad of fresh spinach leaves with apple slices, toasted walnuts, and fruit vinaigrette

♦♦♦

Poached pears with cream

water, if desired, to prevent pasta from sticking.) Add 6 to 8 fresh or frozen tortelli to water; return to boiling. Cook, uncovered, for 6 to 8 minutes or till just tender. Using a slotted spoon, remove tortelli from water and place in a baking pan; cover and keep warm in a 300° oven. Repeat with the remaining tortelli.

6 Meanwhile, for sauce, in a small saucepan melt butter. Add sage leaves; cook and stir over medium heat till butter is lightly browned and leaves are crispy. Watch carefully to avoid over-browning the butter.

7 To serve, place the tortelli on a serving platter; spoon the sauce over the tortelli. If desired, sprinkle with additional nutmeg. Makes 8 to 12 side-dish servings.

Nutrition facts per serving: 321 cal., 11 g total fat (5 g sat. fat), 124 mg chol., 297 mg sodium, 45 g carbo., 3 g fiber, 10 g pro. *Daily values:* 77% vit. A, 24% vit. C, 20% iron.

RED PEPPER LASAGNA

"This recipe is one of my all-time favorites," says Matt.
(See the photograph on page 233.)

4 medium red sweet peppers
1 Tbsp. olive oil
1 28-oz. can crushed tomatoes
½ cup snipped fresh parsley
4 cloves garlic, minced
¾ tsp. black pepper

❖❖❖

⅓ cup butter or margarine
⅓ cup all-purpose flour
½ tsp. ground nutmeg
3 cups milk
1 recipe Homemade Egg Pasta
    (see page 230) or
    12 lasagna noodles

1¼ cups finely shredded
    Parmesan cheese
    Fresh tomato wedges
    (optional)
    Fresh herb sprigs (optional)

1 For red pepper sauce, halve sweet peppers; remove stems, seeds, and membranes. Place peppers, cut side down, on a foil-lined baking sheet. Bake in a 425° oven for 20 to 25 minutes or till skin is bubbly and browned. Wrap peppers in foil; let stand 20 to 30 minutes or till cool enough to handle. Peel skin from peppers. Cut peppers into thin strips.

2 In a large saucepan cook sweet pepper in hot olive oil over medium heat for 1 minute. Stir in undrained tomatoes, parsley, garlic, and black pepper. Bring to boiling; reduce heat. Simmer, uncovered, for 20 minutes, stirring often. Set aside to cool.

3 For béchamel sauce, in a medium saucepan melt butter or margarine. Stir in flour, nutmeg, and ½ teaspoon *salt* till smooth. Add milk all at once. Cook and stir over medium heat till thickened and bubbly. Cook and stir 1 minute more. Set aside to cool.

4 Prepare Homemade Egg Pasta (if using). Roll out dough. Allow dough to dry 1 hour. Cut dough into twelve 12×4-inch strips. To cook homemade pasta, bring a large pot of *salted water* to boiling. (Add 1 teaspoon *cooking oil* to water, if desired, to prevent pasta from sticking.) Add a few strips of homemade pasta to water; return to boiling. Cook, uncovered, 6 minutes or till just tender. Using a slotted spoon,

remove pasta and immediately immerse in *cold water*. Repeat with remaining homemade pasta. (Or, cook lasagna noodles according to package directions; immerse in *cold water*.) Remove cooked pasta with a slotted spoon and drain on a towel; blot dry with another towel.

5 To assemble, grease the bottom of a 3-quart rectangular baking dish. Cover bottom with about one-fourth of the pasta, trimming pasta as necessary. Spread about 1¼ cups of the red pepper sauce over the pasta. Drizzle about ¾ cup of the béchamel sauce over the red pepper sauce; sprinkle with about ⅓ cup of the Parmesan cheese. Repeat twice more with the pasta, red pepper sauce, béchamel sauce, and Parmesan cheese. Top with the remaining pasta and béchamel sauce; sprinkle with the remaining Parmesan cheese.

6 Bake, uncovered, in a 350° oven 30 to 35 minutes or till bubbly and light brown on top. Let stand 10 minutes before serving. If desired, garnish with tomato wedges and herb sprigs. Makes 8 main-dish servings.

▮ TO MAKE-AHEAD ▮

Assemble lasagna as directed. Cover with plastic wrap; refrigerate up to 24 hours. To serve, remove plastic wrap and cover with foil. Bake in a 350° oven 30 minutes. Remove foil. Bake 15 to 25 minutes more or till bubbly.

Nutrition facts per serving: 442 cal., 19 g total fat (7 g sat. fat), 146 mg chol., 786 mg sodium, 49 g carbo., 2 g fiber, 20 g pro. *Daily values:* 54% vit. A, 139% vit. C, 26% calcium, 24% iron.

Top: *Eggplant Rollatini (page 229)*
Above: *Red Pepper Lasagna (page 232)*

Left: *Lamb and Vegetable Platter* (page 228)
Top: *Peppers Stuffed with Chicken and Rice* (page 242)

Page 237: *Granny Cake (page 243)*
Below: *Bourbon and Nut Pie*
(page 242)
Right: *Cola Cake (page 244)*

Page 238: *Squash-Stuffed Tortelli (page 231)*
Top: *Chicken with Porcini Mushrooms (page 227)*
Above: *The Ultimate Minestrone (page 228)*

Above: *Pork Roast with Sweet Potatoes (page 241) and Popover Muffins (page 242)*

DINNER FROM THE HEART

In one Kentucky home, simple Southern cooking means more than meat and potatoes. It's the fuel that fires one growing family every day of the year.

Rosa and Lawrence Robinson celebrated their 55th wedding anniversary in the company of children, grandchildren, and great-grandchildren, all raised on Rosa's family dinners. It's her cooking that joins the limbs of a family tree that sprawls the streets of Louisville, Kentucky. They don't convene for convenience sake, but rather to keep the family whole and wholesome.

"This was home," says Rosa, "and our kids just never stopped coming back for dinner." Rosa's recipes are seldom written down; her pork roast is adapted from her own mother's kitchen, and her Granny Cake is fine-tuned from a church supper. It's food that nourishes, food that holds for late arrivals, food that can stretch to fill a stack of plates (usually eight, sometimes 12). It's also inspiration for future good cooks; already, their great-granddaughter Brittany's favorite toy is a kitchen spoon.

PORK ROAST WITH SWEET POTATOES

Comfort food at its finest, this recipe originated with Rosa's mother. But as with most recipes, Rosa adds a personal touch—this time she added apples and honey.
(See the photograph on page 240.)

1 **3- to 4-lb. boneless pork sirloin roast**
1 **Tbsp. lemon-pepper seasoning**
1 **Tbsp. all-purpose flour**
◆◆◆
⅓ **cup honey**
¼ **cup lemon juice**
1 **Tbsp. brown sugar**
6 **small sweet potatoes, peeled and halved lengthwise**
½ **tsp. ground nutmeg**
◆◆◆
3 **baking apples (such as Golden Delicious or Jonathan), cored and quartered**
2 **small oranges, thinly sliced**

1 Sprinkle pork roast with lemon-pepper seasoning. Sprinkle the top and sides of the roast with the 1 tablespoon flour. Dust a large oven roasting bag with additional *flour* as directed on the package.

2 Place pork roast in bag; tie bag closed. Cut six ½-inch slits in top of bag. Set in a 13×9×2-inch baking pan. Roast in a 375° oven for 1 hour.

3 Meanwhile, in a small mixing bowl stir together the honey, lemon juice, and brown sugar. Slit top of bag and carefully slide roast out of bag, pouring any juices from bag into pan. Place sweet potatoes around roast. Spoon honey mixture over roast and potatoes; sprinkle with nutmeg. Cover and return to oven; roast for 1 to 1¼ hours more or till the meat and potatoes are tender.

4 Arrange apple quarters, cut sides up, atop sweet potatoes. Brush with the honey mixture in the pan. Cut a slit from edge to center in each orange slice and twist; arrange around roast. Return to oven; roast, uncovered, for 15 to 20 minutes more or till apples are just tender.

5 If roast is tied, remove strings. Transfer roast, potatoes, and fruit to serving platter. Makes 8 to 10 main-dish servings.

Nutrition facts per serving: 356 cal., 11 g total fat (4 g sat. fat), 77 mg chol., 473 mg sodium, 38 g carbo., 4 g fiber, 26 g pro. *Daily values:* 121% vit. A, 62% vit. C, 3% calcium, 10% iron.

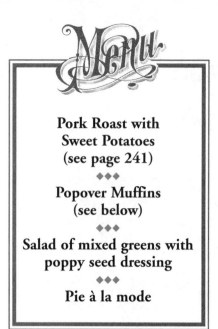

**Pork Roast with
Sweet Potatoes
(see page 241)**

♦♦♦

**Popover Muffins
(see below)**

♦♦♦

**Salad of mixed greens with
poppy seed dressing**

♦♦♦

Pie à la mode

POPOVER MUFFINS

*Like traditional popovers, this
dinner bread has a rich, yet light, taste.
They're a hit with the Robinson family,
especially with meat and potatoes.
(See the photograph on page 240.)*

2 cups all-purpose flour
⅓ cup sugar
1 Tbsp. baking powder
½ tsp. salt
4 eggs
½ cup milk
¼ cup butter-flavored
    shortening, melted

1 Grease twelve 2½-inch
muffin cups; set aside. In a large
mixing bowl stir together the
flour, sugar, baking powder, and
salt. Make a well in the center. In
a medium mixing bowl combine
eggs, milk, and melted shortening; add all at once to flour mixture. Stir with a fork till the dry
ingredients are just moistened.

2 Fill prepared muffin cups
almost full. Bake in a 400° oven

about 15 minutes or till muffins
are golden. Remove from pan.
Serve warm. Makes 12 muffins.

Nutrition facts per muffin: 160 cal., 6 g
total fat (2 g sat. fat), 72 mg chol., 206 mg
sodium, 21 g carbo., 1 g fiber, 4 g pro.
Daily values: 3% vit. A, 9% calcium,
8% iron.

PEPPERS STUFFED WITH CHICKEN AND RICE

*"Food that's nourishing and that can
hold." That's the kind of cooking Rosa
says you'll find in her kitchen. Any
on-the-go family will welcome this dish.
(See the photograph on page 235.)*

1 Tbsp. margarine or butter
½ cup finely chopped celery
1 10¾-oz. can reduced-fat and
    reduced-sodium
    condensed cream of
    mushroom soup
1 cup water or chicken broth
1 single-serving-size envelope
    instant onion soup mix
    (about 1 Tbsp.)
4 cups cubed cooked chicken
3 cups hot cooked rice

♦♦♦

5 large green sweet peppers
    (about 8 oz. each)
1 tsp. lemon-pepper seasoning

♦♦♦

1¼ cups shredded cheddar
    cheese (5 oz.)
⅓ cup chopped pimiento

1 In a large saucepan melt
margarine or butter over medium
heat. Add celery and cook about
5 minutes or till tender. Stir in
condensed mushroom soup,
water or chicken broth, and dry
onion soup mix. Heat till bubbly.
Stir in chicken; heat through. Stir
in rice; remove from heat.

2 To assemble, halve sweet
peppers lengthwise; remove
stems, seeds, and membranes.
Place pepper halves, cut side up,
in a large shallow baking or roasting pan. Divide chicken mixture
among pepper halves. Sprinkle
with lemon-pepper seasoning.

3 Cover peppers loosely with
foil. Bake in a 350° oven about
25 minutes or till peppers are
crisp-tender. Sprinkle with cheese;
top with pimiento. Bake, uncovered, about 5 minutes more or till
cheese is just melted. Makes
10 main-dish servings.

▌ TO MAKE AHEAD ▌

Assemble peppers as directed.
Cover with foil and refrigerate for
up to 24 hours. To serve, bake
peppers, loosely covered with foil,
in a 350° oven about 55 minutes
or till heated through. Top with
cheese and pimiento. Bake,
uncovered, about 5 minutes more
or till cheese is melted.

Nutrition facts per serving: 285 cal., 11 g
total fat (5 g sat. fat), 70 mg chol., 743 mg
sodium, 21 g carbo., 1 g fiber, 23 g pro.
Daily values: 10% vit. A, 55% vit. C, 10%
calcium, 12% iron.

BOURBON AND NUT PIE

*Rosa bakes pies once a week,
four or five at a time. For this
pecan-pie variation, use any
bourbon you prefer.
(See the photograph on page 236.)*

1 recipe Pastry for Single-
    Crust Pie (see recipe and
    tip, page 243)

♦♦♦

3 eggs, slightly beaten
¾ cup light-colored corn syrup
3 Tbsp. granulated sugar

TEST KITCHEN TIP

TOO BUSY TO MAKE PASTRY?

When time is tight, skip the made-from-scratch pastry for Bourbon and Nut Pie and use one of the following: Piecrust mix comes in stick or regular forms. Use 1 stick, or half of an 11- or 9-ounce package for a 9-inch pie. Just prepare the stick or mix according to package directions and roll it out.

Refrigerated pastry saves time because it's already rolled out. Look for a package of two folded pastry circles in the dairy section of your supermarket. Use 1 circle for a 9-inch pie.

The ultimate in piemaking convenience is a frozen unbaked pastry shell. For Bourbon and Nut Pie, be sure to use the 9-inch deep-dish size.

3 Tbsp. brown sugar
3 Tbsp. butter, softened
1 tsp. vanilla
⅛ tsp. salt
½ cup finely chopped pecans
⅓ cup bourbon

♦♦♦

1 6-oz. pkg. (1 cup) semisweet chocolate pieces
1½ cups pecan halves

1 Prepare Pastry for Single-Crust Pie. On a lightly floured surface, roll out dough to 12-inch circle. Line a 9-inch pie plate with pastry. Trim to ½ inch beyond edge. Fold under extra pastry and flute edge. Do not prick pastry.

2 For filling, in a large mixing bowl combine the eggs, corn syrup, granulated sugar, brown sugar, butter, vanilla, and salt; mix well. Stir in the chopped pecans and bourbon.

3 Pat chocolate pieces lightly onto bottom of pastry shell. Pour filling atop chocolate pieces. Arrange pecan halves atop filling.

4 Bake in a 350° oven about 1 hour or till a knife inserted near the center comes out clean. Cover edges of pie loosely with foil the last 30 minutes to prevent over-browning. Serves 10.

Pastry for Single-Crust Pie: Stir together 1¼ cups *all-purpose flour* and ¼ teaspoon *salt*. Cut in ⅓ cup *shortening* till pieces are the size of small peas. Using 4 to 5 tablespoons *cold water* total, sprinkle 1 tablespoon water over part of the mixture; gently toss with a fork. Push to side of bowl. Repeat till all is moistened. Form into a ball.

Nutrition facts per serving: 506 cal., 31 g total fat (5 g sat. fat), 73 mg chol., 153 mg sodium, 52 g carbo., 2 g fiber, 6 g pro. *Daily values:* 6% vit. A, 3% calcium, 19% iron.

GRANNY CAKE

Another name for this moist, fruity cake is Hummingbird Cake. (See the photograph on page 237.)

3 cups all-purpose flour
2 cups granulated sugar
1 tsp. baking soda
1 tsp. ground nutmeg
½ tsp. salt
½ tsp. ground cloves
¾ cup butter or margarine
3 eggs
2 cups mashed ripe bananas
1 8-oz. can crushed pineapple
2 tsp. vanilla
1 cup finely chopped pecans
Paper doily (optional)
Powdered sugar (optional)
Red grapes (optional)

1 Grease and flour a 10-inch tube pan. In a medium mixing bowl stir together flour, granulated sugar, baking soda, nutmeg, salt, and cloves; set aside.

2 In a large mixing bowl beat butter or margarine with an electric mixer on medium speed for 30 seconds. Add eggs, bananas, undrained pineapple, and vanilla. Beat till combined. Add flour mixture. Beat on low speed till combined. Beat on medium speed for 1 minute. Fold in pecans.

3 Spread batter in the prepared pan. Bake in a 325° oven for 70 to 75 minutes or till a wooden toothpick inserted near the center comes out clean. Cool cake in pan on a wire rack for 10 minutes. Remove cake from pan. Cool completely.

4 If desired, decorate cake with a powdered-sugar design. Place doily atop cake. Spoon some powdered sugar into a sieve or sifter and sift over the doily to fill cutout designs. Carefully remove and discard the doily. If desired, serve cake with grapes. Makes 12 to 16 servings.

Nutrition facts per serving: 481 cal., 19 g total fat (8 g sat. fat), 84 mg chol., 328 mg sodium, 74 g carbo., 2 g fiber, 6 g pro. *Daily values:* 13% vit. A, 12% vit. C, 2% calcium, 13% iron.

Cola Cake

Rosa's grandchildren love this sweet treat. They'd eat seconds and thirds if she'd let them. (See the photograph on page 236.)

- 2⅓ cups all-purpose flour
- 2 cups sugar
- 1 tsp. baking soda

♦♦♦

- 1 cup cola
- ⅔ cup butter or margarine
- 2 Tbsp. unsweetened cocoa powder
- 2 eggs
- ½ cup buttermilk
- 2 tsp. vanilla
- 1½ cups tiny marshmallows

♦♦♦

- 1 recipe Cocoa Topping (see below)

1 Grease and flour a 13×9×2-inch baking pan. In a large mixing bowl stir together flour, sugar, and baking soda; set aside.

2 In a medium saucepan bring cola, butter, and cocoa powder to boiling over medium heat. Add hot mixture to flour mixture; stir till just combined. Add eggs, buttermilk, and vanilla; stir till combined. Gently stir in marshmallows (they will float to top).

3 Pour batter into prepared pan. Bake in a 350° oven 30 minutes or till a wooden toothpick inserted near the center comes out clean. Transfer cake in pan to a wire rack. Immediately spread Cocoa Topping over cake. Cool completely. Makes 16 servings.

Cocoa Topping: In a medium saucepan bring ½ cup *butter or margarine*, ¼ cup *unsweetened* cocoa powder, and ¼ cup *cola* to boiling. Add 2½ cups sifted *powdered sugar* and 1 teaspoon *vanilla*. Mix with a wire whisk. Stir in 1 cup chopped *nuts*.

Nutrition facts per serving: 419 cal., 19 g total fat (9 g sat. fat), 63 mg chol., 233 mg sodium, 60 g carbo., 1 g fiber, 5 g pro. *Daily values:* 13% vit. A, 4% calcium, 9% iron.

Old-Fashioned Gingerbread

- 1½ cups all-purpose flour
- ½ tsp. baking powder
- ½ tsp. baking soda
- ½ tsp. ground cinnamon
- ⅛ tsp. ground cloves

♦♦♦

- ½ cup shortening
- ¼ cup packed brown sugar
- 1 egg
- ½ cup molasses
- 2 tsp. grated fresh gingerroot or ¾ tsp. ground ginger
- Sweetened whipped cream* (optional)

1 Grease an 8×8×2-inch baking pan. Combine flour, baking powder, soda, cinnamon, cloves, and ½ teaspoon *salt.*

2 Beat shortening with an electric mixer 30 seconds. Add brown sugar; beat till combined. Add egg, molasses, and gingerroot; beat 1 minute. Alternately add flour mixture and ½ cup *boiling water,* beating on low speed after each addition just till combined. Pour into prepared pan.

3 Bake in a 350° oven 30 to 35 minutes or till a toothpick inserted in center comes out clean. Cool slightly. Serve warm with sweetened whipped cream, if desired. Makes 9 servings.

Note: Make the sweetened whipped cream by adding 2 tablespoons *sugar* and 1 teaspoon *vanilla* to 1 cup *whipping cream;* whip to soft peaks.

Nutrition facts per serving: 247 calories, 12 g total fat (3 g sat. fat), 24 mg chol., 98 mg sodium, 32 g carbo., 1 g fiber, 3 g pro. *Daily values:* 1% vit. A, 3% calcium, 12% iron.

Meet the Molasses Family

Light-flavored molasses: This maple-syrup-colored molasses is made by reducing and blending sugarcane juices into a syrup. Most cooks favor this type, especially for baking, because of its lighter, sweeter flavor. Add to plain yogurt or hot cereal as a sweetener.

Dark-flavored molasses: For a robust flavor and a darker color, try dark-flavored molasses anywhere you'd use light. This type is a by-product of sugar making, so some sugar has been removed. Use dark-flavored molasses to complement savory dishes such as casseroles, baked beans, and meat sauces.

Blackstrap molasses: Sold in health food stores as a concentrated source of iron, blackstrap molasses has a pungent, intensified flavor. Because most of the sugar has been removed, this type of molasses isn't really considered a sweetener.

NOVEMBER
Together at Thanksgiving

IN THIS CHAPTER

30-minute recipes indicated in RED.
Low-fat recipes indicated with a ♥.

As families gather and give thanks, begin the day's feast with a plateful of nibbles such as Citrus Shrimp Bruschetta and Ham and Cheese Crisps. Fragrant homemade breads are showstoppers, whether as a warm breakfast wake-up such as Raisin-Pumpkin Twist or as dinner accompaniments such as Potato Buns served alongside the turkey. You can make both of them days ahead. Cookies herald the season, and now's the time to stash away batches of Chocolate-Pistachio Wreaths and Nutcracker Cookies along with ribbon-trimmed jars of spicy chutneys so you ease into the holidays with perfect gifts at the ready in your cupboard.

TOMATO-OLIVE SPIRALS

Hot roll mix gives you a headstart on these crowd-pleasing appetizers. (See the photograph on page 275.)

1 16-oz. pkg. hot roll mix
❖❖❖
½ cup oil-packed dried tomatoes
1 8-oz. pkg. cream cheese, softened
1 3-oz. pkg. cream cheese, softened
½ cup finely chopped pitted ripe olives
¼ cup chopped green onions
1 egg yolk, slightly beaten
1 tsp. cracked black pepper
½ tsp. dried oregano or thyme, crushed (optional)
❖❖❖
1 slightly beaten egg
1 Tbsp. water

1 Prepare the hot roll mix according to package directions. After kneading, divide the dough into thirds; cover and let rest for 5 minutes. Grease a large baking sheet; set aside.

2 For filling, drain tomatoes, reserving oil. Chop the tomatoes. In a mixing bowl combine the tomatoes, cream cheese, olives, green onions, egg yolk, pepper, and, if desired, oregano or thyme. Stir in enough reserved tomato oil (about 1 tablespoon), if necessary, to make a filling that is easy to spread.

3 On a lightly floured surface, roll each portion of dough into a 14×11-inch rectangle. Spread a third of the filling atop each rectangle to within ½ inch of edges (filling amount will seem generous). Roll up dough tightly from long sides. Seal seams. Place, seam side down, on the prepared baking sheet. Cover and let dough rise till nearly double (about 30 to 40 minutes).

4 Using a sharp knife, slash tops making 3 or 4 diagonal cuts, about ¼ inch deep. Combine the egg and water; brush onto rolls. Bake in a 375° oven about 25 minutes or till golden. Carefully remove rolls from baking sheet and cool on a wire rack. Serve warm or at room temperature. Slice with a serrated knife. Makes 3 loaves (72 spirals).

■ TO MAKE AHEAD ■

Prepare and bake bread as directed; cool completely. Wrap loaves individually in heavy foil and freeze for up to 3 months. To reheat, bake each wrapped loaf in a 300° oven about 30 minutes or till heated through.

Nutrition facts per spiral: 44 cal., 2 g total fat (1 g sat. fat), 14 mg chol., 58 mg sodium, 5 g carbo., 0 g fiber, 1 g pro. *Daily values:* 2% vit. A, 1% vit. C, 1% iron.

HAM AND CHEESE CRISPS

Shape and freeze these easy puff pastry appetizers days or weeks ahead, then bake just before serving.

1 17¼-oz. pkg. frozen puff pastry (2 sheets)
2 Tbsp. honey
2 Tbsp. Dijon-style mustard
❖❖❖
¼ cup grated Romano or Parmesan cheese
6 oz. thinly sliced cooked ham
❖❖❖
1 egg
2 tsp. water

1 Let folded pastry stand at room temperature for 20 minutes to thaw. Line baking sheets with parchment or plain brown paper. In a small bowl stir together the honey and mustard. Set the baking sheets and honey-mustard mixture aside.

2 On a lightly floured surface, unfold 1 sheet of pastry. Spread with half of the honey-mustard mixture. Sprinkle with *half* of the cheese; top with *half* of the sliced ham. Starting at one long edge, roll pastry, jelly-roll style, to the center. Repeat from the opposite edge, forming 2 rolls that meet in the center.

3 With a sharp knife, cut the pastry roll crosswise into ½-inch-thick slices. (If the roll is too soft to slice easily, chill for a few minutes.) Arrange the slices 2 inches apart on the prepared baking sheets. Repeat with remaining pastry, honey-mustard mixture, cheese, and ham.

4 Combine egg and water; brush onto pastries. Bake pastries in a 400° oven for 15 to 18 minutes or till golden and crisp. Remove from baking sheet; cool on a wire rack. Serve warm or at room temperature. Makes 40.

■ TO MAKE AHEAD ■

Prepare crisps as directed, except do not brush with egg-water mixture and do not bake. Place the baking sheet in freezer till pastries are solid. Transfer frozen pastries to freezer containers or bags. Freeze for up to 1 month. Bake frozen pastries as directed.

Nutrition facts per crisp: 67 cal., 4 g total fat (0 g sat. fat), 8 mg chol., 121 mg sodium, 5 g carbo., 0 g fiber, 2 g pro. *Daily values:* 1% vit. C.

CITRUS SHRIMP BRUSCHETTA

Bruschetta (broo-SKEH-tah) is an Italian word for cooking over coals. It also refers to appetizers of toasted, thinly sliced bread, seasoned and topped with flavorful cheeses, herbs, and condiments.

30 **medium fresh or frozen shrimp in shells**

♦♦♦

1 **15¼-oz. can crushed pineapple (juice pack), well drained**
2 **Tbsp. orange marmalade**
2 **Tbsp. snipped fresh cilantro**
2 **tsp. grated gingerroot**
¼ **tsp. bottled hot pepper sauce**

♦♦♦

1 **8-oz. loaf French bread (baguette-style) (8 inches long)**
½ **of an 8-oz. tub cream cheese (about ½ cup)**
    Fresh cilantro leaves (optional)

1 Thaw shrimp, if frozen. Remove shells, leaving tails intact; devein shrimp. In a large saucepan cook shrimp, uncovered, in boiling *lightly salted water* for 1 to 3 minutes or till shrimp turn pink. Drain; cover and chill.

2 For topping, in a small mixing bowl stir together the pineapple, marmalade, snipped cilantro, gingerroot, and hot pepper sauce. Set aside.

3 Just before serving, thinly slice the bread into 30 slices, about ¼ inch thick. Place on the unheated rack of a broiler pan; broil 3 to 4 inches from the heat for 2 to 3 minutes or till lightly toasted on both sides, turning once. Spread one side with cream cheese. Top with pineapple mixture and a shrimp. Broil for 2 to 3 minutes more or till heated through. If desired, garnish each with a cilantro leaf. Serve immediately. Makes about 30.

Nutrition facts per bruschetta: 53 cal., 2 g total fat (1 g sat. fat), 22 mg chol., 78 mg sodium, 7 g carbo., 0 g fiber, 3 g pro. *Daily values:* 2% vit. A, 2% vit. C, 1% calcium, 3% iron.

NESTED PUFFS WITH TOMATO CHUTNEY

⅓ **cup dried tomatoes (not oil-packed)**
1 **small tart cooking apple, peeled, cored, and finely chopped (¾ cup)**
⅓ **cup finely chopped onion**
⅓ **cup finely chopped cooked ham**
¼ **cup finely chopped red sweet pepper**
3 **Tbsp. brown sugar**
3 **Tbsp. apple cider vinegar**
2 **Tbsp. finely chopped raisins**
½ **tsp. dried basil, crushed**
1 **clove garlic, minced**
½ **tsp. crushed red pepper**

♦♦♦

1 **17¼-oz. pkg. frozen puff pastry (2 sheets), thawed**

1 For tomato chutney, place dried tomatoes in a small bowl; add *boiling water* to cover. Let stand 10 minutes. Drain tomatoes, reserving 2 tablespoons soaking liquid. Finely snip or chop softened tomatoes. In a small saucepan combine tomato pieces, apple, onion, ham, sweet pepper, brown sugar, vinegar, raisins, basil, garlic, crushed red pepper, and reserved liquid. Bring to boiling; reduce heat. Simmer, uncovered, 15 minutes, stirring occasionally. Cover and let stand at room temperature for 30 minutes. Cover and chill till ready to use.

2 Line baking sheets with parchment paper or plain brown paper. Set baking sheets aside. Roll each sheet of pastry into a 15×10-inch rectangle. Using a sharp knife, cut each rectangle into fifteen 10×1-inch strips.

3 Take a strip, 1 end in each hand, and twist ends in opposite directions 3 or 4 times. Coil the twisted strip on prepared baking sheet, forming into a rosette. Tuck the end under. Repeat with remaining strips, placing them about 2 inches apart. Using your thumb or 2 fingers, make an indentation in the center of each pastry. Spoon about 2 teaspoons chutney into each indentation.

4 Bake in a 425° oven for 10 to 15 minutes or till golden brown. Remove from the baking sheet. Serve warm. Makes 30.

Nutrition facts per puff: 97 cal., 6 g total fat, (4 g sat. fat), 17 mg chol., 132 mg sodium, 9 g carbo., 0 g fiber, 1 g pro. *Daily values:* 6% vit. A, 3% vit. C, 3% iron.

ROAST TURKEY WITH ROSEMARY-SOURDOUGH STUFFING

To shorten the roasting time by 30 to 45 minutes, roast an unstuffed bird and cook the stuffing alongside.

1 **8- to 12-lb. turkey**
   Salt (optional)
   ♦♦♦
1 **recipe Rosemary-Sourdough**
   Stuffing (optional)
   (see right)
   Cooking oil or melted
   margarine or butter
   ♦♦♦
   Fresh rosemary (optional)
   Fresh marjoram (optional)

1 Rinse turkey; pat dry with paper towels. If desired, rub salt inside the body cavity.

2 If stuffing turkey, do not stuff till just before cooking. To stuff, spoon some of the Rosemary-Sourdough Stuffing loosely into the neck cavity. Pull the neck skin to back and fasten with a small skewer. Loosely spoon stuffing into the body cavity. (Place any remaining stuffing in a casserole and refrigerate till the bird is almost done.) If there is a band of skin across the tail, tuck drumsticks under the band. If there is no band, tie drumsticks securely to the tail. Twist wing tips under the back.

3 Place the turkey, breast side up, on a rack in a shallow roasting pan. Insert a meat thermometer into the center of one of the inside thigh muscles. The bulb should not touch the bone.

4 Cover turkey with foil, leaving air space between turkey and foil. Roast in a 325° oven for 3 to 3½ hours for stuffed bird or 2¾ to 3¼ hours for an unstuffed bird. Baste occasionally with pan drippings, if desired, to moisten and flavor meat. When the turkey is two-thirds done, cut the band of skin or string between the drumsticks so the thighs will cook evenly. Uncover the turkey the last 45 minutes of cooking to let the turkey brown. Continue roasting until meat thermometer registers 180° to 185°. Add the stuffing in the casserole to the oven; bake till heated through, allowing 40 to 45 minutes for the entire stuffing recipe.

5 When the turkey is done, the drumsticks should move easily in their sockets and the thickest parts of the drumsticks should feel extremely soft when pressed. The stuffing should be at least 165°. The turkey meat should be fork tender and juices should run clear when a thigh is pierced with a fork.

6 When the turkey is done, remove it from the oven and cover it with foil. Let stand for 20 minutes before carving. If desired, garnish platter with fresh rosemary and marjoram. Store leftover turkey and stuffing separately as soon as possible after serving. Makes 14 to 22 servings.

Nutrition facts per serving without stuffing: 174 cal., 8 g total fat (2 g sat. fat), 81 mg chol., 57 mg sodium, 0 g carbo., 0 g fiber, 24 g pro. *Daily values:* 5% vit. A, 1% calcium, 11% iron.

ROSEMARY-SOURDOUGH STUFFING

Sourdough adds a pleasant tang to traditional stuffing. To dry the bread for stuffing, see the note on page 249.

3 **cups sliced assorted fresh**
   mushrooms (8 oz.),
   such as shiitake, brown,
   or white
1 **cup sliced celery**
1 **cup chopped onion**
½ **cup margarine or butter**
¼ **cup snipped fresh parsley**
1 **tsp. dried rosemary, crushed**
½ **tsp. pepper**
   ♦♦♦
8 **cups dry sourdough bread**
   cubes*
½ **to ¾ cup chicken broth**

1 In a large saucepan cook the mushrooms, celery, and onion in hot margarine or butter till tender; remove from heat. Stir in parsley, rosemary, and pepper.

2 Place dry bread cubes in a large bowl. Add mushroom mixture. Drizzle with enough broth to moisten, tossing lightly. Use to stuff one 8- to 12-pound turkey. Or, bake separately in a casserole, covered, in a 325° oven for 40 to 45 minutes or in a 375° oven for 20 to 30 minutes or till heated through. (If the stuffing is baked inside the turkey, the temperature of the cooked stuffing should register at least 165° in the center.) Makes 8 to 12 servings.

*Note: To make dry bread cubes for stuffing, cut the bread into ½-inch square pieces. (You'll need 12 to 14 slices of bread for 8 cups of dry cubes.) Spread in a single layer in a 15½×10½×2-inch baking pan. Bake in a 300° oven for 10 to 15 minutes or till dry, stirring twice; cool. The bread will continue to dry and crisp as it cools. (Or, let bread stand, loosely covered, at room temperature for 8 to 12 hours.)

Nutrition facts per serving: 279 cal., 14 g total fat (3 g sat. fat), 0 mg chol., 544 mg sodium, 34 g carbo., 1 g fiber, 6 g pro. *Daily values:* 15% vit. A, 9% vit. C, 5% calcium, 14% iron.

TURKEY: SMART WAYS TO STUFF IT

Play-It-Safe Stuffing
Good stuffing begins with prudent preparation—mix the stuffing just before you stuff and roast. Pack it loosely into neck and body cavities.

To roast, place the stuffed bird in an oven that's preheated to at least 325°. When juices run clear, check temperature in center of stuffing and innermost part of thigh. The stuffing must reach a temperature of 165°, and the meat must be 180° for safe eating.

Thawing Fast and Safe
Be sure your bird is completely thawed before stuffing or roasting. (If the center is still frozen, it may not cook evenly.) To thaw a whole frozen turkey, place the wrapped bird on a tray in the refrigerator for 1 to 5 days. Allow 24 hours for every 5 pounds. Or, place it in a sink of cold water. Change the water every 30 minutes. Allow 30 minutes per pound. Do not thaw at room temperature or in warm water. Remove the giblets and neck. Rinse bird and pat dry with paper towels. Do not stuff the bird until you're ready to roast it.

Preparing the Bird
To stuff, spoon some stuffing loosely into neck cavity. (Allow no more than ¾ cup stuffing per pound of turkey.) Pull the neck skin over stuffing; fasten to back with a short skewer. Loosely spoon stuffing into the body cavity; do not pack. Spoon any remaining stuffing into a casserole; cover and chill till ready to roast. If you prefer not to stuff your turkey, place quartered onions and celery in the body cavity to add flavor. Pull the neck skin to the back; fasten with a short skewer. Tuck the drumsticks under the band of skin that crosses the tail. If there isn't a band, tie the drumsticks to the tail. Twist the wing tips under the back.

Turkey Roasting Guide

Type of turkey	Ready-to-cook weight	Oven temperature	Roasting time
Stuffed whole turkey (open roasting)	8 to 12 lb.	325°	3 to 3½ hours
	12 to 14 lb.	325°	3½ to 4 hours
	14 to 18 lb.	325°	4 to 4¼ hours
	18 to 20 lb.	325°	4¼ to 4¾ hours
	20 to 24 lb.	325°	4¾ to 5¼ hours
Stuffed whole turkey (in oven cooking bag)	12 to 16 lb.	350°	2½ to 3 hours
	16 to 20 lb.	350°	3 to 3½ hours
	20 to 24 lb.	350°	3½ to 4 hours

For unstuffed turkeys of the same weight, reduce the total cooking time by 15 to 30 minutes.

Menu

Roast Turkey with Rosemary-Sourdough Stuffing (see page 248)

✦✦✦

Honey-Dijon Gravy (see below)

✦✦✦

Cranberry sauce

✦✦✦

Glazed Carrot and Parsnip Coins (see page 251)

✦✦✦

Whole wheat rolls with butter

✦✦✦

Fruit pie with light cream

HONEY-DIJON GRAVY

Plan to cook this homemade gravy from the roasting pan juices before carving your turkey.

Pan drippings from roast turkey

✦✦✦

¼ **cup all-purpose flour**
1 **to 1½ cups chicken broth**
2 **tsp. Dijon-style mustard**
2 **tsp. honey**
  Dash salt (optional)
  Dash pepper (optional)

1 After transferring turkey to a serving platter, pour pan drippings into a large measuring cup; scrape the browned bits from the pan into the cup. Skim fat from the drippings, reserving ¼ cup fat.

2 Place reserved fat in a medium saucepan. Stir in flour. Add enough broth to remaining drippings in the measuring cup to equal 2 cups. Add all at once to the flour mixture. Cook and stir over medium heat till thickened and bubbly. Stir in Dijon-style mustard and honey. Cook and stir for 1 minute more. Season to taste with salt and pepper. Makes 8 to 10 servings.

Nutrition facts per serving: 87 cal., 7 g total fat (2 g sat. fat), 7 mg chol., 226 mg sodium, 4 g carbo., 0 g fiber, 2 g pro. *Daily values:* 2% iron.

SWEET POTATO-PEAR BISQUE

Canned sweet potatoes and pears let you skip the usual precooking needed for vegetables in creamy soups.

2¼ **cups chicken broth**
1 **medium onion, chopped (½ cup)**
1 **tsp. snipped fresh thyme or ½ tsp. dried thyme, crushed**

✦✦✦

1 **16- to 18-oz. can sweet potatoes, drained**
1 **8¼-oz. can pear halves (juice pack)**
1 **cup half-and-half or light cream**
⅛ **tsp. pepper**
1 **recipe Pepper Croutons (see right)**
  Fresh thyme (optional)

1 In a large saucepan combine *1 cup* of the broth, onion, and snipped thyme. Bring to boiling; reduce heat. Simmer, covered, 5 minutes or till onion is tender. Do not drain. Cool slightly.

2 Transfer broth mixture to a blender container or a food processor bowl. Add sweet potatoes. Cover and blend or process till smooth. Return sweet potato mixture to saucepan. Add undrained pears to blender container; cover and blend till smooth. Add blended pears to saucepan. Stir remaining broth, the half-and-half or light cream, and pepper into saucepan. Cook and stir till heated through.

3 To serve, ladle the soup into bowls. Top with Pepper Croutons. If desired, garnish with fresh thyme. Makes 8 to 10 side-dish servings.

Pepper Croutons: In a mixing bowl stir together 2 tablespoons melted *margarine or butter* and ¼ teaspoon *pepper*. Add 2 cups *French or wheat bread* cut into ½-inch cubes (about four ½-inch-thick slices French bread or 3 slices wheat bread). Stir till coated. Spread bread cubes in a single layer in a shallow baking pan. Bake in a 300° oven for 10 minutes; stir. Bake 10 minutes more or till crisp and toasted; cool. Makes about 1½ cups.

Nutrition facts per serving: 184 cal., 7 g total fat (3 g sat. fat), 11 mg chol., 372 mg sodium, 26 g carbo., 2 g fiber, 5 g pro. *Daily values:* 52% vit. A, 26% vit. C, 5% calcium, 7% iron.

GLAZED CARROT AND PARSNIP COINS

To shortcut mealtime preparation, cook the carrots and parsnips a day ahead, then reheat them in the balsamic vinegar glaze.

1½ **lb. medium carrots and/or parsnips, peeled**
◆◆◆
2 **Tbsp. olive oil**
¼ **cup packed brown sugar**
2 **Tbsp. balsamic vinegar or white wine vinegar**
1 **tsp. cornstarch**
  Dash salt
  Pepper

1 Slice carrots and/or parsnips ¼ inch thick. In a medium saucepan cook the carrots and/or parsnips, covered, in a small amount of *boiling salted water* for 7 to 9 minutes or till crisp-tender. Drain the vegetables; remove from the pan.

2 In the same saucepan combine the olive oil, brown sugar, balsamic or white wine vinegar, cornstarch, and salt. Stir over medium heat till slightly thickened. Add the carrots and/or parsnips. Cook, uncovered, about 2 minutes or till vegetables are glazed, stirring frequently. Season to taste with pepper. Makes 8 side-dish servings.

Nutrition facts per serving: 91 cal., 4 g total fat (0 g sat. fat), 0 mg chol., 71 mg sodium, 15 g carbo., 3 g fiber, 1 g pro.
Daily values: 192% vit. A, 4% vit. C, 2% calcium, 5% iron.

BASIL PEAS AND MUSHROOMS

Shiitake mushrooms add an earthy flavor to this side dish of peas and carrot. If shiitake mushrooms are unavailable at your grocery store, you can substitute white or another variety of fresh mushrooms.

1 **medium carrot, sliced (½ cup)**
2 **cups shelled fresh peas or frozen loose-pack peas**
◆◆◆
1 **cup sliced fresh white mushrooms**
1 **cup sliced fresh shiitake mushrooms**
2 **green onions, cut into ½-inch pieces (¼ cup)**
1 **Tbsp. margarine or butter**
1 **Tbsp. snipped fresh basil or ½ tsp. dried basil, crushed**
¼ **tsp. salt**
  Dash pepper

1 In a medium saucepan cook the carrot, covered, in a small amount of boiling salted water for 3 minutes. Add the peas. Cook about 4 minutes more or till carrot and peas are crisp-tender. Drain the vegetables; remove from the pan.

2 In the same saucepan cook the mushrooms and green onions in margarine or butter over medium heat till tender. Stir in the basil, salt, and pepper. Add the carrot and peas; heat through. Serve immediately. Makes 4 side-dish servings.

Nutrition facts per serving: 92 cal., 3 g total fat (1 g sat. fat), 0 mg chol., 233 mg sodium, 13 g carbo., 3 g fiber, 4 g pro.
Daily values: 48% vit. A, 15% vit. C, 2% calcium, 11% iron.

SAVORY PUMPKIN SPOON BREAD

Delightful served alongside turkey and stuffing, this not-so-sweet puddinglike bread makes a superb dessert as well. For dessert, sprinkle it with powdered sugar and serve it with apples that have been sautéed in butter.

  Margarine or butter
1 **medium onion, finely chopped (½ cup)**
2 **Tbsp. margarine or butter**
1½ **cups milk**
¾ **cup yellow cornmeal**
1 **cup canned pumpkin**
1 **tsp. sugar**
½ **tsp. baking powder**
½ **tsp. salt**
¼ **tsp. pepper**
3 **egg yolks, beaten**
3 **egg whites**

1 Grease a 1½-quart soufflé dish using margarine or butter; set aside. In a medium saucepan cook onion in 2 tablespoons hot margarine till tender. Meanwhile, combine milk and cornmeal; add to saucepan. Cook and stir till mixture is thick. Stir in pumpkin, sugar, baking powder, salt, and pepper; remove from heat. Stir 1 cup of hot mixture into egg yolks; return all to saucepan. Beat egg whites with an electric mixer on medium speed to stiff peaks; fold into pumpkin mixture.

2 Turn mixture into prepared dish. Bake in a 325° oven 55 to 60 minutes or till a knife inserted near center comes out clean. Serve immediately. Serves 6.

Nutrition facts per serving: 187 cal., 8 g total fat (2 g sat. fat), 111 mg chol., 317 mg sodium, 22 g carbo., 2 g fiber, 7 g pro.
Daily values: 115% vit. A, 4% vit. C, 10% calcium, 11% iron.

POTATO BUNS

Partially bake these old-fashioned buns ahead of time, then brown them right before dinner.
(See the photograph on page 274.)

1½ cups buttermilk
⅔ cup water
¼ cup sugar
2 Tbsp. margarine or butter
1½ tsp. salt
¾ cup instant mashed potato flakes
½ cup thinly sliced green onions or ⅓ cup snipped fresh chives

◆◆◆

4¼ to 4¾ cups all-purpose flour
2 pkg. active dry yeast

◆◆◆

All-purpose flour

1 In a medium saucepan combine buttermilk, water, sugar, margarine or butter, and salt. Bring just to boiling (mixture may appear curdled). Remove from heat. Stir in potato flakes; let stand about 5 minutes or till temperature is 120° to 130°. Stir in green onions or chives.

2 In a large mixing bowl stir together *1½ cups* of the all-purpose flour and the yeast. Add potato mixture. Beat with an electric mixer on low to medium speed for 30 seconds, scraping bowl constantly. Beat on high speed for 3 minutes. Using a wooden spoon, stir in as much of the remaining 4¼ to 4¾ cups of all-purpose flour as you can.

3 On a lightly floured surface, knead in enough of the remaining flour to make a moderately stiff dough that is smooth and elastic (6 to 8 minutes total). Shape into a ball. Place in a lightly greased bowl; turn once to grease the surface of dough. Cover and let rise in a warm place till double (45 to 60 minutes).

4 Punch dough down. Turn out onto a lightly floured surface. Divide in half. Cover and let rest for 10 minutes. Grease 2 large baking sheets. Divide each half of dough into 12 pieces. Shape into balls. Lightly dip tops of balls into the additional all-purpose flour. Arrange on the prepared baking sheets so balls don't touch (about 2 inches apart). Cover; let rise till almost double (30 minutes).

5 Bake buns in a 375° oven for 14 to 16 minutes or till golden brown. Remove buns from baking sheets and cool slightly on a wire rack. Serve warm. Makes 24 buns.

Nutrition facts per bun: 106 cal., 1 g total fat (0 g sat. fat), 1 mg chol., 163 mg sodium, 20 g carbo., 1 g fiber, 3 g pro. *Daily values:* 1% vit. A, 2% vit. C, 1% calcium, 7% iron.

Brown 'n' Serve Buns: Prepare buns as directed, except bake in a 325° oven for 10 minutes (rolls should not brown yet). Remove buns from baking sheets; cool on wire racks. Place buns in a freezer container or bag and freeze for up to 3 months.

To serve, thaw frozen buns in open container or bag at room temperature for 10 to 15 minutes. Arrange buns on ungreased baking sheets. Bake, uncovered, in a 375° oven for 12 to 14 minutes or till golden brown.

SWISS-CARAWAY BREAD

Bake this quick bread as a loaf or, even quicker, as drop biscuits.
(See the photograph on page 274.)

3 cups all-purpose flour
2 tsp. baking powder
1 tsp. caraway seed
½ tsp. baking soda
¼ tsp. salt
2 eggs
1 8-oz. carton plain yogurt
½ cup milk
⅓ cup margarine or butter, melted
1½ cups shredded fontina or Swiss cheese (6 oz.)
¼ tsp. caraway seed

1 Grease and flour a 9×5×3-inch loaf pan; set aside. In a large mixing bowl stir together the flour, baking powder, 1 teaspoon caraway seed, the baking soda, and salt.

2 In another mixing bowl beat eggs slightly; stir in the yogurt, milk, and melted margarine or butter. Add to flour mixture along with fontina or Swiss cheese. Stir just till moistened (batter will be thick). Turn batter into the prepared loaf pan. Sprinkle with ¼ teaspoon caraway seed.

3 Bake in a 350° oven 1 to 1¼ hours or till a wooden toothpick inserted near center comes out clean. Cool for 10 minutes in pan on a wire rack. Remove from pan. Cool on the wire rack for at least 1 hour. Serve warm or cool. Makes 1 loaf (18 servings).

Nutrition facts per serving: 157 cal., 7 g total fat (3 g sat. fat), 36 mg chol., 240 mg sodium, 16 g carbo., 1 g fiber, 6 g pro. *Daily values:* 9% vit. A, 10% calcium, 7% iron.

Swiss-Caraway Biscuits: Prepare bread as directed on page 252, except drop dough by well-rounded tablespoonsful onto greased baking sheets. Do not sprinkle with additional caraway seed. Bake in a 450° oven about 12 minutes or till golden. Makes 18 to 20 biscuits.

HONEY-SEED ROLLS

This recipe earned Kathy Berkey of Whitehouse, Ohio, $200 in the magazine's monthly contest.

1 1-lb. loaf frozen white or whole wheat bread dough, thawed
1 egg yolk, beaten
2 Tbsp. honey
1 Tbsp. olive oil
¼ to ⅓ cup shelled sunflower seeds, poppy seed, sesame seed, caraway seed, and/or fennel seed

1 Grease twelve 2½-inch muffin cups; set aside. On a lightly floured surface, roll dough into a 12×10-inch rectangle. Stir together egg yolk, honey, and oil; brush mixture onto dough. Sprinkle with desired seed. Roll up dough from a long side; seal seam. Slice dough crosswise into twelve 1-inch-thick pieces. Place in the prepared muffin cups. Cover; let rest 20 minutes.

2 Bake rolls, uncovered, in a 350° oven about 20 minutes or till golden. Remove from muffin cups. Cool slightly on a wire rack. Serve warm. Makes 12 rolls.

Nutrition facts per roll: 130 cal., 3 g total fat (0 g sat. fat), 18 mg chol., 19 mg sodium, 20 g carbo., 0 g fiber, 3 g pro. *Daily values:* 2% vit. A, 4% calcium, 2% iron.

CARAMEL APPLE BREAKFAST PUDDING

2 large apples
¾ tsp. ground cinnamon

♦♦♦

½ cup packed brown sugar
2 Tbsp. light-colored corn syrup
2 Tbsp. margarine or butter
¼ cup pecan pieces

♦♦♦

3 beaten eggs
1¼ cups milk
1 tsp. vanilla
¼ tsp. ground nutmeg
8 to 10½-inch-thick slices Italian or French bread

1 Peel, core, and slice apples (should have 2 cups). In a small saucepan combine apple slices and ¼ cup *water*. Bring to boiling; reduce heat. Cook, covered, over medium-low heat 5 to 7 minutes or till tender, stirring occasionally. Drain; transfer apples to a small bowl. Gently stir cinnamon into cooked apples; set aside.

2 In the same small saucepan combine brown sugar, corn syrup, and margarine or butter. Cook and stir over medium heat till the mixture just comes to a boil. Pour the mixture into a 2-quart square baking dish. Sprinkle pecans over all.

3 Combine the eggs, milk, vanilla, and nutmeg. Arrange *half* the bread slices in the baking dish atop caramel mixture, trimming bread to fit. Spoon apples evenly over bread. Arrange remaining bread slices on top. Carefully pour egg mixture over bread, pressing bread down gently to moisten slices. Cover; chill 3 to 24 hours.

4 Bake, uncovered, in a 325° oven for 40 to 45 minutes or till a knife inserted near center comes out clean. Remove from oven; run a knife around edge to loosen. Let stand 15 minutes. Carefully invert pudding onto a platter. Spoon any remaining caramel mixture in dish over pudding. Cut into triangles. Serve warm or cool. Makes 8 servings.

Nutrition facts per serving: 208 cal., 7 g total fat (2 g sat. fat), 83 mg chol., 168 mg sodium, 31 g carbo., 0 g fiber, 5 g pro. *Daily value:* 9% vit. A, 7% calcium, 8% iron.

KEEPING BREAD FRESH

Assuming you're lucky enough to have leftover homemade bread, you can keep it fresh by storing it properly.

♦ Completely cool the bread, then place it in an airtight container or bag. Store it in a cool, dry place for 2 to 3 days. Do not refrigerate leftover unfilled yeast bread because it will grow stale more quickly.

♦ To freeze up to 3 months, place the completely cooled, unfrosted bread in a freezer container or bag. Thaw the wrapped bread at room temperature for 2 hours. Frost sweet yeast breads after thawing.

LOFTY LOAVES

Most baking procedures, including those for yeast breads, must be adapted for high altitudes. Flours are drier at high altitudes, so they absorb more liquid. Also, the higher the altitude, the faster the bread dough may rise. Because this can cause the final loaf to be coarse in texture, only let the dough rise until nearly double. If you want to give the yeast flavor more time to develop, punch the dough down once, and let it rise a second time.

PRIZE TESTED RECIPE WINNER

CHEESY PIZZA BREAD

This recipe earned Cinnamon Culpepper of Rossville, Georgia, $100 in the magazine's monthly contest.

1 6½-oz. pkg. pizza crust mix
❖❖❖
2 Tbsp. margarine or butter, melted
1 clove garlic, minced, or ½ tsp. dried minced garlic
½ tsp. dried Italian seasoning, crushed
¼ tsp. seasoned salt
1 cup shredded mozzarella cheese (4 oz.)

1 Grease a 12-inch pizza pan; set aside. Prepare the pizza crust mix according to the package directions. Pat dough into the prepared pizza pan.

2 In a small bowl combine margarine or butter, garlic, Italian seasoning, and seasoned salt. Brush mixture onto the pizza dough. Sprinkle with the mozzarella cheese. Bake in a 450° oven 12 to 15 minutes or till golden brown. Makes 10 to 12 servings.

Nutrition facts per serving: 116 cal., 5 g total fat (2 g sat. fat), 6 mg chol., 244 mg sodium, 14 g carbo., 0 g fiber, 5 g pro. *Daily values:* 4% vit. A, 6% calcium, 4% iron.

CHOCOLATE-WALNUT SWIRL LOAVES

Take advantage of your bread machine—it makes preparing this mocha-flavored dough super simple.

½ cup milk
¼ cup water
2 eggs
2 Tbsp. margarine or butter
2 cups bread flour
1 cup whole wheat flour
⅓ cup sugar
½ tsp. salt
½ tsp. instant coffee crystals
½ tsp. ground cinnamon
½ tsp. vanilla
1 pkg. active dry yeast
1 6-oz. pkg. (1 cup) semisweet chocolate pieces
❖❖❖
¼ cup chopped walnuts
1 tsp. shortening

1 Add the milk, water, eggs, margarine or butter, bread flour, whole wheat flour, sugar, salt, coffee crystals, cinnamon, vanilla, yeast, and ½ cup of the semisweet chocolate pieces to the bread machine according to manufacturer's directions. Prepare dough using manufacturer's cycle directions. When cycle is complete, remove dough from machine.

2 Punch dough down. Divide dough in half. Cover and let rest for 10 minutes. Grease two 8×4×2-inch loaf pans; set aside.

3 On a lightly floured surface, roll each half of dough into a 10×7-inch rectangle. Sprinkle each rectangle with 2 tablespoons each semisweet chocolate pieces and walnuts, pressing in lightly. Roll up jelly-roll style, starting from a short end. Seal seams and ends. Place each shaped loaf, seam side down, in prepared pans. Cover and let rise till nearly double (about 1½ hours).

4 Bake in a 350° oven about 30 minutes or till bread sounds hollow when lightly tapped. If necessary, to prevent overbrowning, cover with foil the last 10 minutes. Remove from pans; cool slightly on wire racks. In a saucepan melt together remaining chocolate pieces and shortening. Drizzle chocolate over loaves. Makes 2 loaves (32 servings).

CONVENTIONAL METHOD

In a large mixing bowl combine 1½ cups of the bread flour, the yeast, and cinnamon. In a saucepan heat and stir milk, water, margarine or butter, sugar, salt, coffee crystals, and ½ cup of the semisweet chocolate pieces till warm (120° to 130°) and margarine almost melts. Add the milk mixture, eggs, and vanilla to the flour mixture. Beat with an electric mixer on low speed for

30 seconds, scraping bowl constantly. Beat on high speed for 3 minutes. Using a wooden spoon, stir in the whole wheat flour and as much of the remaining ½ cup bread flour as you can. (It may be necessary to increase bread flour by as much as ½ cup.)

Turn dough out onto a lightly floured surface. Knead in enough bread flour to make a moderately soft dough that is smooth and elastic (3 to 5 minutes total). Shape into a ball. Place in a lightly greased bowl; turn once to grease surface. Cover and let rise in a warm place till double (about 1¼ hours).

Punch down dough. Cover; let rest 10 minutes. Shape, let rise, bake, and glaze as directed on page 254.

Nutrition facts per serving: 97 cal., 4 g total fat (0 g sat. fat), 14 mg chol., 48 mg sodium, 15 g carbo., 1 g fiber, 3 g pro. *Daily values:* 4% iron.

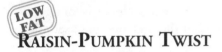

Raisin-Pumpkin Twist

Your bread machine makes the dough, then you shape and bake it. If you don't have a bread machine, follow the traditional yeast dough directions that follow.
(See the photograph on page 274.)

¾ cup canned pumpkin
2 tsp. finely shredded orange peel
⅓ cup orange juice
3 Tbsp. sugar
3 Tbsp. margarine or butter
1 egg
3 cups all-purpose flour
1 pkg. active dry yeast
1½ tsp. pumpkin pie spice

¾ tsp. salt
¾ cup raisins

♦♦♦

1 Tbsp. milk
1 tsp. poppy seed

1 In a bread machine combine all ingredients except raisins, milk, and poppy seed. Prepare dough using the manufacturer's dough cycle directions. Add the raisins later in the cycle, after about 20 minutes. When the cycle is complete, remove dough from the machine.

2 Punch dough down. Turn out onto a lightly floured surface. Divide dough into 3 equal portions. Cover and let rest for 10 minutes. Lightly grease a baking sheet; set aside. Shape each portion into a thick rope 16 inches long.

3 On the prepared baking sheet line up the ropes, 1 inch apart. Starting in the middle, loosely braid by bringing the left rope underneath the center rope; lay it down. Next bring the right rope under the new center rope; lay it down. Repeat braiding to the end. On the other end, braid by bringing alternate ropes over center rope to the center. Press the rope ends together to seal; tuck under. Cover and let rise till nearly double (about 30 minutes).

4 Brush milk onto loaf. Sprinkle with poppy seed. Bake in a 350° oven for 25 to 30 minutes or till bread sounds hollow when you tap the top. If necessary, cover loosely with foil the last 10 to 15 minutes of baking to prevent overbrowning. Cool on a wire rack. Makes 1 loaf (16 servings).

In a large mixing bowl combine *1½ cups* of the all-purpose flour, the yeast, and pumpkin pie spice. In a saucepan heat and stir orange juice, sugar, margarine or butter, and salt till warm (120° to 130°) and margarine or butter is almost melted. Add warm mixture to flour mixture; add egg and pumpkin. Beat with an electric mixer on low speed for 30 seconds, scraping the bowl constantly. Beat on high speed for 3 minutes. Stir in orange peel and raisins. Using a spoon, stir in as much of 1¼ to 1¾ cups flour as you can. Turn dough out onto a lightly floured surface. Knead in remaining flour to make a moderately stiff dough that is smooth and elastic (6 to 8 minutes total). Shape into a ball. Place in a lightly greased bowl; turn once to grease the surface. Cover and let rise in a warm place till double (about 30 minutes). Shape and bake as directed.

Nutrition facts per serving: 142 cal., 3 g total fat (1 g sat. fat), 13 mg chol., 131 mg sodium, 26 g carbo., 1 g fiber, 3 g pro. *Daily values:* 28% vit. A, 6% vit. C, 1% calcium, 9% iron.

Raisin-Pumpkin Rolls: Prepare dough as directed, except after punching dough down, divide into 18 pieces. Lightly grease eighteen 2½-inch muffin cups. Shape each piece of dough into a ball; place a ball in each muffin cup. With floured scissors, snip top in half, then snip again to make 4 points. Let rise in a warm place till nearly double (about 20 minutes). Bake in a 375° oven for 12 to 15 minutes or till golden brown. Makes 18 rolls.

ALMOND BREAKFAST ROUND

Snip rings of dough before letting the dough rise in the refrigerator overnight. You'll love waking up to this ready-to-bake treat any day of the year. (See the photograph on page 275.)

 1 pkg. active dry yeast
⅓ cup warm water
   (105° to 115°)
2½ cups all-purpose flour
 1 cup whole wheat flour
¼ cup packed brown sugar
½ tsp. salt
½ tsp. ground cardamom or
   nutmeg
½ cup cold margarine or butter
 2 eggs, beaten
½ cup milk
½ tsp. almond extract
   ◆◆◆
½ cup ground almonds
 3 Tbsp. brown sugar
 2 Tbsp. granulated sugar
½ tsp. ground cardamom or
   allspice
   ◆◆◆
 2 Tbsp. margarine or butter,
   melted
   ◆◆◆
   Milk (optional)
   Coarse sugar (optional)

1 In a small mixing bowl stir together yeast and warm water; set aside. In a large mixing bowl stir together all-purpose flour, whole wheat flour, the ¼ cup brown sugar, salt, and the ½ teaspoon cardamom or nutmeg. Using a pastry blender, cut in the cold margarine or butter till mixture resembles fine crumbs. Stir in the softened yeast, eggs, milk, and almond extract till combined. Cover and refrigerate 1 to 2 hours or till dough is easy to handle.

2 For filling, stir together ground almonds, the 3 tablespoons brown sugar, the granulated sugar, and the ½ teaspoon cardamom or allspice; set aside.

3 Turn dough out onto lightly floured surface. Divide into 3 portions. Shape each portion into a ball. Cover and let rest for 10 minutes. Line a 12-inch pizza pan or large baking sheet with foil; grease foil. Gently roll each portion into a 10-inch circle. Place a dough circle on prepared pizza pan or baking sheet. Brush with *half* of the melted margarine or butter; sprinkle with half of the filling. Cover with another circle of dough. Brush with remaining margarine; sprinkle with remaining filling. Top with last circle.

4 Using kitchen shears or a sharp knife, cut the stack of dough into 12 wedges, cutting only to within 1 inch of center. Carefully lift each wedge and turn over twice to create a twist in each piece. Cover with plastic wrap; chill 2 to 24 hours before baking.

5 Let bread stand at room temperature for 20 minutes before baking. If desired, brush with milk and sprinkle with coarse sugar. Bake in a 350° oven for 30 to 35 minutes or till bread sounds hollow when tapped. Carefully transfer foil with bread to a cooling rack. Transfer round to a serving platter; cut into wedges. Serve warm. Serves 12.

Nutrition facts per serving: 284 cal., 13 g total fat (2 g sat. fat), 36 mg chol., 219 mg sodium, 36 g carbo., 3 g fiber, 7 g pro. *Daily values:* 13% vit. A, 3% calcium, 13% iron.

CHEESE DANISH COFFEE CAKE

 1 1-lb. loaf frozen white bread
   dough, thawed
   ◆◆◆
½ of an 8-oz. pkg. reduced fat
   cream cheese (Neufchâtel),
   softened
½ cup ricotta cheese
 1 egg
¼ cup granulated sugar
¼ cup chopped almonds
½ tsp. finely shredded orange
   peel
¼ tsp. almond extract
   ◆◆◆
½ cup sifted powdered sugar
¼ tsp. vanilla
   Milk or water
 2 Tbsp. sliced almonds,
   toasted

1 Grease a 9×1½-inch round baking pan. Divide bread dough in half. On a lightly floured surface, roll half of the dough out to a 9-inch circle. Place dough circle in the prepared pan; set aside.

2 For filling, in a small mixing bowl beat together the cream cheese, ricotta cheese, egg, granulated sugar, chopped almonds, orange peel, and almond extract with an electric mixer till combined. Spread over dough in pan. Cut remaining dough into 24 pieces. Scatter pieces randomly but evenly over filling. Cover; let rise in warm place till nearly doubled (about 30 minutes).

3 Bake in a 350° oven for 40 to 45 minutes or till browned. Let cool in pan for 5 minutes. Invert to remove and place coffee cake right side up on a wire rack. Cool slightly.

4 Meanwhile, combine powdered sugar, vanilla, and *2 teaspoons* milk or water. Gradually add more milk or water, ½ teaspoon at a time, till icing is easy to drizzle. Drizzle atop warm coffee cake; sprinkle with sliced almonds. Makes 8 servings.

Nutrition facts per serving: 280 cal., 8 g total fat (3 g sat. fat), 39 mg chol., 84 mg sodium, 39 g carbo., 0 g fiber, 9 g pro. *Daily values:* 8% vit. A, 10% calcium, 3% iron.

MULLED CRANBERRY CIDER

1 small orange
8 cups cranberry-raspberry drink
¼ cup packed brown sugar
6 inches stick cinnamon
1 teaspoon whole cloves
1 star anise (optional)
   Orange peel strips (optional)

1 Remove orange peel; cut into strips. Squeeze juice from orange, discarding seeds and pulp. In large saucepan combine orange juice, fruit drink, and brown sugar. In an 8-inch square of 100-percent-cotton cheesecloth, combine orange peel, cinnamon, whole cloves, and, if desired, star anise.

2 Bring up corners of cheesecloth and tie with cotton string. Add to saucepan. Bring mixture to boiling; reduce heat. Cover and simmer 10 minutes. Remove and discard spices. Serve warm. Garnish with more orange peel, if desired. Makes 10 (6-ounce) servings.

Nutrition facts per serving: 53 cal., 0 g total fat, 0 mg chol., 8 mg sodium, 12 g carbo., 9 g fiber, 0 g pro. *Daily Values:* 152% vit. C, 1% calcium, 2% iron.

NO FAT

PINEAPPLE-ORANGE MARMALADE

Light and aromatic, this intriguing blend can't be found in a supermarket.

1 orange
1 small lime
1 cup orange juice
   ◆◆◆
2 medium ripe pineapples (about 4 lb. total)
4 cups sugar

1 Wash orange and lime. Remove peels and white membrane from fruit; set aside. Cut peels into very thin strips. In a saucepan combine peels and orange juice. Bring to boiling; reduce heat. Cover and simmer for 20 minutes; do not drain.

2 Meanwhile, section orange and lime over bowl to catch juices. Add sections and juice to pan. Return to boiling; reduce heat. Simmer, covered, 10 minutes. Transfer to a 6- or 8-quart pot.

3 Peel, core, and finely chop pineapple (you should have 4 cups). Add pineapple to orange mixture. Return to boiling; reduce heat. Cook, uncovered, over medium-low heat about 20 minutes or till lime peel is extremely tender and pineapple is soft, stirring occasionally. Add sugar, stirring till dissolved. Bring to a full rolling boil, stirring frequently. Reduce heat to medium and boil gently, uncovered, till mixture sheets off a metal spoon or reaches 220° on a jelly thermometer, stirring frequently to prevent sticking. (This will take 20 to 25 minutes.)

THE CLEVER COOK

SPICE BAG SUBSTITUTE

Whenever you're making warm spiced drinks, such as cider or mulled wine, use a coffee filter for your spice bag. Add the whole spices to the coffee filter and fasten with a plastic twist tie. Make a pin hole in the filter to release air.

Mary Ellen Chapman
Cox's Mill, West Virginia

4 Ladle hot marmalade into hot, sterilized half-pint canning jars, leaving ½-inch headspace. Wipe jar rims with a clean, damp cloth. Place prepared lids on jars. Add screw bands, tightening according to the manufacturer's directions. Process the filled jars in a boiling-water canner for 5 minutes (start timing when water boils). Remove the jars from the canner; cool jars on racks. Store in a cool, dry place. Refrigerate after opening. Makes about 5 half-pints (80 one-tablespoon servings).

■ SERVING SUGGESTION ■

Our taste panelists loved this breakfast spread on biscuits and scones, but it dresses up almost any bread at breakfast time.

Nutrition facts per tablespoon: 51 cal., 0 g total fat, 0 mg chol., 0 mg sodium, 13 g carbo., 0 g fiber, 0 g pro. *Daily values:* 7% vit. C.

PROCESSING MADE PERFECT

To ensure the quality and safety of home-cooked relishes, condiments, and marmalades, you should process them in a boiling-water canner unless the recipe indicates that they are to be refrigerated or frozen. Any large pot can be used for the canner as long as it has a rack (any heatproof rack can be used—even a trivet). It must also have a tight-fitting lid and be deep enough to allow enough room for 1 inch of water to boil briskly over tops of the jars.

◆ For gift-giving, you may be tempted to use unusual containers to preserve these accompaniments, but they may not seal properly. Instead, look for canning jars that are more decorative and can be used with standard canning methods. Also, use only new canning lids. (Screw bands can be reused if they are not bent or rusty.) Clean jars are important. Wash the empty jars in hot, soapy water, then rinse well. Sterilize the jars by immersing them in boiling water for at least 10 minutes. Prepare the jar lids and screw bands according to the jar manufacturer's directions.

◆ Prepare only as much food as you will need to fill the jars. Keep all of your working surfaces and utensils clean and sterilized, and allow enough time to complete the preparation once you've started. Once the food to be preserved is prepared, carefully fill each jar, making sure to leave the recommended headspace (the space—usually about ½ inch—between the top of the food and rim of the jar).

◆ To process in the boiling-water canner, heat the water, covered, in the canner, plus heat some additional water in a teakettle or saucepan. When the water in the canner is hot, position the rack in the canner and fill the jars. Any trapped air can be released by working a thin rubber spatula down the sides of the jars. Add more liquid to the jars, if necessary, to adjust the headspace to the proper level.

Wipe the jars, screw bands, and lids with a clean, damp cloth. Adjust the lids and tighten the screw bands according to the instructions. Then place the jars in the rack as each one is filled. Be sure to position the filled jars in the rack so that they don't touch each other.

◆ After placing the last jar on the rack, add boiling water from the teakettle or saucepan to reach 1 inch over jar tops. Replace cover and return water to just boiling. Begin processing timing when water is boiling, keeping the water at a gentle boil during processing. Follow processing times called for in the individual recipes.

◆ When processing is completed, carefully remove each jar and place on a towel or rack to cool. Leave space between the jars to allow air to circulate between them. The jars will take 12 to 24 hours to completely cool.

◆ When jars are cool, check the seal on each jar. Do this by gently pressing the center of each lid. If the lid does not stay down, the jar isn't properly sealed. Check for any flaws in the seal, such as misaligned or ill-fitting lids or screw bands.

◆ If a jar is not sealed, the contents do not need to be discarded if refrigerated and used within two or three days. They also can be reprocessed within 24 hours, in a new jar with a clean lid, and for the full length of time. If the level of liquid in a jar has dropped slightly, but the jar has a tight seal, the contents are still safe, although the food not covered by liquid may discolor.

◆ Wipe the cooled jars with a clean damp cloth. Remove, wash, and dry the screw bands. Label all jars before storing, including the contents, date, and batch number, if necessary. Keep the jars stored in a cool, dark, dry place for up to a year.

DRIED FRUIT CONSERVE

When is a preserve a conserve? When it includes two or more fruits (one being a citrus); nuts are usually in the ingredient list, too.

- 3 cups water
- 2 cups sugar
- 2 6-oz. pkg. mixed dried fruit bits
- ¾ cup dried tart red cherries, snipped
- 1 medium unpeeled orange, chopped and seeded

◆◆◆

- ½ cup chopped pitted dates
- 1 Tbsp. lemon juice
- ½ tsp. ground cardamom
- ½ cup slivered almonds, toasted and chopped

1 In a 4-quart pot combine the water, sugar, dried fruit bits, cherries, and orange. Bring mixture to boiling; reduce heat. Cook, covered, about 15 minutes or till dried fruits are tender.

2 Stir in the dates, lemon juice, and cardamom. Return to boiling; reduce heat. Cook, uncovered, about 12 minutes more or till mixture is thickened but some liquid remains, stirring frequently (you should have about 6 cups mixture). Stir in almonds; cook 2 minutes more.

3 Ladle hot conserve into hot, sterilized half-pint canning jars, leaving ½-inch headspace. Wipe jar rims with a clean, damp towel. Place prepared lids on jars. Add screw bands according to the manufacturer's directions. Process the filled jars in a boiling-water canner for 15 minutes (start timing when water boils). Remove the jars from the canner; cool jars on racks. Store in a cool, dry place. Refrigerate after opening. Makes 6 half-pints (96 one-tablespoon servings).

■ SERVING SUGGESTION ■

This conserve tastes luscious on firm-textured toasted bread such as whole wheat. Also, try it on a bagel along with the traditional cream cheese. Or, use it as a glaze for meats and poultry.

Nutrition facts per tablespoon: 36 cal., 0 g total fat, 0 mg chol., 3 mg sodium, 9 g carbo., 0 g fiber, 0 g pro.
Daily values: 1% vit. A, 1% vit. C.

HONEY-PEAR PRESERVES

If you have pots of fresh herbs growing in your kitchen, use a little rosemary to flavor these honey-laced fruit preserves. Otherwise, purchase the fresh rosemary in the produce section of your local supermarket.

- 2 to 3 lb. firm, ripe pears (such as Bartlett or Bosc)
- 1 unpeeled lemon, quartered and extra-thinly sliced
- 1½ cups sugar
- ½ cup honey
- 1 tsp. snipped fresh rosemary

1 Core, peel, and finely chop enough pears to measure 4 cups. In a 4-quart pot combine pears, lemon, sugar, and honey. Bring to boiling over medium heat, stirring till sugar dissolves. Stir in rosemary. Cook for 20 to 25 minutes or till mixture is thickened and sheets off a metal spoon, stirring frequently.

2 Ladle hot preserves into hot, sterilized half-pint canning jars, leaving ½-inch headspace. Wipe jar rims; adjust lids. Process the filled jars in a boiling-water canner for 10 minutes (start timing when water boils). Remove the jars from the canner; cool jars on racks. Store in a cool, dry place. Refrigerate after opening. Makes about 3 half-pints (48 one-tablespoon servings).

Nutrition facts per tablespoon: 47 cal., 0 g total fat, 0 mg chol., 0 mg sodium, 12 g carbo., 1 g fiber, 0 g pro.
Daily values: 4% vit. C.

APRICOT-CRANBERRY RELISH

Cook this sparkling ruby relish a day or two before your big feast.

- 1 cup water
- ¾ cup sugar
- 2 cups fresh cranberries
- ½ cup snipped dried apricots
- ¼ cup orange marmalade
  Shredded orange peel (optional)

1 In a medium saucepan combine water and sugar. Bring to boiling, stirring to dissolve sugar. Boil rapidly for 5 minutes. Add cranberries. Return just to boiling; reduce heat. Boil gently over medium heat 3 to 4 minutes or till most of the skins pop, stirring occasionally. Stir in apricots and marmalade. Remove from heat; serve warm or chilled. (Add a small amount of *water,* if necessary, to reach desired consistency.) If desired, garnish with orange peel. Makes 9 side-dish servings.

Nutrition facts per serving: 116 cal., 0 g total fat, 0 mg chol., 3 mg sodium, 30 g carbo., 2 g fiber, 0 g pro.
Daily values: 5% vit. A, 6% vit. C, 3% iron.

DECORATING YOUR JARS

To make your gift of homemade jam, jelly, or preserves look as special as it tastes, trim the canning jars with ribbons and decorative labels. Or, remove the screw bands and place a small, lacy doily or fabric swatch with a pinked edge over the sealed lids before replacing the screw bands. Arrange each jar in a ready-made gift bag along with an elegant relish server or jam spreader, and your gift from the kitchen is sure to be a hit.

NO FAT

CRANBERRY-KUMQUAT RELISH

Instead of the usual orange, cranberry teams with kumquats and a pinch of ginger for unexpected zip.

- 4 cups cranberries (1 lb.)
- 1½ cups fresh kumquats (8 oz.), seeded and coarsely chopped
- 1¼ cups granulated sugar
- 1¼ cups packed brown sugar
- 1 cup orange juice
- 2 tsp. grated gingerroot or ½ tsp. ground ginger
- ½ cup coarsely chopped walnuts

1 In a 4-quart pot combine cranberries, kumquats, granulated sugar, brown sugar, orange juice, and gingerroot or ground ginger. Bring mixture to boiling; reduce heat. Simmer, uncovered, over medium-low heat for 10 minutes, stirring frequently. Stir in nuts.

2 Ladle hot relish into hot, sterilized half-pint canning jars, leaving ½-inch headspace. Wipe jar rims with a clean, damp cloth. Place the prepared lids on jars. Add screw bands, tightening according to the manufacturer's instructions. Set each jar into a boiling-water canner as it is filled, making sure the jars do not touch each other. Process the filled jars in a boiling-water canner for 10 minutes (start timing when water boils).

3 Remove jars from the canner; cool on racks. Store in a cool, dry place. Refrigerate after opening. Makes about 5 half-pints (80 one-tablespoon servings).

SERVING SUGGESTION

Use instead of cranberry sauce with your holiday turkey or ham and the leftovers.

Nutrition facts per tablespoon: 36 cal., 0 g total fat, 0 mg chol., 2 mg sodium, 8 g carbo., 0 g fiber, 0 g pro.
Daily values: 5% vit. C.

NO FAT

GREEN APPLE-JALAPEÑO CHUTNEY

The heat level can vary among jalapeño peppers, so if your peppers taste particularly hot, you may want to use fewer of them.

- 1½ lb. ripe green or yellow apples, such as Crispin, Granny Smith, Golden Delicious, or Newtown Pippin
- 1 large papaya (about 1 lb.), peeled, seeded, and cut up
- 2 medium onions, cut up
- 1 medium red sweet pepper, cut up
- 8 small fresh jalapeño peppers, seeded and cut up (about ½ cup)*

◆◆◆

- 1¼ cups cider vinegar or white vinegar
- 1¼ cups sugar
- ½ cup raisins
- 1 Tbsp. dry mustard
- ½ tsp. salt

1 Wash, core, and cut up the apples. Use a food processor to chop the apples, papaya, onions, red sweet pepper, and jalapeño peppers, processing the ingredients in about five batches. Or, finely chop the fruits and vegetables with a sharp knife. (You should have about 6 cups total chopped mixture.)

2 In a 4-quart pot combine the chopped fruits and vegetables, cider vinegar or white vinegar, sugar, raisins, mustard, and salt. Bring the mixture to boiling, stirring to dissolve sugar; reduce heat. Simmer, uncovered, 30 minutes, stirring occasionally.

3 Ladle the hot chutney into hot, sterilized half-pint canning jars, leaving ½-inch headspace. Wipe jar rims with a clean, damp cloth. Place prepared lids on jars. Add screw bands, tightening according to the manufacturer's directions. Set each jar into a boiling water canner as it is filled, making sure the jars do not touch each other. Process in the canner for 10 minutes (start timing when the water boils).

4 Remove jars from canner; cool on racks, allowing space between jars. Store in a cool, dry place. Refrigerate after opening.

Makes about 7 half-pints (112 one-tablespoon servings).

*Note: Because jalapeño peppers contain volatile oils that can burn skin and eyes, avoid direct contact with the peppers as much as possible. Wear plastic or rubber gloves. If your bare hands touch the chili peppers, wash your hands and nails well with soap and water.

◼ SERVING SUGGESTION ◼

Spoon this spicy blend over grilled chicken or seafood, or stir a spoonful into a dressing for fruit salads.

Nutrition facts per tablespoon: 17 cal., 0 g total fat, 0 mg chol., 39 mg sodium, 4 g carbo., 0 g fiber, 0 g pro.
Daily values: 3% vit. C.

DRIED TOMATO-MANGO CHUTNEY

Mango is the fruit traditionally used in Indian chutneys, but cutting it can be a challenge, especially if you've never done it before. Follow the directions in the note at the end of the recipe to make seeding and cutting a breeze.

2   cups water
3   medium onions, coarsely
      chopped (1½ cups)
2   medium mangoes, seeded,*
      peeled, and coarsely
      chopped (2 cups)
1   cup dried tomatoes
      (not oil-packed), snipped
      (about 2 oz.)
½   cup raisins
½   to ¾ tsp. crushed red pepper
½   cup packed brown sugar
⅓   cup balsamic vinegar or red
      wine vinegar
1   Tbsp. white vinegar

1 In a 3-quart saucepan combine water, onions, mangoes, dried tomatoes, raisins, and crushed red pepper. Bring mixture to boiling; reduce heat. Simmer, uncovered, about 15 minutes or till tomatoes are tender, stirring occasionally. Add brown sugar and vinegars. Boil gently, uncovered, about 20 minutes or till most of the liquid is absorbed, stirring occasionally. Cool slightly; transfer to storage containers. Cover and store in the refrigerator up to 4 weeks or freeze up to 12 months. Makes about 3 cups (48 one-tablespoon servings).

*Note: To remove the mango fruit from the large, flat seed in the center, slide a sharp knife lengthwise next to the seed along one side of the mango, cutting all the way through. Repeat on the other side of the seed, cutting 2 large pieces away from the seed. Then cut away all of the fruit that remains around the seed. Remove the peel from all the pieces.

◼ SERVING SUGGESTION ◼

Try this chutney with roast pork or beef.

Nutrition facts per tablespoon: 26 cal., 0 g total fat, 0 mg chol., 26 mg sodium, 7 g carbo., 0 g fiber, 0 g pro.
Daily values: 3% vit. A, 5% vit. C, 1% iron.

CRANBERRY-MACADAMIA BARS

Bar cookies are a sweet solution when you don't have time to shape and bake. (See the photograph on page 279.)

1¼   cups all-purpose flour
¾   cup sugar
½   cup butter

½   cup finely chopped
      macadamia nuts, hazelnuts
      (filberts), or pecans
      ◆◆◆
1¼   cups sugar
2   beaten eggs
2   Tbsp. milk
1   tsp. finely shredded orange
      peel
1   tsp. vanilla
½   cup finely chopped
      macadamia nuts, hazelnuts
      (filberts), or pecans
1   cup finely chopped
      cranberries
½   cup coconut

1 In a mixing bowl stir together the flour and the ¾ cup sugar. Cut in butter till mixture resembles coarse crumbs. Stir in ½ cup nuts. Press flour mixture onto the bottom of an ungreased 13×9×2-inch baking pan. Bake in a 350° oven for 10 to 15 minutes or till the crust is light brown around the edges.

2 Meanwhile, combine the 1¼ cups sugar, eggs, milk, orange peel, and vanilla. Beat till combined. Pour over the hot crust. Sprinkle with ½ cup nuts, cranberries, and coconut.

3 Bake in the 350° oven for 30 minutes more or till golden. Cool slightly in the pan on a wire rack. Cut into 24 bars; cut bars in half diagonally while warm. Cool completely. Makes 48 bars.

Nutrition facts per bar: 88 cal., 4 g total fat (2 g sat. fat), 14 mg chol., 23 mg sodium, 12 g carbo., 0 g fiber, 1 g pro.
Daily values: 2% vit. A, 1% iron.

MAKING COOKIES WITH MARGARINE

The firmness of your cookie dough will vary depending on whether you use butter or margarine. If you use margarine, it will depend on what type of margarine it is. To ensure the best cookies every time, use only butter or use margarine that contains at least 60 percent vegetable oil. Do not use the "extra light" spreads that contain only about 40 percent oil.

NUTCRACKER COOKIES

Treat your kids to visions of dancing sugarplum fairies, with cookie cutters based on the holiday ballet classic. Look for cookie cutters in the shape of dancers, soldiers, trees, stars, rocking horses, candles, and bells in specialty cookware shops.
(See the photograph on page 279.)

1½ cups all-purpose flour
 1 cup whole wheat flour
 ½ tsp. baking soda
 ½ tsp. ground cardamom or
     1 tsp. ground cinnamon
        ◆◆◆
 ½ cup butter
 ½ cup packed brown sugar
 1 egg
 ⅓ cup honey
 1 tsp. vanilla
 1 recipe Meringue Powder
     Glaze (see above right)

1 In a medium mixing bowl stir together all-purpose flour, whole wheat flour, baking soda, and cardamom or cinnamon.

2 In a large mixing bowl beat butter 30 seconds. Add brown sugar; beat till fluffy. Add egg, honey, and vanilla; beat well. Beat in as much of the flour mixture as you can. Stir in remaining flour mixture. Divide dough in half. Cover; chill at least 2 hours or till dough is easy to handle.

3 On a lightly floured surface, roll out dough to between ⅛- and ¼-inch thickness. Cut with assorted cutters. Place on a cookie sheet. Bake in a 375° oven 5 to 6 minutes or till edges are light brown. Remove immediately and cool on a wire rack. Decorate with Meringue Powder Glaze. Makes about 72 (3- to 4-inch) cookies.

Meringue Powder Glaze: In a medium mixing bowl stir together ¼ cup *warm water* and 2 tablespoons *meringue powder*. Stir in 2 cups sifted *powdered sugar* till combined. Gradually stir in about 1½ cups sifted *powdered sugar* to make a smooth glaze that is easy to spread. (It should have a flowing consistency and be too thin to hold ridges when spread.)

TO MAKE AHEAD

Bake and cool cookies as directed. Do not glaze. Place in layers separated by waxed paper in a freezer container and freeze for up to 1 month. To serve, thaw for 15 minutes. Decorate with glaze.

Nutrition facts per cookie with glaze: 55 cal., 1 g total fat (1 g sat. fat), 3 mg chol., 25 mg sodium, 10 g carbo., 0 g fiber, 1 g pro. *Daily values:* 1% vit. A, 1% iron.

CHOCOLATE-PISTACHIO WREATHS

To one basic dough, add two different flavors—chocolate and pistachio—to roll and twist into cookie wreaths.
(See the photograph on page 279.)

 ¾ cup butter
 ¾ cup granulated sugar
 ¼ tsp. baking powder
 1 egg
 1 tsp. vanilla
1¾ cups all-purpose flour
        ◆◆◆
 ¼ cup finely chopped pistachio
     nuts
 ¼ tsp. almond extract
 3 Tbsp. unsweetened cocoa
     powder
 2 Tbsp. milk
        ◆◆◆
 ½ cup sifted powdered sugar
 1 to 2 tsp. milk
     Red paste food coloring
     Chopped pistachio nuts
     (optional)

1 In a large mixing bowl beat the butter with an electric mixer on medium to high speed about 30 seconds or till softened. Add the granulated sugar and baking powder. Beat till combined, scraping the sides of the bowl occasionally. Beat in the egg and vanilla. Beat in as much of the flour as you can. Using a wooden spoon, stir in any remaining flour.

2 Remove half of the dough from the bowl. In a small mixing bowl combine this dough with the ¼ cup pistachio nuts and almond extract; cover and set aside. Stir the cocoa powder and the 2 tablespoons milk into dough remaining in bowl. Cover and chill both portions of dough about 30 minutes or till dough is easy to handle or for up to 2 days.

3 On a lightly floured surface, shape each half of the dough into a 12-inch-long log. Cut each log into twenty-four ½-inch-thick pieces. With your hands, roll each piece into a 6-inch-long rope. Place a light and a dark rope side by side and twist together 5 to 6 times. Shape twisted rope into a circle, gently pinching where ends meet. Place 2 inches apart on ungreased cookie sheets.

4 Repeat with the remaining dough, leaving 2 inches between cookies. Bake in a 375° oven for 8 to 10 minutes or till edges are light brown. Cool on cookie sheet about 1 minute. Remove cookies and cool thoroughly on a wire rack.

5 For icing, in a small mixing bowl combine the powdered sugar and enough milk to make of piping consistency. Stir in food coloring to reach desired color. Decorate by piping a red bow on each wreath. If desired, sprinkle with additional pistachio nuts. Makes about 24 cookies.

TO MAKE AHEAD

Bake and cool cookies as directed. Do not ice. Place in layers separated by waxed paper in a freezer container and freeze for up to 1 month. To serve, thaw for 15 minutes. Decorate with icing.

Nutrition facts per cookie: 128 cal., 7 g total fat (4 g sat. fat), 24 mg chol., 65 mg sodium, 16 g carbo., 0 g fiber, 2 g pro. *Daily values:* 5% vit. A, 1% calcium, 4% iron.

PECAN SNAPS WITH ESPRESSO-CREAM FILLING

The filled cookies make tempting additions to holiday cookie trays, especially when the cookie edges are brushed with melted chocolate.

¼ **cup packed brown sugar**
3 **Tbsp. butter or margarine, melted**
2 **Tbsp. dark-colored corn syrup or light-flavored molasses**
1 **Tbsp. coffee liqueur or coffee**
½ **cup extra-finely chopped pecans**
¼ **cup all-purpose flour**
♦♦♦
3 **oz. semisweet chocolate, melted (optional)**
♦♦♦
1 **cup whipping cream**
¼ **cup sifted powdered sugar**
4 **tsp. instant espresso coffee powder**

1 Lightly grease a cookie sheet or line with parchment paper. In a small mixing bowl stir together brown sugar, melted butter or margarine, corn syrup or molasses, and coffee liqueur or coffee. Stir in pecans and flour till combined. Drop batter from a level teaspoon 3 inches apart, or a level tablespoon 5 inches apart, on the prepared cookie sheet. (Bake only 4 or 5 cookies at a time.) Bake in a 350° oven for 7 to 8 minutes for smaller cookies and 8 to 10 minutes for larger cookies or till cookies are bubbly and a deep golden brown.

2 Cool cookies on the cookie sheet for 1 to 2 minutes or till set. Quickly remove cookies, 1 at a time. Place each cookie, upside down, on a heatproof surface. Immediately roll each cookie around a metal cone or the greased handle of a wooden spoon. When the cookie is firm, slide the cookie off the cone or spoon and cool completely on a wire rack. (If cookies harden before you can shape them, reheat them in the oven about 1 minute or till softened.) If desired, carefully brush the top edge of cones with melted semisweet chocolate. Use a light touch, as the cookies are fragile and break easily.

3 Up to 30 minutes before serving, in a large mixing bowl beat whipping cream, powdered sugar, and espresso coffee powder with an electric mixer on low speed till stiff peaks form. Pipe or spoon some of the filling into each cookie. Makes about 30 small or 11 large cookies.

TO MAKE AHEAD

Bake, shape, and cool cookies as directed. Arrange in a single layer in a freezer container and freeze for up to 1 month. To serve, thaw cookies for 15 minutes. Beat the filling and fill the cookies.

Nutrition facts per small cookie with filling: 68 cal., 5 g total fat (3 g sat. fat), 14 mg chol., 16 mg sodium, 5 g carbo., 0 g fiber, 0 g pro. *Daily values:* 4% vit. A, 1% iron.

GINGERED FRUIT EN PAPILLOTE

Make individual portions of this fruit combo or a one-dish casserole.

½ cup dried tart red cherries, dried blueberries, raisins, or currants
¼ cup orange liqueur or orange juice
  Parchment paper
2 Tbsp. margarine or butter, melted
4 cups thinly sliced, peeled peaches, nectarines, or apples

◆◆◆

¼ cup packed brown sugar
2 Tbsp. finely chopped crystallized ginger
½ tsp. finely shredded orange peel
4 Tbsp. margarine or butter

◆◆◆

½ cup Crème Fraîche (optional) (see right)
  Candied Orange Peel (optional) (see right)

1 In a small saucepan combine dried fruit and orange liqueur or orange juice; heat just to boiling. Remove from heat; let stand 5 minutes. Drain fruit and discard liquid. Set the fruit aside.

2 To assemble bundles, cut four 20×10-inch rectangles from parchment paper. Brush both sides of the 4 paper rectangles with the 2 tablespoons melted margarine or butter.

3 Mound peach, nectarine, or apple slices on the right half of the rectangles, leaving about 2 inches of parchment paper showing around the edges. Top with the drained, dried fruit.

4 In a small mixing bowl stir together brown sugar, ginger, and orange peel. Sprinkle brown sugar mixture over fruit. Place *1 tablespoon* margarine or butter on each mound of fruit. Then fold the left half of the paper rectangles over the fruit, matching edges. To seal each package, starting at 1 side of the rectangle, fold the edges together in a triple fold. Fold only 1 side at a time to ensure a tight seal. Then twist the 4 corners to close the package.

5 Place the bundles on an ungreased 15×10×1-inch baking pan. Bake in a 400° oven for 18 to 20 minutes or till paper puffs up and fruit is tender (carefully open paper to check doneness).

6 To serve, cut bundles open by slashing a large X on top of each, then pull back the paper. Transfer bundles to dessert plates. If desired, serve with Crème Fraîche and garnish with Candied Orange Peel. Makes 4 servings.

Nutrition facts per serving: 358 cal., 17 g total fat (3 g sat. fat), 0 mg chol., 207 mg sodium, 50 g carbo., 3 g fiber, 2 g pro. *Daily values:* 39% vit. A, 19% vit. C, 2% calcium, 3% iron.

Gingered Fruit en Casserole: Prepare fruit as directed, except omit the paper and 2 tablespoons melted margarine or butter. Place sliced fruit in an 8×8×2-inch baking dish or 9-inch quiche dish. Top with the drained, dried fruit. Sprinkle with brown sugar mixture. Dot with the 4 tablespoons margarine or butter. Bake, covered, in a 375° oven for 30 to 35 minutes or till fruit is tender. Stir before serving. To serve, spoon fruit mixture into dessert dishes

and, if desired, serve with Crème Fraîche and garnish with Candied Orange Peel.

CRÈME FRAÎCHE

¼ cup whipping cream (not ultra-pasteurized)
¼ cup dairy sour cream

1 In a mixing bowl stir together the whipping cream and sour cream. Cover with plastic wrap. Let stand at room temperature for 2 to 5 hours or till the mixture thickens. When thickened, cover and chill in the refrigerator till serving time or for up to 1 week. Stir before serving. Makes ½ cup.

CANDIED ORANGE PEEL

2 medium oranges or lemons, 4 medium tangerines, or 1 grapefruit

◆◆◆

1⅓ cups sugar
⅓ cup water

◆◆◆

  Sugar (about ¼ cup)

1 Cut the peels of desired fruit into quarters, cutting through the peels to pulp. Using a spoon, loosen the peel from the pulp, leaving the white membrane attached to the peel. (Reserve pulp for another use.)

2 Place fruit peel in a 2-quart nonmetal bowl. Add enough *cold water* to cover. If necessary, place a plate in the bowl to keep the peel submerged. Let stand overnight.

3 Drain the peel. Rinse with *cold water.* Place peel in a 2-quart saucepan. Cover with cold water. Bring to boiling; drain. Repeat boiling and draining the peel 3 more times. Drain peel; cool thoroughly.

4 Cut the fruit peel into ⅛- to ¼-inch-wide strips. In the same saucepan combine the 1⅓ cups sugar and ⅓ cup water. Bring to boiling, stirring constantly to dissolve sugar. Add the peel; return to boiling. Reduce heat and cook, uncovered, over medium-low heat (mixture should boil at a moderate, steady rate over the entire surface) till peel is almost translucent, stirring occasionally. This should take 15 to 20 minutes. *Do not overcook.*

5 Using a slotted spoon, remove peel from syrup and place on a wire rack with waxed paper placed underneath. Discard the syrup. Cool peel till lukewarm. While peel is still slightly sticky, roll it in additional sugar to coat. Dry on the rack for 1 to 2 hours. Place in an airtight container and store in a cool, dry place up to 1 week or in the freezer for up to 6 months. Makes about 2 cups.

BROWN BUTTER TART WITH RASPBERRIES

  1 recipe Sweet Tart Pastry
     (see right)
◆◆◆
  3 eggs
1¼ cups sugar
  ½ cup all-purpose flour
  1 tsp. vanilla or 1 vanilla bean,
     split lengthwise
  ¾ cup butter

  2 cups raspberries or
     blackberries*
  2 Tbsp. currant jelly

1 For pastry shell, on a lightly floured surface, use your hands to slightly flatten the Sweet Tart Pastry dough. Roll dough from center to edges, forming a 12-inch circle. Wrap pastry around the rolling pin. Then unroll pastry onto a 10-inch tart pan with a removable bottom. Ease pastry into the tart pan, being careful not to stretch it. Press the pastry into the fluted sides of tart pan and trim edges. Set the unbaked pastry shell aside.

2 In a large mixing bowl use a rotary beater or a wire whisk to lightly beat eggs just till mixed. Then stir in sugar, flour and, if using, liquid vanilla. Set egg mixture aside.

3 In a heavy medium saucepan combine the butter and, if using, vanilla bean. Cook over medium-high heat till the butter turns the color of light brown sugar. Remove from heat. Remove and discard the vanilla bean. Slowly add the browned butter to the egg mixture, stirring till mixed. Pour into the unbaked pastry shell.

4 Bake in a 350° oven about 35 minutes or till the top is crisp and golden brown. Cook completely in pan on a wire rack.

5 To serve, remove sides of the tart pan. Arrange fruit on top of the tart. In a small saucepan heat currant jelly till melted. Brush melted jelly over the fruit. Makes 8 servings.

*Note: To substitute nectarines or plums for the berries, pit and thinly slice 2 medium *nectarines or* 4 medium *plums.* Place fruit slices in an 8-inch skillet; add enough *water* just to cover and 2 tablespoons *sugar.* Bring mixture to boiling; reduce heat. Simmer, covered, about 4 minutes or just till fruit is tender. Using a slotted spoon, remove fruit and place on paper towels. Arrange the drained fruit in a decorative pattern on top of tart. Then brush with melted jelly.

Nutrition facts per serving: 559 cal., 32 g total fat (19 g sat. fat), 210 mg chol., 317 mg sodium, 64 g carbo., 2 g fiber, 6 g pro. *Daily values:* 38% vit. A, 12% vit. C, 2% calcium, 12% iron.

SWEET TART PASTRY

1¼ cups all-purpose flour
  ¼ cup sugar
  ½ cup cold butter
◆◆◆
  2 beaten egg yolks
  1 Tbsp. water

1 In a medium mixing bowl stir together flour and sugar. Cut in butter till pieces are the size of small peas.

2 In a small mixing bowl stir together egg yolks and water. Gradually stir egg yolk mixture into flour mixture. Using your fingers, gently knead the dough just till a ball forms. If necessary, cover with plastic wrap and chill for 30 to 60 minutes or till dough is easy to handle.

PUMPKIN NAPOLEONS

For a sweeter note, drizzle the tops with powdered sugar icing instead of sprinkling with powdered sugar.

½ **of a 17¼-oz. pkg. frozen puff pastry (1 sheet)**

❖❖❖

1 **3-oz. pkg. cream cheese, softened**
¾ **cup sifted powdered sugar**
½ **tsp. pumpkin pie spice**
1 **cup canned pumpkin**
⅓ **cup whipping cream**
Powdered sugar

1 Let puff pastry thaw according to package directions; unfold sheet. Using a sharp knife, cut lengthwise and crosswise into thirds, forming 9 rectangles. Place on an ungreased baking sheet. Bake in a 425° oven 10 minutes or till puffed and golden. Transfer to a rack; cool.

2 In a large mixing bowl beat the cream cheese, ¾ cup powdered sugar, and pumpkin pie spice with an electric mixer on low to medium speed till combined. Beat in pumpkin. Wash beaters. In a small mixing bowl beat whipping cream on medium speed to stiff peaks. Fold whipped cream into pumpkin mixture. Cover and chill at least 1 hour.

3 To serve, using the tines of a fork, carefully split puff pastry rectangles in half horizontally. Spread with pumpkin mixture. Replace tops. Sprinkle with powdered sugar. Makes 9 servings.

Nutrition facts per serving: 227 cal., 15 g total fat (4 g sat. fat), 23 mg chol., 135 mg sodium, 21 g carbo., 1 g fiber, 2 g pro. *Daily values:* 67% vit. A, 2% vit. C, 1% calcium, 3% iron.

TEST KITCHEN TIP

MAKING YOUR OWN PUMPKIN PULP

It's easy to make your own pumpkin pulp if you have the time. Cut a medium pumpkin (about 6 pounds) into 5-inch-square pieces. Remove the seeds and fibrous strings. Arrange the pieces in a single layer, skin side up, in a large shallow baking pan. Cover with foil. Bake in a 375° oven for 1 to 1½ hours or till tender. Scoop the pulp from the rind. Working with part of the pulp at a time, place pulp in a blender container or food processor bowl. Cover and blend or process till smooth. Place pumpkin in a cheese-cloth-lined strainer; press out any liquid. Makes about 2 cups.

PRIZE TESTED RECIPE WINNER

PUMPKIN CHARLOTTE

This recipe earned Maria F. Gugliotti of Waterbury, Connecticut, $100 in the magazine's monthly contest.

2 **3-oz. pkg. ladyfingers, split (24 total)**

❖❖❖

2 **3-oz. pkg. cream cheese, softened**
2 **Tbsp. granulated sugar**
1¾ **cups whipping cream**
2 **Tbsp. powdered sugar**

❖❖❖

2 **4-serving-size pkg. instant vanilla pudding mix**
½ **tsp. ground cinnamon**
¼ **tsp. ground ginger**
¼ **tsp. pumpkin pie spice**
1 **15-oz. can pumpkin**
1 **cup milk**

❖❖❖

½ **cup apricot jam, melted (optional)**
¼ **cup whipping cream**
Pumpkin pie spice (optional)

1 Chill a mixing bowl and beaters. For crust, line the bottom of a 9-inch springform pan with ladyfingers, cutting to fill spaces. Trim bottoms of the remaining ladyfingers slightly to stand in pan. Place ladyfingers, round side out, against pan sides; set aside.

2 For cream cheese filling, beat cream cheese and granulated sugar with an electric mixer on medium speed till combined. In a chilled bowl beat 1¾ cups cream and powdered sugar till soft peaks form; reserve ½ cup. Fold remaining into cheese mixture.

3 For pumpkin filling, stir together pudding mixes, cinnamon, ginger, and ¼ teaspoon pumpkin pie spice. Add pumpkin and milk; beat till thick. Fold in reserved ½ cup whipped cream.

4 Spread the cream cheese filling evenly onto the bottom of prepared pan. Carefully spread pumpkin layer over cream cheese layer. Cover and chill overnight.

5 Remove sides from pan; place the charlotte on a platter. If desired, brush sides with melted jam. Beat ¼ cup whipping cream to soft peaks; spoon atop each serving. If desired, sprinkle with additional pumpkin pie spice. Makes 12 servings.

Nutrition facts per serving: 516 cal., 22 g total fat (13 g sat. fat), 123 mg chol., 1,040 mg sodium, 78 g carbo., 1 g fiber, 5 g pro. *Daily values:* 105% vit. A, 4% vit. C, 7% calcium, 9% iron.

PUMPKIN FRUITCAKE

This recipe earned Judy K. Myers of Hays, North Carolina, $200 in the magazine's monthly contest.

1 cup granulated sugar
1 cup packed brown sugar
¾ cup shortening
2 eggs
2½ cups all-purpose flour
2 tsp. baking soda
2 tsp. ground cinnamon
1 tsp. ground cloves
1 tsp. ground nutmeg
1 15-oz. can pumpkin
1 cup raisins
1 cup chopped pecans
1 cup chopped maraschino
    cherries

♦♦♦

Orange juice (optional)
Coarse sugar (optional)
1 recipe Cream Cheese Butter
    (optional) (see above right)

1 Grease and flour a 10-inch fluted tube pan; set aside. In a large mixing bowl beat sugars, shortening, and eggs with an electric mixer on medium speed for 2 minutes, scraping bowl. In a medium mixing bowl combine flour, soda, cinnamon, cloves, nutmeg, and ¼ teaspoon *salt*. Add

flour mixture and pumpkin alternately to shortening mixture, beating on low speed after each addition till combined. Stir in raisins, nuts, and cherries.

2 Turn batter into prepared pan. Bake in a 350° oven 1 hour or till cake tests done. Cool on a wire rack 10 minutes. Remove from pan. Cool completely. If desired, brush cake with juice, sprinkle with coarse sugar, and top each slice with Cream Cheese Butter. Serves 14 to 16.

Cream Cheese Butter: Beat two 3-ounce packages softened *cream cheese,* ¼ cup softened *butter,* and 1 teaspoon *vanilla* till light and fluffy. Gradually add 1¼ cups sifted *powdered sugar,* beating well. Cover and chill. Let stand at room temperature 30 minutes before serving.

Nutrition facts per slice without butter: 400 cal., 17 g total fat (4 g sat. fat), 30 mg chol., 235 mg sodium, 60 g carbo., 3 g fiber, 4 g pro. *Daily values:* 68% vit. A, 4% vit. C, 3% calcium, 15% iron.

CRANBERRY-PEAR CAKE

Serve it plain as a coffee cake or with whipped cream for a luscious dessert. (See the photograph on page 277.)

½ cup butter
4 eggs
2½ cups all-purpose flour
1 Tbsp. baking powder
1¼ cups granulated sugar
1½ tsp. vanilla
¼ cup buttermilk or milk
3 cups peeled and coarsely
    chopped pears and/or
    apples
1 cup cranberries, coarsely
    chopped

Powdered sugar
Fresh kumquats (optional)
Rose leaves (optional)

1 Grease and flour a 10-inch fluted tube pan or a 13×9×2-inch baking pan; set aside. Let butter and eggs stand at room temperature 30 minutes. In a mixing bowl combine flour, baking powder, and ¼ teaspoon *salt*. In a large mixing bowl beat butter with an electric mixer on medium speed 30 seconds. Gradually add granulated sugar, 2 tablespoons at a time, beating on medium to high speed 6 minutes total. Add vanilla. Add eggs, 1 at a time, beating 1 minute after each addition and scraping bowl often. Beat in buttermilk or milk. Gradually add flour mixture to butter mixture, beating on low to medium speed just till combined. Fold in pears and/or apples; fold in cranberries. Spoon batter into the prepared pan; spread evenly.

2 Bake in a 350° oven 50 to 55 minutes for tube pan or 40 to 45 minutes for 13×9×2-inch pan or till a toothpick inserted near center comes out clean. Cool on rack 15 minutes. Remove cake from tube pan or leave in baking pan. Cool on rack. Sprinkle with powdered sugar. If desired, garnish with kumquats and rose leaves. Makes 12 to 16 servings.

*Note: If you use rose leaves for a garnish, check to see that they have been grown without pesticides and wash them first.

Nutrition facts per serving: 305 cal., 10 g total fat (5 g sat. fat), 92 mg chol., 240 mg sodium, 51 g carbo., 3 g fiber, 5 g pro. *Daily values:* 10% vit. A, 6% vit. C, 9% calcium, 11% iron.

PUMPKIN CHEESECAKE

½ **cup finely crushed graham crackers**
¼ **cup finely crushed gingersnaps**
2 **Tbsp. finely chopped pecans**
1 **Tbsp. all-purpose flour**
1 **Tbsp. powdered sugar**
2 **Tbsp. butter or margarine, melted**

◆◆◆

2 **8-oz. pkg. cream cheese, softened**
1 **cup granulated sugar**
3 **eggs**

◆◆◆

1 **15-oz. can pumpkin**
1 **egg**
¼ **cup milk**
½ **tsp. ground cinnamon**
¼ **tsp. ground ginger**
¼ **tsp. ground nutmeg**

◆◆◆

½ **cup whipping cream**
Toasted chopped pecans

1 For crust, in a medium bowl combine the crushed graham crackers, crushed gingersnaps, 2 tablespoons pecans, flour, powdered sugar, and melted butter or margarine. Press evenly onto the bottom of a 9-inch springform pan; set aside.

2 In a large mixing bowl beat together cream cheese and granulated sugar with an electric mixer on medium speed till fluffy. Add 3 eggs all at once, beating on low speed just till combined.

3 Place 1 cup of the cream cheese mixture in a medium bowl. Add pumpkin, 1 egg, milk, cinnamon, ginger, and nutmeg. Beat on low speed just till combined. Pour pumpkin mixture into prepared

pan. Top with the cream cheese mixture. With a knife or thin metal spatula, gently swirl through the layers to marble.

4 Place springform pan on a shallow baking pan. Bake in a 350° oven 40 to 45 minutes or till center appears set when shaken. Cool on a wire rack 15 minutes. Loosen crust from sides of pan. Cool 30 minutes more; remove sides of pan. Cool completely. Cover; chill at least 4 hours.

5 Before serving, beat the whipping cream to stiff peaks. Pipe or spoon into mounds atop cheesecake. Sprinkle with pecans. Makes 12 to 16 servings.

Nutrition facts per serving: 326 cal., 22 g total fat (13 g sat. fat), 132 mg chol., 195 mg sodium, 27 g carbo., 1 g fiber, 6 g pro. *Daily values:* 104% vit. A, 2% vit. C, 5% calcium, 10% iron.

TOFFEE-APPLE CHEESECAKE

Try the lower-fat version on page 269 of our decadent rich, creamy original. (See the photograph on the cover and on page 278.)

1¼ **cups finely chopped toasted walnuts***
⅔ **cup all-purpose flour**
⅓ **cup butter or margarine, melted**

◆◆◆

2 **8-oz. pkg. cream cheese, softened**
1 **14-oz. can (1¼ cups) sweetened condensed milk**
½ **cup frozen apple juice concentrate, thawed, or**
¼ **cup frozen apple juice concentrate, thawed, plus**
¼ **cup apple brandy**

3 **eggs**
½ **cup finely chopped, peeled apple**

◆◆◆

1 **or 2 medium red and/or yellow apples, such as Jonathan or Golden Delicious, cored and cut into thin slices**

◆◆◆

¼ **cup caramel ice cream topping**
White Chocolate Leaves (optional) (see right)
Apple Rose (optional) (see right)

1 For crust, in a medium mixing bowl combine chopped walnuts and flour. Stir in melted butter or margarine. Press evenly onto the bottom and 2 inches up the sides of an 8- or 9-inch springform pan; set aside.

2 For filling, in large mixing bowl beat cream cheese with an electric mixer on low speed till fluffy. Gradually beat in sweetened condensed milk. Add juice concentrate and eggs; beat on low speed just till combined. Stir in finely chopped apple. Pour into the prepared pan.

3 Place springform pan in a shallow baking pan. Bake in a 375° oven 45 to 50 minutes for the 8-inch pan or 35 to 40 minutes for 9-inch pan or till center appears nearly set when shaken.

4 Cool in pan on a wire rack for 15 minutes. Loosen crust from sides of pan. Cool for 30 minutes more; remove sides of pan. Cool cheesecake completely.

5 In a skillet poach apple slices in *boiling water* about 1 minute or till soft; drain. Cover and chill cheesecake and apples separately in the refrigerator for at least 4 hours or overnight.

6 Before serving, arrange apple slices atop cheesecake. Drizzle with warmed caramel topping. If desired, garnish with White Chocolate Leaves and an Apple Rose. Makes 12 servings.

*Note: To toast walnuts, spread nuts in a thin layer in a shallow baking pan. Bake in a 375° oven 10 minutes or till golden brown, stirring twice. Watch carefully so the nuts do not burn. Cool.

White Chocolate Leaves: Melt 6 ounces *vanilla-flavored candy coating* over low heat, stirring constantly; cool. Stir in 3 tablespoons *light-colored corn syrup.* Turn mixture out onto a large sheet of waxed paper. Let stand at room temperature for 3 to 24 hours or till dry to the touch. Gently knead for 10 to 15 strokes or till mixture is smooth and pliable. If mixture is too soft, chill in the refrigerator about 15 minutes or till easy to handle (or knead in enough *powdered sugar* to make the mixture stiffen). Store any unused mixture in a sealed plastic bag at room temperature for 3 to 4 weeks (mixture will stiffen with storage; knead mixture till it is pliable before using). Flatten mixture slightly; place between 2 sheets of waxed paper dusted with *powdered sugar.* Roll to ⅛-inch thickness. Using leaf-shape cutters, cut into shapes. Use a toothpick to draw veins on leaves. Curve leaves as desired.

Apple Rose: Starting at the corner of an extra-thin fresh *apple slice,* roll up diagonally to form a cone shape for the rose center. Press on additional slices, curving around center to make thin petals. Add petals to make a rose.

Nutrition facts per serving: 451 cal., 30 g total fat (14 g sat. fat), 120 mg chol., 251 mg sodium, 38 g carbo., 1 g fiber, 10 g pro. *Daily values:* 26% vit. A, 2% vit. C, 12% calcium, 9% iron.

Low-Fat Toffee-Apple Cheesecake: For crust, stir together ¾ cup crushed *graham crackers,* 2 tablespoons *sugar,* 2 tablespoons *all-purpose flour,* and 2 tablespoons melted *margarine or butter.* Press onto the bottom of the 8- or 9-inch springform pan. Bake crust in a 375° oven for 7 minutes. Cool on a wire rack.

For filling, substitute *reduced-fat cream cheese (Neufchâtel)* for regular cream cheese, *fat-free sweetened condensed milk* for regular sweetened condensed milk, and ¾ cup *refrigerated or frozen egg product,* thawed, for eggs. Continue as directed. Serves 12.

Nutrition facts per serving: 303 cal., 12 g total fat (6 g sat. fat), 29 mg chol., 256 mg sodium, 40 g carbo., 1 g fiber, 9 g pro. *Daily values:* 18% vit. A, 1% vit. C, 12% calcium, 5% iron.

MOCHA PEARS

Soak canned pears in coffee-flavored syrup, then top with yogurt and chocolate before serving.

- **2 16-oz. cans or one 29-oz. can pears in heavy syrup (12 pear halves)**
- **2 tsp. instant coffee crystals**
- **1 tsp. vanilla**

¾ cup vanilla yogurt
Chocolate curls or miniature semisweet chocolate pieces

1 Drain pears; reserve syrup. Place pears in a bowl; set aside. In a saucepan combine syrup and coffee. Bring to boiling; reduce heat. Simmer, uncovered, 15 minutes or till slightly thickened and reduced to ½ cup. Stir in vanilla. Pour syrup over pears. Cover; chill several hours, turning pears once.

2 To serve, place 2 pear halves into each of 6 dessert dishes. Top each serving with some of the syrup, 2 tablespoons yogurt, and some chocolate. Makes 6 servings.

Nutrition facts per serving: 168 cal., 2 g total fat (1 g sat. fat), 2 mg chol., 30 mg sodium, 37 g carbo., 1 g fiber, 2 g pro. *Daily values:* 1% vit. A, 3% vit. C, 4% calcium, 2% iron.

TROPICAL NUT TORTE

Be sure to bake the meringue on the torte the full 15 minutes so the egg white is thoroughly cooked.

2 **Tbsp. all-purpose flour**
1 **tsp. baking powder**
4 **eggs**
¾ **cup sugar**
2 **cups macadamia nuts or almonds**
½ **cup flaked coconut**

◆◆◆

1 **recipe Coconut and Banana Cream Filling (see right)**
1 **recipe Meringue (see right)**
 Mango slices (optional)

1 Grease and flour two 8×1½-inch round baking pans; set aside. In a small bowl combine flour and baking powder; set aside. In a blender container or food processor bowl, place eggs and sugar. Cover and blend or process till smooth. Add nuts and coconut. Blend 1 minute or till nearly smooth. Add flour mixture. Blend just till combined.

2 Spread batter evenly into the prepared baking pans. Bake in a 350° oven 20 minutes or till lightly browned. Cool in pans on wire racks 10 minutes. Remove from pans. Cool on racks.

3 Place a cake layer on a large ovenproof plate. Spread with cooled Coconut and Banana Cream Filling. Place second cake layer on top. Prepare Meringue. Immediately frost sides and top with Meringue. Bake in a 350° oven 15 minutes. Cool slightly before serving. If desired, garnish with mango. Cover leftovers and chill to store. Makes 10 servings.

Coconut and Banana Cream Filling: In a small skillet melt 1 tablespoon *butter* over medium heat. Stir in 1 tablespoon *brown sugar.* Add half of a medium *banana,* thinly sliced. Cook and stir for 2 to 3 minutes or till brown sugar is dissolved; set aside.

In a small saucepan combine 2 tablespoons *granulated sugar* and 1 tablespoon *all-purpose flour.* Stir in ½ cup purchased *coconut milk* and 1 beaten *egg yolk* till thoroughly combined. Cook and stir over medium heat till thickened and bubbly. Cook and stir 2 minutes more. Remove from heat; stir in banana mixture. Cover; cool without stirring.

Meringue: Allow 4 *egg whites* to stand at room temperature for 30 minutes. In a large mixing bowl combine egg whites, ½ teaspoon *vanilla,* and ¼ teaspoon *cream of tartar.* Beat with an electric mixer on medium speed about 2 minutes or till soft peaks form (tips curl). Gradually add ½ cup *granulated sugar,* 1 tablespoon at a time, beating on high speed about 4 minutes or till mixture forms stiff, glossy peaks and sugar dissolves. Use immediately.

■ TO MAKE AHEAD ■

You can bake and freeze cake layers up to a month ahead. The filling can be made and chilled overnight; let it stand at room temperature before using. The only thing you can't do is prepare meringue ahead of time; it needs to be made just before baking.

Nutrition facts per serving: 414 cal., 28 g total fat (8 g sat. fat), 110 mg chol., 100 mg sodium, 38 g carbo., 3 g fiber, 7 g pro. *Daily values:* 8% vit. A, 5% calcium, 9% iron.

HAZELNUT-CAPPUCCINO TORTE

Every holiday dessert table needs a chocolate choice. Why not one with a little coffee, too? (See the photograph on page 276.)

1 **8-oz. pkg. semisweet chocolate, cut up**
1⅓ **cups milk chocolate pieces (8 oz.)**
1 **cup whipping cream**
2 **Tbsp. instant coffee crystals**

◆◆◆

5 **eggs**
¼ **cup coffee liqueur or coffee**
1 **tsp. vanilla**
½ **cup all-purpose flour**
¼ **cup sugar**
1 **cup chopped toasted hazelnuts (filberts) or almonds**

◆◆◆

1 **recipe Mocha Cream (see page 271)**
 Chocolate-covered coffee beans (optional)

1 In a heavy saucepan heat semisweet chocolate, milk chocolate, whipping cream, and coffee crystals over low heat till chocolate is melted, stirring constantly. Cool to room temperature.

2 Grease and flour the bottom and sides of a 9-inch springform pan; set aside. In a large mixing bowl beat eggs, coffee liqueur or coffee, and vanilla with an electric mixer on low speed till combined. Add flour and sugar. Beat on medium to high speed 8 minutes (batter should be light and slightly thickened). Fold about one-fourth egg mixture into chocolate mixture. Fold chocolate mixture into remaining egg mixture. Fold in nuts.

3 Spread batter into the prepared pan. Bake in a 325° oven for 40 to 45 minutes or till slightly puffed around the outer edge (center will be slightly soft). Cool the cake in the pan on a wire rack for 20 minutes. Loosen sides. Remove sides of pan. Cool for 3 to 4 hours more. Cover and chill for up to 24 hours.

4 To serve, let cake stand at room temperature 30 minutes. Cut cake into wedges and top each serving with Mocha Cream and, if desired, garnish with chocolate-covered coffee beans. Makes 12 to 16 servings.

Mocha Cream: In a chilled small mixing bowl beat ½ cup *whipping cream* and 2 tablespoons *coffee liqueur* with the chilled beaters of an electric mixer on medium to high speed just till stiff peaks form.

Nutrition facts per serving: 445 cal., 31 g total fat (12 g sat. fat), 130 mg chol., 58 mg sodium, 38 g carbo., 1 g fiber, 7 g pro. *Daily values:* 19% vit. A, 8% calcium, 10% iron.

CREAM-FILLED CARAMEL CAKE ROLL

½ **cup all-purpose flour**
1 **tsp. baking powder**
◆◆◆
4 **eggs, separated**
½ **tsp. vanilla**
⅓ **cup granulated sugar**
½ **cup granulated sugar**
    Powdered sugar
◆◆◆
1 **egg**
⅔ **cup granulated sugar**
1 **5-oz. can (⅔ cup) evaporated milk**

¼ **cup margarine or butter**
½ **cup chopped toasted hazelnuts (filberts)**
½ **cup chopped toasted almonds**
½ **cup chopped toasted pecans**
◆◆◆
1 **recipe Sweetened Whipped Cream Frosting (see right)**

1 Grease and lightly flour a 15×10×1-inch baking pan. Combine flour and baking powder. Set aside.

2 In a medium bowl beat egg yolks and vanilla with an electric mixer on high speed 5 minutes or till thick and lemon-colored. Gradually add the ⅓ cup sugar, beating on high speed till sugar is almost dissolved. Thoroughly wash the beaters. In a large mixing bowl beat the egg whites on medium to high speed till soft peaks form (tips curl). Gradually add the ½ cup sugar, 2 tablespoons at a time, beating on medium to high speed till stiff peaks form (tips stand straight).

3 Fold about 1 cup of the egg white mixture into egg yolk mixture. Then fold all of the egg yolk mixture into remaining egg white mixture. Sprinkle flour mixture over egg mixture. Gently fold in just till combined.

4 Spread batter evenly into the prepared pan. Bake in a 375° oven for 12 to 15 minutes or till top springs back when lightly touched. Immediately loosen cake from pan. Invert cake onto a towel sprinkled with powdered sugar. Trim ⅛ inch from cake edges. Roll up warm cake and

towel, jelly-roll style, starting from a short side; cool.

5 For nut filling, in a small saucepan beat the whole egg just till mixed. Stir in ⅔ cup sugar, evaporated milk, and margarine or butter. Cook and stir over medium heat about 6 minutes or till thickened and bubbly. Stir in nuts; cool.

6 Gently unroll cake. Spread nut filling on cake to within ½ inch of edges. Spread 1 cup Sweetened Whipped Cream Frosting on top of nut filling to within 1 inch of edges of cake. Roll up cake, without towel, jelly-roll style, starting from a short side. Transfer to a large platter.

7 Spoon remaining Sweetened Whipped Cream Frosting into a decorating bag fitted with a medium round tip (about ¼-inch opening). Pipe frosting on top of cake roll in a decorating pattern. Serves 10.

Sweetened Whipped Cream Frosting: In a 1-cup glass measure combine 1 tablespoon *cold water* and ½ teaspoon *unflavored gelatin*. Place measuring cup in saucepan of *boiling water*. Cook and stir about 1 minute or till the gelatin is completely dissolved.

In a bowl beat 1 cup *whipping cream* and 2 tablespoons *sugar* with an electric mixer on medium speed while drizzling the gelatin into the cream mixture till stiff peaks form.

Nutrition facts per serving: 445 cal., 28 g total fat, (9 g sat. fat), 143 mg chol., 202 mg sodium, 44 g carb., 2 g fiber, 8 g pro. *Daily values:* 31% vit. A, 11% calcium, 8% iron.

ALMOND CRUNCH PUMPKIN PIE

For the pumpkin layer that covers the rich praline bottom, you can use 1½ teaspoons pumpkin pie spice instead of the individual spices.

1 recipe Pastry for Single-Crust Pie (see below right)

♦♦♦

¼ cup finely chopped almonds or pecans
¼ cup packed brown sugar
2 Tbsp. butter, softened
1 tsp. finely shredded orange peel

♦♦♦

2 eggs, beaten
1 16-oz. can (1¾ cups) pumpkin
¾ cup packed brown sugar
1 Tbsp. all-purpose flour
1 tsp. ground cinnamon
½ tsp. ground nutmeg
¼ tsp. ground ginger
1 12-oz. can (1½ cups) evaporated milk or 1½ cups half-and-half or light cream
Whipped cream (optional)

1 Prepare and roll out Pastry for Single-Crust Pie. Line a 9-inch pie plate with pastry. Trim and flute edge of pastry. Do not prick shell. Line pastry with a double thickness of foil. Bake pastry shell in a 450° oven for 8 minutes. Remove foil.

2 For praline layer, in a small mixing bowl stir together almonds, ¼ cup brown sugar, butter, and orange peel. Spoon mixture into the hot, partially baked pastry shell, spreading it over bottom as butter melts. Bake 5 to 6 minutes more or till shell is set and dry and praline is bubbly.

3 For filling, combine eggs, pumpkin, ¾ cup brown sugar, flour, cinnamon, nutmeg, and ginger. Gradually stir in the evaporated milk; mix well.

4 Reduce oven temperature to 375°. Place partially baked pastry shell on oven rack. Pour pumpkin filling into pastry shell. To prevent overbrowning, cover edge of pie with foil. Bake 25 minutes. Remove foil. Bake 20 to 25 minutes more or until a knife inserted near center comes out clean. Cool on a wire rack before serving. Refrigerate within 2 hours; add cover for longer storage. If desired, serve with whipped cream. Makes 8 servings.

Nutrition facts per serving: 373 cal., 19 g total fat (7 g sat. fat), 73 mg chol., 167 mg sodium, 47 g carbo., 2 g fiber, 8 g pro. *Daily values:* 133% vit. A, 6% vit. C, 13% calcium, 17% iron.

PASTRY FOR SINGLE-CRUST PIE

1¼ cups all-purpose flour
¼ tsp. salt
⅓ cup shortening

♦♦♦

4 to 5 tablespoons cold water

1 In a medium mixing bowl combine flour and salt. With a pastry blender, cut in shortening till pieces are size of small peas.

2 Sprinkle *1 tablespoon* of the water over part of mixture and gently toss with a fork. Push moistened dough to side of bowl. Repeat, using 1 tablespoon of water at a time, till all is moistened. Form dough into a ball.

3 On a lightly floured surface, use your hands to slightly flatten dough. Roll out dough from center to edges, forming a 12-inch circle. Transfer pastry to a 9-inch pie plate; ease into pie plate, being careful not to stretch it. Trim pastry to ½ inch beyond edge of pie plate. Fold under extra pastry. Flute edges. Do not prick shell. Bake as directed in recipe.

ALMOND-BRIE SPREAD

Serve this creamy three-ingredient spread with fresh fruit, crackers, or French bread. (See the photograph on page 273.)

2 4½-oz. rounds Brie cheese
2 Tbsp. cream sherry or milk
3 Tbsp. sliced almonds, toasted

1 Using a vegetable peeler or a small paring knife, cut the thin white covering from chilled cheese. Place the cheese in a mixing bowl; let stand at room temperature about 1 hour or till softened. Beat with an electric mixer on medium speed for 1 minute. Add sherry or milk. Beat till light and smooth. Chop *2 tablespoons* of the almonds; stir into cheese mixture.

2 Serve immediately or cover and chill overnight or till serving time. If chilled, let stand at room temperature for 30 to 45 minutes before serving. Sprinkle with remaining almonds. Makes about 1¼ cups.

Nutrition facts per tablespoon: 51 cal., 4 g total fat (2 g sat. fat), 13 mg chol., 80 mg sodium, 0 g carbo., 0 g fiber, 3 g pro. *Daily values:* 2% vit. A, 2% calcium.

Above: *Almond-Brie Spread (page 272)*

Top: *Tomato-Olive Spirals (page 246)*
Above: *Almond Breakfast Round (page 256)*
Page 274, clockwise from top: *Potato Buns (page 252) and Swiss-Caraway Biscuits (page 253),*
Swiss-Caraway Bread (page 252), Raisin-Pumpkin Twist (page 255)

Above: *Hazelnut-Cappuccino Torte (page 270)*
Right: *Cranberry-Pear Cake (page 267)*

Above: *Toffee-Apple Cheesecake (page 268)*
Page 279, clockwise from top: *Nutcracker Cookies (page 262), Chocolate-Pistachio Wreaths (page 262), Cranberry-Macadamia Bars (page 261)*

Cranberry-Date Pie (page 281)

CRANBERRY-DATE PIE

*Your stitch in time is
using refrigerated piecrust to make
a stunning lattice pie top.
(See the photograph on page 280.)*

1¾ **cups granulated sugar**
¼ **cup all-purpose flour**
½ **cup water**
3 **cups cranberries**
1 **cup chopped pitted dates**
    ◆◆◆
1 **15-oz. pkg. folded
    refrigerated unbaked
    piecrusts (2 crusts)**
    ◆◆◆
1 **Tbsp. coarse sugar (optional)**

1 For filling, in a medium saucepan stir together granulated sugar and flour; stir in water. Stir in cranberries. Bring to boiling; reduce heat. Cook and stir over medium heat till bubbly and almost all cranberry skins pop. Remove from heat; stir in dates. Let cool for 10 minutes.

2 Place 1 piecrust in a 9-inch pie plate according to package directions. On a lightly floured surface, cut remaining crust into ½-inch-wide strips.

3 Spread cooled filling in pastry shell. To make a lattice top, cross 2 strips in the center of the pie. Add strips in alternate directions, weaving under and over the other pastry strips. Trim pastry. Fold strips under bottom pastry to make a smooth raised edge. Flute edge. If desired, sprinkle pastry with coarse sugar. Cover the edge loosely with foil.

4 Bake on a baking sheet in a 375° oven for 25 minutes. Remove foil; bake for 20 to 25 minutes more or till crust is golden. Cool on a wire rack. Makes 10 servings.

Nutrition facts per serving: 403 cal., 12 g total fat (0 g sat. fat), 12 mg chol., 170 mg sodium, 74 g carbo., 3 g fiber, 2 g pro. *Daily values:* 7% vit. C, 2% iron.

HOLIDAY TRIFLE

*Layer the fruit, cream, and crumbled
cookies in assorted goblets and
set them out on a serving tray lined
with holiday greenery.*

8 **oz. mascarpone cheese**
1 **cup whipping cream**
⅓ **cup sweet Marsala wine,
    cream sherry, or orange
    juice***
2 **Tbsp. powdered sugar**
2 **cups crumbled soft
    coconut macaroon
    cookies (about ½ of a
    13¾-oz. pkg.)**
    ◆◆◆
3 **oranges, peeled and
    sectioned**
2 **cups fresh raspberries**
2 **cups seedless green grapes,
    halved**
    ◆◆◆
    **Fresh raspberries (optional)
    Fresh mint leaves (optional)**

1 In a medium mixing bowl combine mascarpone; whipping cream; (orange peel, if using orange juice option); *2 tablespoons* of the Marsala, sherry, or orange juice; and powdered sugar. Beat just till mixture has thickened to almost puddinglike consistency. (Do not overbeat; mixture should not form soft peaks.) Place the macaroons in a medium mixing bowl. Toss with the remaining Marsala, sherry, or orange juice.

THE CLEVER COOK

PATCHWORK PIECRUSTS

When my frozen or refrigerated piecrusts have cracks before prebaking, I patch them by sprinkling a spoonful of crushed vanilla wafers or graham cracker crumbs into the cracks. This keeps the filling from seeping through and making the crust soggy. And, it's almost impossible to see the repair when the pie is served.

Deborah Schum
Litchfield, Illinois

2 In another bowl combine orange sections, the 2 cups raspberries, and grape halves.

3 Divide half of the fruit mixture among 10 goblets or dessert dishes. Divide half of the macaroon mixture among the goblets atop the fruit. Then top with half of the mascarpone mixture. Repeat layers. Chill for 1 to 2 hours. If desired, garnish with a few additional raspberries and mint leaves. Makes 10 servings.

*Note: If you use orange juice instead of wine, add ½ teaspoon finely shredded *orange peel* to the cheese mixture for a flavor boost.

Nutrition facts per serving: 346 cal., 25 g total fat (12 g sat. fat), 61 mg chol., 30 mg sodium, 29 g carbo., 2 g fiber, 7 g pro. *Daily values:* 11% vit. A, 32% vit. C, 3% calcium, 2% iron.

PEAR TART

Fresh pears get a rosy blush when poached in the red wine mixture.

1 recipe Rich Tart Pastry (see right)

♦♦♦

1 recipe Pastry Paint (see right) or milk and sugar

♦♦♦

3 medium pears
½ cup dry red wine
½ cup water
2 Tbsp. sugar
6 whole cloves

♦♦♦

1 8-oz. pkg. cream cheese, softened
½ cup dairy sour cream
¼ cup honey
¼ cup finely chopped crystallized ginger

1 Prepare Rich Tart Pastry; remove about one-fourth of the pastry and set aside. On a lightly floured surface, roll out the remaining pastry from center to edges, forming a 13×10-inch rectangle. Ease the pastry rectangle into an 11×8-inch rectangular tart pan with a removable bottom. (Or, roll out the pastry into a 12-inch circle. Ease pastry into a 10-inch round tart pan with a removable bottom.)

2 Press the pastry into the fluted sides of the tart pan and trim edges. Using the tines of a fork, prick bottom and sides of pastry generously. Line pastry shell with a double thickness of foil. Bake in a 450° oven for 10 minutes. Remove foil. Bake for 5 minutes more or till golden. Cool in pan on a wire rack.

3 Roll reserved pastry to ⅛-inch thickness. Using a knife or cookie cutter, cut leaf shapes. Make vein marks with the tip of a knife or wooden pick. Decorate with Pastry Paint or brush with milk and sprinkle with sugar. Arrange the leaf shapes on a baking sheet. (If desired, before placing pastry cutouts on baking sheet, cover the baking sheet with crumpled foil for a rolling surface so the leaves don't bake flat.) Bake in a 450° oven for 3 to 5 minutes or till cutouts are golden; cool.

4 Peel, halve, and core pears. Place pear halves, flat side down, on cutting board. Make about 7 lengthwise cuts in each pear half, starting about ½ inch from the stem end and cutting to the bottom. In a large skillet combine red wine, water, 2 tablespoons sugar, and cloves. Bring to boiling. Carefully add the pear halves, flat sides down, to wine mixture. Spoon wine mixture over pears. Return to boiling; reduce heat. Simmer, covered, for 10 to 15 minutes or till pears are tender, occasionally spooning liquid over halves. Using a slotted spoon, carefully remove the pears from the liquid; drain and chill pears. Discard cooking liquid.

5 For filling, stir together the softened cream cheese, sour cream, honey, and ginger. Spread filling evenly on bottom of baked crust. Cover and chill for up to 2 hours.

6 Just before serving, pat pears dry with paper towels and carefully arrange on cheese mixture, fanning cuts. Top the tart with the baked pastry leaves. Makes 10 servings.

Rich Tart Pastry: In a medium mixing bowl combine 1½ cups *all-purpose flour* and ⅓ cup *sugar*. Using a pastry blender, cut in ½ cup *butter* till pieces are the size of small peas. In a small bowl combine 2 *egg yolks* and 2 tablespoons *cold water*. Gradually stir egg yolk mixture into flour mixture. Add additional *cold water* if necessary, 1 tablespoon at a time, till all of the dough is moistened. Using your fingers, gently knead the dough just till a ball forms.

Pastry Paint: In a small mixing bowl stir together 1 slightly beaten *egg yolk* and 1 teaspoon *water*. Place half of the mixture in another small bowl. To each bowl, stir in a few drops of *food coloring*, making 2 different shades of green. Using a small, clean brush, paint mixture onto pastry leaves.

▌ TO MAKE AHEAD ▐

Bake the pastry shell a day ahead and store tightly covered overnight. Poach, drain, and chill pears till ready to serve. Prepare and chill filling overnight. Assemble tart no more than 2 hours before serving.

Nutrition facts per serving: 368 cal., 21 g total fat (13 g sat. fat), 97 mg chol., 179 mg sodium, 40 g carbo., 2 g fiber, 5 g pro. *Daily values:* 27% vit. A, 5% vit. C, 4% calcium, 13% iron.

DECEMBER
Dinners with Distinction

30-minute recipes indicated in RED.
Low-fat recipes indicated with a ♥.

*D*inners served by
candlelight with
polished silver and
gleaming china call for
spectacular recipes.
Masterpiece Beef Roast
and Prosciutto-Stuffed
Turkey Breast fit the
bill. Accompaniments
such as Piquant
Potatoes and Pepper-
Cheddar Yorkshire
Pudding take these
meals to new heights.
For the finale, count on
flaky fruit pies and
plum pudding, and
start traditions by
serving White Chocolate
Pie or Lemon Curd
Tarts. Don't miss our
rich assortment of
cookie and candy
recipes—Peppermint
Creams and Turkish
Delight candies, and
Macaroons, Lebkuchen,
and Speculaas cookies
are just a few.

Holiday Frittata
(see below right)

❖❖❖

Minty Winter Compote
(see below)

❖❖❖

**Christmas Morning
Cinnamon Rolls**
(see right)

❖❖❖

**Orange juice with a
splash of champagne**

mixture, sugar, and snipped mint. Bring just to boiling; reduce heat. Simmer, covered, for 5 minutes. Strain, discarding mint; cool.

2 Combine pineapple, grapefruit, orange peel and slices, and kiwifruit; set aside. Pour strained syrup over fruit; cover and chill 2 hours or overnight. To serve, stir in pomegranate seeds; garnish with fresh mint. Serves 6.

Nutrition facts per serving: 101 cal., 0 g total fat, 0 mg chol., 2 mg sodium, 26 g carbo., 2 g fiber, 1 g pro.
Daily values: 2% vit. A, 93% vit. C, 2% calcium, 4% iron.

MINTY WINTER COMPOTE

See the photograph on page 315.

1 15½-oz. can pineapple chunks (juice pack)
2 Tbsp. sugar
2 Tbsp. snipped fresh mint or 1½ tsp. dried mint, crushed

❖❖❖

1 Tbsp. finely slivered grapefruit peel
2 red grapefruit, peeled, halved, and sliced ¼ inch thick
1 Tbsp. finely slivered orange peel
2 oranges, peeled, halved, and sliced ¼ inch thick
1 kiwifruit, peeled and sliced ¼ inch thick
¼ cup pomegranate seeds
Fresh mint leaves

1 Drain pineapple, reserving juice; add enough water to pineapple juice to make 1 cup. In a saucepan combine reserved juice

HOLIDAY FRITTATA

See the photograph on page 315.

1 Tbsp. cooking oil
1 cup fresh or frozen broccoli flowerets
½ of a large red sweet pepper, seeded and thinly sliced
¼ cup chopped onion
½ tsp. dried Italian seasoning, crushed

❖❖❖

10 eggs, beaten, or 2½ cups refrigerated or frozen egg product, thawed
2 Tbsp. milk

❖❖❖

2 Tbsp. finely shredded Parmesan cheese
Curly endive (optional)

1 In a 10-inch skillet heat oil over medium heat. Add broccoli, sweet pepper, onion, Italian seasoning, ¼ teaspoon *salt,* and ⅛ teaspoon *pepper.* Cook and stir 4 to 5 minutes or till crisp-tender.

2 Combine eggs or egg product and milk. Pour over vegetable mixture. As eggs begin to set, run a spatula around edge of skillet, lifting egg mixture to allow uncooked portions to flow underneath. Continue cooking and lifting edges till eggs are nearly set (surface will be moist).

3 Remove skillet from heat; sprinkle with cheese. Cover; let stand 3 to 4 minutes or till set. If desired, garnish with curly endive. Makes 6 main-dish servings.

Nutrition facts per serving: 168 cal., 11 g total fat (3 g sat. fat), 357 mg chol., 230 mg sodium, 4 g carbo., 1 g fiber, 12 g pro.
Daily values: 24% vit. A, 47% vit. C, 6% calcium, 10% iron.

CHRISTMAS MORNING CINNAMON ROLLS

See the photograph on page 314.

3½ to 4 cups all-purpose flour
1 pkg. active dry yeast
1 cup milk
⅓ cup margarine or butter
⅓ cup sugar
1 egg

❖❖❖

2 Tbsp. margarine or butter, softened
¾ cup packed brown sugar
2 tsp. ground cinnamon
½ cup raisins
½ cup chopped nuts

❖❖❖

4 tsp. half-and-half or light cream

1 Combine *1½ cups* of the flour and yeast; set aside. In a saucepan heat milk, ⅓ cup margarine or butter, sugar, and ½ teaspoon *salt* till warm (120° to

JEWELS OF THE POMEGRANATE

Whoever coined the phrase "beauty is more than skin deep" may have had the pomegranate in mind. This ancient fruit has been a star of Middle Eastern menus since biblical times. Although the Romans called it the "apple of many seeds," it looks more like a petrified tomato. Hidden beneath its hard, leathery skin, however, are dozens of crunchy, translucent, scarlet seeds embedded in white membranes. Biting into these crisp kernels releases a ruby juice that's refreshingly sweet and tangy.

Vital Statistics. Pomegranates are available August through November. Or, look for bottled juice in Middle Eastern food markets year-round. Pomegranates are the size of a small grapefruit. Choose fruit with a rich, red skin bearing no signs of shriveling. They should feel heavy for their size; buy the largest you can find. You can refrigerate the whole fruit up to 3 months. Or, you can freeze the seeds in airtight containers up to 3 months.

Peel and Reveal. To peel fruit, cut out blossom end; remove as much white pith as possible, but leave seeds intact. Score skin in quarters from stem to blossom end; gently break apart along those lines. (Do not cut into seeds—juices will release, and they are prone to staining.)

Bend back the rind and pull out the seeds, discarding the white membrane. Use seeds immediately or cover and refrigerate.

Many Uses for Many Seeds. These jewel-like seeds boast enticing texture, color, and a tart-sweet flavor that can boost many a dish from so-so to spectacular. Use them as you would use nuts to garnish fruit, vegetable, lettuce, grain, and pasta salads. Or, stir them into prepared side dishes such as bulgur, wild rice, lentils, and couscous.

Sprinkle these bright sequins atop cream soups, ice cream, and sorbet. The seeds also add zest to sauces for game, pork, and fowl, especially those prepared with Mexican and Middle Eastern spices such as cumin, turmeric, ginger, and cinnamon.

Use the juice in sorbets and ices, smoothies, and other beverages, or to add a tasty plus to salsas and salad dressings. To make juice, place seeds in a blender or food processor container; cover and process till pulverized. Strain, then enjoy in cold drinks—anything from cocktails to lemonade—and sauces or desserts.

130°) and margarine is almost melted. Add to flour mixture along with egg. Beat with an electric mixer on low speed 30 seconds, scraping bowl. Beat on high speed 3 minutes. Stir in as much of the remaining flour as you can.

2 Turn dough out onto a lightly floured surface. Knead in enough remaining flour to make a moderately soft dough that is smooth and elastic (3 to 5 minutes total). Shape dough into a ball. Place dough in a lightly greased bowl; turn once. Cover and let rise in a warm place till double (1 to 1½ hours).

3 Punch dough down. Turn out onto a lightly floured surface. Cover; let rest 10 minutes. Grease a 13×9×2-inch baking pan; set aside. Roll dough into 18×10-inch rectangle. Spread with softened margarine or butter. Combine brown sugar and cinnamon; sprinkle onto dough. Sprinkle with raisins and nuts. Tightly roll up, jelly-roll style, starting from a long side. Pinch seams to seal.

4 Cut dough crosswise into 12 even slices. Arrange slices, cut sides down, in the prepared baking pan. Cover and let rise till nearly double (about 30 to 40 minutes). (Or, cover with oiled waxed paper, then with plastic wrap. Chill in the refrigerator for 2 to 24 hours. Before baking, let stand for 20 minutes at room temperature. Uncover and puncture any surface bubbles with a greased wooden toothpick.)

5 Brush rolls with half-and-half or light cream. Bake in a 350° oven for 25 to 30 minutes or till golden. Invert rolls onto a wire rack or serving platter. Cool slightly. Makes 12 rolls.

Nutrition facts per roll: 319 cal., 12 g total fat (2 g sat. fat), 20 mg chol., 192 mg sodium, 49 g carbo., 2 g fiber, 6 g pro. *Daily values:* 10% vit. A, 1% vit. C, 4% calcium, 15% iron.

CHRISTOLLEN BREAD

Germans have baked this rich, fruit-filled bread at Christmastime ever since the Middle Ages. (See the photograph on page 314.)

4¾ to 5¼ cups all-purpose flour
  2 pkg. active dry yeast
  1 tsp. ground cardamom
1¼ cups milk
  ½ cup sugar
  ½ cup margarine or butter
  ¾ tsp. salt
  1 egg
  1 cup diced mixed candied
      fruits and peels
  1 cup raisins
  ¾ cup chopped walnuts
  1 Tbsp. finely shredded
      lemon peel
    Milk

1 In a large mixing bowl combine *2 cups* of the flour, yeast, and cardamom. In a saucepan heat and stir milk, sugar, margarine or butter, and salt till warm (120° to 130°) and margarine or butter is almost melted. Add to flour mixture along with egg. Beat with an electric mixer on low speed 30 seconds, scraping bowl. Beat on high speed 3 minutes. Using a wooden spoon, stir in fruits and peels, raisins, nuts, and lemon peel. Stir in as much of the remaining flour as you can.

2 Turn dough out onto a lightly floured surface. Knead in enough remaining flour to make a moderately soft dough that is smooth and elastic (3 to 5 minutes total). Shape into a ball. Place in a greased bowl; turn once. Cover and let rise in a warm place till double (about 1 to 1½ hours).

3 Punch dough down. Turn out onto a lightly floured surface. Divide in half; divide each half into thirds. Cover; let rest for 10 minutes. Meanwhile, grease 2 baking sheets.

4 With hands, roll each piece into a 1-inch-thick rope about 15 inches long. Line up 3 ropes, 1 inch apart, on a prepared baking sheet. Starting from middle, loosely braid by bringing left rope under center rope; lay it down. Then bring right rope under new center rope; lay it down. Repeat to end. On other end, braid by bringing outside ropes alternately over center rope to center. Press rope ends together to seal. Repeat braiding with remaining 3 ropes on the other prepared baking sheet. Cover and let rise till nearly double (about 1 hour).

5 Brush loaves with milk. Bake in a 350° oven for 20 to 25 minutes or till golden and loaves sound hollow when tapped. If necessary, cover with foil the last few minutes to prevent over-browning. Remove from baking sheets and cool on a wire rack. If desired, toast the slices. Makes 2 loaves (32 servings).

Nutrition facts per serving: 157 cal., 5 g total fat (1 g sat. fat), 7 mg chol., 92 mg sodium, 25 g carbo., 1 g fiber, 3 g pro. *Daily values:* 4% vit. A, 1% calcium, 6% iron.

DILL-WHEAT BREAD

2¾ to 3¼ cups all-purpose flour
  1 pkg. active dry yeast
  2 tsp. dried dillweed
  ¼ tsp. pepper

1¾ cups water
  3 Tbsp. margarine or butter
  2 Tbsp. packed brown sugar
1½ tsp. salt
  2 cups whole wheat flour
    Milk

1 In a large mixing bowl combine *2 cups* of the all-purpose flour, the yeast, dillweed, and pepper; set aside. In a medium saucepan heat and stir water, margarine or butter, brown sugar, and salt till warm (120° to 130°) and margarine or butter is almost melted. Add to flour mixture and beat with an electric mixer on low to medium speed for 30 seconds, scraping bowl. Beat on high speed for 3 minutes. Using a wooden spoon, stir in whole wheat flour and as much of the remaining all-purpose flour as you can.

2 Turn dough out onto a lightly floured surface. Knead in enough remaining all-purpose flour to make a moderately stiff dough that is smooth and elastic (6 to 8 minutes total). Shape into a ball. Place in a lightly greased bowl; turn once to grease surface. Cover and let rise in a warm place till double (about 1 hour).

3 Punch dough down. Turn out onto a lightly floured surface. Divide dough in half. Shape each half into a ball. Cover and let rest for 10 minutes. Meanwhile, grease 2 baking sheets.

4 With floured fingers, make a hole in the center of each ball of dough. Stretch dough to form a circle about 8 inches in diameter, with an opening in the center about 4 inches across. Place circles on prepared baking sheets.

5 Using kitchen scissors, cut slits diagonally at about 1¼-inch intervals from outside about two-thirds of the way to the center of each circle of dough. Stretch center again, if necessary, to maintain 4-inch opening. Cover and let rise in a warm place till nearly double (about 30 to 45 minutes).

6 Bake in a 350° oven 25 to 30 minutes or till bread sounds hollow when tapped. Immediately brush tops of loaves with milk. Transfer to wire racks to cool. Makes 2 loaves (32 servings).

Nutrition facts per serving: 75 cal., 1 g total fat (0 g sat. fat), 0 mg chol., 114 mg sodium, 14 g carbo., 1 g fiber, 2 g pro. *Daily values:* 1% vit. A, 5% iron.

PEPPER-PARMESAN BREAD

5¼ to 5¾ cups all-purpose flour
½ cup grated Parmesan cheese
2 pkg. active dry yeast
1½ tsp. fresh ground black
    pepper
1 tsp. salt
¼ tsp. garlic powder
2 cups warm water
    (120° to 130°)
    ◆◆◆
Cornmeal
1 cup grated Parmesan cheese
    ◆◆◆
1 slightly beaten egg white
1 Tbsp. water

1 In a large mixing bowl combine *2 cups* of the flour, the ½ cup Parmesan cheese, yeast, pepper, salt, and garlic powder; add the warm water. Beat with an electric mixer on low speed for 30 seconds, scraping bowl. Beat on high speed for 3 minutes. Using a wooden spoon, stir in as much of the remaining flour as you can.

2 Turn the dough out onto a lightly floured surface. Knead in enough of the remaining flour to make a stiff dough that is smooth and elastic (8 to 10 minutes total). Shape into a ball. Place dough in a lightly greased bowl, turning once to grease surface. Cover and let rise in a warm place till double (1 to 1½ hours).

3 Punch down; turn out onto a lightly floured surface. Divide in half. Cover and let rest 10 minutes. Grease a baking sheet; sprinkle with cornmeal. Roll out half the dough into a 15×12-inch rectangle. Sprinkle *½ cup* of the 1 cup Parmesan cheese atop dough in a narrow row, 3 inches from and parallel to a long side of the rectangle. Starting from the opposite long side, roll up tightly jelly-roll style. Moisten edges and seal well; taper ends. Repeat with remaining dough and cheese.

4 Place the loaves, seam sides down, on the prepared baking sheet (cheese should be at the top of the loaves). Cover and let dough rise till nearly double (about 45 minutes).

5 Stir together the egg white and the 1 tablespoon water. Brush mixture over loaves. Using a sharp knife, make 5 or 6 diagonal cuts, about ¼ inch deep, across tops of the loaves.

6 Bake in a 375° oven for 40 to 45 minutes or till the loaves sound hollow when tapped with your finger. For a crispier crust, brush the loaves again with the egg-white mixture after 20 minutes of baking. If necessary, cover loaves loosely with foil the last 15 minutes of baking to prevent overbrowning. Transfer loaves to a wire rack; cool. Makes 2 loaves (40 servings).

Nutrition facts per serving: 75 cal. 1 g fat (1 g sat.), 3 mg chol., 125 mg sodium, 12 g carbo.,1 g fiber, 3 g pro. *Daily values:* 4% calcium, 5% iron.

Onion-Cheese Tarts

Nonstick spray coating
1 **15-oz. pkg. folded**
   refrigerated unbaked
   piecrust (2 crusts)

◆◆◆

3 **cups thinly sliced onions**
   (about 3 large)
2 **Tbsp. margarine or butter**
½ **tsp. dried thyme, crushed**

◆◆◆

2 **eggs, beaten**
⅓ **cup milk**
   Dash salt
   Dash pepper

◆◆◆

¼ **cup crumbled semisoft goat**
   cheese or feta cheese, or
   shredded Swiss cheese or
   cheddar cheese (1 oz.)

1 Spray four 4½-inch tart pans with nonstick spray coating. Unfold pastry. If necessary, on a lightly floured surface flatten the pastry with a rolling pin. Cut two 5½-inch circles from each pastry round. Fit into prepared tart pans, trimming edges. Place pans on a baking sheet; *do not prick*. Line each pastry with a double thickness of foil. Bake in a 450° oven for 8 minutes. Remove foil. Bake 4 minutes more or till pastry is dry but not brown; remove from oven. Reduce the oven temperature to 350°.

2 Meanwhile, in a large skillet cook onions in margarine or butter over medium heat about 10 minutes or till very tender, stirring occasionally. Stir in thyme. Divide onions among the pre-baked crusts.

3 Combine the eggs, milk, salt, and pepper. Pour over onion

in crusts. Bake, uncovered, in the 350° oven about 20 minutes or till nearly set. Sprinkle with cheese. Bake 5 minutes more or till set. Let stand 5 minutes before carefully removing from pans. To serve, cut each tart in half. Makes 8 side-dish servings.

Nutrition facts per serving: 317 cal. 20 g fat, 72 mg chol., 294 mg sodium, 29 g carbo., 1 g fiber, 5 g pro.
Daily values: 6% vit. A, 4% vit. C, 2% calcium, 2% iron.

Prosciutto-Stuffed Turkey Breast

This recipe earned Lisa Alado of Philadelphia $200 in the magazine's monthly contest.

2 **tsp. olive oil or cooking oil**
½ **cup thinly sliced leek**
½ **cup soft bread crumbs,**
   toasted
⅓ **cup pine nuts, toasted**
¼ **cup grated Parmesan cheese**
2 **Tbsp. snipped fresh sage or**
   2 tsp. dried sage, crushed
2 **Tbsp. snipped fresh parsley**

◆◆◆

1 **4½- to 5-lb. whole turkey**
   breast

◆◆◆

4 **oz. thinly sliced prosciutto**
   or cooked ham
2 **tsp. olive oil or cooking oil**

◆◆◆

2 **Tbsp. all-purpose flour**
1⅓ **cups reduced-sodium**
   chicken broth
¼ **cup dry white wine**
1 **Tbsp. snipped fresh sage or**
   1 tsp. dried sage, crushed

1 For stuffing, in a medium skillet heat 2 teaspoons oil. Add leek and cook till tender. Remove from heat. Stir in the bread crumbs, nuts, Parmesan cheese, sage, and parsley. Set aside.

2 Rinse turkey; pat dry. Remove skin in 1 piece; set aside. Remove bone; split breast into 2 equal pieces. Place breast halves, skin sides down, on plastic wrap, giving 1 a half-turn so the 2 halves form a square. Cover with plastic wrap. Pound with the flat side of a meat mallet to ½-inch thickness (breasts should form a rectangle).

3 To stuff, arrange prosciutto or ham atop turkey. Spoon stuffing atop. Starting with a side that is parallel to seam, roll up turkey and stuffing. Wrap skin around turkey. Tie with string. Place on a rack in a roasting pan. Brush with 2 teaspoons oil. Insert a meat thermometer into center. Bake in a 375° oven for 1¼ to 1½ hours or till 170° and no longer pink. Remove turkey from pan, reserving 2 tablespoons drippings. Cover turkey and let stand for 10 minutes.

4 For gravy, spoon reserved drippings into a medium saucepan. Stir in flour. Stir in broth and wine. Add sage. Cook and stir till thickened and bubbly. Cook and stir 2 minutes more. Serve with turkey. Makes 12 servings.

Nutrition facts per serving: 244 cal., 12 g total fat (2 g sat. fat), 61 mg chol., 341 mg sodium, 4 g carbo., 0 g fiber, 30 g pro.
Daily values: 2% vit. C, 4% calcium, 12% iron.

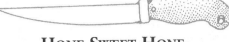

HONE SWEET HONE

It's true: All good cooks should put a little bit of themselves into their cooking. But you don't want to take this maxim literally. If prep work in your kitchen has gone from the "nick of time" to the "time of nicks," you could be ready for a little honing of your knife safety skills.

SHARPER IS SAFER

A cook's best friend and most important utensil is a sharp knife. You might not notice, but as your knives slowly become dull, the amount of time you spend cutting and chopping increases. Plus, most kitchen accidents are knife-related, and dull knives are the usual culprits. Dull knives have to be forced to perform, and when forced, they have a tendency to slip.

The most important thing you can do to ensure safety with knives is to purchase good knives. A good knife is heavy and well-balanced compared to a flimsy knife, which may bend or snap. Poorly constructed knives also have a hard time maintaining their edge, and they can warp over time. A good, forged (not stamped) knife with high carbon content and a molded handle will last forever if cared for properly.

ON THE BOARD

Always use a cutting board. Kitchen counters and knives were not meant for each other, and using a knife on one invites slipping and sliding. Hard plastic and marble are better boards for working pastry, not chopping and slicing. Harder boards quickly dull a knife and cause it to slip more easily. Another point to consider is how you hold the food to be cut. Curl your fingertips slightly, with your thumb tucked under, to keep them out of the way of the blade.

KEEPING IT SHARP

With the right knives and the right surface, you are two-thirds of the way to knife safety. Now you need to keep your knives sharp. Grinding wheels put on the best edge, but few of us have a diamond-faced grinding wheel on our kitchen counter. But there are many others tools available, such as steels, whetstones, and hand sharpeners, to keep knives sharp.

STEEL AND STONE

Many knife sets include a steel, a long sharpening rod. Don't rely solely on a steel to sharpen knives. It should be used for quick rehoning. Excessive use of a steel will fold or crumble the edge of a knife. Steels take a little extra skill to work with. To use a steel, hold it in one hand, with the knife in your other hand at a 20-degree angle to the steel. Draw the knife's blade edge over the steel, starting from the base of the blade and working to the tip with a slicing motion that goes across and down at the same time. Applying only a little pressure, use careful, even strokes as if peeling a carrot.

The sharpening stone, or whetstone, uses the same motions as described for the steel. Fix the stone securely on the countertop; with both hands, hold knife gently against stone. Starting from base of knife, draw blade edge along stone, working to the tip using a slicing motion. Keep sharpening stones oiled with food-grade mineral oil. Other oils can ruin the stone.

HAND SHARPENERS

Manual and electric hand sharpeners have improved greatly, and there are many user-friendly ones on the market. Since sharpeners vary greatly, be sure to follow the operating instructions to the letter.

THE TEN COMMANDMENTS OF KNIFE SAFETY

1. Keep knives sharp! A dull blade is more dangerous than a sharp one.

2. Use knives only for cutting and slicing, not as can openers or screwdrivers.

3. Always use an appropriate, firmly fixed cutting surface. A damp towel under a cutting board will keep it from sliding around the countertop.

4. Use the right knife for the right job–paring knives for paring, boning knives for boning, etc.

5. Never soak a dirty knife in a suds-filled sink. Hand-clean only.

6. Always hold a knife by the handle. Use "drawing" motions to cut and slice, using almost the entire length of the blade.

7. Hold and store knives in blade-down position. Always cut away from yourself.

8. Store knives with the blade covered, if possible. Knife racks, sheaths, or blocks are best.

9. Never wash knives in a dishwasher. It can dull blades, loosen rivets, and cause cracks in handles.

10. If you drop a knife, let it come to a complete rest before attempting to pick it up.

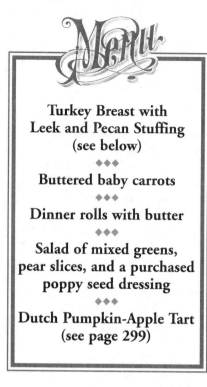

**Turkey Breast with
Leek and Pecan Stuffing**
(see below)

♦♦♦

Buttered baby carrots

♦♦♦

Dinner rolls with butter

♦♦♦

**Salad of mixed greens,
pear slices, and a purchased
poppy seed dressing**

♦♦♦

Dutch Pumpkin-Apple Tart
(see page 299)

TURKEY BREAST WITH LEEK AND PECAN STUFFING

1 2½- to 3½-lb. turkey breast
    portion with skin
⅔ cup thinly sliced leeks
½ cup chopped onion
¼ cup margarine or butter
⅓ cup chopped toasted pecans
1 Tbsp. snipped fresh thyme,
    or ½ tsp. dried thyme,
    crushed
5 cups dry bread cubes*
¼ to ⅓ cup chicken broth

♦♦♦

2 tsp. cooking oil
1 12-oz. jar turkey or chicken
    gravy
1 Tbsp. frozen orange juice
    concentrate, thawed

1 Remove the bone from turkey breast portion, if present. Wash turkey; pat dry. In a large saucepan cook and stir leeks and onion in hot margarine or butter

5 minutes or till tender. Remove from heat. Stir in pecans, thyme, and ⅛ teaspoon *pepper*. Add bread cubes. Toss with enough chicken broth to moisten.

2 Spoon stuffing into bottom of a lightly greased shallow roasting pan. Place turkey breast atop stuffing. Brush skin lightly with oil. Insert meat thermometer. Roast in a 325° oven for 1 to 1¼ hours or till meat thermometer registers 170° and the stuffing registers 165°. Meanwhile, in a medium saucepan combine gravy and orange juice concentrate. Heat through. Serve with turkey and stuffing. Serves 6 to 8.

*Note: For dry bread cubes, use 10 slices bread, cut into cubes. Place in a shallow roasting pan and bake in a 325° oven for 12 to 15 minutes or till lightly toasted. Cool on a wire rack.

Nutrition facts per serving: 405 cal., 19 g total fat (3 g sat. fat), 59 mg chol., 699 mg sodium, 28 g carbo., 3 g fiber, 31 g pro. *Daily values:* 9% vit. A, 11% vit. C, 7% calcium, 22% iron.

PORTLY GAME HENS

2 1¼- to 1½-lb. Cornish game
    hens,* split
¾ cup thinly sliced celery
¾ cup chopped onion
¼ cup margarine or butter
½ cup finely snipped pitted
    prunes
¼ tsp. pepper
5 cups dry bread cubes (see
    *Note above)
2 Tbsp. port wine
2 to 4 Tbsp. water
⅓ cup currant jelly
2 Tbsp. port wine

1 Rinse Cornish game hen halves; pat dry. Season lightly with *salt* and *pepper*. Cook celery and onion in margarine or butter till tender; remove from heat. Stir in prunes and the ¼ teaspoon pepper. In a bowl combine bread cubes and onion mixture. Add 2 tablespoons port wine; drizzle with enough water to moisten, tossing lightly. Transfer to a 2-quart square baking dish.

2 Place hens, cut sides down, atop stuffing. Melt jelly; stir in 2 tablespoons port wine. Brush hens with half of the jelly mixture. Cover and roast in a 375° oven for 50 minutes. Uncover, brush with remaining jelly mixture. Roast, uncovered, 10 to 15 minutes more or till hens are tender and no longer pink. Makes 4 servings.

*Note: If you wish, substitute 4 chicken breasts halves for game hens; roast, covered, 35 minutes. Uncover; continue as directed.

Nutrition facts per serving: 653 cal., 32 g total fat (7 g sat. fat), 100 mg chol., 449 mg sodium, 56 g carbo., 4 g fiber, 35 g pro. *Daily values:* 18% vit. A, 7% vit. C, 7% calcium, 16% iron.

MASTERPIECE BEEF ROAST

*God rest ye merry gentlemen!
With savory roast beef on the table,
and maybe Yorkshire pudding,
merriment's almost assured.
(See the photograph on page 313.)*

1 4- to 6-lb. beef rib roast
2 Tbsp. olive oil
1 Tbsp. dried minced onion
2 tsp. bottled minced garlic

1 Cut 1-inch-deep pockets on fat side of roast at 3-inch intervals. If desired, sprinkle roast with *salt* and *pepper*. In a small bowl combine the olive oil, onion, and garlic. Rub mixture onto roast and into pockets.

2 Place meat, fat side up, in a 15½×10½×2-inch roasting pan. Insert a meat thermometer into the thickest portion of meat without touching fat or bone. Roast in a 325° oven for 1¾ to 2 hours for medium rare (145°), 2¼ to 2½ hours for medium (155°), or 2¾ to 3 hours for well done (165°). Note that temperature will rise 5° on standing.

3 Transfer to serving platter; cover with foil. Let stand at least 15 minutes before carving. Makes 10 to 12 servings.

Nutrition facts per serving: 296 cal., 18 g total fat (7 g sat. fat), 91 mg chol., 83 mg sodium, 1 g carbo., 0 g fiber, 31 g pro. *Daily values:* 1% vit. C, 1% calcium, 19% iron.

HERBED ROAST LAMB WITH BLACK BEANS

This recipe earned Ellen Burr of Truro, Massachusetts, $100 in the magazine's monthly contest.

1 5- to 6-lb. bone-in leg of
   lamb
2 cloves garlic, peeled and
   sliced
1 medium lime, halved
1 recipe Herb Rub (see right)

♦♦♦

COOKING WITH THERMOMETERS

Cooking thermometers eliminate the guesswork from determining when your food is cooked. You'll need different types for different uses.

♦ **Candy or Deep-Fat Frying:** Clipped onto the side of pans, this type of thermometer measures the temperature of candy mixtures, some frostings, and syrups. It also tells when the liquid is just right for yeast breads or when fat is ready for frying. The face shows the degrees and candymaking stages, such as thread, soft-ball, and hard-crack (see "Degrees of Candymaking," page 304).

♦ **Instant-Read:** This type gauges the temperature of cooked foods. Insert the point into meats, fish, sauces, poultry, meringues, and other dishes to make sure the food is safely cooked and to your liking.

♦ **Meat:** The pointed end of this thermometer makes it easy to push into meat and poultry. The face usually is marked with degrees and the stages of doneness. For accurate readings, insert it into the thickest part of a meat roast or whole bird without touching fat or bone.

♦ **Microwave:** Measuring the temperature of liquids and poultry during microwave cooking requires a thermometer made with less metal. Some microwave ovens come with a probe programmed to cook foods to a certain temperature.

1 cup chopped onion
2 15-oz. cans black beans,
   rinsed
1 4½-oz. can diced green chili
   peppers, rinsed and
   drained
1 4-oz. jar chopped pimiento,
   drained
¼ cup snipped fresh cilantro
1 Tbsp. red wine vinegar

1 Trim fat from lamb. Cut slits in lamb; insert garlic. Squeeze lime juice over lamb; rub the surface with Herb Rub. Place on a rack in a roasting pan; insert meat thermometer into the thickest portion of meat without touching bone. Roast in a 325° oven for 2 to 3 hours or till 145° to 155°.

2 Skim fat from juices. In a saucepan combine 2 tablespoons juices and onion; cook till tender. Stir in remaining ingredients. Bring to boiling; reduce heat. Cook, uncovered, 5 minutes. Serve with lamb. Serves 10 to 12.

Herb Rub: Combine 1 teaspoon *dried oregano*, crushed, 1 teaspoon *ground coriander*; ½ teaspoon *dried thyme*, crushed; ½ teaspoon *ground cumin*; ½ teaspoon *chili powder*; and ¼ teaspoon *salt*.

Nutrition facts per serving: 242 cal., 8 g total fat (3 g sat. fat), 80 mg chol., 362 mg sodium, 15 g carbo., 4 g fiber, 32 g pro. *Daily values:* 26% vit. C, 5% calcium, 22% iron.

PEPPER-CHEDDAR YORKSHIRE PUDDING

In Britain, Christmas is not Christmas without roast beef, and beef is not beef without a savory Yorkshire pudding served at its side. (See the photograph on page 313.)

Pan drippings from a 4- to 6-lb. beef rib roast

❖❖❖

4 eggs
2 cups milk
1¾ cups all-purpose flour
¼ tsp. salt
¼ tsp. pepper
½ cup finely shredded, extra-sharp cheddar cheese (2 oz.)

1 After removing roast from oven, measure pan drippings. If necessary, add *cooking oil* to drippings to make ¼ cup; divide drippings and pour into two 8×8×2-inch or 9×9×2-inch square pans. Place pans in a 450° oven about 2 minutes or till slightly hot.

2 In a mixing bowl combine eggs and milk. Add flour, salt, and pepper. Beat with a rotary beater or whisk till smooth. Divide egg mixture evenly between the pans; stir into drippings in pans. Bake in the 450° oven about 25 minutes or till puffed and brown. Sprinkle with cheese. Cut into squares; serve at once with roast. Makes 8 to 10 side-dish servings.

Nutrition facts per serving: 246 cal., 13 g total fat (6 g sat. fat), 126 mg chol., 173 mg sodium, 23 g carbo., 1 g fiber, 10 g pro. *Daily values:* 10% vit. A, 1% vit. C, 11% calcium, 10% iron.

PIQUANT POTATOES

Less is more: Lemon and chives are all it takes to turn simple potatoes into splendid eating. (See the photograph on page 313.)

2 lb. whole tiny new potatoes (about 16), halved
2 Tbsp. margarine or butter
1 tsp. finely shredded lemon peel
1 Tbsp. lemon juice
Few dashes white pepper or black pepper
2 Tbsp. snipped fresh chives

1 In a large saucepan cook potatoes in boiling water, covered, for 10 to 12 minutes or just till tender; drain in a colander. Add margarine or butter to saucepan; heat and stir till melted. Remove from heat. Stir in lemon peel, lemon juice, and pepper. Add potatoes, tossing gently to coat. Transfer to a serving bowl. Sprinkle with chives. Makes 8 side-dish servings.

Nutrition facts per serving: 136 cal., 3g total fat (1 g sat. fat), 0 mg chol., 42 mg sodium, 25 g carbo., 1 g fiber, 3 g pro. *Daily values:* 3% vit. A, 26% vit. C, 1% calcium, 12% iron.

HERRING SALAD (HARINGSLA)

Dutch fanciers of herring devour the fresh fish with gusto throughout summer. But in the cold days that follow, herring pickled in vinegar and spices is used to make this hearty salad.

2 medium red-skinned potatoes
¼ cup reduced-calorie mayonnaise or salad dressing

4 tsp. sweet pickle juice

❖❖❖

Lettuce leaves
2 cups pickled herring
4 small sweet pickles (gherkins), sliced
½ of a small red onion, thinly sliced
1 16-oz. can sliced beets, chilled, drained, and cut into strips
Fresh dill sprigs (optional)

1 In a saucepan cook unpeeled potatoes, covered, in *boiling salted water* for 20 to 25 minutes or till just tender. Drain and cool. Carefully cut into slices; cover and chill. For dressing, in a small bowl stir together mayonnaise or salad dressing and pickle juice; cover and chill.

2 In 6 individual salad bowls lined with lettuce leaves, combine herring, pickles, and onion; cover and chill. To serve, arrange potatoes and beets atop the herring mixture. Serve with dressing. If desired, garnish with dill. Makes 6 side-dish servings.

Nutrition facts per serving: 231 cal., 10 g total fat (2 g sat. fat), 5 mg chol., 781 mg sodium, 28 g carbo., 2 g fiber, 7 g pro. *Daily values:* 10% vit. A, 16% vit. C, 4% calcium, 16% iron.

FOUR-ONION SOUP

It's the intriguing combination of leeks, onions, garlic, and chives that flavors this pot. By pureeing the blend, we've created a creamy texture that also makes this onion soup distinctive.

¼ cup margarine or butter
3 cups thinly sliced leeks (white part only)

4½ cups thinly sliced onions
(6 medium)
2 Tbsp. minced garlic
(12 cloves)
1 Tbsp. sugar
5½ cups chicken broth
1 tsp. dried thyme, crushed
¼ tsp. pepper

◆◆◆

½ cup chicken broth
2 Tbsp. all-purpose flour
2 slightly beaten egg yolks
¼ cup Marsala wine or sweet
sherry (optional)
1 cup half-and-half or light
cream

◆◆◆

Baguette-style French bread
slices, toasted
Fresh chives (optional)
Fresh thyme (optional)

1 In a large pot melt margarine or butter. Stir in leeks, onions, garlic, and sugar. Cook, covered, over medium-low heat about 10 minutes or till tender, stirring occasionally. Remove ¾ cup of the onion mixture; set aside. Add the 5½ cups chicken broth, dried thyme, and pepper to remaining mixture in pan. Bring to boiling; reduce heat. Simmer, covered, over low heat for 20 minutes.

2 Remove from heat; cool slightly. Transfer a third of the mixture to a blender container or food processor bowl. Cover and blend or process mixture till smooth. Repeat with remaining mixture. Return all of the pureed mixture to the pot.

3 In a small bowl stir together the ½ cup chicken broth and the flour till smooth. Stir in egg yolks.

Gradually add 1 cup of the hot soup to egg mixture; stir mixture into remaining soup. Cook and stir over medium-high heat till thickened and bubbly. If desired, add Marsala or sherry. Add reserved onion-leek mixture. Cook and stir for 1 minute more; reduce heat. Stir in half-and-half or light cream. Cook and stir till heated through; *do not boil.*

4 To serve, ladle into a large soup tureen or 6 individual bowls. Top each serving with a toasted baguette slice. If desired, sprinkle with chives and thyme. Makes 6 main-dish servings.

▮ TO MAKE AHEAD ▮

Prepare soup up through the point of adding the half-and-half or light cream. Remove from heat. Cool slightly; cover and refrigerate soup for up to 24 hours. To serve, cook and stir soup till heated through; *do not boil.*

Nutrition facts per serving: 253 cal., 16 g total fat (5 g sat. fat), 87 mg chol., 893 mg sodium, 20 g carbo., 3 g fiber, 9 g pro. *Daily values:* 25% vit. A, 13% vit. C, 9% calcium, 13% iron.

SAVORY SPROUTS AND APPLES

Brussels sprouts become holiday fare when spruced up with spicy mustard and sweet apples; Jonathans or Rome Beauties are good choices. (See the photograph on page 313.)

4 cups fresh Brussels sprouts
(about 1 lb.) or two 10-oz.
pkg. frozen Brussels
sprouts

◆◆◆

½ cup finely chopped onion
1 Tbsp. margarine or butter
⅓ cup apple cider or apple
juice
2 Tbsp. Dijon-style or coarse-
grain brown mustard
¼ tsp. salt
⅛ tsp. pepper
2 small apples, unpeeled,
cored, and thinly sliced

1 Halve any large sprouts. In a large saucepan cook fresh Brussels sprouts, covered, in *boiling, lightly salted water* over medium heat about 10 minutes or till just tender. (Or, cook frozen Brussels sprouts according to package directions.) Drain; return to saucepan to keep warm.

2 Meanwhile, in a medium skillet cook onion in hot margarine or butter over medium heat 5 minutes or till tender. In a small bowl stir together apple cider or apple juice, mustard, salt, and pepper; stir into onion mixture. Add apple slices; cook, uncovered, for 2 to 3 minutes more or till apple is crisp-tender, stirring gently once or twice.

3 Add the onion-apple mixture to the Brussels sprouts in the saucepan, tossing gently to coat. Transfer to a serving dish. Makes 8 side-dish servings.

Nutrition facts per serving: 70 cal., 2 g total fat (0 g sat. fat), 0 mg chol., 192 mg sodium, 13 g carbo., 3 g fiber, 2 g pro. *Daily values:* 6% vit. A, 68% vit. C, 2% calcium, 5% iron.

AIOLI IS A-OK

Garlic is as good as seven mothers, the old saying goes—so consider aioli a whole village worth of comfort givers. Aioli (pronounced ay-OH-lee), a French inspiration, is simply a thick, rich mayonnaise pumped up with lots of garlic. It's delicious slathered on firm French bread or hard-boiled eggs. Stir it into soups such as fish-based bouillabaisse or anoint grilled meat, fish, and veggies with the delectably potent condiment. Aioli is particularly satisfying when used with chicken, tuna, summer sweet corn, and cold boiled potatoes.

AIOLI

Purists use a mortar and pestle to puree the garlic and blend in the oil. We're equally happy with the speedy version modern kitchen appliances produce. And it's perfectly safe to dip right in if you use egg product rather than the traditional raw egg.

  4 **large cloves garlic, minced**
  ¼ **cup refrigerated or frozen egg product, thawed**
  1 **to 2 Tbsp. lemon juice**
  ¼ **tsp. salt**
  ¼ **cup olive oil or salad oil**

1 In a blender container or food processor bowl, combine garlic, egg product, lemon juice, and salt. Cover and blend or process for 5 seconds or till combined. With blender or processor running, gradually add the oil in a thin, steady stream. When necessary, stop machine and use a rubber scraper to scrape sides.

2 Place in a covered container and refrigerate till ready to serve. Store for up to 3 days in the refrigerator. If the mixture begins to separate, stir before serving. Makes about 1 cup.

Nutrition facts per tablespoon: 94 cal., 10 g total fat (1 g sat. fat), 0 mg chol., 40 mg sodium, 0 g carbo., 0 g fiber, 1 g pro. *Daily values:* 1% vit. C.

Hot-and-Spicy Aioli: Add ½ to 1 teaspoon *crushed red pepper* before blending or processing.

Green-Onion Aioli: Add 2 tablespoons sliced *green onion* before blending or processing. Serve with cold chicken or pork, or as a dip for raw vegetables.

Dill Aioli: Add 2 tablespoons snipped *fresh dillweed* before blending or processing. This is great with cold fish or potatoes.

MULLED CIDER

Cardamom, allspice, and cinnamon smell like Christmas in the making. (See the photograph on page 318.)

  8 **cups apple cider or apple juice**
  2 **to 4 Tbsp. packed brown sugar**
  2 **cardamom pods, cracked (about ½ tsp. seed)**
  1 **tsp. whole allspice**
         ◆◆◆
    Cinnamon sticks (optional)

1 In a large saucepan combine the apple cider or juice and brown sugar. For the spice bag, cut a double thickness of 100-percent-cotton cheesecloth into a 6- or 8-inch square. Place cardamom seeds and whole allspice in the center of cloth. Bring up corners; tie with a clean string. Add spice bag to cider mixture in saucepan.

2 Bring the mixture to boiling; reduce heat. Simmer, covered, for at least 10 minutes. Discard spice bag. To serve, pour cider into a large punch bowl or mugs. If desired, garnish with the cinnamon sticks. Makes 8 (8-ounce) servings.

Nutrition facts per serving: 135 cal., 0 g total fat , 0 mg chol., 8 mg sodium, 37 g carbo., 0 g fiber, 0 g pro. *Daily values:* 4% vit. C, 1% calcium, 8% iron.

MULLED WINE

Sugar and spice and everything nice go into this soul-warming sipper.

  1½ **cups water**
  ½ **cup sugar**
  2 **oranges, sliced**
  10 **whole cloves**
  2 **4-inch cinnamon sticks**
         ◆◆◆
  1 **750-ml. bottle dry red wine***
  ¼ **cup brandy**

1 In a large saucepan combine water, sugar, and *half* of the orange slices. To make a spice bag, cut a double thickness of 100-percent-cotton cheesecloth into a 6- or 8-inch square. Place cloves and cinnamon sticks in center of cloth. Bring up corners and tie together with a clean string. (Or, place cloves in a tea strainer.) Add spice bag to mixture in saucepan.

2 Bring mixture to boiling; reduce heat. Simmer, uncovered, for 10 minutes. Remove and discard orange slices and spices. Add wine and brandy. Cook, uncovered, over medium heat till heated through. *Do not allow to boil.* To serve, pour wine into a large punch bowl or mugs. Garnish with remaining orange slices. Makes 8 (4-ounce) servings.

*Note: It is not necessary to use expensive wine for this recipe. Any type of burgundy will do.

Nutrition facts per serving: 148 cal., 0 g total fat, 0 mg chol., 62 mg sodium, 18 g carbo., 1 g fiber, 1 g pro.
Daily values: 29% vit. C, 1% calcium, 3% iron.

SPICED PECANS AND CHERRIES

2 **Tbsp. Worcestershire sauce**
2 **Tbsp. margarine or butter, melted**
½ **tsp. ground red pepper**
½ **tsp. garlic powder**
½ **tsp. ground cumin**
½ **tsp. seasoned salt**
¼ **tsp. dried oregano, crushed**
3 **cups pecan halves**

◆◆◆

1½ **cups dried tart red cherries**

1 Stir together Worcestershire sauce, margarine or butter, red pepper, garlic powder, cumin, seasoned salt, and oregano. Add pecan halves, tossing to coat.

2 Spread mixture into a 13×9×2-inch baking pan. Bake in 350° oven for 15 minutes; stir every 5 minutes. Stir in cherries. Bake about 5 minutes more or till pecans are toasted. Spread on paper towels to cool. Store in an airtight container. Makes 4 cups.

Nutrition facts per serving: 187 cal., 15 g total fat (1 g sat. fat), 0 mg chol., 63 mg sodium, 13 g carbo., 2 g fiber, 2 g pro.
Daily values: 9% vit. A, 2% vit. C, 3% iron.

RUMTOPF

Spoon some of this spirited fruit over ice cream or pound cake when you're ready to celebrate. (See the photograph on page 317.)

1½ **cups packed brown sugar**
4 **large pears, cored and cut up**
4 **medium nectarines or peeled peaches, pitted and sliced; or one 16-oz. pkg. frozen unsweetened peach slices, thawed**
2 **cups seedless red grapes, halved (optional)**
1 **medium pineapple, peeled, cored, and cut up**

◆◆◆

2½ **to 3 cups rum**

1 Combine brown sugar and 1 cup *water.* Cook and stir over medium-low heat till sugar is dissolved; cool. In a 4-quart-tall, nonmetal crock or jar combine fruit; pour in syrup mixture.

2 Add enough rum to cover the fruit; stir gently to combine. Store, covered, in a cool place overnight. Place in the refrigerator and store, covered, for up to 4 months, stirring occasionally, using portions as desired.* Let fruit stand at room temperature 30 minutes before serving. Makes about 3 quarts mixture (24 servings).

*Note: To replenish Rumtopf, add 2 cups chopped *fruit* and ½ cup packed *brown sugar* to replace every 2 cups of fruit and syrup removed (the top layer of fruit may darken during storage). Store in the refrigerator.

Nutrition facts per serving: 148 cal., 0 g total fat, 0 mg chol., 1 mg sodium, 24 g carbo., 1 g fiber, 0 g pro.
Daily values: 1% vit. A, 11% vit. C, 1% iron.

PICK A PIE PLATE

You need to use standard glass or dull metal pie plates if you want your pies as nicely browned on the bottom as they are on the top. Shiny metal pie pans—which do work just fine for crumb-crust pies—can cause the bottom pastry crust to turn out soggy.

Check the size of ceramic or pottery pie plates; they may not be standard. A standard-size plate holds about 3¾ cups liquid. You may need to adjust the amount of filling and the baking time.

Disposable foil pie pans usually are smaller than standard pie plates; foil deep-dish pie pans are closer to the norm.

LOW FAT

LEMON CURD TARTS

A lemon-lover alert: These intensely tangy tarts are more addictive than the potato chip. We dare you to eat just one!
(See the photograph on page 317.)

1¼ cups all-purpose flour
⅓ cup granulated sugar
2 tsp. finely shredded lemon peel
½ cup cold butter
1 egg yolk, beaten
2 Tbsp. cold water

◆◆◆

⅔ cup granulated sugar
1 Tbsp. cornstarch
2 tsp. finely shredded lemon peel
½ cup lemon juice
¼ cup water
2 Tbsp. butter

◆◆◆

3 egg yolks, beaten

◆◆◆

Powdered sugar (optional)
Lemon peel curls (optional)

1 In a medium bowl combine flour, the ⅓ cup sugar, and 2 teaspoons lemon peel. Cut in the ½ cup cold butter till mixture is crumbly. In a bowl combine the beaten egg yolk and 2 tablespoons cold water. Gradually stir yolk mixture into flour mixture. Gently knead the dough just till a ball forms. If necessary, cover with plastic wrap and chill for 30 to 60 minutes or till easy to handle.

2 Meanwhile, for lemon curd, in a medium saucepan stir together the ⅔ cup sugar and the cornstarch. Stir in the 2 teaspoons lemon peel, lemon juice, the ¼ cup water, and the 2 tablespoons butter. Cook and stir over medium heat, uncovered, till thickened and bubbly.

3 Slowly stir about half the lemon mixture into the 3 beaten egg yolks. Return all of the egg mixture to the saucepan; stir to combine. Bring to boiling; reduce heat. Cook and stir for 2 minutes more. Transfer to bowl. Cover surface with plastic wrap; chill while pastry shells bake.

4 For tassies, divide chilled dough into 36 pieces. Press 1 piece onto bottom and up sides of a 1¾-inch tassie pan; repeat with remaining pieces.* Bake in a 375° oven for 8 to 10 minutes or till golden. (Or, for mini-tart shells, divide chilled dough into 24 pieces. Press 1 piece onto bottom and up sides of a 2¼-inch mini-tart pan; repeat with remaining pieces.* Place pans on a baking sheet; prick with a fork. Bake in a 375° oven for 12 to 14 minutes or till golden.)

5 Cool in pans on a wire rack; unmold. Spoon a rounded teaspoon of lemon curd into each tassie or a scant tablespoon into each tart; cover with plastic wrap and chill for up to 2 hours before serving. Before serving, if desired, decorate with sifted powdered sugar and lemon peel. Makes 36 tassies or 24 mini tarts.

***Note:** If necessary, keep part of the dough chilled as you bake the pastries.

▌ TO MAKE AHEAD ▐

Prepare dough as directed. Wrap in plastic wrap and freeze for up to 1 month. Thaw dough in the refrigerator 1 day before working with it. Once baked, the tart shells may be stored in a covered container at room temperature for up to 4 days or frozen for several weeks. Store lemon curd in the refrigerator for up to 1 week.

Nutrition facts per tassie: 72 cal., 4 g total fat (2 g sat. fat), 32 mg chol., 33 mg sodium, 9 g carbo., 0 g fiber, 1 g pro. *Daily values:* 6% vit. A, 3% vit. C, 1% iron.

CHOCOLATE-HAZELNUT PIE

This recipe earned Sally Cracroft of Paonia, Colorado, $100 in the magazine's monthly contest.

¾ cup all-purpose flour
⅓ cup very finely chopped hazelnuts
3 Tbsp. brown sugar
⅓ cup butter or margarine, melted

❖❖❖

1 8-oz. pkg. cream cheese, softened
¾ cup semisweet chocolate pieces, melted and cooled
⅓ cup granulated sugar
2 Tbsp. milk
1 cup whipping cream

❖❖❖

¼ cup semisweet chocolate pieces
2 Tbsp. butter or margarine
1 cup frozen loose-pack unsweetened red raspberries, thawed
2 Tbsp. light corn syrup
Fresh mint (optional)

1 Combine flour, nuts, and brown sugar. Stir in butter; toss to mix. Press onto bottom and up sides of 9-inch pie plate for firm, even crust. Bake in a 425° oven 8 to 10 minutes or till brown; cool.

2 For filling, combine cream cheese, ¾ cup chocolate pieces, granulated sugar, and milk; beat with an electric mixer on medium speed till smooth. Wash beaters. In a chilled bowl beat whipping cream till soft peaks form; fold into cream cheese mixture. Spread

mixture into cooled crust. Cover; chill several hours or overnight.

3 Before serving, melt ¼ cup chocolate pieces and 2 table-spoons butter; drizzle onto pie. For sauce, in a blender container or food processor bowl, combine raspberries and corn syrup; cover and blend till nearly smooth. If desired, press sauce through a sieve to remove seeds. Serve with pie. If desired, garnish with *raspberries* and mint. Serves 10.

Nutrition facts per serving: 427 cal., 32 g total fat (16 g sat. fat), 80 mg chol., 168 mg sodium, 34 g carbo., 1 g fiber, 5 g pro. *Daily values:* 28% vit. A, 5% vit. C, 5% calcium, 10% iron.

BANANA TART WITH MACADAMIA CRUST

This recipe earned Koula Mitchell of Carmel, Indiana, $200 in the magazine's monthly contest.

½ cup butter or margarine
1½ cups all-purpose flour
¼ cup sugar
2 egg yolks
½ tsp. vanilla
1 cup shredded coconut
⅓ cup finely chopped unsalted macadamia nuts, toasted

❖❖❖

½ cup whipping cream
4 oz. white chocolate baking squares, chopped
⅓ cup sugar
3 Tbsp. cornstarch
1 Tbsp. all-purpose flour
1 cup milk
1 cup half-and-half or light cream

2 egg yolks, beaten
1 tsp. vanilla
½ cup whipping cream
3 ripe bananas, sliced

1 Lightly grease an 11-inch tart pan with a removable bottom. Beat butter 30 seconds. Add ¾ *cup* of the flour, ¼ cup sugar, 2 egg yolks, and ½ teaspoon vanilla; beat till combined. Stir in the remaining ¾ cup flour, coconut, and nuts. Press into bottom and up sides of prepared pan. Bake in a 350° oven for 10 to 12 minutes or till golden. Remove from oven; cool. Remove sides of pan.

2 Combine ½ cup whipping cream and white chocolate. Cook and stir over low heat till chocolate is melted; set aside. In a medium saucepan combine ⅓ cup sugar, cornstarch, and 1 table-spoon flour. Gradually stir in milk and half-and-half. Cook and stir over medium heat till thickened and bubbly. Cook and stir 2 minutes more. Gradually stir 1 cup of hot mixture into 2 beaten egg yolks. Return all to pan. Bring to a gentle boil; reduce heat. Cook and stir 2 minutes. Remove from heat. Stir in chocolate mixture. Stir in 1 teaspoon vanilla; cool.

3 Beat ½ cup whipping cream till soft peaks form. Fold into cooled mixture. Arrange bananas atop crust. Spread with filling. Cover; chill several hours or overnight. If desired, top with *dessert topping, kiwifruit,* and additional *nuts.* Serves 12 to 16.

Nutrition facts per serving: 435 cal., 28 g total fat (16 g sat. fat), 128 mg chol., 59 mg sodium, 42 g carbo., 2 g fiber, 6 g pro. *Daily values:* 30% vit. A, 7% calcium, 8% iron.

PRETTY PIE PASTRIES

The edge that you put on your piecrust serves two purposes: to look good and to keep the pie filling sealed in. Making it look good is as easy as a few pinches, presses, tucks, and twists.

Rope-shaped edge: Trim and fold under the edge of the pastry for a single-crust, double-crust, or lattice-top pie. Then crimp around the edge of the pastry by pinching it. When pinching, push forward on a slant with a bent finger and pull back with your thumb.

Cutout edge: Line the pie plate with pastry, and trim pastry to the edge of the pie plate. Roll pastry scraps until they are thin. Use a knife or canape cutter to cut the pastry scraps into the desired shapes. Brush the edge of the pastry shell with water. Arrange the pastry cutouts on the edge of the pastry shell, and press lightly to secure the cutouts.

Twisted edge: Line the pie plate with pastry, and trim pastry to the edge of the plate. Brush the edge of the pastry shell with water. Loosely twist two ½-inch-wide strips of pastry dough around the edge of the pastry shell. As a strip runs out, seal another strip to it by pressing the ends together. Secure the twist by lightly pressing the bottom pastry strip against the edge of the pastry shell.

MINCEMEAT-PEAR PIE

Most mincemeat no longer contains minced meat and suet. These days you may purchase prepared mincemeat in jars. Our version pushes the envelope even further by tempering the savory spice filling with fresh pears. For winter baking, Bosc pears are a good choice. (See the photograph on page 316.)

3 **cups thinly sliced, peeled, and cored pears**
1 **27-oz. jar mincemeat (2⅔ cups)**
1 **Tbsp. lemon juice**
1 **15-oz. pkg. folded refrigerated unbaked piecrusts (2 crusts)**
◆◆◆
Milk (optional)
Coarse sugar (optional)
1 **recipe Hard Sauce (see page 299) (optional)**

1 For filling, in a mixing bowl stir together pears, mincemeat, and lemon juice. Line a 9-inch pie plate with 1 of the piecrusts. Transfer filling to pastry-lined pie plate; flute edge. Cover edge of pie with foil. Bake in a 375° oven 25 minutes; remove foil. Bake 20 to 25 minutes more or till pastry is golden. Cool on a wire rack.

2 Meanwhile, on a lightly floured surface, with a knife or cookie cutter, cut remaining piecrust into stars or other decorative shapes. Place cutouts on an ungreased cookie sheet. If desired, brush with milk and sprinkle with coarse sugar. Bake alongside pie about 10 minutes or till golden. Transfer cutouts to a wire rack; cool. To serve, arrange cutouts atop pie. If desired, serve with Hard Sauce. Makes 8 servings.

Nutrition facts per serving: 478 cal., 16 g total fat (0 g sat. fat), 15 mg chol., 490 mg sodium, 82 g carbo., 2 g fiber, 3 g pro. *Daily values:* 5% vit. C, 3% calcium, 11% iron.

Mincemeat-Pear Tarts: Divide each unbaked piecrust into 4 portions (8 pieces total). Shape 6 portions into balls. Roll out each ball between pieces of waxed paper to 6-inch circles. Ease each into a 4- to 4½-inch tart pan. Flute edges or trim evenly with tart pans.

Divide filling among tart shells (about ¾ cup per tart). With a knife or cookie cutter, cut remaining piecrust portions into stars or other decorative shapes. Place cutouts atop tarts. If desired, brush cutouts with milk and sprinkle with sugar.

Bake in a 375° oven for 35 to 40 minutes or till pastry is golden and filling is bubbly. Makes 6 tarts (12 servings).

HARD SAUCE

Scooped atop a wedge of warm fruit pie or a slice of steaming plum pudding, this buttery sauce melts down into tasty goodness.

¾ cup butter
1¼ cups sifted powdered sugar
3 Tbsp. brandy, rum, or
   orange juice
½ tsp. vanilla

1 In a medium mixing bowl beat butter and sifted powdered sugar with an electric mixer on medium speed till fluffy. Beat in brandy, rum, or orange juice and vanilla. Store, covered, in refrigerator for up to 2 weeks. Let stand at room temperature 30 minutes before serving. Makes 1¼ cups.

Nutrition facts per tablespoon: 90 cal., 7 g total fat (4 g sat. fat), 18 mg chol., 70 g sodium, 6 g carbo., 0 g fiber, 0 g pro. *Daily values:* 6% vit. A.

DUTCH PUMPKIN-APPLE TART

This layered apple and pumpkin crumb-topped tart fills the pan, so be sure your tart pan measures 11 inches.

1¼ cups all-purpose flour
⅓ cup sugar
½ cup butter or margarine
¼ cup chopped macadamia
   nuts or walnuts
1 egg yolk
2 Tbsp. milk
1 medium tart cooking apple,
   peeled, cored, and thinly
   sliced (about 1 cup)
♦♦♦
2 eggs, lightly beaten
1 15-oz. can pumpkin

1 cup evaporated milk
½ cup sugar
½ tsp. ground cinnamon
½ tsp. ground ginger
¼ tsp. ground cloves
   Whipped cream (optional)

1 In a medium bowl combine the flour and ⅓ cup sugar. Using a pastry blender, cut in butter or margarine till mixture resembles coarse crumbs. Remove ½ cup of the crumb mixture for topping; stir in nuts and set aside. Add egg yolk and milk to remaining mixture, tossing with a fork till all is moistened but still crumbly. With floured hands, pat mixture into the bottom and up the sides of an 11×1-inch tart pan with removable bottom. Bake in a 400° oven for 10 minutes. Remove from oven. Arrange apple slices over bottom of crust.

2 In a medium bowl stir together the eggs, pumpkin, evaporated milk, ½ cup sugar, cinnamon, ginger, and cloves. Spread pumpkin mixture evenly over apples in pan. Bake in a 400° oven for 15 minutes or till nearly set. Sprinkle with crumb topping. Return to oven and bake for 10 to 15 minutes more or till a knife inserted near center comes out clean. Cool in pan on a wire rack.

3 To serve, remove sides of pan. Cut into wedges and top with whipped cream, if desired. Store any leftovers in the refrigerator for up to 2 days. Makes 16 servings.

Nutrition facts per serving: 187 cal., 10 g total fat (5 g sat. fat), 60 mg chol., 86 g sodium, 23 g carbo., 1 g fiber, 4 g pro. *Daily values:* 68% vit. A, 2% vit. C, 5% calcium, 7% iron.

COTTAGE CHEESE TARTS

⅔ cup cream-style cottage
   cheese
2 cups all-purpose flour
¼ cup ground toasted almonds
1 Tbsp. sugar
½ tsp. salt
½ cup butter or margarine
4 to 5 Tbsp. cold water
♦♦♦
½ cup canned pie filling
   (apple, peach, apricot, or
   raisin) (cut up larger
   pieces of fruit as necessary)
   Milk
⅓ cup sliced almonds

1 Sieve cottage cheese. Stir together flour, ground almonds, sugar, and salt. Cut in butter till pieces are size of small peas. With a fork stir in cottage cheese. Sprinkle 1 tablespoon cold water over part of the mixture, tossing to mix. Repeat with remaining water till all is moistened. Form into 2 balls.

2 Grease baking sheets. On lightly floured surface, roll out half of the dough to a 9×9-inch rectangle. Cut into nine 3-inch squares. Spoon a rounded teaspoon of pie filling into center of each square; brush edges with water. Fold each square in half to form triangles; seal edges with tines of fork. Prick tarts; brush with milk and sprinkle with sliced almonds. Place tarts on prepared baking sheets. Repeat with remaining dough. Bake in a 375° oven 25 to 30 minutes or till golden. Makes 18 tarts.

Nutrition facts per tart: 129 cal., 7 g total fat (4 g sat. fat), 15 mg chol., 146 g sodium, 13 g carbo., 1 g fiber, 3 g pro. *Daily values:* 5% vit. A, 1% vit. C, 1% calcium, 5% iron.

WHITE CHOCOLATE PIE

2 3-oz. pkg. cream cheese, softened
3 Tbsp. sugar
1 cup whipping cream

❖❖❖

¾ cup vanilla milk pieces
1 tsp. finely shredded orange peel
1 Graham Cracker Crust (see right)

❖❖❖

2 cups fresh raspberries and/or quartered strawberries
¼ cup vanilla milk pieces
¼ tsp. shortening
1 oz. semisweet chocolate
¼ tsp. shortening

1 In a medium mixing bowl beat cream cheese and sugar till fluffy; set aside. Wash beaters. In a chilled bowl beat whipping cream to soft peaks; set aside.

2 In a small saucepan melt the ¾ cup vanilla milk pieces over very low heat, stirring constantly. Add the warm melted pieces to the cream cheese mixture and beat till fluffy. Stir in orange peel. Fold in the whipped cream. Spread evenly in Graham Cracker Crust. Cover and chill pie at least 3 hours or overnight.

3 Up to 1 hour before serving, top pie with berries. In a small saucepan over very low heat, melt the ¼ cup vanilla milk pieces and ¼ teaspoon shortening, stirring till smooth. Cool slightly. Repeat melting and cooling with the semisweet chocolate and ¼ teaspoon shortening. Drizzle melted mixtures separately atop fruit. Makes 8 to 10 servings.

Graham Cracker Crust: In a mixing bowl combine ⅓ cup melted *butter or margarine*, ¼ cup *sugar* and 1¼ cups finely crushed *graham crackers*. Toss to mix well. Press mixture onto bottom and sides of a 9-inch pie plate. Bake in a 375° oven for 4 to 5 minutes or till edge is lightly browned. Cool on a wire rack before filling.

Nutrition facts per serving: 493 cal., 35 g total fat (21 g sat. fat), 86 mg chol., 244 mg sodium, 42 g carbo., 2 g fiber, 5 g pro. *Daily values:* 29% vit. A, 13% vit. C, 8% calcium, 7% iron.

PLUM PUDDING

Fresh plums in December? Not in the olden days, so this traditional British Christmas pudding uses dried plums—prunes—instead.
(See the photograph on page 316.)

1½ cups pitted prunes, snipped
½ cup brandy or orange juice
1 medium apple, peeled and finely shredded
¾ cup chopped walnuts
½ cup diced mixed candied fruits and peels
1 Tbsp. finely shredded orange peel

❖❖❖

3 cups all-purpose flour
1 tsp. ground cinnamon
½ tsp. baking soda
½ tsp. salt
½ tsp. ground ginger
½ tsp. ground nutmeg

❖❖❖

1½ cups packed brown sugar
½ cup butter or margarine, softened
3 eggs
1¼ cups milk

❖❖❖

1 recipe Hard Sauce (see page 299) (optional)

1 In a medium mixing bowl soak prunes in brandy or orange juice, covered, in a cool place for 2 hours or overnight, or till most of the liquid is absorbed. Do not drain. Stir shredded apple, walnuts, candied fruits and peels, and orange peel into prune mixture; set aside.

2 Grease and flour a 12-cup fluted tube mold or pan. In a large mixing bowl stir together the flour, cinnamon, baking soda, salt, ginger, and nutmeg; set aside.

3 In another large mixing bowl beat together brown sugar and butter or margarine with an electric mixer on medium speed till well combined. Add eggs, 1 at a time, beating on low speed just till combined. *Do not overbeat.* Add flour mixture alternately with milk, beating on low speed after each addition just till combined. Fold in prune mixture.

4 Spread batter into prepared mold. Lightly grease a square of foil; cover mold with foil, greased side down. Press foil tightly against the rim of mold. Place mold on a rack in a deep kettle containing 1 inch of *simmering water*. Cover kettle; steam over low heat for 1½ to 2 hours or till a toothpick inserted near center comes out clean, adding *boiling water* if necessary. Remove from kettle. Cool 15 minutes. Carefully invert and remove pudding from mold. Cool slightly on wire rack. If desired, serve warm with Hard Sauce. Makes 18 servings.

Prepare pudding as directed, except cool completely. Wrap pudding in 100-percent-cotton cheesecloth moistened with additional *brandy or orange juice.* Wrap tightly with foil and store in refrigerator for up to 2 weeks. To reheat, unwrap pudding and remove cheesecloth; return pudding to the mold or pan. Cover tightly with foil and place on a rack in kettle containing 1 inch of *simmering water.* Cover kettle; steam over low heat for 30 to 40 minutes or till heated through.

Nutrition facts per serving: 290 cal., 10 g total fat (4 g sat. fat), 50 mg chol., 171 mg sodium, 44 g carbo., 2 g fiber, 5 g pro. *Daily values:* 10% vit. A, 2% vit. C, 4% calcium, 12% iron.

BATTENBERG CAKE

The British royals trace their roots back to Germany, and so does this cake. It was a favorite of Queen Victoria's daughter, Beatrice, whose married name, Battenberg, became Anglicized to Mountbatten. We've reduced the traditional four layers to three. (See the photograph on page 320.)

2 **16-oz. pkg. pound-cake mix**
   Red paste food coloring

   ◆◆◆

2 **Tbsp. orange juice**
½ **cup seedless red raspberry jam**
2 **Tbsp. light-colored corn syrup**

   ◆◆◆

2 **7-oz. pkg. marzipan**
   Sifted powdered sugar

   ◆◆◆

   Sugared Raspberries and Mint Leaves (see right) (optional)

1 Grease and flour two 9×5×3-inch loaf pans; set aside. Prepare cake mixes according to package directions (prepare each batter separately; do not make a double batch at one time). Spread batter from 1 mix in a prepared pan. Stir enough food coloring into second batter to tint it pink; spread in second pan. Bake cakes according to package directions or till cakes spring back when lightly touched. Cool in pans on a wire rack for 10 minutes; remove from pans and cool completely.

2 To assemble, trim crusts from the sides, ends, and top of each cake to make evenly shaped loaves. Trim loaves again so each measures 7½×4×1½ inches. Cut the plain loaf into 4 evenly shaped logs measuring 7½×1×¾ inches. Cut pink loaf into 5 logs measuring 7½×1×¾ inches. Assemble cake using 5 pink logs and 4 plain logs. (Use remaining cake pieces for other desserts.)

3 Drizzle the 9 logs with orange juice; set aside. In a small saucepan combine the jam and corn syrup. Heat and stir till jam is melted and mixture is smooth; set aside.

4 In a bowl combine marzipan; knead with hands to soften. Sprinkle both sides of marzipan with powdered sugar; roll marzipan between 2 sheets of waxed paper to a 12×8-inch rectangle. (If desired, roll marzipan to a 15×8-inch rectangle; trim off 3 inches from a short side and use to cut small shapes for garnishes.) Brush off excess powdered sugar.

5 Remove top sheet of waxed paper. Place a plain-colored cake log crosswise in center of marzipan sheet. Brush jam mixture on all sides of cake log. Place pink logs on each side of first log and brush them with jam. For second layer, place another pink log on top of the plain log and plain logs atop the first pink logs, brushing all sides with jam. Repeat layering with remaining cake logs, alternating colors to make a checkerboard pattern. Press cake logs together. Bring marzipan up over sides of cake, with edges meeting at top of cake and covering long sides but not ends. Crimp edges of marzipan to seal; decorate top with marzipan trimmings as desired. Carefully transfer to a serving plate. Trim cake and marzipan to make each end even. Cover and let cake stand several hours or overnight before serving.

6 To serve, slice cake. If desired, garnish with Sugared Raspberries and Mint Leaves. Makes 8 to 10 servings.

Sugared Raspberries and Mint Leaves: Place 2 teaspoons *dried egg whites* (available in cake decorating stores) and ¼ cup *water* in a 6-ounce custard cup; stir together with a wire whisk or fork. Place *superfine or granulated sugar* in a shallow dish. Using a pastry brush, brush egg white mixture onto fresh *raspberries* and *mint leaves;* roll in sugar. Allow to dry on a wire rack.

Nutrition facts per serving: 450 cal., 17 g total fat (7 g sat. fat), 66 mg chol., 136 mg sodium, 69 g carbo., 2 g fiber, 6 g pro. *Daily values:* 10% vit. A, 3% vit. C, 11% calcium, 9% iron.

VIENNESE CHOCOLATE TORTE

For a luscious garnish, sprinkle curls made of white chocolate and semisweet chocolate atop the torte before serving.

3 oz. unsweetened chocolate
1 cup water
2¼ cups all-purpose flour
1½ tsp. baking soda
½ tsp. salt

♦♦♦

½ cup margarine or butter
2 cups granulated sugar
1 tsp. vanilla
3 eggs
1 cup buttermilk
1 recipe Chocolate Mousse (see right)
1 recipe White Chocolate Ganache (see top right)

1 Grease and flour two 9×1½-inch round baking pans. In a small saucepan heat and stir chocolate and water till chocolate melts; cool. In a bowl combine flour, soda, and salt; set aside.

2 In a large mixing bowl beat margarine or butter with an electric mixer on medium to high speed till softened. Add sugar and vanilla; beat till mixed. Add eggs, 1 at a time, beating well after each. Combine chocolate mixture and buttermilk. Alternately add flour and chocolate mixtures, beating on low to medium speed after each addition just till combined.

3 Pour batter into prepared pans. Bake in 350° oven 30 to 35 minutes or till a wooden toothpick inserted in centers comes out clean. Cool in pans on wire racks 10 minutes. Remove from pans. Cool completely on wire racks.

4 To assemble, split cake layers in half. Spread ¾ cup Chocolate Mousse on each layer; stack layers. Frost sides of cake with White Chocolate Ganache. Cover and refrigerate up to 1 day. Before serving, let stand 30 minutes at room temperature. Serves 16.

Chocolate Mousse: In saucepan melt 2 cups s*emisweet chocolate pieces.* Beat together ¼ cup *water* and 4 *egg yolks.* Gradually stir *half* of chocolate into yolk mixture. Return to saucepan. Cook and stir over medium heat till bubbly and slightly thickened.

Remove from heat. Stir in ½ teaspoon *ground cinnamon* and ½ teaspoon *vanilla;* cool. Fold chocolate mixture into 1 cup *whipping cream,* whipped.

White Chocolate Ganache: Heat 1 cup *whipping cream* till simmering. Remove from heat; add one 6-ounce package *white baking bar,* chopped, stirring till melted. Stir in 1 teaspoon *vanilla.* Cover with plastic wrap. Chill for 3 to 6 hours. To frost cake, beat with electric mixer on medium speed just till soft peaks form. Do not overbeat.

Nutrition facts per serving: 529 cal., 31 g total fat (12 g sat. fat), 135 mg chol., 304 mg sodium, 62 g carbo., 1 g fiber, 7 g pro. *Daily values:* 30% vit. A, 7% calcium, 13% iron.

MOCHA TRUFFLE ROLL

A sinfully rich and silky smooth mocha butter filling generously fills this chocolate cake roll.

⅓ cup all-purpose flour
¼ cup unsweetened cocoa powder
¼ tsp. baking soda
¼ tsp. salt

♦♦♦

4 egg yolks
½ tsp. vanilla
⅓ cup granulated sugar

♦♦♦

4 egg whites
½ cup granulated sugar

♦♦♦

Sifted powdered sugar
1 recipe Mocha Truffle Filling (see page 303)
Unsweetened cocoa powder

1 Grease and lightly flour a 15×10×1-inch jelly-roll pan. In a mixing bowl stir together flour, ¼ cup cocoa powder, baking soda, and salt. Set pan and flour mixture aside.

2 In a small bowl beat egg yolks and vanilla with an electric mixer on high speed about 5 minutes or till thick and lemon-colored. Gradually add ⅓ cup granulated sugar, beating till sugar is almost dissolved. Wash beaters.

3 In a large bowl beat egg whites on medium to high speed till soft peaks form (tips curl). Gradually add ½ cup granulated sugar, about 2 tablespoons at a time, beating till stiff peaks form (tips stand straight). Fold yolk mixture into whites. Sprinkle flour mixture over egg mixture; fold in gently, just till combined. Spread the batter evenly in the prepared pan.

4 Bake in 375° oven for 12 to 15 minutes or till cake springs back when lightly touched. Immediately loosen edges of cake; turn out onto a towel sprinkled with sifted powdered sugar. Starting with a narrow end, roll up cake and towel together. Cool on a wire rack.

5 Unroll cake. Spread Mocha Truffle Filling onto cake to within 1 inch of edges. Reroll cake. Chill till serving time. Sprinkle with cocoa powder and additional *powdered sugar* before serving. Makes 10 servings.

Mocha Truffle Filling: Dissolve 1 teaspoon *instant coffee crystals* in 2 tablespoons *hot water.*

Beat ½ cup *margarine or butter* with an electric mixer on medium to high speed till softened. Mix ½ cup *unsweetened cocoa powder and* 1½ cups *sifted powdered sugar.* Alternately add cocoa powder mixture and 3 tablespoons *pasteurized egg product* to margarine or butter, beating after each addition. Beat in coffee mixture, adding additional *hot water,* if necessary, to make filling of spreading consistency.

Nutrition facts per serving: 288 cal., 13 g total fat (2 g sat. fat), 85 mg chol., 226 mg sodium, 39 g carbo., 0 g fiber, 5 g pro. *Daily values:* 24% vit. A, 7% calcium, 9% iron.

BAVARIAN MINT FROSTING

An everyday chocolate cake becomes special enough for holidays when spread with this creamy mint frosting.

   1   **10-oz. pkg. semisweet mint-flavored chocolate pieces**
  ½   **cup margarine or butter**
  ¾   **cup dairy sour cream**
  3¾ **cups sifted powdered sugar**

◆◆◆

1 In a heavy saucepan heat chocolate and margarine or butter over low heat till melted. Transfer to a mixing bowl; cool 5 minutes. Stir in the sour cream. Add powdered sugar, beating with an electric mixer till frosting is of spreading consistency.

2 Frost cake. If desired, decorate with *chocolate curls.* Store cake, covered, in the refrigerator. Makes 3 cups (enough for two 9-inch round cakes).

Nutrition facts per tablespoon: 82 cal., 4 g total fat (1 g sat. fat), 2 mg chol., 24 mg sodium, 12 g carbo., 0 g fiber, 0 g pro. *Daily values:* 3% vit. A, 1% iron.

ORANGE-CREAM CHEESE FROSTING

This smooth, citrus-flavored frosting complements white or carrot cake.

   2   **3-oz. pkg. cream cheese**
  ½   **cup margarine or butter**
  ¼   **cup frozen orange juice concentrate**

◆◆◆

  4½ **cups sifted powdered sugar**

1 Allow cream cheese and margarine or butter to soften. In a mixing bowl beat cream cheese and margarine or butter with an electric mixer on medium speed till fluffy. Add juice concentrate; beat till combined.

2 Gradually beat in 2 cups of the powdered sugar. Beat in enough of the remaining powdered sugar to make the frosting easy to spread.

3 Frost cake. Store cake, covered, in the refrigerator. Makes 3 cups (enough for two 9-inch round cakes).

Nutrition facts per tablespoon: 68 cal., 3 g total fat (1 g sat. fat), 4 mg chol., 33 mg sodium, 10 g carbo., 0 g fiber, 0 g pro. *Daily values:* 3% vit. A.

CHOCOLATE-PEANUT BUTTER FROSTING

4¾ cups sifted powdered sugar
    (1 lb.)
⅔ cup boiling water
½ cup unsweetened cocoa
    powder
½ cup creamy peanut butter
1 tsp. vanilla

1 In a mixing bowl combine powdered sugar, boiling water, cocoa, peanut butter, and vanilla. Beat with an electric mixer on low to medium speed till combined. Cool for 30 minutes.

2 Spread frosting onto cake. Makes 2½ cups (enough for two 9-inch round cakes or one 13×9-inch cake).

Nutrition facts per tablespoon: 69 cal., 2 g total fat (0 g sat. fat), 0 mg chol., 16 mg sodium, 13 g carbo., 0 g fiber, 1 g pro. *Daily values:* 1% iron.

FRENCH SPICE CAKE

This honey cake traces its roots to the kitchens of 15th-century France. More like a dense bread than a cake, a slice goes well with a handful of nuts and dried fruits.
(See the photograph on page 316.)

1 cup honey
1 cup boiling water
2 tsp. finely shredded lemon
    peel
3½ cups all-purpose flour
1 cup sugar
1 tsp. baking powder
1 tsp. ground cinnamon
½ tsp. baking soda
¼ tsp. salt
¼ tsp. ground cloves

3 beaten eggs
½ cup cooking oil
♦♦♦
Whipped cream (optional)

1 Grease and flour a 10-inch fluted tube pan; set aside. In a small mixing bowl stir together honey, boiling water, and lemon peel; set aside. In a large mixing bowl stir together flour, sugar, baking powder, cinnamon, baking soda, salt, and cloves. Add the warm honey mixture to flour mixture, stirring with a wooden spoon till nearly smooth. Stir together the beaten eggs and cooking oil; add to batter and stir just till combined.

2 Pour batter into the prepared tube pan. Bake in a 325° oven about 50 minutes or till a wooden toothpick inserted near center comes out clean. Cool in pan on a wire rack for 10 minutes. Remove from pan and cool completely. Wrap and store overnight. If desired, serve with whipped cream. Makes 18 servings.

Nutrition facts per serving: 249 cal., 7 g total fat (1 g sat. fat), 36 mg chol., 97 mg sodium, 44 g carbo., 1 g fiber, 3 g pro. *Daily values:* 1% vit. A, 2% calcium, 8% iron.

VANILLA FUDGE

Our Test Kitchen gave this fudge a 10: Creamy, smooth, and with lots of vanilla flavor, it's a pleasant change from the chocolate classic.
(See the photograph on page 319.)

2 cups sugar
1 5-oz. can evaporated
    milk (⅔ cup)
⅓ cup milk
⅛ tsp. salt

TEST KITCHEN TIP

DEGREES OF CANDYMAKING

Before you start making holiday candies, it's a good idea to check the accuracy of your candy thermometer. To calibrate your thermometer, put it in a pan of boiling water for a few minutes then read the temperature. If the thermometer registers above or below 212°, calculate the difference; then add or subtract that number to or from the temperature specified in your recipe, and cook to the newly calculated temperature. For example, if the thermometer registers 210°, cook the candy 2 degrees lower than the recipe specifies.

¼ cup butter
1 tsp. vanilla
♦♦♦
Broken nuts (optional)

1 Line an 8×4×2-inch loaf pan with foil, extending foil over edges of pan. Butter foil; set aside.

2 Butter the sides of a heavy 2-quart saucepan. In saucepan combine sugar, evaporated milk, milk, and salt. Cook and stir over medium-high heat to boiling. Carefully clip a candy thermometer to the side of the pan. Cook and stir over medium-low heat to 238°, soft-ball stage (this should take 25 to 35 minutes).

3 Immediately remove saucepan from heat. Add butter and vanilla, but *do not stir*. Cool, without stirring, to 110° or lukewarm (about 55 minutes). Remove candy thermometer from saucepan. Using a wooden spoon, beat vigorously till fudge becomes very thick and just starts to lose its gloss (about 10 minutes total).

4 Immediately spread fudge into prepared pan. Score into 1-inch squares while warm. If desired, top each square with a nut. When candy is firm, lift it out of pan. Cut into squares. Place in an airtight container and store in the refrigerator. Makes about 1 pound (32 servings).

Nutrition facts per 1-inch square: 70 cal., 2 g total fat (1 g sat. fat), 6 mg chol., 30 mg sodium, 13 g carbo., 0 g fiber, 0 g pro. *Daily values:* 1% vit. A, 1% calcium.

Turkish Delight

The Turkish name for this candy means "rest for the throat," which is perfect for December's feasts. Kids love the way it jiggles. (See the photograph on page 319.)

1½　cups sugar
3　envelopes unflavored gelatin
¾　cup cold water
1　tsp. lemon juice
1　tsp. strawberry flavoring or
　　¾ tsp. rose water*
1 to 2　drops red food coloring
◆◆◆
⅔　cup sifted powdered sugar

1 Grease an 8×4×2-inch loaf pan; set aside. In a 1-quart saucepan combine the 1½ cups sugar and gelatin; add water and lemon juice. Cook and stir over low heat till dissolved. Remove from heat. Add strawberry flavoring or rose water; tint mixture pink with food coloring. Cool to room temperature.

2 Pour mixture into the prepared pan. Cover and chill 2 hours or overnight or till firm. Sift some powdered sugar onto a sheet of waxed paper. Loosen edges of candy with a knife; invert pan onto the sifted sugar. (If the candy does not easily separate from the pan, dip pan for just a few seconds into a larger pan of warm water, then invert.)

3 Cut candy into 24 to 32 bite-size pieces. Turn to coat all sides with remaining powdered sugar. Place each piece in a paper candy cup. Store, refrigerated, in an airtight container for up to 1 week. Toss candy in additional *powdered sugar* before serving, if necessary. Makes 24 to 32 candies.

***Note:** You can find rose water in health-food stores and Middle Eastern specialty shops.

Nutrition facts per candy: 63 cal., 0 g total fat, 0 mg chol., 1 mg sodium, 15 g carbo., 0 g fiber, 1 g pro.

Peppermint Creams

Treat this mixture like a sugar-cookie dough, rerolling and recutting scraps and decorating as your fancy dictates. (See the photograph on page 318.)

2½　cups sifted powdered sugar
4　tsp. dried egg whites*
2　Tbsp. water

10 to 12　drops peppermint extract
　　Paste food coloring (optional)

1 In a large mixing bowl stir together *1½ cups* of the powdered sugar and the dried egg whites. Add water, peppermint extract, and food coloring, if desired. Beat with an electric mixer on low speed till smooth. Gradually add as much of the remaining powdered sugar as you can, beating on low speed till combined. Knead in any remaining powdered sugar (mixture should be extremely stiff and not sticky).

2 Divide mixture in half. Wrap 1 portion in plastic wrap; set aside. Sprinkle a little additional *powdered sugar* onto a piece of waxed paper. Place the unwrapped portion of the mixture on sugared paper; sprinkle with a little more *powdered sugar* to prevent sticking. Roll out to ¼-inch thickness. Cut into bite-size shapes with a small cookie or hors d'oeuvre cutter, rerolling scraps as necessary. Line a baking sheet with waxed paper; place candies on paper. Repeat with remaining dough. Cover loosely with a towel; let dry overnight. Store in an airtight container. Makes about 60 candies.

***Note:** You can find dried egg whites in stores where cake decorating supplies are sold.

Nutrition facts per candy: 17 cal., 0 g total fat, 0 mg chol., 1 mg sodium, 4 g carbo., 0 g fiber, 0 g pro.

MACAROONS

A chocolate drizzle brings these dainty coconut cookies up to dress code for the holiday cookie platter. (See the photograph on page 319.)

3 egg whites
1 cup sugar
2 cups flaked coconut
   (about 5 oz.)

   ❖❖❖

1 oz. semisweet chocolate
2 tsp. shortening

1 Grease a cookie sheet; set aside. In a large mixing bowl beat egg whites with an electric mixer on high speed till soft peaks form (tips curl). Gradually add sugar, a tablespoon at a time, beating till stiff peaks form (tips stand straight). Fold in coconut.

2 Drop by rounded tea-spoonful 2 inches apart onto the prepared cookie sheet. Bake in a 325° oven 20 minutes or till edges are light brown. Cool the cookies on a wire rack. Store in an airtight container.

3 To serve, in a small sauce-pan heat and stir chocolate and shortening over low heat till melt-ed and smooth. Cool slightly. Transfer chocolate mixture to a self-sealing plastic bag; seal. Cut a small hole in a corner of the bag; pipe chocolate through hole over cookies. Let stand till chocolate is set. Makes about 45 cookies.

Nutrition facts per cookie: 38 cal., 1 g total fat (1 g sat. fat), 0 mg chol., 4 mg sodium, 6 g carbo., 0 g fiber, and 0 g pro.

LEBKUCHEN

The good cooks of Nuremberg, Germany, pulled out all the stops when creating this holiday cookie, adding their cache of candied fruits and almonds to the rich, honey-sweetened dough. The traditional cookies were pressed into large, decorative molds; we've sliced ours into smaller diamonds for ease in storing and snacking. (See the photograph on page 319.)

1 cup honey
1 cup packed brown sugar

   ❖❖❖

4½ cups all-purpose flour
1 Tbsp. ground cinnamon
1 tsp. baking powder
1 tsp. ground nutmeg
2 eggs
½ cup butter, softened
1 cup diced mixed candied
   fruits and peels
1 cup slivered almonds

   ❖❖❖

Whole blanched almonds
(optional)

1 In a medium saucepan warm honey and brown sugar over low heat, stirring till dissolved; remove from heat. Set aside to cool.

2 Meanwhile, stir together flour, cinnamon, baking powder, and nutmeg; set aside. Place honey mixture in a large bowl. With an electric mixer on medi-um speed, beat in eggs, 1 at a time, and butter. Add candied fruits and peels and slivered almonds; beat on low speed till combined. Add flour mixture; beat till dough is smooth. Cover and refrigerate overnight.

3 On a lightly floured surface, roll out half the dough at a time to ⅛- to ¼-inch thickness. Cut into 1½-inch diamonds with a knife. If desired, press a whole almond in the center of each dia-mond. (Or, cut into desired shapes with cookie cutters.) Arrange cookies on a cookie sheet. Bake in a 350° oven for 10 to 12 minutes or till golden. Transfer cookies to a wire rack to cool. Store in an airtight container or in the freezer for 6 weeks. Makes about 96 cookies.

Note: To soften slightly, store cookies with a quartered *apple* in an airtight container at room temperature for a few days.

Nutrition facts per cookie: 59 cal., 2 g total fat (1 g sat. fat), 7 mg chol., 16 mg sodium, 10 g carbo., 0 g fiber, 1 g pro.
Daily values: 1% vit. A, 2% iron.

SUGAR COOKIE ORNAMENTS

You might want to bake the cookies a day ahead so your family can enjoy an afternoon of decorating these edible ornaments. To wrap each cookie ornament in a homemade gift box, see the directions in the tip on page 307.

1 recipe Vanilla Cutouts
   (see page 307)

   ❖❖❖

1 recipe Royal Icing, tinted as
   desired (see page 307)

1 For 3-dimensional orna-ments, prepare Vanilla Cutouts dough and chill. Working with a fourth of the dough at a time, roll out on a lightly floured surface to ⅛-inch thickness.

DECORATED GIFT BOXES

Present a Cookie Ornament (see page 306) in a festively decorated box. To add the embellishments, cover a plain box (about 6 inches square without lid) with decorative paper. Using double-faced tape, adhere paper lace doilies to the side of the box, allowing the doily ends to extend over the top of the box. You can fold the doily over the top of the box to act as a lid. Loosely stuff the box with tissue paper and carefully add the ornament.

2 Using a sharp paring knife, cookie cutters, or fluted pastry wheel, cut dough into rounds, squares, diamonds, or Christmas tree shapes that are about 3 to 4 inches wide. Make at least 2 of each shape, as you'll need to put them together later.

3 Arrange the shapes on ungreased cookie sheets. Cut half of the cookies in half from top to bottom, but *do not separate.* Using a drinking straw, poke a hole off-center at the top of each whole cookie. Bake in a 375° oven for 8 to 10 minutes or till edges are light brown. Carefully cut apart halved cookies. Transfer to a wire rack, keeping cookie pairs together; cool thoroughly.

4 For each ornament, decorate cookies (whole and halves) with Royal Icing. Let dry.

5 To assemble, pipe icing onto cut edge of a matching cookie half; attach cookie half to a whole cookie of the same size and shape; let dry. Add icing; attach the second matching cookie half to the other side of the whole cookie. (For easier handling, you may want to lean the fully assembled ornament against a cup.) Let dry completely. Run a ribbon or yarn through the hole of each cookie, forming a loop large enough for hanging on a tree. Makes about 40 ornaments.

VANILLA CUTOUTS

Enjoy a nibble or two as these come out of the oven. Once assembled as ornaments, the cookies and frosting will probably be too firm to eat.

4 **cups all-purpose flour**
1 **tsp. baking powder**
¾ **tsp. ground cardamom**
½ **tsp. salt**

◆◆◆

1 **cup butter or margarine**
1 **cup sugar**
⅔ **cup light corn syrup**
1 **Tbsp. vanilla**

◆◆◆

1 **beaten egg**

1 In a medium mixing bowl stir together flour, baking powder, cardamom, and salt; set aside.

2 In a saucepan combine butter or margarine, sugar, and corn syrup. Cook and stir over medium heat till margarine is melted and sugar is dissolved. Pour into a large mixing bowl. Stir in vanilla. Cool 5 minutes.

3 Add egg; mix well. Add flour mixture to egg mixture; mix well. Divide dough in half. Cover; chill at least 2 hours or overnight. (If the dough chills overnight, let stand for 5 to 10 minutes at room temperature before rolling.) Continue as directed on page 306 for Sugar Cookie Ornaments.

Nutrition facts per cookie: 120 cal., 5 g total fat (3 g sat. fat), 18 mg chol., 88 mg sodium, 18 g carbo., 0 g fiber, 1 g pro. *Daily values:* 4% vit. A, 1% calcium, 5% iron.

ROYAL ICING

Thanks to meringue powder, this frosting "glues" the cookie ornament pieces together. Look for the powder with candymaking supplies or check out a local candy shop.

3 **Tbsp. meringue powder**
6 **Tbsp. warm water**
1 **1-lb. pkg. powdered sugar, sifted**
1 **tsp. vanilla**
½ **tsp. cream of tartar**

1 In a large mixing bowl combine meringue powder and warm water. Beat lightly with a fork till combined. Add powdered sugar, vanilla, and cream of tartar. Beat with an electric mixer on high speed for 7 to 10 minutes or till extremely stiff. Use immediately. As you work, cover the bowl with wet paper towels to prevent the icing from getting too firm. Makes about 3 cups.

Nutrition facts per tablespoon: 37 cal., 0 g total fat (0 g sat. fat), 0 mg chol., 0 mg sodium, 9 g carbo., 0 g fiber, 0 g pro.

SPECULAAS

Dutch bakers got the name for this crisp cookie from the Latin word for "mirror" (pronounced SPEC-oo-lahs). When they pressed the dough into a wooden mold, the cookie mirrored its shape. We took a little baker's license and used fanciful cookie cutters. (See the photograph on page 319.)

    4 cups all-purpose flour
    4 tsp. baking powder
    1 Tbsp. ground cinnamon
    1 tsp. ground ginger
    1 tsp. ground nutmeg
    1 tsp. ground cloves
    ½ tsp. salt
    1 cup butter
 1½ cups granulated sugar
    2 eggs
    2 tsp. finely shredded lemon
       peel
    2 tsp. finely shredded orange
       peel
    ⅓ cup milk
       ◆◆◆
    1 recipe Powdered Sugar Icing
       (see right) (optional)

1 Combine flour, baking powder, cinnamon, ginger, nutmeg, cloves, and salt; set aside. Beat butter with an electric mixer on medium speed for 30 seconds. Add granulated sugar and beat about 4 minutes or till fluffy. Add eggs and lemon and orange peels; beat on medium speed till combined. Add about one-third of the flour mixture and beat on low speed till combined. Beat in milk. Beat in as much of the remaining flour mixture as you can. Using a wooden spoon, stir in any remaining flour mixture. Divide dough into 4 portions. Cover; chill about 1 hour or till easy to handle.

2 On a lightly floured surface, roll out dough, 1 portion at a time, to ⅛-inch thickness. Using cutters, cut into desired shapes. Arrange cookies 1 inch apart on an ungreased cookie sheet.

3 Bake in a 350° oven for 8 to 10 minutes or till golden. Cool on a wire rack. If desired, decorate with Powdered Sugar Icing. For the snowflake design as pictured on page 319, use a fine paintbrush to apply icing. When icing is dry, store in an airtight container. Makes about 65 cookies.

Nutrition facts per cookie: 71 cal., 3 g total fat (2 g sat. fat), 14 mg chol., 69 mg sodium, 10 g carbo., 0 g fiber, 1 g pro. *Daily values:* 2% vit. A, C, 2% calcium, 2% iron.

FAVORITE SUGAR COOKIES

If you have a carton of eggnog in the wings, use a bit to enrich these cookies. Otherwise, milk and vanilla can stand in nicely. (See the photograph on page 318.)

    ⅓ cup butter
    ⅓ cup shortening
    2 cups all-purpose flour
    1 egg
    ¾ cup granulated sugar
    1 Tbsp. dairy eggnog or milk*
    1 tsp. baking powder
       ◆◆◆
    1 recipe Powdered Sugar Icing
       (see above right) (optional)

1 Beat butter and shortening for 30 seconds. Add about *half* of the flour, the egg, granulated sugar, eggnog or milk, and baking powder. Beat till combined. Beat in remaining flour. Divide dough in half. Cover and chill 3 hours.

2 On a lightly floured surface, roll out half the dough at a time to ⅛-inch thickness. Using cookie cutters, cut into desired shape. Arrange cookies 1 inch apart on an ungreased cookie sheet.

3 Bake in a 375° oven for 7 to 8 minutes or till edges are firm and bottoms are very light brown. Cool on a wire rack. If desired, frost with Powdered Sugar Icing. Store in an airtight container. Makes about 40 cookies.

*Note: If using milk, add 1 teaspoon *vanilla.*

Powdered Sugar Icing: Combine 2 cups sifted *powdered sugar* and 2 tablespoons *eggnog or milk.* Stir in additional *eggnog or milk* till of drizzling consistency. If desired, tint with *food coloring.*

Nutrition facts per cookie: 74 cal., 4 g total fat (2 g sat. fat), 11 mg chol., 29 mg sodium, 9 g carbo., 0 g fiber, 1 g pro. *Daily values:* 1% vit. A, 1% calcium, 2% iron.

CRANBERRY SHORTBREAD

Traditionally, these Scottish teatime treats were baked as a large round. The edge was scalloped to resemble the sun's rays (in otherwise short supply in dreary December). (See the photograph on page 318.)

 2½ cups all-purpose flour
    ½ cup sugar
    1 cup butter
    ½ cup finely snipped dried
       cranberries*

1 Combine flour, sugar, and ¼ teaspoon *salt.* Cut in butter till mixture resembles fine crumbs.

Stir in cranberries. Form dough into a ball and knead till smooth. Divide into 2 equal portions.

2 To make wedges, on an extra-large ungreased cookie sheet, pat or roll out each dough portion to an 8-inch circle. (If two 8-inch circles don't fit on baking sheet, use two smaller sheets. Rearrange sheets halfway through baking time.) Using your fingers, press to make a scalloped edge. With a knife, cut each circle into 16 pie-shaped wedges. Leave wedges in the circle shape.

3 Bake in a 325° oven 25 to 30 minutes or till bottom just starts to brown and center is set. Cut into wedges again while warm. Cool on cookie sheet 5 minutes; transfer to a wire rack. Makes 32 wedges.

***Note:** To finely snip cranberries, toss the cranberries in a bowl with 1 tablespoon of the flour. Place cranberries and flour in a blender container. Cover and blend for 30 seconds or till cranberries are finely "snipped."

Nutrition facts per wedge: 101 cal., 6 g total fat (4 g sat. fat), 15 mg chol., 75 mg sodium, 11 g carbo., 0 g fiber, 1 g pro. *Daily values:* 5% vit. A, 2% iron.

VANILLA-NUT CRESCENTS

Vanilla sugar is one of life's little luxuries. It's easy to justify, for the classy bean flavors heaps of sugar. (See the photograph on page 319.)

1　cup butter
½　cup vanilla sugar* or
　　granulated sugar
1½　cups all-purpose flour

1½　cups almonds or hazelnuts
　　(about 6 oz.), ground

◆◆◆

Colored sugar (optional)

1 In a medium mixing bowl beat butter with an electric mixer on medium speed for 30 seconds. Add vanilla sugar; beat till fluffy. Beat in as much of the flour as you can with the mixer. Using a wooden spoon, stir in ground nuts and remaining flour till combined. Form dough into a ball. If necessary, wrap in plastic wrap and chill about 1 hour or till easy to handle.

2 Form the dough into 1-inch balls, then roll by hand into 2½-inch lengths. Place 1 inch apart on ungreased baking sheets, curving to form crescents. If desired, sprinkle crescents with colored sugar.

3 Bake in a 350° oven for 10 to 12 minutes or till bottoms are slightly golden. Cool on the cookie sheet 1 minute; transfer to a wire rack (cookies will deflate slightly). Cool completely. Store in an airtight container. Makes about 50 cookies.

***Note:** To make vanilla sugar, split a *vanilla bean* lengthwise; immerse in a jar with 2 cups *granulated sugar.* Cover and let stand for 1 week. (Use extra vanilla sugar to replace the sugar in other recipes or in beverages.)

Nutrition facts per cookie: 70 cal., 5 g total fat (2 g sat. fat), 9 mg chol., 35 mg sodium, 5 g carbo., 0 g fiber, 1 g pro. *Daily values:* 3% vit. A, 1% iron.

Pasta Dinner

*Surprise your family and friends with this menu that puts an
upbeat spin on traditional Italian cuisine.*

**Mesclun (spring greens) with diced
Roma tomatoes, chopped fresh mozzarella,
and Herbed Vinaigrette (page 98)**

◆◆◆

Zucchini Lasagna with Walnuts (page 89)

◆◆◆

Onion and Olive Focaccia (page 206)

◆◆◆

Chocolate Fudge Cheesecake (page 220)

The day before:
◆ Prepare and bake the cheesecake;
cool, cover, and chill.
◆ Make cheesecake topping; chill.
◆ Prepare vinaigrette; chill.

Several hours before:
◆ Make and bake the bread.

1½ hours before:
◆ Prepare and bake lasagna.*
◆ Arrange salad ingredients on plates
(do not add vinaigrette); cover and chill.

Just before serving:
◆ Drizzle vinaigrette over salads.
◆ Spread topping on cheesecake.

*If you prefer, follow the make-ahead
directions and prepare the lasagna
up to 1 month ahead.

A Farmer's Market Celebration

*After you've collected some of the freshest peak-season produce at the farmer's market, invite
in some guests for this spectacular meal to showcase your finds.*

**Spring Greens and Vegetable Salad
(page 98)**

◆◆◆

Eggplant Rollatini (page 229)

◆◆◆

Crusty French rolls or a sliced baguette

◆◆◆

Fresh Summer Fruit Tart (page 146)

The day before:
◆ Prepare Eggplant Rollatini according to
the make-ahead directions.
◆ Prepare the dressing for the
salad; cover and chill.

4 hours before:
◆ Make and bake tart shell; set aside.
◆ Prepare filling for tart; cover and chill.

30 minutes before:
◆ Bake Eggplant Rollatini.
◆ Prepare salad (do not add dressing);
cover and chill.

Just before serving:
◆ Add dressing to salad.
◆ Assemble tart.

Bistro Dinner

Create the atmosphere—light the candles, turn on the tunes, pour some wine— and sit down to bistro-style fare with all the comforts of home.

Warm Winter Salad (page 67)

◆◆◆

French Farmhouse Garlic Chicken (page 28)

◆◆◆

Hot mashed potatoes

◆◆◆

Sliced cooked zucchini

◆◆◆

Potato Buns (page 252)

◆◆◆

Apple-Cherry Pecan Tart (page 217)

3 hours before:
◆ Make and bake the buns.*
◆ Make the tart.

1 hour before:
◆ Toss greens; cover and chill.

40 minutes before:
◆ Slice the zucchini; set aside.
◆ Prepare the chicken.
◆ Cook and mash the potatoes.

Just before serving:
◆ Cook the zucchini.
◆ Finish preparing salad.

Between courses:
◆ Cut tart into wedges; top with whipped cream.

*To make these buns up to 3 months ahead, follow recipe for Brown 'n' Serve Buns (page 252).

Come Coffee with Me

Whatever the morning occasion may be, your club for bridge or coffee with friends, when it's your turn to hostess, serve an array of coffeehouse specialties.

Vanilla Biscuits (page 74)

◆◆◆

Tangerine-Vanilla Curd (page 74)

◆◆◆

Lemon-Poppy Seed Biscotti (page 208)

◆◆◆

Ricotta Fruit Dip (page 71)

◆◆◆

Assorted fresh fruit

◆◆◆

Mocha Java (page 54) or coffee

Up to 2 weeks before:
◆ Prepare Tangerine Vanilla Curd; cover and chill.

The day before:
◆ Make and bake the biscotti; cover.
◆ Prepare dip; cover and chill.

45 minutes before:
◆ Make and bake the biscuits.
◆ Clean fruit and arrange on a platter.

Just before serving:
◆ Make Mocha Java or coffee.

Simple Summertime Supper

Summer days and simple times go hand in hand, so pull together your family and enjoy the pleasure of preparing and sharing this easy-to-fix supper.

Fish Tacos with Mango Salsa (page 108)

◆◆◆

Mixed Citrus Salad (page 66)

◆◆◆

Ice cream with Caramel Crunch Ice-Cream Sauce (page 116)

◆◆◆

Purchased cookies

1 hour before:
◆ Make salsa; cover and chill.*
◆ Prepare grill.
◆ Peel and section fruit for salad; cover and chill.
◆ Make dressing for salad.
◆ Heat tortillas and grill fish.

Just before serving:
◆ Arrange salad.
◆ Assemble tacos.

Between courses:
◆ Make sauce for ice cream.

*This salsa is simple enough to put together minutes before mealtime, but you can mix it up to 24 hours ahead and cover and chill till needed.

Sunday Morning Breakfast

Make Sunday the morning to kick back and relax with good company over good breakfast.

Farmer's Casserole (page 45)

◆◆◆

Almond Breakfast Round (page 256)

◆◆◆

Winter-Bright Pear Compote (page 16)

◆◆◆

Fruit juice and/or coffee

The day before:
◆ Prepare casserole according to the make-ahead directions.
◆ Make and shape dough for Almond Breakfast Round; cover and chill.

1 hour before:
◆ Let Almond Breakfast Round stand at room temperature, then bake.
◆ Bake casserole.
◆ Make compote.

Just before serving:
◆ Prepare juice and/or coffee.

Above, clockwise from top:
Pepper-Cheddar Yorkshire Pudding (page 292),
Piquant Potatoes (page 292),
Savory Sprouts and Apples (page 293),
Masterpiece Beef Roast (page 290)

Top: *Christollen Bread (page 286)*
Above: *Christmas Morning Cinnamon Rolls*
(page 284)
Page 315: *Holiday Frittata (page 284),*
Minty Winter Compote (page 284)

Above: *Rumtopf (page 295)*
Right: *Lemon Curd Tarts (page 296)*
Page 316, clockwise from top left:
Plum Pudding (page 300),
Mincemeat-Pear Pie (page 298),
French Spice Cake (page 304)

Above: *Mulled Cider (page 294)*
Pages 318–319, clockwise from top
right: *Speculaas (page 308)*,
Macaroons (page 306),
Turkish Delight (page 305),
Vanilla Fudge (page 304),
Lebkuchen (page 306),
Peppermint Creams (page 305),
Cranberry Shortbread (page 308),
Favorite Sugar Cookies (page 308),
Vanilla-Nut Crescents (page 309)

Above: *Battenberg Cake (page 301)*

GLOSSARY

Almond paste: Almond paste is made from almonds that have been finely ground and combined with sugar. It can be used for fillings in coffee cakes and pastries. For best results in baking, check the ingredient label and select an almond paste made without syrup or liquid glucose.

Arborio rice: A short-grained rice used in Italian risottos because it contributes to the creamy quality of the dish yet remains firm and chewy. Look for Arborio rice in Italian markets, specialty stores, and large supermarkets.

Belgian endive: A small cone-shaped salad green with 5- to 6-inch, slender leaves that are tightly packed. The leaves are creamy white with pale yellow tips. The slightly bitter flavor of Belgian endive complements mild lettuces when mixed in salads. Look for tightly packed heads that are firm and unblemished and leaves that are creamy white with pale yellow tips. Refrigerate in a plastic bag for up to 3 days.

Blood orange: A variety of orange with blushing orange-red skin and reddish orange meat. It is small in size but possesses an intense orange flavor. Look for blood oranges from December through July (the supply is limited). Select well-formed fruit that is heavy for its size. Store for up to 3 weeks in your refrigerator.

Bok choy: A variety of Chinese cabbage with long celerylike white stalks and large deep green leaves. Crisp like celery, bok choy has a sweet, mild cabbagelike flavor. The leaves and stalks can be used either raw or cooked. Choose bok choy that has crisp leaves and firm stalks. Avoid stalks with wilted, mushy leaves. Store bok choy in a plastic bag in the refrigerator. Use within a few days. Trim the base and pull the stalks apart. Discard any ragged or discolored leaves. Slice or chop the stalks and shred the leaves.

Broccoli raab: A vegetable with 6- to 9-inch, leafy dark green stalks and clusters of small buds that look similar to those on broccoli. The stems and the leaves have a somewhat sharp and bitter flavor. Broccoli raab is sold in loose bunches. Look for small, sturdy stems and fresh-looking dark green leaves. Keep broccoli raab in a plastic bag in the refrigerator for up to 4 days.

Bulgur: A parched, cracked wheat product. Bulgur is dark tan in color with a delicate nutty flavor. Bulgur absorbs twice its volume in water when soaked. Because bulgur is precooked, it cooks quickly or needs only a brief soaking before using. Look for bulgur in the aisle with the rice in supermarkets. If you can't find bulgur, you might try cracked wheat, which is a similar product. Store bulgur in an airtight container in a cool, dry place for up to 6 months. Or, it may be stored indefinitely in the freezer.

Carambola (star fruit): A small oval fruit with deep lengthwise grooves, waxy-looking bright yellow skin, and juicy, sweet yellow meat. Carambola tastes like a combination of lemon, pineapple, and apple. Its flavor ranges from sweet to slightly tart. Carambola is nicknamed star fruit because when it is sliced crosswise, the slices are shaped like stars. Select firm, shiny-skinned golden fruit. Fruit with more green than gold will taste extremely tart. Ripen fresh carambolas with green-tinged skin at room temperature. Refrigerate fully yellowed fruit in a covered container or plastic bag about 1 week.

Cherimoya: A fist-sized tropical fruit that is heart-shaped and has a patterned pale green outer skin. Cherimoyas have a creamy white interior with large black seeds. When ripe, this fruit has a creamy, almost custardlike texture. It tastes like a combination of bananas and papaya with a tinge of pineapple. Cherimoyas sold in supermarkets usually are pale green and quite firm. When ripe, some cherimoyas turn a dull brownish green. A ripe cherimoya should be slightly soft. Refrigerate ripe fruit for up to 2 days. If the fruit is not ripe, ripen it by leaving it at room temperature, turning the fruit occasionally, until the skin turns a dull brownish green. Serve cherimoyas raw. Halve the fruit, then remove the seeds. Cube or slice the fruit, or spoon extra-soft fruit right from the skin. Mix cherimoyas into fruit salads or compotes.

Chèvre cheese: Any cheese made from goat's milk. These cheeses often have a distinctive tangy flavor and are made in a number of shapes, such as logs and cones. Chèvre comes plain or coated with herb or edible ash.

continued

Chinese cabbage: A name given to both a specific variety of Oriental cabbage and to a category that includes bok choy. The variety known as Chinese cabbage has elongated, tightly curled leaves with large white ribs and slightly frilly pale green tips. It is crunchy and a little sweeter than head cabbage, with a slight zestiness. Avoid heads with discolored, wilted leaves. Refrigerate in a plastic bag for up to 4 days.

Couscous: A grain product in the shape of tiny beads. Made from ground semolina, it is a staple in North African cooking and can either be used in recipes or as a mild-tasting side dish in place of rice. It is found in the rice or pasta section of the supermarket and at specialty stores.

Crystallized ginger: Also known as candied ginger, crystallized ginger is a confection rather than a spice. Bits of gingerroot are cooked in a sugar syrup, then coated with sugar. Store in a cool, dry, dark place.

Escarole: A variety of endive with elongated and irregularly shaped, flat green leaves with slightly curled edges. Escarole has a firm, chewy texture, mildly bitter flavor, and can be eaten raw or cooked. Serve escarole raw in salads. Its slightly bitter flavor is best when mixed with mild lettuces. Or, serve escarole warm in wilted salads. Its firm leaves make it an excellent choice for wilting. Pick heads with a crisp, fresh texture; avoid those with discoloration. Refrigerate, tightly wrapped, for up to 3 days.

Feta cheese: A soft, crumbly white cheese with a sharp, salty flavor. Feta is made from cow's, sheep's, or goat's milk, and is cured in salt brine. It is an important ingredient in Greek cooking.

Fontina cheese: A semisoft to firm-textured cheese, depending on the age. Fontina cheese has small holes, an ivory color, and a wax rind. It has a pleasant aroma with a delicate to full flavor.

Gorgonzola cheese: A type of blue cheese made from cow's milk and streaked with greenish veins. Gorgonzola has a softer, creamier, and less pungent flavor than most blue cheeses.

Guava: An oval tropical fruit with yellow to green skin and meat that ranges from off-white to red. Guavas have tiny edible seeds and a taste similar to pineapple and lemon. Guavas grow from 1 to 4 inches in diameter. Fresh guavas generally are available most of the year except in early spring. Left to ripen on trees until they fall, guavas found in supermarkets typically will be ripe and ready to eat. Don't purchase any guava that is overly soft or has bruises. If necessary, ripen guavas at room temperature until they are slightly soft and fragrant. Then refrigerate for up to 4 days.

Leek: A member of the onion family that resembles an oversize green onion with overlapping wide green leaves, a fat white stalk, and shaggy roots. Leeks have a subtle onion flavor. Use them as you would onions. Leeks are available year-round. Look for healthy-looking leeks with crisp green leaves. Avoid leeks that are larger than 1½ inches in diameter because they will be less tender. Refrigerate leeks in a plastic bag for up to 5 days.

Mango: An oval, round, or kidney-shaped tropical fruit with green to yellow skin tinged with red, depending on the variety. Mangoes have a deep golden yellow meat, with a large, flat, oval white seed. The fruit has a spicy peach flavor, but is more perfumy than a peach and extremely juicy. Mangoes are available from March through September. When ripe, mangoes should be fully colored, smell fruity, and feel fairly firm when pressed gently. Avoid extremely soft or bruised fruit or fruit with blemishes. Store mangoes at room temperature to ripen. Refrigerate them as soon as they are ripe and use them within 4 or 5 days. Since the meat of the mango holds tightly to the seed, an easy way to remove the meat is to make a cut through the mango, sliding a sharp knife next to the seed along one side of the mango. Repeat on the other side of the seed, resulting in two large pieces. Then cut away all of the meat that remains around the seed. Remove the peel on all pieces and cut up or puree the meat.

Mesclun: A mixture of piquant and delicate baby lettuces grown in rows next to each other and harvested at the same time. The number and proportion of lettuce varies, but it always is a combination of flavors, textures, and colors. If you can't find mesclun, a mixture of Bibb lettuce, arugula, radicchio, and curly endive makes a good substitute.

Orzo: A tiny dried pasta, shaped like grains of rice. Also called rosamarina, orzo can be added to soups and stews or served as a side dish. Look for it with other dried pastas in supermarkets.

Papaya: A melonlike, pear-shaped fruit with greenish yellow to yellow-orange skin and golden orange meat. The seed cavity has tiny black seeds. Papayas taste like a cross between peaches and melons. They are fragrant and extremely sweet with a creamy spoonable consistency. Papayas weigh about 1 pound each. Choose fruit that is at least half yellow and feels somewhat soft when pressed. The skin should be smooth and free from bruises or soft spots. A firm papaya can be ripened at room temperature for 3 to 5 days until mostly yellow to yellow-orange. Store a ripe papaya in the refrigerator for up to 1 week. Peel papayas, then halve and scoop out seeds. Slice, chop, or puree papayas, or use the hollowed-out fruit shells as serving containers. Because papaya contains the enzyme papain, the fruit must be cooked before using in a gelatin mixture. Cooking deactivates the enzyme, which would prevent gelatin from setting up.

Pine nut: The small seed from one of several pine tree varieties. The pine nut, which has a sweet, faint pine flavor, also is known as pignolia and piñon. The small creamy white nut can be slender and pellet-shaped or more triangular. Pine nuts turn rancid quickly, so refrigerate them in an airtight container for up to 2 months or freeze them for up to 6 months.

Plum tomato: A small to medium oval tomato. Also called Italian tomatoes, these red or yellow tomatoes are thick and meaty with small seeds, little juice, and a mild, rich flavor. Roma tomatoes are a common variety. All varieties are especially good for canning and sauces. Look for plump, well-shaped tomatoes that are fairly firm-textured and bright-colored. Avoid bruised, cracked, or soft tomatoes. To ripen, store at room temperature in a brown paper bag or in a bowl with other fruits. Don't stand them in the sun to ripen or they will become mushy. When ripe, tomatoes yield slightly to gentle pressure.

Prosciutto: Like ham, prosciutto is from the hog's leg. Salt-curing draws out the moisture. Unlike ham, the cured pork is air-dried, not smoked. The result is a somewhat sweetly spiced, rose-colored meat with a sheen. Serve slices of prosciutto for a luncheon meat or wrap them around melon balls for an appetizer. Use small amounts in pasta, sauces, and meat dishes. Prosciutto is salty, so taste the dish before adding salt. Sliced prosciutto dries out quickly and should be used within a day or frozen for longer storage.

Saffron: The dried, threadlike reddish orange filaments of a special variety of purple crocus. Used as a spice, saffron threads impart a bright yellow color, bittersweet flavor, and an exotic aroma to classic dishes. Because the delicate filaments must be carefully picked by hand, saffron is the world's most expensive spice. Saffron is sold as a powder and in the tiny strands called threads.

Shallot: A petite member of the onion family. Shallots are formed in the same way as garlic with a head made up of several cloves. A thin, papery skin of reddish brown to yellow-brown covers off-white meat that is tinged with green or purple. Shallots have a mild, delicate flavor and tender texture. They can be eaten raw or cooked. Look for firm, well-shaped shallots that are not sprouting. Avoid wrinkled or shriveled shallots. Store in a cool, dry place for up to 1 month.

Tahini (sesame paste): A smooth paste made from sesame seeds and used as an ingredient to flavor Middle Eastern dishes and as a spread for bread. Look for it in the baking section of large supermarkets and specialty stores.

Toasted sesame oil: A thick, aromatic reddish brown oil, made from toasted sesame seeds, that is used to flavor Oriental dishes. Because it has a strong flavor, use sesame oil sparingly. You can use it with cooking oil for stir-frying but never use it alone for frying.

Tomatillo: A small olive green fruit covered with a thin, papery brown husk, which is removed before using. Their texture is like that of a firm tomato with lots of seeds, and their flavor is rather acidic with hints of lemon and apple. Tomatillos are popular in Mexican cooking. Fresh tomatillos are available year-round. Look for firm tomatillos with tight-fitting, dry husks. Avoid shriveled and bruised ones. Refrigerate fresh tomatillos for up to 10 days. Canned, husked tomatillos also are available.

INDEX

EMERGENCY SUBSTITUTIONS

IF YOU DON'T HAVE:	SUBSTITUTE:
1 teaspoon baking powder	½ teaspoon cream of tartar plus ¼ teaspoon baking soda
1 tablespoon cornstarch (for thickening)	2 tablespoons all-purpose flour
1 package active dry yeast	1 cake compressed yeast
1 cup buttermilk	1 tablespoon lemon juice or vinegar plus enough milk to make 1 cup (let stand 5 minutes before using); or 1 cup plain yogurt
1 cup whole milk	½ cup evaporated milk plus ½ cup water; or 1 cup water plus ⅓ cup nonfat dry milk powder
1 cup light cream	1 tablespoon melted butter or margarine plus enough whole milk to make 1 cup
1 cup dairy sour cream	1 cup plain yogurt
1 whole egg	2 egg whites, 2 egg yolks, or 3 tablespoons frozen egg product, thawed
1 cup margarine	1 cup butter; or 1 cup shortening plus ¼ teaspoon salt, if desired
1 ounce semisweet chocolate	3 tablespoons semisweet chocolate pieces; or 1 ounce unsweetened chocolate plus 1 tablespoon granulated sugar
1 ounce unsweetened chocolate	3 tablespoons unsweetened cocoa powder plus 1 tablespoon cooking oil or shortening, melted
1 cup corn syrup	1 cup granulated sugar plus ¼ cup liquid
1 cup honey	1¼ cups granulated sugar plus ¼ cup liquid
1 cup molasses	1 cup honey
1 cup granulated sugar	1 cup packed brown sugar or 2 cups sifted powdered sugar
1 cup beef broth or chicken broth	1 teaspoon or 1 cube instant beef or chicken bouillon plus 1 cup hot water
2 cups tomato sauce	¾ cup tomato paste plus 1 cup water
1 cup tomato juice	½ cup tomato sauce plus ½ cup water
¼ cup fine dry bread crumbs	¾ cup soft bread crumbs, ¼ cup cracker crumbs, or ¼ cup cornflake crumbs
1 small onion, chopped (⅓ cup)	1 teaspoon onion powder or 1 tablespoon dried minced onion
1 clove garlic	½ teaspoon bottled minced garlic or ⅛ teaspoon garlic powder
1 teaspoon lemon juice	½ teaspoon vinegar
1 teaspoon poultry seasoning	¾ teaspoon dried sage, crushed, plus ¼ teaspoon dried thyme or marjoram, crushed
1 teaspoon dry mustard (in cooked mixtures)	1 tablespoon prepared mustard
1 tablespoon snipped fresh herb	½ to 1 teaspoon dried herb, crushed
1 teaspoon dried herb	½ teaspoon ground herb
1 teaspoon grated gingerroot	¼ teaspoon ground ginger
1 teaspoon apple pie spice	½ teaspoon ground cinnamon plus ¼ teaspoon ground nutmeg, ⅛ teaspoon ground allspice, and dash ground cloves or ginger
1 teaspoon pumpkin pie spice	½ teaspoon ground cinnamon plus ¼ teaspoon ground ginger, ¼ teaspoon ground allspice, and ⅛ teaspoon ground nutmeg